Adobe® Premiere® 6.5 Bible

Adele Droblas and Seth Greenberg

WILEY
Wiley Publishing, Inc.

Adobe® Premiere® 6.5 Bible

Published by
Wiley Publishing, Inc.
909 Third Avenue
New York, NY 10022
www.wiley.com/compbooks

Library of Congress Control Number: 2002111060

ISBN: 0-7645-1830-5

Printed in the United States of America

10 9 8 7 6 5 4 3 2 1

1B/SQ/RR/QS/IN

Distributed in the United States by Wiley Publishing, Inc.

Distributed by CDG Books Canada Inc. for Canada; by Transworld Publishers Limited in the United Kingdom; by IDG Norge Books for Norway; by IDG Sweden Books for Sweden; by IDG Books Australia Publishing Corporation Pty. Ltd. for Australia and New Zealand; by TransQuest Publishers Pte Ltd. for Singapore, Malaysia, Thailand, Indonesia, and Hong Kong; by Gotop Information Inc. for Taiwan; by ICG Muse, Inc. for Japan; by Intersoft for South Africa; by Eyrolles for France; by International Thomson Publishing for Germany, Austria, and Switzerland; by Distribuidora Cuspide for Argentina; by LR International for Brazil; by Galileo Libros for Chile; by Ediciones ZETA S.C.R. Ltda. for Peru; by WS Computer Publishing Corporation, Inc., for the Philippines; by Contemporanea de Ediciones for Venezuela; by Express Computer Distributors for the Caribbean and West Indies; by Micronesia Media Distributor, Inc. for Micronesia; by Chips Computadoras S.A. de C.V. for Mexico; by Editorial Norma de Panama S.A. for Panama; by American Bookshops for Finland.

For general information on Hungry Minds' products and services please contact our Customer Care department within the U.S. at 800-762-2974, outside the U.S. at 317-572-3993 or fax 317-572-4002.

For sales inquiries and reseller information, including discounts, premium and bulk quantity sales, and foreign-language translations, please contact our Customer Care department at 800-434-3422, fax 317-572-4002 or write to Wiley Publishing, Inc., Attn: Customer Care Department, 10475 Crosspoint Boulevard, Indianapolis, IN 46256.

For information on licensing foreign or domestic rights, please contact our Sub-Rights Customer Care department at 650-653-7098.

For information on using Wiley Publishing's products and services in the classroom or for ordering examination copies, please contact our Educational Sales department at 800-434-2086 or fax 317-572-4005.

For press review copies, author interviews, or other publicity information, please contact our Public Relations department at 650-653-7000 or fax 650-653-7500.

For authorization to photocopy items for corporate, personal, or educational use, please contact Copyright Clearance Center, 222 Rosewood Drive, Danvers, MA 01923, or fax 978-750-4470.

About the Authors

Adele Droblas is an artist, writer, and computer consultant. She has produced digital video clips that appear on the Web for her clients.

Seth Greenberg is a computer consultant, programmer, and author. He has worked as a television producer and scriptwriter.

Credits

Acquisitions Editor
Mike Roney

Project Editor
Timothy J. Borek

Technical Editor
Dennis R. Short

Copy Editor
Beth Taylor

Editorial Manager
Rev Mengle

Senior Vice President, Technical Publishing
Richard Swadley

Vice President and Publisher
Mary Bednarek

Project Coordinator
Regina Snyder

Graphics and Production Specialists
Beth Brooks, Melanie DesJardins, LeAndra Johnson, Jeremey Unger

Quality Control Technicians
Carl Pierce, Andy Hollandbeck, Charles Spencer

Permissions Editors
Laura Moss and Carmen Krikorian

Media Development Specialist
Angela Denny

Media Development Coordinator
Sarah Cummings

Proofreading and Indexing
TECHBOOKS Production Services

Special Help
Jill Mazurczyk

To our family and to Angelique and Laurence, the stars of our videos, who make every day and every night shine.

Foreword

These are very exciting times for those of us who are involved with desktop digital video! We're in the midst of a digital video revolution, very much like the desktop publishing revolution that took the world by storm in the 1980s. Look at the evidence: Today's digital cameras are as good as BetaCam at about one-fifth the price; Computer CPUs are fast enough to handle the demands of desktop video; nonlinear editing software (NLE) is robust and has professional features; RAM and fast hard drive storage are cheap; operating systems are more reliable; and modern video subsystem technologies (DirectX, QuickTime, and so on) have the professional features required. All of these factors combined make creating broadcast-quality video on the desktop or laptop feasible. Not only is it feasible, it is even affordable on a hobbyist budget!

With the recent release of Adobe Premiere 6.5, we have added some really big new features, and improved workflow and performance. The biggest new feature in terms of changing how people work is the new Real-Time Preview feature. Premiere's implementation is comprehensive and the only limitation is the available processing power. Anything that you can do in Premiere (transitions, filters, transparency, motion, titling, and so on — even third-party filters) can now be previewed in real time, with no need to render first! The new Adobe Title Designer allows creating professional broadcast-quality title sequences, and comes with over 150 templates and styles. The Adobe MPEG Encoder is a full-featured exporter for MPEG-1 and MPEG-2 files to be used for VCD, SVCD, and DVD. We've also included some new professional-quality audio filters, additional After Effects plug-ins, and more. Premiere is compatible with the widest variety of OSes — Mac OS 9, Mac OS X, Windows 98 SE, Windows 2000, Windows Me, and Windows XP.

We've worked hard to design Premiere to integrate well with the other Adobe applications. In Adobe Premiere, integration is excellent with Adobe After Effects, Photoshop, Illustrator, and GoLive. Seamlessly and efficiently working with the other Adobe applications is Premiere's single greatest competitive advantage. The integration is so good, and so important in the video production workflow, that rather than directly comparing Premiere to a competitor NLE, you have to consider the entire suite of Adobe applications. Each successive release of these Adobe products improves the overall integration. Here are a few examples of how these applications work together: Files from Photoshop and Illustrator can be used in Premiere and After Effects, layers intact (name, position, visibility, even Adjustment Layers and blending modes are preserved); Premiere projects can be opened in After Effects for further compositing work; Photoshop plug-ins can be used in Premiere, After Effects, and Illustrator; Premiere supports After Effects plug-ins; Edit Original allows opening files used in Premiere or After Effects in the application that created them and after they are saved, they're updated in Premiere or After Effects; Illustrator or Photoshop paths can be pasted into After Effects and used as masks or even keyframe data for position or visual effects; Premiere and After Effects can save movies with URLs, Chapter points, and even frame target references that can be used in GoLive.

Premiere was designed to fit into the workflow of a single-person shop, or into that of a team of creative professionals across a company, even in mixed-platform environments. It has also been designed with Adobe's award-winning user interface, sharing common keyboard shortcuts and tabbed palettes. This translates to comfort and familiarity for new Premiere users who have used other Adobe applications, resulting in a gentler learning curve.

Variety and capabilities of available NLE systems have never been greater. Adobe Premiere's versatility and popularity have allowed it to grow to the point where it offers more choices for hardware, third-party effects software, and training materials than any other NLE. Premiere has been designed to work on video content for CD, DVD, Web, and broadcast, including HDTV.

The CPUs are so fast in today's computer systems that new hardware is being designed so that much of the processing of digital-video is being done on the CPU instead of on a dedicated video card. What's so exciting about this is that the processors are going to keep getting faster, and that means the speed of video processing will scale each time the CPU is upgraded (with no necessary changes to the software).

The Web allows us to easily communicate — to share ideas and seek our fortune on a global basis. There is no question that motion and sound make Web sites more exciting, memorable, and dynamic. In today's fiercely competitive environment, businesses with an online presence are looking to interactive animations and streaming audio and video content to help them build compelling sites to keep visitors longer. Not long ago, we had low-frame-rate, postage-stamp-sized video that took ages to download. Today, with better streaming technology and the increased bandwidth in the home and workplace, Web video is very compelling. We will see more events being streamed live and archived for on demand viewing. Streaming Video Hosting services previously only accessible by big companies due to the cost, are beginning to offer affordable rates to individual people. The Adobe suite of applications offers you everything you need to develop, deploy, and manage high-impact Web sites so you can take advantage of these exciting times.

Microsoft and Apple now support DV via the OHCI standard at the operating system level (by DirectX and QuickTime respectively). Premiere uses QuickTime and DirectX to communicate with and control DV devices, offering professional features like tape logging and batch capture on consumer budgets. Premiere's DV support is wide and deep: NTSC, PAL; 4:3, 16:9; non-square pixel support; wide variety of DV devices supported for frame accurate device control; DV transmitting when render-scrubbing and full-quality playback. For the Web, Adobe has partnered with RealNetworks, Microsoft, and Apple to deliver excellent streaming Web video export capabilities from right inside Premiere. Video compression is a complex process, and wrong choices along the way can cause less desirable results and waste precious time. In Premiere, we've provided numerous presets to help you through the process for good results with little or no knowledge of video compression. For our advanced users, the details are just below the surface and easily revealed if desired, allowing experimentation and fine-tuning. With Premiere 6.5, it has never been easier to go from shooting digital video to delivering it on tape, the Web, CD or DVD.

Welcome to Adobe Premiere and the world of digital video. Here, we live on the bleeding edge, constantly pushing our gear and software to their limits. This makes for a thrilling, but at times bumpy, ride. I'd like to invite you to join our community, where you'll meet others on this journey, and have an opportunity to help shape the future of Premiere:

If you think of a great idea for how Premiere can be improved, we would love to hear from you. Please include lots of detail and send us an email: premierewishlist@adobe.com. Our interface designers, product managers, and engineers read all of these, but please do not expect a personal response.

Try the Adobe User to User Forums at `www.adobe.com/support/forums/main.html` where you can lurk or actively participate in discussions about digital video, creative solutions to problems, special techniques, and so on. Forums are offered for each Adobe application and by platform.

Finally, once you've got some work you are proud of, we'd love to see it! You can even submit it to us (`www.adobe.com/motion/firstperson/demoreel.html`) for possible inclusion on our prestigious customer demo reel to be used at industry trade shows and events.

Adele, Seth, and Wiley did an amazing job with the *Adobe Premiere 6 Bible,* and have done it again with this updated version covering Premiere 6.5. They've been able to take Premiere, a very deep and powerful program, and break it into logical sections then tell you what you need to know. It is a powerful reference tool, and also encourages browsing to learn new techniques. The *Adobe Premiere 6.5 Bible* not only covers using Premiere in detail, but also will teach you how to get the most out of the entire suite of Adobe products.

Bruce Bowman

Adobe Premiere Product Manager
Adobe Systems

Preface

As you read these words, a revolution in desktop video is taking place. One of the main causes of the revolution is the advent of the digital video camera, which digitizes high-quality video directly in the camera. After the signal has been digitized, it can be transferred directly over a cable to a personal computer. After your computer gets hold of the video, you need Adobe Premiere to help you creatively shape it into a compelling desktop video production.

Adobe Premiere combines power and ease of use to provide a complete authoring environment for producing desktop digital video productions. By using Premiere, you can capture video directly from your camcorder into Premiere's capture window. After you've captured or imported video and sound, you can assemble your clips into a production by simply clicking and dragging a video clip from one window to another. Placing clips and reassembling them is almost as easy as snapping together the cars in a child's toy railroad train set. Creating transitions that dissolve one scene into another or wipe one scene away to reveal another is simply a matter of dragging an icon representing the transition between the two clips. To fine-tune your work, Premiere provides numerous digital editing tools — some similar to those available in professional editing studios; others only possible through digital magic. After you've finished editing, you can output your digital movie with settings for the Web, videotape, or CD-ROM. If you've ever tried creating a video production by using traditional videotape hardware, Adobe Premiere will revolutionize the way that you work.

Who Should Read This Book

The *Adobe Premiere 6.5 Bible* is for multimedia producers, Web designers, graphic designers, artists, filmmakers, and camcorder users — anyone interested in using his or her computer to create desktop video productions or to output desktop video to videotape, CDs, or the Web. As you read through the *Adobe Premiere 6.5 Bible,* you'll soon see that it is more than just a reference to virtually all the features in Adobe Premiere. The book is filled with short tutorial exercises that help you understand concepts and put into practice the key Premiere features covered in a chapter. You'll find this book an indispensable bible as you learn to use Adobe Premiere (and as a useful reference book after you've mastered the Premiere program's key features). So don't wait another moment — start reading and learning what you can do with your creative visions.

How This Book Is Organized

If you read the *Adobe Premiere 6.5 Bible*'s chapters in order, you'll gradually become an expert at using Adobe Premiere. However, we expect that most readers will jump in and out of chapters as needed or as their interest moves from subject to subject. Throughout the book, we've included numerous step-by-step tutorials to guide you through the process of creating video sequences by using many Adobe Premiere features. As you work, you'll find numerous clips on the CD-ROM that will aid you in quickly and efficiently creating short examples that illustrate and help explain chapter topics.

Note: For updated information on digital video, check out our Web sites: `www.droblas.com` and `www.bonitavida.com`.

The *Adobe Premiere 6.5 Bible* is broken down into seven main parts, each described in the following sections.

Part I: Getting Started with Premiere

Part I provides an introduction to as well as an overview of Adobe Premiere. Chapter 1 includes a getting-started tutorial that introduces you to the basics of creating a desktop video production by using Adobe Premiere. Chapter 2 provides an overview of the Premiere interface: its menus, palettes, and tools. Chapter 3 introduces you to the Premiere program's basic project settings, and Chapter 4 shows you how to capture video directly into Premiere from a digital video camcorder or an analog camcorder.

Part II: Editing with Premiere

Part II provides a thorough look at the basics of putting together a digital video production. Chapter 5 shows you how to use the Premiere Timeline to assemble a video production. Chapter 6 continues editing essentials, providing a look at the Premiere audio features. Chapter 7 rounds out this part with a discussion of how to use the Premiere program's transitions to smooth changes from one clip to another.

Part III: Working with Type and Graphics

Part III is dedicated to type and graphics. This part shows you how to use the new Premiere Title Designer window and titling tools. You'll learn how to create Titles with styles, templates and logos. How to create rolling and scrolling credits as well as how to create titles with drop shadows. You'll also learn how to create graphics by using the Premiere 6.5 Title Designer window, Adobe Illustrator, and Adobe Photoshop. Chapters 8 and 9 cover creating type and graphic effects. Chapter 8 also provides several examples of using transparency effects with static and moving text.

Part IV: Advanced Techniques and Special Effects

Part IV covers advanced editing techniques and special effects. Chapter 10 covers the sophisticated editing features in Premiere, such as 3- and 4-point edits. It also provides a discussion of using the Premiere program's Rolling Edit and Ripple Edit tools as well as using its Slip and Slide editing tools. Chapter 10 also covers precise frame-by-frame editing by using the Trim view of the monitor window. Chapter 11 reviews every effect in the Premiere Video Effects palette, while Chapter 12 covers all the Premiere program's transparency effects. If you want to create motion effects in Premiere, check out Chapter 14, which provides a thorough look at the Motion dialog box. Chapter 15 takes you on a guided tour and show you how to enhance your video by using both Adobe Premiere and Adobe Photoshop.

Part V: Outputting Digital Video from Premiere

After you've learned how to create a digital video production in Premiere, your next concern is how to output your work in the best possible manner. This part covers all the bases. Chapter 16 reviews the Premiere settings for exporting QuickTime and AVI movies. Chapters 17 and 18 describe how to obtain the best possible quality when outputting a movie to the Web. Chapter 19 provides a discussion of outputting to videotape; while Chapter 20 covers outputting to CD-ROM as well as using Premiere with Macromedia Director.

Part VI: Premiere and Beyond

The chapters in this section (Chapter 21–26) provide a look at using Premiere with different software packages, such as Adobe Photoshop, Adobe Illustrator, and Adobe After Effects. Chapter 21 provides a look at how you can use Adobe After Effects to edit Premiere projects. Chapter 22 shows you how to create alpha channels in Photoshop that can be used in Premiere; it also shows you how to edit Premier Filmstrip files in Photoshop and export them back into Premiere. Chapter 23 shows how to create graphics and text by using Adobe Illustrator. These graphics and texts are then imported and used in Adobe Premiere, many times as masks. Chapters 24 and 25 deal with working with Adobe After Effects. In Chapter 24, you learn how to import a Premiere project into After Effects and create sophisticated masks by using After Effects. In Chapter 25, you also learn how to use the After Effects powerful motion paths and how to create composite video clips. The last chapter in this part, Chapter 26, provides a look at third-party plug-ins that add to Premiere's special effects generating power.

Part VII: Appendixes

The *Adobe Premiere 6.5 Bible* appendixes provide a hardware overview geared to nontechnical users, a resource guide, and a guide to the *Adobe Premiere 6.5 Bible* CD-ROM. The appendixes also feature a section on how to license QuickTime from Apple Computer. If you are going to distribute a Premiere movie on a CD-ROM as a

QuickTime movie, you'll probably want to include QuickTime; therefore, you'll need to obtain a software license from Apple Computer. The hardware overview appendix provides a look at computer systems and IEEE 1394/FireWire ports, and it also provides a short guide to DV camcorders and audio. The resource appendix provides a Web guide for digital video and sound equipment as well as the Web addresses for magazines and publishers specializing in video, audio, and lighting.

Things to Note

The *Adobe Premiere 6.5 Bible* is a cross-platform book. When keyboard instruction for Mac and Windows differ, Macintosh keyboard commands are provided first; Windows keyboard commands are given next. For instance: To save your file, press Command+S/Ctrl+Z. Here are some other conventions in this book that you should note.

Key combinations

When keyboard instructions call for pressing several keys simultaneously, the keys are separated by a plus sign. For example: To deselect all clips in the Timeline, press Command/Ctrl+Shift+A.

Mouse instructions

When the text specifies to click an item, move the mouse pointer over the item and click once. Windows users always click the left mouse button unless instructed otherwise. If the text specifies double-click, click the mouse twice without moving the mouse.

Menu commands

When the text specifies steps for executing a menu command, the menu and the command are separated by an arrow symbol, such as Timeline⇨Preview. When submenus are specified, you'll often see an arrow separating each menu command. For instance, to import a file into Premiere, you'll see the instructions written as File⇨Import⇨File.

Acknowledgments

Thanks to Adobe Systems for creating products that allow us to express our creative visions. Thanks also to Steve Jobs, whose vision it was to make a computer that allows us to be creative by allowing us to combine type, artwork, photographs, sound, and video into a masterpiece.

A special thanks to Daniel Brown, Marcus Chang, Matt Douglas, Kristen Chang, Patty Stoop, Wendy Shobloom, Barabara Rice, Eric Lundblade, and Amacker Bullwinkle at Adobe Systems for their help.

Thanks to everyone at Wiley Publishing, Inc., especially Mike Roney who helped get the *Adobe Premiere 6.5 Bible* off the ground and kept us on schedule. Thanks to Will Pesce and Stephen Kippur for believing in us. Thanks also to Tim Borek and Beth Taylor for doing such a careful and meticulous job. Thanks, too, to the art people and everyone who helped put the CD-ROM together — Angie Denny, Carmen Krikorian, and Sarah Cummings.

Thanks to Dennis Short for his job in tech editing the *Adobe Premiere 6.5 Bible.*

Thanks to Constance di Preta and Tracey Tannenbaum from Digital Vision for supplying us with digital stock clips for use in the CD-ROM that accompanies the book. Thanks also to Rachel Branch at Sony for lending us a Sony digital camcorder, which we used throughout the book. Thanks also to Lisa Lorik at Eastman Kodak for the use of a digital camera, which we also used to capture images for the book.

Thanks to Midnight Sun Music for letting us videotape them while they where performing. A glimpse of their performance can be found in Chapter 12 and on the CD-ROM. Thanks to all the people (family, friends, especially our musician and computer friends, the children of today, who are the future, and to all those people we have met that radiate peace and happiness for all) who have touched our lives and inspired us to want to capture those wonderful moments that life has to offer. For links to some inspiring sites, go to bonitavida.com. Hopefully, *Adobe Premiere 6.5 Bible* will help you capture those special moments in your life and allow you to share them with friends and loved ones. We hope you enjoy *Adobe Premiere 6.5 Bible.*

A letter came to us from Buenos Aires, Argentina. The words in the letter touched many lives. Here are some of the words that have moved us. We share them with you verbatim:

> Don't save anything for a special occasion. Every day that you live is a special day . . . I have learned that life should be filled with experiences to enjoy, not just to live by. Today I save nothing . . . The words, someday and one of these days are disappearing from my vocabulary. If it is worth seeing it, listening to it or doing it, I want to see it, listen to it and do it . . . Tomorrow we all take for granted . . . It is the small things that one does not do, the ones that make me mad . . . And every day I say to myself, this day is a special day. Every day, hour, every minute is special . . . Don't be too lazy or too busy to take a few moments to touch someone's life, talk to a friend, tell a loved one you love them or too busy to do something special to help this world be a brighter, happier, kinder place . . . If you think, one of these days, then one of these days may be far away or one of these days may never happen.

Peace on Earth.

Adele and Seth

Contents at a Glance

Contents

Part II: Editing with Premiere 91

Getting Started with Premiere

PART

I

In This Part

CHAPTER 1

Premiere Quickstart

In This Chapter

Welcome to the world of Adobe Premiere and digital video. For both experts and beginners alike, Adobe Premiere 6.5 packs the power you need to create sophisticated digital video productions. You can create digital movies, documentaries, sales presentations, and music videos directly from your desktop computer or laptop. Your digital video production can be output to videotape or the Web, or you can integrate it into projects in other programs, such as Adobe After Effects, Adobe Live Motion, Macromedia Director, and Macromedia Flash.

This chapter introduces you to the basics of Adobe Premiere: understanding what it is and what you can do with it. This chapter also provides a simple Quickstart project to get you acquainted with the Adobe Premiere production process. You'll see how easy it is to load digital video clips and graphics into an Adobe Premiere project and to edit them into a short presentation. After you've completed the editing process, you'll export the movie as either a QuickTime or Windows Media movie for use in other programs.

What You Can Do with Premiere

Whether you need to create a simple video clip for the Web or a sophisticated documentary or presentation, Premiere has the tools you need to create a dynamic video production. In fact, the best way to think about Premiere is to visualize it as a complete production facility. You'd need a roomful of videotape and special effects equipment to do everything that Premiere can do.

Here's a short list of some of the production tasks that you can accomplish with Premiere:

- ✦ Edit digital video clips into a complete digital video production.
- ✦ Capture video from a digital camcorder or videotape recorder.
- ✦ Capture audio from a microphone or audio recording device.
- ✦ Load stock digital graphics, video, and audio clips.
- ✦ Create titles and animated title effects, such as scrolling or rolling titles.
- ✦ Integrate files from different sources into your production. Premiere loads not only digital video and audio files, but also Adobe Photoshop, Adobe Illustrator, JPEG, and TIFF graphics.
- ✦ Create special effects, such as distortions, blurring, and pinching.
- ✦ Create motion effects in which logos or graphics move or bounce across the screen.
- ✦ Create transparency effects. You can superimpose titles over backgrounds or use color, such as blue or green, to mask the background from one image so that you can superimpose a new background.
- ✦ Edit sound. Premiere enables you to cut and assemble audio clips as well as create sophisticated audio effects, such as cross fades and pans.
- ✦ Create transitions. Premiere can create simple dissolves from one scene to another, as well as a host of sophisticated transition effects, such as page curl and curtain wipes.
- ✦ Output files in a variety of digital formats. Premiere can output QuickTime and Video for Windows files, which can be viewed directly in other programs, as well as streamed over the Web. Premiere also features Web-specific file formats, such as animated GIF. You can also use Premiere's Advanced RealMedia Export command to export your clips to RealVideo format for the Web.
- ✦ Output files to videotape.
- ✦ Output Edit Decision Lists. Edit Decision Lists can be used by professional production houses to recreate your digital production on videotape.

Figure 1-1 shows frames from a short Premiere project called America and the Timeline that represents it.

Figure 1-1: Frames from a Premiere project with its Timeline

How Premiere Works

To understand the Premiere production process, you need a basic understanding of the steps involved in creating a conventional videotape production in which the production footage is *not* digitized. In traditional, or *linear*, video production, all production elements are transferred to videotape. During the editing process, the final production is electronically edited onto one final or *program* videotape. Even though computers are used while editing, the linear or analog nature of videotape makes the process very time-consuming; during the actual editing session, videotape must be loaded and unloaded from tape or cassette machines. Time is wasted as producers simply wait for videotape machines to reach the correct editing point. The production is usually assembled sequentially. If you want to go back to a previous scene and replace it with one that is shorter or longer, all subsequent scenes must be rerecorded to the program reel.

Nonlinear video-editing programs such as Premiere have revolutionized the entire process of video editing. Digital video and Premiere eliminate many of the time-consuming production chores of traditional editing. When using Premiere, you don't need to hunt for tapes or to load and remove them from tape machines. When producers use Premiere, all production elements are digitized to disk. An icon in Premiere's Project window represents each element in a production, whether it is a video clip, a sound clip, or a still image. The final production is represented by icons in a window called the Timeline. The focal point of the Timeline are its video and audio *tracks*, which appear as parallel bars that stretch from left to right across the timeline. When you need to use a video clip, sound clip, or still image, you simply click it in the Project window and drag it to a track in the Timeline window. You can place the items of your production down sequentially, or drag them anywhere to different tracks. As you work, you can access any portion of your production by clicking in the desired portion in the Timeline window with the mouse. You can also use the mouse to click either the beginning or end of a clip and shorten or extend the clip's duration.

To fine-tune your edits, you can view and edit the clips frame by frame in the Timeline window. You can also set in and out points in the Clip or Monitor window. Setting an *in point* affects where a clip starts playing, and setting an *out point* affects where a clip stops playing. Because all clips are digitized (and no videotape is involved), Premiere can quickly adjust the final production as you edit.

The following list summarizes some of the digital-editing magic that you can perform in Premiere by simply dragging clips in the Timeline:

- **Rolling edit.** As you click and drag to add frames to the clip in the Timeline, Premiere automatically subtracts from the frames in the next clip. As you click and drag to remove frames, Premiere automatically adds back frames from the next clip in the Timeline.
- **Ripple edit.** As you add or subtract frames, Premiere automatically adds to or subtracts from the entire program's duration.
- **Slip edit.** Dragging a clip to the left or right automatically changes in and out points without changing the program duration.
- **Slide edit.** Dragging a clip to the left or right keeps its duration intact but changes the in or out points of the preceding or succeeding clip.

Cross-Reference Chapters 5 and 10 both provide in-depth discussion of Premiere editing techniques.

As you work, you can easily preview edits, special effects, and transitions. Changing edits and effects is often a simple matter of changing in and out points. There's no hunting down the right videotape or waiting for the production to be reassembled on tape. When all of your editing is completed, you can export the file to videotape or create a new digital file in one of several formats. You can export it as many times as you want, in as many different file formats as you want. Furthermore, if you want to add more special effects to your Premiere projects, you can easily import them into Adobe After Effects. You can also integrate your Premiere movie into a Web page using Adobe GoLive.

Cross-Reference Adobe After Effects is covered in Chapter 21 and 24. Adobe GoLive is discussed in Chapter 17.

Your First Video Production

The following sections provide a Quickstart tutorial that leads you step by step through the basics of video production in Premiere.

In this project, you'll create a video project called Nite Out. Figure 1-2 shows frames of the production in Premiere's Timeline window. The production begins with a title created in Adobe Title Designer, viewed over an opening scene of people walking in the city. After a few seconds, a dissolve transitions to the scene of diners in a restaurant. Soon the dining scene dissolves into one showing kitchen workers preparing food. The project ends with another title superimposed over the last scene.

Figure 1-2: Scenes from the Nite Out project

Starting a Premiere project

A Premiere digital video production is called a *project* instead of a video production. The reason for this is that Premiere not only enables you to create the production, but it enables you to create and store titles, transitions, and effects. Thus, the file you work in is much more than just a production — it's truly a project.

Your first step in creating a digital video production in Premiere is to create a new project. Here's how:

1. **To load Premiere, double-click the Adobe Premiere icon.** When you load Premiere, the program automatically assumes that you want to create a new project.
2. **To create a new project, double-click the Premiere icon to load the program.** Windows users can also choose Premiere in the Adobe Group after clicking the Start button. If Premiere is already loaded, you can create a new project by choosing File ➪ New Project.

Note

If Premiere is already loaded and you already have a project onscreen, you need to close that project because you can only have one project open at a time.

Specifying Project Settings

Before you can start importing files and editing, you must set certain options. The Load Project Settings dialog box appears whenever you create a new project (see Figure 1-3). This dialog box enables you to quickly use predetermined video and audio settings. The most important project settings determine the frame rate (frames per second) and the frame size (viewing area) of your project as well as how the digital video will be compressed.

Cross-Reference

For a detailed description of project settings, see Chapter 3.

As a general rule, you normally choose project settings that match your source footage. For this example, you can choose whether to create a project from digital video (DV) footage with a frame size of 720 x 480 at 29.9 frames a second, or from footage that consumes less hard drive space. This footage has a frame size of 160 x 120 pixels and plays at 25 frames per second. If you're running Premiere at the minimum system requirements, you may want to create the production with these files.

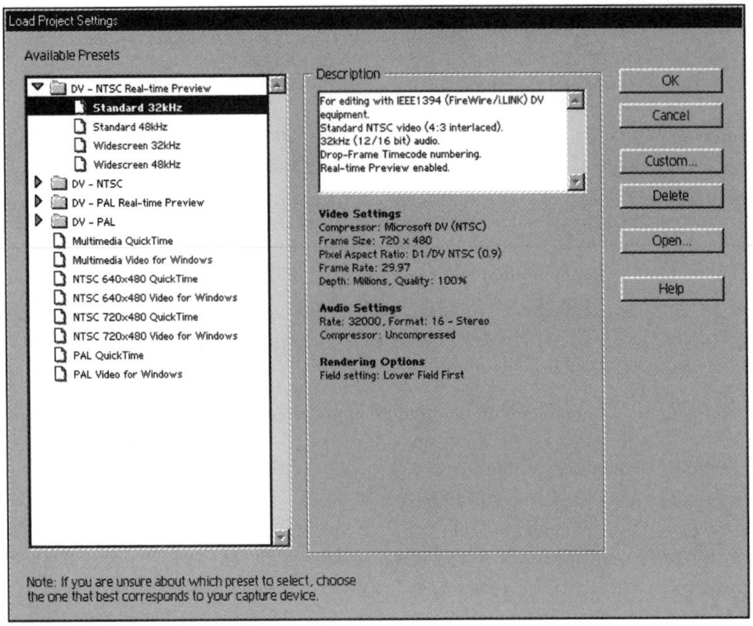

Figure 1-3: Use the Load Project Settings dialog box to pick project presets.

- If you want to use the DV files, click the DV– NTSC Real-time preview folder and then click the Standard 32kHz choice. This setting is used for footage shot with a DV camera. It adheres to the National Television System Committee (NTSC) standards used for broadcast TV in the United States.

- If you want to use the lower-resolution files, click the Multimedia QuickTime choice. After you select the QuickTime preset, click OK to create the new project. The footage files that we use are 160 x 120 and play at 25 frames per second. Thus, your next step is to change the project settings to match the frame size and frame rate of the video footage. To do this, choose Project ➪ Project Settings ➪ Video. In the Project Settings dialog box, set the frame size to in the horizontal field (h) to 160. Automatically Premiere enters 120 into the vertical resolution field (v) because the default setting is for a 4:3 aspect ratio. Next, change the frame rate field to 25. After you've made the changes, click OK. Premiere warns you that the Video Settings have been changed. It also mentions that preview files will be deleted. Don't worry about this. Simply click OK.

After you've selected the preset, click OK to create the new project. Premiere then opens the Project, Timeline, and Monitor windows, along with two palette groups.

Setting a Workspace

When you start Premiere for the first time, a dialog box opens in which you must choose your default workspace. After you make your choice, Premiere sets up windows and palettes geared to your specific needs. You must choose between A/B Editing and Single-Track Editing.

If you are new to Premiere or don't have any editing experience, your best bet is to choose Edit: A/B workspace. The examples in this chapter feature the A/B Editing workspace. This workspace assumes that you will often edit by dragging clips to the Timeline with your computer's mouse. In this workspace, the Video 1A and Video 1B tracks offer a visual representation of how clips overlap when transitions are created. In this workspace, your program plays in the Monitor window in Single View. In Single View, one program monitor is displayed.

Users with professional editing experience who plan to make sophisticated edits may wish to choose the Single-Track Editing workspace from the Timeline pop-up menu. In this workspace, tracks Video 1A and 1B are combined into one track. In this workspace, the Monitor window opens in Dual View. In Dual View, source clips appear in the left side of the Monitor window; program material placed in the Timeline appears in the right side of the window. No matter which choice you make, you always change the workspace by choosing Window ➪ Workspace ➪ A/B Editing or Window ➪ Workspace ➪ Single Track Editing.

Importing production elements

You can use video, audio, and still images in your Premiere projects, as long as they are in a digital format. Table 1-1 lists the major file formats that Premiere supports. All media footage, or *clips*, you want to use in your project must first be saved to disk. Even if your video is stored on a digital camcorder, it still must be transferred to disk. Premiere can capture the digital video clips and automatically store them in your projects. Analog media such as motion picture film and VHS videotape must first be digitized before Premiere can use it. In this case, Premiere, in conjunction with a capture board, can capture your clips directly into a project.

Cross-Reference

For more information about capturing video and audio, see Chapter 4.

Table 1-1
Supported Files in Adobe Premiere

Media	***File Formats***
Video	QuickTime (MOV) and Video for Windows (AVI)
Audio	AIFF, WAV, AVI, and MOV
Still images, and Sequence	TIF, JPEG, BMP (Windows only), GIF, PICT, (Mac only), Filmstrip, Illustrator, and Photoshop

After the Premiere windows open, you're ready to import the various graphic and sound elements that will comprise your digital video production. All the items that you import are stored in the Project window. An icon represents each item. Next to the icon, Premiere displays whether the item is a video clip, an audio clip, or a graphic.

When importing files into Premiere, you can choose whether to import one file, multiple files (by pressing and holding the Shift key), or an entire folder. If desired, you can even import one project into another, using the File ⇨ Import ⇨ Project command.

Here's how to load the production elements for the Nite Out project:

1. **Choose File ⇨ Import ⇨ Folder.**
2. **Open the Tutorial Projects folder on the *Adobe Premiere 6.5 Bible* CD-ROM.** If you want to load the DV files, select the Nite Out folder in the Chapter 1 folder and then click OK. If you want to load the multimedia files that consume less hard disk space, select the Multimedia folder. The DV filenames end with an *f* and the multimedia files end with a *p*.
3. **Double-click the Nite Out or the Multimedia folder in the Project window.** If you loaded the multimedia files, you need to import the sound clip from the Nite Out folder by choosing File ⇨ Import File.
4. **Assign an alias to each clip.** You'll then be able choose the clip using its alias rather than its filename. To create an alias, click the clip in the Project window and then choose Clip ⇨ Set Clip Alias. In the Set Clip Name Alias dialog box, type the name for the clip. Here are the filenames for the low-res and DV clips and the aliases to use. As you rename the clips, Premiere rearranges them alphabetically:
    - Name the audio clip (705001.aif) **Background Music.**
    - Name clip 705008 **Diners.**
    - Name clip 7005009 **Chefs.**
    - Name clip 705029 **Walkers.**

Figure 1-4 shows the Project window with all the low-resolution clips needed to create the Nite Out project clip.

The Nite Out project requires the following files:

- ✦ A video clip showing shadows of people walking in the city (Walkers)
- ✦ A video clip of people out in a restaurant (Diners)
- ✦ A video clip of chefs working in a restaurant (Chefs)
- ✦ Two title files created using templates from Adobe Title Designer
- ✦ A sound clip of background music

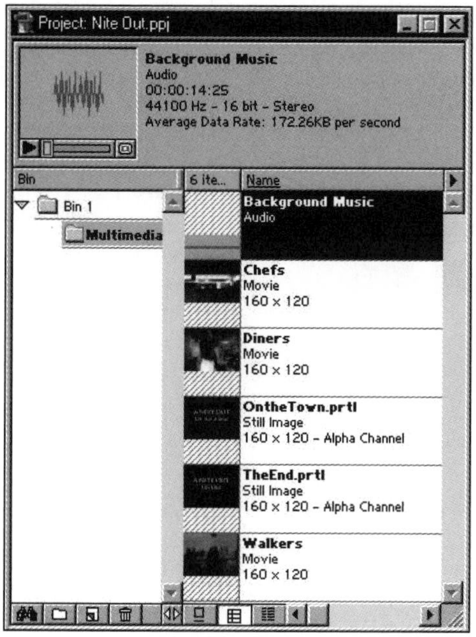

Figure 1-4: The Project palette with the items needed to create the Nite Out project

Cross-Reference

Creating titles in Premiere is discussed in Chapter 8.

Viewing clips in the Project window

Before you begin assembling your production, you may want to view a clip or graphic, or listen to an audio track. You can obtain a thumbnail preview of any of the clips in the Project window by clicking the clip. The preview appears at the upper-left corner of the Project window. If you are previewing a video or audio clip, a small triangle (Play button) appears below the preview. Click the Play button to see a preview of a video clip or to hear an audio clip. If you prefer, you can click and drag the slider next to the Play button to gradually view the clip.

Note

Double-clicking the clip in the Project window opens the clip in the Clip window. You can preview the clip here by clicking Play (black triangle).

Using a storyboard

Before diving headfirst into a video production, consider planning your production first by creating a *storyboard.* A storyboard is a simple visual representation of your production, often resembling a series of cartoons with descriptions underneath the visuals.

Premiere's storyboard feature enables you to import clips into a storyboard window or to drag clips into a Storyboard window to help you in your pre-production planning. Figure 1-5 shows a simple storyboard we created for our *Nite Out* project. Viewing it should give you an idea of how the production will be edited.

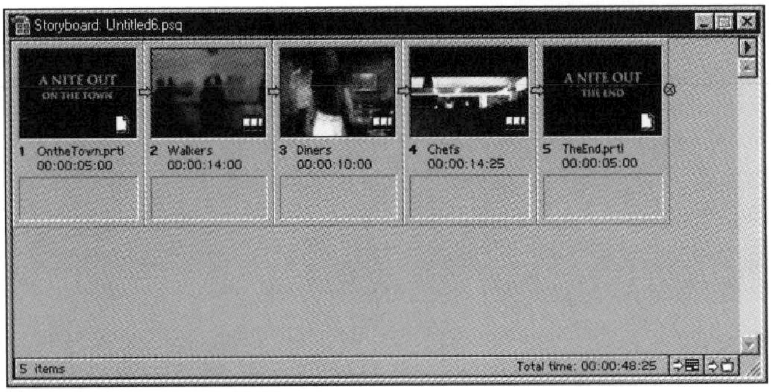

Figure 1-5: Using a storyboard can help in your pre-production planning.

Here's how to create your own storyboard:

1. **Choose File ➪ New ➪ Storyboard.**
2. **Drag clips from the Project window into the Storyboard window.** If clips haven't been loaded yet, you can load them directly into the Storyboard window by choosing File ➪ Import File or File ➪ Import Folder. At any point, you can click and drag in the Storyboard window to rearrange the graphics.
3. **To add descriptive text to the storyboard, double-click in the white rectangular area below each image.**
4. **To save your storyboard, choose File ➪ Save from the Storyboard window.**

Tip You can have Premiere automatically place the items from the Storyboard window to the Timeline window by choosing Automate to Timeline from the Storyboard options menu (the right-pointing arrow in the upper-right corner of the Storyboard window).

Assembling production elements

After you import all of your production elements, you need to place them in the Timeline window so that you can start assembling your project. The Timeline window displays a visual overview of your entire production. Using the mouse, you can edit, rearrange, and create transitions in the Timeline window.

Placing clips in the Timeline

To move an item from the Project window to the Timeline window, simply click it in the Project window and then drag it to a track in the Timeline window. The item then appears in the Timeline as an icon. The duration of the clip or graphic is represented by the length of the clip in the Timeline.

Arranging clips in the Timeline

You'll spend a great deal of time positioning clips in the Timeline while editing your production. Premiere's Selection and Range Select tools help you assemble your program's clips in the order you want.

Here's how to work select and move clips:

- **Single clip.** Click the Selection tool (the arrow icon in the upper-left corner of the Timeline). Next, click in the middle of the clip in the Timeline. To quickly activate the Selection tool, press V on your keyboard. With the clip selected, click and drag it to the desired location.
- **Multiple clips.** Click the Range Select tool (the empty dotted-line square icon in the toolbox location to the right of the Selection tool in the toolbox). Next, click and drag over the clips that you want to select. Press M to cycle through the Selection tools to select the Range Select tool using your keyboard.

Figure 1-6 displays the Timeline window for the *Nite Out* project. The Title appears in the Video 2 track. We put it here because it enables us to create a transparency effect in which we fade in the title text over background video. The Walkers video clip appears in track Video 1A. Notice that the next clip (the Diners clip) appears in the Video 1B track. These two tracks are used to help show transitions that include elements from tracks Video 1A and Video 1B. Between the two tracks is a transition track to which transitions are dragged from the Transitions palette. The project also ends with a transition to a scene of chefs working in a kitchen, before the final title appears.

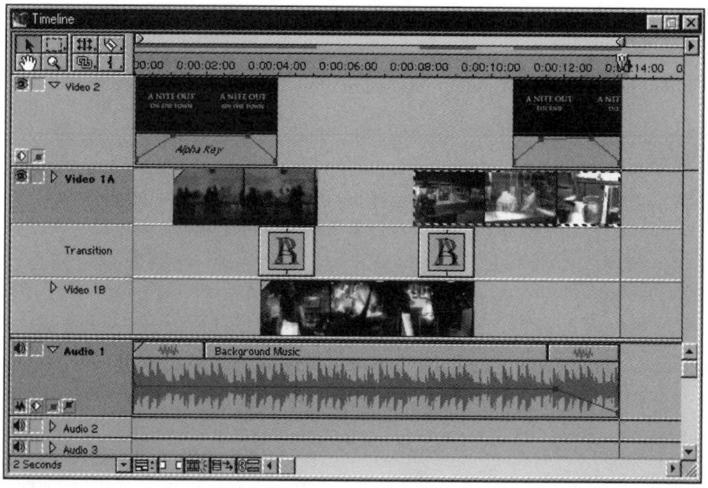

Figure 1-6: The Timeline window with the items for the Nite Out video clip

Changing the time zoom level

Most Premiere users create their video projects at 15 to 30 frames per second. Viewing all of these frames on the Timeline quickly consumes Timeline space. As you work, you'll probably want to switch time intervals back and forth between viewing individual frames and viewing frames by seconds.

To switch time intervals on the Timeline, click the Timeline Zoom level pop-up menu at the lower-left corner of the Timeline. Figure 1-7 shows the Timeline Zoom level pop-up menu. To see each frame in the production as an individual unit on the Timeline, click 1 Frame in the pop-up menu. To switch time intervals to view 1-second intervals, choose 1 Second in the pop-up menu. Choosing 1 Second gives you a good sense of how long each clip is and how long transitions will be. When 1 Second is chosen, each tick mark on the Timeline represents half a second.

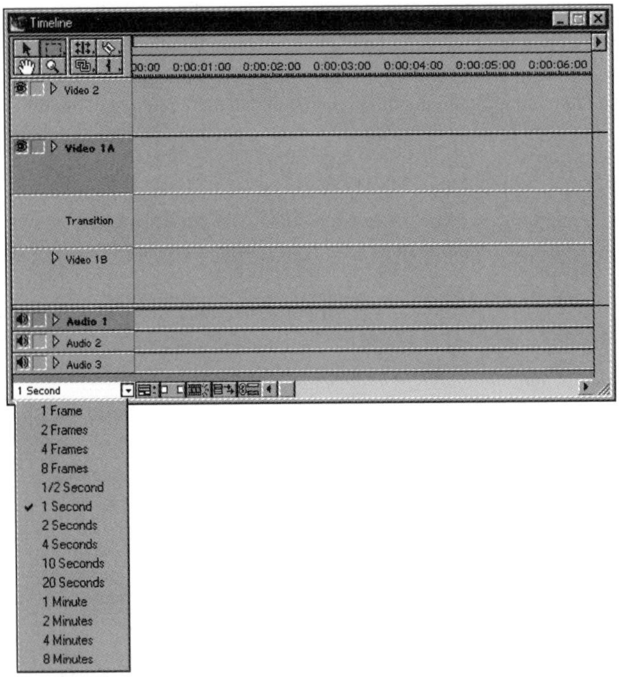

Figure 1-7: The Timeline window with the Zoom level pop-up menu

Tip

You can also use the Navigator palette to change the Timeline Zoom level. See Chapter 2 to learn about the Navigator palette.

Adding the title to the Timeline

Start the production process by adding the opening title to the Timeline. The title includes an *alpha channel*, which allows the background video to be seen beneath the title. The title was created from a template in Adobe Title Designer. (To access Adobe Title Designer, choose File ➪ New ➪ Title.) We placed the title in the Video 2 track because it enables you to easily fade in the text over the video in lower tracks. The diagonal line immediately below the track represents the fade-in effect.

Cross-Reference

See Chapter 8 to learn more about Adobe Title Designer.

The following steps explain how to add the title to the Timeline window, fading it in and out:

1. **Click the Nite Out title in the Project window and drag it into the Video 2 track.**
2. **Reduce the length of the title to 4 seconds by clicking and dragging left on the right end of the title.** Use the time readout at the top of the Timeline as a guide.
3. **Expand the Video 2 track to view its opacity control.** To expand the track, click the Display Opacity Rubberbands icon (small triangle at the left of track Video 2). The red rubberband line enables you to control the title text's transparency.
4. **Click the red line about a second into the title.** This creates an anchor point.
5. **Drag the left end point down to the bottom of the track (see Figure 1-8).**
6. **Repeat Steps 4 and 5 a second before the title ends.**

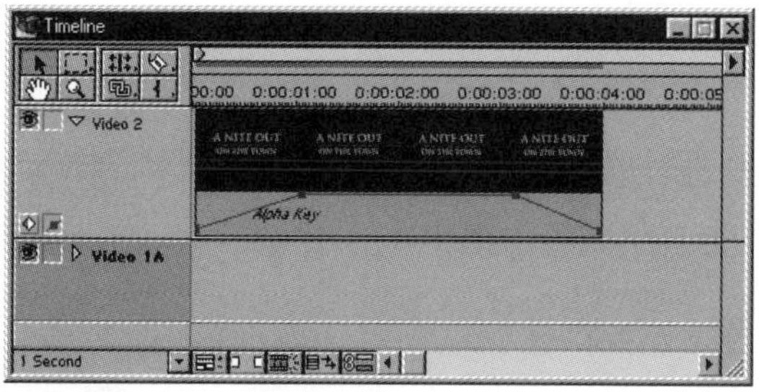

Figure 1-8: The Opacity rubberband controls the fade-in of the title text.

Note

To remove a control point, click and drag it off the red rubberband line.

7. **Save your work by choosing File ➪ Save.** Name your file **Nite Out**.

Note

If you don't see tracks Video 1A and Video 1B, your workspace is probably set to Single Track Editing. To view the Video 1A and 1B tracks, choose Window ➪ Workspace ➪ A/B Editing.

Trimming clips in the Timeline window

You can edit a clip in several ways. We'll start simply editing the first clip by clicking and dragging its out point in the Timeline. Before editing a clip, you may want to view it.

To view a video clip, do one of the following:

✦ Double-click the video clip in the Project window. When the Clip window appears, click the Play button to view the clip.

✦ Double-click the video clip in the Timeline window. In the Clip window, click the Play button to view the clip.

The following steps explain how to add the first video clip to the Timeline window: The first clip is the Walkers clip. If you haven't viewed the clip, you can play a thumbnail version of it in the project window. Click it in the Project window and then click the left arrow button at the top of the Clip window. Also note that the clip is 14 seconds long. We only need 4 seconds of it.

1. **Drag the Walkers clip from the Project window into the Video 1A track.** Position the clip so that it starts about at the vertical line where the title fade-in ends — about 1 second on the Timeline.
2. **Change the zoom level to 2 seconds.** When you place the clip, Premiere sends you to its end point on the Timeline. Zooming to 2 seconds makes editing a bit easier.
3. **Position the mouse pointer at the end of the clip.** The cursor changes to a bracket.
4. **Click and drag to the left to shorten the clip.** Make the clip about 4 seconds long so that it ends on the 9-second mark (00:00:09:00) on the Timeline.

Previewing in the Monitor window

To look at the video production so far, you can preview the program in the Monitor window. Make sure that the Monitor window is open by choosing Window ➪ Show Monitor (see Figure 1-9).

Click the Play In to Out button at the bottom of the Monitor window. As soon as you click, the video clip rewinds and begins playing in the window. To stop the clip, press the spacebar or click the Stop button.

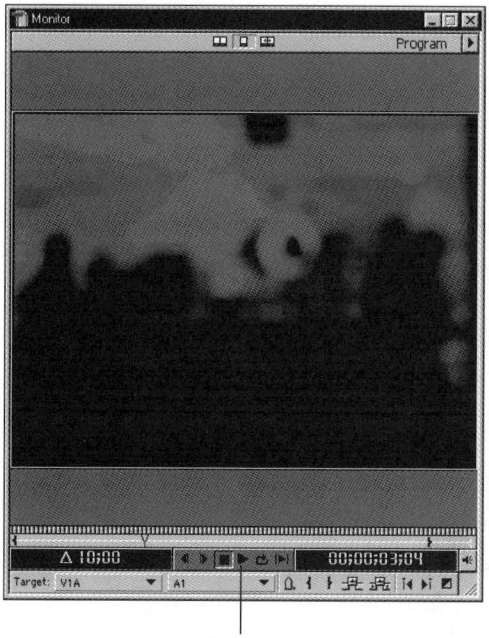

Figure 1-9: The Monitor window's Play button

Editing in the Clip window

The clip window provides precise controls for editing clips. Using the Clip window, you can easily navigate to specific frames and then mark in or out points. After you apply the in and out points, you can drag the clip directly to the Timeline. If the clip is already in the Timeline, it adjusts to the settings used in the clip window.

Here you'll set the in and out points in the Clip window. To learn about the different ways to edit a video clip, see Chapters 5 and 10.

1. **Drag the Diners clip to track Video 1B in the Timeline.** Place it below the end of the previous clip. Place the clip in 1B, so you can eventually create a transition between tracks Video 1A and Video 1B.
2. **Position the Diners clip so it begins about two seconds before the Walkers clip ends.** This should be on the 6-second tick mark on the Timeline.
3. **Double-click the clip in the Timeline window.** This opens the clip in the Clip window, shown in Figure 1-10.

Note

Clips open in the Clip window, when the Monitor window is set to Single View (the default setting for the A/B Workspace). If the Monitor is set to Dual View, double-clicking a clip opens it in the left (Source) side of the Monitor window. The button controls in the Source section of the Monitor window are very similar to those in the Clip window.

Figure 1-10: You can use the Clip window to edit clips.

4. **Play the clip by clicking the Play button.** The scene eventually shows a waitress handing out menus. Before you edit the clip's in and out points, you need to go to the precise frame that you want to edit.

5. **To move to specific areas in the clip, click in the tread area below the video window.** After you click, the scrub tool (Triangle icon) moves to the point that you clicked. To gradually move through the frames with the mouse, click and

drag the Scrub tool, or click and drag in the tread area. To forward or backward move frame-by-frame, click either of the two arrow buttons to the left of the Stop button.

6. **Now click and drag in the tread area or drag the Scrub tool to the right to move toward the end of the clip.** At about 6 seconds and 2 frames, the scene switches to a long shot of the waitress handing out menus.
7. **Either by clicking and dragging or by entering the precise location using your keyboard, position the clip at 00;00;06;24.**
8. **Click the Mark Out button (see Figure 1-10).**

Note

To clear an in or out point, press Option/Alt, while clicking the in or out point.

9. **To edit the clip, click the Apply button.** The Apply button appears in the Clip window after you click the in point button. After you click, you'll see the length of the clip change in the Timeline window.

Note

Although you edited the clip in the Timeline, the original clip in the Project window remains the same. At any point in time, you can re-edit the clip to return the missing parts.

Creating a transition

Now view your production by previewing it in the Monitor window. To start the preview from the beginning of the Timeline, click the Play In to Out button in the Monitor window. As you watch the preview, notice that the cut from the Walkers clip to the Diners clip is quite abrupt. To smooth the flow of the production, you can add a *transition* between the two tracks.

Cross-Reference

For more information on using transitions, turn to Chapter 7.

Here's how to add a Cross Dissolve transition to your project:

1. **Open the Transitions options by choosing Window ⇨ Show Transitions palette, if it is not already open.**
2. **In the Transitions palette, open the Dissolve folder by double-clicking it.**
3. **Preview the Cross Dissolve effect by double-clicking it.** The Cross Dissolve Settings dialog box appears (see Figure 1-11). An animated preview is shown in the lower-right corner. You can also create your own preview by clicking and dragging the slider beneath the Start area. Click Cancel to close the dialog box.

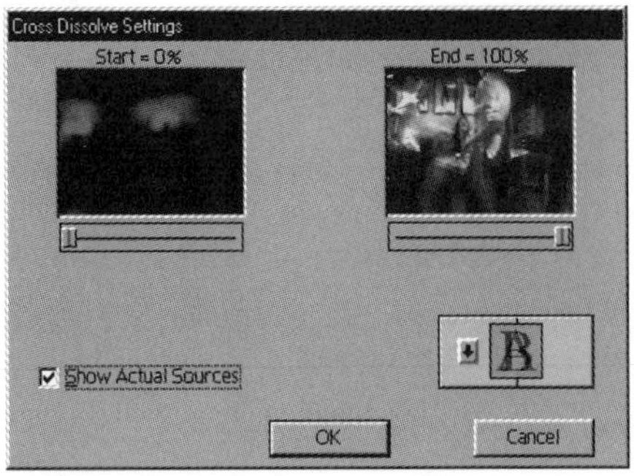

Figure 1-11: The Cross Dissolve Settings dialog box previews the curtain effect.

4. **To place the transition onscreen, click and drag it to the Transition track.** Place it at the point where the clip in the Video 1A track ends, and the clip in track Video 1B begins.

Previewing the transition

You can create a manual preview of the transition effect by double-clicking the Transition icon in the Transition palette. In the Cross Dissolve dialog box, select the Show Actual Sources check box. When the Show Actual Sources check box is selected, the Walking clip appears at the left side of the dialog box. Click the slider beneath the Walking clip, and you'll see the dissolve transition to the Diners clip.

Premiere 6.5 includes a Real-Time Preview feature that enables you to view transitions and video effects as you work. If you are working with the DV files and chose the project preset with Real-Time preview, press Enter to preview your project. If you are working with the Multimedia files, or if you didn't see the transition, Premiere needs to *render* your work area. To render the work area and preview it, press Shift+Return/Enter or choose Timeline ⇨ Render Work Area.

Editing the Chefs clip

Next you will add the Chefs clip to the program and edit it in the Clip window.

1. **Click the Chefs clip in the Project window and then drag it to Timeline track Video 2A.**
2. **Double-click the Chefs clip with the Selection tool to display the Clip window.**
3. **Set the in point.** Click and drag in the *scrubbing area* (the area below the preview and above the Play button) to choose a frame about little more than 3 seconds into the clip. Click the Mark In button.
4. **Set the out point.** Click and drag in the scrubbing area to find a point about 4 seconds into the clip. Watch the time readout at the bottom-right of the window to pick the frame. When you have found the frame you want, click the Mark Out button.

5. **To complete the edit, click the Apply button.**

Adding another dissolve

Now create another transition — this time between the Diners clip and the Chefs clip.

1. **Open the Dissolve folder in the Transition palette.**
2. **Drag the cross-dissolve transition into the Transition channel between tracks Video 1A and Video 1B.**
3. **Use the Selection tool to tighten the edits so that about one second of the flag appears during the beginning of the dissolve, and one second of the cloud appears at the end of the dissolve.** If desired, you can stretch the length of the dissolve by clicking and dragging on either edge of the Dissolve Clip icon.

Adding the last title

Your next step is to add the end title to the Video 2 track.

1. **Drag the TheEnd title image from the Project window to Video 2 track.** Position the Title clip so that it begins about 2 seconds before the end of the Chefs clip in the Video 1A track.
2. **Drag the clip's end point to make its duration 3 seconds long or select the Title and choose Clip ⇨ Duration.** In the Clip Duration Dialog box, set the display to 00;00;03;00 and click OK.
3. **Fade the title text in and out as you did for the opening title.** Use Figure 1-6 as a reference.

Previewing the fade-in

Now, you only need to preview the fade-in effect, without previewing the entire production. As mentioned earlier, the yellow bar above the Timeline indicates just which area will be previewed. As you work, you can preview just the new effects that you want to see.

Here's how to change the area that is previewed:

1. **Scroll in the Timeline so that only the title area appears in the middle of the window.**
2. **Double-click in the Timeline preview area (the yellow area above the Timeline).** The yellow Timeline preview area shrinks to the width of the current window.
3. **Using the mouse, drag the left end of the Timeline preview to the left so that it begins just before the Title clip appears in the Timeline.**
4. **Drag the right end of the Timeline preview so that it ends just after the end of the Title sequence.**

5. **Press the Return/Enter key or choose Timeline ➪ Preview.** If you don't see the transparency effect, render the area by pressing Shift+Return/Enter.

Adding and fading in the audio track

Now that the majority of editing is complete, it's time to add the audio track. Fortunately, the Timeline treats audio much the same as it treats video. To place the audio track in the Timeline, follow these steps:

1. **Listen to the Background Music clip by double-clicking it in the Project window.** After the clip opens in the Monitor window, click the Play button.
2. **Drag the Background Music clip from the Project window to the Audio 1 track in the Timeline window.** Line the beginning of the audio track with the beginning of the video track.
3. **Expand the Audio 1 track by clicking the triangle icon at the far left of the track.**
4. **Click the Display Volume Rubberbands icon (the red square).**
5. **Click the red rubberband line to create an anchor point about two seconds before the clip ends.**
6. **Click and drag the end of the red rubberband downward so that it gradually moves down.**
7. **Preview your project to see the production and hear the fade-out.** If you want to fine-tune the effect, use the mouse to edit the Rubber Band icon beneath the audio track.

Cross-Reference

See Chapter 6 to learn more about Premiere's audio features.

Fine-tuning the project

The project you've worked on is a simple introduction to editing in premiere. Feel free to enhance, change, and re-edit as you desire. If you want, create a fade up from black or fade out to black. You can create pure black video and place it in a video track. To create black, choose File ➪ New ➪ Black Video. This command places the black video clip into the Project window. From there you can drag it into the time line. If you want to fade in or out, place it in track Video 2.

Exporting your first movie

When you finish editing your movie, you can export it in a variety of different formats. Premiere enables you to export movies in video formats such as QuickTime, RealVideo, and Advanced Windows Media, as well as formats for DVD discs. The export format for your project was set when you created your project. (The export format was specified by the preset you originally chose. You can quickly view the export format and other settings by choosing Project ➪ Settings View). However, as the next section explains, you can change these settings before you export the final movie.

Exporting a Windows Media file

If you are a Windows user, you may wish to export your project in Windows Media format. This format can be read by most Windows users, and can be used for projects that appear on the Web. To export your movie in Windows media format, follow these steps

1. **Choose File ➪ Export Timeline ➪ Advanced Windows Media.** The Advanced Windows Media Export Plug-in Dialog box appears (see Figure 1-12).
2. **Click a profile.** For example, if you want to create your project for a 56 Kbps modem, click that profile. If you want to output the project for a Local Area Network, choose one of those profiles.
3. **Select a destination folder in which to store the finished Windows Media file.** In the Destination section, click the button with three dots on it. This opens the Save As dialog box where you can navigate to the folder area where you wish to save your file.
4. **Name your file and then click Save.**
5. **When you return to the Windows Media dialog box, click OK.**

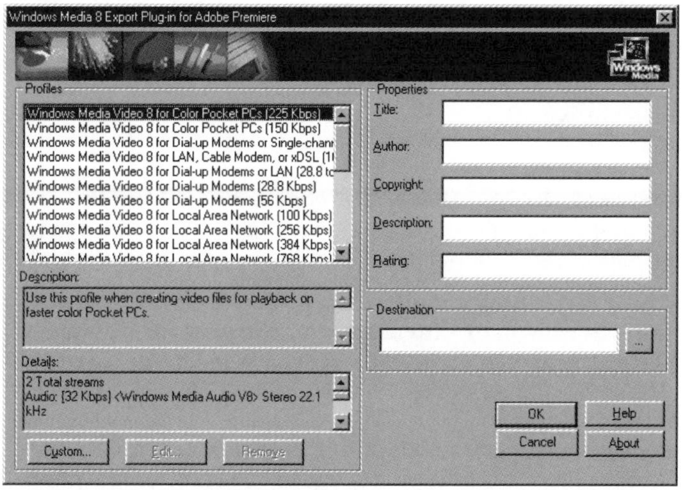

Figure 1-12: This plug-in optimizes your finished Windows Media movie file for your target audience.

Exporting a QuickTime movie

Both Mac and Windows users can export Premiere projects as QuickTime movies. QuickTime is widely used on the Web and can be imported into other programs such as Macromedia Director and Macromedia Flash. Depending upon the final destination of your project, you may want to change the frame size and frame rate of our video before exporting. For example, if you want to export a file composed of DV footage to a multimedia project, you'll probably want to reduce the DV frame size from 720 x 480 to a smaller size that fits comfortably into your production.

Here are the steps for exporting your project as a QuickTime movie:

1. **Choose File ➪ Export Timeline ➪ Movie.** The Export Movie dialog box appears.
2. **To view export settings in the Export Movie Settings dialog box, click the Settings button.** If you're a Windows user, choose QuickTime from the File Type drop-down list, as shown in Figure 1-13.

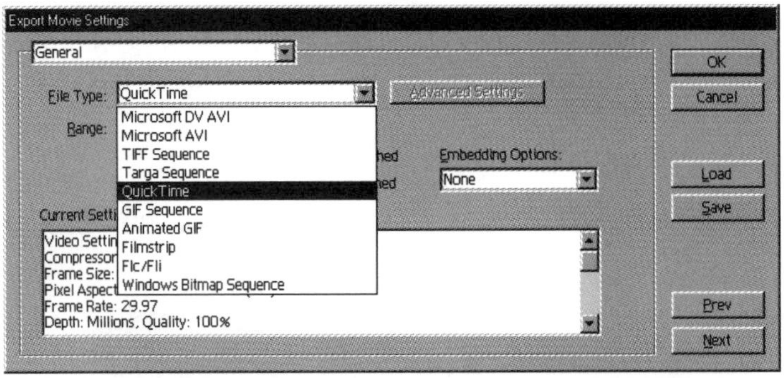

Figure 1-13: Windows users can switch to QuickTime format in the File Type drop-down list.

3. **To switch frame size and frame rate, choose Video from the drop-down list at the top of the dialog box.** The Video Settings dialog box appears. These settings are covered in detail in Chapter 3.
4. **Because you're creating a multimedia project that will play on a computer, select either Sorenson or Cinepak as the compressor.** Optionally, you can change the frame size to 320 x 240 and change the frame rate to 15. If you will be outputting the file for computers with older CD-ROM drives, you will need to lower the data rate to about 250 Kbps. Doing this slows the data rate to prevent frames from being dropped during playback.
5. **After you make your changes, click OK.** Premiere Returns you to the Export Movie dialog box.

6. **In the Export Settings dialog box, type a name for your file.**
7. **Click OK.** Premiere creates the export file and opens it in the Clip window for viewing.

Summary

This chapter gave you a chance to experiment with the basic concepts of editing in Premiere. You learned how to do the following:

- Create a project.
- Add clips to the Timeline.
- Edit clips in the Clip window and in the Timeline.
- Create transitions.
- Preview your production.
- Export your production.

✦ ✦ ✦

CHAPTER 2

Premiere Basics

✦ ✦ ✦ ✦

In This Chapter

Touring Premiere's windows

Touring palettes

Premiere's menu commands

✦ ✦ ✦ ✦

The Adobe Premiere user interface is a combination of a video-editing studio and an electronic image-editing studio. If you're familiar with film, video editing, or audio editing, you'll feel right at home working within Premiere's Project, Monitor, and Audio windows. If you've worked with such programs as Adobe After Effects, Adobe Live Motion, Macromedia Flash, or Macromedia Director, Premiere's Timeline, digital tools, and palettes will seem familiar. If you're completely new to video editing and computers, don't worry; Premiere palettes, windows, and menus are efficiently designed to get you up and running quickly.

To help get you started, this chapter provides an overview of Premiere windows, menus, and palettes. Consider it a thorough introduction to the program's workspace and a handy reference for planning and producing your own digital video productions.

Premiere's Windows

After you first launch Premiere, several windows automatically appear on-screen, each vying for your attention. Why do you need more than one window open at once? A video production is a multifaceted undertaking. In one production, you may need to capture video, edit video, and create titles, transitions, and special effects. Premiere windows help keep these tasks separated and organized for you.

This section provides an overview of the windows that enable you to create the various elements of your digital video project: the Project, Timeline, and Audio Mixer windows. The History, Navigator, Video/Audio Effects, and Transitions palettes float above all other windows. We discuss them separately in the section about Premiere palettes.

Manipulating Premiere windows

Although the Premiere program's primary windows open automatically on-screen from time to time, you may want to close one of them. To close a window, simply click its Close box (Windows users: click the close window *X* icon). If you try to close the Project window, Premiere assumes that you want to close the entire project and prompts you to save your work before closing. If you want to open the Timeline, Monitor, or Audio Mixer windows, choose the Window menu and then click the desired Window name.

The size and elements that actually appear in the Project, Timeline, and Monitor windows can be changed to suit your specific production needs. For example, you can choose to show filenames instead of icons in the Timeline. To change default settings, choose Window ⇨ Window Options. Then choose whether you want to change options for the Project, Timeline, Monitor, or Audio windows.

If you have your windows and palettes set up in specific positions at specific sizes, you can save this configuration by choosing Window ⇨ Workspace Save. After you name your workspace and save it, the name of the workspace appears in the Window ⇨ Workspace submenu. Any time you want to use that workspace, simply click its name.

The Project window

If you've ever worked on a project with many video and audio clips as well as other production elements, you'll soon appreciate the Premiere program's Project window, which is shown in Figure 2-1. The Project window provides a quick bird's-eye view of your production elements and enables you to preview a clip right from the Project window.

As you work, Premiere automatically loads items into the Project window. When you import a file, the video and audio clips are automatically loaded into a Project window *bin* (a folder in the Project palette). If you import a folder of clips, Premiere creates a new bin for the clips, using the folder name as the bin name. When you capture sound or video, you can quickly add the captured media to a Project window bin before closing the clip. Later you can create your own bins by clicking the Create Bin button, at which point you can drag production elements from one bin to another. The Create Item button enables you to quickly create a new title or other production element, such as a color matte (covered in Chapter 13) or bars and tone (used to calibrate color and sound when editing).

If you expand the Project window by clicking and dragging, you can add notes and labels to help easily identify bin elements. This capability is particularly helpful when a clip's filename is not descriptive enough, or if you want to rate the quality of different elements.

Figure 2-1: Premiere's Project window stores production elements.

To keep your production materials well organized, you can create bins to store similar elements. For example, you may create a bin for all sound elements, or a bin for all interview clips. If the bin gets stuffed, you can see more elements at one time by switching from the default thumbnail view to list view, which lists each item, but doesn't show a thumbnail image.

Timeline window

The Timeline shown in Figure 2-2 is the foundation of your video production. It provides a graphic and temporal overview of your entire project. Fortunately, the Timeline is not for viewing only—it's interactive. Using your mouse, you can build your production by dragging video and audio clips, graphics, and titles from the Project window to the Timeline. Using Timeline tools, you can arrange, cut, and extend clips. By clicking and dragging the Work Area markers at either end of the Work Area bar—the yellow bar at the top of the Timeline—you specify the portion of the Timeline that Premiere previews or exports. The thin, colored bar beneath the work area bar indicates whether a preview file for the project exists. A red bar indicates no preview, and a green bar indicates that a video preview has been created. If an audio preview exists, a thinner, light-green bar appears.

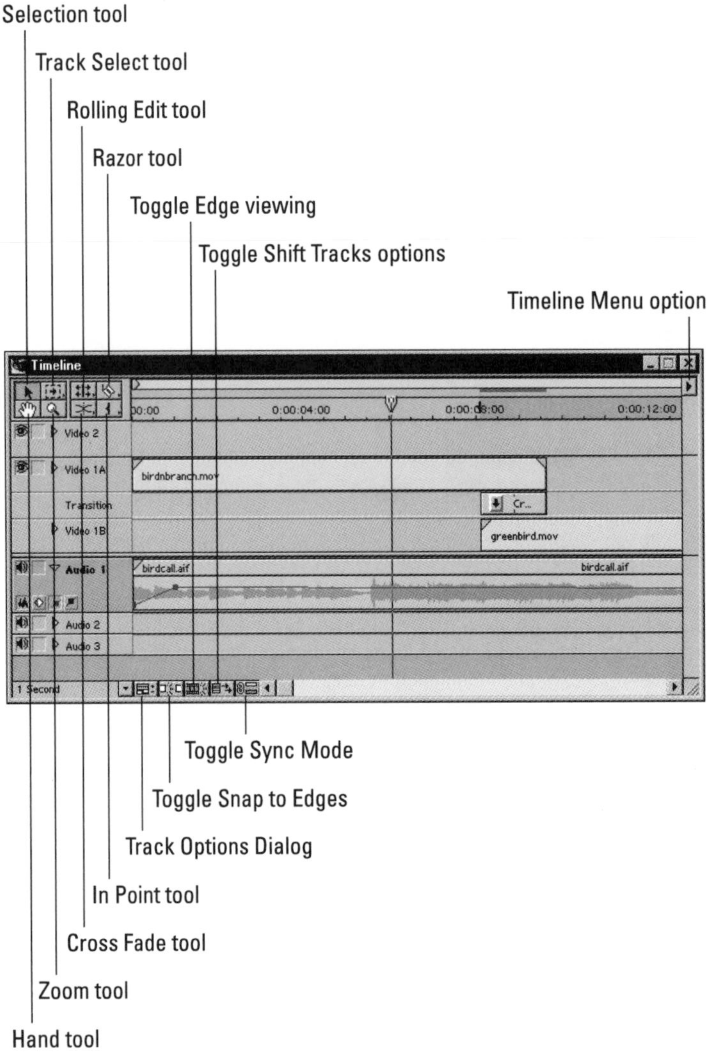

Figure 2-2: The Timeline window provides an overview of your project and enables you to edit clips.

Undoubtedly, the most useful visual metaphor in the Timeline window is its representation of video and audio tracks as parallel bars. Premiere provides multiple, parallel tracks so that you can both preview and conceptualize a production in real time. For instance, parallel video and audio tracks enable you to view video as audio plays. The parallel tracks also enable you to create transparency effects where a portion of one video track can be seen through another. The Video A and Video B tracks can be used for video transitions where one video track dissolves or wipes into another. When you create a transition, a portion of the clip in Video track 1A overlaps a portion of the clip in Video track 1B. Being able to view and control the overlapping area enables you to more easily create and edit transitions.

The Timeline also includes icons for hiding or viewing tracks. Clicking the Eye icon hides a track while you preview your production; clicking it again makes the track visible. Clicking the Speaker icon turns audio tracks on and off. The icons in the upper-left corner are editing tools that you can use to quickly edit scenes. For instance, you can click the Razor Blade tool over a video or audio segment to cut it, and then click the Selection tool to select and move the segments apart.

At the bottom of the window, the Time Zoom Level pop-up menu enables you to change the Timeline's time interval. For example, if you choose one frame as the zoom level, each video frame of your clip appears as a block in the clip. If you want your production to consume less Timeline space, choose to view the Timeline in seconds or minutes.

The other buttons — Track Options Dialog, Toggle Snap to Edges, Toggle Edge Viewing, Toggle Shift Tracks Options, and Toggle Sync Mode — at the bottom left of the window, enable you to change options for syncing tracks and for making edges snap together. These options are discussed in detail in Chapters 5 and 6. Finally, there's more to the Timeline than meets the eye. Clicking the Timeline menu button (right triangle) in the upper-right corner of the window, opens the Timeline menu, enabling you to add video and audio tracks as well as make clip edges snap together.

Monitor window

The Monitor window, shown in Figure 2-3, is primarily used to preview your production as you work. When previewing your work, click the Play button to play the clips in the Timeline and click the Loop button to start from frame one. As you work, you can also click and drag in the *tread area* (serrated lines just below the clip) to *jog*, or scroll, through your footage. Below the tread area is a triangular icon called the *shuttle slider*. You can click and drag the shuttle slider to jump to a specific clip area. As you click, the time readout in the Monitor window indicates your position in the clip. The Monitor window can also be used to set the In and Out points of clips. As discussed in Chapter 1, the In and Out points determine which part of a clip appears in your project.

What Makes a Track Shy?

Shy tracks are video and/or audio tracks that you hide from the Timeline, yet their contents appear in the production and in previews. They're most useful when you want to conserve screen space and concentrate on editing only one or two tracks. To make a track Shy, Command/Ctrl-click the Eye icon at the far left of the track. (This removes the black eyeball in the icon, indicating that the track is shy). Next, choose Hide Shy tracks from the Timeline menu. To show a Shy track, choose Show Shy tracks from the Timeline menu. Reset the track to normal by Command/Ctrl-clicking the Eye icon again.

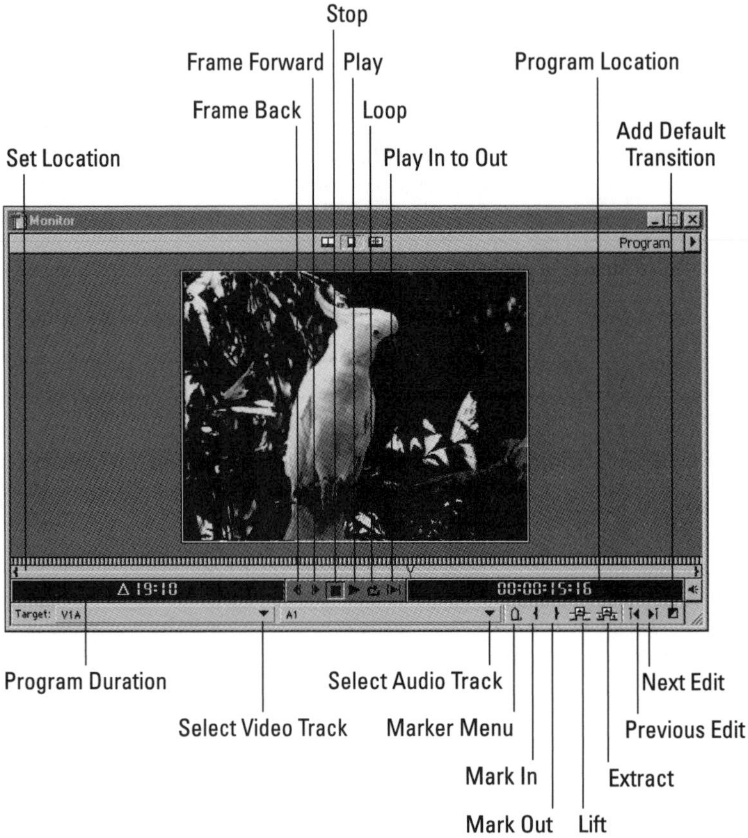

Figure 2-3: The Monitor window can be used to set In and Out points of clips while you edit.

The Monitor window provides three viewing modes:

✦ **Single View.** The window displays one monitor as you preview your production. Using this mode is similar to viewing your production on a television monitor.

✦ **Dual Mode.** The Monitor window is set up similar to a traditional videotape-editing studio. The source clip (footage) appears on one side of the Monitor window, and the program (edited video) appears on the other side of the window. This mode is primarily used when creating three- and four-point edits, which we cover in Chapter 10.

✦ **Trim View.** This mode allows for precision editing of Video track 1A and Video track 1B. One clip appears in one Monitor window, and the other clip appears in the second Monitor window. Precision editing of clips is covered in Chapter 10.

All of the Monitor window modes provide icons (shown in Figure 2-3) that enable you to quickly set In and Out edit points as well as step through the video frames.

Audio Mixer window

The Audio Mixer window, shown in Figure 2-4, enables you to mix different audio tracks, and to create cross fades and pans. (*Panning* enables you to balance stereo channels or shift sound from the left to the right stereo channels, and vice versa). Users of earlier versions of Premiere can appreciate the Audio mixer's capability to work in real time, which means that you can mix audio tracks while viewing video tracks.

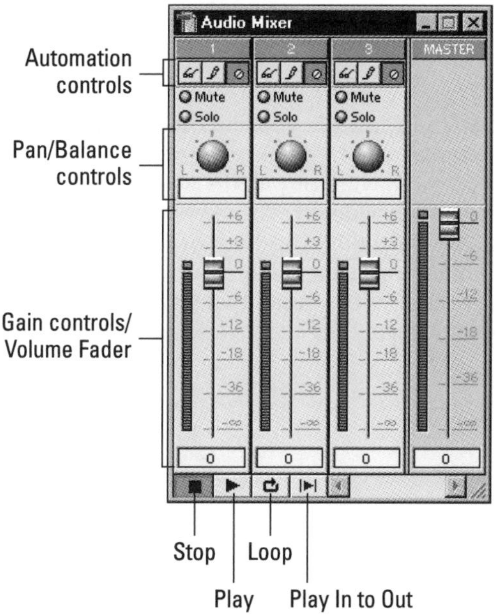

Figure 2-4: Use the Audio Mixer to mix audio and create audio effects.

Using the palette controls, you can raise and lower audio levels for three tracks by simply clicking and dragging the volume fader controls with the mouse. You can also set levels in decibels, by typing a number into the dB level indicator field (at the bottom of the Volume fader area). The round controls enable you to pan or balance audio. The buttons at the top of the Audio Mixer let you play all tracks, pick the tracks that you want to hear, or pick the tracks that you want to mute.

The familiar controls at the bottom of the Audio Mixer window enable you to start and stop recording changes while the audio runs. Chapter 6 provides an in-depth discussion of how to use the Audio Mixer.

Premiere's Floating Palettes

Premiere's Navigator, History, and Transitions *palettes* function differently than Premiere's other windows. Palettes are actually floating windows that never drop below other windows, which makes them readily accessible. In addition, the tabbed format of these windows enables you to keep them in groups that can be split apart and added to.

To activate any palette, just click it. To separate it from its group, click the palette tab and then drag it away from its palette group. To add one palette to another palette group, click the palette's tab and drag it to another group.

The following sections describe each of the palette windows.

Navigator palette

By using the Navigator palette, shown in Figure 2-5, you can quickly change Timeline time intervals. Doing this enables you to quickly see your Timeline as if viewing it up close or far away. In fact, the Navigator palette is actually a tiny version of the Timeline. The Navigator displays video tracks in yellow, audio tracks in green, and transition tracks in blue. As you zoom in and out of the time scale, the Timeline changes, and the viewing area of the Timeline grows or shrinks accordingly. When you zoom in, you can see more of the individual frames in a clip; when you zoom out, the size of the clip shrinks, enabling you to see more of the production without scrolling.

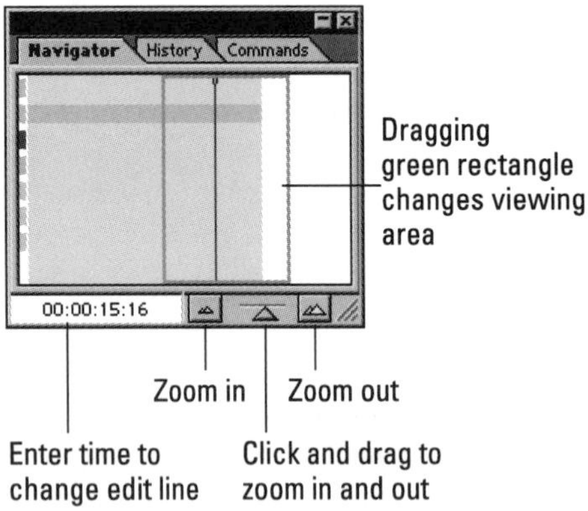

Figure 2-5: Use the Navigator palette to zoom in and out of the Timeline.

Using the Navigator is quite easy. If you want to see a specific part of the Timeline, double-click the timecode area of the Navigator, and then enter the time for the specific part that you wish to view. Press Enter, and the edit line jumps to that portion of your production on the Timeline.

To gradually zoom in or out, click the triangle slider between the two mountain icons at the bottom right of the palette. Clicking and dragging to the right zooms in; clicking and dragging to the left zooms out. To zoom out, click the small mountain icon to the left of the slider. Each click zooms you farther out. To zoom in, click the mountain to the right of the slider. Each click zooms you in.

History palette

Premiere's History palette, shown in Figure 2-6, lets you perform virtually unlimited Undo operations. As you work, the History palette records your production steps. To return to a previous version of your project, just click that history state in the History palette. After you click and begin working again, you rewrite history—all past steps following the state you returned to are removed from the palette as new ones appear. If you want to clear all history from the palette, choose Clear in the History palette's menu (launched by clicking the right triangle). To delete a history state, select it and then click the Delete button (trashcan icon) in the palette.

Figure 2-6: The History palette provides virtually unlimited undo operations.

Caution If you click a history state in the History palette to undo an action and then begin to work, all steps after the one you clicked are removed from your project.

The Commands palette

The Commands palette, shown in Figure 2-7, enables you to execute commands at the click of a button. For example, instead of moving the mouse to the File menu and choosing File ⇨ Import ⇨ File, you can simply click the Import File button in the Commands palette.

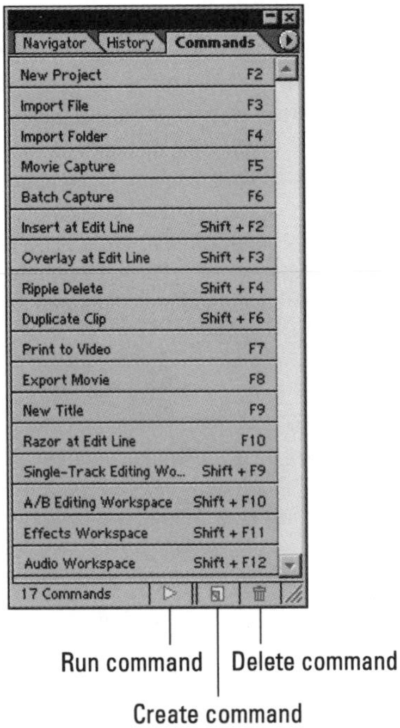

Figure 2-7: Click a button to execute a command.

The Commands palette provides two palette modes: Button mode on and Button mode off. When Button mode is on, you can execute a command by simply clicking its button, or by pressing a function key. When Button mode is off, you can execute a command by clicking its name in the palette, and then clicking Play Command from the palette menu.

Although the Commands palette comes packed with preset commands, you can easily add your own. Here are the steps for adding a command to the palette:

1. **If Button mode is on, turn it off by clicking Button mode in the palette menu.** (Access the palette menu by clicking the arrow at the top right of the palette). If Button mode is on, a check mark appears adjacent to its name.
2. **Click the New Command button at the bottom of the palette or choose Add Command in the Commands palette menu.** Doing this opens the Command options palette.
3. **In the Command options palette, type a name for your new command.** If desired, choose a function key and color from the Function Key and Color pop-up menu.

4. **To assign a menu command to the command, choose a command from one of Premiere's menus.** For example, to add the Save a Copy command, choose File ➪ Save a Copy.
5. **Click OK to close the dialog box.** After the dialog box is closed, Premiere adds the command to the Commands palette.

Info palette

The Info palette provides important information about clips and transitions, and even about gaps in the Timeline. To see the Info palette in action, click a clip, transition, or empty gap in the Timeline. The Info palette shows the clip's (or gap's) size, duration, and starting and ending points, as shown in Figure 2-8.

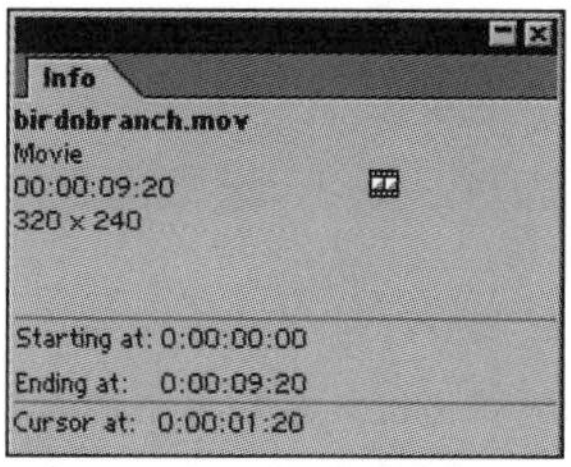

Figure 2-8: The Info palette displays information about clips and transitions.

The Info palette is very handy when doing precise editing, because the palette displays starting and ending points of the clips as you move them in the Timeline.

Effect Controls palette

The Effect Controls palette, shown in Figure 2-9, provides a summary view of all effects applied to a clip. When you click a clip, all effects applied to the clip display in the palette. To change settings for the clip effects, click Setup. That effect's dialog box opens, enabling you to change effect settings. For many effects, the slider controls for the effect actually appear in the Effect Controls palette. Clicking and dragging the slider changes how the effect is applied.

The Video and Audio effects palettes

The Video and Audio effects palettes enable you to quickly apply audio and video effects. Both palettes provide a grab bag of useful effects. For example, the Video palette includes effects that change an image's contrast and distort and blur images. The palette effects are organized into folders. For instance, the Distort folder (see Figure 2-10) features effects that distort clips by bending or pinching them.

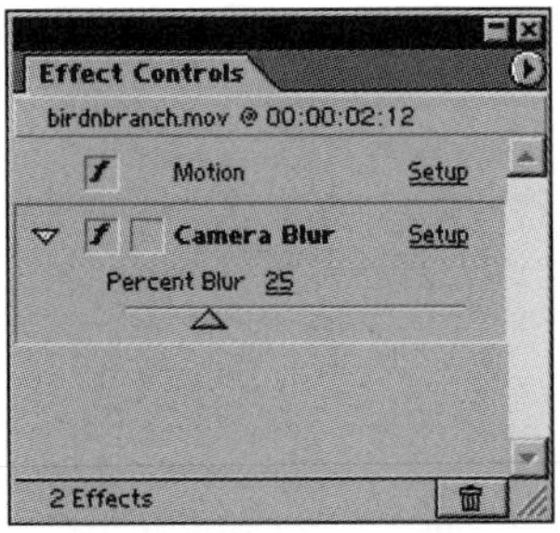

Figure 2-9: The Effect Controls palette enables you to quickly display and edit video and audio effects.

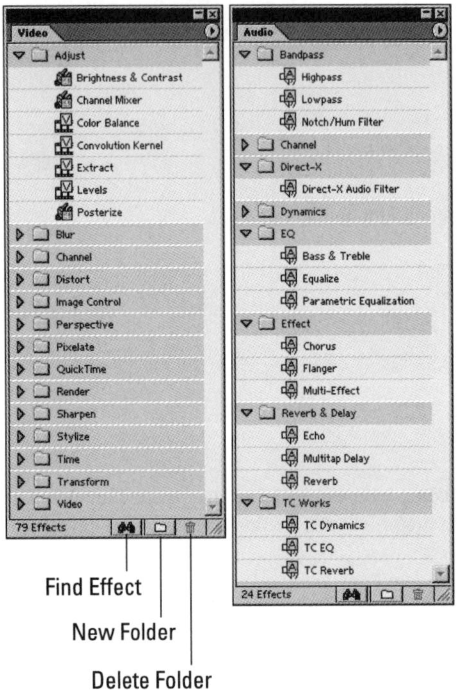

Figure 2-10: Use the Audio and Video effects palettes to apply special effects.

Applying an effect is simple—Just click and drag the effect from its palette to a clip in the Timeline. Typically, doing this opens a dialog box in which you specify options for the effect.

Cross-Reference

See Chapter 11 for more information on using Video effects.

Tip

Both Video and Audio palettes enable you to create your own folders and move effects into them, so that you can quickly access the effects you wish to use in each project.

Transitions palette

Premiere's Transitions palette, shown in Figure 2-11, features more than 70 transitional effects. Some effects, such as the Dissolve group, can provide a smooth transition from one video clip to another. Other transitions, such as page peel, can be used as a special effect to dramatically jump from one scene to another.

Like the Video and Audio palettes, the Transitions palette is organized into folders. If you'll be using the same transitions throughout a production, you can create a folder, name it, and keep the transitions in the custom folder for quick access.

To apply a transition to your program, click and drag the transition effect from its palette into the Transition track, between Video track 1A and Video track 1B. Double-clicking the transition in the track opens a dialog box in which you can specify settings for that transition.

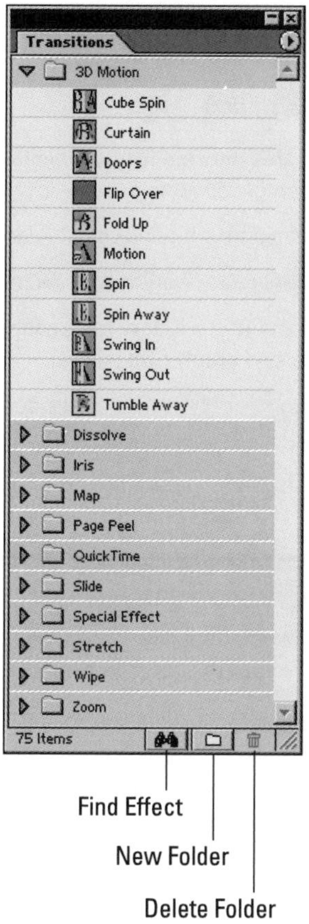

Figure 2-11: The Transitions palette

The Menus

Premiere features seven main menus: File, Edit, Project, Clip, Timeline, Window, and Help. The following sections provide an overview of the different menus and include tables that summarize each menu's commands.

The File menu

The File menu consists of standard Mac and Windows commands such as New, Open, Close, Save, Save As, Revert, and Quit. The menu includes commands for loading movie clips and folders full of files. Table 2-1 summarizes the File menu commands.

Table 2-1
File Menu Commands

Command	*Shortcut Command/Ctrl**	*Description*
New Project	N	Creates new file for new digital video production
New ➪ Bin	/	Creates new bin in Project window
New ➪ Storyboard	Alt+Shift+N	Creates new storyboard window
New ➪ Title		Opens Title window for creating text and graphic titles
New ➪ Universal Counting Leader		Automatically creates countdown clip
New ➪ Bars and Tone		Adds color bar and sound tone to bin in Project window
New ➪ Black Video		Adds pure black video clip to bin in Project window
New ➪ Offline File		Creates offline file that can be used for missing footage in project
New ➪ Color Matte		Creates new color matte in Project window
Open	O	Opens Premiere file
Open Recent Clip		Loads recently used clip from disk
Load Recent Project		Loads recently used Premiere movie
Close	W	Closes Project window
Save	S	Saves file to disk

Command	*Shortcut Command/Ctrl**	*Description*
Save as	Shift+S	Saves file under new name or saves to different disk location; leaves user in newly created file
Save a Copy	Alt+Shift	Creates a copy of the project on disk, but user remains in original
Capture ➪ Batch Capture		Automatically captures multiple clips from the same tape, requires device control
Capture ➪ Movie Capture		Captures clip from videotape
Capture ➪ Stop Motion		Captures still frames from tape, manually or by time lapse
Capture ➪ Audio Capture		Captures audio only
Import ➪ File		Imports video, audio clip, or graphic
Import ➪ Folder		Imports folder into Premiere
Import ➪ Project		Imports Premiere project file
Export Clip		Exports selected clip from Timeline; most choices in submenu are same as Export Timeline
Export Timeline ➪ Movie		Exports movie to disk according to Export Movie settings dialog box
Export Timeline ➪ Stillframe		Exports still frame to disk according to settings in Movie settings dialog box
Export Timeline ➪ Audio		Exports Timeline audio to disk according to settings in Audio Settings dialog box
Export Timeline ➪ Print to Video		Plays Timeline on video screen or centers full screen on computer screen
Export Timeline ➪ Export to Tape		Exports Timeline to videotape
Export Timeline ➪ File List		Creates text file, which lists files used in Timeline
Export Timeline ➪ EDL		Creates Edit Decision List, which can be used by various editing systems to automatically edit videotape according to timecode listing generated by Premiere

Continued

Table 2-1 *(continued)*

Command	***Shortcut Command/Ctrl****	***Description***
Export Timeline ➪ Adobe MPEG Encoder		Exports Timeline in MPEG format (Windows version only)
Export Timeline ➪ Advanced Windows Media		Exports Timeline in Windows Media Formats: WMF, WMA, or ASF (Windows version only)
Export Timeline ➪ Advanced RealMedia Export		Exports Timeline in Real Media format for use on Web
Get Properties for ➪ File		Provides size, resolution, and other digital info about project file
Get Properties for ➪ Selection		Provides size, resolution, and other digital info about selection
Page Setup	Shift P	Choose page options for printing; Windows users can select printer from Page Setup dialog box
Print	P	Prints Project, Timeline, Clip windows; will also print File Properties and Data rate graphs
Quit (Macintosh)/Exit (Windows)	Q	Quits premiere

* Mac users press Command, and Windows users press Ctrl while pressing the key or keys listed in the Shortcut column.

The Edit menu

Premiere's Edit menu consists of standard editing commands, such as Copy, Cut, and Paste, which can be used throughout the program. The Edit menu also provides special paste functions for editing, as well as preferences for Premiere's default settings. Table 2-2 describes the Edit menu commands.

Table 2-2
Edit Menu Commands

Command	***Shortcut Command/Ctrl****	***Description***
Undo	Z	Undoes last action.
Redo	Shift+Z	Repeats last action.

Command	*Shortcut Command/Ctrl**	*Description*
Cut	X	Cuts selected item from screen, placing into clipboard.
Copy	C	Copies selected item into clipboard.
Paste to Fit	Shift+V	Changes Out point of pasted clip so it fits in paste area.
Paste Attributes	Alt+V	Pastes attributes of one clip to another.
Paste Attributes Again	Alt+Shift+V	Allows pasting attributes again.
Clear		Cuts item from screen without saving in clipboard.
Select All	A	Selects all elements in window.
Duplicate Clip	Shift+/	Copies clips.
Find	F	Finds elements in Project window. (Project window must be active.)
Locate Clip	L	Locates selected Timeline clip in Project window.
Edit Original	E	Loads selected clip or graphic from disk so that it can be edited.
Preferences ➪ General/Still image		Sets default startup window; includes options for duration of still images and clip pre-rolls.
Preferences ➪ Auto Save/Undo		Turns Auto Save on and off; sets number of undoes.
Preferences ➪ Scratch Disk/Device Control		Sets which drive will be scratch disk for movies and previews; enables choice of device control.

* Command is for Mac users; Ctrl is for Windows users.

The Project menu

The Project menu provides commands that change attributes for the entire project. The most important commands enable you to set compression, frame size, and frame rate. Table 2-3 describes the Project menu commands.

Table 2-3
Project Menu Commands

Command	*Shortcut Command/Ctrl**	*Description*
Project Settings ➪ General		Sets video movie, timebase, and time display; displays video and audio settings.
Project Settings ➪ Video Settings		Sets video options, such as compression frame size, frame rate and pixel aspect ratio.
Preferences ➪ Audio Settings		Sets output options for audio.
Preferences ➪ Keyframe and Rendering Options		Sets number of keyframes per second; chooses field settings for video output.
Settings Viewer		Displays settings in one easy-to-read screen.
Remove unused clips	U	Removes unused clips from Project window.
Replace clips		Removes preview files from the Timeline.
Automate to timeline		Sequentially places contents of a bin or storyboard into Timeline.
Export bin from Project		Exports bin so that it can be used in other Premiere projects.
Utilities ➪ Batch processing		Renders more than one project. Lets the user leave the computer while batch processing runs overnight.
Utilities ➪ Project trimmer		Project trimmer trims frames, and removes excess frames from project.

* Command is for Mac users; Ctrl is for Windows users.

The Clip menu

The Clip menu provides options that change a clip's motion and transparency settings. It also includes features that aid in editing clips in the Timeline. Table 2-4 describes the Clip menu commands.

Table 2-4
Clip Menu Commands

Command	*Shortcut Command/Ctrl**	*Description*
Properties	Shift+H	Displays file size, resolution, path, and so on about clip.
Set Clip Name alias	H	Allows you to rename selected clip in Project window.
Add clip to project	J	Automatically places clip in Project window.
Insert at Edit line	Shift+,	Automatically adds clip to Timeline at editing point.
Overlay clip at Edit line	Shift+.	Drops clip into area at edit line.
Enable clip on Timeline		Allows clip to be seen in Timeline.
Lock clip in Timeline		Prevents clip in Timeline from being altered.
Unlink audio and video		Separates audio from video track.
Video options ➪ Maintain aspect ratio		Keeps aspect ratio of clip, despite different aspect ratio of project.
Video options ➪ Aspect fill color		If aspect ratio of clip is different from project, image will not fill the screen. Use this command to set the fill color where the image does not appear.
Video options ➪ Transparency		Set transparency (key) options, such as Chroma, Luminance, Blue screen, alpha channel.
Video options ➪ Motion		Create motion effect from clip.
Video options ➪ Frame Hold		Specify settings for making still frame from clip.
Video options ➪ Field options		Sets interlace options, also can set reverse field dominance.
Audio options ➪ Audio gain		Allows change of audio level.
Audio Options ➪ Normal/ Duplicate Left ➪ Duplicate Right Mute/Left Mute Right Swap channels		Stereo controls used when Premiere previews, plays, or exports.

Continued

Table 2-4 *(continued)*

Command	***Shortcut Command/Ctrl****	***Description***
Advanced options ➪ Timecode		Changes frame rate on format of timecode.
Advanced options ➪ Pixel aspect ratio		Changes from square pixels to different DV formats.
Advanced options ➪ Interpret footage		Enables changing speed of clip by changing the frame rate.
Duration	R	Change clip duration.
Clip speed	Shift+R	Speed up or slow down clip.
Open clip	Shift+L	Opens selected clip in project in Monitor window.
Open master clip	Alt+Shift+L	Opens original clip in Monitor window.
Replace with Source		Creates new source clip for selected virtual clip.
Set clip marker		Enables you to set editing point in/out and so on.
Go to clip marker		Enables you to go to a specific clip marker.
Clear clip marker		Clears clip marker.

* Command is for Mac users; Ctrl is for Windows users.

The Timeline menu

The Timeline menu enables you to preview the clips in the Timeline window and to change the number of video and audio tracks that appear in the Timeline window. Table 2-5 describes the Timeline menu commands.

Table 2-5
Timeline Menu Commands

Command	***Shortcut***	***Description***
Preview	Enter	Enables you to preview work area with transitions and effects
Render work area		Creates preview of work area without playing it

Command	***Shortcut***	***Description***
Render audio		Creates preview file of audio without playing it back
Razor at edit line		Cuts project at edit line in Timeline
Ripple delete		Deletes empty space between clips and closes gap
Apply default transition		Applies default transition set in transition palette
Transition settings		Opens transition settings dialog box for selected transition in Timeline
Zoom in	+	Zooms into Timeline by changing time intervals
Zoom out	–	Zooms back from Timeline by changing time intervals
Edge view		Enables you to see change in Monitor window Program view as you drag clip edge when editing In and Out points
Snap to edges		Causes clip edges to snap to each other
Sync selection		Selects linked audio with selected video or video with selected audio in Timeline
Add video track		Adds video track to Timeline
Add audio track		Adds audio track to Timeline
Track options		Adds or deletes tracks from dialog box
Hide shy tracks		Hides tracks marked as shy
Set Timeline marker		Sets a marker in the Timeline
Go to Timeline marker		Jumps edit line to marker in Timeline
Clear Timeline marker		Enables removal of Timeline marker
Edit Timeline marker		Enables editing of Timeline marker

The Window menu

The Window menu enables you to open and close windows and palettes. Most of the commands work identically to each other. Choose the name of the window that you want to open in the menu, and that menu opens. Palettes are opened by choosing Window ➪ Show Navigator, Window ➪ Show Info, and so on. Palettes are hidden by choosing Window ➪ Hide Navigator, Window Hide ➪ Info, and so on.

You can switch Timeline viewing modes by choosing either Window ➪ Workspace ➪ A/B Editing to see Video track 1 as two separate tracks — Video track 1A and Video track 1B — or Window ➪ Workspace ➪ Single Track Editing, to view Video track 1 as one track. Window ➪ Workspace ➪ Effects loads the Effect Controls palette on-screen, along with the Transitions, Video, and Audio effects palettes.

Cross-Reference

To learn more about workspace settings, see Chapter 1.

The Help menu

Premiere's Help menu provides formatted documents that are viewable in a Web browser. Choose Help ➪ Contents to load the main help screen. From this screen, which is shown in Figure 2-12, you can click a topic to learn about it. If you click Index, the alphabet appears. Clicking a letter loads the index listings for terms that begin with that letter. If you click the Search button, you can search for help by first entering a word to search for. For example, if you enter the word edit and click Search, a long list of topics related to the word edit appears. Clicking one of the edit topics brings you to the Help page for that item.

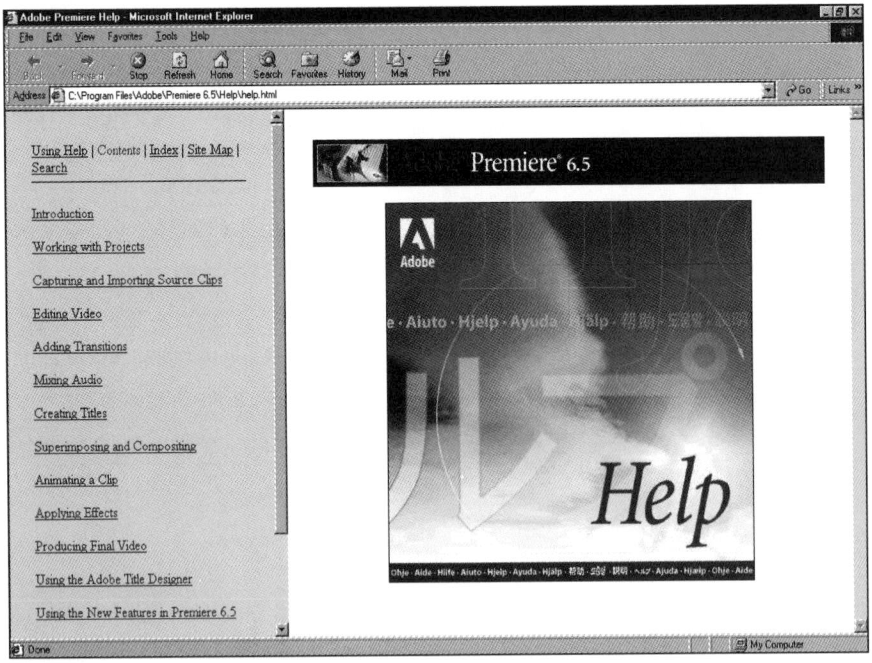

Figure 2-12: Premiere's online help appears in a browser window.

Other Help menu commands access information from the Web. Choose Help ⇨ Adobe Online to access Adobe's Web site. Choose Help ⇨ Support or Updates to download information from Adobe. To register your version of Premiere online, choose Help ⇨ Registration.

Summary

Premiere's windows, menus, and palettes provide you with an efficient interface and powerful tools to create digital video productions.

- ✦ The Project Window displays production elements.
- ✦ The Timeline window provides a visual display of your project. You can edit audio and video directly in the Timeline.
- ✦ The Monitor window previews your production and can preview edits.
- ✦ The Audio Mixer enables you to mix audio and create audio effects.
- ✦ Premiere's palettes float above other windows, providing production utilities and special effects.

✦ ✦ ✦

CHAPTER 3

Working with Project Settings

✦ ✦ ✦ ✦

In This Chapter

Using analog versus digital video

Understanding video compression

Understanding resolution and bit depth

Understanding compression

Using the project settings

✦ ✦ ✦ ✦

When you first begin creating projects in Premiere, the desktop video terminology and vast number of settings for video, compression capturing, and exporting can seem overwhelming. If you're just getting started with Premiere and are primarily interested in learning the basics of the program, you needn't worry too much about understanding all the commands in all the program's project-setting dialog boxes. However, if you don't understand such terms as *frame rates, frame size,* and *compression*—terms used in Premiere's project-setting dialog boxes—you're likely to be frustrated when you attempt to output your production.

This chapter provides an overview of key desktop video concepts. It also provides a guide to the different dialog boxes in which you designate the startup settings for Premiere projects. For the most part, these are settings that Premiere uses while you are importing and editing in Premiere. Settings for capturing video are covered in Chapter 4. Project settings for exporting video are covered later in Part V of this book.

What is Digital Video?

In the past few years, the term *digital video* has taken on a variety of new meanings. To the consumer, digital video may simply mean shooting video with the latest video camera from Canon, Sony, or JVC. A digital video camera is named as such because the picture information is stored as a digital signal. The camera translates the picture data into digital signals and saves it on tape in much the same way that your computer saves data to a hard drive.

Older video-recording systems store information in an analog format on tape. In analog format, information is sent in waves rather than as specific individual bits of data.

In Premiere, a digital video *project* usually contains video, still images, and audio that has been *digitized*, or converted from analog to digital format. Video and audio information stored in digital format from digital video cameras can be transferred directly to a computer through an IEEE 1394 port. (Although Apple Computer's trade name for the IEEE port is *FireWire*, and Sony's is i.LINK, the specifications are identical.) Because the data is already digitized, the IEEE 1394 port provides a fast means of transferring the data. Using video footage shot on an analog video camera or recorded on an analog video deck, however, requires the additional step of first digitizing the footage. Analog-to-digital capture boards that can be installed in both PCs and Macs generally handle this process. These boards digitize both audio and video. Other types of visual media, such as photographs and slides, also need to be converted to a digital format before Premiere can use them. Scanners digitize slides and still photos, but you can also digitize slides and photos by photographing them with a digital still camera. Scanning an analog image saves the image to the computer's hard drive, where it can then be loaded directly into Premiere. After the project has been fine-tuned, the last step of the digital video production process is to output it to your hard drive or to videotape.

Cross-Reference

See Chapter 4 to learn more about the IEEE 1394 standard and capture boards.

Linear versus nonlinear editing

Digital video provides numerous advantages over traditional analog video. If you use a digital video camera, your video clips are generally superior to analog clips. In digital video, you can freely duplicate video and audio without losing quality. With analog video, on the other hand, you go down a generation each time you copy a clip, thus losing a little quality.

In the context of Premiere, one advantage of digital video is that it enables you to edit video in a *nonlinear* fashion. Traditional video editing requires the editor to assemble a videotape production piece by piece from start to finish in a *linear* manner. In linear editing, each video clip is recorded after the previous clip onto a *program* reel. One problem with a linear system is the time it takes to re-edit a segment or to insert a segment that is not the same duration as the original segment to be replaced. If you need to re-edit a clip in the middle of a production, the entire program needs to be reassembled. The process is similar to creating a necklace with a string of beads. If you want to add beads to the middle of the necklace, you need to pull out all the beads, insert the new ones, and put the old beads back in the necklace, all the while being careful to keep everything in the same order.

In a nonlinear video system, you can freely insert, remove, and rearrange footage. If you reconsider the bead necklace analogy, nonlinear editing enables you to magically pop the beads on the necklace wherever you wish, as if the string didn't exist. Because the image is made up of digital pixels that can be transformed and replaced, digital video enables you to create numerous transitions and effects, which are not possible on a purely analog system. To return to the necklace analogy, a digital system lets you not only insert and replace beads freely, but also change their color and shape at will.

Digital Video Essentials

Before you begin creating a digital video project, it's important to understand some basic terminology. Terms such *as frame rate, compression,* and *frame size* abundantly populate Premiere's dialog boxes. Understanding these terms helps you to make the right decisions as you create new projects and export them to videotape or to your hard drive.

Video frame rates

If you take a strip of motion picture film in your hand and hold it up to the light, you'll see the individual picture frames that comprise the production. If you look closely, you'll see how motion is created: Each frame is slightly different than the previous frame. A change in the visual information in each frame creates the illusion of motion.

If you hold up a piece of videotape to light, you won't see any frames. However, the video camera does electronically store the picture data into individual video frames. The standard frame rate in video is approximately 30 frames per second. (The standard frame rate of film is 24 frames per second.)

Frame rate is extremely important in Premiere, because it helps determine how smooth the motion will be in your project. Premiere enables you to set the frame rate at various speeds. For example, if you capture video directly into Premiere, you can capture the video at approximately 30 frames per second, or you can capture it at a lower frame rate. Higher frame rates provide smoother motion. While you work in your project, you can also set the frame rate. This is the frame rate at which you create the project while you edit. Often you will want the project frame rate to be the same rate as your capture rate. However, you may want to edit at a lower frame rate and export the video at that lower frame rate if you are exporting the project to the Web. By creating a production at a lower frame rate, you enable the production to quickly download to a Web browser.

Frame size

The frame size of a digital video production determines the width and height of your production onscreen. Productions that will be output to videotape need to be created at specific frame sizes. If you are outputting to multimedia or to the Web, you'll want to pick the frame size carefully. A larger frame size creates a larger file that has to be downloaded to a browser. A large frame size viewed over a slow Web connection results in poor playback.

When you create a video production in Premiere, you can freely choose the size of the video frame. In Premiere, frame size is measured in *pixels*, which are the smallest picture element displayed on a computer monitor.

If you create a new project in Premiere and choose one of the settings for NTSC (the U.S. standard) videotape output, Premiere designates 640 x 480 pixels as the frame size. This means that each individual picture is composed of 640 horizontal x 480 vertical pixels. If you pick the European standard (PAL), Premiere chooses a frame size of 768 x 576. If you pick a broadcast NTSC DV (Digital Video) format, Premiere chooses 768 x 576. (The DV PAL setting is 720 x 576.) However, if you pick a multimedia format, Premiere's default setting is 320 x 240. Although you can use this frame size on the Web, you can create a smaller frame size by using Premiere's video setup boxes.

RGB color and bit depth

A color image on the computer screen is created from the combination of red, green, and blue color phosphors. The combination of different amounts of red, green, and blue light enables you to display millions of different colors. In digital imaging programs, such as Premiere and Photoshop, the red, green, and blue color components are often called *channels*. Each channel can provide 256 colors (2^8 — often referred to as 8-bit color because there are 8 bits in a byte), and the combination of 256 red colors x 256 green colors x 256 blue colors results in over 17.6 million colors. This color is often called *24-bit color* (2^{24}).

Although most users will leave Premiere's color setting at 24-bit color, you can reduce the number of colors in a video project, or choose a specific palette of colors to use.

Note

Although television uses a monitor very much like a computer display to provide color, it does not use RGB Color. Instead, television uses a color system called YCC. The Y stands for *luminance*, which essentially controls brightness levels for grayscale or black-and-white images. Both C channels are color channels. YCC was created when television was transitioning between black-and-white and color systems to enable those with black and white systems as well as those with color systems to view the TV signal.

Compression

Larger frame sizes provide greater bit depth, and more frames per second produce a better quality Premiere digital video project. Unfortunately, a full-frame, 24-bit color, 30 frames per second video production requires vast amounts of storage space. You can easily calculate how much hard drive space a full-frame production would take up. Start by multiplying the frame dimensions. Assume that you are creating a project at 640 x 480 pixels. Each pixel needs to be capable of displaying red, green, and blue elements of color, so multiply 640 x 480 x 3. Thus, each frame is approximately 1MB. Thus, one second of video at 30 frames a second is 30MB. (This doesn't even include sound.) A five-minute production consumes about 8GB of storage space.

To reduce the file size of a video project, you can reduce frame size, frame rate, and color bit depth. However, doing so usually results in a tremendous loss in quality. To store more data in less space with a minimum loss of quality, software engineers have created a variety of video compression schemes. The two primary compression schemes are spatial and temporal.

- **Spatial compression.** In spatial compression, computer software analyzes the pixels in an image and then saves a pattern that simulates the entire image.
- **Temporal compression.** Temporal compression works by analyzing the pixels in video frames for screen areas that don't change. Without temporal compression, different frames are saved to disk for each second of video, whether the image on-screen changes or not. Rather than creating many frames with the same image, temporal compression works by creating one keyframe for image areas that don't change. The system calculates the differences between frames to create the compression. For example, for a video that consists of frames of a flower that sometimes blows in the wind, the computer needs to store only one frame for the flower and record more frames only when the flower moves.

When you work with compression in Premiere, you don't choose spatial or temporal compression. Instead, you choose compression settings by specifying a *CODEC*. CODEC stands for compression and decompression. Software manufacturers create codecs. For example, in Premiere, you can choose a codec called Cinepak, which provides temporal compression. When you create, edit, or export your project, you can specify how many keyframes you want to output per second. Another CODEC, Apple Animation, provides spatial compression. When you use this codec, no keyframe choices are provided.

QuickTime, Video for Windows, and MPEG

For your computer to use a video compression system, software, and sometimes hardware, needs to be installed. Both Macs and PCs usually come with video compression software built into their operating systems. QuickTime is the digital video compression system automatically installed with the Mac OS operating system; Video for Windows is the digital video compression system automatically installed in the Windows operating system. QuickTime is also packaged with Premiere, and it can be installed on PCs. Because QuickTime is cross-platform, it is one of the most popular digital video systems for CD-ROM and Web digital video. When you use Premiere, it automatically accesses the QuickTime or AVI software, enabling you to choose from a list of QuickTime or AVI codecs. If you have a capture board installed in your computer, the capture board typically provides a set of codecs from which you can choose.

It's also important to understand that the QuickTime and AVI compression schemes enable you to edit footage into a Premiere project. Other compression systems, such as MPEG (named after the Motion Picture Engineering Group, which oversees the creation of different MPEG file formats), require Premiere to do too much processing to maintain high quality and compressed video — without added hardware. Although you can import an MPEG file into Premiere, the program is not designed to render video in this format without a video board that handles MPEG. The best indicator of this limitation is the fact that no MPEG listings appear in the Project Settings dialog box when you create a project (see Figure 3-1).

Although Premiere provides no MPEG project settings, it enables you to output in MPEG -1 or MPEG-2 format. (Windows users can choose File ➪ Export Timeline ➪ Adobe MPEG Encoder or File ➪ Export Timeline ➪ Adobe MPEG Encoder.) Using the Adobe MPEG encoder is covered in Chapter 16. Mac users who wish to output MPEG files can use Apple's QuickTime Pro. MPEG-2 compression is used to create DVDs, which can provide up to two hours of video with eight tracks of audio. MPEG-1 compression, which can be used on the Web or CD-ROMs, provides VHS quality video. The newest MPEG standard, MPEG-4 (available in QuickTime 6), provides even better compression than MPEG-2 is. Because MPEG-4 is an international standard, it will undoubtedly be one of the chief file formats used to deliver audio and video over the Web.

Note

Video provides so much data that a DV video camera compresses the video even before it is transferred to your computer. The standard compression ratio used is 5:1, which makes the transferred video signal five times smaller than the original video signal.

Understanding Project Settings

After you have a basic understanding of frame rate, frame size, and compression, you can better choose settings when you create a project in Premiere. If you choose your project settings well, you'll produce the best quality video.

You first choose Project settings when you create a new project. The Load Project Settings dialog box shown in Figure 3-1 appears when you first start Premiere, or when you choose File ➪ New Project. The creators of Premiere have streamlined the process of choosing project settings. To get started, you simply need to click one of the available presets. Notice that Premiere provides DV (Digital Video format presets) for NTSC television and the PAL standard. For Web and CD-ROM work, Premiere supplies Multimedia presets. Clicking one of the presets displays the preselected settings for Compression, Frame Size, Pixel Aspect Ratio (discussed later in this chapter), Frame Rate, and Bit Depth, as well as for audio settings. Version 6.5 now offers the Real Time Preview option. Real-time previews enable you to view transitions and effects without first rendering your project, thereby speeding up the editing process. You simply press Enter to preview the selected portion of your project. Although the Real Time Preview check box only appears in the Windows version of Premiere, both Windows and Mac versions provide real-time preview capability. You can learn more about using Real Time Preview both later in this chapter and in Chapter 5.

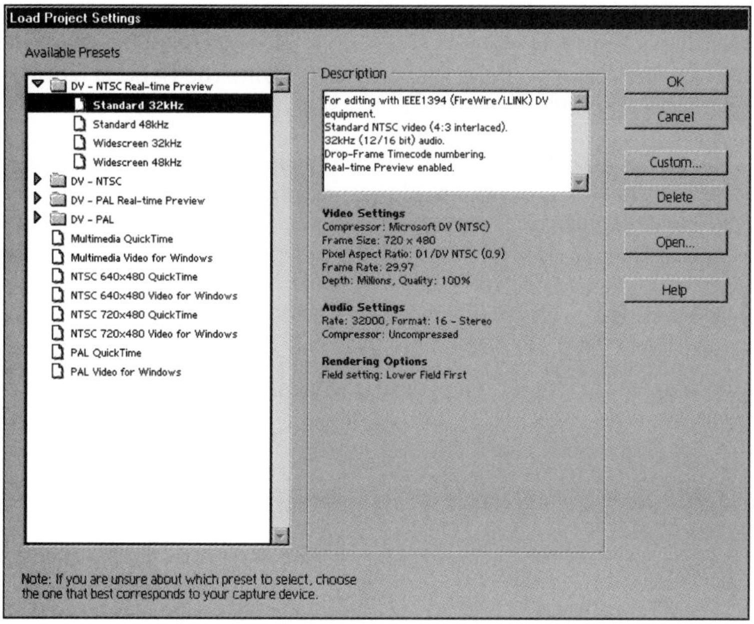

Figure 3-1: The Load Project Settings dialog box includes project presets.

Although the project settings provide an excellent starting point, you may need to change them when you create a project or when you export a project to tape or disc. To change settings in a new project, click the Custom button. To change settings while working on a project, choose Project ➪ Project Settings. When you Export a movie, a Settings button also lets you change settings. To see all settings in a project, choose Project ➪ Settings View. This command opens the Settings Viewer dialog box shown in Figure 3-2. To change project settings from the Settings Viewer, click the Project Settings button.

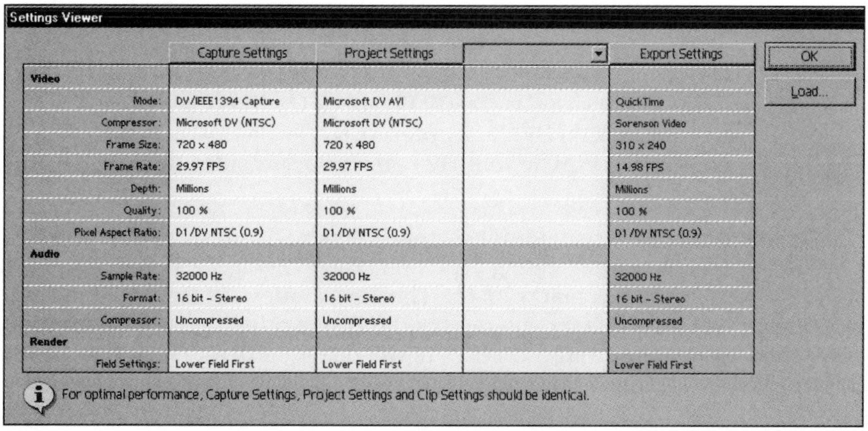

Figure 3-2: The Settings Viewer dialog box provides an overview of all Premiere settings.

No matter which path you take to change project settings, all roads lead to dialog boxes that are divided into five categories: General, Video, Audio, Keyframe and Rendering, and Capture. The sections that follow describe the General Settings, Video, and Keyframe and Rendering dialog boxes.

Cross-Reference

Audio settings are described in Chapter 6 and capture settings are discussed in Chapter 4. See Chapter 17 for more information about the keyframe settings for exporting Premiere projects.

General settings

The General settings section of the Project Settings dialog box, shown in Figure 3-3, provides a summary of the individual project settings. What follows is a description of the choices.

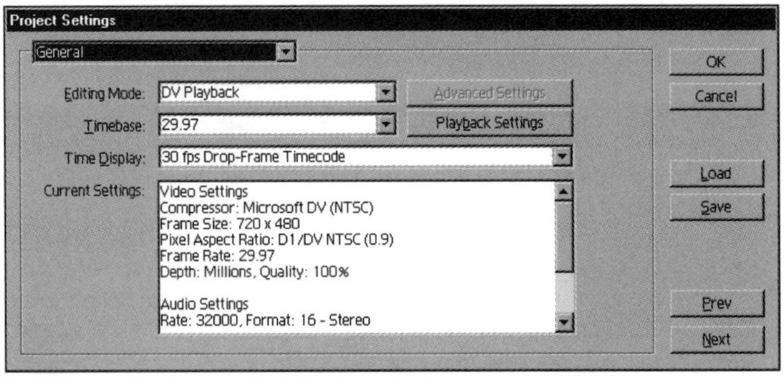

Figure 3-3: The General settings section of the Project Settings dialog box

- ✦ **Editing Mode.** The editing mode is determined by the chosen preset in the Load Project Settings dialog box. The choice here is most likely to be QuickTime, Apple's Desktop Video compression system, or Video for Windows (used by PCs only). The Editing Mode pop-up menu also allows you to set DV playback options. Choose DV Playback and then click the Playback Settings button. This Opens the DV Playback Options dialog box where you can select Playback on DV Camcorder/VCR. Viewing DV playback on a monitor connected to a VCR or your DV Camcorder provides the best preview of your project.
- ✦ **Timebase.** Timebase determines how Premiere divides video frames each second when calculating editing precision. The Timebase also determines the positions of the tick marks on the Timeline window. (If the frame rate does not match the Timebase, Premiere uses the Frame rate.) If you are outputting to video, leave the setting at 29.97, the video standard; for QuickTime, and Video for Windows multimedia and Web projects, choose 30. If you are working with

a production that was captured from film, choose 24, the standard frame rate for film.

Typically, the Timebase matches the capture rate, so if you capture video at 15 frames per second, set the Timebase at 15 frames per second. If you capture video at 30 frames per second and the Timebase at 15 frames per second, Premiere skips every other frame when you are editing.

Futhermore, you should generally choose a Timebase that matches the frame rate in your production. However, to further reduce the file size of a production, you can have a lower frame rate than Timebase. For instance, the Multimedia preset uses a 30-frame Timebase, but the project frame rate is 15 frames per second, and the export rate is 15 frames per second. (If you do change the Frame rate, remember that better quality is achieved by using a Frame rate [such as 15] that is a multiple of the Timebase rate [such as 30]. However, lowering the Frame rate usually produces poorer-quality output.)

✦ **Time Display.** This setting determines how time is displayed during the project. Time is displayed using standard video time readouts. For instance, the time display after the first 29 frames is 00:00:29, the next frame in the video would read out as 00:01:00 (at 30 frames per second), which means 1 second and 00 frames. Here are some recommended settings: For professional video, match the original video. If the original video uses 30, then choose Drop Frame. For Web or CD-ROM production, choose 30 frames per second Non Drop Frame. For PAL projects, use 25 frames per second. For motion picture, choose Feet frame 16 (for 16 mm) or Feet frame 35 (for 35 mm).

✦ **Current Settings.** Shows the current settings

✦ **Advanced Settings.** Available only with specific video boards.

Video settings

The Video settings section of the Project Settings dialog box, shown in Figure 3-4, includes settings specific to the creation of your video project. These settings are described in the following paragraphs.

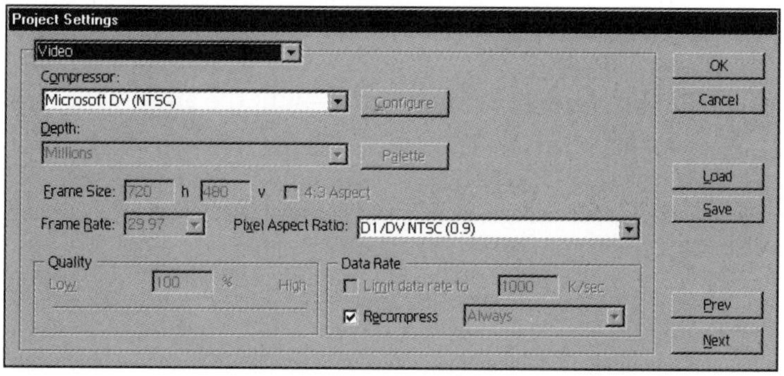

Figure 3-4: The Video settings section of the Project Settings dialog box

✦ **Compressor.** As mentioned earlier, compression is used to store as much data as possible in as little space as possible with a minimum loss of quality. The compressor setting describes the CODEC Premiere uses during Timeline playback. If you capture video into Premiere, you will typically use the same compressor setting as you did when capturing video (such as DV-NTSC or DV-QuickTime). If you are exporting to videotape, you'll typically use the same CODEC again. (The CODECs are set automatically when you choose a preset.)

✦ **Depth.** Specifies the color depth. For the best quality video, leave the color depth set to 24 bit. You can switch to 8 bit if allowed by the current codec chosen in the compressor field. For example, if you chose QuickTime Animation or Cinepak as your CODEC, you can lower the Depth to 256 colors. You can also click the Palette button to load a custom palette from disk.

✦ **Frame Size.** The frame size of your project is its width and height in pixels. The first number represents the frame width, and the second number represents the frame height. Use the default presets for DV-NTSC video (720 x 480). For Web work, you may want to use a smaller frame size than the multimedia default of 320 x 240. If creating a project for the Web or CD-ROM, you can reduce its frame size when exporting your project (discussed Part V later in the book).

As you import clips into your project, you need to understand how Premiere deals with clips that don't match the project frame size. Premiere attempts to automatically convert them to the Frame Size specified in your project settings, which can lead to distortion. For instance, if you create a graphic in Photoshop with different pixel dimensions than those of your project, the image will appear distorted when it is imported into Premiere. If it is impossible to obtain production material that matches frame size, you can prevent distortion by selecting the clip and choosing Clip ⇨ Video Options ⇨ Maintain Aspect Ratio (covered in Chapter 10).

✦ **Frame Rate.** The frame rate is the number of frames per second Premiere uses when it plays back from the Timeline. Typically, the Frame Rate matches the Timebase, but, as mentioned previously, you can set the Frame Rate to be a multiple of the Timebase. For instance, the Timebase could be 30 frames per second with a Frame Rate of 15. Once again, you could reduce the frame rate when exporting your project, if working on a Web or multimedia production.

✦ **Quality.** The quality settings are dependent on which codec is chosen. The higher the quality, the better the video output — but the greater the file size.

✦ **Aspect.** Aspect controls the aspect ratio, horizontal to vertical. The standard video aspect ratio is 4:3. If you are using video clips and change the aspect ratio, you will distort your image. If you are using D1/DV Widescreen (a 1.2-pixel aspect ratio), the frame aspect ratio is 16:9.

- **Pixel Aspect Ratio.** This setting determines the shape of the video pixels — the width to height of one pixel in your image. For analog video and images created in graphics programs or scanned, choose square pixels. The pop-up menu allows you to choose different settings for outputting to videotape. For example, for output to video using DV video, you can choose D1/DV NTSC (0.9); for output to D1/DV Widescreen, choose 1.2; for D1/DV PAL, use 1.0666; for D1/DV PAL Widescreen, use 1.4222. Choose the Anamorphic 2:1 choice if the video was shot on film with an anamorphic lens.
- **Data Rate.** A variety of CODECs enables you to change the data rate to limit the amount of data that is sent to your computer over a given time. This setting helps to ensure that the video output doesn't go beyond the internal transfer capabilities of your computer system during previews. If previews are choppy, you can try reducing the number that appears in the Data Rate K/sec field.
- **Recompress.** If you lower the data rate, select this option to ensure that the lower data rate is maintained. Select Always to recompress every frame; select Maintain data rate to compress only those frames higher than the data rate. This option provides better quality than the Always settings.

Keyframe and Rendering options

The Keyframe and Rendering section of the Project Settings dialog box determines settings for playing back video (see Figure 3-5). Many of these settings are also used when exporting your project. The Rendering Options settings affect playback as you work with Premiere; the Keyframe Options are used when exporting your project. These are discussed in Chapter 16.

Preventing Display Distortion

When rectangular pixels (DV pixel aspect ratios such as .09 or 1.2) that haven't been altered are viewed on a computer monitor (which displays square pixels), images may appear distorted. The distortion does not appear when the footage is viewed on a video monitor instead of on a computer display.

Also, the difference in pixel aspect ratio between computer monitors and DV requires planning if you are integrating graphics created in other programs with a Premiere project. For example, if you create images in Photoshop for NTSC DV projects, create them at 720 x 540 (768 x 576 for PAL). Premiere scales the image to match the project. If you save at 640 x 480, Premiere must upsample (to 720 x 480) when it scales, which can result in poorer quality. If you are outputting 3D animation from your computer and are creating a field-rendered file, Adobe recommends outputting at 640 x 480 to prevent field distortion.

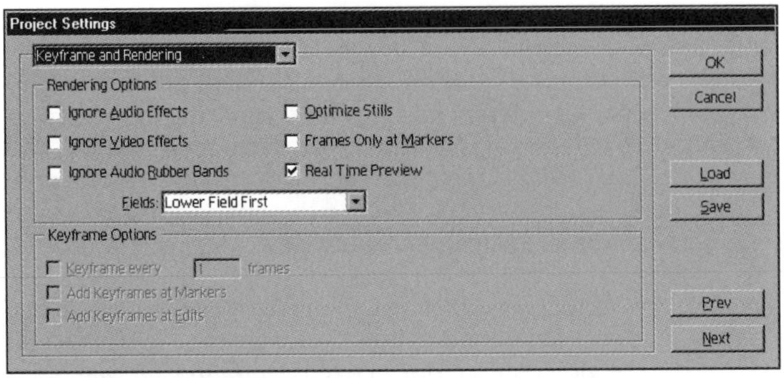

Figure 3-5: The Keyframe and Rendering settings section of the Project Settings dialog box

Rendering options include the following:

✦ **Ignore Audio Effects.** Select this option to prevent audio effects from being previewed when playing back projects from the Timeline.

✦ **Ignore Video Effects.** Select this option to prevent video effects from appearing when playing back from the Timeline.

✦ **Ignore Audio Rubber Bands.** Audio rubberbands can control fade-in and fade-out. Select this option to have Premiere ignore these effects in the Timeline.

✦ **Optimize Stills.** Choosing this option can result in better compression, because Premiere uses only one frame for still frames. For instance, at 30 frames per second, choosing Optimize Stills results in the creation of one frame instead of 30 frames. Choosing this setting may produce choppy playback.

✦ **Frames Only at Markers.** When working in the Timeline, Premiere enables you to tag frames with markers. This option only plays back the frames with markers.

✦ **Preview Settings.** Premiere 6.5 allows a variety of Preview settings that can speed up the preview process. Here are the choices for Mac users.

- **From Disk.** This option creates a preview at the final playback speed by first rendering the preview to a playback file on your hard drive.
- **To Hardware.** Select this option to use a third-party video board to render the playback.
- **To Screen.** When this option is chosen, Premiere creates a real-time preview of your work that enables you to preview video and motion effects and transitions without first rendering the Timeline.

- **Real Time Preview (Windows only).** Select this option to view effects as you work. Enabling this option enables you to preview video and motion effects without first rendering the Timeline. You need only press Enter for the preview to begin playing at the Timeline Edit Line. If you don't choose Real Time Preview, you can toggle between Previewing without effects and Previewing from your hard drive by pressing Shift-Enter

Summary

Premiere provides a nonlinear system of creating desktop video projects. A nonlinear system lets you edit video quickly and efficiently. You can easily edit and insert clips without reassembling your entire project. When you create a new project, you need to specify project settings. In this chapter, you learned the following:

✦ The easiest way to pick project settings is to choose a preset from the Project Settings dialog box.

✦ You can choose which compression system to use, such as Quicktime or Video for Windows, in the General Settings dialog box.

✦ You can change Frame Size, Frame Rate, and Pixel Aspect Ratio in the Video Settings dialog box.

✦ The Keyframe and Rendering dialog box enables you to control how Premiere previews effects while you are working.

✦ ✦ ✦

CHAPTER 4

Capturing Video

✦ ✦ ✦ ✦

In This Chapter

Preparing for video capture

Performing analog to digital capture

Capturing DV video

Adding timecode

Stopping motion capture

✦ ✦ ✦ ✦

The quality of video clips in a Premiere project can often mean the difference between a production that attracts viewers and firmly holds their attention, or one that sends them looking for other sources of information or entertainment. Undoubtedly, one of the primary factors in determining the quality of source material is how the video is *captured* on a computer hard drive.

If you have a capture board, or peripheral card, that digitizes analog video, you may be able to access the capture board directly from Premiere to digitize video. If you have an IEEE 1394 port, you may also be able to use Premiere's Movie Capture window to transfer clips directly from your DV video camera. Depending upon the sophistication of your equipment, and the quality requirements of your production, you may be able to capture all of your video source material by using Premiere.

This chapter focuses on the process of capturing video and audio using Premiere. It leads you step-by-step through the process of using Premiere's Movie Capture window to capture videotape. If your equipment enables *device control*, you are able to start and stop a camcorder or tape deck directly from Premiere. You may also be able to set up a batch capture session in which Premiere automatically seeks out and captures multiple clips during one session.

Getting Started

Before you get started capturing video for a production, you should first realize that the quality of the final captured footage depends on the sophistication of your digitizing equipment and the speed of the hard drive that you are using to capture the material. Much of the equipment sold today can provide quality suitable for the Web or in-house corporate video. However, if your goal is to create very high-quality video productions and transfer them to videotape, you should analyze your production needs and carefully assess exactly what hardware and software configuration best suits your needs.

Fortunately, Premiere can capture audio and video using low-end and high-end hardware. Capture hardware, whether high- or low-end, usually falls into two categories.

✦ **FireWire/IEEE1394.** Apple Computer created the IEEE 1394 primarily as a means of quickly sending digitized video from video devices to a computer. In Apple computers, the IEEE 1394 board is called a FireWire port, and most Macs come with the board built-in. Several other manufacturers, including Sony (Sony calls its IEEE 1394 port an i.LINK port) and Dell, sell computers with IEEE pre-installed.

If your computer has an IEEE 1394 port, you can copy digitized data directly from a DV camcorder to your computer. As mentioned in Chapter 3, DV camcorders actually digitize and compress the signal as you shoot. Thus, the IEEE 1394 port is a conduit between the already digitized data and Premiere. If your equipment is Premiere compatible, you are able to use Premiere's Movie Capture window to start, stop, and preview the capture process. If you have an IEEE 1394 board in your computer, you may be able to start and stop a camcorder or tape deck from within Premiere; this is called *device control.* With device control, everything is controlled from Premiere. You can cue up the video source material to specific tape locations, record timecode, and set up batch sessions, which enable you to record different sections of videotape automatically in one session.

✦ **Analog to digital capture boards.** These boards take an analog video signal and digitize it. Some computer manufacturers, such as Apple Computer, have sold models with these boards built directly into the computer. On the PC, most analog to digital capture boards are add-ins that must be installed in the computer. More expensive analog to digital capture boards permit device control, enabling you to start and stop a camcorder or tape deck as well as cue it up to the tape location that you want to record.

Note

Analog boards capture video using square pixels. If you mix square pixel graphics or files with footage that are output in NTSC DV format (which uses non-square pixels at 720 x 480), the square pixel footage is distorted. To avoid this problem, save square pixel files that will be output at 720 x 480 DV format at 720 x 540 or 640 x 480 (for PAL formats use 768 x 576). Premiere automatically scales files captured or saved at 640 x 480 or 720 x 540 frame sizes so that the frame size, pixel and frame aspect ratios match that of your project without distortion. If possible, use 720 x 540 instead of 640 x 480, because you obtain better quality when Premiere reduces, rather than enlarges the image.

Making the right connection

Before you begin the process of capturing video or audio, make sure that you've read all relevant documentation supplied with the hardware. Many boards include plug-ins so that you can capture directly into Premiere (rather than capturing it using capture software and then importing it into Premiere).

✦ **Analog to digital.** Most analog to digital capture boards use Composite Video or S-Video systems. Some boards provide both composite and S-video. Hooking up a composite system usually entails connecting a cable with three RCA jacks from the video and sound output jacks of your camcorder or tape deck to the video and sound input jacks of your computer's capture board. The S-video connection provides video output from your camcorder to the capture board. Typically, this means simply connecting one cable from the camcorder or tape decks S-video output jack to the computer's S-video input jack. Some S-video cables have an extra jack for sound as well.

✦ **The IEEE/FireWire connection.** Making the connection to your computer's IEEE 1394 port is easy. Simply plug the IEEE 1394 cable into the DV In/Out jack of your camcorder, and plug the other end into the IEEE 1394 jack of your computer. Despite the simplicity, be sure to read all documentation. The connection may not work unless you supply external power to your DV cameras. The transfer may not work on the DV camera's batteries alone.

Note

IEEE 1394 cables for desktop and laptop computers are usually different, and not interchangeable. Furthermore, an IEEE 1394 cable that connects an external FireWire hard drive to a computer may be different from an IEEE 1394 cable that connects a computer to a camcorder. Before purchasing an IEEE 1394 cable, make sure you've got the right cable for your computer.

Shopping for video capture cards

If you're interested in exploring the ins and outs of video capture boards, look no further than the Web. One of the best places to start your investigation is `http://dvguide.sharbor.com/head-to-head`. This site provides a comparison-shopping guide listing video board specs for more than 50 boards from a variety of manufacturers. The site lists important board features such as CODECs, compression rates, and input/output ports.

To use this site, you first click the names of two different cards that you want to compare. Next, click Compare, and the screen shows a side-by-side comparison of the different boards. For instance, the DV storm board by Canopus provides DV CODECS for other video formats. It captures at a frame resolution of 720 x 480 and includes an IEEE 1394 port as well as an S-video jack. Audio inputs are stereo RCA and stereo mini-jacks with a sustained data rate of 3.6MB per minute. You can pick from low-end boards such as the Canopus EZDV card, which provides IEEE 1394 capturing and playback, to more sophisticated boards such as the Canopus DV Storm SE, which provides DV in/out as well as analog output (composite and S-video). The card also provides frame-accurate deck control as well as real-time output of effects and titles. The card also outputs MPEG files. The dvguide Safe Harbor site also lists high-end cards such as the Pinnacle DC 2000/DV, which lists for about $2,000 in the U.S. This board ships with several software packages, including Adobe Premiere. Apart from Premiere, the bundled software includes programs to create CDs as well as numerous video effects. The DC 2000 is a dual-stream card, which means that it can accept two video streams, enabling it to create on-the-fly transitions and effects.

For more information about video capture cards, you also want to check out the Web sites of manufacturers such as Matrox, Canopus, and Pinnacle Systems. Some of the Web sites feature reviews from computer and video magazines. The Canopus Web site even enables you to download PDF versions of card installation instructions.

Troubleshooting video drivers

Before you start the capture process, you should ensure that your computer has the correct digital video drivers installed. Premiere's video capture commands will only work on PCs if Microsoft DV drivers are installed. Sony installs its own drivers on its desktop and laptop models. These drivers enable Sony computer users to capture video directly to their computers using Sony's capture software. If Sony's drivers are installed on your computer, you will not be able to capture video in Premiere. Fortunately, Adobe's Web site provides a simple solution. You can download a program called SonySwitcher that enables you to quickly switch from the Sony DV drivers to the Microsoft DV drivers. You can later use the software to switch back to Sony's driver. You can download the software at `www.adobe.com/support/downloads`. Scroll to the Premiere section and then click the Windows link. Listed among the downloads is the SonySwitcher. You'll need to download the file. After you've uncompressed the file, double-click the Sonyswitcher.exe file to open the window shown in Figure 4-1. Finally, click Switch and you're ready to go.

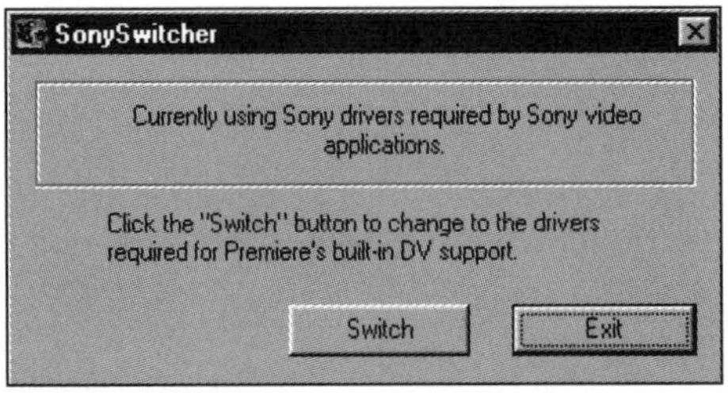

Figure 4-1: The Sony Switcher software switches PCs to Microsoft DV drivers.

Starting the Capture Process

Before you get started capturing video and audio, it's important to understand that many settings in Premiere depend upon the actual equipment you have installed in your computer. It's also important to understand that the dialog boxes that appear when capturing, change depending upon the hardware and software installed in your computer. The dialog boxes that appear in this chapter may vary from what you see on your computer, but the general steps for capturing video and audio are pretty much the same. However, if you have a capture board that digitizes analog video, the setup process is different than if you have a FireWire port installed in your computer. The following sections describe how to set up Premiere for both systems.

Note: To ensure that your capture session is successful, be sure to read all manufacturers read me files and documentation. Know exactly what is installed in your computer.

Setting the scratch disk

Whether you are capturing digital video or digitizing analog video, one of your first steps should be to insure that Premiere's *scratch disk* is set up properly. The scratch disk is the disk used to actually perform the capture. Make sure that the scratch disk is the fastest one connected to your computer, and that the hard drive is the one with the most amount of free space. To access the correct dialog box, choose File ➪ Preferences ➪ Scratch Disk and Device Control, or click the Edit button in the Preferences section of the Movie Capture dialog box (File ➪ Movie Capture). In the Capture Movie field in the Scratch Disk section of the dialog box, choose the hard disk that you wish to use for capturing video and audio in the Captured Movies pop-up menu.

Capturing analog video

If you are capturing video with a capture board that digitizes analog video, you do not need to create a Project onscreen before the capture session. You can access Premiere Capture settings directly from the program's Capture dialog box.

To open the capture dialog box, choose File ➪ Capture ➪ Movie Capture. After Premiere opens the Movie Capture window shown in Figure 4-2, the capture settings are shown onscreen in the dialog box. If these settings are correct, you're ready to capture. However, even if you do not need to change the settings, reviewing and understanding the different options available is a good idea.

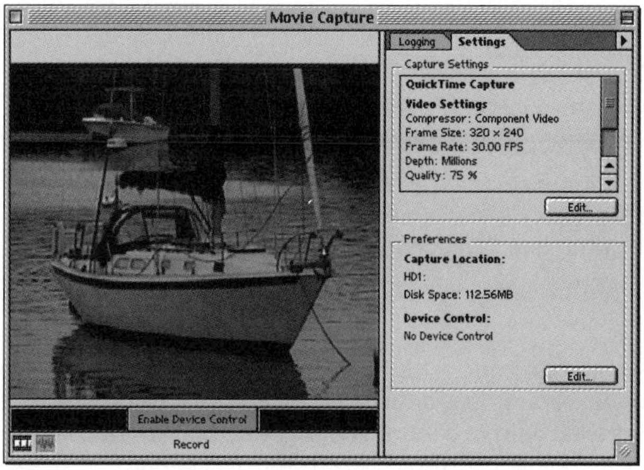

Figure 4-2: Capture Settings can be viewed in the Movie Capture window.

Note that the Capture Location is designated in the bottom-right side of the dialog box. If you want to change this, you can click the Edit button in the Preferences section. This action opens the Scratch Disk and Device Control sections of the Preferences dialog box settings.

Changing capture settings

If you want to view or change capture settings, click the Edit button in the Movie Capture window. If the Movie Capture window is not open, you can change settings by choosing Project ➪ Project Settings ➪ Capture. Doing so opens the Capture section of the Project Settings dialog box, shown in Figure 4-3. The options in the Capture section are described in the following list:

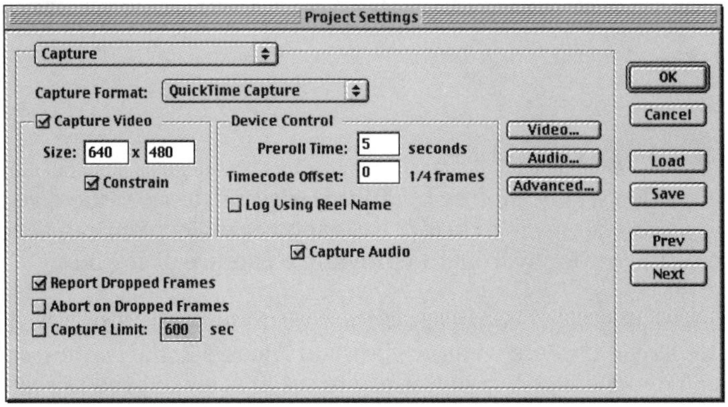

Figure 4-3: The Capture section of the Project Settings dialog box

- ✦ **Capture Format.** The choices that appear here depend upon your capture board. Some boards only provide one choice. Choose the setting recommended by your capture board manufacturer.
- ✦ **Capture Video.** Leave this check box selected to capture video. Deselect only if you wish to capture audio without video.
- ✦ **Size.** Enter the frame dimensions for your capture session. Smaller dimensions produce smaller files. However, note that you can capture video at a larger frame size than the one you use for the final export.
- ✦ **Capture Audio.** Leave this selected to capture audio. Deselect only if you want to capture video without audio.
- ✦ **Report Dropped Frames.** Selecting this option provides an on-screen report detailing which frames were dropped during the capture. Frames are frequently dropped if the hard drive cannot support the capture rate. Some capture boards may not allow capturing at 30 frames a second.

✦ **Abort on Dropped Frame.** Select this option if you want to have Premiere stop the capture process if the frames are dropped.

✦ **Capture Limit.** This enables you to set a time limit for the capture session. After the time limit expires, the capture stops.

Device control setting

If your hardware allows device control, these settings are available. If your hardware does not allow device control, these settings are dimmed onscreen.

✦ **Preroll Time.** Enter the duration in seconds before capture starts. Typically, you want the tape deck or camera to get *up to speed* before the In point of the capture. Refer to camera and tape deck documentation for specifics.

✦ **Log Using Reel Name.** If you are using Batch capture, enter the reel name here. The Batch capture process is described later in this chapter.

Assigning video settings

The Capture section of the Project Settings dialog box, previously shown in Figure 4-1, provides general capture settings. You may want to change specific settings such as the capture frame rate, or what compressor to use.

To view or change video settings for your capture board, click Video in the Capture section of the Project Settings dialog box (Figure 4-3). This opens the Video dialog box, shown in Figure 4-4.

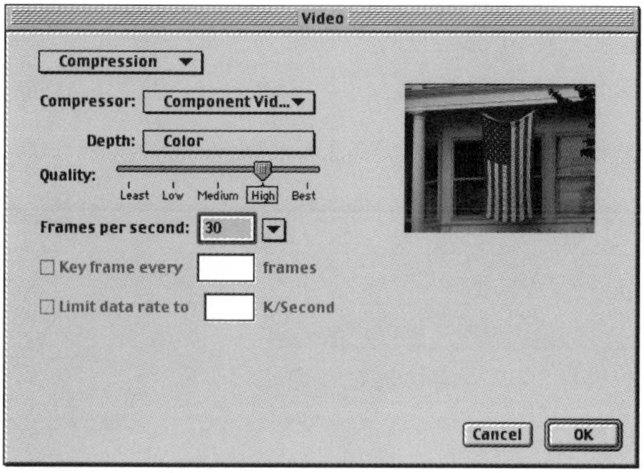

Figure 4-4: The Video dialog box with compression settings

The pop-up menu, at the top of the Video dialog box, controls dialog box options. The following sections provide a review of the choices.

Compression settings

When Compression appears, you can choose the compression CODEC, color depth, quality, and frames per second. You may be able to obtain higher-quality video by increasing the number of frames per second, or by choosing a compression CODEC that provides less compression — however, this creates larger files. If you haven't experimented with capture settings, start by choosing the defaults preset by your board manufacturer or those settings recommended by your board manufacturer.

Note The choices shown in the video dialog box depend on the hardware that you use.

Image settings

If you set the pop-up menu to Image, the Video dialog box changes to the options shown in Figure 4-5. The choices enable you to correct video during the capture session. The Hue slider enables you to adjust colors, Saturation enables you to adjust color intensity, and Brightness enables you to control lightness and darkness. Use the Sharpness slider to sharpen the image. Only change the default settings if your clip is soft, or needs to be color corrected. If you change the settings, you can return to the default settings by clicking the Defaults button.

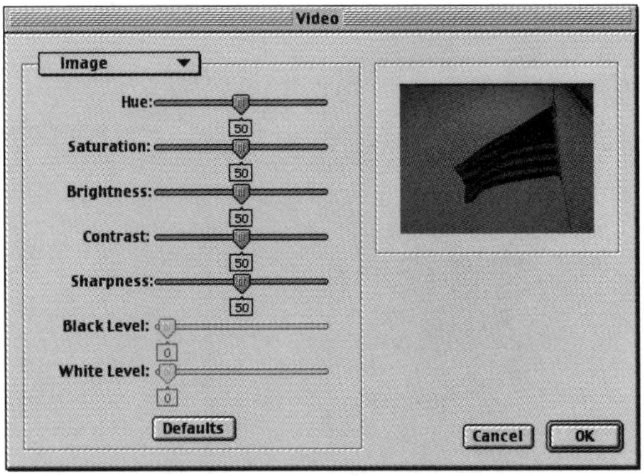

Figure 4-5: The Video Settings dialog box with Image settings

Source settings

Choosing the Source pop-up menu changes the dialog box settings to those shown in Figure 4-6. After you choose this option, information about the capture card and capture settings appears. The choices in the Input pop-up menu depend upon the card you are using. For instance, you may be able to switch between video formats such as composite, S-video, and component. The format menu enables you to switch between video systems such as NTSC, PAL, or SECAM. In Figure 4-6, the Built-in choice in the Digitizer field indicates that the capture board is built into the computer.

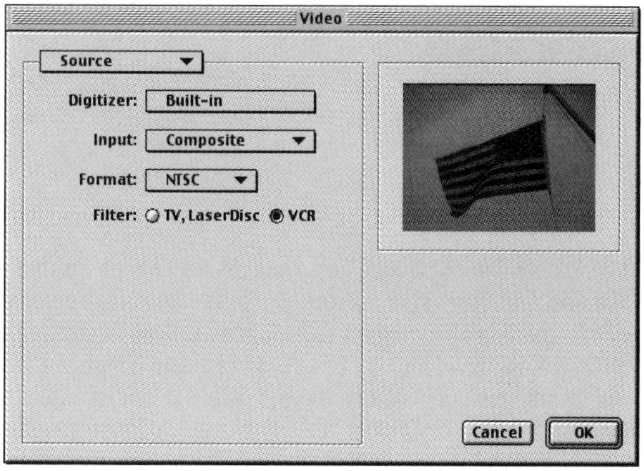

Figure 4-6: The Video dialog box with Source settings

After you've reviewed or changed video settings, click OK in the Video dialog box. This returns you to the Capture dialog box.

Assigning audio settings

To change or review audio settings for a capture session, click the Audio button in the Capture section of the Project Settings dialog box. Like the video settings dialog box, the audio choices change, depending upon the selected item in the pop-up menu at the top of the screen. No matter what settings are chosen, the Sound dialog box always enables you to turn the speaker on or off, as well as control volume and gain. These settings are always active; you turn on your camera or tape deck and set audio levels before you start recording.

Compression settings

When Compression is selected in the Sound dialog box, as shown in Figure 4-7, the settings change to enable you to choose a compression CODEC in the Compressor pop-up menu. Compression reduces file size. However, choosing the wrong compressor may adversely affect quality.

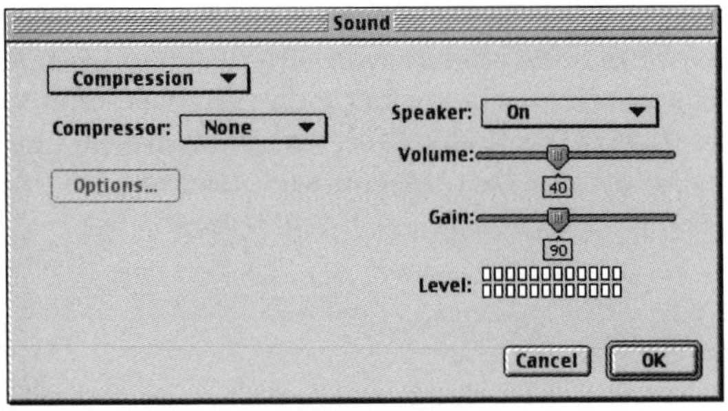

Figure 4-7: The Sound dialog box with Compression settings

Sample settings

When Sample is chosen in the Sound dialog box, the settings, shown in Figure 4-8, change to enable you to pick a sample rate. The sample rate is the number of times per second that sampling occurs during the conversion from analog to digital data. You can choose between 8 bits and 16 bits, and between Mono and Stereo. Larger sample rates and higher bit rates or stereo provide better quality but create larger files. For most purposes, a sample rate of 22.050 kHz with 16 bits and mono should provide good quality sound, although you can reduce file size further, if required.

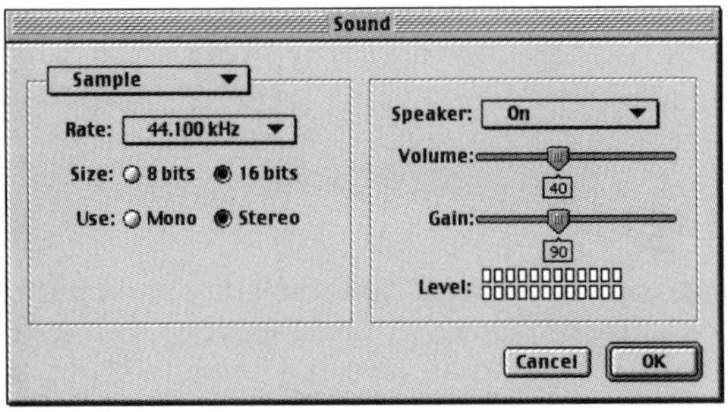

Figure 4-8: The Sound dialog box with Sample settings

Source settings

The Source setting in the Sound dialog box, shown in Figure 4-9, enables you to specify the source of the sound. The choices that appear in the input screen depend on your hardware settings. Many users with IEEE 1394 boards see *DV Audio* as the choice under Device, and *Two channels* under input. Users with built-in analog capture boards probably see *Built-in* as the choice and *RCA in* as input (indicating that RCA phono connectors are used to connect the computer to the camcorder or VCR). If the source is set incorrectly, sound won't be recorded when you capture video.

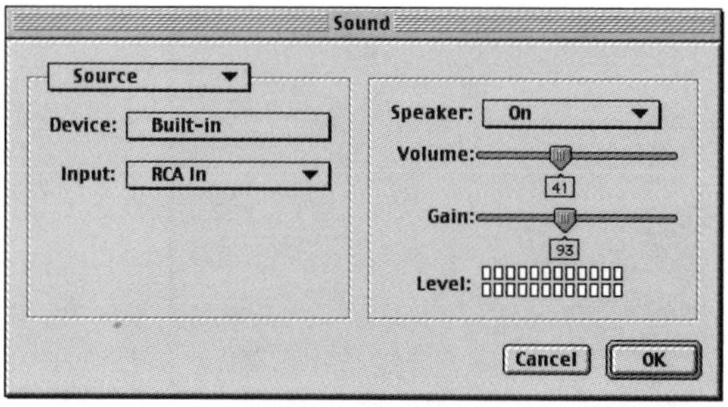

Figure 4-9: The Sound dialog box with Source settings

Adjusting digital video capture settings

If you want to capture video from a DV camera or DV tape deck, the Capture preparation process is different than it is from analog video. Because DV cameras compress and digitize, the capture dialog box for DV is primarily used just to start and stop recording. However, to ensure the best quality capture, you must create a project before the capture session.

Note: To prevent dropped frames during a DV capture session, your hard drive should be able to sustain a 3.6MB per second data rate.

Before beginning a DV capture session, make sure that the connection between your source (DV camera or DV tape deck) and computer is set up properly. For the transfer to operate, your system also needs a DV CODEC. The CODEC may be installed in your system as software, or a chip that communicates with the FireWire or i.LINK port.

Note: AVI capture files are limited in file size between 1 and 2GB.

1. **Choose File ⇨ New Project.** At this point, you must choose either a DV preset or one recommended by your board manufacturer. The Project Settings dialog box with DV presets is shown in Figure 4-10.
2. **Choose Edit ⇨ Preferences ⇨ Scratch Disks and Device Control to make sure that the capture location is set to the correct hard disk.**
3. **Choose Project ⇨ Project Settings ⇨ Capture.** The Capture screen appears.
4. **Click Video.** The Video dialog box appears.
5. **Click the pop-up menu and choose Source.** Your screen should look similar to Figure 4-6.

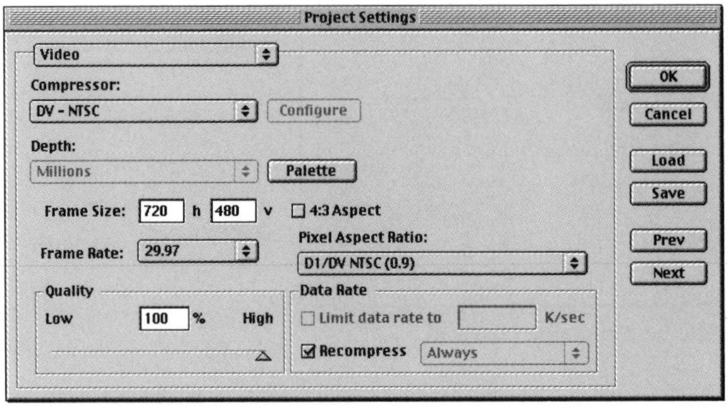

Figure 4-10: The DV-NTSC chosen as one of the Project settings

6. **In the Digitizer menu, choose the correct digitizer.** The proper choice may already be selected. For many users, the choice is DV-NTSC. If you made any changes click OK.
7. **Leave all settings in the Movie Capture window alone.** They were set when you created your project.

Capturing Video in the Movie Capture Window

If your system does not allow device control, you can capture video by turning on your tape deck or camera and viewing the footage in the Movie Capture window. By manually starting and stopping the camera or tape deck, you can preview the source material. Here are the steps to follow:

1. **Make sure that all cables are properly connected.**
2. **Choose File ⇨ Capture ⇨ Movie Capture.** You can change the window size by clicking and dragging the lower-right edge of the window.
3. **In the Movie Capture window menu, select Fit Image in Window to view the clip at the correct aspect ratio.**
4. **Set the camera or tape deck to Play mode.** You should see and hear the source clip, as shown in Figure 4-11.
5. **Three or four seconds before the section that should be recorded, click the Record button in the Movie Capture window.**
6. **To stop recording, press ESC.** When the recording stops, the File Name dialog box appears.

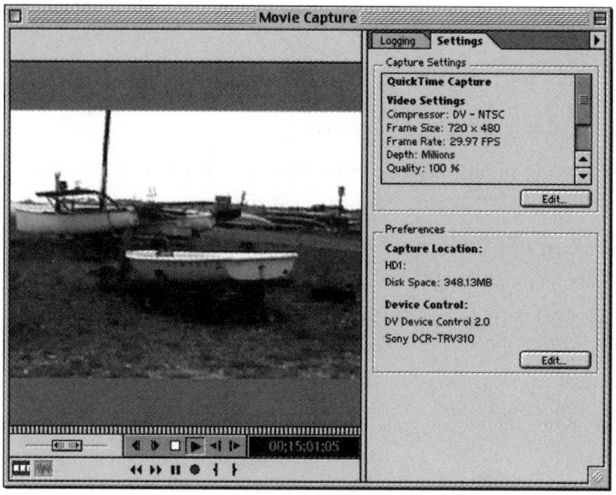

Figure 4-11: Capture screen set for DV capture

7. **Type a filename for the clip.** Optionally, you may type additional comments in the Comments box.
8. **Click OK to save the file.**

If you had a Premiere project open when capturing, the captured clip appears in the Project window. If no Project is open, the clip opens in a Clip window.

After the capture session, a Properties window opens. Among other items, this window describes the frame size, pixel depth, pixel aspect ratio, average data rate, how many (if any frames) were dropped, and displays the average recorded frame rate.

Capturing with device control

During the capture session, device control enables you to start and stop a camera or tape deck directly from Premiere. To work with device control, you need a capture board that supports device control as well as a frame-accurate tape deck (that is controlled by the board). If device control is supported by your system, you may also be able to import timecode and automatically generate a batch list to batch capture clips automatically.

Cross-Reference

See the section "Adding Timecode to a Clip" to learn more about timecode.

Before starting a device control capture session, make sure that all cables are setup properly and all settings, as described in the previous sections, are correct. Here are the steps:

1. **Choose File ➪ Capture ➪ Movie Capture.**
2. **If Premiere requests a reel name, type the reel name.** When you place a new tape in your source device, you may be asked to enter a reel name.
3. **Click the on-screen controls to move to the point that you want to start capturing video.**
4. **Click either the Mark In icon or the Set In button.** See Figure 4-12.

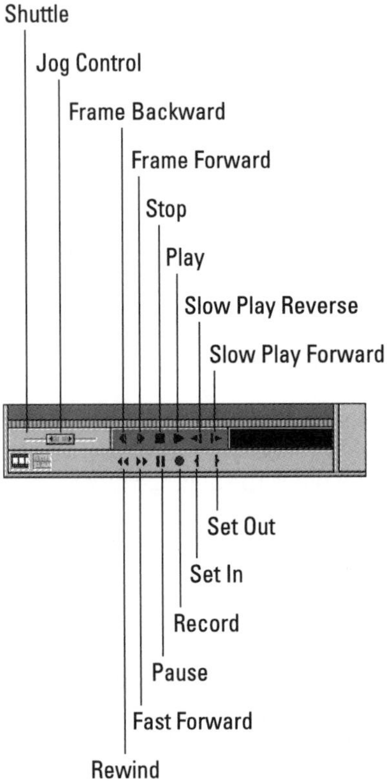

Figure 4-12: Device control icons

5. **Click the on-screen controls to move to the point that you wish to start capturing video.**

6. **Click either the Mark Out icon or the Set Out button.** At this point you can preview the clip. To preview the clip, Option-click (Windows users Alt-click) the Play button. If you wish to rewind the tape, you can play to the In point by Option-clicking (Windows users, Alt-click) the Mark In button. If you want to play to the Out point, Option-click (Windows users Alt-click) the Out button.

Tip

Click and drag the jog control area (the serrated line at the top of Figure 4-12) to the left to rewind one frame; click and drag to the right to advance one frame. Drag the Shuttle control to change speed as you view the footage.

7. **To begin capturing, click the Record button in the Capture Screen.** Optionally, click the Capture In/Out button on the Logging tab. Premiere starts the pre-roll and begins the capture session at the In point, and ends it at the Out point.

8. **When the Filename dialog box appears, type a name for the clip.** If a project is open, the clip automatically appears in the Project window.

Performing a batch capture

If your capture board supports device control, you can set up a *batch capture list* in Premiere's Batch Capture dialog box, shown in Figure 4-13. A batch capture list contains all the In and Out points of the clips you want to capture. You can create this list manually or by using device control.

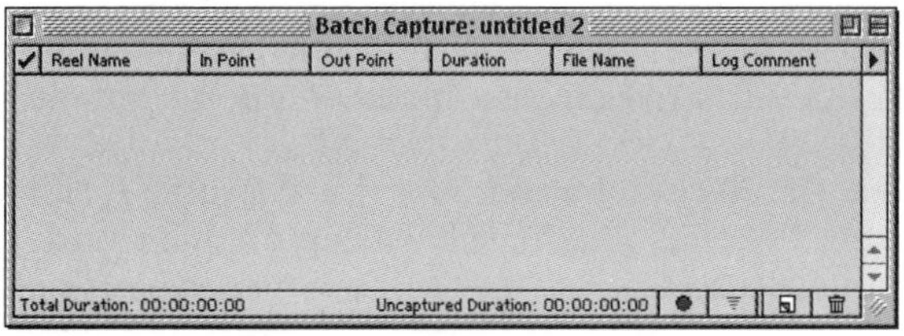

Figure 4-13: The Batch Capture dialog box

Creating a batch capture list manually

To create a batch capture list of clips that you specify manually, follow these steps:

1. **Choose File ➪ Capture ➪ Batch Capture.** The Batch Capture dialog box appears.

2. **Click the Add New Item button.** The clip Capture Parameter dialog box, shown in Figure 4-14, opens.

3. **Type an In point, Out point, and a filename for the clip.**

4. **Click OK.** The clip's information is added to the Batch Capture log. When you add a clip, a black diamond appears indicating that the clip needs to be captured. To turn off the diamond, simply click it.

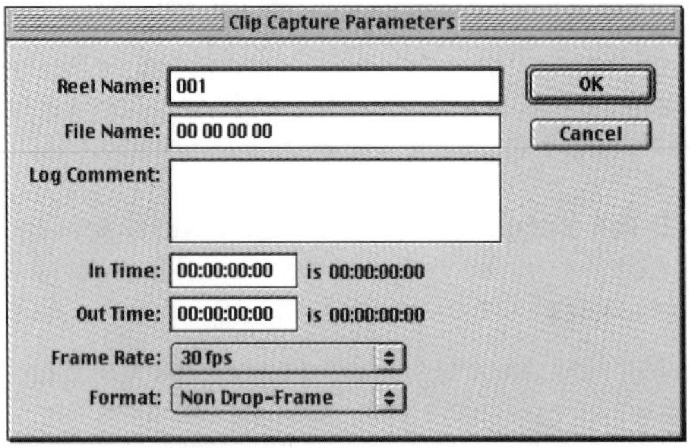

Figure 4-14: The Clip Capture Parameters dialog box

5. **For each clip that you want captured, repeat Steps 2–4.**
6. **Choose File ➪ Save to save the Batch Capture list.** You can reload the list later when you want to begin the capture session.

Tip

Before capturing, you can check the capture settings by choosing Recording Setting in the Batch Capture pop-up menu. Choosing the Handles command opens the Capture Handles dialog box, which enables you to set the number of frames before each In and Out point. You can also import or export a text file.

7. **To capture the clips, click the Record button.** After the capture session, a check mark appears next to the clips that have been captured and an X appears if the clip was not captured.

Creating a batch capture list with device control

If you want to create a batch capture list but do not want to type in the In and Out points of all clips, you can use Premiere's Movie Capture window to do the job for you. Here are the steps:

1. **Open the batch capture window by choosing File ➪ Capture ➪ Batch Capture.**
2. **Open the Movie Capture window by choosing File ➪ Capture ➪ Movie Capture.**
3. **Click the Logging tab and type a reel name.**
4. **Use the capture control icons to locate the portion of the tape that includes the section you want to capture.**

5. **Click the Mark In button.** The In point appears in the Logging tab's In field.
6. **Use the Capture control icons to locate the clip's Out point.**
7. **Click the Mark Out button.** The Out point appears in the Out field.
8. **Click the Login/Out button and enter a file name for the clip (unless you wish to use the default name provided).** If desired, type comments in dialog box and then click OK.
9. **For every clip you want to capture, repeat Steps 4–8.**
10. **Close the Movie Capture window.**
11. **Choose File ➪ Capture ➪ Batch Capture.** The Batch Capture window appears, listing the In and Out points.
12. **To start the recording process, click the Record button.**

Note

You can open multiple batch capture lists by choosing File ➪ Open. This way you can compare capture sessions.

Adding Timecode to a Clip

High-end video cameras and mid-range DV cameras can record timecode to videotape (often called SMPTE timecode for the Society of Motion Picture and Television Engineers). The timecode provides a frame accurate readout of each videotape frame in Hour: Minute: Second: Frame format. Timecode is used by video producers to move to specific locations on tape and also to set In and Out points. During an edit session, broadcast equipment uses the timecode to create frame accurate edits of the source material onto the final program tape.

When capturing with device control, Premiere captures the timecode, along with the video. When capturing video or importing video, you may wish to use a clip that doesn't have timecode striped on the tape, yet does have the timecode visible (called a window dub). In these cases, you can't actually capture timecode from the clip. However, you can use Premiere to set timecode on the tape. To add timecode to a clip, follow these steps:

1. **To select the clip in the Project window, double-click it to open the clip window.** If you don't want the timecode to start at the beginning of the clip, move to the frame at which you want to begin recording.
2. **Choose Clip ➪ Advanced ➪ Options ➪ Timecode.**
3. **In the Clip Timecode dialog box, shown in Figure 4-15, enter the beginning timecode and the frame rate.**

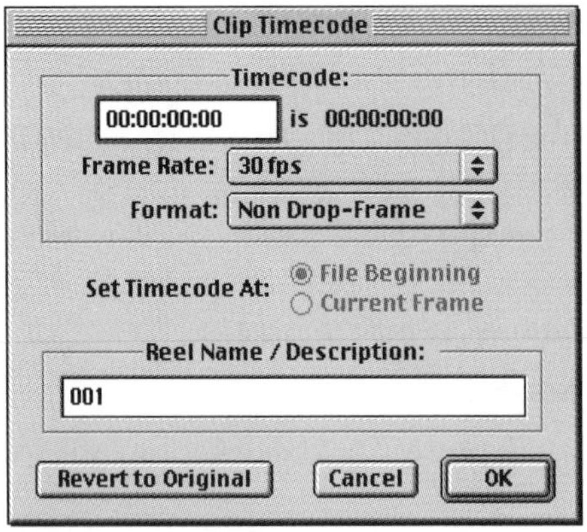

Figure 4-15: Use the Clip Timecode dialog box to set timecode for a clip.

4. **In the Set Timecode At section, specify whether you want the timecode to start at the current frame or the beginning of the clip.**

Drop Frame versus Non-Drop Frame Timecode

SMPTE (Society of Motion Picture and Television engineers) timecode is "striped" (recorded) on tape on a track separate from the video track. Video producers use the timecode as a means of specifying exact In and Out points during edit sessions. When previewing footage, producers often create a "window dub "of the timecode, so that the timecode appears in a window. This enables the producers to view the tape and the timecode at the same time. By default, Premiere uses the SMPTE timecode to display times in this format: hour: minute: second: frame.

If you're new to video or Premiere, this can take some getting used to. For example, the next readout after 01:01:59:29 is 01:02:00:00. This timecode format code is called non-drop frame. However, professional video producers typically use a timecode format called drop frame.

Drop frame timecode is necessary because the NTSC professional video frame rate is 29.97 (not 30 frames a second). Over a long duration the point the .03 time difference between 30 frames and 29.97 frames begins to add up, resulting in inaccurate program times. To solve the problem, professional video producers created a timecode system that would actually visually drop frames in the code without dropping frames in the video. When SMPTE non-drop frame is striped, two frames of every minute are skipped—except for the tenth minute. In drop frame timecode, the frame after 01;01;59;29 is 01;02;00;02. Notice that semicolons are used to designate drop frame from non-drop frame.

If you are not creating video where exact time duration is important, you do not need to use drop-frame timecode. You can capture and use 30 frames per second instead of 29.97 project setting. Furthermore, non-drop frame was created for NTSC video. Do not use it for PAL or SECAM, which use 25 frames per second.

5. Enter a reel number.

6. Click OK.

Capturing Stop Motion Clips

Premiere enables you to create stop motion or time-lapse video captures as well as full-motion capture. When you capture using stop motion, Premiere does not capture every frame sequentially. When you capture using stop-motion, you can tell Premiere how many frames to skip during the capture session. This feature can come in handy if you want to quickly show the passage of an event over time.

Note: Premiere's stop motion feature enables you to capture just one frame of video as well.

1. **To start a stop motion session, choose File ➪ Capture ➪ Stop Motion.** The Stop Motion window opens (see Figure 4-16). You can click and drag the right corner of the dialog box to change the window size (which can be used as the capture size). You can also click and drag a graphic from the Project window into the Stop Motion window to check positioning (to compare the capture size to the size of the graphic).

Figure 4-16: The Stop Motion window

2. **In the Stop Motion menu, choose Recording Settings.** The Recording Settings dialog box appears (see Figure 4-17).

3. **Type in a frame size or click the Record at Current Size radio button (the current window size).**

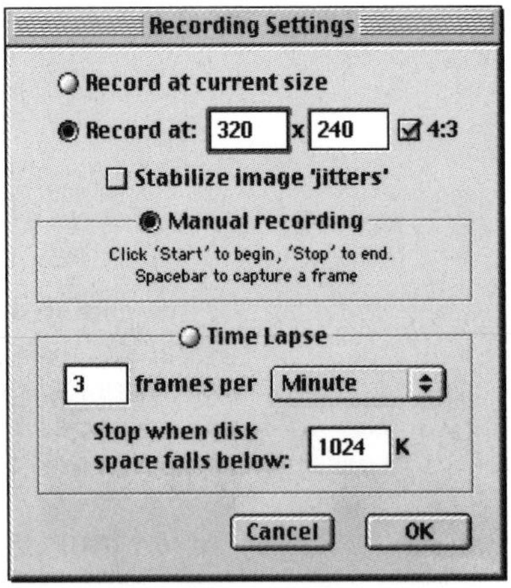

Figure 4-17: The Mac Recording Settings dialog box

4. **Click Stabilize Jitters to help reduce jittery video (Mac only).**
5. **Click Manual recording.** (Windows users click Still Image or Time Lapse. Windows users can also set a frame rate for the capture session.) If you want Premiere to automatically capture using time-lapse mode, click Time Lapse and type the number of frames per minute (or hour or day).

   You may also change the setting in the Stop When Disk Space Falls Below option to automatically stop recording when disk space drops below the number specified in the adjacent field.
6. **Click OK to close the Recording Settings dialog box.**
7. **Choose Video Input from the Stop motion menu.** The Video window is used when capturing video opens. For details, see the section "Assigning Video Settings."
8. **Mac users: Assign any other menu choices available in the Stop motion menu.** Some can be activated during the capture session:
   - **Grab Frames.** Enables you to pick consecutive frames to capture during the stop motion session.
   - **Truncate Movie.** Removes frames after the stop motion is complete.
   - **Show Previous.** Shows the previous frame as a type of ghost image onscreen. This enables you to decide how the next frame looks, as opposed to previous frames. The ghost frame is not recorded.
   - **Remove Background clip.** If you added a background clip, this option is activated and enables you to remove the background clip.

9. **Start your source device — video camera or videotape recorder.**
10. **If you chose the Time Lapse option, click the Start button in the Stop Motion window. Premiere automatically begins capture.** When the capture session is over, click Stop.
11. **If you choose the Manual Recording (Windows: Manual Capture), start the process by clicking Start, then click Step for every frame that you want to capture.**
12. **Choose File ➪ Save to save the clip.**

Capturing Audio

Premiere enables you to capture audio independently of video. When you capture audio, quality is based on the sample rate and bit depth. The *sample rate* is the number of samples taken each second. The *bit depth* is the number of bits (there are 8 bits in a byte of data) per each sample of the actual digitized audio (the minimum bit depth of most audio CODECS is 16). Premiere's audio settings options enable you to specify sample rates and bit depth as well as choose between Mono and Stereo. As you capture, remember that higher bit rates and sample rates create larger files. Remember also that Stereo capturing requires more hard drive space than mono files.

Assigning audio capture settings

Audio capture settings can be changed by opening the Capture Settings dialog box, File ➪ Capture ➪ Movie Settings, or Project ➪ Project Settings ➪ Capture. To change or review audio capture settings, click the Audio button. The options in the Audio Settings dialog box are reviewed in the Audio Settings section. The steps for recording audio for Mac and Windows users are described in the following sections.

Capturing analog audio in Windows

If you are using a PC and have a video or soundboard installed in your computer, you can review or change capture settings for capturing analog audio by choosing File ➪ Capture Audio. A dialog box opens, enabling you to choose the program that you want to use to capture audio. The next time you choose this setting, the program you chose opens automatically. If you don't have a sound-recording program, most Windows users should be able to use SNDRC32.exe, located on most machines in the Windows folder. Sound Recorder, shown in Figure 4-18, enables you to digitize music by clicking the red Record button. To stop recording, click the Stop button and then save your file by choosing File ➪ Save.

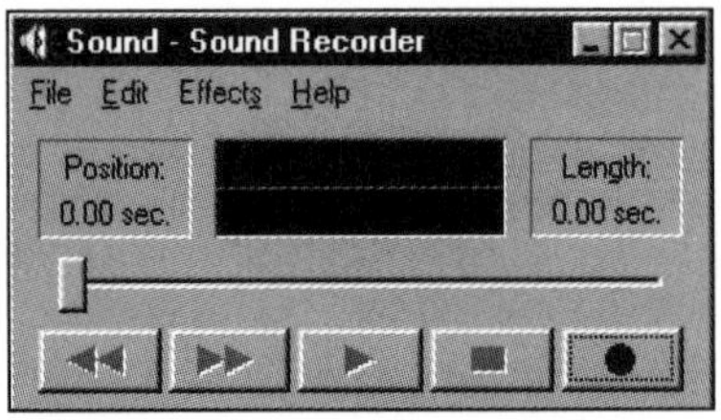

Figure 4-18: The Windows Sound Recorder

Capturing analog audio on the Mac

Mac users with video or soundboards can capture analog audio directly into Premiere by choosing File ➪ Capture ➪ Audio Capture. Doing this opens the Audio Recorder window.

To start recording, turn on the sound device connected to your computer and then click Record. Doing this opens the clip window where you can see the clip being recorded, as shown in Figure 4-18. To stop recording, click the Stop button (the black rectangle).

Figure 4-19: The Mac's Audio Recorder window

Before saving your sound file, you can play back by clicking the Play button (triangle) in the Clip window. You can also set the In and Out points by clicking the Mark In and Mark Out Point buttons in the Clip Window. To save your audio clip, select File ➪ Save.

Summary

Premiere enables you to capture video and audio directly from a video camera or videotape recorder. You can also capture audio from a camcorder or other sound device.

- Before starting a capture session, read all documentation related to your capture hardware.
- Be sure to set up cables properly before the capture session.
- If you are digitizing analog video, specify capture settings in the Capture Settings dialog box (File ➪ Capture ➪ Capture Movie).
- If you are capturing digital video, create a project before the capture session. Use settings recommended by your computer or board manufacturer.
- If your equipment allows device control, you can set up a batch capture session.
- To capture using stop motion, use Premiere's Stop Motion dialog box, File ➪ Capture Stop motion.

✦ ✦ ✦

Editing with Premiere

PART

II

In This Part

CHAPTER 5

Basic Editing with the Timeline, Clip, and Monitor Windows

✦ ✦ ✦ ✦

In This Chapter

Basic editing concepts

Editing in the Timeline

Setting In and Out points in the Timeline

Trimming in the Clip window

Performing Insert and Overlay edits

✦ ✦ ✦ ✦

Editing drives a video program. The careful assembly of sound and video clips can control excitement, tension, and interest. Fortunately, Premiere makes this crucial element of digital video production a logical, creative, and rewarding process rather than a tedious and frustrating one. Premiere's graphical interface — which features its Timeline, Clip, and Monitor windows — combines with its track selection and editing tools to provide a fully integrated and powerful working environment.

This chapter introduces you to the basic techniques of editing in Premiere. It begins with an overview of the editing process and proceeds to basic Timeline editing tasks, such as selecting and moving clips from one part of the Timeline to another. The chapter concludes with a discussion of creating insert and overlay edits by using the Source and Program views in the Monitor window. Premiere's advanced editing techniques are discussed in Chapter 10.

Basic Editing Concepts and Tools

Before you begin editing video in Premiere, you need a basic idea of different techniques that you can use to edit a digital video production. Premiere provides two main areas for editing clips and assembling them — the Timeline window and the

Monitor window. As discussed earlier in this book, the Timeline provides a visual overview of your project. You can begin creating a rough edit by simply dragging clips from the Project window over the Timeline. Using the selection tools in the timeline, you begin arranging the clips in a logical order.

As you work, you can fine-tune your production by performing edits in the Monitor window. When you edit in the monitor window you can set up the Source view to show you a clip that isn't in the Timeline, while the Program view shows you a clip that is already in the Timeline. Using controls in the Monitor window you can insert the source clip into the clip that's already in the Timeline, or *overlay* the source clip so that it replaces a portion of the clip that is in the timeline. The steps and examples in this chapter lead you to the point where you can create insert and overlay edits.

To further fine-tune your editing work, you can use Premiere's editing tools to perform ripple, slide, and slip edits. These, along with more sophisticated monitor editing techniques, such as three- and four-point editing, lifts, and extracts, are discussed in Chapter 10.

As you work, you undoubtedly develop habits that suit the types of productions you are creating. For example, many editing commands feature keyboard shortcuts. You may find it more efficient to set the In and Out points of clips by using keyboard shortcut keys.

Note When you are performing edits, you may find it easier to use keyboard shortcuts. Use the Commands palette to create and display keyboard shortcuts. To display the Commands palette, choose Window ➪ Show Commands.

Creating a storyboard

To better understand your project and to conceptualize the edits that you need, you may want to start the editing process by creating a storyboard. As discussed in Chapter 1, a storyboard is a visual representation of your project created using still images. The Storyboard feature, new in Premiere 6, helps you visualize your project by showing the basic order in which scenes will appear. This is a good place to start when you first begin to assemble your project, because you can arrange clips in the desired order before you have to worry about other edits. Follow these steps to created a storyboard:

1. **Choose File ➪ New ➪ Storyboard.**
2. **Next, drag the items you want to use from the Project window directly to the Storyboard window.**
3. **In the Storyboard window, click and drag the items to rearrange their order.** When you are satisfied with your storyboard, you can have the items from the Storyboard window placed in the Timeline window.
4. **To place Storyboard items into the Timeline, choose Project ➪ Automate to Timeline.** The items in the Timeline window appear in the same order as they do in the Storyboard window.

The workspace

An important consideration before actually editing a project is to plan how you want your workspace set up. To pick a predefined workspace, choose Window ➪ Workspace and then choose from the four choices presented: Single-Track Editing, A/B Editing, Effects, and Audio.

Premiere's Single-Track Editing workspace, shown in Figure 5-1, sets the Timeline window so that you are working with single-track video tracks. Single-Track Editing lets you see more of the Timeline on-screen at once, but it offers less control over transitions. Use Single-Track Editing for projects that primarily consist of cuts, with few transitions, or for rough cuts.

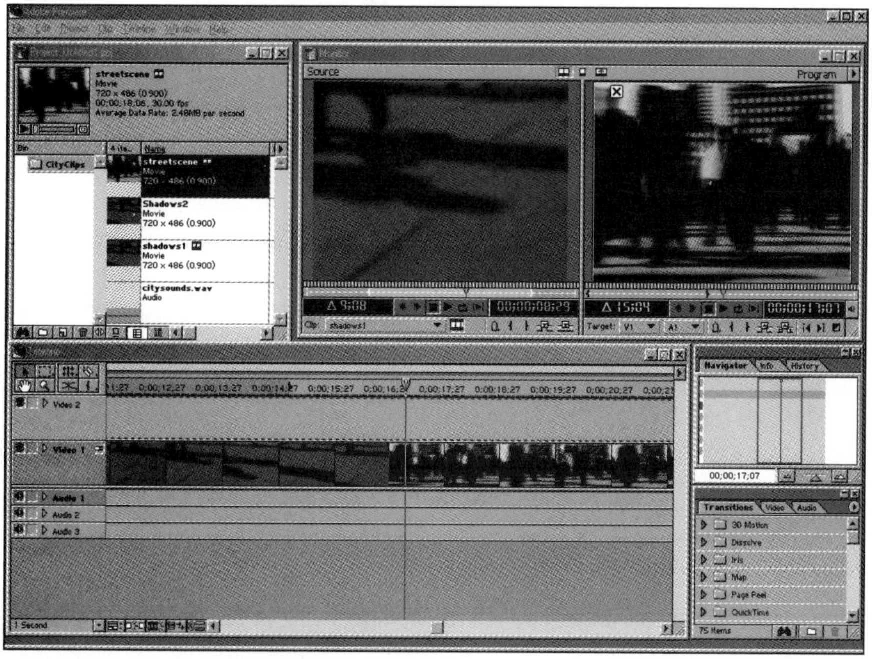

Figure 5-1: Single-Track Editing workspace

In the A/B Editing workspace, shown in Figure 5-2, Video 1 track is expanded into two tracks — Video 1A track and Video 1B track — with a Transition track between them for creating transitions (see Chapter 7 to learn more about creating transitions between clips). This is the most efficient workspace for building a production with many transitions. Many users feel that it is easier to create, edit, and conceptualize transitions using the A/B Editing workspace than the Single-Track workspace.

Figure 5-2: A/B Editing workspace

The Effects workspace, shown in Figure 5-3, is similar to the Single-Track workspace. It features a Video 1 track and Video 2 track, and the Effects Controls palette, along with the Audio and Video effects palette, is displayed. This workspace is useful if you are applying effects to your clips, as described in Part III of this book.

In the Audio workspace, shown in Figure 5-4, the Audio Mixer window is displayed. The Audio workspace is useful when you are working with your project's audio. See Chapter 6 for more on working with audio.

At any point in time, you can change the arrangement of palettes on-screen and save your workspace by choosing Window ➪ Workspace ➪ Save Workspace. This adds your workspace to the options in the Windows ➪ Workspace submenu. When you want to reload your workspace, simply choose Window ➪ Workspace and select your workspace from the menu.

Figure 5-3: The Effects workspace

Figure 5-4: The Audio workspace

Understanding the Timeline Window

To edit efficiently in the Timeline window, shown in Figure 5-5, you should be familiar with all of its features. You need to be able to navigate your way through the Timeline window and zoom in to see close-up views of frames. In this section, you tour the Timeline window and learn how to navigate and master it.

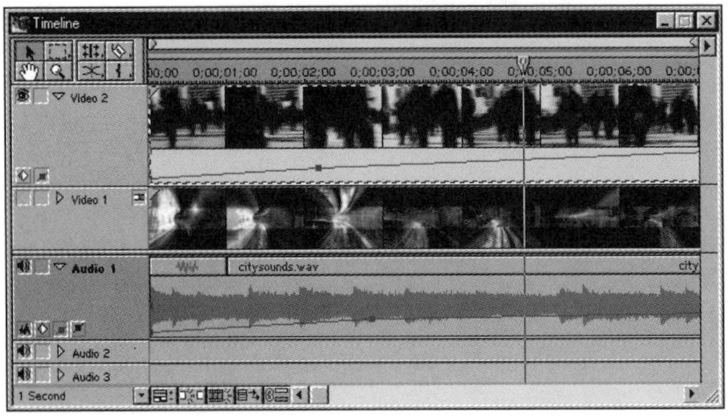

Figure 5-5: The Timeline window

A tour of the Timeline window

The best place to start touring the Timeline window is at the top, where the Work Area band appears. This band simply shows you the entire working area of Premiere. The yellow bar within the Work Area band is called the Work Area bar. The Work Area bar determines the area that Premiere renders when you preview a clip or project. The Work Area markers appear at either end of the Work Area bar. By clicking and dragging the left and right markers, you can change the area onscreen that will be previewed or exported. Below the Work Area bar is the Timeline ruler for the project. Above the Timeline ruler appears the Timeline marker. You can click and drag the timeline marker to view different parts of your project in the Monitor window. To quickly jump to any point in the Timeline, click the mouse at that point in the Timeline ruler.

Tip To reduce the work area to the size of the Timeline window, double-click the Work Area bar. To quickly set the work area to encompass your entire project, Option/Alt-click the Work Area bar.

To the left of the Timeline is a toolbox with various editing tools that enable you to edit and rearrange clips. At the bottom of the Timeline window is the Time Zoom Level pop-up menu. Click in this pop-up menu to change the time or frame increments that appear in the Timeline. For example, if you choose 1 Frame, you can zoom in to view each frame in the clip as a separate entity. Because each frame appears in the Timeline, the Timeline grows, so it can show you more information. If you change the time setting to 1 Second, the Timeline shrinks, as does the size of each clip. When you choose a setting in the Time Zoom Level pop-up menu, the larger tick marks in the Timeline show you the time divisions. For example, if you choose 2 Seconds, the larger tick marks indicate every two seconds of time.

Clicking the first icon to the right of the Time Zoom Level pop-up menu displays the Track Options dialog box shown in Figure 5-6. This dialog box enables you to add or delete tracks. You can also display the Track Options dialog box by choosing Timeline ➪ Track Options. Another way to add tracks is to choose Timeline ➪ Add Video Track or Timeline ➪ Add Audio Track.

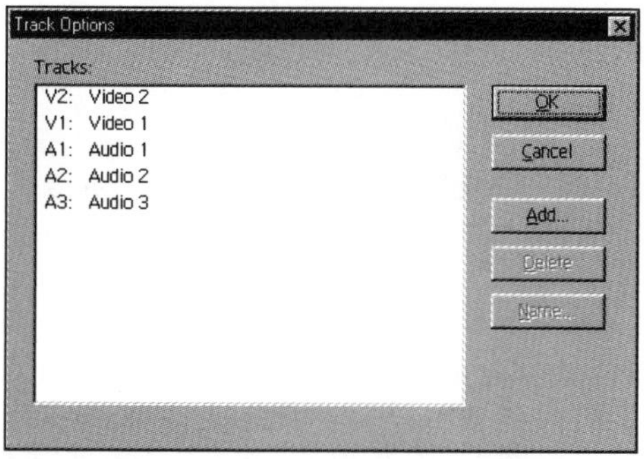

Figure 5-6: Track Options dialog box

In the timeline, an eye icon and an indented square icon appear next to the name of the track. You can click the square icon. After you click, a lock appears, which indicates that the track is locked. A locked clip can't be edited. You can temporarily hide a clip by clicking the eye icon.

You can expand and collapse either a video or audio track by clicking the triangle next to the track name in the Timeline. When the track is expanded, you can see the Track Mode buttons. The buttons enable you to either display fade lines for fading video (changing opacity) or audio (changing volume).

In Single-Track Editing mode, you can also expand the Video 1 track by clicking the Track Mode icon (the rectangle to the right of the track name in the Timeline). This displays two instances of the Video 1 track and a Transition track.

Adjusting track views

When you create a new project, Premiere automatically creates a Video 1 track and a Video 2 track. You can use Video 2 track to superimpose clips over Video 1 track, and you can use Video 1 track to create transitions. As mentioned earlier, you can choose the track view to be in either A/B Editing mode or in Single-Track Editing mode. If you expand the Video 1 track in A/B Editing mode, it converts to the Video 1A track and the Video 1B track with a transition track between them, as seen in Figure 5-2. Only a Video 2 track and a Video 1 track exist in Single-Track Editing mode. No transition track exists, as shown in Figure 5-1.

Navigating Your Way Through the Timeline

You often move from one area to another when working in the Timeline. To move to different parts of the Timeline, you can use the Zoom and Hand tools, or you can use the Navigator palette. If the Time Zoom level pop-up menu is not set to 1 Frame, zooming in enables you to see more frames in your clip. Here's how to use the Zoom and Hand tools (you should have a project on-screen with a clip in the Timeline window):

Note: The Hand and Zoom tools appear in the Toolbox in the Timeline window. They are the first and second tools of the second row of the Toolbox. You can press H on your keyboard to select the Hand tool. You can press Z to select the Zoom tool.

1. **Select the Zoom tool.**
2. **To increase the number of frames that you see in the Timeline, move the Zoom tool toward a clip in the Timeline and click.** Keep clicking to continue increasing the number of frames. Alternatively, with the Zoom tool selected, press and hold the Option/Alt key on your keyboard and click the clip to increase the number of frames or seconds.

To move within the clip in the Timeline, follow these steps:

1. **Select the Hand tool.**
2. **Click and drag to the place you want to see in the clip.**

Here's how to use the Navigator palette:

1. **Choose Window ⇨ Show Navigator to display the Navigator palette.**
2. **Click either the Zoom in or Zoom out button at the bottom of the Navigator palette to zoom in or out.** You can also click and drag the Zoom slider.
3. **To move to a particular place on the Timeline, double-click in the timecode display area (lower left in the Navigator palette), type in a new timecode location, and then press Enter.** Alternatively, you can click and drag the green rectangle in the preview area of the Navigator palette to move back and forth through the Timeline.

Creating shy tracks and exclude tracks

In addition to hiding tracks, you can also *shy* tracks and *exclude* tracks. Marking a track as shy enables you to hide it from the Timeline. After you hide the shy track, it is removed from the Timeline, yet it is still previewed and exported. Using shy tracks enables you to work more efficiently with less visual distractions on-screen.

If you exclude a track, it is removed from the Timeline as well as from previews and all exports. This may be useful, for example, if you want to preview or export a version of the project without a musical audio track.

To mark a track as shy, press and hold the Command/Ctrl key as you click the eye icon next to the name of the track that you want to mark as shy. When you make a track shy, the eye icon is outlined. To hide a shy track, choose Timeline ⇨ Hide Shy Tracks.

To exclude a track, press and hold the Option/Alt key as you click the eye icon next to the name of the track that you want to exclude. The eye icon disappears.

Selecting and moving clips in the Timeline

After you've placed clips in the Timeline, you often need to reposition them as part of the editing process. You can choose to move one clip at a time, or you can move several clips at the same time. (You can also move either the video or audio of a clip independently. To do this you need to temporarily unlink the clip.)

The simplest way to move a single clip is to click it with the Selection tool and move it within the Timeline window. If you want the clip you move to snap to the edge of another clip, make sure the Snap to Edges command is selected. Choose either Timeline ⇨ Snap to Edges or press the Toggle Snap to Edges icon at the bottom of the Timeline window.

If you move a clip on the Timeline that is linked to another clip — such as a video clip that is linked to its audio clip — the linked clips move together. Here's how to temporarily unlink a clip and move it:

1. **To unlink a clip, click the Toggle Sync Mode icon at the bottom of the Timeline window (see Figure 5-5).**
2. **Select either the video or audio portion of the clip with the Select tool.**
3. **Click and drag the selected clip to where you want it to appear in the Timeline.**
4. **To relink the clip, again click the Toggle Sync Mode icon.**

To move several clips simultaneously, you need to select all of the clips that you plan to move. Click and hold the mouse button on the Range Select Tool in the Timeline's toolbox. Point to the desired selection tool and release the mouse button. Here is a description of the selection tools that enable you to quickly select multiple clips and/or tracks The tools are shown in Figure 5-7.

Note

Premiere's Selection tool occupies its own toolbox location, and is not found with the other selection tools. As mentioned earlier, the Selection tool selects the clip that you click. To select different clips in different areas of the Timeline with the Selection tool, press and hold Command/Ctrl as you click.

- **Range Select tool.** Selects only the clips that you click and drag over.
- **Block Select tool.** This tool is used for creating a *virtual clip*—a copy of a specific area of the Timeline—which Premiere creates automatically. On the Timeline the original video clips as well as transitions and effects all appear as one virtual clip that can be copied again and again. You create a virtual clip by first clicking and dragging over the clips that you want to copy with the Block Select tool. After you move the selection to another area of the Timeline, Premiere creates the virtual clip. (For an in-depth discussion of this time-saving feature, turn to Chapter 10.
- **Track Select tool.** Selects everything on a track from the point in the Timeline at which you click to the end of the track. If you move a clip that has been selected with the Track Select tool, only clips on the same track move. If the clip has an audio track associated with it, it won't move.
- **Multitrack Select tool.** Selects everything on all the tracks from the point in the Timeline at which you click to the end of the track, including all clips to the right of your mouse click. If you click and drag with the Multitrack Select tool, all tracks to the right of the mouse click move.

Figure 5-7: The track selection tools

Here's how to select and move multiple clips (you should have a project on screen that has various clips in the Timeline window):

1. **Click and hold the Range Select tool and choose either the Track Select or Multitrack Select tool.**
2. **Click where you want to begin the selection.**

   If you are using the Track Select tool (see Figure 5-8), only clips on the track you clicked are selected. If you select a video track that is linked to an audio track, the tracks are temporarily unlinked.

   If you are using the Multitrack Select tool (see Figure 5-9), all clips on the Timeline after the point at which you clicked are selected.

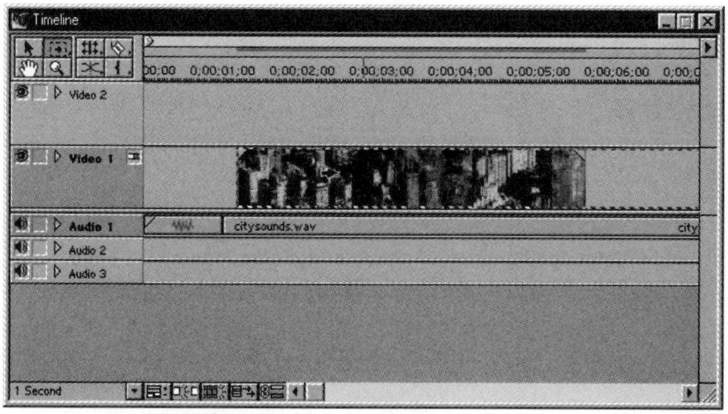

Figure 5-8: Moving a clip with the Track Select tool

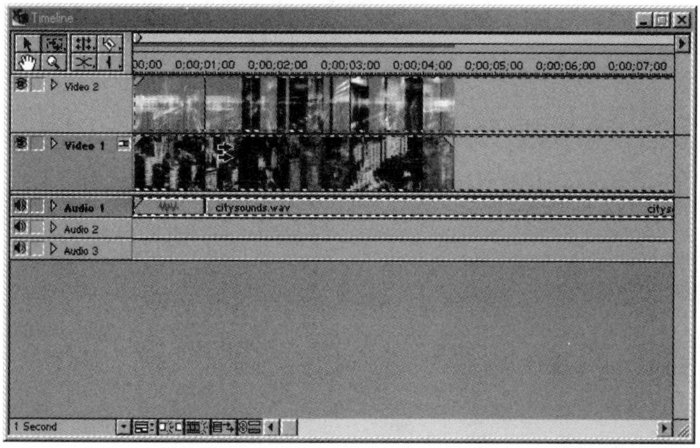

Figure 5-9: Moving a clip with the Multitrack Select tool

To select specific clips by clicking and dragging, use the Range Select tool:

1. **Click and hold the Range Select tool and choose either the Range Select or Block Select tool.**
2. **Click and drag rectangle selection over the clips that you want to select.** The Range Select tool selects all clips that fall within the range you select, as shown in Figure 5-10.

Tip

If you click and drag a clip with the Selection tool between two adjacent clips in the Timeline, Premiere will automatically insert the new clip between the two adjacent clips, automatically moving the clip to the right of the edit.

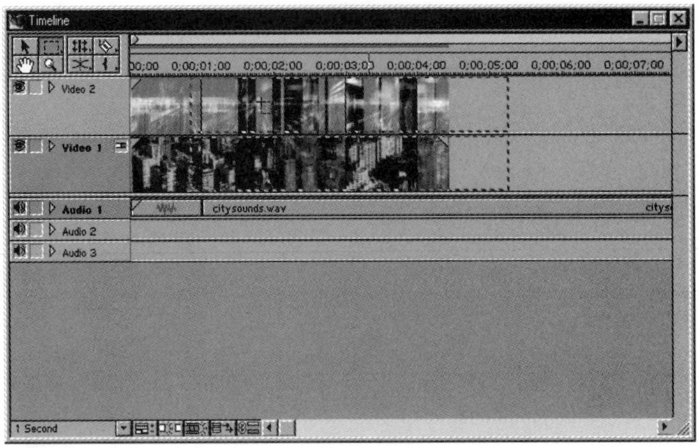

Figure 5-10: Moving a clip with the Range Select tool

Customizing the Timeline window

The Timeline Window Options dialog box enables you to customize the Timeline window. To display the Timeline Window Options dialog box, shown in Figure 5-11, choose Window ⇨ Window Options ⇨ Timeline Window Options.

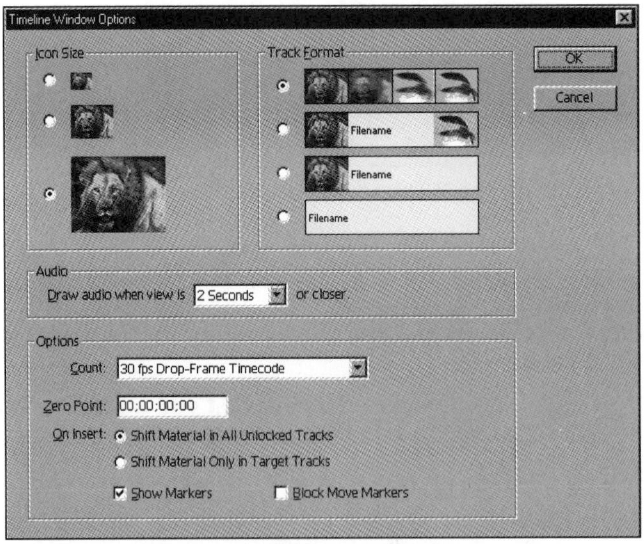

Figure 5-11: The Timeline Window Options dialog box enables you to edit how tracks and clips are displayed.

The Timeline Window Options dialog box features four different sections: Icon Size, Track Format, Audio, and Options.

✦ **Icon Size.** You can click one of the radio buttons in the Icon Size section to change the size of how a clip appears in the Timeline window.

✦ **Track Format.** Clicking one of the radio buttons in the Track Format section changes how a clip is displayed in the track. Clicking the first radio button displays the clip with graphical previews. Clicking the last radio button displays the clip with only the actual filename of the clip to identify it.

✦ **Audio.** Clicking the Audio pop-up menu enables you to set the Timeline zoom level at which an audio waveform becomes visible in the audio track.

✦ **Options.** You can click the Count pop-up menu in the Options section and change the frame rate of your project. In the Options section, you can also set the zero point of the production. By default, the starting point is set to 00:00:00:00. This sets the starting point if you are outputting for timecode.

- **Shift Material in All Unlocked Tracks.** Moves all tracks when you insert a clip in the Timeline.
- **Shift Material Only in Target Tracks.** Select this option if you only want target tracks to move when you insert a clip.
- **Show Markers.** Enables markers to be displayed in the Timeline. You can use markers to identify different areas within the Timeline. Markers are discussed in the next section.
- **Block Move Markers.** Leave this option selected to enable markers in the Timeline to move when you use the Multitrack Select tool or when you execute a ripple edit with Shift Material in All Unlocked Tracks selected. If you deselect this option, Timeline markers remain in place.

Setting In and Out Points in the Timeline Window

When you're familiar with the Timeline, you can easily perform edits. You can edit by either using the Selection tool or setting In and Out points using markers. In and Out points let you specify where transitions should begin or end, where clips should be trimmed or copied, where effects should be applied, and more.

Editing with the Selection tool

One of the simplest ways to edit in the Timeline window is to set In and Out points using the Selection tool. To edit an In or Out point with the Selection tool, follow these steps:

1. **Select the Timeline Selection tool.**
2. **To set a clip's In point, move the Selection tool over the left edge of the clip in the Timeline.** The Selection tool changes to an Edge icon.

3. **Click and drag the edge of the clip to where you want the clip to start playing.**
4. **To a clip's Out point, move the Selection tool over the right edge of the clip in the Timeline.** The Selection tool changes to an Edge icon.
5. **Click and drag the edge of the clip to where you want the clip to stop playing.**

Editing with Timeline markers

You also can set the In and Out points by using the Timeline ➪ Set Timeline Marker ➪ In and Timeline ➪ Set Timeline Marker ➪ Out commands.

Setting In and Out points

Here's how to set In and Out points using menu commands:

1. **Drag the clip from the Project window to a video track in the Timeline window.**
2. **Click and drag the Timeline Edit line marker to where you want your clip to start.**
3. **Choose Timeline ➪ Set Timeline Marker ➪ In.** An In point icon appears on the Timeline at the position of the Timeline Edit line Marker.
4. **Click and drag the Timeline Edit Line marker to where you want your clip to end.**
5. **Choose Timeline ➪ Set Timeline Marker ➪ Out.** An Out point icon appears on the Timeline at the position of the Timeline Edit line marker.

Moving In and Out points

To move In and Out points with the menu command, follow these steps:

1. **Move the Timeline marker to where you want to move either the In or Out point.**
2. **Choose Timeline ➪ Set Timeline Marker ➪ In or Out.** The Timeline marker appears in the newly assigned location.

Note

Before executing the previous steps, create a project and import a clip into it by choosing File ➪ Import. You can use the any of the clips from the Chapter 5 folder on the *Adobe Premiere 6.5 Bible* CD-ROM.

Clearing In and Out points

After making an edit, you may decide to undo your change. You can easily clear Timeline markers with the following menu commands:

✦ To clear both the In and Out points and to start all over again, choose Timeline ➪ Clear Timeline Marker ➪ In and Out.

✦ To clear just the In point, choose Timeline ➪ Clear Timeline Marker ➪ In.

✦ To clear just the Out point, choose Timeline ➪ Clear Timeline Marker ➪ Out.

Editing with the In and Out tools

Here's how to edit using the In and Out tools on the Timeline toolbox:

1. **Click the In Point tool to select it.**
2. **Click where you want the clip to start.** Notice that everything to the left of where you clicked is removed in the Timeline. Only the area to the right of where you clicked remains.

   If you made the In point too far into the clip, select the In Point tool and drag the In point to the left. The section of the clip that was removed from the Timeline reappears.

Note: Moving an In or Out point doesn't delete any of the source file; instead, the In and Out points only tell Premiere which portion of the source file are used.

3. **Select the Out Point tool.** Do this by clicking and holding the In Point tool and then choosing the Out Point tool from the small menu that appears.
4. **Click where you want the clip to end.** Notice that everything to the right of where you clicked disappears. Only the area to the left of where you clicked remains.

   To extend the Out point, select the Out Point tool and click and drag the Out point to the right. The section at the end of the clip that was removed from the Timeline reappears.

Adding Markers

You can add numerical markers to your clip and use them as visual landmarks on the Timeline that you want to quickly return to later. These are especially useful with longer projects.

To add a marker, move the Timeline Marker to where you want to add a marker, and then choose Timeline ➪ Set Timeline Marker ➪ (choose a number).

You can jump to a marker by choosing Timeline ➪ Go To Timeline Marker ➪ (choose an option).

Trimming Using the Clip Window

You can trim a video clip or an audio clip in its Clip window, shown in Figure 5-12. To display the Clip window, double-click a clip in the Timeline window or in the Project window. Double-clicking the clip in the Project window displays the clip so that both video and audio can be edited. If you double-click the clip's video track in the Timeline window, only the video portion appears in the Clip window. If you double-click the audio track of the clip, Premiere displays only the audio part, allowing you to edit only audio.

Figure 5-12: Clips can be trimmed in the Monitor window.

Note You can also choose File ⇨ Open to open a clip in its own window.

When the Clip window appears, you can use the controls shown in Figure 5-12 to view the clip. It's a good idea to view the clip before you edit it. Click the Play button to play the entire clip. You can play the clip continuously by clicking the Loop button. When you find a section you want to edit, you can stop it by clicking the Stop button. When you stop the clip, look at the time readout to see at which frame you have stopped. This can help you when setting In and Out points and when setting markers. If you didn't stop the clip in the correct place, you can use the frame forward and frame backward buttons to slowly locate the frame you want to set as the In point. You can also click and drag in the jogging bar (see Figure 5-12) or the jog tread area to move back and forth through your clip. To make a quick jump in the clip, click the Set location area of the clip.

Note You can jump to a specific frame in a clip by clicking and dragging over the Program Location numerical frame display and typing a specific timecode position. You do not need to type colons or semicolons.

When you reach the In point, click the Mark In button. Now locate the frame that you want to set as the Out point and click the Mark Out button. After you set the In and Out points, you can easily edit their positions by simply clicking and dragging on either of those points. After you've set the In and Out points, note the Time display with the delta symbol in front of it. This number indicates the duration from the In point to the Out point.

If the clip in the Clip window is in the Timeline, you see the length of the clip change. If the clip hasn't been dragged to the Timeline, drag it to the Timeline to see the In and Out points reflect the editing in the Clip window. You may find it convenient to drag the clip directly from the Clip window to the Timeline.

Working with the Monitor Window

The Monitor window can be used for precise editing and trimming. When editing using the Monitor window, you can choose to trim in Single View (Figure 5-13), Dual View (Figure 5-14), or Trim View (Figure 5-15). In Single View mode, the Monitor displays just the edited program (clips on the Timeline). Dual View mode displays a source clip (clip not as yet added to the Timeline) in the left side of the window and the program material (clips on the Timeline) on the right side of the window (placing a clip in the Source section of the Monitor window is covered in the next section). In Trim View mode, the frame to the right and the frame to the left of the edit line are represented in a separate section to provide greater precision for setting In and Out points. To select a view mode for the Monitor, click one of the mode buttons near the top of the Monitor window, or choose Single View, Dual View, or Trim View from the Monitor window's menu.

Figure 5-13: The Monitor window in Single View

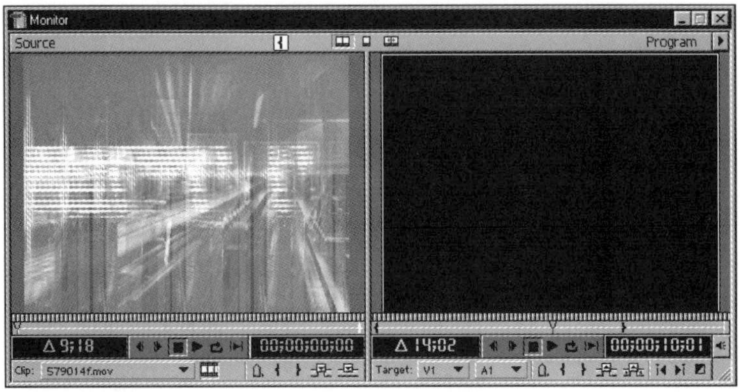

Figure 5-14: The Monitor window in Dual View

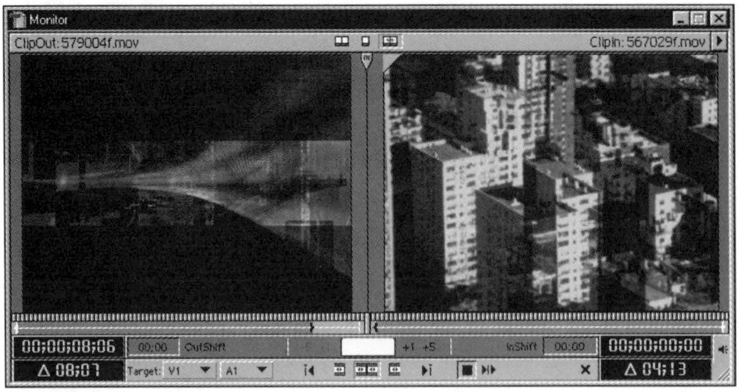

Figure 5-15: The Monitor window in Trim View

The options that appear in the Monitor window vary depending upon what view you are in.

To set the Monitor window options, choose Window ➪ Window Options ➪ Monitor Window Options. The Monitor Window Options dialog box (Figure 5-16) provides three sections: Source Options, Safe Margins, and Trim Mode Options. The Safe Margins enable you to show the video safe zones for movement and for titles. The safe zone markers in the Monitor window indicate the image area that is safely within the monitor viewing area, as well as the image area that might be overscanned. A safe zone is needed because television monitors overscan an image, thus can expand portions of it beyond the screen. In the Monitor Window Options dialog box, you can edit the Action-Safe margin and the Title-Safe margin fields. To view the safe zone markers in the Monitor window, first close the Monitor Window options by clicking OK. Then choose Safe Margins for Source Side and/or Safe Margins for Program Side from the Monitor window menu. When the Safe Zone margins appear in the Monitor window, the inner safe zone is the title-safe area, the outer is the action-safe area.

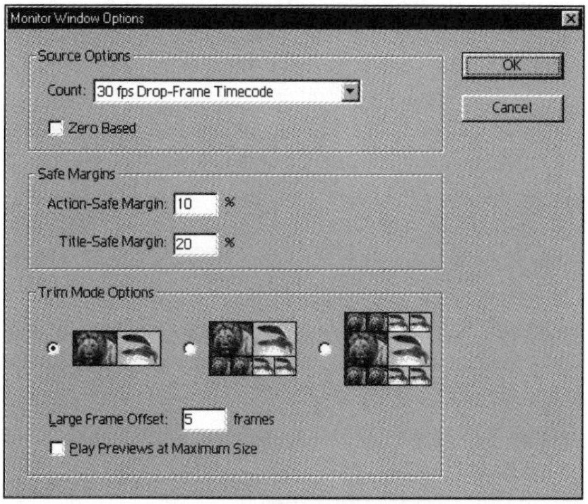

Figure 5-16: The Monitor Window Options dialog box

In most editing situations, you want to view the Monitor window in Dual mode. This enables you to view a source clip (usually not in the Timeline) and the program material (the clip in the Timeline) at the same time. Before you use more sophisticated editing techniques, you should become familiar with the two sections of the Monitor window in Dual mode. Beneath the Source View is the source controller, which enables you to play source clips that haven't been added to the Timeline. The In and Out point icons enable you to set In and Out points of source clips.

Beneath the Program View is the program controller, which enables you to play the program that exists on the Timeline. Clicking the In and Out point icons in the Program View changes the In and Out points of clips already on the Timeline. (You use the program In and Out point icons when you create three-point edits in Chapter 10).

Adding clips to the Timeline using the Monitor window

The Source View of the Monitor window enables you to perform insert and overlay edits. When you perform an *insert edit*, the source clip is inserted into the Timeline at the edit line. If you perform an *overlay edit*, the source clip replaces a section of the program at the Timeline's edit line. For example, assume that you have a clip of a galloping horse in the Timeline. You wish to place a two-second close-up of the jockey on the horse into the clip. If you perform an insert edit, the clip is split at the Timeline edit location, and the jockey is inserted into the clip. The entire Timeline sequence is three seconds longer. If you perform an overlay edit, on the other hand, the three-second jockey footage replaces three seconds of horse footage. An overlay enables you to continue using the audio track that is linked to the galloping horse clip, providing more consistent continuity in the final video.

The following steps show you how to add a clip to the source area of the Monitor window, set which tracks to use on the Timeline for the edit, and then perform an insert or overlay edit:

1. **Choose Window ➪ Monitor to display the Monitor window if it is not onscreen.**
2. **Click Dual View from the Monitor window pop-up menu.** You can also click the Dual View icon to set the Monitor window so that it displays both the Source and Program views.
3. **Click and drag a clip into the Timeline.** This clip appears in the Program section of the Timeline. Assume that this is part of the program you are editing and you now want to insert a clip two seconds into it.
4. **Use the controls in the Monitor window to move to the frame where you want the source clip inserted.** The icons are the same as those in the clip window. You can click the Frame Forward and Frame Backward buttons, or you can use the jogging bar or jogging tread.
5. **Drag a clip from the Project window to the Source section of the Monitor window.** The clip appears in the Monitor window's Source View.

Tip

You can also drag a clip directly from the Clip window to the Source View of the Monitor window.

To view the clip, click the Play button. To use both the video and audio for the clip, there should not be a diagonal line through the Take Video and Take Audio icons. By default, no diagonal line exists. A diagonal line appears only if you click these icons. If the line is present, simply click the icon to toggle the Take Audio or Take Video icon off.

6. **Beneath the Program View, click the first Target pop-up menu so that you can choose the track in which you want the video clip to appear.** Only the video tracks that currently exist on the Timeline for your project appear in the pop-up menu. If you want to use another video track, you need to add a track to the Timeline. To add a track to the Timeline, choose Timeline ➪ Add Video Track.
7. **Beneath the Program View, click the second Target pop-up menu to choose the track in which you want the audio clip to appear.** As with video tracks, only the audio tracks that are currently on your Timeline appear in the pop-up menu. If you want to use another audio track, you need to add an audio track by choosing Timeline ➪ Add Audio Track.
8. **In the Source clip section of the Monitor window, click the Frame Forward and Frame Backward buttons to locate the frames that you want to set as the In and Out points.**
9. **When you reach the In point, click the Mark In button.**
10. **Move to the desired Out point.**
11. **Set the Out point by clicking the Mark Out button.** Now you can perform an insert or an overlay edit.
12. **Perform the insert or overlay edit.** To insert the clip at the Timeline marker line, choose Clip ➪ Insert at Edit line, or click the Insert at Timeline button. After you click, the clip in the Timeline is cut at the frame that you set in the Monitor window. Inserted into the clip is the source clip whose In and Out points you set in the Source window. To overlay the clip, choose Clip ➪ Overlay at Timeline, or click the Overlay button. After you click, the source clip replaces a section of the Timeline.
13. **To view the final edit, click the Play button in the Monitor window.**

Summary

Premiere provides graphical tools to aid in editing a digital video production. The Timeline, the Timeline selection tools, and the Monitor window all come into play when you begin to assemble and fine-tune your production. When you edit in Premiere you can do the following:

- Drag clips to the Timeline from the Project window.
- Use the Timeline selection tools to select and move clips in the Timeline.
- Set In and Out points in the Timeline.
- Set In and Out points in the Clip window or Source View of the Monitor window.
- Perform insert and overlay edits using the Monitor window.

✦ ✦ ✦

CHAPTER 6

Editing Audio

✦ ✦ ✦ ✦

In This Chapter

The role of sound in video

Playing an audio clip

Fading and gaining

Balancing volume

Creating cross fades

Mixing sound using the Audio Mixer

Working with audio effects

Exporting audio clips

✦ ✦ ✦ ✦

Can you imagine what you could do with 99 tracks of audio? You can fade, superimpose, and mix audio tracks in the same way that you can superimpose video tracks. This chapter focuses on what you can do with sound by using Adobe Premiere.

Cross-Reference

For information on editing and trimming sound and/or video clips, see Chapter 5, "Basic Editing Using the Timeline, Clip, and Monitor Windows," and Chapter 10, "Advanced Editing Techniques." For information on superimposing video tracks, turn to Chapter 12, "Superimposing."

This chapter focuses on many of the Premiere program's sound features. It begins with a look at fading sound in and out in the Timeline and progresses to a discussion about the Audio Mixer palette, where you can mix audio tracks in real time — as you hear the sound and view the video in the Monitor window. The chapter concludes with a look at all of the audio effects that appear in the Audio effects palette.

Importance of Sound in Video

Just as a picture tells a thousand words, sound can set the mood for what you are trying to present, or it can be used to capture your audience's attention. Sound is everywhere from the sounds of birds singing and waves crashing, to the sound of rush-hour traffic. The right background music can create a feeling of intrigue, comedy, or mystery. Sound effects can add realism and even add suspense to the visual elements that you present. You can incorporate everyday sounds into your clips that were recorded by using a tape recorder or digital camcorder. After you've recorded your sounds, you can capture the sound onto your computer by plugging your digital camcorder into your computer and using the Premiere program's capture feature. For information on capturing sound, turn to Chapter 4, "Capturing Video."

You can obtain sound clips from music stock agencies, or if you're a musician, you can create your own music by using a sound editing program. You can also make music with an instrument and then digitize it by using a computer.

Playing a Sound Clip

You can choose to play a sound that you have digitized by opening that file, or you can import the sound clip into a project and then play the sound clip from within the project.

Here's how to play a sound by directly opening the sound file:

1. **Choose File ⇨ Open to load a sound file on-screen.** The sound file opens in the Clip window in the form of an audio waveform (see Figure 6-1). An audio waveform visually displays the changes in the sound's *amplitude,* or volume. You can zoom in to the waveform by clicking the Zoom In/Out button at the bottom left-hand side of the Clip window.
2. **To play the sound in the Clip window, click the Play button.**

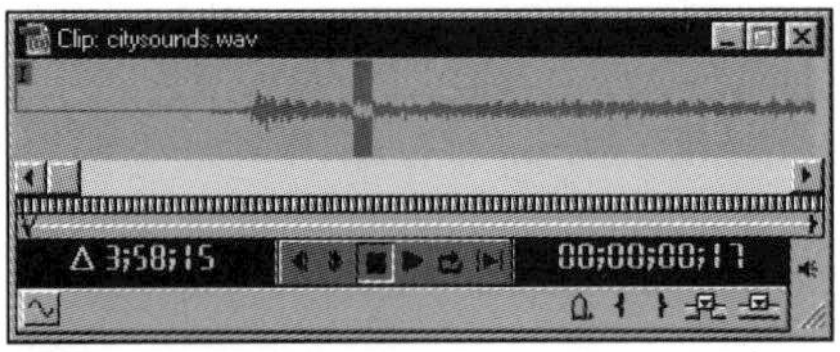

Figure 6-1: An audio waveform in the Clip window

3. **Click the Set Volume button to set the volume of the audio clip.**
4. **Click the Loop button to have the sound continue playing over and over again.**
5. **Click the Stop button to stop the sound.**

The Clip window can also be used to trim an audio clip at the beginning or end of a clip by using the In and Out Point buttons. To play only the edited in and out sound, click the Play In to Out button.

Cross-Reference

For more information on editing a sound, turn to Chapters 5 and 10.

Premiere enables you to also play an audio clip in the Project window. Here's how:

1. **Choose File ➪ New Project to create a new project.**
2. **Choose File ➪ Import ➪ File to import a sound file into your new project. You can also open an existing project with a sound clip already in the Project window.**
3. **In the Project window, click the audio clip that you want to play.**
4. **Click the Play button that appears in the preview at the top of the Project window, shown in Figure 6-2. If the Monitor window is in Dual view, the clip appears in the Monitor window.**

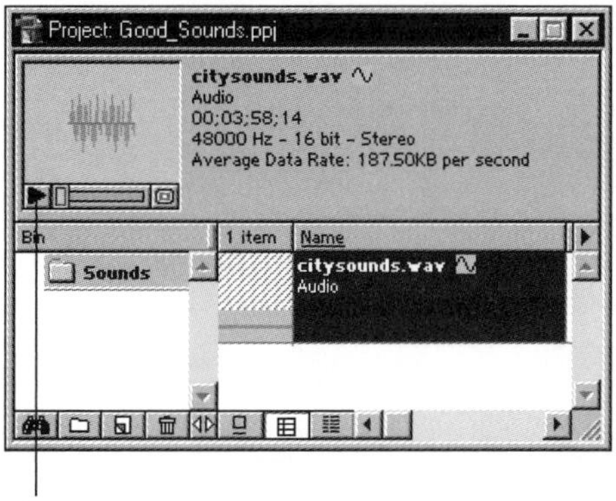

Play button

Figure 6-2: Click the Play button in the clip preview area in the Project window.

You can also play back an audio clip that has been imported into the Timeline window. Follow these steps to do just that:

1. **Choose File ➪ New Project to create a new project.**
2. **Choose File ➪ Import ➪ File to import a sound file into your new project.**
3. **Click the audio clip and drag it from the Project window to Audio track 1 in the Timeline window.** You can also choose to open an existing project with a sound clip already in the Project and Timeline windows.
4. **Double-click the sound clip in the Timeline window.** The sound clip opens in the Clip window.

Note

If your sound clip has video, you'll both see the video and hear the audio when you play the clip, in the Project preview area, the Clip window, or the Monitor window.

With an audio clip in the Timeline window, you can also choose to view the audio clips in audio waveform from within the Timeline window.

Here's how to view the audio waveform of a sound clip in the Timeline window:

1. **Click the Expand/Collapse button (the triangle in front of the word, Audio 1) to expand the audio track.**
2. **Click the Audio Waveform icon to display the audio waveform in the Timeline window, as shown in Figure 6-3.**

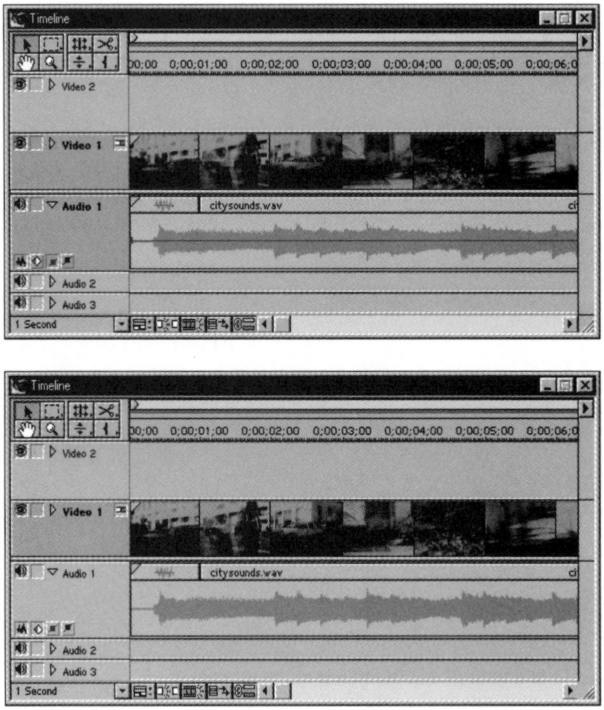

Figure 6-3: An audio waveform in the Timeline window

On the CD-ROM

The CD-ROM includes practice sound clips from Digital Vision's royalty-free CD, *Sounds from the Chill.* The file name of the sound clip used in this chapter is 66501aw.wav. We renamed it citysounds.wav to keep our files organized. You can locate the sound clip in the Chapter 6 folder on the *Adobe Premiere 6.5 Bible* CD-ROM.

Gaining and Fading

One of the most common sound effects is to slowly fade sound in at the beginning of a clip and fade the sound out at the end. You can do this by using the Rubberband option (fade line) that appears when an audio track is expanded. You can also change the volume of a sound in the right and left speakers independently of each other. This is called *panning*, and it can be accomplished by using the Pan Rubberband option. You can change the entire volume of a sound clip by using Premiere's Gain command. The following sections show you how to adjust fade clips in and out and how to pan.

Adjusting sound volume by using the Gain command

The Gain command enables you to change the volume of the entire sound clip by making the volume lower or higher. Here's how to use the Gain command:

1. **Choose File ➪ New Project to create a new project or open a project.**
2. **Choose File ➪ Import to import a sound clip or a video clip with sound.**
3. **Drag the sound clip from the Project window to an audio track in the Timeline window.**
4. **Click the sound clip in the audio track in the Timeline window.**
5. **Choose Clip ➪ Audio Options ➪ Gain.** The Audio Gain dialog box appears (see Figure 6-4).
6. **Type a value in the Gain Value box.** A number greater than 100% increases the sound volume of the clip. A number less than 100 % decreases the sound volume.

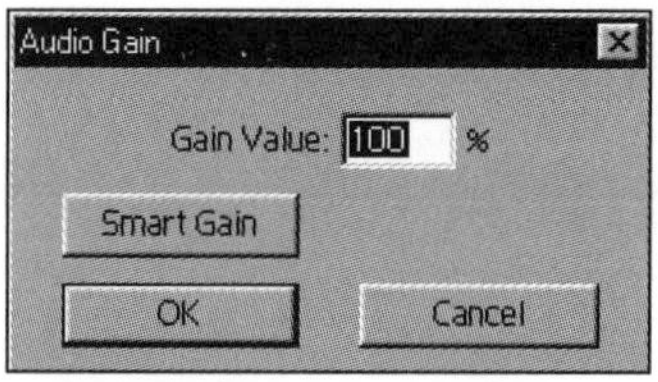

Figure 6-4: The Audio Gain dialog box enables you to increase or decrease a sound's volume.

Fading sound with the volume rubberband

Premiere's red volume rubberband enables you to change the volume of a sound clip at different intervals. The most popular use of the volume rubberband is to fade in a sound clip at the beginning and to fade out a sound clip at the end. When you fade in and out, you decrease the volume of a sound. You can also use the fade line to increase the volume of a sound.

Cross-Reference

For information on using the rubberband line on a video track, turn to Chapter 12, "Superimposing."

Here's how to fade sound in and out:

1. **Choose File ➪ New Project to create a new project or open an existing project with File ➪ Open.**
2. **Choose File ➪ Import ➪ File to import a sound clip or a video clip with sound.**
3. **Drag the sound clip from the Project window to an audio track in the Timeline window.**
4. **Expand the audio track to display the red volume rubberband (see Figure 6-5).** To expand the audio track, click the triangle in front of the word *Audio*. You can show and hide the rubberband in the audio track by clicking the red square (between the blue square and the half white diamond).

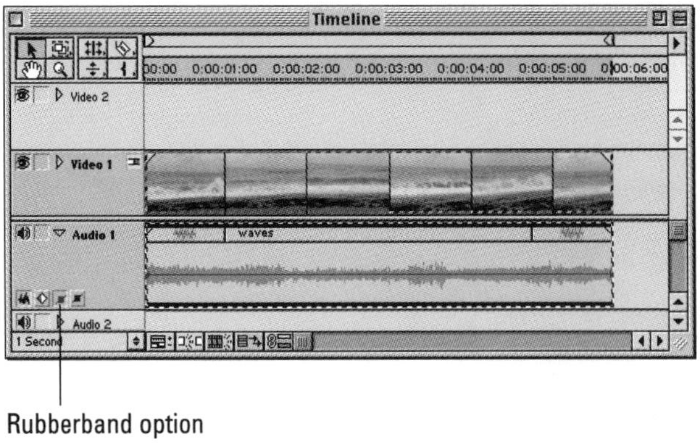

Figure 6-5: The Rubberband option in the Timeline window enables you to fade a sound clip in and out.

5. **Select the Timeline Selection tool if it is not selected.** To select the Selection tool, press V on your keyboard.
6. **Click in the middle of the volume rubberband to create a handle.** This handle serves as a placeholder for the sound to stay at 100 percent of its volume

at the middle of the sound clip. You can use the Info palette to view the percentage of the sound fade as you drag the rubberband. To display the Info palette, choose Window ➪ Show Info.

7. **Drag the red handle at the beginning of the rubberband downward.** This makes the audio clip fade in. Dragging it upward increases the sound.

Tip

Press and hold the Shift key as you drag the volume rubberband downward to fade in 1-percent increments.

8. **Drag the red handle at the end of the rubberband downward to have the audio clip fade out.**

9. **Click the rubberband to add a handle a few seconds back at 100 percent (or more, if you want to increase the volume before the fade).** The clip's volume should now start at 0 percent, fade in up to 100 percent, and then fade back down to 0 percent at the end. Figure 6-6 shows an audio fade line after adding a handle and adjusting the line.

   If you want, you can use the Selection tool to add more handles to the volume rubberband. Adding more handles to it enables you to fade a sound clip in different sections within the sound clip. When you add a handle, the Selection tool turns into a white pointing hand. To delete a handle, move the Selection tool over the handle. The pointer should turn into a gray pointing hand. Make sure that it doesn't turn into a white pointing hand, because this will add a handle and not select one. When the pointer is a gray pointing hand, click the handle and drag it outside the fade area.

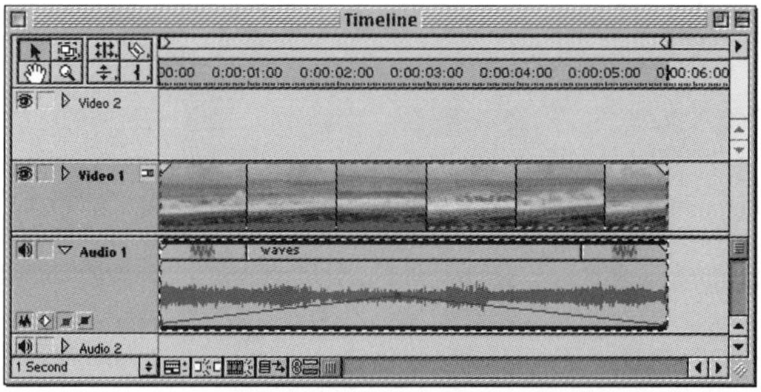

Figure 6-6: Adjusted volume rubberband with handles

10. **To play the sound clip, choose File ➪ Save and then press Enter on your keyboard.**

Using the Fade Adjustment tool on the volume rubberband

You can use the Fade Adjustment and Fade Scissors tools to further adjust an audio fade line. The Fade Adjustment tool and the Fade Scissors tool, as shown in Figure 6-7, appear in the Toolbox at the upper-left side of the Timeline window. The

Fade Adjustment tool moves the fade line at a constant percentage. When you use the Fade Scissors, you add two handles to the fade line. You can use these two handles to separate part of the fade line so that it is not affected.

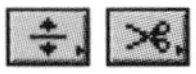

Figure 6-7: The Fade Adjustment and Fade Scissors tools

Before you use the Fade Adjustment tool, make sure that the project you're working on contains an audio clip. The audio clip should be expanded, and the fade line should be displayed. To adjust a clip's volume with the Fade Adjustment tool, follow these steps:

1. **Use the Info palette to view the fade percentage.** To display the Info palette, choose Window ⇨ Display Info.
2. **Click the Fade Adjustment tool.** In the Timeline window, it resides in the second row, third slot of the Toolbox.

Tip

To select the Fade Adjustment tool, press U on your keyboard until the Fade Adjustment tool appears.

3. **Click and drag on the red volume rubberband.** Notice that the rubberband moves as a unit. Alternatively, press V on your keyboard to select the Selection tool and then click the fade line to add handles to the rubberband.
4. **Switch to the Fade Adjustment tool and click between two handles.** The area between two areas moves as a constant and the rest gradually moves, as shown in Figure 6-8.

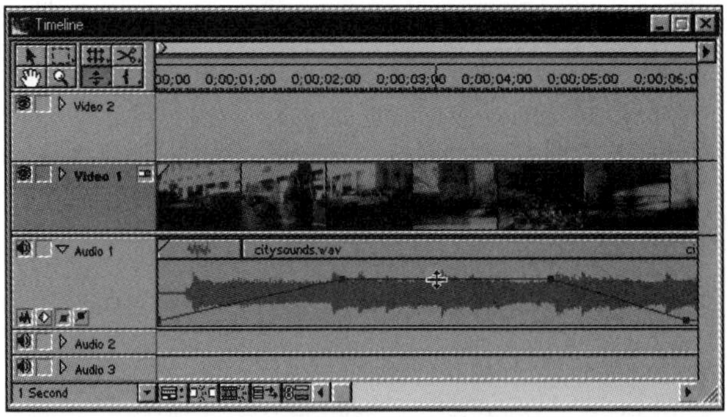

Figure 6-8: The Fade Adjustment tool is used on the volume rubberband.

Using the Fade Scissors tool on the fade line

You can use the Selection tool and the Fade Scissors tool to fade an audio track in and out. Here's how:

1. **Choose File ➪ New Project to create a new project or open an existing project with File ➪ Open.**
2. **Choose File ➪ Import ➪ File to import a sound clip or a video clip with sound.**
3. **Drag the sound clip from the Project window to an audio track in the Timeline window.**
4. **To display the red volume rubberband, expand the audio track and click the red square (see Figure 6-5).** To expand the audio track, click the triangle in front of the word *Audio*. You show or hide the rubberband by clicking the red square in between the blue square and half-white diamond. A red line appears in the sound clip.
5. **Make sure that the volume rubberband does not have any extra handles.** It should have the two default handles that Premiere automatically creates. If it does have extras, click the Selection tool to click and drag them outside of the fade area to delete them.
6. **Click the Fade Scissors tool.** It resides in the first row, fourth slot of the Toolbox in the Timeline window.

Tip: To select the Fade Scissors tool, press C on your keyboard.

7. **With the Fade Scissors tool selected, click in the middle of the rubberband.** Two handles appear side by side.
8. **Press V on your keyboard to switch to the Selection tool.**
9. **Drag the left handle toward the beginning of the rubberband.**
10. **Drag the right handle toward the end of the rubberband.** It should look similar to the one in Figure 6-9.
11. **With the Selection tool still selected, click at the beginning of the rubberband and drag downward.**
12. **Drag the end of the rubberband downward.** Dragging downward makes the sound fade in at the beginning and fade out at the end of the sound clip.

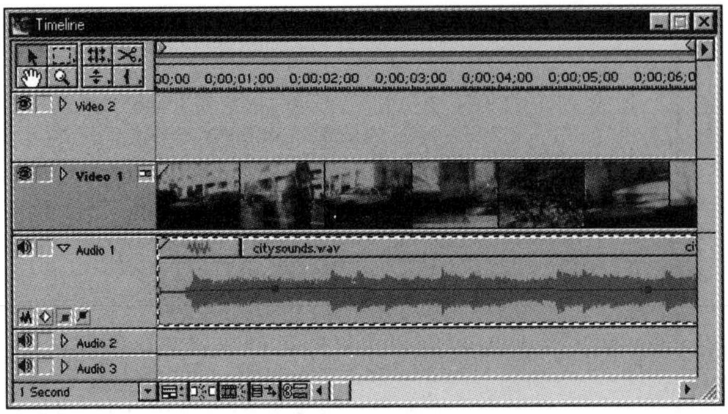

Figure 6-9: Here's how a volume rubberband appears when you fade an audio track in and out.

If you want to create a fade-in and fade-out in another track, you don't have to repeat all the preceding steps; just select the fade line of the audio track with the fade in and out. Then choose Edit ➪ Copy. Next, choose the fade line of the audio track you want to fade in and out, and choose Edit ➪ Paste Attributes. In the Paste Attributes dialog box, set the Content pop-up menu to Normal. The fade in and out is copied to the selected audio track.

Balancing Volume

Premiere enables you to control the balance of the sound for the left and right speakers for sound. Controlling the balance for a sound is sometimes called, Panning. In Premiere, panning is adjusted using the pan line. You control the balance for a stereo sound by using the Clip ➪ Audio Options commands. Both balance and panning can be adjusted using the Audio Mixer palette.

Panning

In this section, you find out how to adjust panning by using the Pan/Balance rubberband. When you pan, you balance the right and left speaker of a sound. With panning, you can set the sound so that it is heard from either the left or right speakers or from both. Panning can be used in a variety of ways. For example, you may want to use panning during a video clip of a car entering a scene. The car can appear slowly while moving into the scene, and the sound of the car can also appear slowly. You can have the sound of the car heard first from one speaker and then from another. To make a dialog more interesting, you can have the dialog in one audio track and have different sounds in a different audio track played on the left and right speakers. On one speaker, you can have a guitar; and on the other, you can have a tambourine sound. Various musicians use panning to create interesting effects. Some songs by the Beatles, Led Zeppelin, and The Who use panning.

Here's how to pan by using the Pan/Balance rubberband:

1. **Choose File ➪ New Project to create a new project or open an existing project with File ➪ Open.**
2. **Choose File ➪ Import ➪ File to import a sound clip or a video clip with sound.**
3. **Drag the sound clip from the Project window to an audio track in the Timeline window.**
4. **Expand the audio track.** To expand the audio track, click the triangle in front of the word Audio.
5. **Click the Pan/Balance Rubberband button.** The Pan/Balance Rubberband button, as shown in Figure 6-10, is the blue square between the red square and the half-white diamond. Click the blue square to display a Pan/Balance rubberband (shown earlier in Figure 6-8). The Pan/Balance line appears as a blue line in the sound clip.

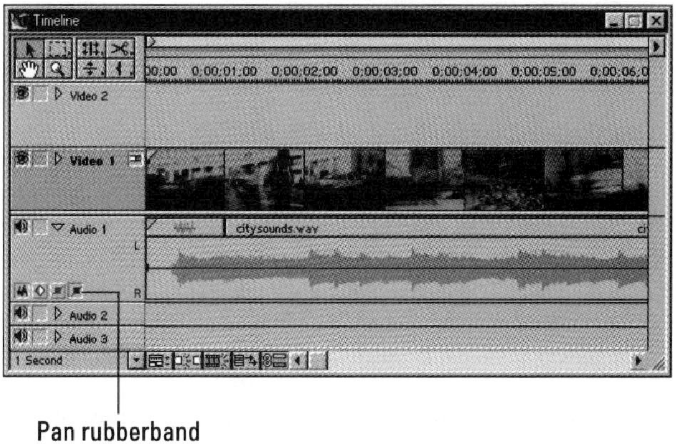

Figure 6-10: The Pan/Balance rubberband in the Timeline window enables you to pan a sound clip.

6. **To set the audio to appear in the left speaker, click and drag the pan line upward. To set the audio to appear in the right speaker, click and drag the pan line downward.** By default, the Pan/Balance rubberband is set to display the audio so that you hear both the left and right sound simultaneously.

Tip: Press and hold the Shift key as you drag the Pan/Balance rubberband to balance a clip in 1-percent increments.

To make the left and right sound appear in different places in the audio track, you need to make handles in the Pan/Balance rubberband. Use the Selection tool to click the Pan line to add handles to the Pan line. Then click and drag up and down within the handles to distribute the sound to the left and right speakers, as shown in Figure 6-11.

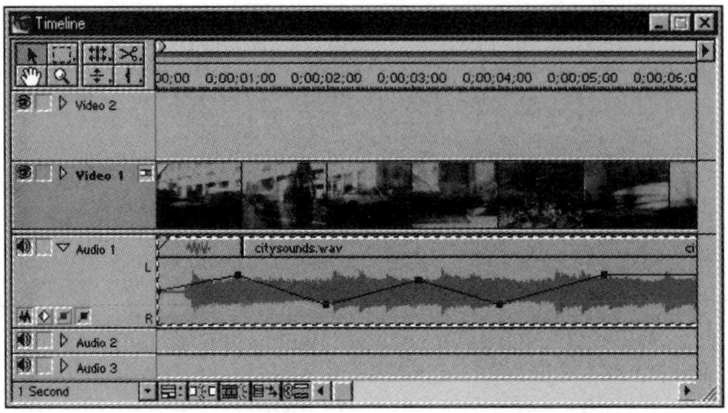

Figure 6-11: Dragging the Pan/Balance Rubberband up and down between handles distributes the sound to the left and right speakers.

Cross-Reference

You can use the Fade Adjustment tool and Fade Scissors tool on the Pan line. For more information on using the Fade Adjustment and Fade Scissors tool, read the previous section, "Fading sound with the volume rubberband."

Balancing stereo

Premiere enables you to adjust which stereo channel is played, left or right. It also enables you to reverse the channels. All this can be done by choosing Clip ➪ Audio Options.

Before proceeding to learn how to use the Clip ➪ Audio Options commands, you need to have a project on-screen with a sound clip in an audio track.

Here's how to set a stereo sound so that it is heard from one channel:

1. **Click the stereo sound clip in an audio track.**
2. **Choose Clip ➪ Audio Options ➪ Right to have the sound heard from only the right channel.**
3. **Choose Clip ➪ Audio Options ➪ Left to have the sound heard from only the left channel.** If you make a mistake and want to start over, choose Clip ➪ Audio Options ➪ Normal to return the sound to its original state.

When a sound or music is recorded, unwanted noises, in either the left or right channel, may also be recorded. When this happens, you may want to mute either channel. Here's how to have one channel muted:

1. **Click a stereo sound clip in an audio track.**
2. **Choose Clip ➪ Audio Options ➪ Mute Left to have the left channel muted.**

3. **Choose Clip ➪ Audio Options ➪ Mute Right to have the right channel muted.** If you make a mistake and want to start over, choose Clip ➪ Audio Options ➪ Normal to return the sound to its original state.

Here's how to swap the left and right channels:

1. **Click a sound clip in an audio track.**
2. **Choose Clip ➪ Audio Options ➪ Swap to swap the left and right channels.** If you make a mistake and want to start over, choose Clip ➪ Audio Options ➪ Normal to return the sound to its original state.

Using the Cross Fade Tool to Fade Audio

The Cross Fade tool, which resides in the Toolbox in the Timeline window, enables you to fade one audio track into another audio track. You can also use the Cross Fade tool to fade one video track with sound into another video track with sound. Here's how to use the Cross Fade tool to fade one audio track into another:

1. **Choose File ➪ New Project to create a new project, or open an existing project with File ➪ Open.**
2. **Choose File ➪ Import ➪ File to import two sound clips.**
3. **Drag the sound clips from the Project window to audio tracks in the Timeline window.** Make sure that the sound clips overlap each other, as shown in Figure 6-12.

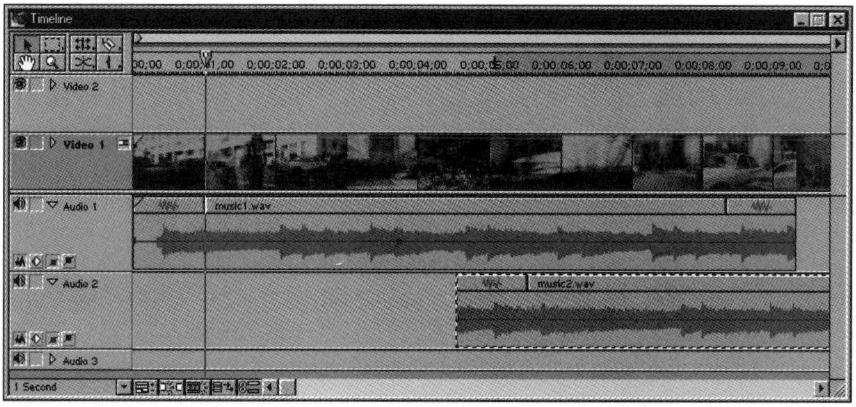

Figure 6-12: You need two overlapping sound clips to create a cross fade.

4. **Select the Cross Fade tool from the Toolbox in the Timeline window.** The Cross Fade tool resides in the second row, third slot of the Toolbox.

Tip

To select the Cross Fade tool, press U on your keyboard until the Cross Fade tool appears.

5. **Click one of the sound clips and then click another to create a cross fade.**

Creating a cross fade from one video clip with sound to another is more complicated. To do so, you first need to temporarily unlink the video and audio clip so that you can move the two independently. A video clip that has its video and audio starting and ending at different points on the Timeline is called a split edit. When the audio ends after the video, it is called an *L-cut.* When the audio starts before the video, it is called a *J-cut* or an audio lead.

Here's how to temporarily unlink video clips with sound and create a cross fade:

1. **Choose File ➪ New Project to create a new project or open an existing project.**
2. **Choose File ➪ Import ➪ File to import two video clips that have audio.**
3. **Drag the video clips from the Project window to video tracks in the Timeline window.**
4. **Click the Toggle Synch Mode button at the bottom of the Timeline window.**
5. **Click one of the clips you want to unlink.** Premiere unlinks the audio and video clips. To relink the clips, just click the Toggle Synch Mode button again before clicking one of the clips.
6. **You can also unlink audio and video clips by clicking the Link/Unlink tool (see Figure 6-13).** The Link/Unlink tool resides in the second row, third slot of the Toolbox.

Figure 6-13: The Link/Unlink tool appears in the lower-left corner of this icon set.

Tip

To select the Cross Fade tool, press U on your keyboard until the Cross Fade tool appears.

7. **With the Link/Unlink tool selected, move the Link/Unlink tool to the edge of either the video or audio track.** The Link icon appears.
8. **Click the mouse to temporarily unlink the video and audio tracks.**

Note

You can link/unlink a video clip with audio by clicking the clip and then choosing Clip ➪ Unlink Audio and Video. To relink the audio and video, you need to use the Link/Unlink tool.

9. **Press the V key to switch to the Selection tool.**
10. **Move the sound and audio tracks to their desired locations.** If you want to create an L-cut, adjust the audio and video clips so that the audio ends after the video clip. If you want to create an audio lead (J-cut), adjust the audio and video clips so that the audio starts before the video.
11. **Press the U key until the Fade Adjustment tool appears.**
12. **With the Cross Fade tool selected, click the audio clips in the audio tracks. A cross fade is created (see Figure 6-14).**

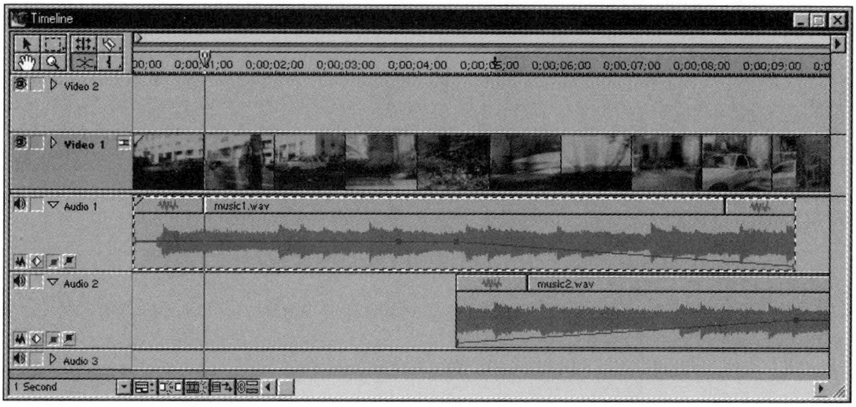

Figure 6-14: Cross fade automatically created by Cross Fade tool

Mixing Audio with the Audio Mixer

The Audio Mixer window, as shown in Figure 6-15, enables you to mix the volume (gain) and the balance (pan) of several sound clips simultaneously. Using the Audio Mixer, you can mix audio in real time as your project plays in the Monitor window. The Audio Mixer features buttons that start and stop audio as well as write the changes to the audio tracks. After an Audio Mixer session, the changes to the track or tracks are visible on the audio track's fade line (visible when the audio track is expanded). To display the Audio Mixer window, choose Window ⇨ Audio Mixer. When the Audio Mixer opens, as shown in Figure 6-15, it appears with controls for three audio tracks and a master track. Three audio tracks appear because, by default, Premiere always creates a new project with three audio tracks. If you add audio tracks to the Timeline window, more tracks appear in the Audio Mixer window. The audio track section of the Audio Mixer window is divided into five sections: Automation, Mute and Solo, Balance, Volume, and Playback.

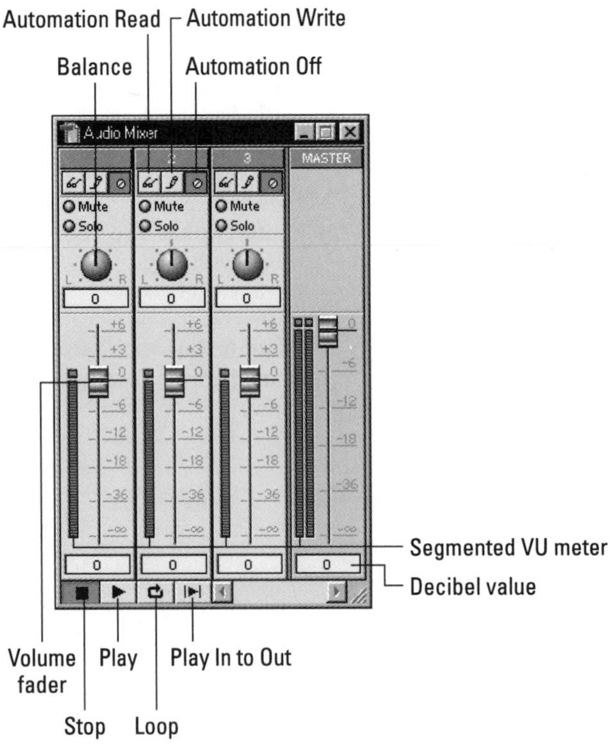

Figure 6-15: The Audio Mixer window facilitates mix balance and volume in various sound clips.

Automation

The Automation options (Automation Read, Automation Write, and Automation Off) determine whether Premiere records the adjustments you make in the Audio Mixer window. To have Premiere record the adjustments, choose Automation Write. Use Automation Read when you want the settings of the Audio Mixer to be read during playback. Use Automation Off when you want the default settings for a sound clip.

Mute and Solo

The Mute and Solo buttons below the Automation options enable you to choose which audio tracks you want to work with and which ones you don't. Click the Mute button for the tracks you don't want to affect and click the Solo button for the audio tracks you want to adjust.

Balance

For each track you can control balance by using the Balance sphere. Stereo can be adjusted from –100 to +100.

Volume

Moving the Volume Fader up or down adjusts the volume. Volume is recorded in decibels (db) from +6 to -95. The decibel volume is displayed in the field below the Volume Fader control. When the volume of an audio track is changed over time by using the Volume Fader control, Premiere places handles on the audio fade line. If you want, you can further adjust the volume by moving the handles. Note that when the Segmented VU meter (to the left of the Volume Fader) turns red, it is warning you that clipping or sound distortion may occur.

Playback

Four icons appear at the bottom left-hand side of the Audio Mixer window. These icons are, Stop, Play, Loop, and Play In to Out. Press the Play button to play an audio clip. Note that the audio clips that are muted will not play. Only the audio clips that have the Solo button selected will play. Click the Automation Read option to play back the adjusted settings. Click the Automation Off button to play back the sound clip's original sound before being edited.

To continue playing a sound over and over again, click the Loop button. To stop playing a sound, press the Stop button. The Play In to Out button enables you to play back just the sound between the edited In and Out points.

The Audio Mixer window options

You can change the options in the Audio Mixer by using the Audio Mixer window options. To display the Audio Mixer Window Options dialog box, Mac users should press and hold the Control key as you click the title bar of the Audio Mixer window. PC users should right-click the Audio Mixer title window. You can also choose Window ⇨ Window Options ⇨ Audio Mixer Window Options to display the Audio Mixer Window Options dialog box.

The Audio Mixer Window Options dialog box, as shown in Figure 6-16, is divided into two sections, Display Options and Automation Write Options.

The Display Options section enables you to choose whether you want to have the Audio Tracks and Master Fader, Audio Tracks Only, or Master Fader Only displayed.

Figure 6-16: The Audio Mixer Window Options dialog box

The Automation Write Options enables you to pick from four different Automation options:

✦ **Touch.** Adjusts the setting while clicking and dragging the mouse. After you stop using the mouse, the option is returned to its original setting.

✦ **Latch.** Locks the settings into position.

✦ **Write.** Records the stored settings.

✦ **Write/Touch.** Uses the Write mode for the next playback and uses the Touch mode for any other playback.

The Enable Automation pop-up menu at the bottom of the dialog box enables you to choose whether to enable both Volume and Pan, enable Volume only, or enable Pan only.

Editing sound with the Audio Mixer track

To record audio adjustments using the Audio Mixer, you first need to have a project on-screen with a few audio clips placed in the Timeline window. Expand the tracks to display the tracks' volume rubberband lines.

Then, follow these steps:

1. **Click and drag the Timeline marker to the area you wish to mix.**
2. **Click the Automation Write button for the track you want to record.** For instance, click the Automation Write button below Audio Mixer track 1 to record changes in Audio track 1.

3. **Click the Solo button for that track and set the other tracks to Mute.**
4. **Click Play in the Audio Mixer.**
5. **When the recording starts, adjust the Volume Fader slider and the Balance.**
6. **To stop recording and write the changes to the audio track(s), click the Stop button.**
7. **Play back what you recorded.** First, click the Automation Read button in the track you are working in. Then, click the Play button. As the track plays, you can see the changes in the audio track volume rubberband.

Using the Audio Effects Palette

The Premiere program's audio effects enable you to enhance and correct audio. The effects provided in the Audio effects palette are similar to many found in professional audio studios.

The Premiere program's Audio Effects palette provides six audio effect folders (Bandpass, Channel, Dynamics, EQ, Effect, and Reverb & Delay), providing a total of twenty different audio effects. The audio effects are found in the Audio Effects palette. The Audio palette works similar to the way the Video palette does. For information on using the Video palette, turn to Chapter 12.

To display the Audio palette, as shown in Figure 6-17, choose Window ➪ Audio Effects. To use an audio effect, just click and drag an audio effect from the Audio palette to an audio track in the Timeline window.

Touring the Audio palette

To view the effects in each folder, either double-click the folder or click the triangle in front of the folder. To see all the effects in all the folders, choose Expand All Folders from the Audio palette pop-up menu. To close all the folders, choose Collapse All Folders. To find an effect, you can click Find from the Audio palette. In the Find dialog box, type the effect you want to find. You can also find an effect by pressing the Find icon at the bottom of the palette.

Ganging Audio Tracks

To *gang* tracks together so that changes you make to one affect one or more of the others, Option-click/right-click the Fade control and choose a gang option. For example, right-click the Fade control for track 1 and choose Gang 1 from the menu; then right-click the fade handle for another track and choose Gang 1 to gang the two tracks together. To ungang, Option-click/right-click again. To temporarily turn off ganging, press the Shift key while using the Audio Mixer.

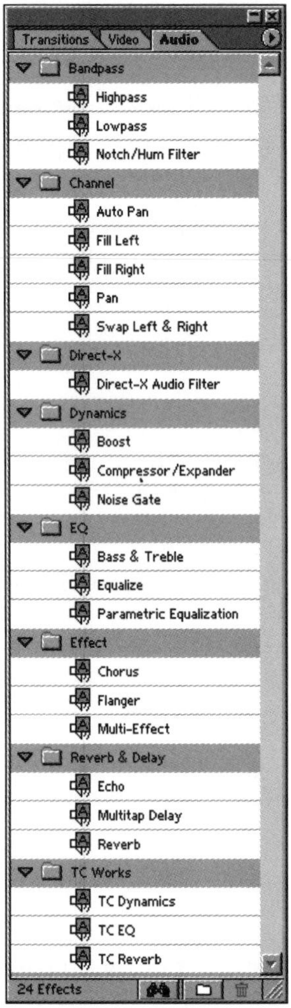

Figure 6-17: The Audio palette enables you to add sound effects to sound clips.

In a project, you may need to use a few effects that are in different folders again and again. If so, you may want to place the effects into one folder. To create a new folder, choose New Folder from the Audio palette pop-up menu. You can also click the New Folder icon at the bottom of the palette. When the New Folder dialog box appears, name the folder. Then drag the effects into the folder. If you want to rename the folder, click the folder and then choose Rename folder from the Audio palette pop-up menu. In the Rename dialog box, name the folder. When you are done with the project, you may want to delete the folder. First, make sure to drag the effects back to the folder they came from. Then click the folder and choose Delete folder from the Audio palette pop-up menu. You can also delete the folder by clicking the Delete icon at the bottom of the palette.

Applying an audio effect

To apply an audio effect to an audio clip, click the effect in the Audio Effects palette and drag it to the audio track in the Timeline. After an effect is applied to an audio track, it appears in the Effect Controls palette (see Figure 6-18). Some audio effects have settings that can adjust how the effect is heard. If the audio effect has a setting, the setting appears in the Effect Controls palette when the effect is expanded. To expand/collapse the effect, click the triangle in front of the effect's name.

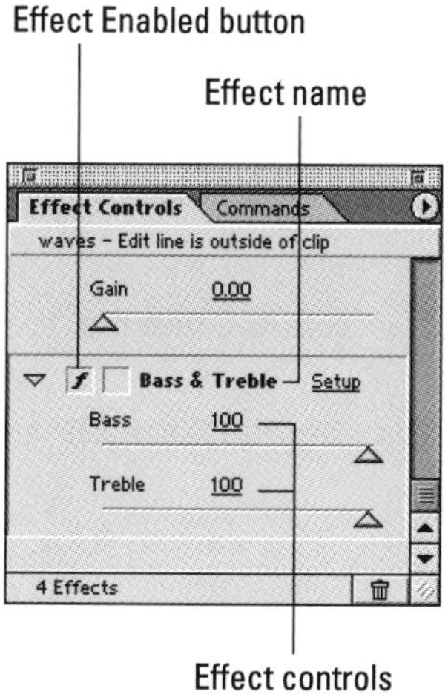

Figure 6-18: The Effect Controls palette

You can adjust the effect in the Effect Controls palette either by moving the sliders in the palette or by pressing the Setup button. When you press the Setup button, a dialog box appears with the settings belonging to that effect. Also in the dialog box is a Preview button, enabling you to preview the sound.

To display the Effect Controls palette, choose Window ➪ Show Effect Controls. Note that you can also drag an audio effect to the Effect Controls palette to apply an effect to an audio track. Just make sure that the audio track you want affected is selected. You can use the Effect Controls palette to delete an effect. To delete an effect, click the effect in the Effect Controls palette and then click the Trash icon at the bottom of the palette. Click the *f* (next to the triangle) to disable the effect temporarily.

Applying an audio effect over time

If you want to change the settings of an effect as an audio clip plays, you need to apply an effect over time and set keyframes where you want to make a change. A *keyframe* stores the effect at a specific point on a line in the Timeline called the keyframe line. Before you can set keyframes in the keyframe line, you need to turn on the Keyframe Enabled button in the Effect Controls palette (next to the effect name).

To apply an audio effect over time, you should have a project open containing an audio clip in an audio track. Then, follow these steps:

1. **Drag an audio effect to the audio clip.**
2. **Choose Window ⇨ Show Effect Controls palette to display the Effect Controls palette.**
3. **Click the Keyframe Enabled button to enable keyframing for that effect.** A stopwatch icon appears.

Note

You can't enable keyframing for the Boost, Fill Left, Fill Right, or Swap Left & Right effect.

4. **Click the Expand/Collapse Track icon (triangle next to the name of the audio track) to expand the audio track.**
5. **Click the Show Keyframe button (the first button after the Show/Hide Audio Waveform button) to display the keyframe line.**
6. **Click and drag the Timeline Marker to the location you want to set a keyframe.**
7. **Click the Add/Delete keyframe box (between the Previous Keyframe and the Next Keyframe) to create a keyframe.**
8. **Now move the Timeline Marker to a new position.** This time, make changes to the audio effect in the Effect Controls palette. Premiere creates a keyframe at the place the Timeline Marker appears.
9. **If you want, repeat the previous step to create a new keyframe.** Repeat the previous step until you create all the keyframes you want. Figure 6-19 shows a keyframe line with various keyframes.

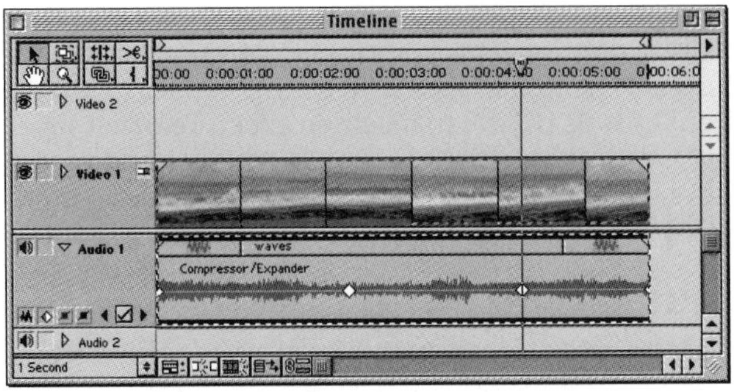

Figure 6-19: The keyframe line with keyframes

10. **To delete a keyframe, move the Timeline Marker over the keyframe you want to delete; then click the check mark in the Add/Delete keyframe box.**

Audio effects described

The best way to become an expert at using the Premiere program's audio effects is to try them. After you apply an audio effect, you can listen to it by clicking the Preview option in the effect's dialog box. Most effects have a dialog box. If an effect doesn't have a dialog box, you can preview the effect by choosing Timeline ➪ Preview.

Bandpass

The audio effects in the Bandpass folder are Highpass, Lowpass, and Notch/Hum filter.

Highpass

The Highpass effect is used to filter out low-frequency sounds. When you choose the Highpass effect, you can click the Setup button to display the Highpass Filter Settings dialog box, as shown in Figure 6-20. The dialog box enables you to click the Preview sound checkbox, so that you can preview the sound as you are adjusting it.

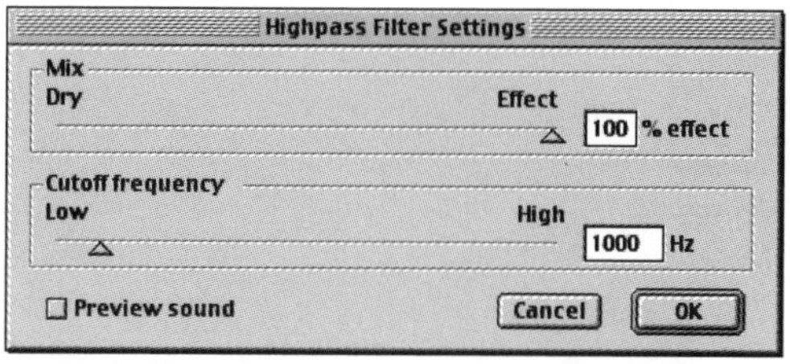

Figure 6-20: The Highpass Filter Settings dialog box

The Mix slider enables you to choose whether you want the effect to be strong or soft. Drag the Mix slider toward Dry to make the effect soft. To make the effect strong, drag the slider toward Effect. You can move the Cutoff Frequency slider toward either Low or High.

Lowpass

The Lowpass effect is used to delete high-frequency sounds. The Lowpass effect is similar to Highpass. The Lowpass Filter Settings dialog box, as shown in Figure 6-21, is also very similar to Highpass, which filters out low-frequency sounds.

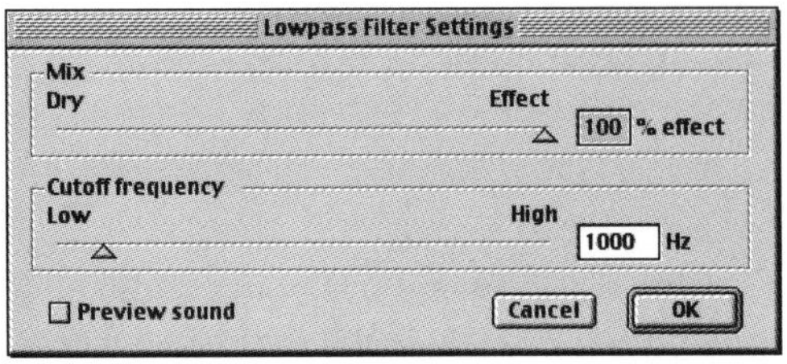

Figure 6-21: The Lowpass Filter Settings dialog box

Notch/Hum filter

The Notch/Hum filter is used to remove power line hum. In the Notch/Hum Filter Settings dialog box, as shown in Figure 6-22, use the slider to indicate the AC power-line frequency for the country you are in. For the United States, the frequency is 60.

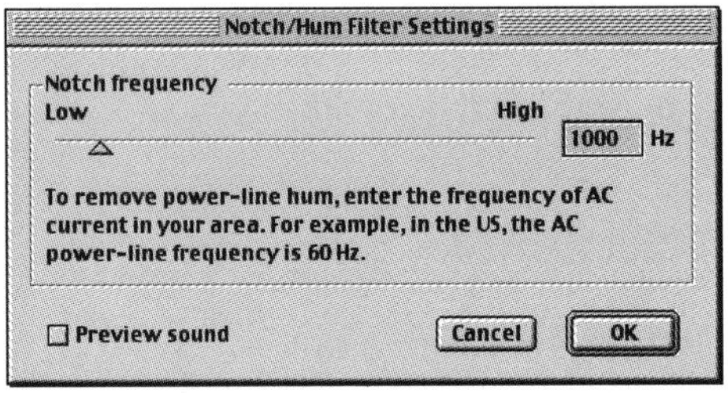

Figure 6-22: The Notch/Hum Filter Settings dialog box

Channel

The audio effects in the Channel folder enable you to adjust how the left and/or right speaker channel is heard. The audio effects in the Channel folder are Auto Pan, Fill Left, Fill Right, Pan, Swap Left & Right.

Auto Pan

The Auto Pan effect creates a cyclical pan from left to right. You can control the pan by using the Depth and Rate sliders in the Auto Pan Settings dialog box, as shown in Figure 6-23. The Depth slider enables you to choose from a narrow to a wide pan. The Rate slider adjusts the rate at which the pan moves from left to right.

Fill Left

The Fill Left effect places the audio clip in the left channel.

Fill Right

The Fill Right effect places the audio clip in the right channel.

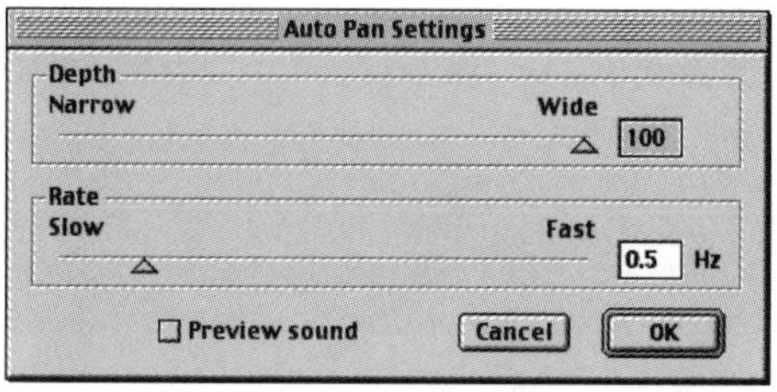

Figure 6-23: The Auto Pan Settings dialog box

Pan

The Pan effect enables you to control whether you want the sound to be heard from the left or right channel. Drag the Pan Setting slider in the Pan Settings dialog box (as shown in Figure 6-24) to the right to set the sound to the right channel. Drag the Pan Setting slider to the left to set the sound to the left channel.

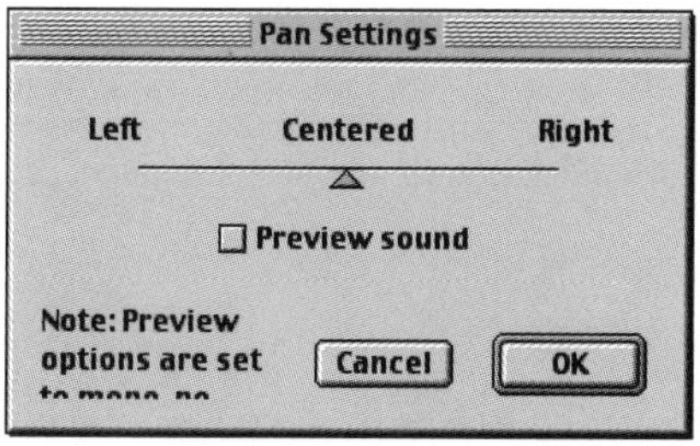

Figure 6-24: The Pan Settings dialog box

Swap Left & Right

The Swap Left & Right effect swaps the left and right channels.

Dynamics

The audio effects in the Dynamics folder can pull the low sounds up and the high sounds down. The effects in the Dynamics folder are Boost, Compressor/Expander, and Noise Gate.

Boost

The Boost effect increases low-frequency sound, while leaving the high sounds alone. For more frequency control, use the Compressor/Expander effect.

Compressor/Expander

The Compressor/Expander effect controls dynamic range. Dynamic range is the difference between the highest and lowest frequency. The Compressor/Expander effect enables you to either compress or expand a sound. To compress a sound, you raise the soft sounds, leaving the highs alone. Therefore, compression decreases the gap between low and high sounds, while expansion increases the difference.

By using the Compressor/Expander Settings dialog box, as shown in Figure 6-25, you can adjust the Ratio, Threshold, and Gain sliders. As you make adjustments, the Output and Input sound level chart (shown in the dialog box) for either compressor or expander is affected.

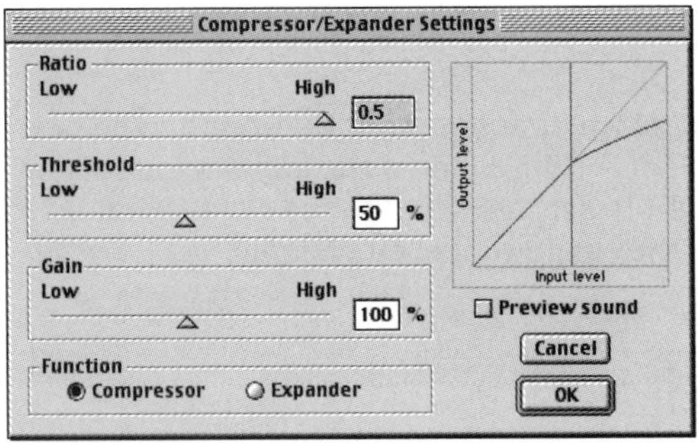

Figure 6-25: The Compressor/Expander Settings dialog box

Noise Gate

Noise Gate enables you to remove some unwanted noises from your sound clip. Use the Threshold and Decay time sliders in the Noise Gate Settings dialog box, as shown in Figure 6-26, to adjust the effect.

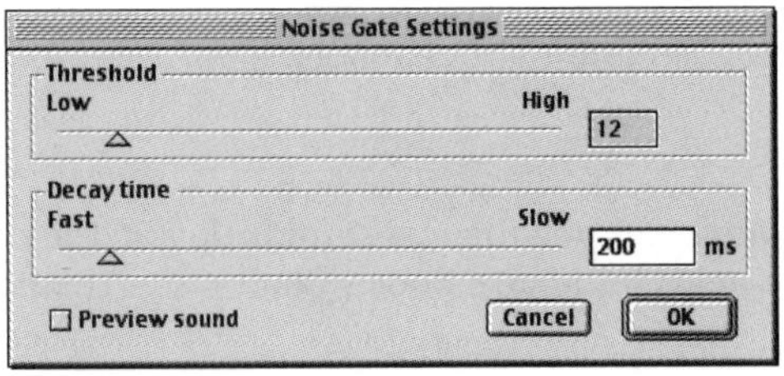

Figure 6-26: The Noise Gate Settings dialog box

EQ

The audio effects in the EQ folder are Bass & Treble, Equalize, and Parametric Equalization.

Bass & Treble

Bass & Treble settings enable you to cut or boost an audio frequency. In the Bass & Treble Settings dialog box, as shown in Figure 6-27, moving the Bass slider affects the low frequencies in an audio clip. Moving the Treble slider, affects the high frequency of an audio clip. Clicking the Flat button resets the Bass and Treble sliders. For more tone control, use either the Equalize or Parametric Equalizer effect.

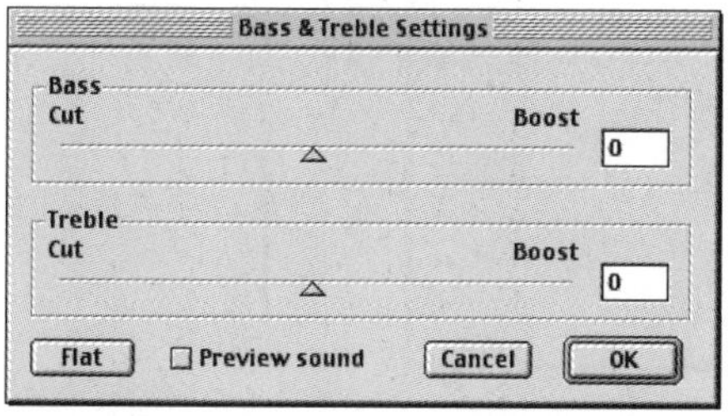

Figure 6-27: The Bass & Treble Settings dialog box

Equalize

Clicking the sliders in the Equalize Settings dialog box, as shown in Figure 6-28, enables you to enhance tonal quality by lowering or raising the audio signal at different frequencies. To set the tone back to where it originally was, click the Flat button. For more precise tonal adjustments, use the Parametric Equalizer command.

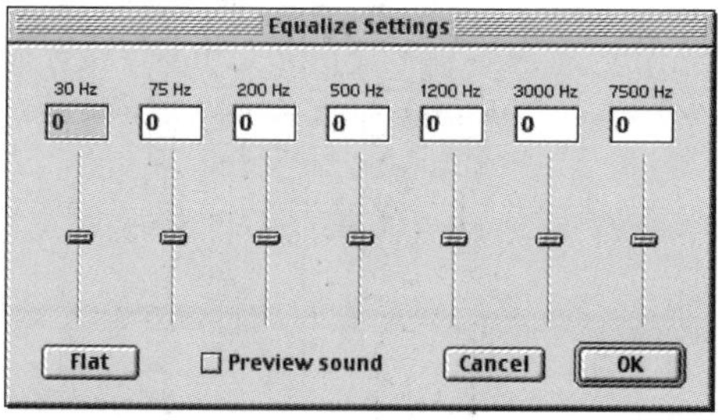

Figure 6-28: The Equalize Settings dialog box

The Parametric Equalizer

The Parametric Equalizer is the most precise effect you can use to enhance tonal control. By using this effect, you can set the frequency range for three separate bands The Equalize command does not enable you to set the frequency range. In the Parametric Equalization Settings dialog box, as shown in Figure 6-29, you can set the Frequency, Bandwidth, and Boost/Cut for Bands 1, 2, and 3.

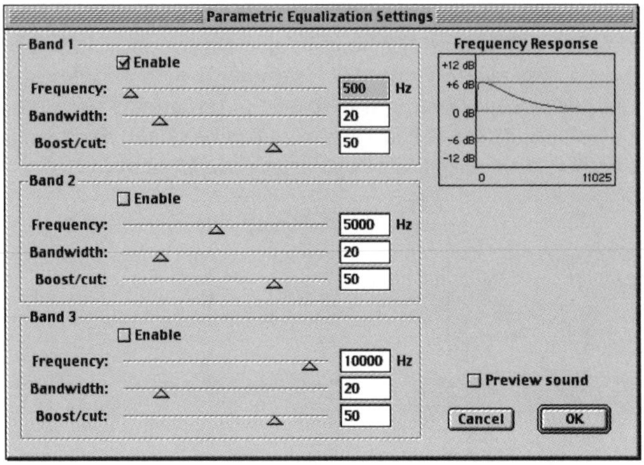

Figure 6-29: The Parametric Equalize Settings dialog box

Effect

The audio effects in the Effect folder are Chorus, Flanger, and Multi-Effect.

Chorus

The Chorus effect can be used to add depth to an audio clip. The Chorus effect creates a copy of the audio clip that is slightly different from the original sound. In the Chorus Settings dialog box, as shown in Figure 6-30, you can move the Mix slider to mix the original (Dry) sound with the copy (Effect). The Depth slider controls the delay of the sound effect. Setting a high value for Regeneration creates a Flanger effect (an inversion effect that adds depth and wavering to the audio, which sometimes sounds like a swooshing sound within the audio). The Rate controls the rate at which the sound is heard.

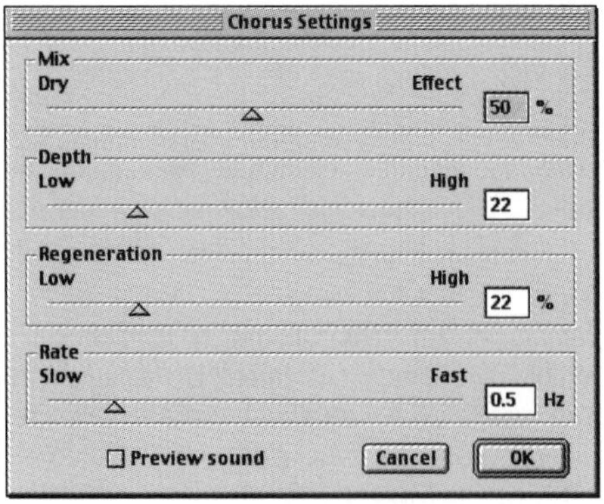

Figure 6-30: The Chorus Settings dialog box

Flanger

The Flanger Settings dialog box, as shown in Figure 6-31, is similar to the Chorus dialog box. In both dialog boxes, you can set the sliders (Mix, Depth, and Rate) so that you create a low or high effect.

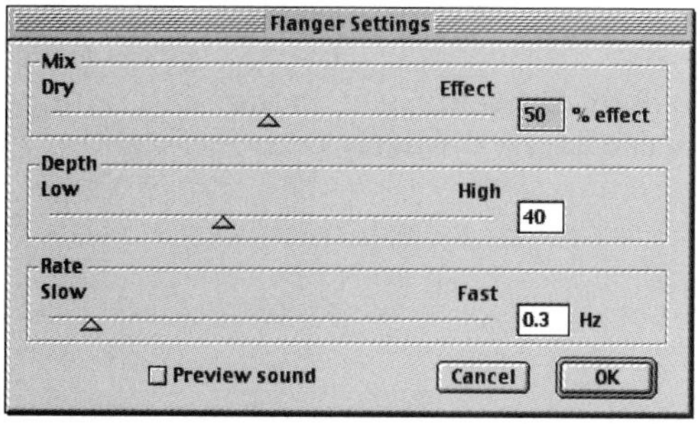

Figure 6-31: The Flanger Settings dialog box

Multi-Effect

The Multi-Effect can be used to create echo and chorus. You can use the Multi-Effect Settings dialog box, as shown in Figure 6-32, to set Delay and Modulation. The Modulation (modulation is a change in the attributes of the audio wave) area of the dialog box alters the delay time using cycles of sound. The Rate enables you to set how fast the audio is modulated. The Intensity controls whether you apply a small or large amount of modulation to the audio. The Waveform section enables you to choose a waveform for the modulation.

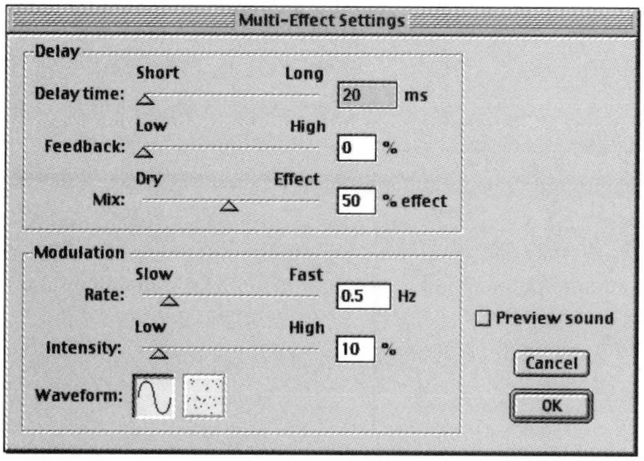

Figure 6-32: The Multi-Effect Settings dialog box

Reverb & Delay

The audio effects in the Reverb & Delay folder enable you to change the audio so that it feels like you are listening to it from either a small room or from a large hall. The audio effects in the Reverb & Delay folder are Echo, Multitap Delay, and Reverb.

Echo

The Echo effect plays again with a slightly different effect. In the Echo Settings dialog box, as shown in Figure 6-33, you can adjust the delay of the echo and whether the echo will be soft or loud.

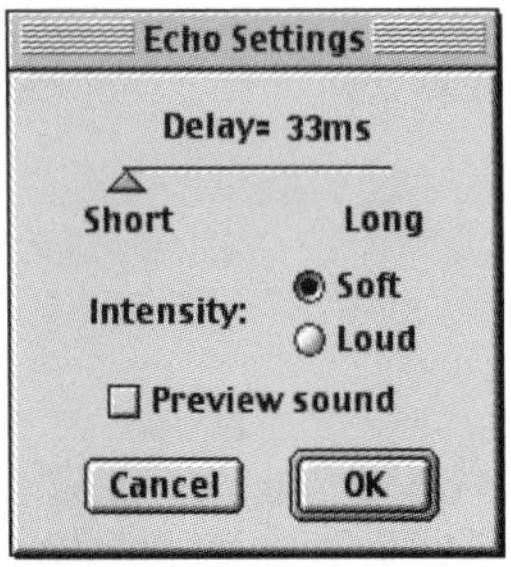

Figure 6-33: The Echo Settings dialog box

Multitap Delay

The Multitap Delay Settings dialog box, as shown in Figure 6-34, enables you to use four taps (tap is a delay effect) to control the overall delay effect. You can synch taps to a music clip by using the Musical Time Counter section. Set the tempo of the music in *bpm*, beats per minute. Click the note the music is based on.

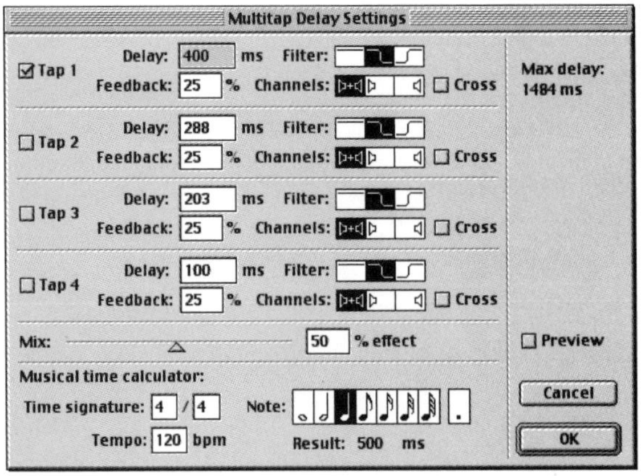

Figure 6-34: The Multitap Delay Settings dialog box

In the dialog box, click a tap checkbox to activate a tap delay effect. Enter a delay time in the delay field. The delay is the time between the audio and the delay. Click in the filter icon to remove low or high frequencies. The Feedback percentage controls the percentage of delay fed back to the original audio.

Use the Channels icon only with Stereo audio clips to specify which channel governs the effect. The Cross option can be used to create echoes, by creating a feedback in the opposite channel of a delay.

The Musical Time Calculator at the bottom of the dialog box is designed to help you calculate delay if you want to synchronize the Multitap filter effect with music. Enter the time signature, such as 4/4, the tempo in beats per minutes, and then click a note.

Reverb

In the Reverb Settings dialog box, as shown in Figure 6-35, you can choose whether you want your sound to appear as though it is in a medium or large room. The Mix slider enables you to control how much effect is added to the sound. At the Dry setting, the audio alone is heard. Decay controls how long it takes for the effect to finish. The Diffusion slider diffuses the audio, making the audio appears as if it is coming from a distance. The Brightness setting enables you to choose how much of the original sound is maintained. The term brightness is used because the more brightness, the brighter or more lively the sound. The Algorithm enables you to pick your audio locale: a large room or a medium room.

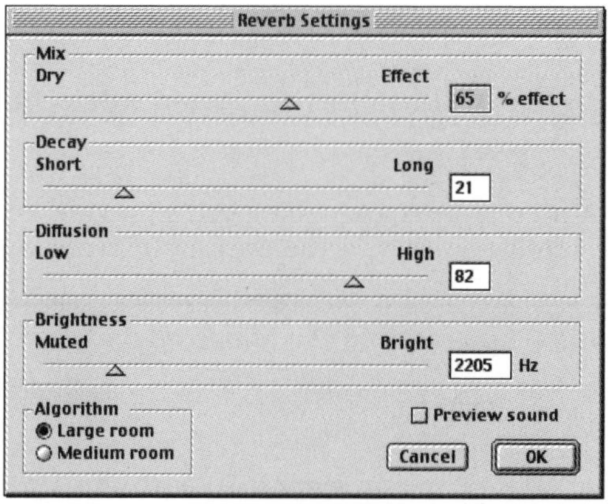

Figure 6-35: The Reverb Settings dialog box

Using the TC Works Filters

If you installed the Windows version of Premiere using the standard installation option, you can find the TC Works filter folder in the Audio Effects folder. The TC Works filters created by TC Works of Germany include TC Dynamics, TC EQ, and TC

Reverb. One of the chief advantages of using the TC Works filters is their real-life audio interface, shown in Figure 6-36. Using your mouse, you can operate the filter controls as if you were using real studio equipment. All of the filters include a preview button that enables you to preview the effects in real time. In other words, you can change settings and hear the changes as the audio plays. Each filter also provides access to a help module that explains the different controls for each of the filters.

Figure 6-36: The TC Works Dynamic filter provides a real-life interface.

Exporting Sound Files

You can build a preview of your project so that you can view the entire project with all its video clips, audio clips, effects, and/or transitions. After you've built a preview of the entire project, you can also choose to export one or more edited audio clips as an AIFF file.

Here's how to preview all the edited audio and video clips in an entire project:

1. **On-screen, you should have a project with edited audio and video clips.**
2. **Choose File ➪ Save.**
3. **Choose Timeline ➪ Preview.** A prompt appears, telling you a preview is being built. When Premiere is done building a preview, the preview appears in the Monitor window.
4. **To replay the preview, click the Play button in the Monitor window.**

Here's how to export one audio clip as an AIFF file:

1. **Select the audio track with the audio clip you want to export.**
2. **Choose File ➪ Export Clip ➪ Audio.** The Export Audio dialog box appears.
3. **Type a name for your audio file.**

4. **Click the Settings button.**
5. **In the Export Audio Settings dialog box, set the File Type pop-up menu to AIFF File.** You can set the Range pop-up menu to edit In and Out points of the sound clip or the entire sound clip.
5. **Click the General pop-up menu and choose Audio.** In the Audio section, you can set the Rate (in Hz) and the Format (8 bit or 16 bit, Mono or Stereo).
6. **Click OK to close the dialog box.**
7. **Click Save to save the selected audio as an AIFF file.**

Follow these steps to export the audio clips in the Timeline:

1. **If you want just a work area to be exported, move the yellow preview bar over that area.**
2. **Choose File ⇨ Export Timeline ⇨ Audio.** The Export Audio dialog box appears.
3. **Type a name in the Export Audio dialog box.**
4. **Click the Settings button.**
5. **In the Export Audio Settings dialog box, set the File Type pop-up menu to AIFF File.** You can set the Range pop-up menu to Work Area or Entire project.
6. **In the Export Audio Settings dialog box, click Audio in the General menu.** In the Audio section, you can set the Rate (in Hz) and the Format (8 bit or 16 bit, Mono or Stereo).
7. **Click OK to close the dialog box.**
8. **Click Save to create an AIFF file.**

Here's how to export an entire project:

1. **Choose File ⇨ Export Timeline ⇨ Movie.** The Export Movie dialog box appears.
2. **Name your project.**
3. **Click Settings.**
4. **In the Export Movie Settings dialog box, choose the options you want.**
5. **Click OK to close the dialog box.**
6. **In the Export Movie dialog box, click Save to save your project.**

Summary

Premiere provides numerous features for adjusting and editing audio. You can control fade-ins and fade-outs in the Timeline, you can use Audio tools in the Timeline's Toolbox, and you can create many professional audio effects by using the Premiere program's Audio mixer.

✦ By using the rubberband icons in the audio tracks, you can fade in and fade out and adjust the volume of audio clips.

✦ You can adjust audio gain by choosing Clip ➪ Audio Options ➪ Gain.

✦ Use the Timeline's Cross Fade tool to create cross fades.

✦ To create panning and mixing effects, use the Premiere Audio mixer, which enables you to mix audio in real time.

✦ Use the effects in the Premiere Audio Effects palette to enhance and correct audio.

✦ ✦ ✦

CHAPTER 7

Creating Transitions

✦ ✦ ✦ ✦

In This Chapter

✦ ✦ ✦ ✦

A cut from one scene in your video production to another provides an excellent transition for action clips or for clips that move the viewer from one locale to another. However, when you want to convey the passage of time or create an effect in which a scene gradually transforms into the next, a simple cut just won't do. To artistically show passage of time, you may want to use a *cross dissolve* — which gradually fades one clip in over another. For a more dramatic and abrupt effect, you can use a *clock wipe* in which one scene is rotated on-screen, as if it were swept into the frames by the hands of a clock.

Whether you're trying to turn night into day, day into night, youth into age — or simply wake up your audience with a startling special effect that bridges one scene to another, you should find what you're looking for in the Adobe Premiere Transitions palette.

Touring the Transitions Palette

Adobe Premiere's Transitions palette stores over 75 different transitional effects. To view the Transitions palette and see a list of the transition categories, choose Window ⇨ Show Transition. As shown in Figure 7-1, the Transitions palette keeps all of the transitions organized into folders. To view the contents of a transition folder, double-click the folder or click the triangle icon to the left of the folder. When the folder opens, the triangle icon points down. Click the downward-pointing triangle icon to close the folder or double-click the folder again.

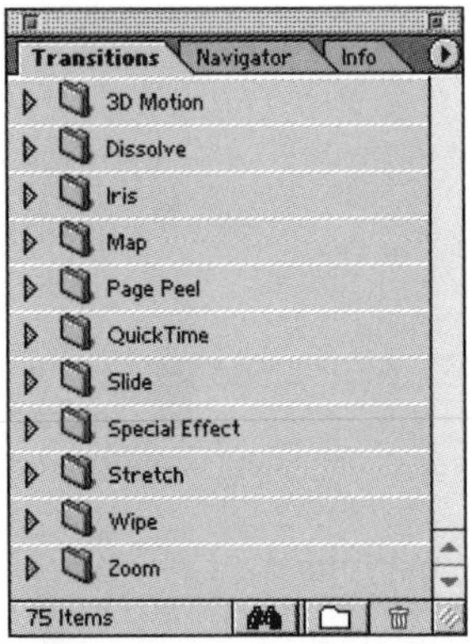

Figure 7-1: The Transitions palette contains over 75 different transitional effects.

Using the Transitions palette menu

The Transitions palette menu helps you locate transitions and keep them organized. To view the Transitions palette menu, shown in Figure 7-2, click the triangle icon at the top right of the palette.

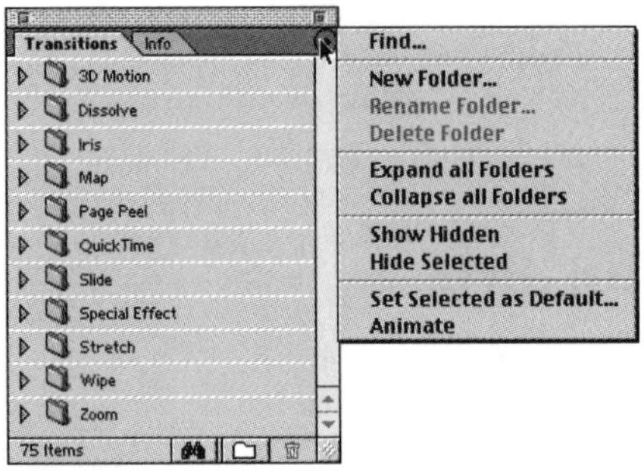

Figure 7-2: The Transitions palette menu items

Following is a description of the menu choices found in the Transitions palette menu:

✦ **Find.** Enables you to search for a transition by name. Clicking Find opens the Find Transitions dialog box where you can enter the name of the transition you want to find. You needn't type in the full name. For example, type the word cross (with the open folder option selected), and the Find command opens the Dissolve folder and selects the Cross Dissolve transition. Type the word Invert, and the Find command finds the Random Invert transition.

- **New Folder.** Choose this command to create a new folder to keep the transitions that you are using grouped together. After you create the folder, you can click and drag transitions into the folder.
- **Rename Folder.** Enables you to rename the selected folder in the Transitions palette.
- **Delete Folder.** Enables you to delete the selected folder in the Transitions palette.
- **Expand all Folders.** Reveals the contents of each folder by expanding each one.
- **Collapse all Folders.** Closes all folders in the Transitions palette.
- **Show Hidden.** Shows folders that are hidden in the palette. When Show Hidden is activated, a check mark appears next to the choice. Click again, and the hidden folders are hidden again and the check mark disappears.
- **Hide Selected.** Hides selected transitions in the palette. (You can Shift+click to select more than one transition to hide.)
- **Set Selected as Default.** Sets the selected transition as Premiere's default transition. (Use of this feature is described later in this chapter.)
- **Animate.** Animates the icons in the Transitions palette, providing a miniature preview of each transition.

A/B and Single-Track Editing

Premiere enables you to create transitions in two Timeline modes: A/B Editing or Single-Track.

Tip

With a project onscreen, you can set your workspace to either A/B Editing or Single-Track Editing by choosing Window ➪ Workspace ➪ Single-Track Editing or Window ➪ Workspace ➪ A/B Editing. To change just the Timeline window to either A/B Editing or Single-Track Editing, click the Timeline window pop-up menu and choose either A/B Editing or Single-Track Editing.

The A/B Editing mode is named after the A and B rolls used in film editing, in which the movie is edited using two reels of film (A and B), instead of one. In this mode, Video track 1 is divided into tracks Video track 1A and Video 1B. Between the two tracks is a transition track. To apply a transition using this mode, one clip is placed in Video track 1A, another is placed in Video track 1B, and the transition is placed between them in the transition track. When the final project is exported, the three different tracks are combined into one movie with a transition between the two clips.

In Single-Track Editing mode, which is similar to traditional video editing, the transition is dragged between two clips in the track. The transition uses the extra frames at the Out point of the first clip, and the extra clips at the In point of the second clip as the transitional area. Using this technique, it is harder to judge how the transition will appear as you edit, and it is more time-consuming to set up.

Creating transitions with A/B tracks

The easiest way to apply a transition is to place one video clip in Video track 1A and another in Video track 1B. Then place the transition between the two tracks, as shown in Figure 7-3. In Figure 7-4, you can see the actual transition occurring in frames of the final video clip.

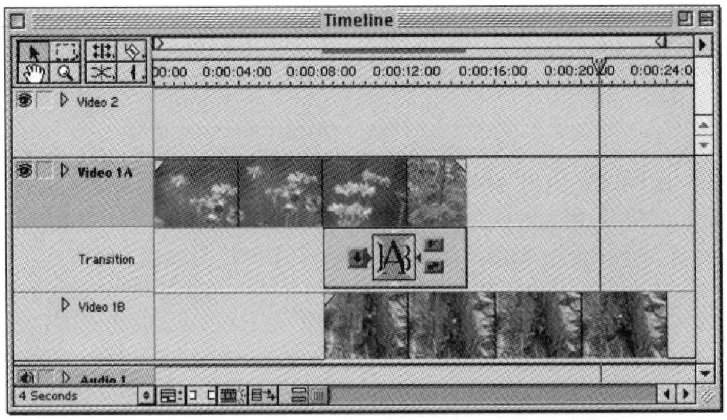

Figure 7-3: The Timeline window in A/B Editing mode, with two video clips and a transition between the two

Here's how to apply a transition in A/B Editing mode:

1. **Before following the steps, create a new project by choosing, File ⇨ New Project.** In the Load Project Settings dialog box, set the setting to Multimedia. Click OK to create a new project.
2. **In the Timeline menu, make sure that A/B Editing is selected.**
3. **Choose File ⇨ Import ⇨ File to import two video clips.** In the Import dialog box, click a file to import. Premiere provides separate methods for Mac and Windows users who want to import more than one file at a time from the same folder: Mac users should press and hold the ⌘ key while selecting files, and PC users should press and hold the Ctrl key when selecting files.
4. **When you've finished selecting files, click the Open button to import the file(s) into the Project window.**

On the CD-ROM

If you want, you can load the clips used in Figure 7-3 (rockclimber.mov and yellowflowers.mov) from the Chapter 7 folder, that is in the Tutorial Projects folder, which is on the CD-ROM that accompanies this book. For an alternative choice in video clips, in the Chapter 7 folder you will also find Digital Vision's Electro clip# 579018f.mov and Electro clip# 579019f.mov.

5. **To set the Timeline window to A/B Editing mode, click the Timeline pop-up menu and choose A/B Editing.** You should now see Video track 1A, the Transitions track, and Video track 1B.

Figure 7-4: Frames from a project with the Doors transition between two clips

6. **Drag one video clip from the Project window to Video track 1A.**
7. **Drag the other video clip from the Project window into Video track 1B.**
8. **Use the Selection tool to drag the clip in Video track 1A and Video track 1B so that they overlap, as seen in Figure 7-3.** The overlapping frames are used by the transition to show the last frames of one clip and the first frames of the next clip. Thus, if you want a two-second transition, make sure that the last second of Video track 1A overlaps the first second of Video track 1B.
9. **Pick a transition from the Transitions palette and drag it into the Transition track between the two overlapping tracks.** For example, click the Doors transition found in the 3D Motion folder and then drag it to the Transition track into the area where Video track 1A and 1B overlap, as seen in Figure 7-3.

Note

It's easier to place transitions if you have the Snap to Edges model selected in the Timeline pop-up menu. When you place the transition, it snaps into place between the clips.

10. **If you want to change the duration of the transition, select the Selection tool and move the pointer over the left or right transition edge.** Click and drag to extend the transition or to shorten it.
11. **To display a transition's dialog box, double-click the transition's icon in the Transition track.** In the transition's dialog box, notice that there is an A and a B box, as seen in the left dialog box in Figure 7-5.
12. **Click the Show Actual Sources option.** Notice that the A and B boxes are replaced with the video clips from Video track 1A track and Video track 1B, as seen in right dialog box shown in Figure 7-5.
13. **Click and drag the sliders below the video clip images to see a preview of the transition.**

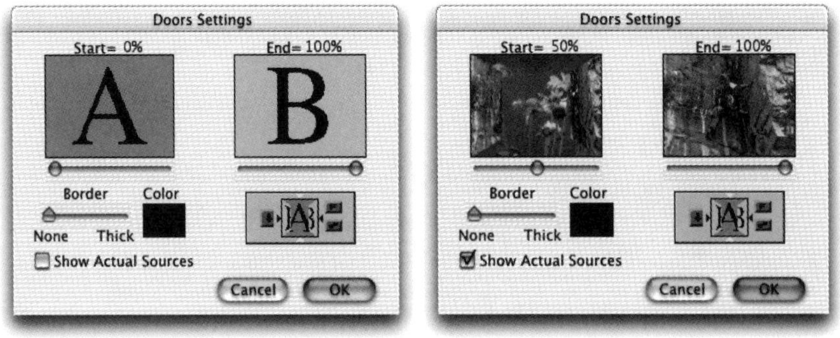

Figure 7-5: The Doors Settings dialog box before and after displaying video clips from Video track 1A and 1B

14. To view the transition in the Monitor window, choose Timeline ➪ Preview or press Enter. Premiere then asks you to save your work. Save your work. When Premiere has finished building a preview, the preview appears in the Monitor window.

Tip To preview just the transitional area of your project, move the left and right Work Area Markers so that the Work Area Bar (preview area bar at the top of the Timeline window) appears only over the transition. To see the Timeline window with callouts, refer to Chapter 5.

Applying a transition in Single-Track Editing mode

Although it's more intuitive to create transitions in Premiere's A/B Editing mode, you can also create transitions if you are editing in a single track. When you use Premiere's Single-Track editing, extra frames beyond the Out point of one clip and the extra frames before the In point of the next clip are used as the transitional area (if no extra frames are available, Premiere enables you to repeat ending or beginning frames). Figure 7-6 shows a sample Timeline with transitions using Single-Track editing. In the Timeline window, you see that we used six different transitions (Pinwheel, Multi-Spin, Swirl, Iris Star, Paint Spatter, and Iris Square) on three different backgrounds (a blobs sequence, a still image called Colorful spheres, and another still image called Chalk mode).

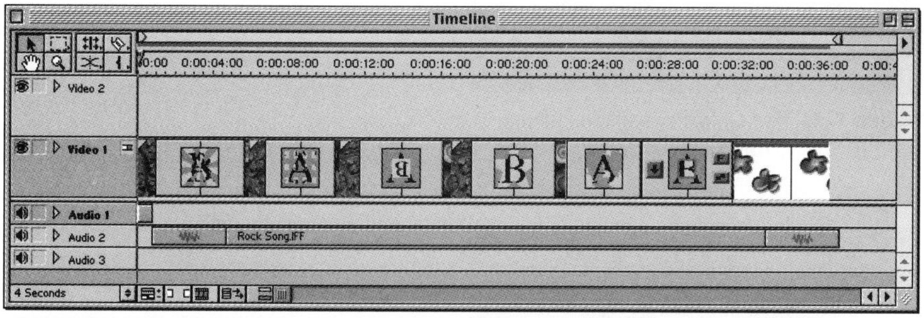

Figure 7-6: The Timeline window with transitions using Single-Track editing

A frame from the blobs sequence is seen in Figure 7-7. Figures 7-8 and 7-9 show the Colorful spheres and Chalk Mode images used in the Timeline window. These images are on the Chapter 7 folder in the CD-ROM that accompanies this book.

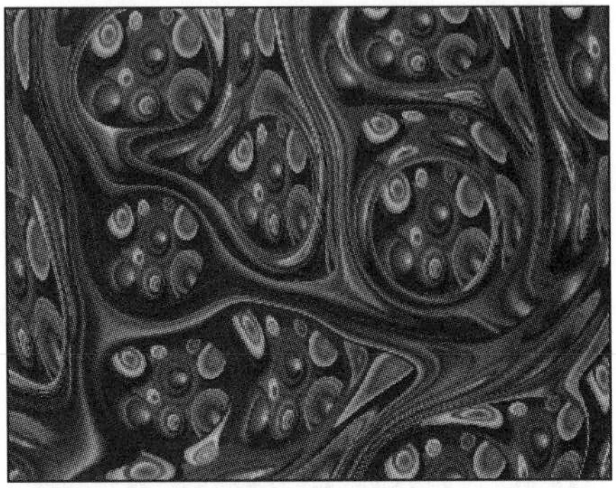

Figure 7-7: A frame from the blobs sequence used in the Timeline window

Figure 7-8: The Colorful spheres image used in the Timeline window

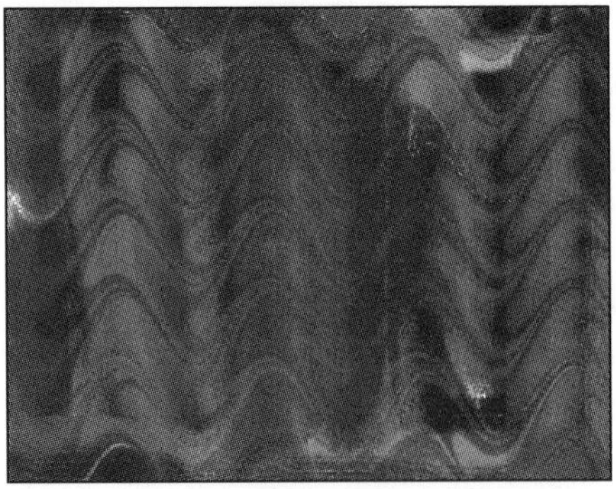

Figure 7-9: The Chalk mode image used in the Timeline window

Figures 7-10 through 7-15 show frames from a Pinwheel, Multi-Spin, Swirl, Iris Star, Paint Spatter, and Iris Square transition using the Blobs sequence and the Colorful Spheres image.

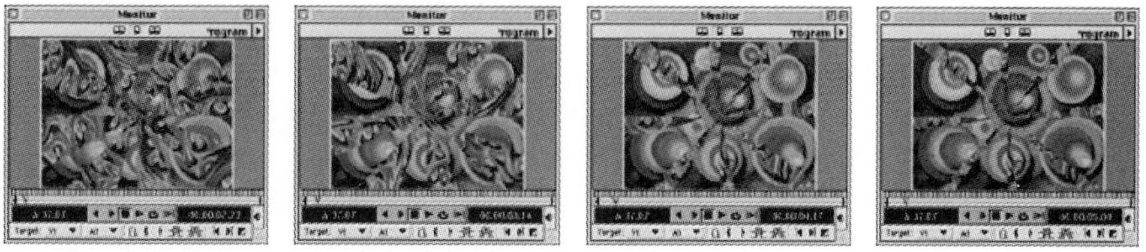

Figure 7-10: Frames from the Pinwheel transition using the Blobs sequence and the colorful spheres image

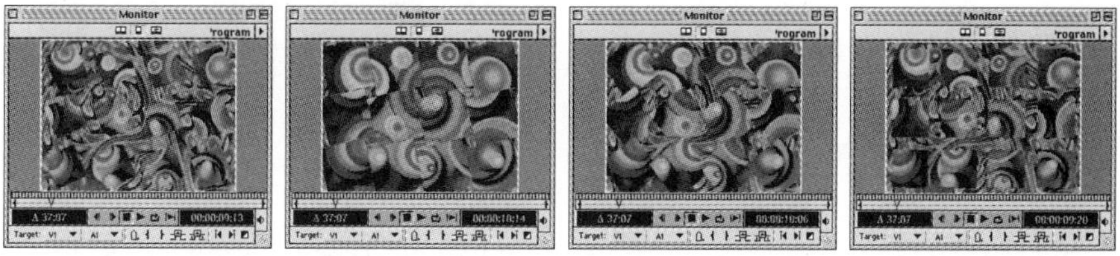

Figure 7-11: Frames from the Multi-Spin transition using the Blobs sequence and the colorful spheres image

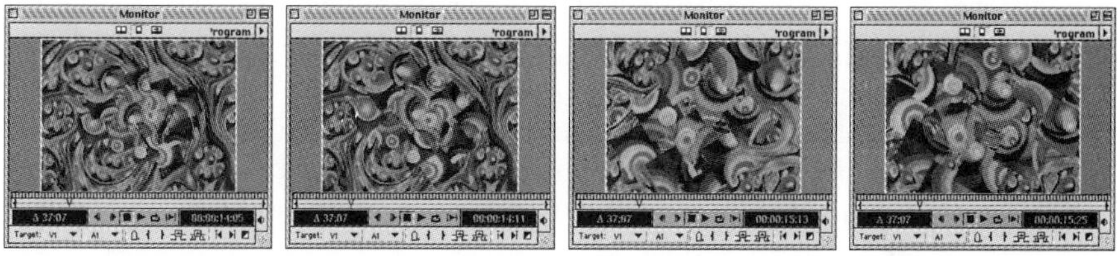

Figure 7-12: Frames from the Swirl transition using the Blobs sequence and the colorful spheres image

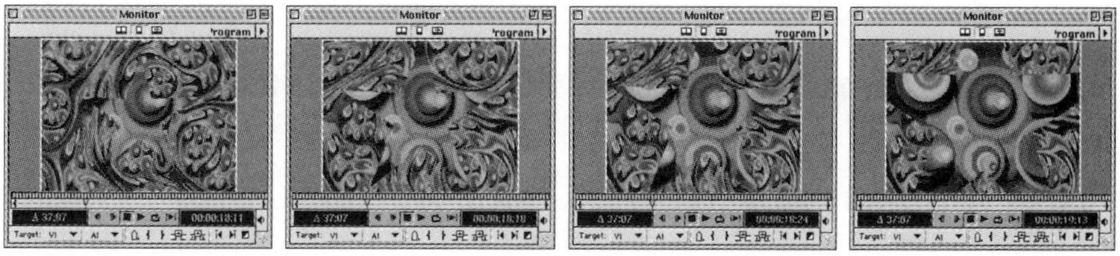

Figure 7-13: Frames from the Iris Star transition using the Blobs sequence and the colorful spheres image

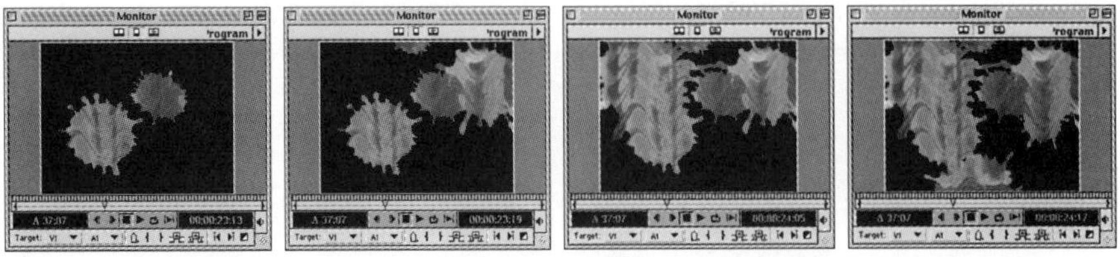

Figure 7-14: Frames from the Paint Splatter transition using the Blobs sequence and the colorful spheres image

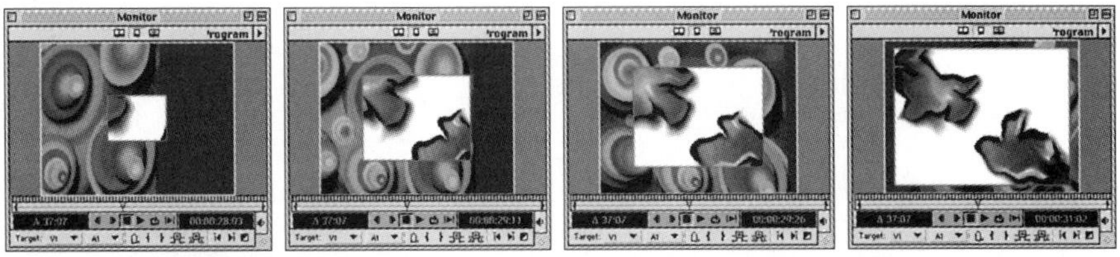

Figure 7-15: Frames from the Iris Square transition using the Blobs sequence and the colorful spheres image

Here are the steps for creating a transition in Single-Track Editing mode:

1. **Create a new project by choosing File ➪ New Project.** In the Load Project Settings dialog box, set the setting to Multimedia. Click OK to create a new project.
2. **In the Timeline pop-up menu, choose Single-Track Editing.** You should now have just Video 1 track. When you are in Single-Track Editing mode, note that in the Timeline window there appears a rectangular white and black clip icon next to the word Video 1 (see Figure 7-6). The rectangular white and black clip icon designates that you are in Single-Track Editing mode.
3. **Choose File ➪ Import ➪ File to import images or video clips. Choose File ➪ Import ➪ Folder to import a folder.** In the Import dialog box, select the file or folder you want to import.

On the CD-ROM

If you want, you can import the images used in Figure 7-6 (a blobs sequence folder, a blob.psd still image called Colorfulspheres.psd, and another still image called Chalkmode.psd). The images are found in the Chapter 7 folder, that is in the Tutorial Projects folder in the CD-ROM that accompanies this book.

4. **Drag one clip from the Project palette into Video track 1 of the Timeline. Then drag another clip next to it.** Set the Out point of the first clip and the In point of the second clip. The first clip should have extra frames that extend beyond the Out point. The second clip should have extra frames that extend beyond the In point. These extra frames are used by Premiere to determine the length of the transition. When you set the In and Out points, each clip

should have an equal number of extra frames. The extra frames determine the length of the transition. For example, to create a 30-frame dissolve, each clip should have 15 extra frames in each clip. You can set In and Out points by either using the Selection tool, Timeline markers, Clip window, or Monitor window. For more information on setting In and Out points, turn to Chapter 5.

5. **Now pick a transition from the Transition palette and place it over the area where the two clips meet.** Premiere highlights the area where the transition occurs and then places the transition within the track. If the number of extra frames for each clip is not sufficient to create the transition, Premiere opens the Fix Transition dialog box. In the Fix Transition dialog box, you can change the duration of the transition or click a radio button to have Premiere repeat the last and first frames of the clips to accommodate the transition.

Tip

f you press the Option key (Alt for Windows users) while dragging a transition over Video track 1, Premiere automatically opens the Fix Transition dialog box, enabling you to set the duration of the transition. The Fix Transition dialog box also enables you to choose whether you want the transition to be placed over the center of the cut, the start of the cut, or the end of the cut.

Tip

If you move a transition edge, you may also move the edge of a clip. To move a transition edge without affecting any clips, Mac users press ⌘ (Windows users press Ctrl), while you click and drag the Transition edge.

6. **To see the overlapping areas and the transition displayed below the first clip and above the next clip, click the Track mode icon — just to the right of Video track 1.**

7. **Save your work by choosing File ➪ Save.**

8. **Preview the transition by choosing Timeline ➪ Preview or press Enter.**

Editing Transitions settings

Many of the transitions include settings options that enable you to change how a transition appears on-screen. For example, after you apply a transition, you can edit the transition direction by simply clicking the arrow in the transitions thumbnail in the Transitions palette. By default, a clip transitions from the first clip to the second (A to B). Occasionally, you might wish to create a transition in which scene B transitions to scene A — even though scene B appears after scene A. To switch the transition directions, click the arrow in the Thumbnail. B to A transitions display an arrow pointing upward instead of downward.

For more control over a transition, double-click the transition's thumbnail in the Timeline. This opens the Transition Settings dialog box for the transition (see Figure 7-16). To see a preview of the transition effect, click and drag the A or B slider. To see the actual clips previewed in the palette, select the Show Actual Sources check box and then click and drag the sliders.

Many transitions enable you to reverse the effect. For example, the Curtain Transition in the 3D Motion folder normally applies the transition with Clip A onscreen; the curtain opens to display clip B. However, by clicking the R button (for Reverse) at the bottom of the palette, you can make the curtain close to reveal Clip B. The Doors Transition is quite similar. Normally the Doors open to reveal Clip B. If you click the R button, the doors close to reveal Clip A.

Several transitions also enable you to smooth the effect or create a soft-edge effect by applying anti-aliasing to the transitions. To smooth the effect, click the anti-alias button shown in Figure 7-16.

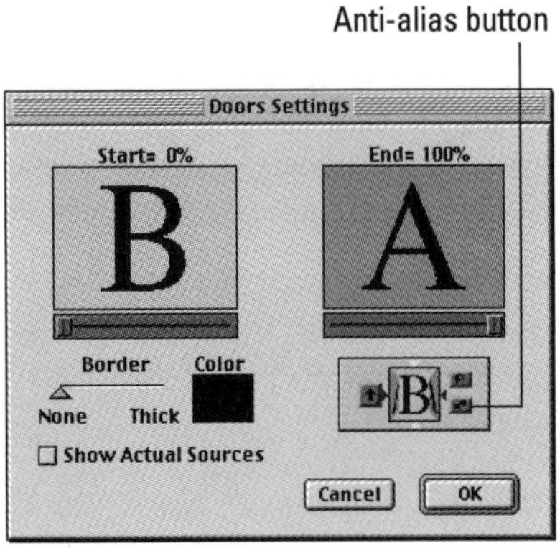

Figure 7-16: The Doors Settings dialog box and its settings

Creating a Default Transition

If you are applying the same transition many times throughout a project, you can set a default transition. After you've specified a default transition, you can easily apply it without having to drag it to the Timeline from the Transitions palette.

Here are the steps for creating a default transition:

1. **If the Transitions palette is not opened, open it by choosing Window ➪ Show Transitions.**
2. **In the Transitions palette, click the transition that you want to set as the default.**
3. **In the Transitions palette menu, choose Set Selected as Default.** Doing this opens the Default Effect palette shown in Figure 7-17.
4. **In the Default Effect dialog box, enter the duration and an alignment setting from the Effect Alignment pop-up menu.**
5. **Click OK to close the dialog box.**

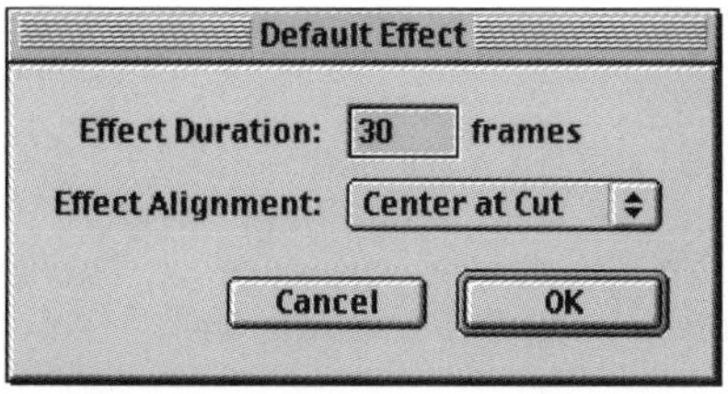

Figure 7-17: The Default Effect dialog box and its settings

Note: The default transition remains the default transition for all Premiere projects until you choose another default transition.

Applying a Default Transition

To use a default transition, organize the clips in Video track 1A and Video track 1B as you would for a normal transition. If you are using Single-Track editing, position the clips so that the In and Out points meet in the single track.

✦ If the Transition track is visible, you can set the default transition by pressing ⌘+Option+Shift (PC users press Ctrl+Alt+Shift) and clicking in the Transition track.

✦ Alternatively, if extra frames exist between the two clips, you can click the Apply Default Transition button in the Monitor window. (Use this technique for Single-Track editing.)

Tip: You can apply the default transition with the monitor window open by pressing ⌘/Ctrl+D.

Replacing and Deleting Transitions

After you've created a transition, you may decide that it doesn't quite provide the effect you originally intended. Fortunately, replacing or deleting transitions is easy:

✦ To replace one transition with another, simply click and drag one transition from the Transitions palette over the transition that you want to replace in the Timeline. The new transition replaces the old transition.

✦ To delete a transition, simply select it with the mouse and then press the Delete key. (PC users can also press Backspace.)

Transitions Review

Premiere's Transition palette provides 11 different transition folders: 3D Motion, Dissolve, Iris, Map, Page Peel, QuickTime, Slide, Special Effect, Stretch, Wipe, and Zoom. Each folder features its own set of eye-catching transitions. This section features a tour of virtually every transition in each folder, along with examples of some of the transitions.

Note

To aid in describing the transitions, we call the clip in Video track A, *Clip A*; the clip in Video track B is called *Clip B*. In the following sections, we describe how Clip A transitions to Clip B. However, note that many transitions can be reversed so that Clip B transitions to Clip A.

3D Motion

The 3D Motion folder features 11 transitions: Cube Spin, Curtain, Doors, Flip Over, Fold Up, Motion, Spin, Spin Away, Swing In, Swing Out, and Tumble Away. Each one of the transitions includes motion as the transition occurs.

Cube Spin

The Cube Spin transition uses a spinning 3D cube to create the transition from Clip A to Clip B. In the Cube Spin Settings dialog box, you can set the transition to be from left to right, right to left, top to bottom, or bottom to top. Drag the Border slider to the right to increase the border color between the two video tracks. Click the color swatch if you want to change the border color.

Curtain

The Curtain transition simulates a curtain that opens to reveal Clip B replacing Clip A. The Curtain dialog box can be seen in Figure 7-18.

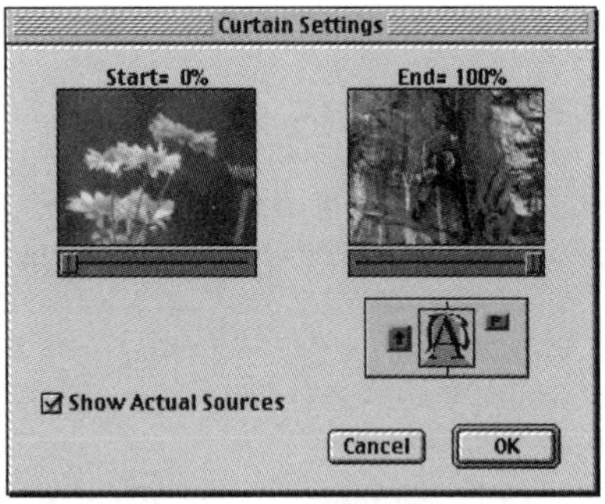

Figure 7-18: The Curtain Settings dialog box

Doors

The Doors transition simulates opening a door. What's behind the door? Clip B, (replacing Clip A). You can have the transition move from left to right, right to left, top to bottom, or bottom to top. The Door Settings dialog box, shown in Figure 7-19, includes a Border slider. Drag the Border slider to the right to increase the border color between the two video tracks. Click the color swatch if you want to change the border color.

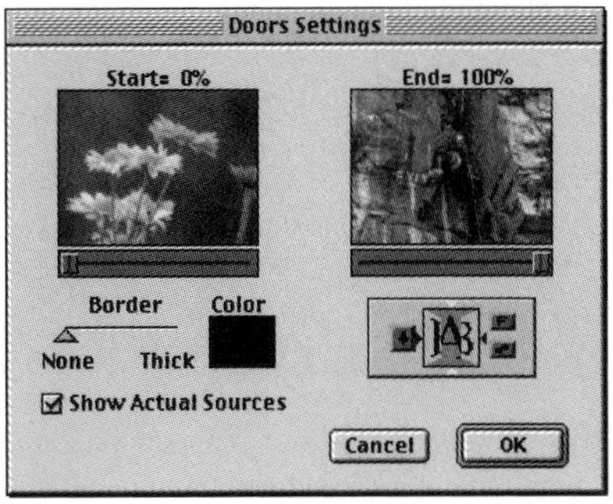

Figure 7-19: The Doors Settings dialog box

Flip Over

The Flip Over transition flips Clip A along its vertical axis to reveal Clip B. Click the Custom Settings button in the Flip Over Settings dialog box to set the number of bands and cell color.

Fold Up

The Fold Up transition folds up Clip A (as if it were a piece of paper), to reveal Clip B.

Motion

The Motion Settings transition dialog box, shown in Figure 7-20, shows Clip B as a small ever-growing rectangle that tumbles across the screen. If you click the Custom Settings button, you can load motion settings saved from the Premiere Motion Settings dialog box.

Spin

Spin is very similar to the Flip Over transition, except that Clip B spins onto the screen, rather than flipping, to replace Clip A. Figure 7-21 shows the Spin Settings dialog box.

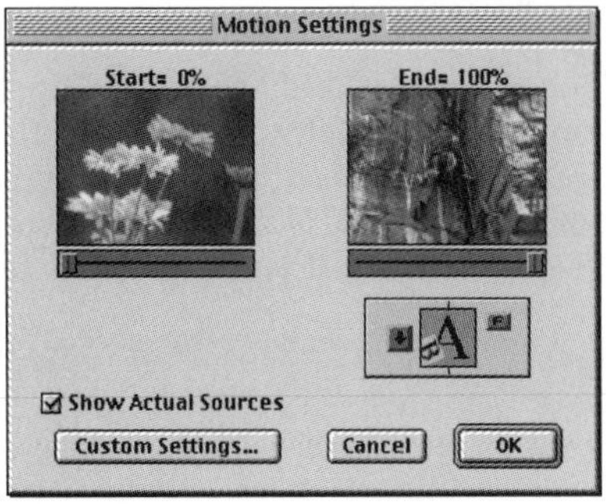

Figure 7-20: The Motion Settings dialog box

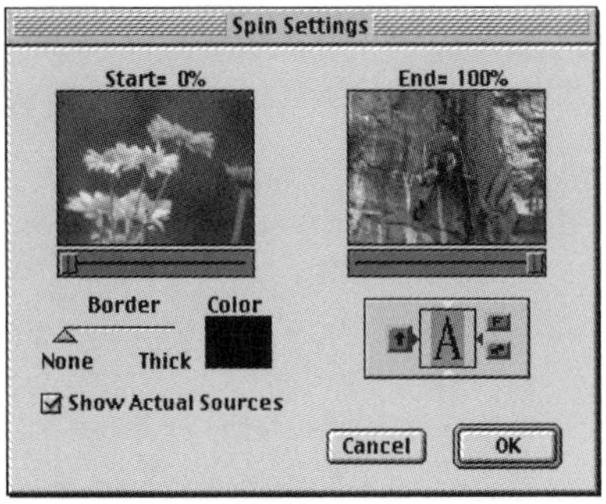

Figure 7-21: The Spin Settings dialog box

Spin Away

In the Spin Away transition, Clip B spins on-screen similar to the Spin transition. However, in Spin Away, Clip B consumes more of the frame than the Spin transition.

Swing In

In the Swing In transition, Clip B swings onto the screen from screen left, like a gate shutting from the inside.

Swing Out

In the Swing Out transition, Clip B swings onto the screen from screen left, like a gate shutting from the outside.

Tumble Away

In the Tumble Away transition, Clip A spins and gradually becomes smaller as it is replaced by Clip B.

Dissolve

The Dissolve transition gradually fades in one video clip over another. Five dissolve transitions exist: Additive Dissolve, Cross Dissolve, Dither Dissolve, Non-Additive Dissolve, and Random Invert.

Additive Dissolve

The Additive Dissolve transition creates a fade from one clip to the next. The Additive Dissolve Settings dialog box is shown in Figure 7-22.

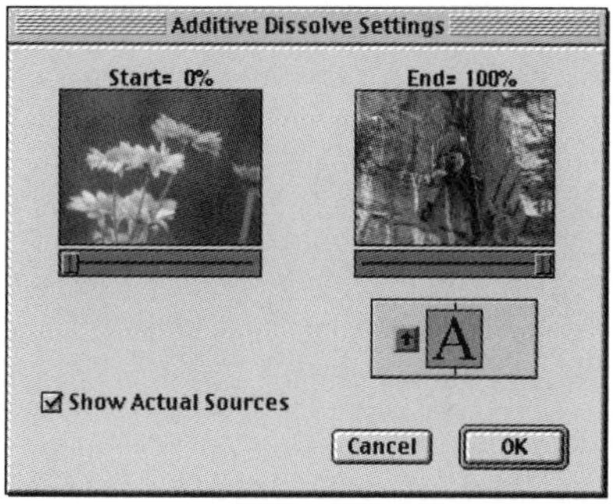

Figure 7-22: The Additive Dissolve Settings dialog box

Cross Dissolve

In this transition, Clip B fades in before Clip A fades out. The Cross Dissolve Settings dialog box is shown in Figure 7-23.

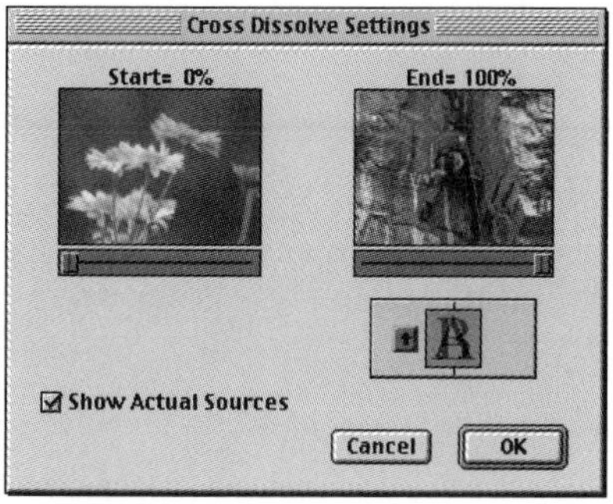

Figure 7-23: The Cross Dissolve Settings dialog box

Dither Dissolve

In the Dither Dissolve transition, Clip A dissolves to Clip B as tiny dots appear on-screen. The Dither Dissolve Settings dialog box is shown in Figure 7-24.

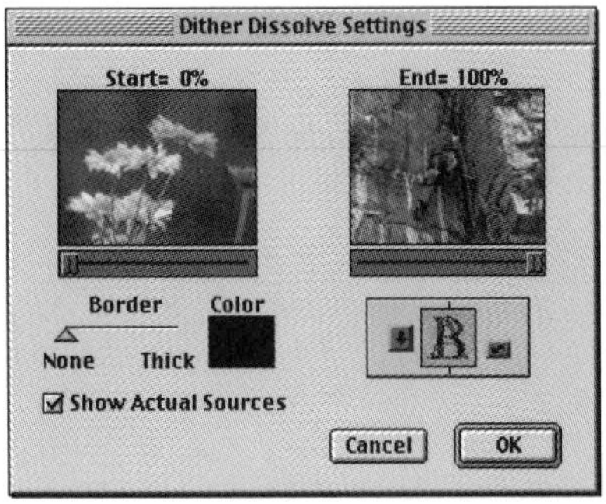

Figure 7-24: The Dither Dissolve Settings dialog box

Non-Additive Dissolve

In this transition, Clip B gradually appears in colored areas of Clip A.

Random Invert

In the Random Invert transition, random dot patterns appear as Clip B gradually replaces Clip A.

Iris

The Iris transitions all begin or end at the center point of the screen. The Iris transitions are Iris Cross, Iris Diamond, Iris Points, Iris Round, Iris Shapes, Iris Square, and Iris Star.

Iris Cross

In this transition, Clip B gradually appears in a cross that grows bigger and bigger until it takes over the full frame. The Iris Cross Settings dialog box is shown in Figure 7-25.

Iris Diamond

In this transition, Clip B gradually appears in a diamond that gradually takes over the full frame.

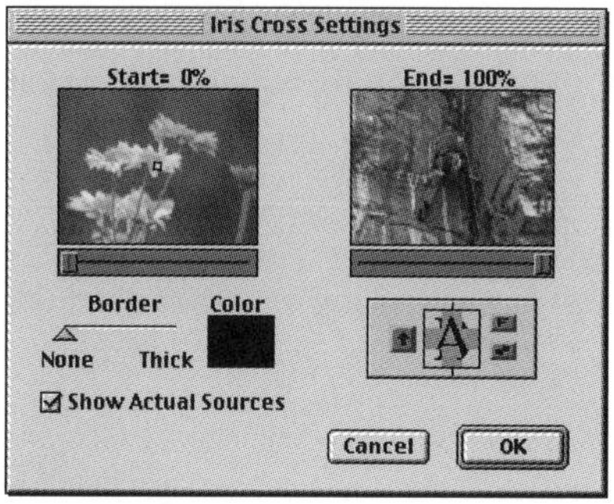

Figure 7-25: The Iris Cross Settings dialog box

Iris Points

In this transition, Clip B appears in the outer edges of a large cross, with Clip A in the cross. As the cross becomes smaller, Clip B gradually comes full screen.

Iris Round

In the Iris Round transition Clip B gradually appears in an ever-growing circle that gradually consumes the full frame.

Iris Shapes

In this transition, Clip B gradually appears inside of three diamonds (with the default settings) that gradually grow and consume the frame. The Iris Shapes Settings dialog box is shown in Figure 7-26. Click the Custom Settings button to pick the number of shapes and the shape type.

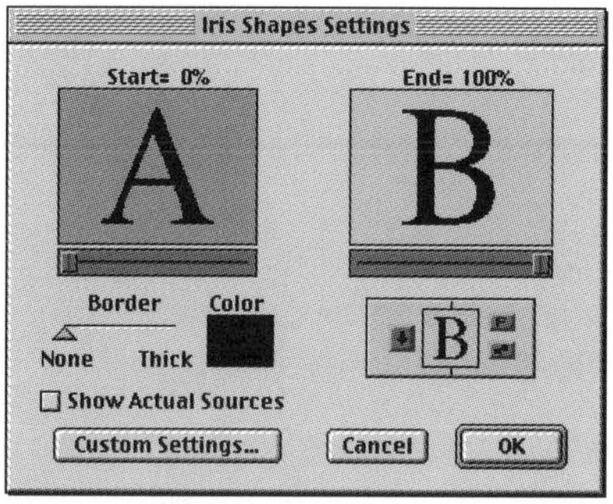

Figure 7-26: The Iris Shapes Settings dialog box

Iris Square

In this transition, Clip B gradually appears in an ever-growing square that gradually consumes the full frame.

Iris Star

In this transition, Clip B gradually appears in an ever-growing star that gradually consumes the full frame.

Map transitions

The Map transitions remap colors during the transition. The available Map transitions are Channel Map and Luminance.

Channel Map

The Channel Map transition enables you to create unusual color effects by mapping image channels to other image channels. To use this transition, click the Custom Settings button in the Channel Map Settings dialog box. Doing this opens the Channel Map Setting dialog box, shown in Figure 7-27. In this dialog box, select the channel from the pop-up menu and choose whether to invert the colors. Click OK and then preview the effect in the transition dialog box.

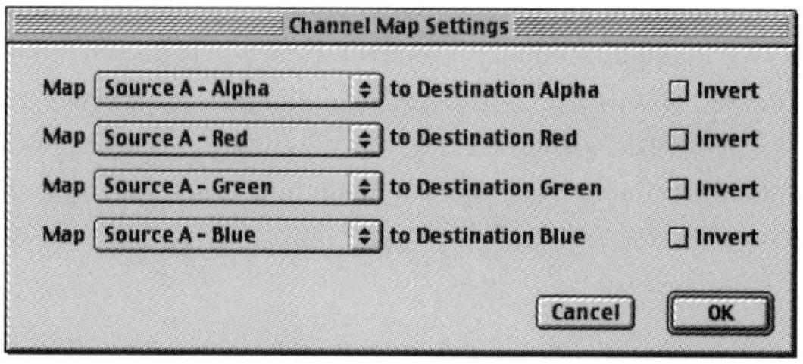

Figure 7-27: The Channel Map Settings dialog box after clicking the custom button

Luminance Map

The Luminance Map transition replaces the brightness levels of one clip with another. Figure 7-28 shows the Luminance Map Settings dialog box.

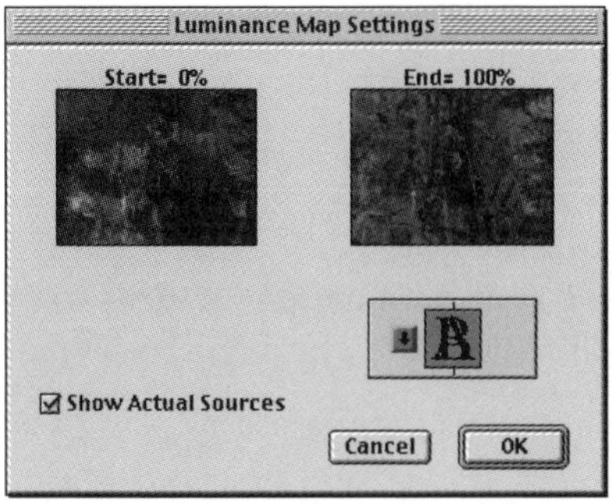

Figure 7-28: The Luminance Map Settings dialog box

Page Peel

The transitions in the Page Peel folder simulate one page of a book turning to reveal the next page. On the first page is Clip A; and on the second page is Clip B. This transition can be quite striking, as Premiere renders the image in Clip A curled onto the back of the turning page.

Center Peel

Center Peel creates four separate page curls that rip out of the center of Clip A to reveal Clip B. Figure 7-29 shows the Center Peel Settings dialog box.

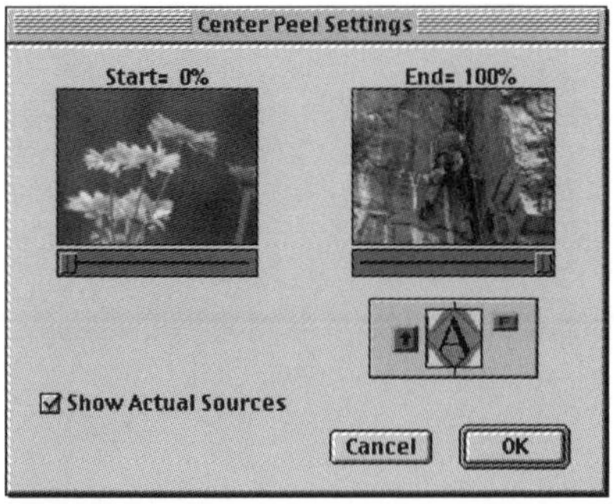

Figure 7-29: The Center Peel Settings dialog box

Page Peel

This transition is a standard peel where the page curls from the upper-left of the screen to the lower-right, to reveal the next page.

Page Turn

With the Page Turn transition, the page turns, but doesn't curl. As it turns to reveal Clip B, you see Clip A reversed on the back of the page.

Peel Back

In this transition, the page is peeled back from the middle to the upper-left, then to the upper-right, then lower-right, then lower-left.

Roll Away

In this transition, Clip A rolls from left to right off the page (with no curl) to reveal Clip B.

QuickTime

The QuickTime transitions are provided as part of the Apple's QuickTime package installed with Premiere. To apply a transition, drag the QuickTime transition to the Transition track and then click the Custom button. Choose from the following list of transitions found in the dialog box shown in Figure 7-30: Alpha Compositor, Chroma Key, Fade, Explode, Gradient Wipe, Implode, Iris, Matrix Wipe, Push, Radial, Slide, Wipe, and Zoom.

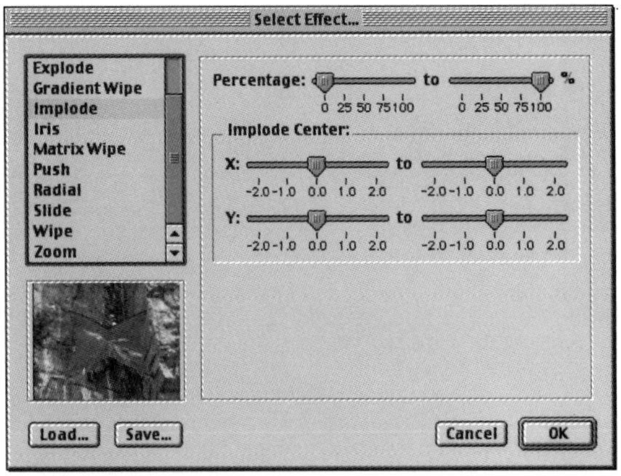

Figure 7-30: The Select Effect dialog box with a list of QuickTime transitions

After you click the transition name, the Select Effect dialog box appears, enabling you to choose settings for the different effects. Click OK to apply the effect.

Slide

The Slide transitions enable you to slide clips in and out of the frame to provide transitional effects.

Band Slide

In this transition, rectangular bands appear from screen right and screen left, gradually replacing Clip A with Clip B. The Band Slide dialog box is shown in Figure 7-31. Click the Custom button to choose how many band slides you want.

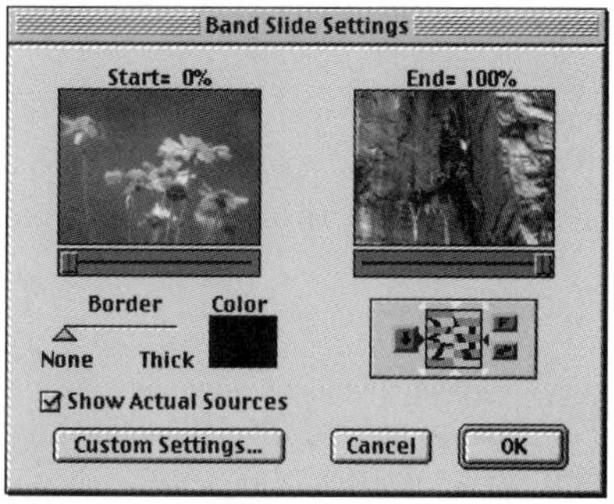

Figure 7-31: The Band Slide Settings dialog box

Center Merge

In this transition, Clip A gradually shrinks and squeezes into the center of the frame as it is replaced by Clip B.

Center Split

In the Center Split transition, Clip A is split into four quadrants and gradually moves out of the frame as it is replaced by Clip B.

Multi-Spin

In the Multi-Spin transition, Clip B gradually appears in tiny spinning boxes that grow to reveal the entire clip. Click the Custom Settings button in the Multi-Spin Settings dialog box to set the horizontal and vertical values.

Push

In this transition, Clip B pushes Clip A across the frame.

Slash Slide

In this transition, diagonal slashes filled with pieces of Clip B gradually replace Clip A. Click the Custom Settings button in the Slash Slide Settings dialog box to set the number of slashes.

Slide

In the Slide transition, Clip B gradually slides over Clip A.

Sliding Bands

In this transition, Clip B begins in a compressed state, and then gradually stretches across the frame to replace Clip A.

Sliding Boxes

In the Sliding Boxes transition, vertical bands composed of Clip B gradually move across the screen to replace Clip A.

Split

In this transition, Clip A splits apart from the middle to reveal Clip B behind it. The effect is like opening two sliding doors to reveal the contents of a room.

Swap

In the Swap transition, Clip B swaps places with Clip A. The effect almost looks as if one clip move lefts or right then behind the previous clip.

Swirl

In the Swirl transition, Clip B swirls onto the screen to replace Clip A. Click the Custom Settings button in the Swirl Settings dialog box to set the horizontal, vertical, and rate amount.

Special Effects

The transitions in the Special Effects folder are a grab bag of transitions that create special effects, many of which change colors or distort images. The Special Effects transitions are: Direct, Displace, Image Mask, Take, Texturizer, and Three-D.

Direct

The Direct transition is actually a cut. Place the transition between tracks Video 1A and Video 1B, and the scene cuts from A to B with audio from track A. By clicking and dragging on the transition edge, you can control the In and Out points of Clip B without actually editing Clip B. The transition is most useful when you need to drop in a short piece of video. In other words the you can have clip A play and use the Direct Transition to create a short insert edit to clip B before the program returns to clip A.

Displace

In the Displace transition, the colors in Clip B create an image distortion in Clip A. Clicking the Custom button enables you to change the Scale setting. The lower the Scale, the larger the displacement. If the displacement would cause the image to stretch beyond the frame, the Wrap Around option tells Premiere to wrap the pixels to the other side of the frame. The Repeat Pixels option repeats the pixels along the image edges instead of wrapping them on the other side of the frame. The Custom mode of the Displace Settings dialog box is shown in Figure 7-32.

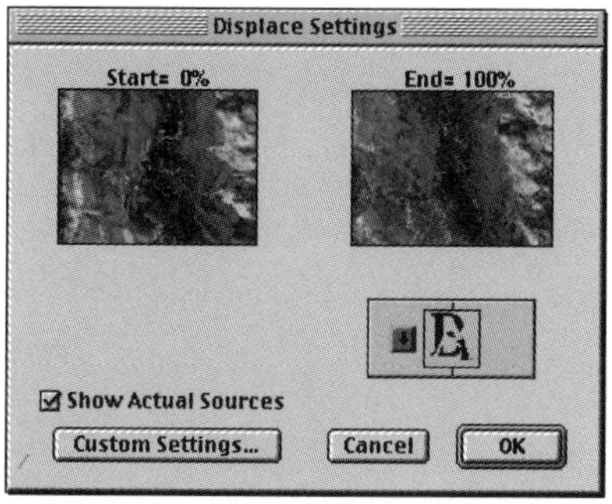

Figure 7-32: The Displace Settings dialog box after clicking the Custom Settings button

Image Mask

This transition uses a black-and-white mask image to determine how the transition appears. When you apply this transition, the Image Mask Settings dialog box immediately appears. Click the Select Image button to select a black-and-white image to use as a mask. Clip B is seen through white areas of the Mask. Clip A is seen through black areas of the mask.

Note: If you select a grayscale image to use as a mask, the transition converts all pixels below 50% black to white, and all pixels above 50% black to black. This can result in a very aliased (jaggy) transition if the mask image is not carefully chosen.

Take

The Take Transition is similar to Direct, providing a cut from Clip A to B. If you click and drag the end of the transition beyond Clip B, Premiere inserts black rather than returning to Clip A.

Texturizer

The Texturizer transition maps color values from Clip B into Clip A. The blending of the two clips can create a textured effect.

Three-D

The Three-D transition distorts the colors in Clips A and B creating a composite between the two images. The brightness values of Clip A applied to Clip B can create a three-dimensional effect. The Three-D Settings dialog box is shown in Figure 7-33.

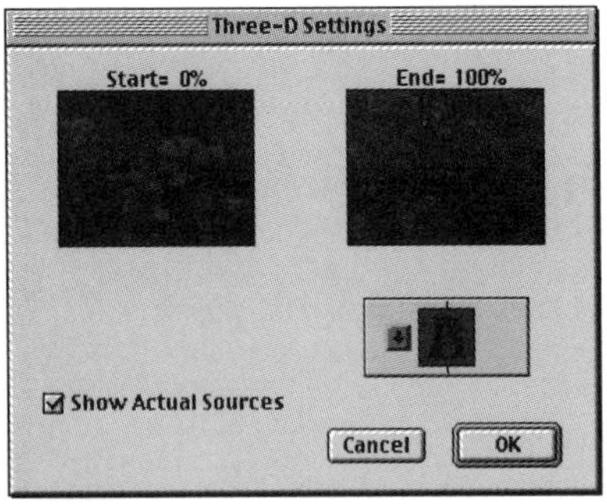

Figure 7-33: The Three-D Settings dialog box

Stretch transitions

The Stretch transitions provide a variety of effects that usually stretch at least one of the clips during the effect.

Cross Stretch

This transition is more like a 3D cube transition than a stretch. When the transition occurs, the clips appear as if on a cube that turns. As the cube turns, Clip B replaces Clip A.

Funnel

In this transition, Clip A is gradually transformed into a triangular shape and then sucked out the point of the triangle to be replaced by Clip B.

Stretch

In the Stretch transition, Clip B starts compressed and then gradually stretches across the frame to Clip A. The Stretch Settings dialog box is shown in Figure 7-34.

Stretch In

Clip B appears over Clip A stretched, but then gradually unstretches. The Stretch In Settings dialog box is shown in Figure 7-35.

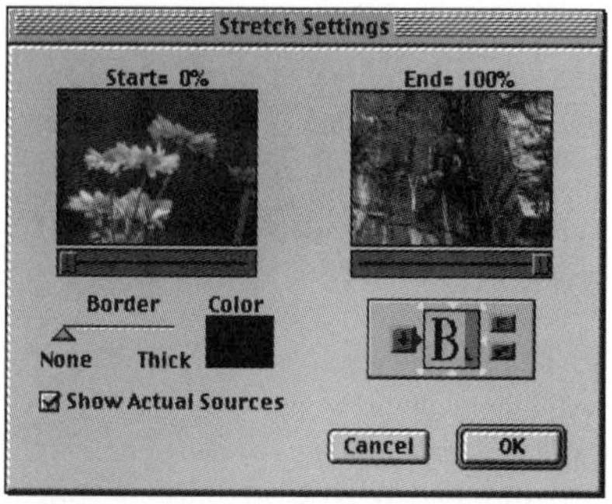

Figure 7-34: The Stretch Settings dialog box

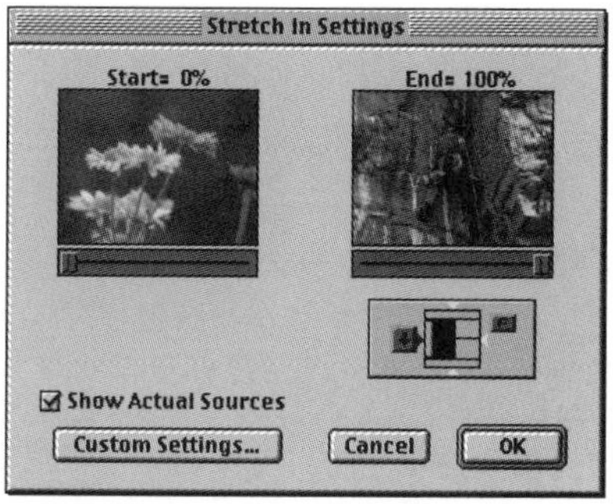

Figure 7-35: The Stretch In Settings dialog box

Stretch Over

In this transition, Clip B appears over Clip A in a thin, elongated stretch but then gradually unstretches.

Wipe transitions

The Wipe transitions wipe away different parts of Clip A to reveal Clip B. Many of the transitions provide a very modern-looking digital effect.

Band Wipe

In the Band Wipe transition, rectangular bands from screen left and screen right gradually replace Clip A with Clip B.

Barn Doors

In this transition, Clip A opens to reveal Clip B. The effect is more like sliding doors than barn doors that swing open.

Checker Wipe

In the Checker Wipe transition, a checkerboard pattern of 12 squares slides across the screen with Clip B in it.

Checkerboard

In the Checkerboard transition, a checkerboard pattern with Clip B in the pattern gradually replaces Clip A. This effect provides more squares than the Checker Wipe transition. The Checkerboard Settings dialog box is shown in Figure 7-36.

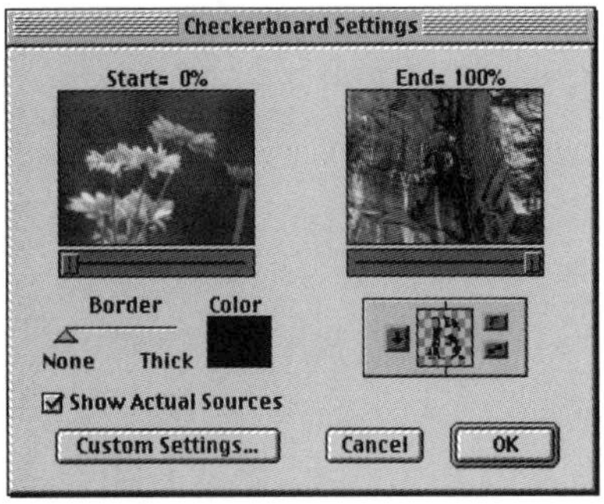

Figure 7-36: The Checkerboard Settings dialog box

Clock Wipe

In this transition, Clip B appears on screen gradually revealed in a circular motion. It's as if the rotating hand of a clock is sweeping the clip on screen.

Gradient Wipe

In this transition, Clip B gradually wipes across the screen using the brightness values of a user-selected grayscale image to determine which image areas in Clip A to replace. When using this wipe, you can load a grayscale image by first clicking the Custom button. When the wipe appears, image areas of Clip B corresponding to the black areas and dark areas of Clip A show through first. After clicking the Custom button, you can also click and drag the softness slider to soften the effect.

Inset

In this transition, Clip B appears in a small rectangular box in the upper-left corner of the frame. As the wipe progresses, the box grows diagonally until Clip B replaces Clip A.

Paint Splatter

In the Paint Splatter transition, Clip B gradually appears in splashes that look like splattered paint.

Pinwheel

In this transition Clip B gradually appears in a growing star that gradually consumes the full frame.

Radial Wipe

In the Radial Wipe transition, Clip B is revealed by a wipe that begins horizontally across the top of the frame and sweeps through an arc clockwise, gradually covering Clip A.

Random Blocks

In this transition, Clip B gradually appears in tiny boxes that appear randomly on-screen.

Random Wipe

In this transition, Clip B gradually appears in small blocks that gradually drop down the screen.

Spiral Boxes

In the Spiral Boxes transition, a rectangular border moves around the frame gradually replacing Clip A with Clip B.

Venetian Blinds

In this transition, Clip B appears as if seen through Venetian blinds that open gradually and reveal Clip B's full frame.

Wedge Wipe

In the Wedge Wipe transition, Clip B appears in a pie wedge that becomes larger, gradually replacing Clip A with Clip B.

Wipe

In this simple transition, Clip B slides in from left to right replacing Clip A. The Wipe Settings dialog box is shown in Figure 7-37.

Zig-Zag Blocks

In this transition, Clip B gradually appears in horizontal bands that move from left to right and right to left down the screen. The Zig-Zag Blocks Settings dialog box is shown in Figure 7-38.

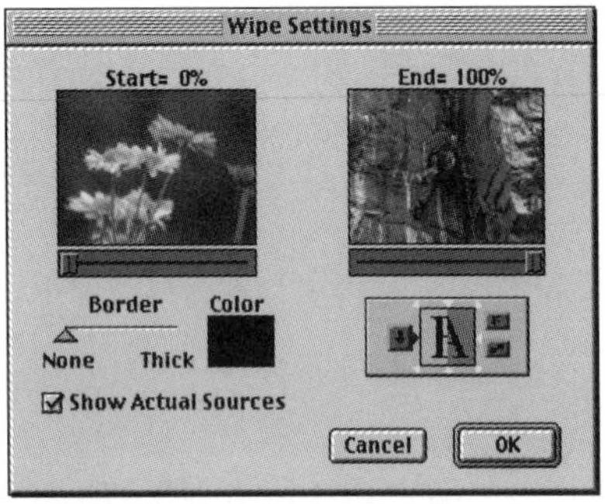

Figure 7-37: The Wipe Settings dialog box

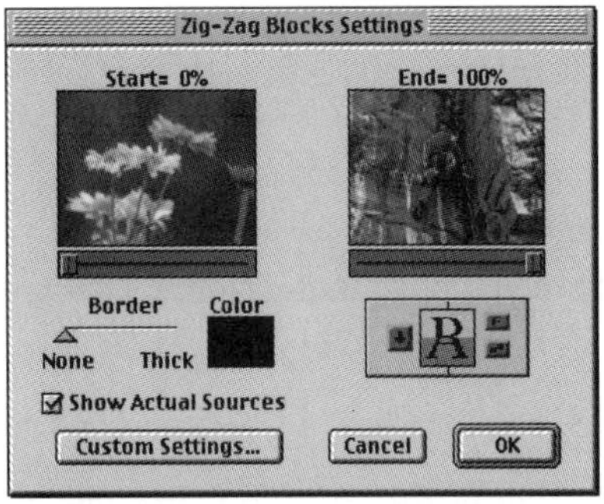

Figure 7-38: The Zig-Zag Blocks Settings dialog box

Zoom transitions

The Zoom transitions provide effects in which the entire clip zooms in or out, or boxes zoom in and out to replace one clip with another.

Cross Zoom

The Cross Zoom transition zooms into Clip B, which gradually grows to consume the full frame. The Cross Zoom Settings dialog box is shown in Figure 7-39.

Zoom

In this transition, Clip B appears as a tiny dot, then gradually enlarges to replace Clip A.

Zoom Boxes

In this transition, tiny boxes filled with Clip B gradually enlarge to replace Clip A.

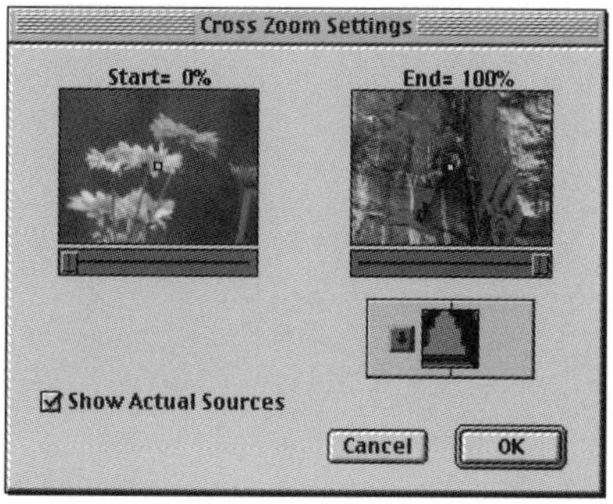

Figure 7-39: The Cross Zoom Settings dialog box

Zoom Trails

In the Zoom Trails transition, Clip A gradually shrinks (a zoom-out effect), leaving trails as it is replaced by Clip B.

Gallery of Transitions in Premiere

Adobe Premiere's Transitions palette stores over 75 different transitional effects. To view the Transitions palette and see a list of the transition categories, choose Window ⇨ Show Transition. This section provides a gallery of dialog boxes described in this chapter (Figures 7-40 through 7-91) of various transitions that are available to the Premiere user.

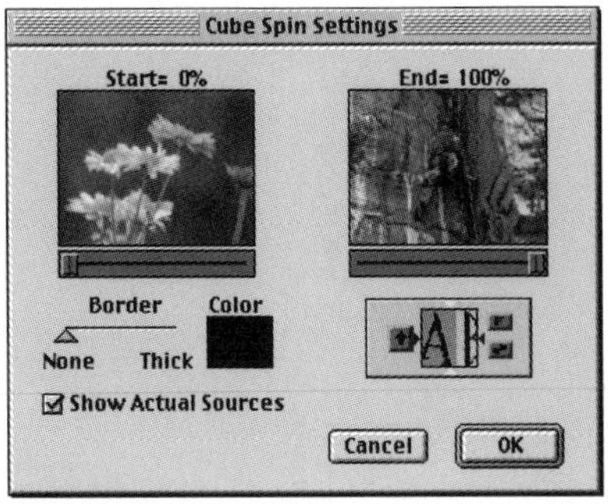

Figure 7-40: The Cube Spin Settings dialog box

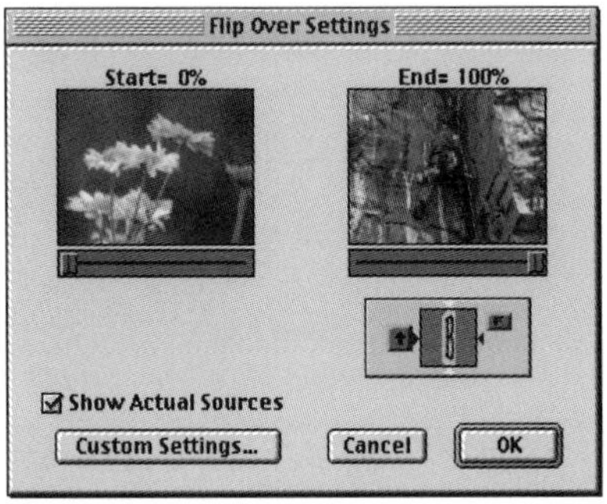

Figure 7-41: The Flip Over Settings dialog box

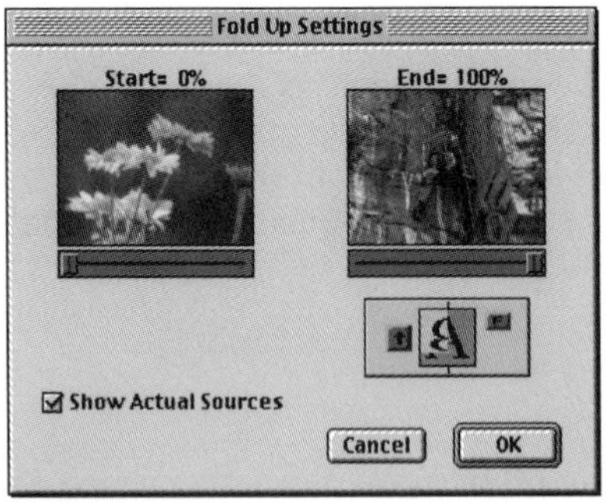

Figure 7-42: The Fold Up Settings dialog box

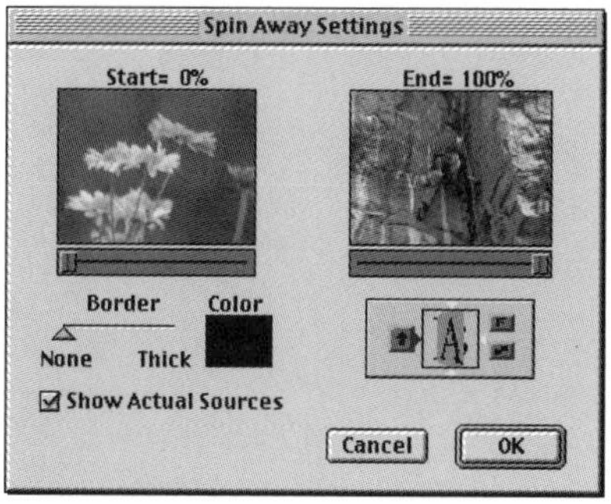

Figure 7-43: The Spin Away Settings dialog box

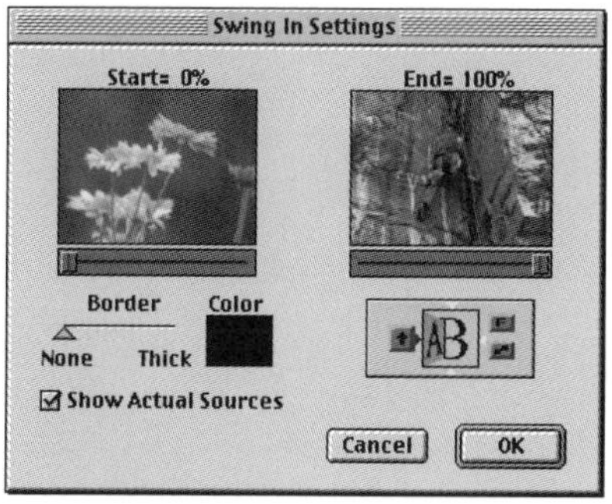

Figure 7-44: The Swing In Settings dialog box

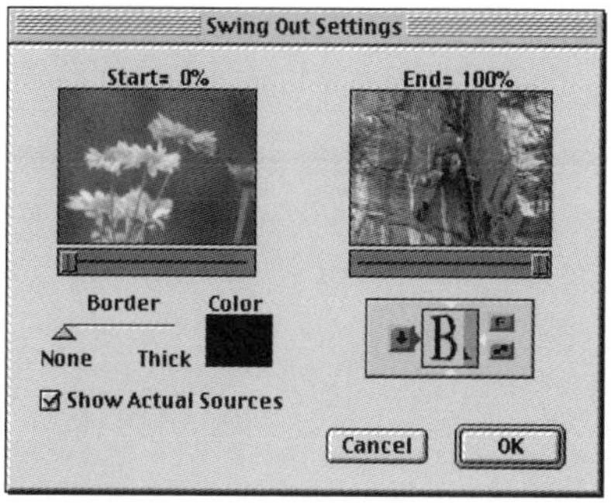

Figure 7-45: The Swing Out Settings dialog box

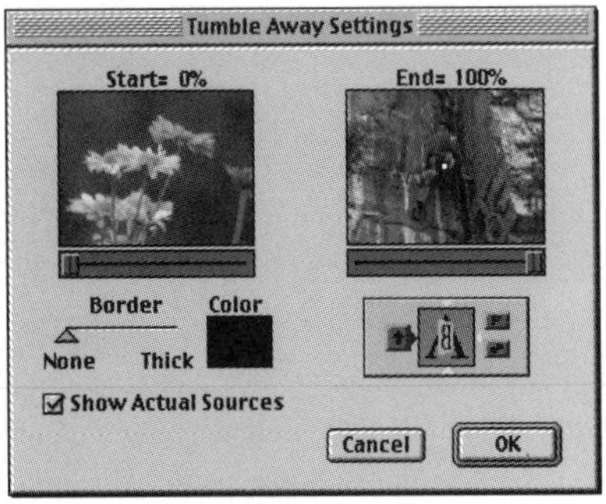

Figure 7-46: The Tumble Away Settings dialog box

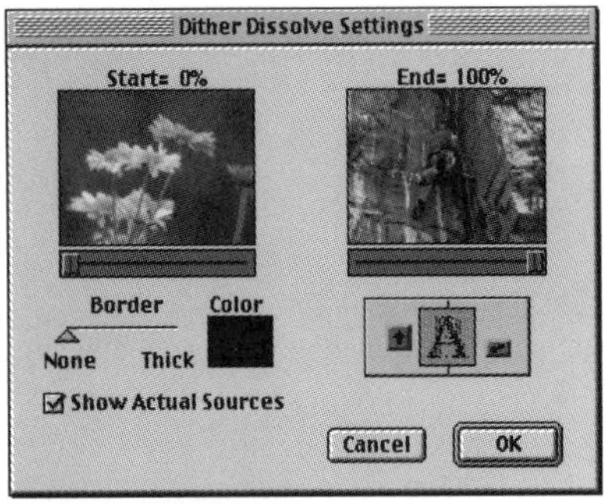

Figure 7-47: The Dither Dissolve Settings dialog box

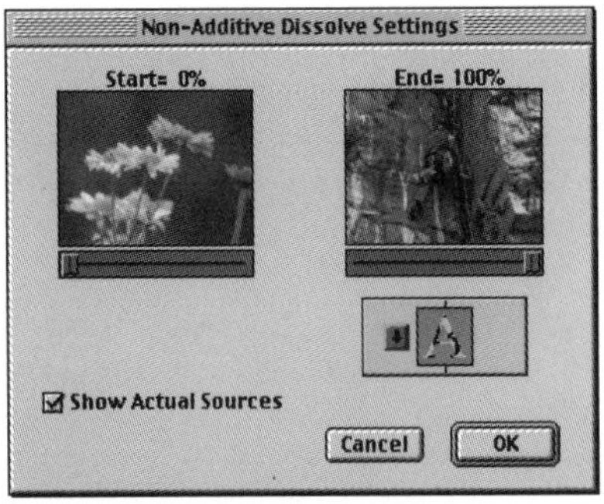

Figure 7-48: The Non-Additive Dissolve Settings dialog box

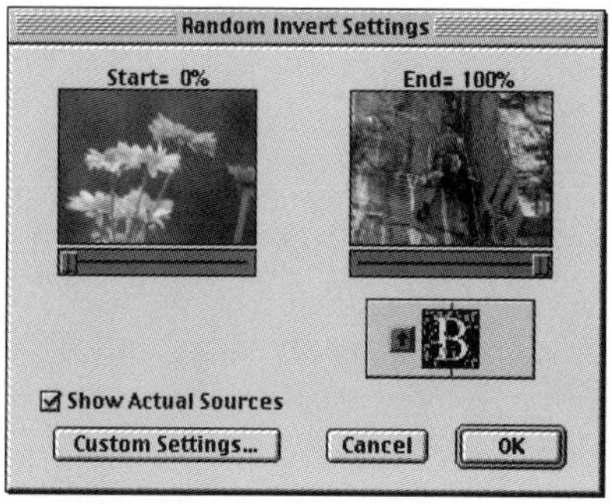

Figure 7-49: The Random Invert Settings dialog box

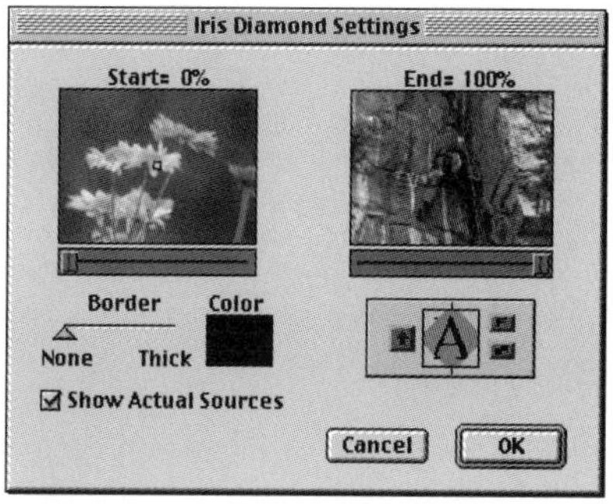

Figure 7-50: The Iris Diamond Settings dialog box

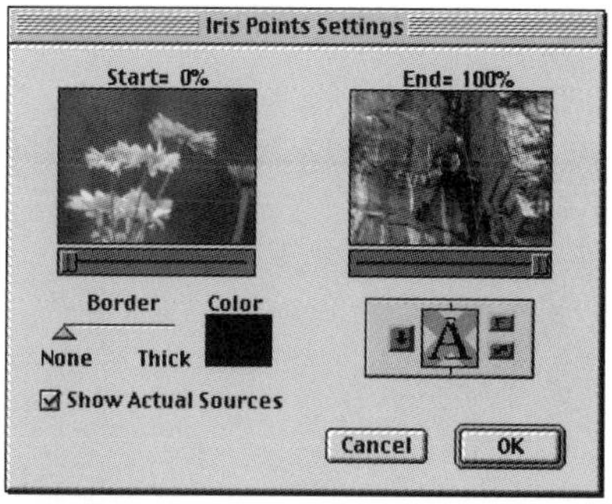

Figure 7-51: The Iris Points Settings dialog box

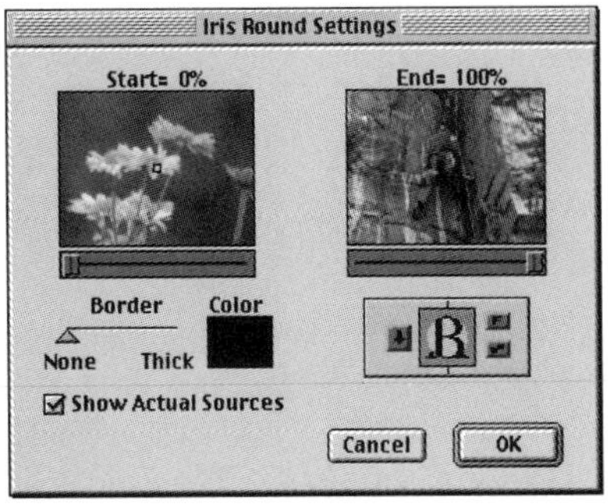

Figure 7-52: The Iris Round Settings dialog box

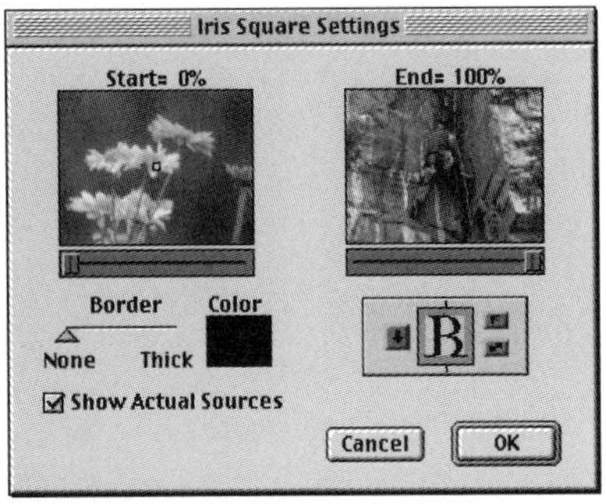

Figure 7-53: The Iris Square Settings dialog box

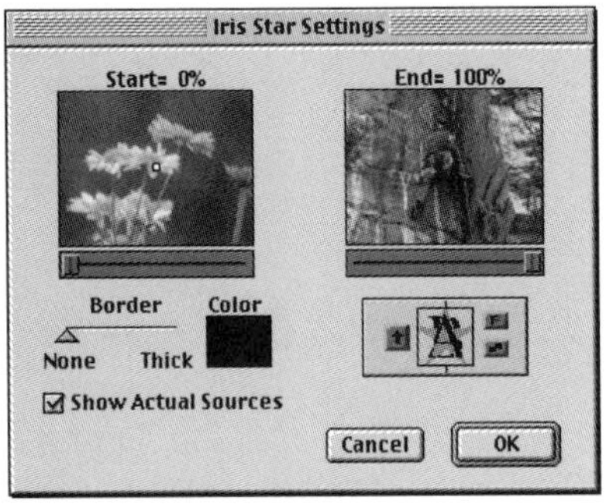

Figure 7-54: The Iris Star Settings dialog box

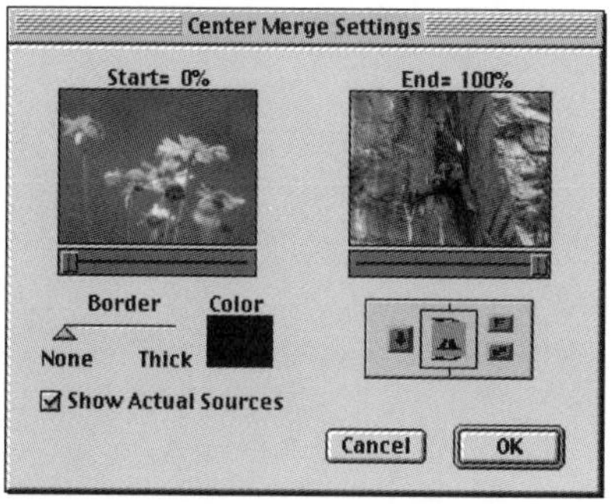

Figure 7-55: The Center Merge Settings dialog box

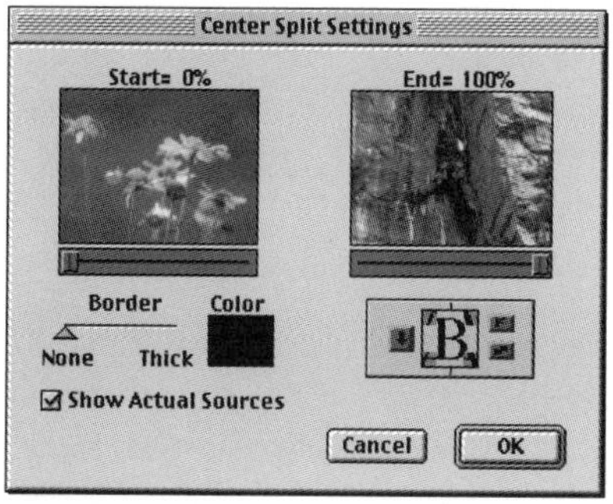

Figure 7-56: The Center Split Settings dialog box

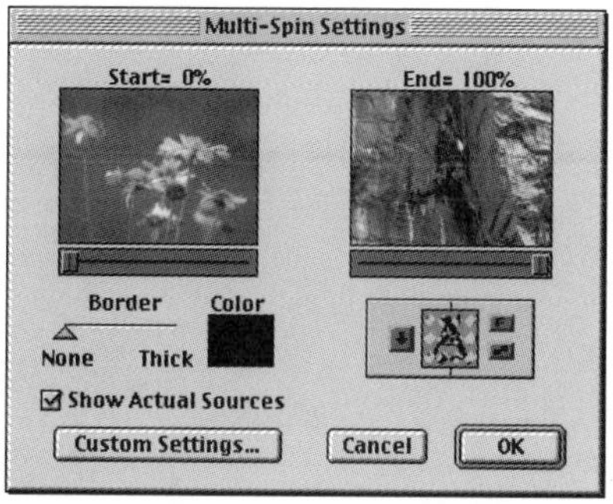

Figure 7-57: The Multi-Spin Settings dialog box

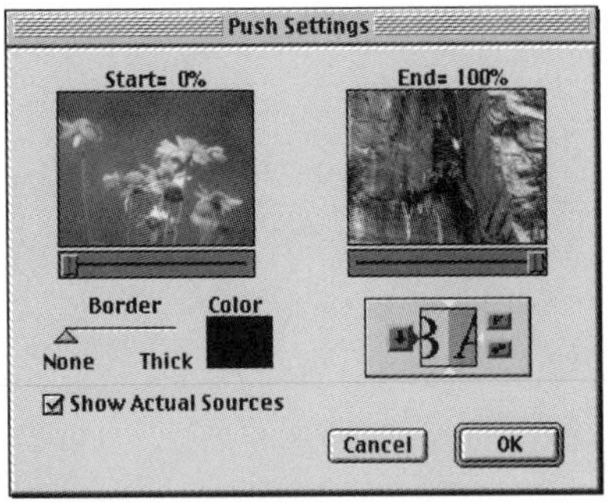

Figure 7-58: The Push Settings dialog box

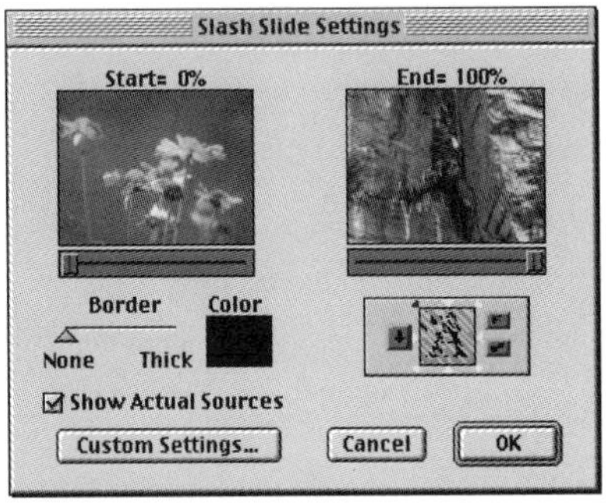

Figure 7-59: The Slash Slide Settings dialog box

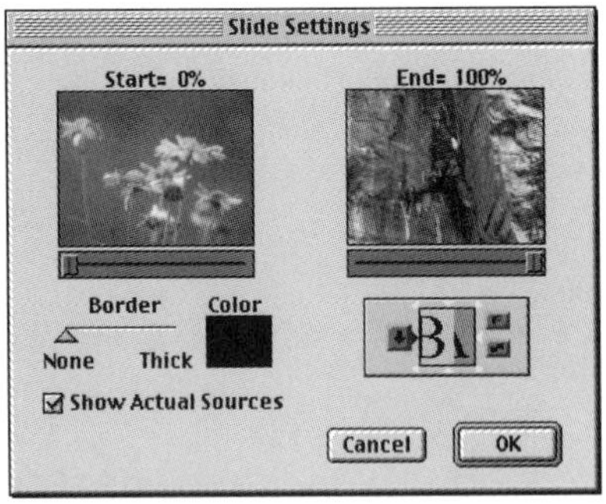

Figure 7-60: The Slide Settings dialog box

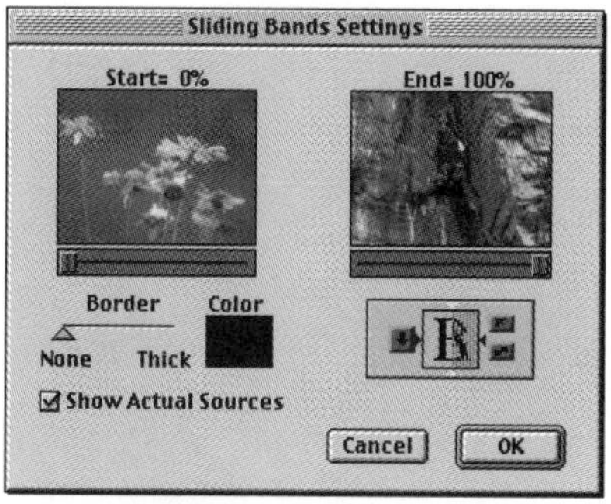

Figure 7-61: The Sliding Bands Settings dialog box

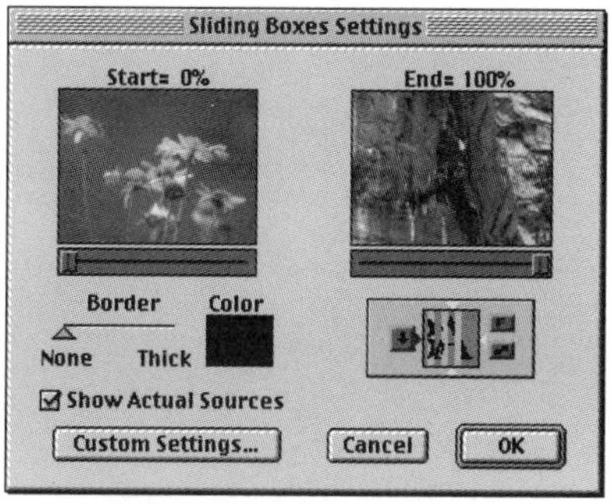

Figure 7-62: The Sliding Boxes Settings dialog box

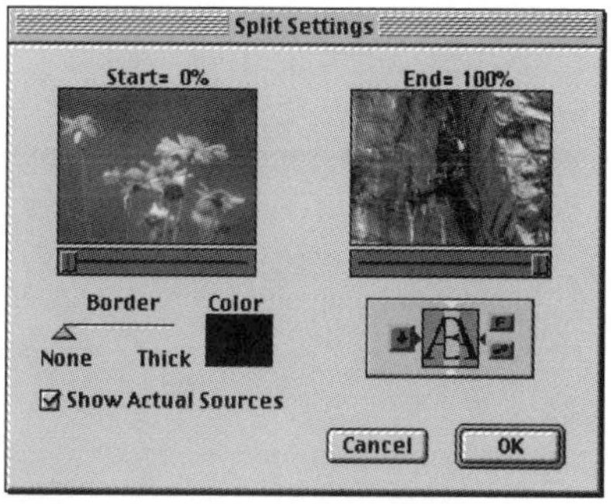

Figure 7-63: The Split Settings dialog box

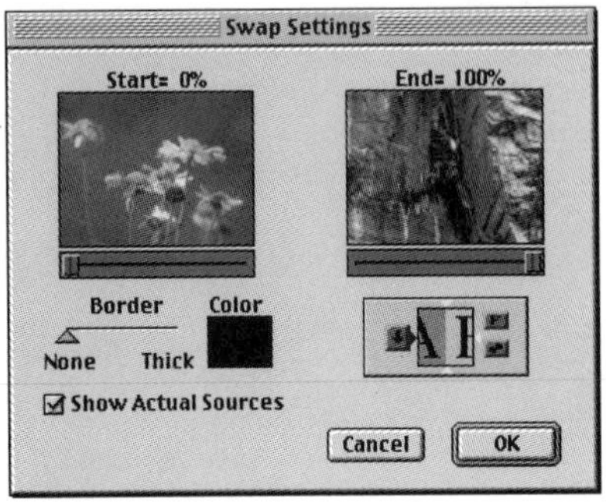

Figure 7-64: The Swap Settings dialog box

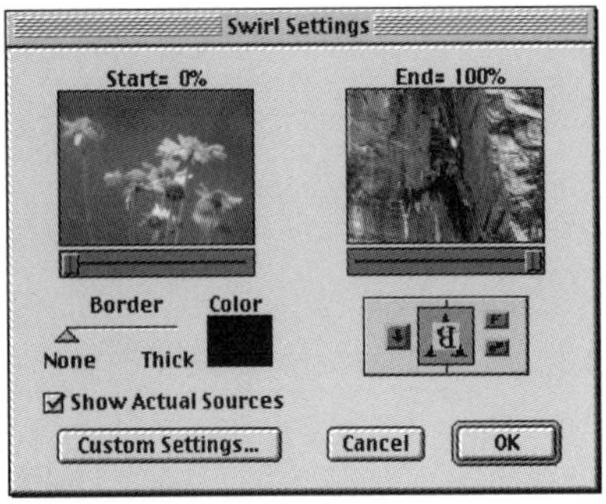

Figure 7-65: The Swirl Settings dialog box

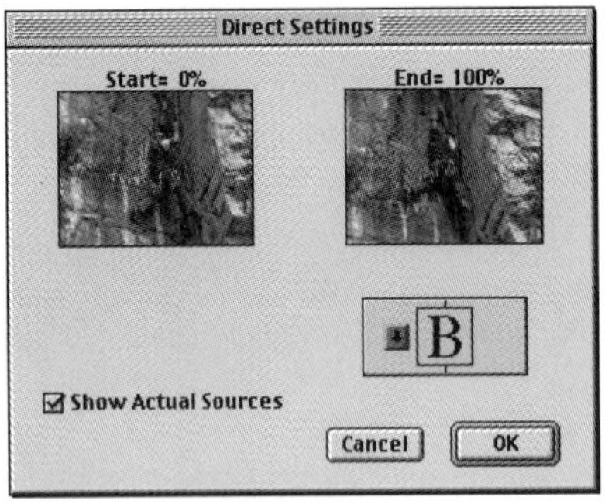

Figure 7-66: The Direct Settings dialog box

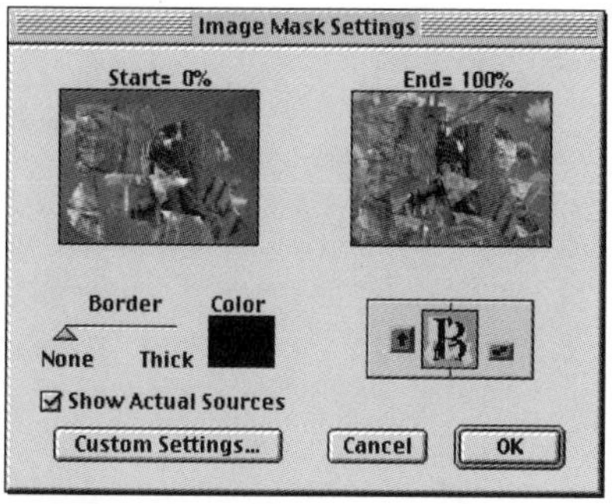

Figure 7-67: The Image Mask Settings dialog box

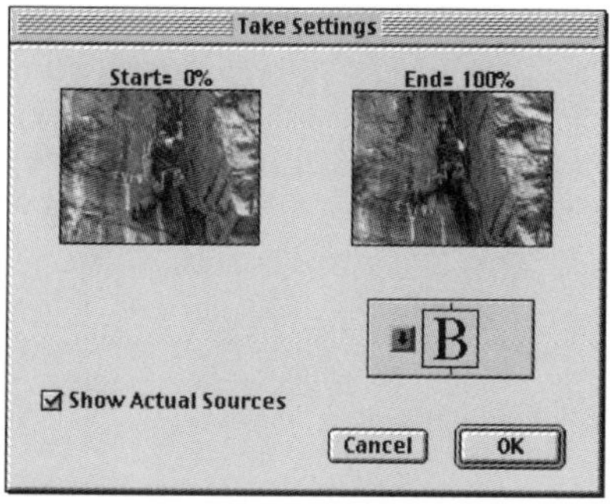

Figure 7-68: The Take Settings dialog box

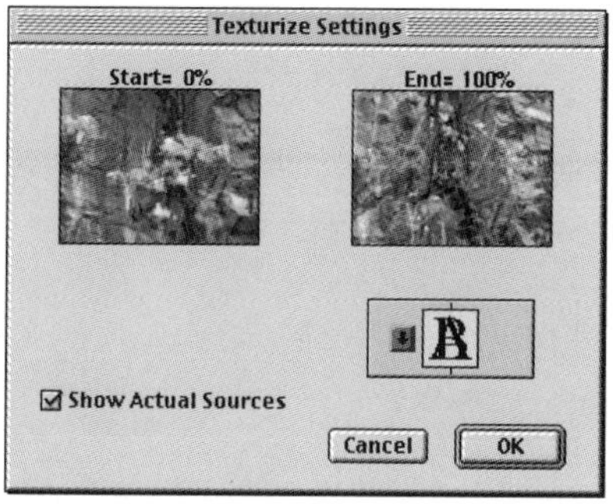

Figure 7-69: The Texturize Settings dialog box

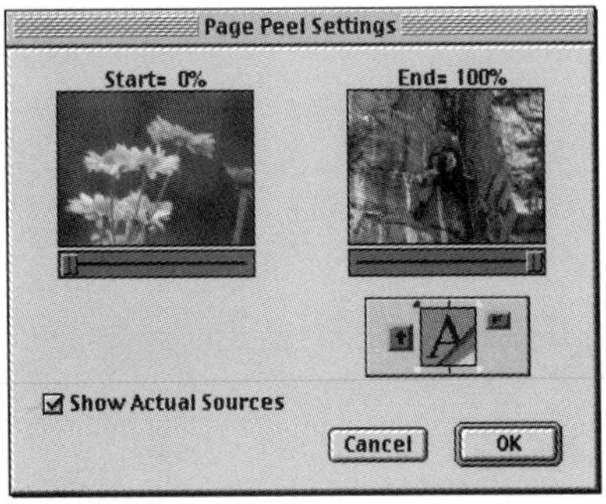

Figure 7-70: The Page Peel Settings dialog box

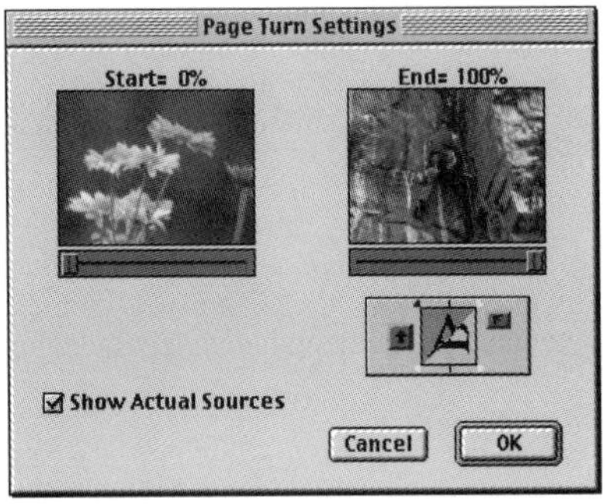

Figure 7-71: The Page Turn Settings dialog box

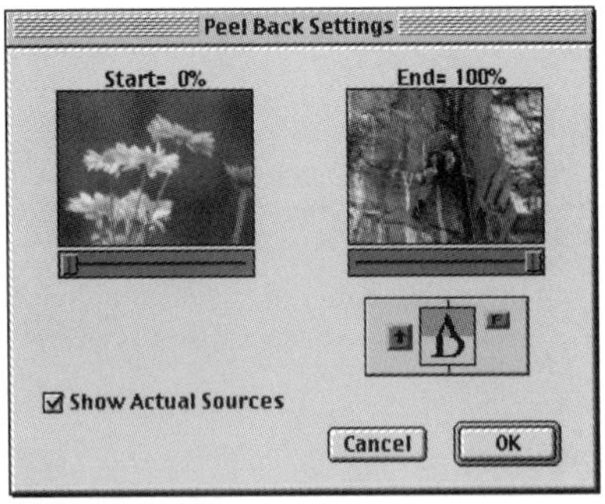

Figure 7-72: The Peel Back Settings dialog box

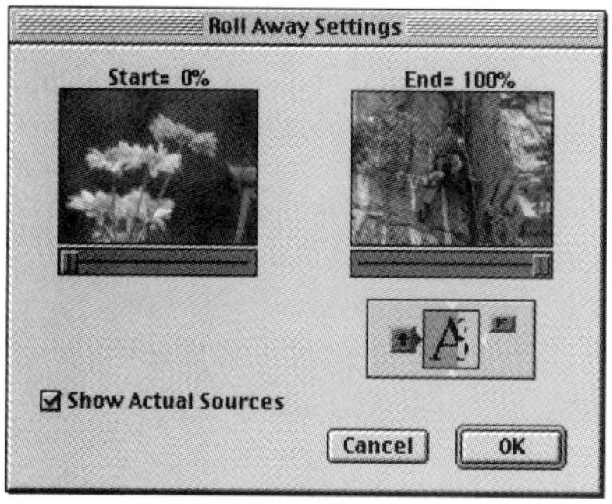

Figure 7-73: The Roll Away Settings dialog box

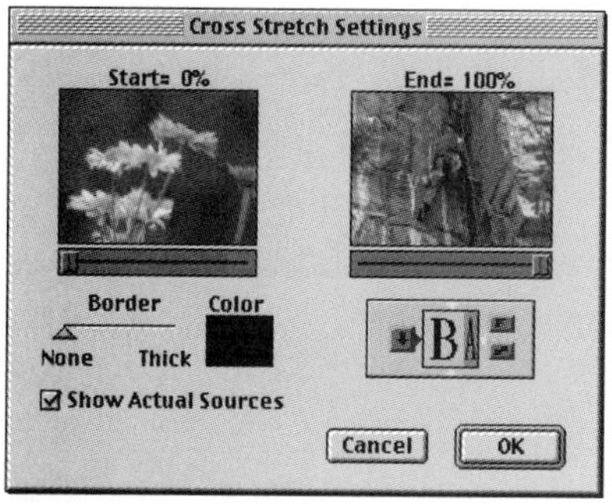

Figure 7-74: The Cross Stretch Settings dialog box

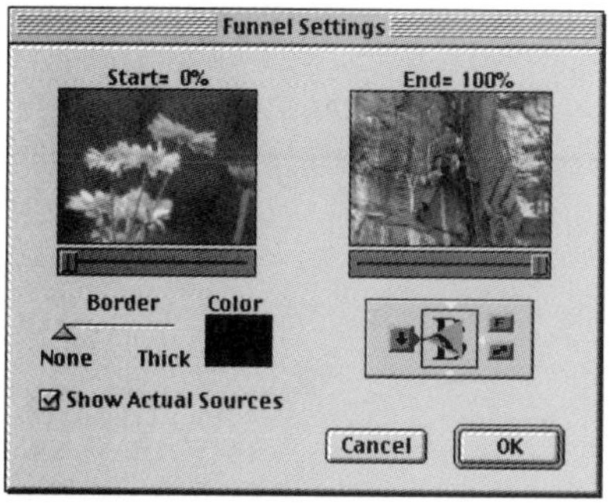

Figure 7-75: The Funnel Settings dialog box

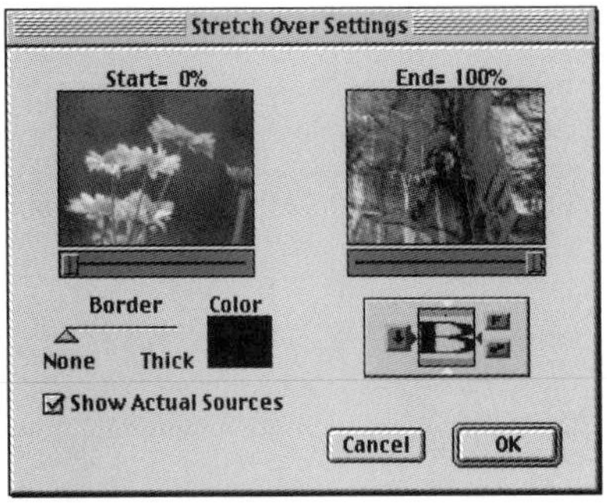

Figure 7-76: The Stretch Over Settings dialog box

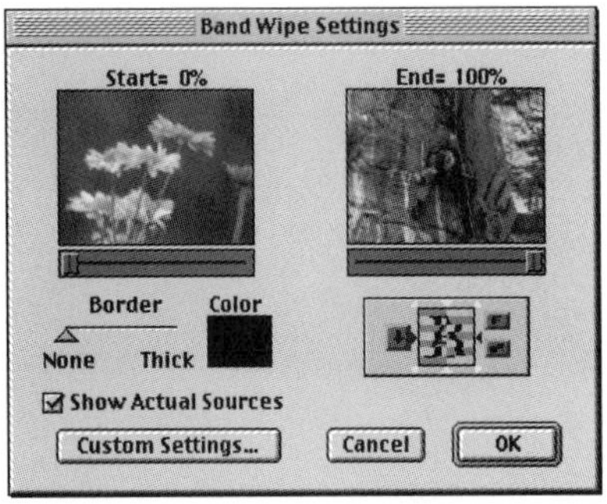

Figure 7-77: The Band Wipe Settings dialog box

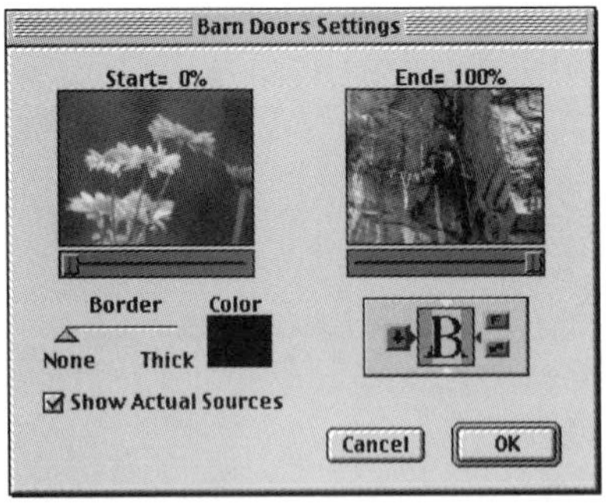

Figure 7-78: The Barn Doors Settings dialog box

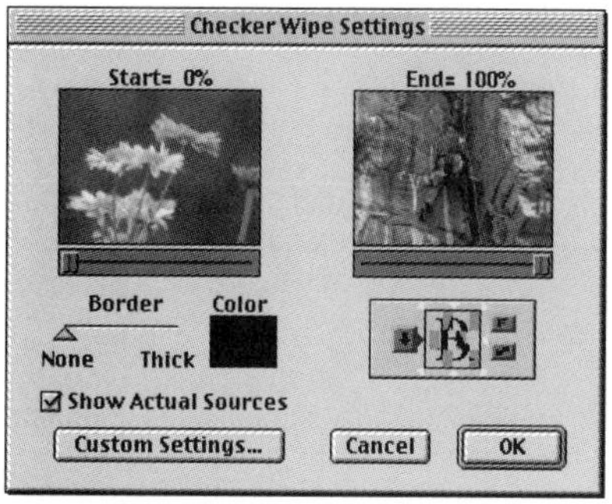

Figure 7-79: The Checker Wipe Settings dialog box

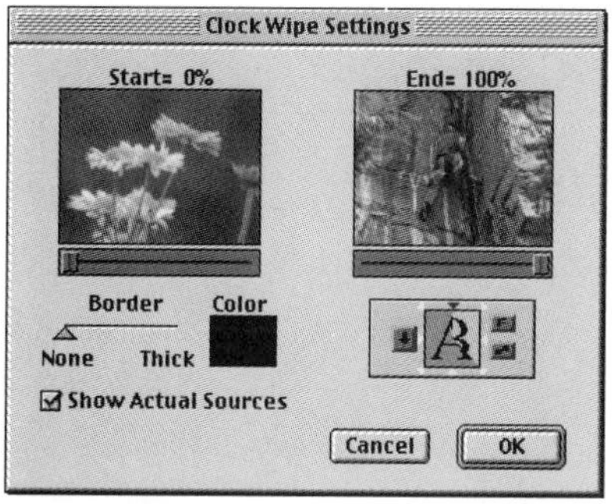

Figure 7-80: The Clock Wipe Settings dialog box

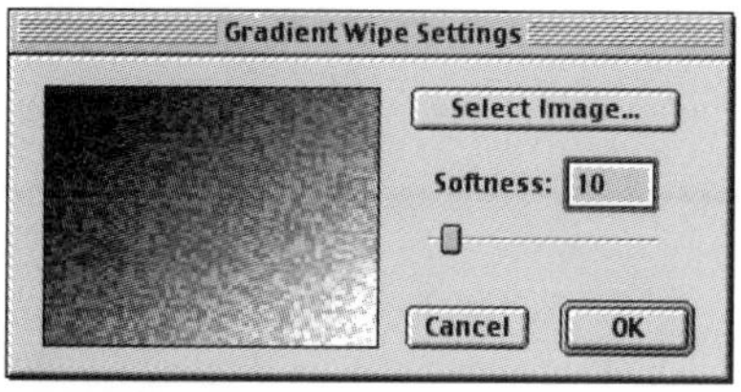

Figure 7-81: The Gradient Wipe Settings dialog box

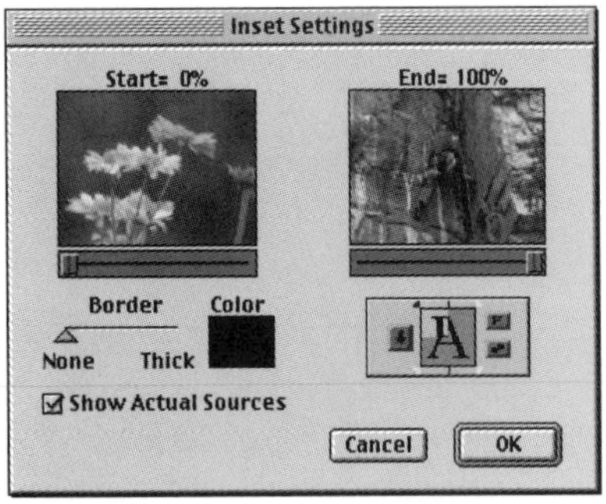

Figure 7-82: The Inset Settings dialog box

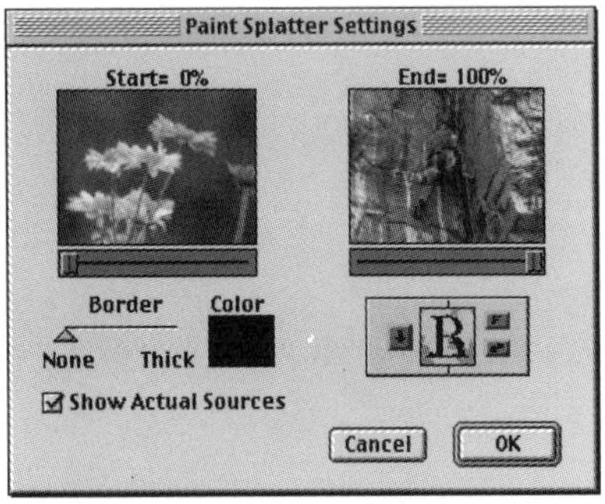

Figure 7-83: The Paint Splatter Settings dialog box

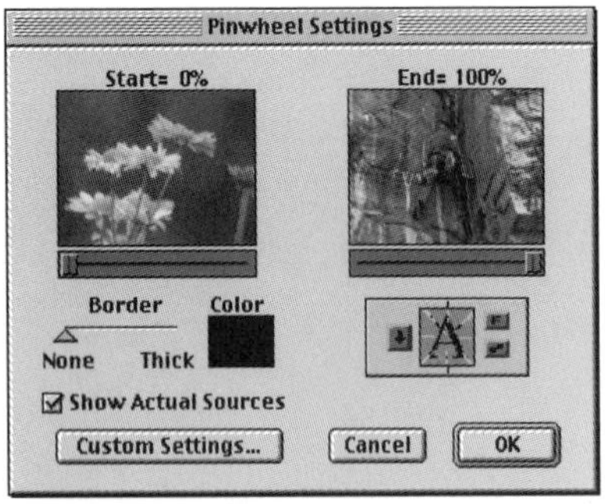

Figure 7-84: The Pinwheel Settings dialog box

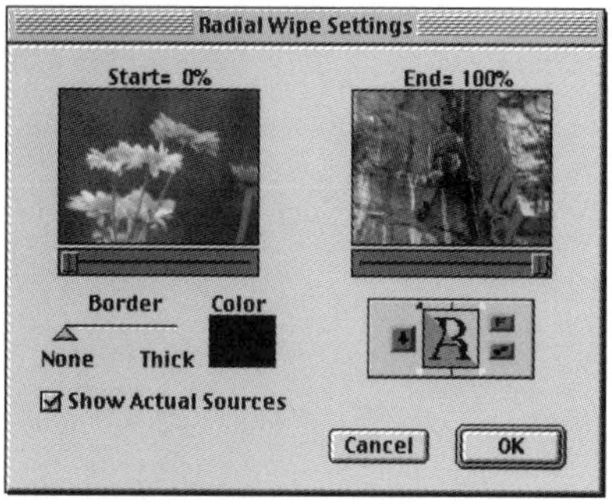

Figure 7-85: The Radial Wipe Settings dialog box

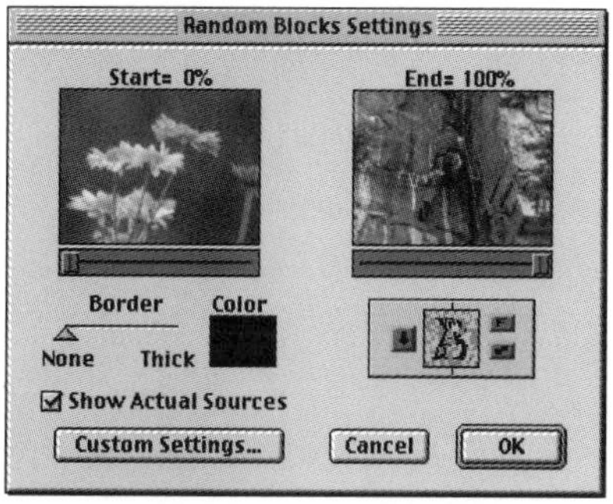

Figure 7-86: The Random Blocks Settings dialog box

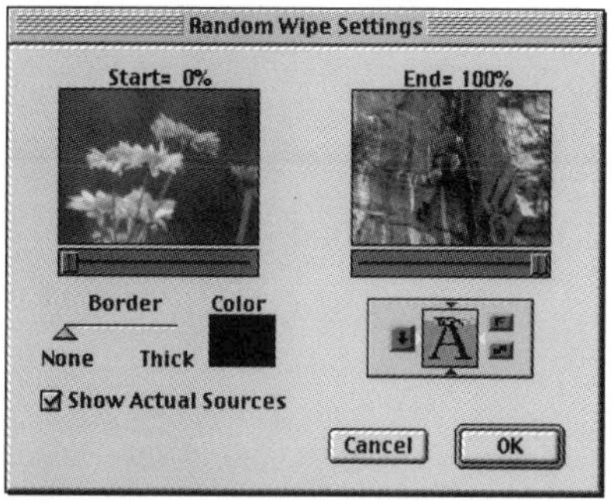

Figure 7-87: The Random Wipe Settings dialog box

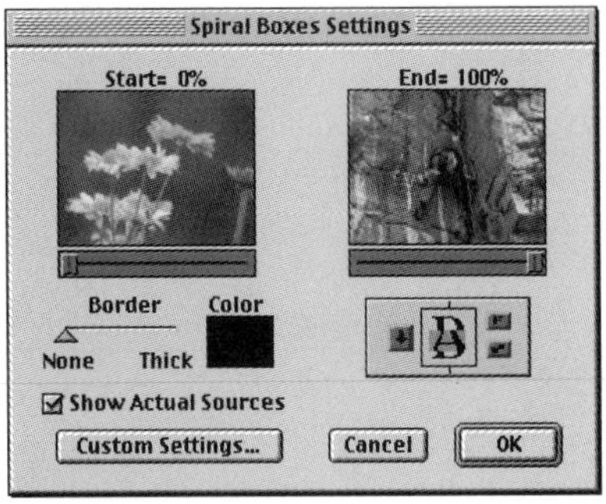

Figure 7-88: The Spiral Boxes Setting dialog box

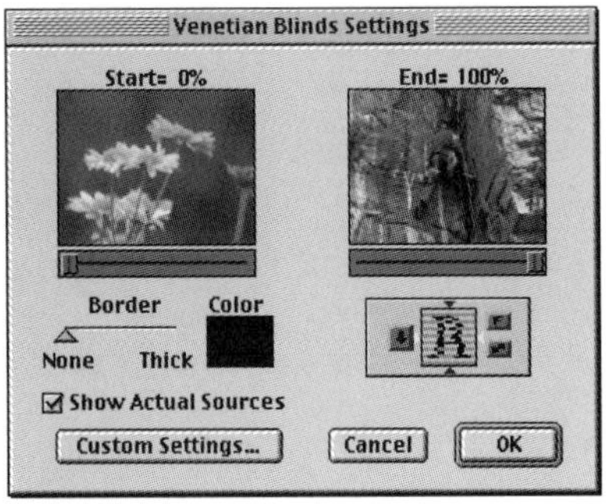

Figure 7-89: The Venetian Blinds Settings dialog box

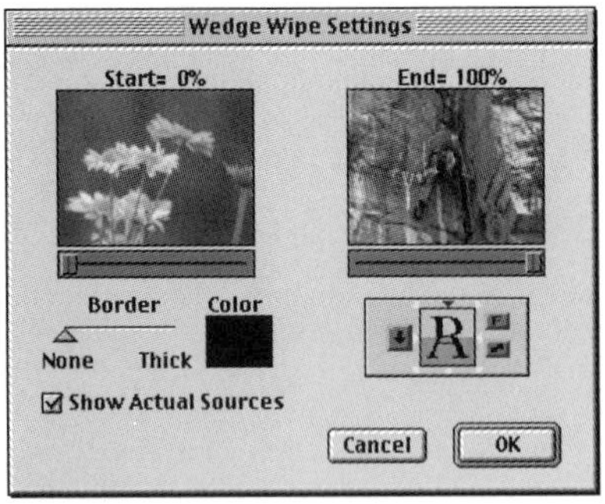

Figure 7-90: The Wedge Wipe Settings dialog box

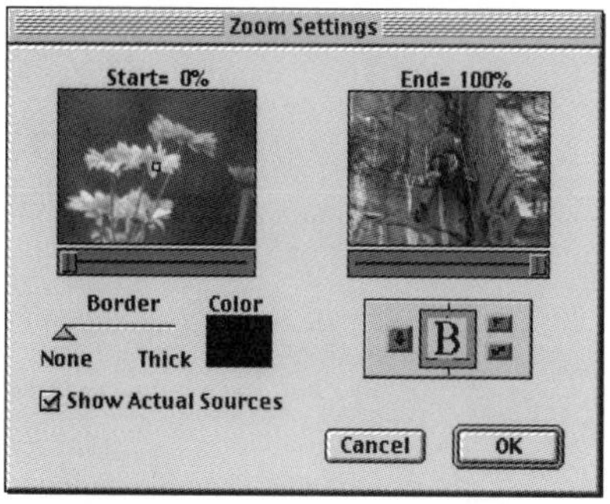

Figure 7-91: The Zoom Settings dialog box

Summary

Premiere's Transitions provide a variety of transitions that can be used to smooth the flow from one clip to another.

- ✦ To add a transition between two clips in A/B Editing mode, drag the transition from the Transitions palette to the Transitions track.
- ✦ To edit a transition, double-click the Transition thumbnail in the Timeline.
- ✦ To replace one transition with another, click and drag the new transition over the old transition.
- ✦ To specify a default transition, select the transition in the Transitions palette and then choose Set Selected as Default in the Transitions palette menu.

✦ ✦ ✦

Working with Type and Graphics

P A R T

III

✦ ✦ ✦ ✦

In This Part

✦ ✦ ✦ ✦

CHAPTER 8

Creating Titles and Graphics with Adobe Title Designer

✦ ✦ ✦ ✦

In This Chapter

Exploring the Adobe Title Designer window and Title menu commands

Creating and stylizing type

Creating gradients and drop shadows

Working with styles and templates

Creating rolling and scrolling titles

Creating graphic objects

Creating a logo

✦ ✦ ✦ ✦

Titles can help turn day into night, night into day; summer into fall and fall into winter. Used effectively, titles at the beginning of a production can help build expectations, introduce a subject, establish a mood, and, of course, provide the title of the production. Throughout a video production, titles can provide transitions between one segment and another; they can help introduce speakers and locales, or reveal their names. Titles used with graphics can help convey statistical, geographical, and other technical information. At the end of the production, you can use titles to give yourself and your production crew the credit you so richly deserve for your creative efforts.

Although titles can be created in graphics programs, such as Adobe Photoshop and Adobe Illustrator, you may find that Premiere's Title window offers all the titling capabilities you need for many productions without ever leaving the Premiere environment. As you'll soon see, Adobe Title Designer not only enables you to create text and graphics, but it also enables you to create drop shadows and animation effects with crawling and scrolling text.

This chapter provides a step-by-step look at how to create production titles using Adobe Title Designer, new to Adobe Premiere 6.5. We then show you how to integrate your titles into your digital video productions.

Exploring the Adobe Title Designer Window

The Adobe Title Designer window provides a simple and efficient means of creating text and graphics that can be used for video titles in Premiere projects.

To display the Adobe Title Designer window, you first need to load Premiere and create a new project. When creating a new project, make sure to use the aspect ratio and frame size you want your title drawing area to have. The title drawing area takes on the aspect ratio and frame size of the existing project. The *aspect ratio* is the ratio of screen width to screen height. For example, if you plan to output your Premiere project to a QuickTime movie that is 320 x 240 pixels, set the frame size of your project to 320 x 240. By having the title and the output dimensions the same, you ensure that your titles appear exactly where you want them to be in your final production. The standard aspect ratio for digital video is 4:3. Use a different aspect ratio only if you are outputting your production using nonstandard dimensions. For example, you can create a digital video production at 240 x 320, rather than 320 x 240. If so, your production's aspect ratio would be 3:4.

Creating a simple title

To familiarize you with the core tools and features of Adobe Title Designer, the following steps guide you through the process of creating and saving a simple title clip for use in a Premiere project.

1. **Choose File ➪ New Project to create a new project.** The Load Project Settings dialog box appears.
2. **Click a project preset to assign project settings.** As you select a preset, notice the frame size in the description area. If you want, you can click the Custom button to display the New Project Settings dialog box. In the New Project Settings dialog box, click the pop-up menu and select Video to display the Frame Size height and width. If needed, change the height and width and then click OK to create a new project. After creating a new project but before creating a new title, you can still change the frame size by choosing Project ➪ Project Settings ➪ Video. In the Project Settings dialog box, make the change and then click OK. For more information on Premiere digital video project settings, turn to Chapter 3.
3. **Choose File ➪ New ➪ Title to create a new title.** The Adobe Title Designer window appears, as shown in Figure 8-1. The drawing area of the title is the same size as the project frame size. If you plan on outputting your titles to film

or videotape, you should display the safe title margin and safe action margin areas. To do so, choose Title ➪ View ➪ Safe Title Margins and Title ➪ View ➪ Safe Action Margin. You can also click the Show Safe Title Margins and Show Safe Action Margins check box in the Preferences Titler dialog box.

The tools and drawing area in the Adobe Title Designer window resemble those found in simple drawing and painting programs. The window is divided into the following areas:

- **Main toolbar.** Edit these options to specify whether you are creating still, crawling, or rolling text, using a template, and whether to show a video clip in the background.
- **Toolbox.** The graphic and text tools are grouped vertically here, along the left side of the window.
- **Object Style.** The settings in this area enable you to stylize text and graphic objects.
- **Transform.** The settings in this area enable you to transform text and graphic objects.

4. **Click the Horizontal Title tool (the arrow below the Selection tool) and move the mouse to the center of the drawing area.**
5. **Click the mouse and type Title.**
6. **Format your text in the Object Style area.** This area contains the Properties, Fill, Strokes, and Shadow text options. For example, to change the following parameters:
   - **Font or font size.** Click the triangle in front of the word Properties to expand the Properties section. Click the Font menu to change the font, and click and drag on the Font Size value to change the font size. For more information on stylizing type, turn to the "Creating and Stylizing Type" section.
   - **Font color.** Click the triangle before the word Fill to expand the Fill section. Leave the Fill Type menu set to Solid and click the Color Swatch next to the Color option. When the Color Picker dialog box appears, click a color and then click OK. The new color is applied to the title text. For more information on working with color in the Adobe Title Designer window, turn to the "Using Color" section later in this chapter.
7. **To save and name the Adobe Title Designer window, choose File ➪ Save.** The Title file is saved to your hard drive and placed in the current project's Project window. If you want to place the title file into your project, all you need to do is close the Title window and then drag the title file from the Project window to a video track in the Timeline window.

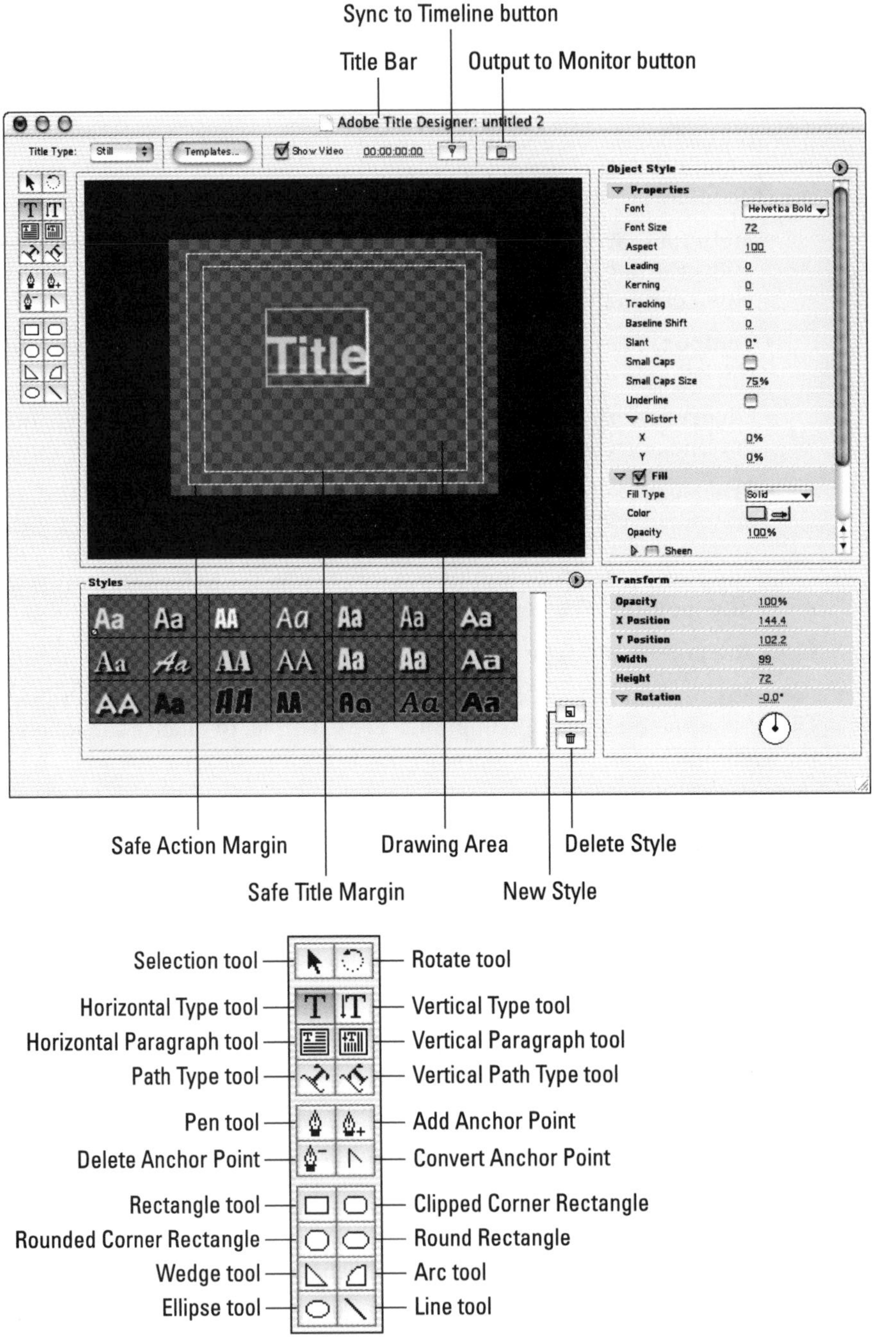

Figure 8-1: Use Adobe Title Designer to create text and graphics for production titles.

Touring the Adobe Title Designer window tools

The Toolbox in the Adobe Title Designer window enables you to create graphics and text. Table 8-1 reviews the tools and other graphic controls.

Table 8-1
Adobe Title Designer Window Toolbox Items

Shortcut Key	*Name*	*Description*
V	Selection tool	Selects objects so that they can be moved or resized (stretched or shrunk); can also be used to select text before changing text attributes.
I	Rotation Tool	Allows you to rotate text.
T	Horizontal Type tool	Creates type horizontally.
T	Vertical Type tool	Creates type vertically.
T	Horizontal Paragraph tool	Creates wrapped text horizontally.
T	Vertical Paragraph tool	Creates wrapped text vertically.
T	Path text tools	Creates text along a path.
P	Pen tool	Creates curved shapes using Bézier curves.
P	Add Anchor Point tool	Adds anchor points to path.
P	Delete Anchor Point too	Deletes anchor points from path.
P	Convert Anchor Point	Converts curved point to corner point and vice versa.
Y	Rectangle tool	Creates rectangles.
R	Clipped Corner Rectangle tool	Creates rectangles with dog-eared corner.
R	Rounded Corner Rectangle tool	Creates rectangles with round corners.
W	Wedge tool	Creates triangular shapes.
A	Arc tool	Creates curved shapes.
E	Ellipse tool	Creates ellipses.
L	Line tool	Creates lines.

Using the Title menu

Premiere's Title menu enables you to change the settings of many of the tools in the Title window and to change the visual attributes of text and graphic objects. For example, you can use the Title menu to set the font, size, and style of the text that you create in the Adobe Title Designer window. You can also use it to set the speed and direction of rolling title text. Table 8-2 summarizes the Title menu commands. The Title menu appears only when the Adobe Title Designer window is open on-screen.

Table 8-2
The Title Menu Commands

Menu Command	***Description***
Font	Changes typeface.
Size	Changes size of text.
Type Alignment	Sets text to flush left, flush right, or centered.
Orientation	Sets text to be horizontal or vertical.
Word Wrap	Sets text to wrap, when it reaches the safe title margin.
Tab Stops	Enables you to create tabs within a textbox.
Templates	Enables you to apply, create, and edit templates.
Roll/Crawl Options	Provides options for setting direction and speed of rolling and crawling text.
Logo	Enables you to insert logos in the entire Adobe Title Designer drawing area as a background, in a portion of the drawing area or within a textbox.
Transform	Enables you to change the position, scale, rotation, and opacity of an object or text.
Select	Enables you to select from a stack of objects, the first object above, next object above, next object below, last object below.
Arrange	Enables you to bring selected objects to the front, back, forward or backward of a stack of objects.
Position	Moves object so that it is either horizontally or vertically centered, or to the lower third part of the Adobe Title Designer drawing area. The lower third position is frequently used for text that must be read without covering up the on-screen image.
Align Objects	Enables you to align selected objects horizontally, left, right, or centered and vertically, top, bottom, or centered.
Distribute Objects	Enables you to distribute selected objects horizontally, left, right, centered, or even spacing and vertically top, bottom, centered, or even spacing.
View	Enables you to view safe title margin, safe action margin, text baselines, and tab markers.

Saving, Closing, and Opening a Title

After you've created some stunning text and/or graphics in the Adobe Title Designer window, save it so that you can use it in one of your Premiere projects. If you save your title, you can always load the title into any project. You can even create one title as a template and then load it, edit the text and graphics, and save it under a new name.

Caution You can place one title in multiple projects but editing the title contents causes Premiere to replace every instance of the title in your projects with the newly edited version.

To save your title, choose File ➪ Save. In the Save File As dialog box, type a name for your title and choose the location where you want to save it. To close the Title window, choose File ➪ Close or choose the close box icon.

Note When you save a title, the title is placed in the Project window of the current project on-screen.

When you want to load your title file back into the Adobe Title Designer window, choose File ➪ Open. Choose the file from the correct folder and then click Open to load the file. After the file is loaded you can place it into an existing Premiere project.

Tip Double-clicking a title clip in the Project windows opens that title in the Adobe Title Designer window.

Creating and Stylizing Type

Premiere's horizontal and vertical Type tool works very much like Type tools in graphic programs. Creating text, selecting and moving it, and stylizing fonts works very much the same as most other Type tools. Changing type color and adding shadows is somewhat different but very simple when you get the hang of it. The Path Type tools even enable you to create text along a Bézier path.

Cross-Reference Creating text along a path with the Path type tools, along with creating Bézier paths and shapes with the Pen tool, is covered later in this chapter in the section "Working with the Bézier Tools."

Using the Horizontal and Vertical Type tools

Text in video productions should be clear and easy to read. If viewers need to strain their eyes to read your titles, they'll either stop trying to read them or they'll ignore the video and audio as they try to decipher the text on-screen.

Premiere's Type tools provide the versatility that you need to create clear and interesting text. Not only can you change size, font, and color, but by using the Object Style options in the Adobe Title Designer window, you can also create drop shadows and emboss effects.

Premiere's Type tools enable you to place type anywhere in the Adobe Title Designer window drawing area. As you work, Premiere places each block of text within a text *bounding box* that can easily be moved, resized, or deleted.

Here's how to create horizontal and vertical text:

1. **Choose File ➪ New Project to create a new project.** Set the preset to the size of your Title and production.
2. **Choose File ➪ New ➪ Title to create a new title.** The Adobe Title Designer window appears. The Title Type pop-up menu should be set to Still because you are creating still text rather than rolling or crawling text.

Cross-Reference

To learn how to create rolling and crawling text, turn to the section "Creating Rolling and Crawling Text" later in this chapter.

3. **Click either the Horizontal Type or Vertical Type tool in the Toolbox.** The Horizontal Type tool creates text horizontally from left to right, and the Vertical Type tool creates text vertically.
4. **Drag the I-beam cursor to where you want your text to appear and then click the mouse.** A blinking cursor appears.

Note

Select the Horizontal Paragraph and Vertical Type Paragraph tool to create horizontal and vertical text that wraps.

5. **Type your title text.** If you make a mistake and want to delete the last character you typed, press Delete/Backspace. Figure 8-2 shows text being entered in a bounding box.

Note

You can choose Edit ➪ Undo to undo your last entry.

Editing with the Type tools

If you want to edit text after you finish using the Type tool, you must reselect the text with the Type tool. Move the I-beam cursor over the characters that you want to edit and then click. The blinking cursor appears where you clicked; you can then start editing your text. To select all the text within a textbox, you can choose Edit ➪ Select All.

If you are using the Horizontal or Vertical Type tool and you want to create a new line, press Enter and then begin typing. Before you press Return/Enter, make sure that the I-beam cursor is set to where you want the new line to begin.

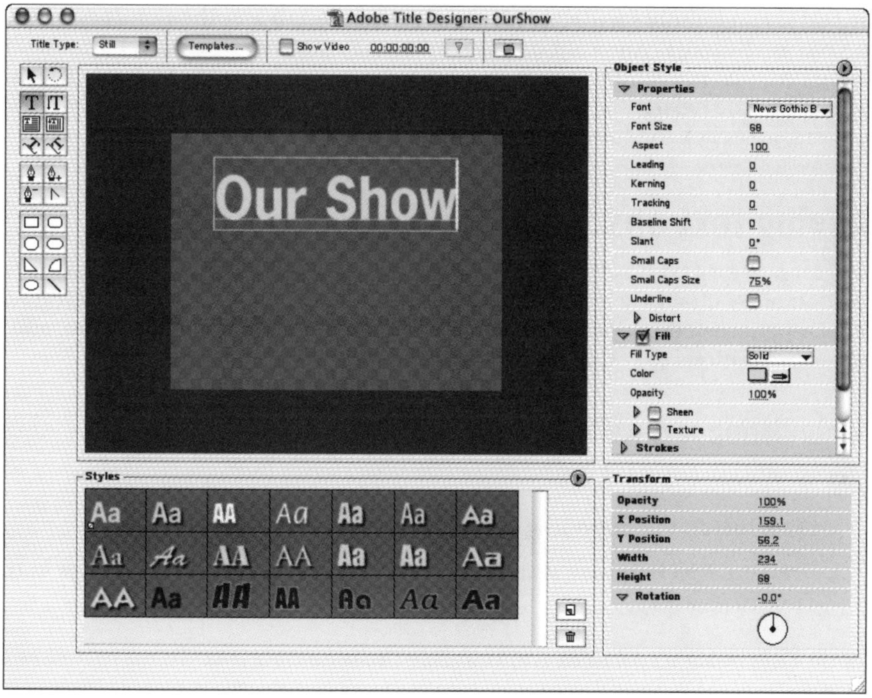

Figure 8-2: Text created with Premiere's Horizontal Type tools

Wrapping text

The Horizontal and Vertical Type tools do not automatically wrap text to the next line. If you want to have Premiere automatically wrap text created with the Horizontal and/or Vertical tool, choose Title ⇨ Word Wrap. The Horizontal and Vertical Paragraph Type tools automatically wrap text to the next line. To use the Horizontal and Vertical Paragraph Type tools, select the tool from the Toolbox. Move the tool to the drawing area, click and drag to create a textbox, and begin typing. Notice that as you type, the text automatically wraps to the next line.

Using tabs

You can add spacing between words and align them left, center, or right using tabs. Tabs can help make your titles (or rolling and crawling text) more readable. To apply tabs to your text, you need to use the tab ruler in the Tab Stops dialog box. Before you display the tab ruler, you may want to display the tab markers. By displaying tab markers, Premiere has lines appear where you set your tab marks. By displaying the tab markers as lines, you can better visualize how your tabs will appear within your text. To display tab marks, choose Title ⇨ View ⇨ Tab Markers. To display the tab ruler, choose Title ⇨ Tab Stops. To create a tab, just click the ruler with the either the left, center, or right tab selected. To move a tab, click and drag on it. To apply the tab, click OK to close the Tab Stops dialog box. Then move the text beam in front of where you want to apply a tab and then press the Tab key on your keyboard. If you want to change the tabs after you've closed the Tab Stops dialog box, just reopen the Tab Stops dialog box and then click and drag the tab on the ruler to the desired location. The text is automatically updated. To delete tab markers, just click the tab and drag it off the ruler.

Moving text onscreen

You can move a text box by using the Selection tool, choosing Title ➪ Transform ➪ Position or by changing the X and Y Position in the Transform section of the Adobe Title Designer window. You can also use the Selection tool, the Title menu, and Transform options to rotate the textbox on-screen.

Manipulating text with the Selection tool

You can quickly move the type's bounding box. Here's how:

1. **Click inside the bounding box with the Selection tool.**
2. **Drag the text to a new location.** The X and Y Position values change in the Transform area.

Adobe Title Designer enables you to resize the bounding box. To do so, follow these steps:

1. **Using the Selection tool, move the Selection tool over one of the bounding box handles.** The cursor changes to a small, straight line with two arrows at either end of it.
2. **Click and drag to increase or decrease the bounding box and text size.** Notice in the Transform section that the Width, Height, X Position, and Y Position values change.

Adobe Title Designer enables you to rotate a bounding box using the Selection tool. To do so, follow these steps:

1. **Move the Selection tool over one of the bounding box handles.**
2. **When the cursor icon changes to a small, curved line with two arrows at either end of it, click and drag to rotate the bounding box and text size.** Notice that the Rotation value in the Transform section changes.

Note

To rotate a bounding box, you can use the Rotate tool in the Toolbox. To use the Rotate tool, click on it in the Toolbox. Then move it to the bounding box and click and drag in the direction you want to rotate the textbox.

Manipulating text with the Transform values

You can use the Transform values to move, resize, and rotate a bounding box. Before you can move, resize, or rotate a bounding box, you must select the bounding box by clicking inside it with the Type tool or the Selection tool.

- **Moving a bounding box.** Click and drag to the right or left, on the X and Y Position values to change them. To move the textbox in increments of ten, press and hold the Shift key as you drag to the right or left on the X and Y Position values.
- **Resizing a bounding box.** In the Transform section, click and drag to the right or left on the Width and Height values to change them. Pressing the Shift key as you drag left or right, increases the values in increments of ten.
- **Rotating a bounding box.** Click the Rotation value and drag to the right or left to change it. Dragging left rotates the box counterclockwise, and dragging right rotates the box clockwise.

Manipulating text with the Title menu

Before you can move, resize, or rotate a bounding box, you must select it. If it is not already selected, click inside the textbox with either the Type tool or the Selection tool.

- **Moving the bounding box.** Choose Title ➪ Transform ➪ Position. In the Position dialog box, type in a value for the X and Y Position and then click OK. The Title ➪ Position command enables you to move the box horizontally center, vertically center, and to the lower third area.
- **Resizing the bounding box.** Choose Title ➪ Transform ➪ Scale. In the Scale dialog box, type in a scale percentage. You can choose to scale uniformly or nonuniformly. Finally, click OK.
- **Rotating the bounding box.** Choose Title ➪ Transform ➪ Rotation. In the Rotation dialog box, type in the degrees you want to rotate the textbox and then click OK.

As you move, resize, and rotate the textbox, notice that the options in the Transform section change.

Changing text attributes

When you first type with the Type tool, Premiere places the type on-screen in its default font and size. You can change type attributes by changing the Properties in the Object Style section of the Adobe Title Designer window or using the menu commands found in the Title menu. The Properties section allows you not only to change font and font size, but it also allows you to set the aspect ratio, kerning, tracking, leading, baseline shift, slant, small caps, and add an underline. You can use the Type menu to change font and size, and you can also change the type orientation from horizontal to vertical, and vice versa.

Changing font and size attributes

You can use both the Title menu and the Properties options in the Adobe Title Designer window to change the font and size of your type. Adobe Title Designer offers three basic techniques for editing font and size attributes.

To change the font and size text attributes before typing, follow these steps:

1. **Click a Type tool.**
2. **Click where you want the text to appear.**
3. **Change the settings for font and size by using the Title ⇨ Font command and Title ⇨ Size command.** You can also change the font and size from the Font pop-up menu in the Properties section in the Type Designer window. As you type, the new text you type features the attributes of the current font and size settings.

To change individual characters or words, try this:

1. **Select the text with the Type tool by clicking and dragging over the character.**
2. **Change type attributes using either the Title menu commands or the Properties options in the Object Style area of the Adobe Title Designer window.**

Tip

To browse through the font available, choose Title ⇨ Font ⇨ Browse. In the Font Browser dialog box, click the down arrow to see a preview of the fonts. The character display in the Font Browser dialog box can be replaced by changing the letters in the Font Browser field in the Preferences Titler dialog box.

If you want to change all text in a text block, click the text with the Selection tool. Then change the font and size text attributes.

Changing spacing attributes

Typically, a typeface's default *leading* (space between lines), *kerning* (space between two letters), and *tracking* (space between various letters) provides sharp, readable type on-screen. If you begin using large type sizes, however, white space between lines and letters may look awkward. If this happens, you can use Premiere's leading, kerning, and tracking controls to change spacing attributes.

Here's how to change leading:

1. **Use either the Horizontal Paragraph or Vertical Paragraph Type tool to create more than one line of text in the drawing area of the Adobe Title Designer window.**
2. **Click and drag left or right on the Leading value.** Increase the leading value to add space between each line. Decrease the leading value to remove space between each line. If you want to reset spacing to its original leading, type **0** in the Leading field. The Leading field is in the Properties section of the Adobe Title Designer window.

You can also change the spacing between lines by using Baseline Shift. Changing the Baseline Shift moves a text up or down: Here's how:

1. **Use the Horizontal or Vertical Type tool to create more than one line of text.**
2. **Click and drag on the Baseline Shift value to change it.** Increasing the Baseline shift, moves the baseline of the text up. Decreasing the baseline moves the baseline of the text down.

Here's how to change kerning:

1. **Use a Type tool to create a word in the Adobe Title Designer window.**
2. **Click between the two letters whose spacing you want to change.**
3. **Increase or decrease the kerning values in the Properties section of the Adobe Title Designer window.** As you increase kerning value, the space between letters increases. If you decrease kerning value, the space between the letters decreases.

Here's how to change tracking:

1. **Use a Type tool to create a word or two in the Adobe Title Designer window.**
2. **Click and drag over the text with the Type tool.**
3. **Increase or decrease tracking value in the Properties section of the Adobe Title Designer window.** Increasing the tracking value increases the spacing between the letters. Decreasing the tracking value decreases the spacing between the letters.

Changing other text attributes

Some of the other text attributes allow you to change the look and feel of the text. These are the Aspect, Slant, Distort, Small Caps, and Underline. Figure 8-3 shows text before and after applying the Aspect, Slant, and Distort attributes.

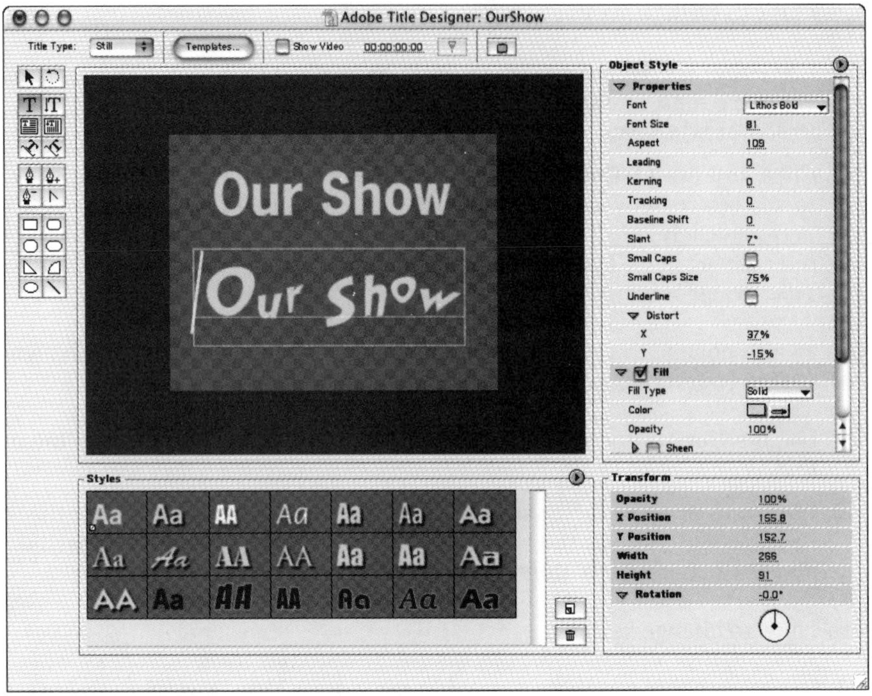

Figure 8-3: Text before changing attributes, after changing Aspect, Slant, and Distortion

Here's how to change the look and feel of your text using some of the text attributes in the Properties section of the Type Designer window:

1. **Select a font and font size.**
2. **Type a word using the Horizontal Type tool.**
3. **Click and drag to the right and left on the Aspect value to increase or decrease the horizontal scale of the text.**
4. **To slant the text to the right, click and drag on the Slant value to the right. To slant the text to the left, click and drag on the Slant value to the left.**
5. **To distort the text, click the X and Y values in the Distort section.**
6. **If you want to underline or convert the text or convert the text to small caps, click the option's check box.** Doing so selects the option.

Using Color

The colors you choose for text and graphics can add to the mood and sophistication of your video project. Using the Premiere color tools, you can pick colors as well as create gradients from one color to another. You can even add transparency effects that show background video frames through text and graphics.

How do you know what colors to pick when creating titles? The best guide is to use colors that stand out from background images. When watching broadcast television, pay special attention to titles. You'll often notice that many television producers simply use white text against a dark background; or they'll use bright text with drop shadows to prevent the titles from looking flat. If you are creating a production that includes many titles — such as *lower thirds* (graphics at the bottom of the screen often providing information such as the names of speakers), keep the text the same color throughout the production to avoid distracting the viewer.

Choosing color with the Color Picker

Any time you select a color in Premiere, you are using Premiere's Color Picker. Picking colors in Premiere can be as simple as clicking the mouse. To see how easy it is to pick a color in Premiere, open the Color Picker, shown in Figure 8-4, by double-clicking the Solid Fill Color swatch. Click the Fill triangle to expand the Fill section and display the Color Swatch. For the Solid Fill Color Swatch to appear, the Fill Type pop-up menu should be set to Solid. (The Fill section is found in the Object Style section of the Adobe Title Designer window.)

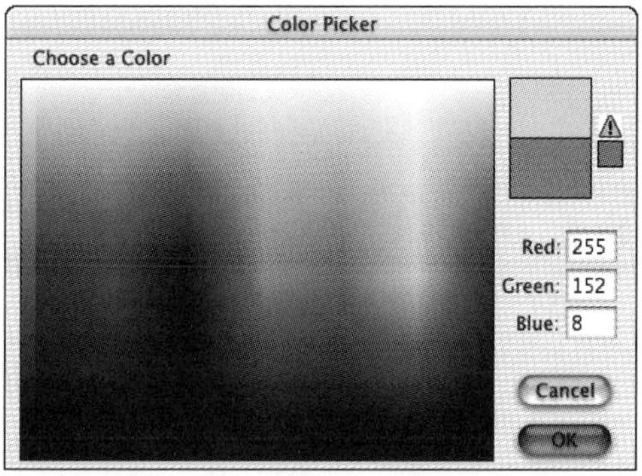

Figure 8-4: Use Premiere's Color Picker to select colors.

You can pick colors for text and graphic objects in the Color Picker window by clicking in the main color area of the dialog box, or you can enter specific RGB values. As you work in the Color Picker, the color that you are creating is previewed in the bottom swatch in the upper-right of the Color Picker dialog box. The top swatch displays the original color. If you want to return to the original color, simply click the top color swatch.

If you pick a color that falls beyond the NTSC video color gamut, Premiere displays a gamut warning signal that looks like a yellow triangle with an exclamation mark in it (shown in Figure 8-4). To drop the color back to the nearest NTSC color, simply click the gamut warning signal.

Note

PAL and SECAM video feature larger color gamuts than NTSC video does. You can ignore the gamut warning if you are not using NTSC video.

Understanding RGB colors

Computer displays and television video monitors create colors by using the red, green, and blue color model. In this model, adding different values of red, green, and blue light creates millions of colors.

Premiere's Color Picker simulates adding light by enabling you to enter values into its Red, Green, and Blue fields. The concept is illustrated in Table 8-3.

The largest number that can be entered into one of the color fields is 255, and the smallest is zero. Thus, Premiere enables you to create over 16 million colors (256 x 256 x 256). When each RGB value equals zero, no light is added to create colors; the resulting color is black. If you enter 255 in each of the RGB fields, you create white.

To create different shades of gray, make all field values equal. R 50, G 50, B 50 creates a dark gray; R 250, G 250, B 250 creates a light gray.

Table 8-3
The Color Values for RGB Colors

Color	*Red Value*	*Green Value*	*Blue Value*
Black	0	0	0
Red	255	0	0
Green	0	255	0
Blue	0	0	255
Cyan	0	255	255
Magenta	255	0	255
Yellow	255	255	0
White	255	255	255

Choosing color using the Eyedropper tool

Apart from the Color Picker, the most efficient way of picking colors is to click a color with the Eyedropper tool. The Eyedropper tool automatically copies the color you click into the Color swatch. Therefore, you can recreate a color with one click of the mouse, rather than wasting time experimenting with RGB values in the Color Picker.

You can use the Eyedropper tool to do the following:

✦ Select a color from a type or graphic object in the drawing area.

✦ Select a specific color from a logo, style, or template.

✦ Copy a specific color from a video clip in the background of the Adobe Title Designer window.

The Eyedropper tool can be very handy when selecting colors from a video clip, logo, style, or template. Here's how to use the Eyedropper tool:

1. **Create a New Project using the presets you want your title to have.**
2. **If you want to use the Eyedropper tool to select a color from a video frame (shown in Figure 8-5), you need to import a video clip into your project by choosing File ⇨ Import ⇨ File.**
3. **Drag the video clip from the Project window to the Timeline window.**

On the CD-ROM

The video clip that appears in Figure 8-5 is in the Chapter 8 folder on the CD-ROM that accompanies this book. The video clip is from Digital Vision's NightMoves (#705018).

4. **Choose File ⇨ New ⇨ Title to create a new title.**
5. **To display the video clip in the Adobe Title Designer window, click the Show Video check box to display the video clip.**
6. **Click and drag in the Timeline location area to display the frame you want to appear in the background of the Adobe Title Designer drawing area.** Notice that the Fill, Strokes, and Shadow sections all have Eyedropper tools. Using the Fill Eyedropper tool changes the Fill Color Swatch. Using the Strokes Eyedropper tool changes the Strokes Color Swatch. Using the Shadow Eyedropper tool changes the Shadow Color Swatch. Click the Eyedropper tool you want to use.

Note

To import a graphic file as the background or as a logo into the Adobe Title Designer window drawing area, choose Title ⇨ Logo ⇨ Insert Logo. To import a template into the drawing area of the Adobe Title Designer window, use the Template button.

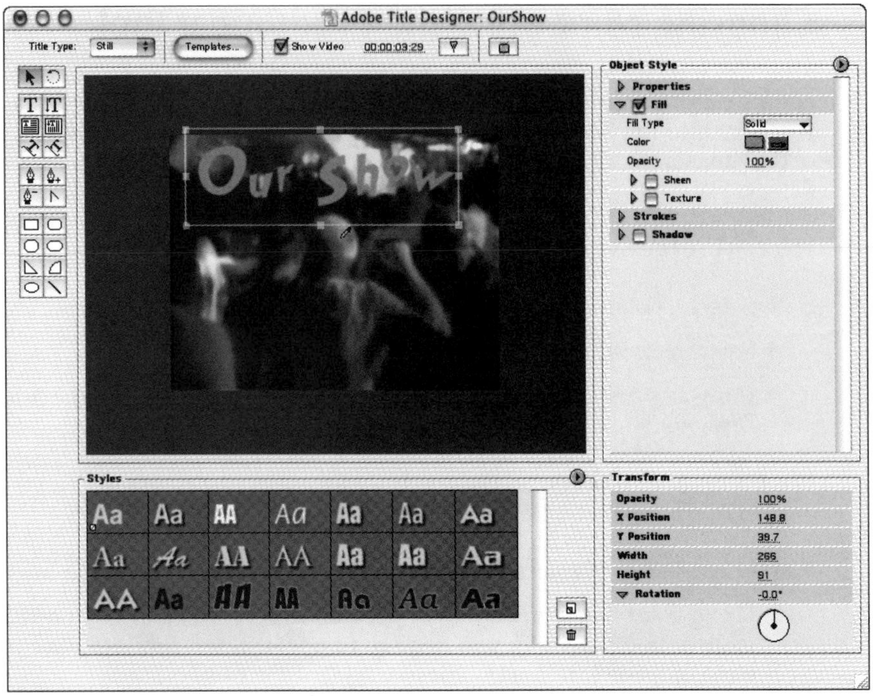

Figure 8-5: Use the Eyedropper tool to select colors from a frame of a video clip.

7. **Move the Eyedropper tool over the color you want to select and click the mouse.** The Color Swatch changes to the new color.

Applying solid colors to text and graphics

After you've created a graphic object or some text, applying a solid fill color using Premiere's Color Picker is quite simple. Here's how:

1. **Use a Type tool to create a text object or use a Graphic tool to create a graphic object on-screen.** You can use the Selection tool to select a text or graphic object already on-screen.
2. **Verify that a check mark appears in front of the Fill option in the Properties section.** Deselecting the Fill check box option removes the fill. Keep the Fill option selected.
3. **Click the triangle in front of the Fill option to display the options.**

4. **Set the Fill Type pop-up menu to Solid.**
5. **Double-click the Color Swatch.** Doing so opens the Color Picker.
6. **Pick your new color and close the Color Picker.** You can also use the Eyedropper tool to pick a color from an object in the drawing area or from a video clip in the background.
7. **To make the color translucent so that you can see through it, reduce the Opacity percentage.** The lower the opacity, the more translucent the object. You can change the opacity percentage by using either the Opacity field in the Object Style section or in the Transform section. You can also use the Title ➪ Transform ➪ Opacity command. By lowering the opacity in an object, you can create interesting graphic effects where portions of objects below show through the object above.

Applying highlights and textures with text and graphic objects

You can also add a highlight and/or a texture to the fill and stroke of text or a graphic object. To add a highlight, use the Sheen option.

Adding a highlight

Follow these steps to create a sense of light and shadow in your text or graphic:

1. **With an object selected, click the Sheen check box.**
2. **Click the triangle in front of the Sheen check box to display the Sheen options.**
3. **Double-click the Color Swatch to pick a color.** You can also use the Eyedropper tool to pick a color from an object onscreen or from a background video clip.
4. **Click and drag on the Size value to change the size of the highlight.** Drag to the right to increase the size. Drag to the left to decrease the size.
5. **Click and drag on the Angle value to change the value of the highlight.**
6. **Click and drag on the Offset value to move the highlight up or down.** Increasing the offset value moves the highlight up and decreasing the offset value moves the offset down.
7. **Change the Opacity value to make the highlight translucent.** Reducing the Opacity value makes the highlight more translucent.

Adding a texture to text or graphics

You can easily make text and graphics more realistic by applying a texture. Follow these steps:

1. **With an object selected, click the Texture check box.**
2. **Click the triangle in front of the Texture check box to display the Texture options.**
3. **Click the Texture Swatch to display the Load a Texture dialog box, as shown in Figure 8-6.**
4. **In the Load a Texture dialog box, pick a texture from the Premiere 6.5 Texture folder.**
5. **Click Open to apply the texture to the selected object.** Figure 8-7 shows the selected object with the texture applied to it.

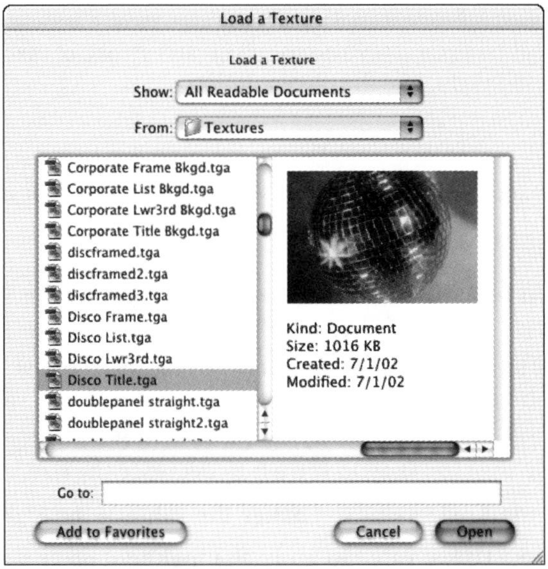

Figure 8-6: The Load a Texture dialog box enables you to load a texture onto a selected object.

Note

You can create your own textures. You can use Photoshop to save any bitmap file and save it in jpeg format. Or you can use Premiere to output a frame from a video clip.

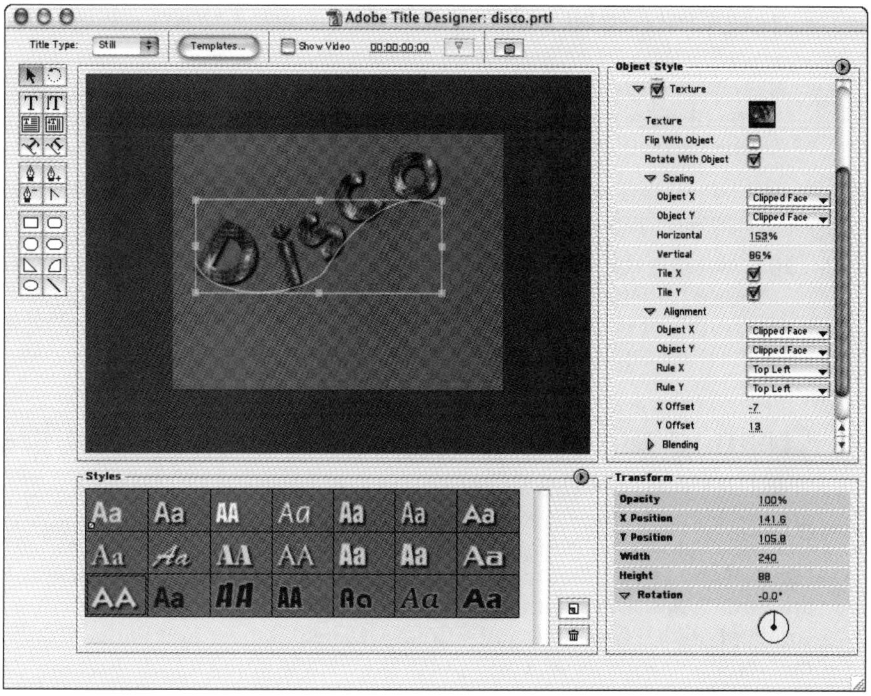

Figure 8-7: A texture applied to a text object created with the Path Text tool

6. Specify optional settings:

- **Flip With Object or Rotate With Object.** Premiere flips and/or rotates a texture with the object.
- **Scaling.** Premiere scales the texture. First, click the triangle in front of the option and then click and drag on the Horizontal and Vertical values.
- **Tile X and Tile Y.** Specifies whether you want the texture to be tiled to an object.
- **The Object X and Object Y** pop-up menu in the Scaling section determines how the texture is stretched along the X and Y axis. There are four choices from the pop-up menu — Clipped Face, Arbitrary, Face, and Extended Character. The choice you pick determines how the texture is stretched. By default the Clipped Face option is selected.
- **The Object X and Object Y** pop-up menu in the Alignment section determines how the texture is aligned to the object. There are four choices from the pop-up menu: Clipped Face, Arbitrary, Face, and Extended Character. The choice you pick determines how the texture is aligned. By default the Clipped Face option is selected.
- **The Rule X and Rule Y** check boxes in the Alignment section determine how the texture is aligned. Choose Top Left, Center, or Bottom Right.

7. **To offset a texture, click and drag the X and Y Offset values in the Alignment section.**

8. **To blend the texture with the fill color, click and drag on the Mix value in the Blending section.** Decreasing the Mix increases the fill color and decreases the texture.

9. **The Fill Key and Texture Key check boxes in the Blending section allow for transparency of the object to be considered.**

10. **Lowering the Alpha Scale value, in the Blending section, makes the object more translucent.** The Composite Rule pop-up menu allows you to pick which channel is going to be used in determining the transparency. Clicking the Invert Composite check box inverts the alpha values.

Creating and applying gradients to text and graphics

Premiere's color controls enable you to apply gradients to text and graphic objects created in the Adobe Title Designer window. A gradient, which is a gradual blend from one color to another, can help add interest and depth to otherwise flat color. Used effectively, gradients can also help simulate lighting effects in graphics. There are three types of gradients you can create in the Type Designer window; Linear Gradient, Radial Gradient, and 4 Color Gradient. Linear and Radial Gradients are created from two colors. The 4 Color Gradient is created from four colors. Figure 8-8 shows a graphic created using gradients. To create the kite object, in Figure 8-8, we used the 4 Color Gradient. To learn how to create a diamond shape using the Graphic tools in the Adobe Title Designer window, turn to the "Working with the Bézier tools" section). The highlight area in the middle of the kite was created using the Sheen option. To the text inside the kite object, we applied a linear gradient.

Here's how to create a linear and radial gradient:

1. **Select or create text or a graphic object with the Selection tool.**

Note

If you want to apply a gradient to specific letters in a text block, select the text by clicking and dragging over it with the Type tool.

Note

If you are outputting to video, gradients created in small text may make the text unreadable on a television monitor.

2. **The Fill check box should be selected and the triangle in front of the check box should be facing downwards.** Do so, if it isn't.

3. **From the Fill pop-up menu choose either Linear Gradient or Radial Gradient.**

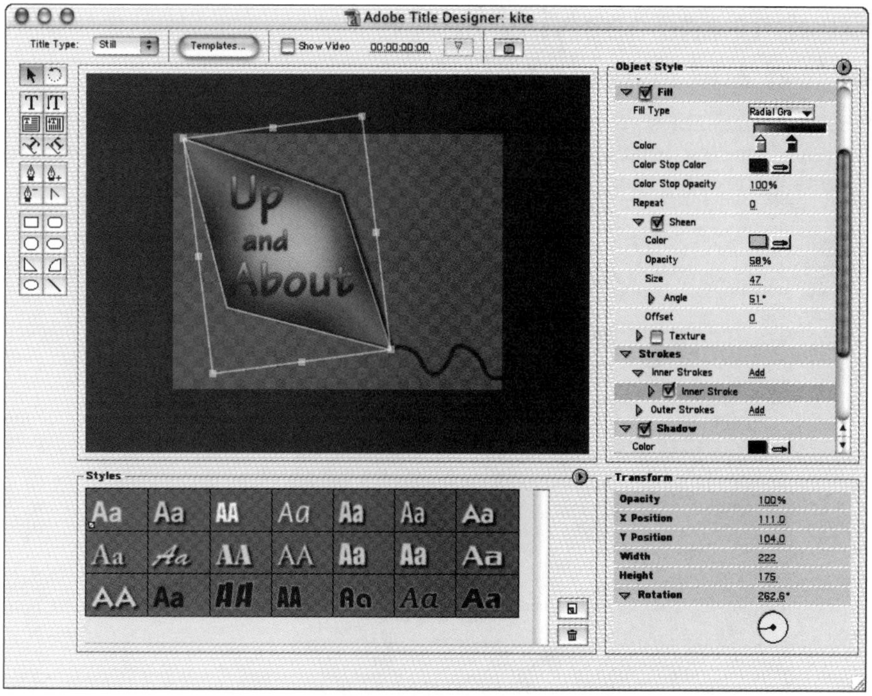

Figure 8-8: Graphic object and text created using gradients

4. **To set the start and ending colors of the gradients, use the Gradient Start and End Color Swatches.** They are the two tiny rectangles below the gradient bar. Pick the starting gradient color by double-clicking the Gradient Start Color Swatch. When the Color Picker opens, pick a color. Double-click the Gradient End Color Swatch. When the Color Picker opens, pick an ending gradient color.

Moving the Gradient Start and End Color Swatch

You can move the Gradient Start Color Swatch and the Gradient End Color Swatch. Moving the swatches changes how much color of each swatch is applied to the gradient.

The Color Stop Color Swatch allows you to change the color of the selected color swatch. The Color Stop Opacity allows you to change the opacity of the selected color swatch. The selected color swatch is the color swatch with a black triangle above it.

To change the angle in a linear gradient, click and drag on the Angle value.

To increase the number of repeats in the linear or radial blend, click and drag on the Repeat value.

Creating and applying bevels to text and graphic objects

Premiere 6.5 enables you to create some really cool bevels in the Adobe Title Designer window. You can add a three-dimensional effect to your text and graphic objects by beveling them, as shown in Figure 8-9.

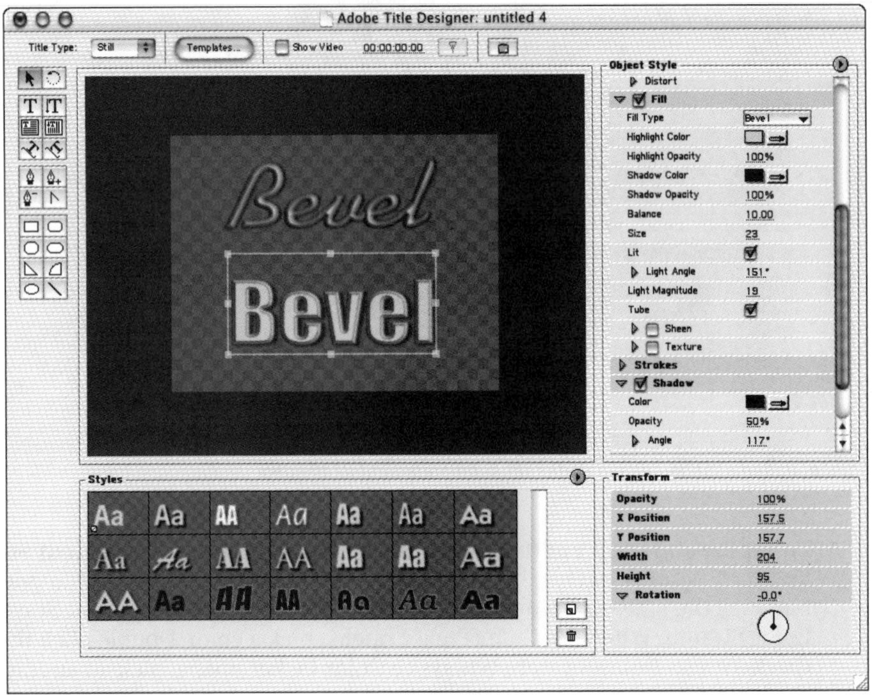

Figure 8-9: Graphic object created with a bevel

Here's how to bevel an object:

1. **Select or create text or a graphic with the Selection tool.**
2. **The Fill check box should be selected and the triangle in front of the check box should be facing downwards.** Do so, if it isn't.
3. **From the Fill pop-up menu choose Bevel.**
4. **Double-click the Highlight Color Swatch or use the Eyedropper tool to pick a highlight color.** Then click the Shadow Color Swatch or the Eyedropper tool to pick a shadow color.

5. **Click and drag the Size slider to the right to increase the bevel size.**
6. **To increase or decrease the highlight color, click and drag on the Balance value.** Increasing the highlight color, decrease shadow color, and vice versa.
7. **To make your bevel look more decorative, click the Tube check box.** Notice that a tubular border appears between the highlight and shadow area.
8. **Click the Lit check box to increase the bevel effect and make the object more three-dimensional.** Click and drag on the Light Angle value to change the angle of the light. Click and drag on the Light Magnitude value to increase or decrease the amount of light.
9. **If you want to make the bevel translucent, click and drag to the left on either the Highlight Opacity or Shadow Opacity value.**

Applying shadows to text and graphics

To add a finishing touch to your text or graphic object, you may want to add a shadow to it. You can add either an inner or outer stroke to an object. Here's how:

1. **In the Adobe Title Designer window, select text or a graphic with the Selection tool.**

Note

If you want the selected object to fill but with a shadow, set the object's Fill Type to Ghost Fill.

2. **Click the Shadow check box to select it.**
3. **To see all the Shadow options, click the triangle in front of the Shadow option, so that it is facing downwards.**
4. **Click and drag on the Size value to set the size of the shadow.**
5. **Click and drag on the Distance and Angle values to move the shadow to the desired location.**
6. **Click and drag on the Spread value to soften the edges of the shadow.**
7. **Double-click the Color Swatch to change the color for the drop shadow. You can also use the Eyedropper tool to pick a color from a background video clip or template.**
8. **Reduce the Opacity value if you want to make the shadow translucent.**

Note

Don't let a shadow fool you. If you are changing the opacity of an object that has a solid shadow, the opacity effect you desire may not be possible until you remove the shadow or make the shadow transparent.

Applying strokes to text and graphics

To separate the fill color from the shadow color, you may want to add a stroke to it. You can add either an inner or outer stroke to an object. Here's how:

1. **In the Adobe Title Designer window, select text or a graphic with the Selection tool.**

Note: If you want the selected object to have a stroke, but no fill or shadow, set the object's Fill Type to Eliminate Fill. This way you can use the selected object as a frame.

2. **Click the triangle in front of the Strokes option so that it is facing downwards.**
3. **Click Add next to either Inner Strokes and/or Outer Strokes option to add either inner or outer strokes to the selected object.**

Note: You can click the Object Style menu — the tiny circle with an arrow surrounding it — to add, delete, or move a stroke.

4. **Click the Stroke Type pop-up menu to pick a stroke type.**
5. **Click and drag the Size value to change the stroke size.**
6. **Click and drag in the Angle value to change the angle of the Depth and Drop Face stroke type.**
7. **Click the Fill Type pop-up menu to pick a fill type.**
8. **Double-click the Color Swatch to pick a color for the drop shadow.** You can also use the Eyedropper tool to pick a color from a background video clip or template, and so on.
9. **Reduce the Opacity value if you want to make the stroke translucent.**

Using Styles

Although setting text attributes is quite simple, sometimes finding the right combination of font, size, style, kerning, and leading can be time-consuming. After you've spent the better part of an hour fine-tuning text attributes to one text block, you may want to apply the same attributes to other text in the Adobe Title Designer window or to other text that you've previously saved. You can save attributes and color using styles.

The Premiere Adobe Title Designer enables you to save and load preset styles for text and graphics. Thus, instead of picking font, size, and color each time you create a title, you can apply a style name to the text, and have all of the attributes applied at once. Using one or two styles throughout your project helps insure consistency. If you don't want to create your own Styles, you can use the preset styles appearing at the bottom of the Adobe Title Designer. All you need to do to apply a style is select the text and click the style swatch that suits your needs.

The styles section introduces you to a new interface feature of Adobe Premiere 6.5. The choices for styles are hidden from the screen but accessible by clicking the Styles menu — the tiny circle with an arrow surrounding it. The Styles menu is shown in Figure 8-10. Clicking the Styles menu arrow opens up commands that allow you to create styles, save them to disk, and change the way styles appear on-screen.

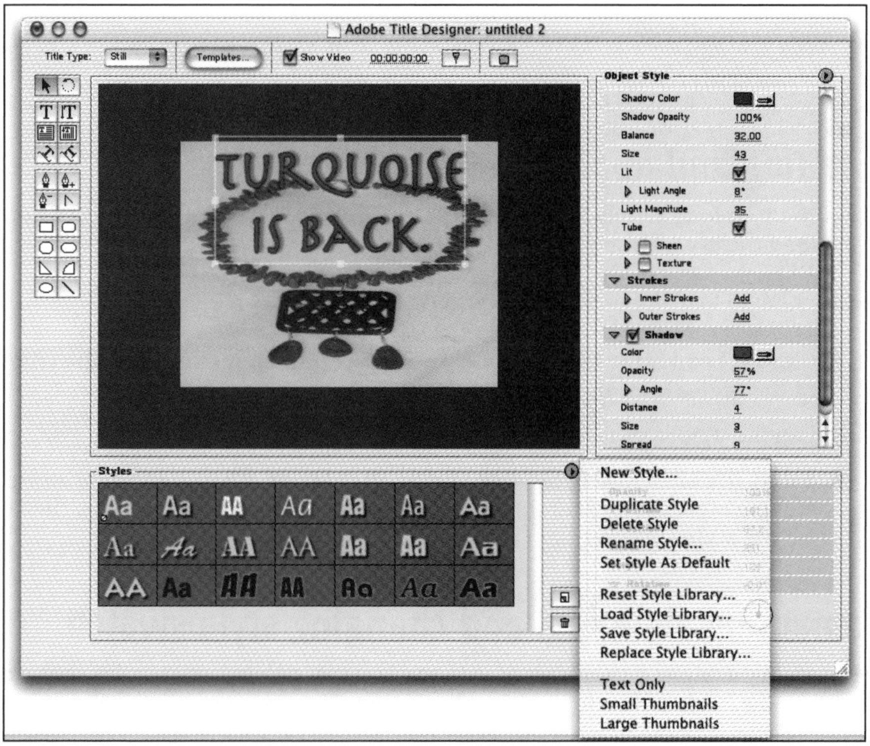

Figure 8-10: The Styles menu displays styles and available style library options.

Here's how to create a style:

1. **Create the text using attributes that you have in the style.**
2. **Choose Name Style from the Styles menu, or you can click the New Style button (above the Delete Style button).**
3. **Enter a name for the style and then click OK.** You'll see either a swatch of the new style or the style name will appear in the Styles area.

Styles only remain during the current Premiere project session. If you want to use a style again, you must save the styles into a style file. Here's how to save a style file:

1. **Select the name of the style you want to save or select its thumbnail.**

Note: You can also start by selecting each object containing the style that you want to save.

2. **Choose Save Style Library from the Styles menu.**
3. **Enter a name for the style and designate its location on your hard drive.**
4. **Click Save.** Premiere saves the file using a .prtl file extension.

Note: You can replace a pre-existing style name with a new style by choosing Replace Styles rather than save styles.

Loading and applying styles

If you want to load a style from the hard drive to use in a new Premiere session, you must load the style library before you can apply it.

Here's how to load styles from the hard drive:

1. **Choose Load Style Library from the Styles pop-up menu. Click the triangle in the Styles section to display the Styles pop-up menu.**
2. **Use the mouse to navigate to the hard drive location containing your style.**
3. **Select the style and then click Open.** After styles are loaded, you can easily apply a style by clicking the text or object and then simply clicking the swatch for the style that you want to apply.

Renaming, deleting, and changing style swatch

You can duplicate styles and rename them. You can delete saved styles that you don't need to use anymore. You can also change the way the style swatches appear in the Adobe Title Designer window.

Here's how to duplicate, rename, and delete styles:

1. **Choose Duplicate Style from the Styles menu.**
2. **To rename a style, first select it and then choose Rename Style from the Styles menu.**
3. **In the dialog box that appears type a new name.**
4. **To delete a style, select it and choose Delete Style from the Styles menu.**

If you feel the style swatches consume too much screen space, you can change the display of styles so that they appear as text or as small icons. To change the display, simply click the Styles menu and then choose either Text only, Large Thumbnails, or Small Thumbnails.

Note: You can use the Preferences Titler dialog box to change the characters that appear in the style swatch.

Placing a Title in a Project

To use the titles you create in the Adobe Title Designer window, you need to add them to a Premiere project. When you save a Title, Premiere automatically adds the title to the Project window of the current project. After the title is in the Project window, you add titles to the Timeline window much the same way as you add video clips and other graphics(by dragging and dropping them from the Project window to the Timeline window. Titles can either be placed in the Video 2 Track or the Video 1 track of the Timeline window. Typically, you add a title to the Video 2 track so that the title or title sequence appears over the video clips in the Video 1 track. If you want to have a Title file gradually transition into a video clip, place the Title file in the Video 1A track and a video clip in the Video 1B track.

You can add a pre-existing title to a project on-screen by importing it into a project. Here's how to add a title to the Project window by using the Import command:

1. **Choose File ⇨ Open to open the project file that you want to work with.**
2. **Choose File ⇨ Import ⇨ File to import the title file that you want to use.**

   You should have the title file in the Project window of the project file.
3. **Drag the Title file from the Project window to the Timeline window.** If the Timeline window is not open, you can open it by choosing Window ⇨ Timeline.
4. **After you add your title to a video track in the Timeline window, you'll probably want to save and preview your project.** In the Timeline window, move the work area bar over the area you want to preview. Then open the Monitor window (choose Window ⇨ Monitor). Premiere plays the video clip in the Monitor window. Press Enter to build and preview the video clip with the title over it. To see the preview again, click the play button in the Monitor window. (For more information about previewing Premiere projects, see Chapter 3.)

Tip: After you place a title file into a project, you can edit the title file by double-clicking it. When you double-click, the Adobe Title Designer window appears.

Adding a Background to a Title Clip

In this section, you'll create a new project. In the project, you'll import a video clip to use behind the title you create using the Premiere 6.5 Adobe Title Designer window. Then you'll save the title and place it in your production. Figure 8-11 shows the Premiere layout of a production created using a title superimposed over a video clip. In the Monitor window, you can see the Title file, superimposed over the video clip. In the Timeline window, the Title file is selected. The Effects Control palette displays that the Transparency option is selected for the Title file. Setting the Transparency option allows you to see a video clip below the Title file. Notice that in the Timeline window the Title file appears in the Video 2 track, the video clip appears in the Video 1 track, and a sound clip appears in the Audio 1 track. By placing a Title file in the Video 2 track, Premiere allows you to set a transparency setting.

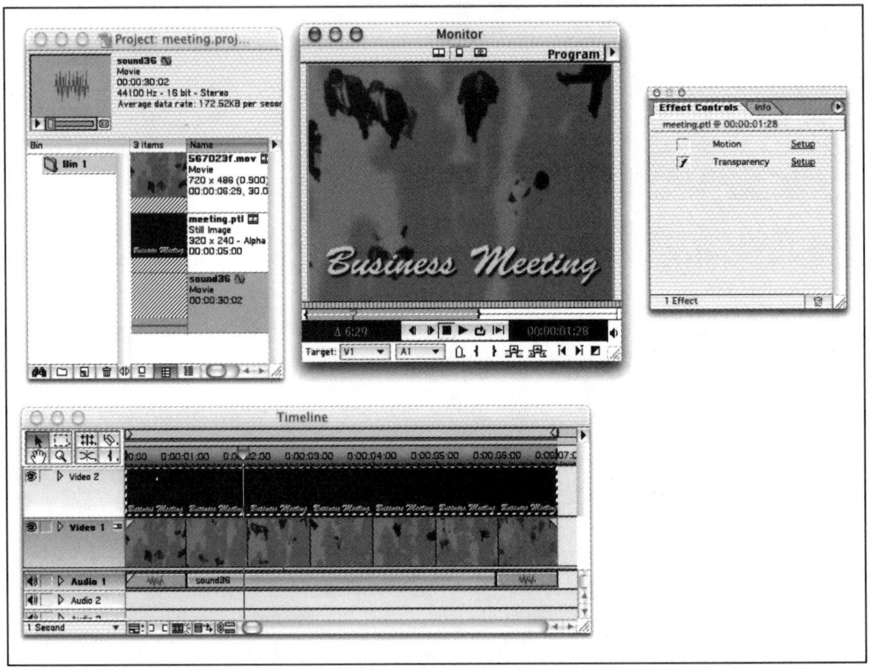

Figure 8-11: The production layout of a Premiere project with a Title superimposed over a video clip

Here are the steps to create a title and to overlay it onto a video clip:

1. **Choose File ➪ New Project, to create a project.** Make sure that you use the proper preset. For practice purposes, use Multimedia.
2. **Choose File ➪ Import ➪ File to import the video clip you want to appear behind the title.**

On the CD-ROM

If you want, you can use the video clip that appears in Figure 8-11. It is found in the Meeting folder, inside the Chapter 8 folder, in the Tutorial Projects folder, that is on the CD-ROM that accompanies this book. The video clip is from Digital Vision's CityLife CD-ROM (# 567023).

3. **Choose Window ⇨ Workspace ⇨ Single-Track Editing to set the workspace to single-track editing.** To change just the Timeline window to Single-Track editing, click the Timeline pop-up menu and choose Single-Track Editing.
4. **Drag the video clip from the Project palette to the Video 1 track in the Timeline window.**
5. **Choose File ⇨ New ⇨ Title to create a new title.**
6. **Click Show Video check box to display the video clip in the drawing area of the Adobe Title Designer window.** Premiere places the frame in the background where the Timeline marker is located. To use a different frame in the video clip, move the Timeline Marker in the Timeline window and then click Sync to Timeline button, or you can click and drag the Timeline values to the right of the Show Video check box.

Note

If you are outputting to video or film, choose Type ⇨ View ⇨ Safe Title Margins and Type ⇨ View ⇨ Safe Action Margins. If you are outputting to the Web, you don't need to select these options.

7. **Click the Type tool and move the I-beam cursor to the drawing area and type** Business Meeting **(as shown in Figure 8-12) or whatever else you may prefer.**
8. **Choose a style.** You can change the text attributes, color, and shadow as desired.
9. **Save the title and name it by choosing File ⇨ Save.** The Title is saved to your drive and in the Project palette of the project.
10. **Drag the title you just saved from the Project palette to the Video 2 track of the Timeline window.** Move the Title into position. We moved the title shown in Figure 8-11 so that it lines up with the video clip in the Video 1 track.
11. **If you need to extend the title so that it matches the length of the video clip, click the left side of the title in the Timeline window and drag to the left.**

Note

You can change the duration of a title by clicking the title in the Timeline window and choosing Clip ⇨ Duration. In the Clip Duration dialog box, type in the new duration.

12. **To set the Transparency option, you can either choose Clip ⇨ Video Options ⇨ Transparency Setting or click Setup next to Transparency in the Effect Controls palette.** In the Transparency Settings dialog box, the Key Type pop-up menu should be set to Alpha Channel, as shown in Figure 8-13.

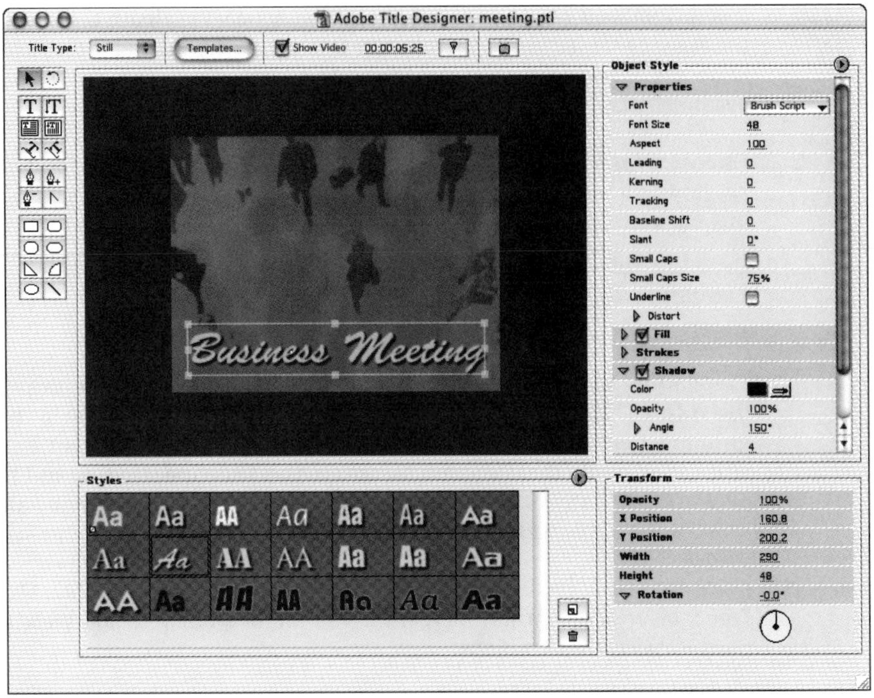

Figure 8-12: The Adobe Title Designer window for the production shown in Figure 8-11

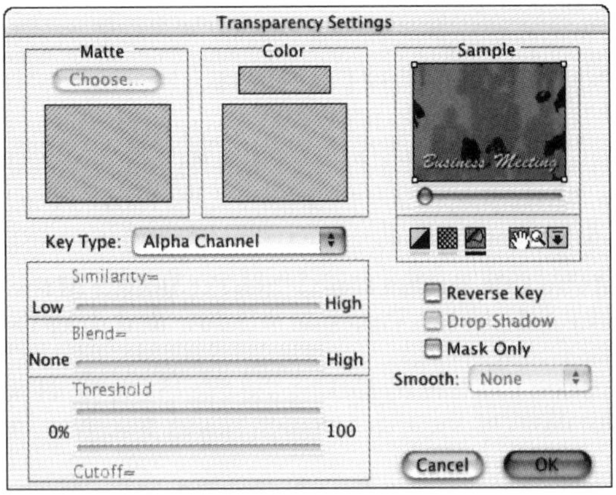

Figure 8-13: Select Alpha Channel as the key type.

Note

You can animate your title, by choosing either Clip ➪ Video Options ➪ Motion or click Setup next to Motion in the Effect Controls palette. In the Motion Settings dialog box, you can make adjustments in the dialog box, or you can click OK. For more information on using the Motion Settings dialog box, turn to Chapter 14.

13. **To add sound to your clip, choose File ➪ Import ➪ File.** Locate the sound you want to import. When the sound clip is in the Project window, click and drag it to Audio Track 1 of the Timeline window. If the sound clip is too long, you can cut it using the Razor tool. For more information on editing sound, refer to Chapter 6.

On the CD-ROM

If you want, you can use the sound clip that appears in Figure 8-11. You can find it in the Meeting folder, inside the Chapter 8 folder, in the Tutorial Projects folder, that is on the CD-ROM that accompanies this book. The sound clip is from Digital Vision's CityLife UrbanMoods CD-ROM (Sound 36).

14. **Save the project and press Enter to build a preview of the project.**
15. **Display the Monitor window, if it is not already open by choosing Window ➪ Monitor.** Click the Play button to play the project.

Working with Logos

Logos can be imported into the Adobe Title Designer window and used either in a portion or in the entire area of the drawing area. A logo can be either a graphic or a photograph. In Figure 8-14, we created a title by importing a texture in the background and a photograph into the center of the drawing area.

Here's how to import a logo into a title:

1. **Choose File ➪ New Project to create a new project.** For practice purposes use the Multimedia preset.
2. **Choose File ➪ New ➪ Title to create a new title.**
3. **In the Adobe Title Designer window, choose Title ➪ Logo ➪ Insert Logo.** In the Load Logo dialog box, shown in Figure 8-15, pick a file to import into the Adobe Title Designer drawing area. You can either use one of the logos in the Logo or Texture folder that comes with Premiere, or you can make your own by using Adobe Illustrator and/or Adobe Photoshop.

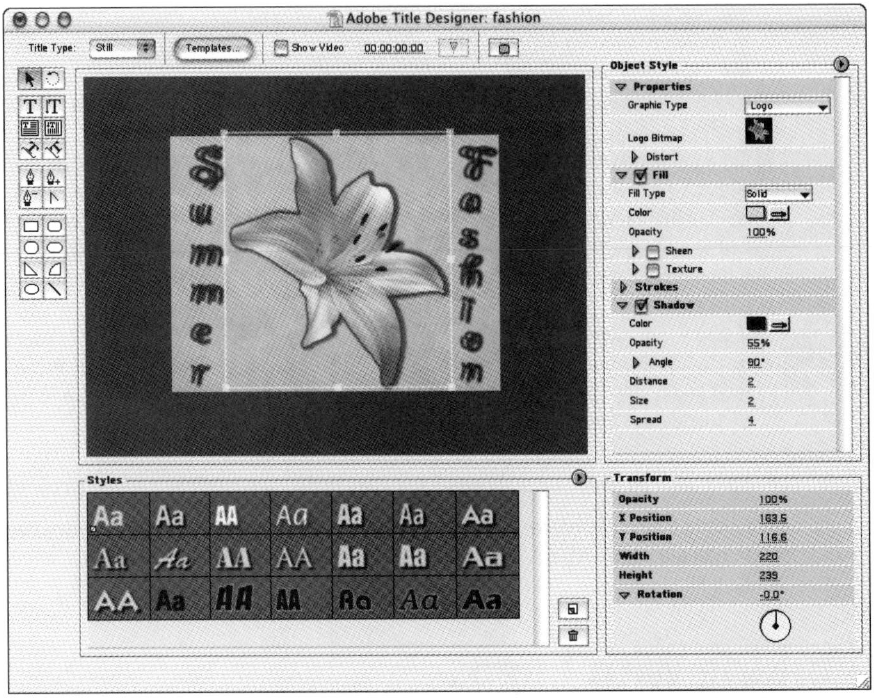

Figure 8-14: A title created by importing a texture in the background and a photograph in the center of the drawing area

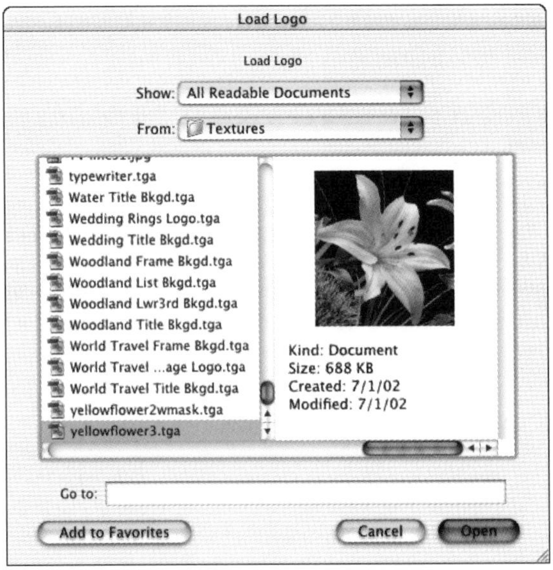

Figure 8-15: The Load Logo dialog box enables you to choose which logo you want to insert into the drawing area of the Adobe Title Designer window.

Note

To insert a logo in a textbox, double-click the textbox with the Selection tool. Then choose Title ⇨ Logo ⇨ Insert Logo into Text.

4. **To change the logo in the drawing area to a different graphic, click the box to the right of Logo Bitmap in the Properties section.** When the dialog box appears, pick a file.
5. **After the logo is in the drawing area, you can move, resize, and rotate it with the Selection tool.** You can also use the Transform commands in the dialog box or the Title menu.
6. **To restore the logo to its original settings, choose Title ⇨ Logo ⇨ Restore Logo Size or Title ⇨ Logo ⇨ Restore Logo Aspect Ratio.**

Using Templates

Creating titles using pre-existing styles and templates can help speed up the time it takes to create a Premiere project. Creating a Title using a template is easy.

Here is how to use a template:

1. **Choose File ⇨ New Project to create a new project. Use the Multimedia preset for practice.**
2. **Choose File ⇨ New ⇨ Title to create a new title.**
3. **In the Adobe Title Designer window, click the Templates button or choose Title ⇨ Templates.** In the Template dialog box that appears, pick a template from one of the template folders. Then click Apply to apply the template to the drawing area.

You can use the Templates pop-up menu in the Templates dialog box to save a title as a template, rename, and delete a template, plus other options. Here's how:

1. **Create a new title or open an existing title.**
2. **Click the Templates button in the Adobe Title Designer window.**
3. **Click the triangle in the Templates dialog box to display the Templates menu, shown in Figure 8-16.**
4. **To save the title on-screen as a template, choose Save as a template.**
5. **To rename or delete a template, click the template you want to change and then pick Rename Template or Delete Template from the Templates menu.**
6. **To import a file as a template, select a file and then choose Import File as Template.**

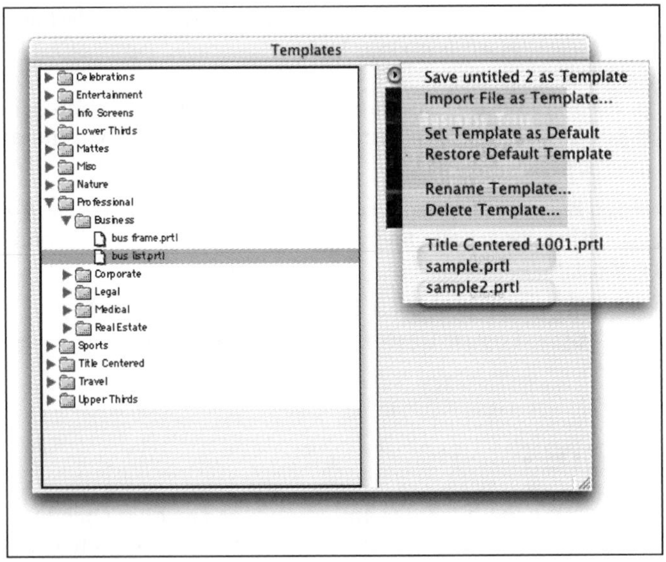

Figure 8-16: The Templates menu enables you to save a title onscreen as a template.

After the template is in the Adobe Title Designer window, you can change it how you want. Click and drag over the text in the template with the Type tool to edit the text. If you want, you can also change the style of the text. You can select items in the template with the Selection tool and move them to a new position. You can also change the fill style and color.

Using a Title Created From a Template

In this section, you create a project using two different titles using templates. One title will go at the beginning of the project in the Video 1A track; the other title will go on the Video 2 track, at the end of the project. The first template will be used as an opening screen, which will gradually fade out to a video clip and the second one will be used as a closing screen. Figure 8-17 shows the Premiere screen for the project. Figure 8-18 shows frames from the final video clip created using the Premiere project, shown in Figure 8-17.

Figure 8-17: A Premiere project created using two titles that were created using templates

Here's how to create a project using two titles created from templates:

1. **Choose File ⇨ New Project to create a project.** Make sure that you use the proper preset. For practice purposes, use Multimedia.
2. **Choose Window ⇨ Workspace ⇨ A/B Editing to set the workspace to A/B editing mode.**
3. **Choose File ⇨ New ⇨ Title to create a new title.**
4. **In the Adobe Title Designer window, click the Templates button or choose Title ⇨ Templates.** In the Template dialog box that appears, pick a template from one of the template folders. There are two types of templates you can choose. The first one is a template with a background and no transparent area, and the second type has a transparent area in the template. For the project, you need to create two titles, one with a solid background and one with no transparent areas. Start by creating the title with a solid background. Click the bus list.prtl file that is located in the Business folder, within the Professional folder. A preview of the bus list.prtl file appears in the Templates dialog box, as shown in Figure 8-19. Click Apply to for the bus list template to appear in the drawing area of the Adobe Title Designer dialog box, as shown in Figure 8-20.

Figure 8-18: Frames from the final video clip created using the Premiere project shown in Figure 8-17

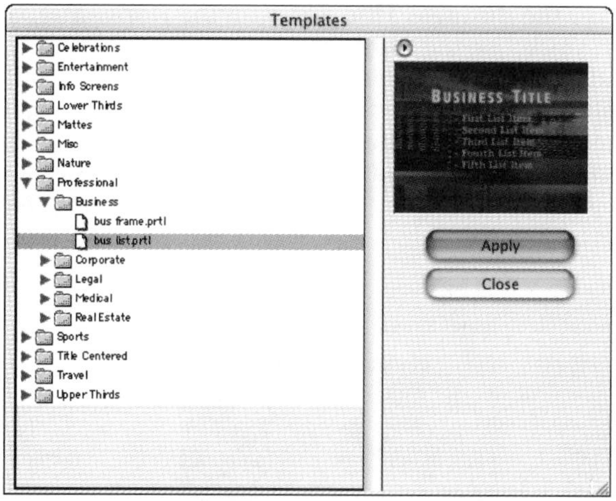

Figure 8-19: A preview of the bus list.prtl file appears in Templates dialog box.

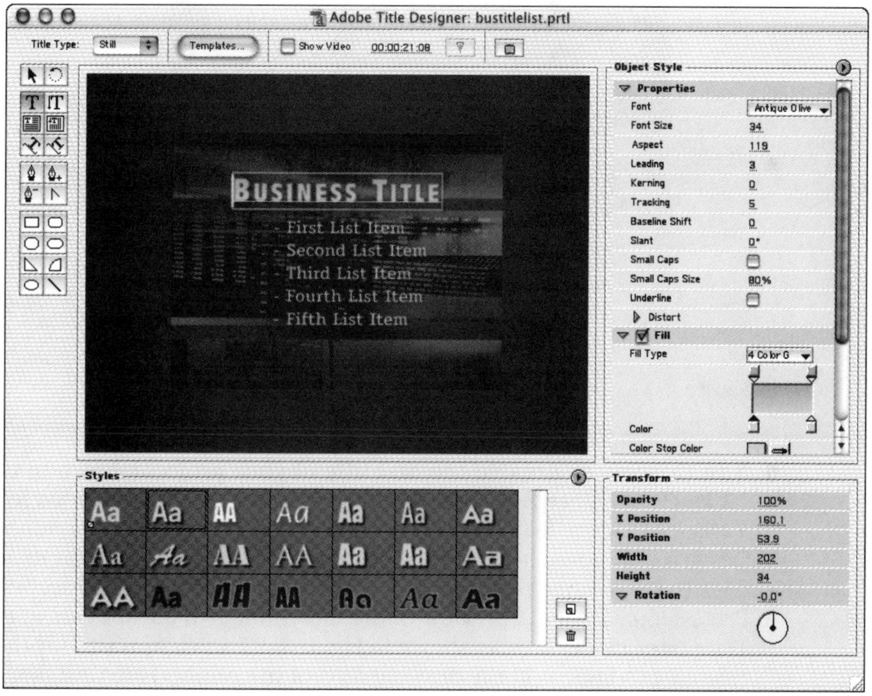

Figure 8-20: The bus list.prtl template appears in the Adobe Title Designer dialog box.

5. **Click and drag over the Business Title text with the Horizontal Type tool and type** Going to Work. Use the Horizontal Type tool to click and drag over the first bullet and type, **Make Success Your Target**. Then click and drag over the other bullets and delete the text. With the Selection tool, move the text to the bottom-right corner of the drawing area, as shown in Figure 8-21. When you are done, choose File ⇨ Save to save the title to your hard drive and have Premiere place it in the Project window of the project on-screen.

Figure 8-21: The template from Figure 8-20 after editing the text

6. **Now that you've created the first title of your project (shown in the Video 1A track in Figure 8-17), create the second title project (shown in the Video 2 track in Figure 8-17) by choosing File ⇨ New ⇨ Title.** In the Adobe Title Designer window, click the Templates button. In the Templates dialog box, click the bus frame.prtl file that is located in the Business folder within the Professional folder. A preview of the bus frame.prtl file appears in the Templates dialog box, as shown in Figure 8-22. Click Apply to for the bus list template to appear in the drawing area of the Adobe Title Designer dialog box, as shown in Figure 8-23. Click and drag over the Business Title text with the Horizontal Type tool and type **Going Home**. Use the Horizontal Type tool to click and drag over the Subtitle Goes Here text and type, **Make Success Your Target**, as shown in Figure 8-24. When you are done, choose File ⇨ Save to save the title to your hard drive and have Premiere place it in the Project window of the project on-screen.

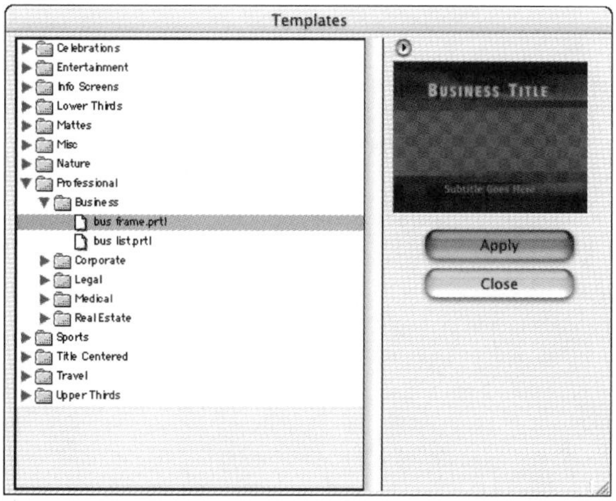

Figure 8-22: The bus frame.prtl template appears in the Templates dialog box.

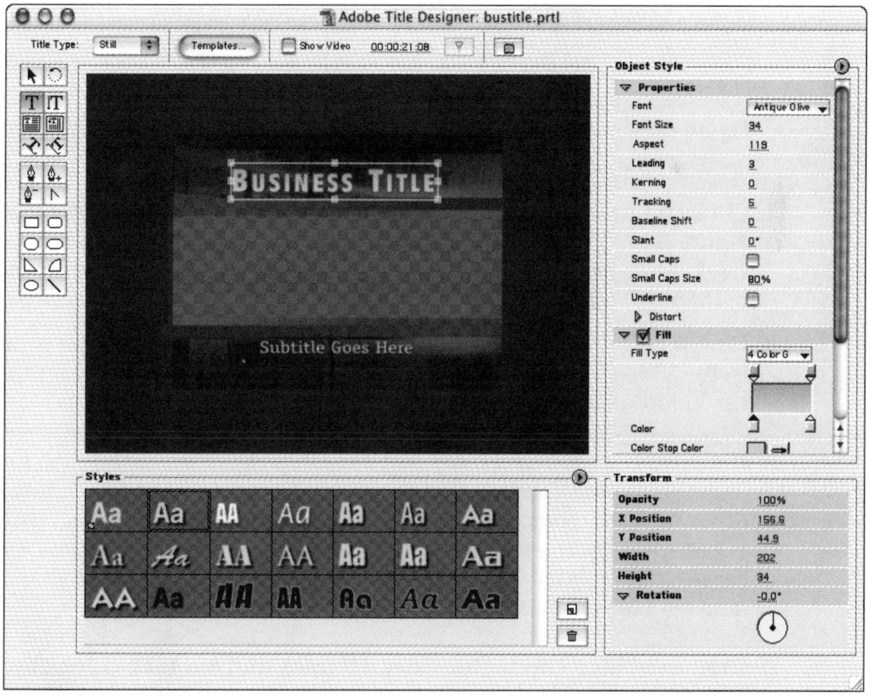

Figure 8-23: Editing the bus frame.prtl template in Adobe Title Designer

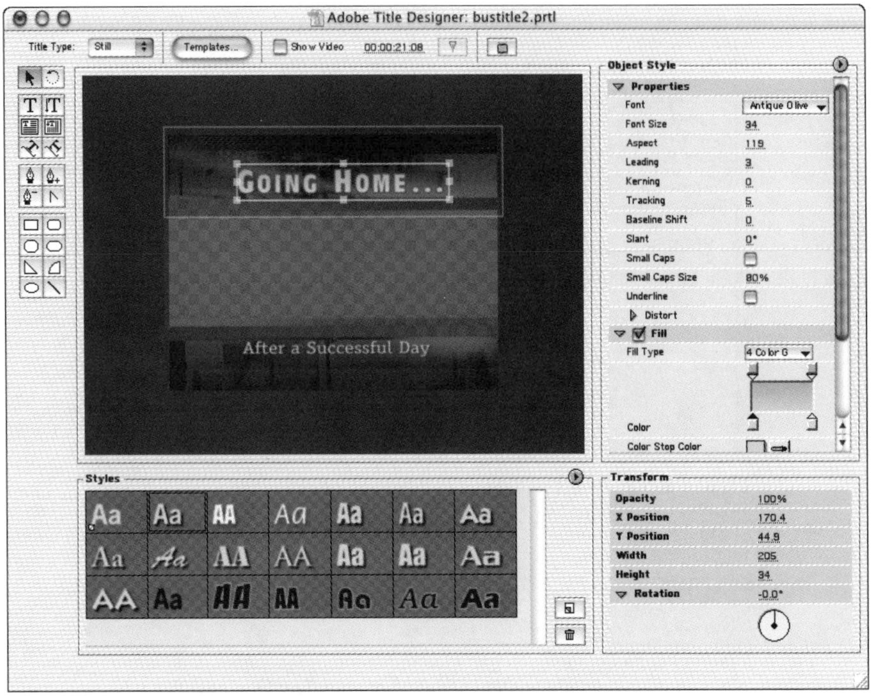

Figure 8-24: The template from Figure 8-23 with edited text

7. **Click and drag the first Title you created to the Video 1A track, as shown in Figure 8-17.** Then click and drag the second Title you created to the Video 2 track, as shown in Figure 8-17. To extend the title duration, click and drag end of the title and drag left.

8. **Choose File ➪ Import ➪ File to import the video clip that you want to appear in the Video 1B track.** Then import the video clip that you want to appear in the Video 1A track.

On the CD-ROM

The video clips and sound clip that appear in Figure 8-17 are found in the Work folder, inside the Chapter 8 folder, in the Tutorial Projects folder, that is on the CD-ROM that accompanies this book. To import the entire folder, choose File ➪ Import ➪ Folder. The video clips (567007.mov and 567030.mov) are from Digital Vision's CityMix. The sound clip (665002aw.wav) is from Digital Vision's Sounds from the Chill CD-ROM.

9. **Drag one video clip to the Video 1B track and another video clip to the Video 1A track, as shown in Figure 8-17.** We put video clip 567007.mov in the Video 1B track and video clip 567030.mov to the Video 1A track.

10. **In the Transitions palette, click and drag on the triangle in front of the Dissolve folder.** Drag two Dissolve transitions to the Transition track. Drag one Dissolve transition between the first title and the first video clip and another Dissolve transition above the end of the video clip in the Video 1B track and below the beginning of the video clip in the Video 1A track. For more information on using transitions turn to Chapter 7.

11. **To fade the title in the Video 2 track, click the triangle in front of the words "Video 2" to expand the Video Track.** To fade the title in, use the Selection tool to create a handle (shown in Figure 8-17). Then click and drag at the beginning of the fade line and drag down. To fade the video clip out, use the Selection tool to create another handle (shown in Figure 8-17). Then click and drag at the end of the fade line and drag down. For more information on fading video clips, turn to Chapter 12.

12. **To make the transparent area of the Title file in the Video 2 track transparent.** Click Setup, next to Transparency in the Effect Controls palette. The Key Type pop-up menu in the Transparency Settings dialog box should be set to Alpha Channel.

13. **To add sound to your project, click and drag the sound clip from the Project window to Audio 1 of the Timeline window.** If the sound is too long, use the Razor tool to cut the sound. For more information on editing sound clips, turn to Chapter 6.

14. **Choose File ⇨ Save to save your project.** Press Enter to preview your project.

Rolling and Crawling Titles

If you'll be creating production credits or a long sequence of text, you'll probably want to animate the text so that it scrolls up or down or crawls left or right across the screen. Premiere's Adobe Title Designer provides just what you need — it enables you to create smooth attractive titles that stream across the screen.

Here are the steps for creating scrolling or crawling text:

1. **Create a new project or load a project.**

2. **Create a new title by choosing File ⇨ New ⇨ Title.**

Note If you want to place a graphic in the background of the scrolling titles, you can either choose Title ⇨ Logo ⇨ Insert Logo or click the Show Video check box, as discussed earlier in this chapter.

3. **To roll text vertically up or down, choose Roll from the Title Type pop-up menu. To make the text crawl across the screen, choose Crawl.**

4. **Select a Type tool.** Position the cursor in the area where you want the titles to appear and then click. Start typing the text that you want to scroll across the screen. For scrolling text, press Enter to add new lines. Figure 8-25 shows scrolling text. Notice that a scroll bar appears to the right of the drawing area in the Adobe Title Designer window.

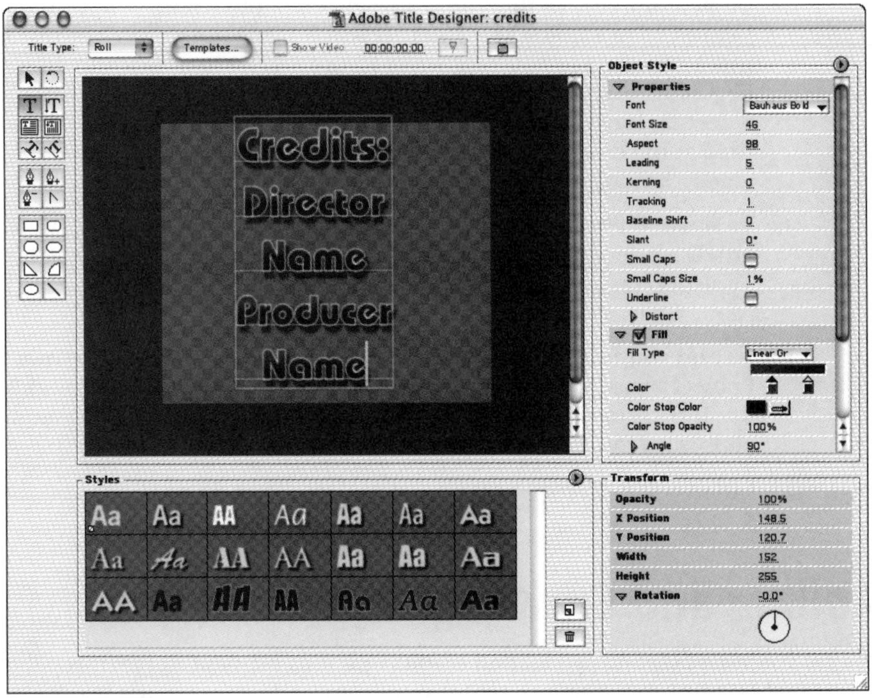

Figure 8-25: When you create scrolling text in the Adobe Title Designer window, a scrolling bar appears to the right of the drawing area.

5. **Use the techniques described earlier in this chapter to stylize the text that you want to Roll or Crawl.** If you want to reposition or resize the bounding box, click outside the box. The Text window disappears and is replaced by a bounding box with four handles. To move the box, click in the middle and drag it to reposition it on-screen. To resize the box, click one of the four handles and drag with the mouse. Enter the text that you want to scroll across the screen.

6. **Set the Rolling and Crawling options by choosing Title ➪ Roll/Crawl Options.** In the Roll/Crawl Options dialog box (shown in Figure 8-26), the options provide choices to customize the roll or crawl. The options provide the following effects:

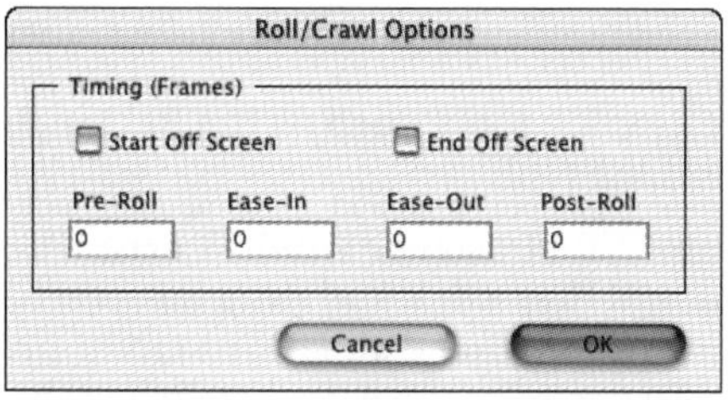

Figure 8-26: The Roll/Crawl Options dialog box

- **Start off screen:** Choose this option to have the roll/crawl effect begin with the text off screen.
- **End off screen:** Choose this option to have the roll/crawl effect end with the text off screen.
- **Pre-roll:** If you want the text to appear motionless before the animation begins, enter the number of static frames in this field.
- **Ease in:** Enter the number of frames that you want to ramp up or gradually accelerate until normal playing speed.
- **Ease out:** Enter the number of frames that you want the titles to ramp down or gradually slowdown to a complete stop.
- **Post roll:** If you want the text to appear motionless after the animation ends, enter the number of static frames in this field.

7. **Choose a Rolling and Crawling option from the Roll/Crawl Options dialog box.** Then click OK to close the dialog box. After you've created your titles, a vertical scroll bar appears indicating rolling titles; a horizontal bar appears if you have created horizontal titles.

Note

You can create templates from your rolling and scrawling text. To save the rolling or scrawling title on-screen as a template, click the Templates button. In the Templates dialog, click the triangle to display the Templates pop-up menu. Choose Save as a template and then click Apply to save the Title on-screen as a template.

8. **Choose File ⇨ Save to save the Title.** After you create the title, drag the icon from the Project window on to the Timeline window to see the scrolling or rolling type put to action.

Creating Basic Graphics

Premiere's graphics tools enable you to create simple shapes, such as lines, squares, ovals, rectangles, and polygons. You can find these basic graphic tools in the lower portion of the Toolbox (the last four rows). They are the Rectangle, Clipped Corner Rectangle, Rounded Corner Rectangle, Wedge, Arc, Ellipse, and Line tools.

Here are the steps for creating a rectangle, a rounded rectangle, an ellipse, or a line:

1. **Select one of Premiere's basic graphic tools, such as the Rectangle, Rounded Rectangle, Ellipse, or Line tool.**
2. **Move the pointer into the Adobe Title Designer window area where you wish to have the shape appear and then click and drag on-screen to create the shape.** To create a perfect square, rounded square, or circle, press the Shift key as you click and drag. To create a line at 45-degree increments, press the Shift key while dragging with the Line tool. Press and hold the Option key on a Mac or the Alt key on a PC to create an object from its center out.
3. **As you drag, the shape appears on-screen.** Release the mouse after you finish drawing the shape.
4. **To change a graphic from one shape to another, click the Graphic Type pop-up menu and make a selection.** The Graphic Type pop-up menu is located inside the Properties section within the Object Style area of the Type Designer window.
5. **To distort a graphic shape, change the X and Y values in the Distort section.** The Distort section is located below the Graphic Type section.
6. **Click the Graphic Type pop-up menu to transform an object into another.**

Transforming Graphics

After you create a graphic shape in Premiere, you may want to resize or move it. The following sections provide step-by-step instructions on how to move and resize graphic shapes.

Moving graphic objects

To move a graphic object, follow these steps:

1. **Click the Selection tool and click a graphic shape to select it.**

Note

If you have various shapes on-screen overlapping each other and are having difficulty selecting a specific shape, you may want to use one of the Title ➪ Select commands and/or the Title ➪ Arrange commands.

2. **With the Selection tool activated, click and drag the shape to move it.** As you move the graphic, notice that the X and Y position in the Transform section of the Type Designer window changes.
3. **If you want, you can change the position of a graphic shape by changing either the X Position or the Y Position in the Transform section of the Designer Type window or by using the Title ➪ Transform ➪ Position command.**

4. **To Premiere center a graphic horizontally, vertically, or in the lower-third section of the Adobe Title Designer area, choose one of the Title ➪ Position commands.**

Note

If you have various shapes selected on-screen, and are having difficulty distributing or aligning them horizontally or vertically, you may want to use one of the Title ➪ Align Objects commands or the Title ➪ Distribute Objects commands.

Resizing graphic objects

Follow these steps to resize and rotate an object:

1. **Click the Selection tool.**
2. **Resize the shape by moving the mouse pointer to one of the shape's handles.** When the icon changes to a line with arrows at either end of it, click and drag on the shape's handle to enlarge to reduce the graphic shape. As you resize the graphic, notice that the X and Y position and the Width and Height values in the Transform section of the Type Designer window change.

Note

Pressing and holding the Shift, while resizing a shape with the Selection tool, keeps the shape's proportions. Press and hold the Option key on a Mac or the Alt key on a PC as you resize with the Selection tool to create an object from its center out.

3. **If you want, you can change the size of a graphic shape by changing the Width or Height in the Transform section of the Type Designer window or by using the Title ➪ Transform ➪ Scale command.**
4. **Rotate the shape by moving the mouse pointer to one of the shape's handles.** When the icon changes to a curved line with arrows at either end of it, click and drag on the shape's handle to rotate the graphic shape. As you rotate the graphic, notice that the Rotation value, in the Transform section of the Type Designer window changes.
5. **If you want, you can change the rotation of a graphic shape by changing the Rotation in the Transform section of the Type Designer window or by using the Title ➪ Transform ➪ Rotation command.**
6. **You can also rotate an object by using the Rotate tool in the Toolbox.**

Stylizing Graphic Objects

After you've created a graphic object, you may want to change the attributes and stylize it. You change the fill color, fill style, opacity, stroke, and size and apply a shadow to it. You can also change the shape of a graphic. All these effects can be changed using the options in the Object Style section of the Type Designer dialog box.

Changing the fill color

Here's how to change the fill color of an object:

1. **Use the Select tool to select the graphic shape you want to change.**
2. **Click the Fill Type pop-up menu and pick a fill style.**

Note: For more information on picking a color and fill style turn to the section on using colors in the section, "Understanding Color in the Adobe Title Designer window."

3. **Double-click the Color Swatch and pick a color from Premiere's Color Picker.**
4. **If desired, you can change the opacity to make your object translucent.** Decreasing the Opacity value makes your object more translucent.
5. **You can also add a sheen (a highlight) or texture to your object.** You can add sheen by clicking the Sheen check box. You can add texture by clicking the Texture check box. Then click on the triangle before the Sheen and/or Texture section to display the options.

Adding a shadow

Here's how to add a shadow to your object:

1. **Use the Select tool to select the graphic shape you want to change.**
2. **Click the Shadow box to add a check box.** Then click the triangle in front of the check box to expand the Shadow section.
3. **By default the shadow color is black. If you want to change the shadow color, double-click the Shadow Color Swatch to change the color.** If you have either a video clip or a graphic in the background of the Adobe Title Designer window, you can use the Eyedropper tool to change the shadow color to one of the colors in the background. Just click the Eyedropper tool and click the color to which you want to change the Shadow Color Swatch.
4. **Use the Size, Distance, and Angle options to customize the magnitude and direction of the shadow.** To soften the edges of the shadow, use the Spread and Opacity options.
5. **To remove the shadow, click the Shadow check box.**

Applying a stroke

Here's how to add a stroke to your object:

1. **Select the filled object with the Selection tool.**
2. **Click the triangle before Strokes to expand the Strokes section.**

3. **To add a stroke using the default settings, click Add after the words Inner Strokes and/or Outer Strokes.**
4. **To customize the inner stroke or outer stroke, click the triangle before Inner Stroke and Outer Stroke.**
5. **Pick a stroke type and size.** Then pick a fill type and fill color. If you want, you can add a sheen and pattern.
6. **To remove a stroke, click the Inner Stroke and/or Outer Stroke check box.**

Working with the Bézier Tools

Premiere features a Pen tool (as found in Adobe Illustrator), a curve-drawing tool that enables you to create freeform shapes with round and/or corner edges. These freeform polygon shapes are created from anchor points, lines, and curves. You can edit these Bézier shapes by using the Selection tool to move anchor points or by using the Add Anchor Point or Delete Anchor point tools to add or delete anchor points. You can also use the Convert Anchor Point tool for rounding the corners of polygons or for making rounded corners, pointed corners. For example, you can transform large triangles into mountains or many small triangles into waves.

Note Before you start the following sections, you should have the Adobe Title Designer window open.

Here's how to use the Pen tool to create a line:

1. **Select the Pen tool.**
2. **Move the Pen tool to the left side of the Adobe Title Designer work area and then click the mouse to establish an anchor point.**
3. **To create a straight line, move the Pen tool to the right side of Adobe Title Designer work area and then press and hold the Shift key as you click the mouse.** Now you have two anchor points connected by a straight line.
4. **If you click again, the Pen tool will keep creating anchor points and lines.** To have the Pen tool stop creating anchors, click the Select tool. If you accidentally created an extra anchor point, you can delete it, by selecting it with the Delete Anchor Point tool.

Here's how to convert a rectangle into a diamond:

1. **Select the Rectangle tool.**
2. **Move the Rectangle to the Adobe Title Designer drawing area. Then click and drag to create a rectangle.**
3. **Notice that the Graphic Type pop-up menu is set to Rectangle, change to Closed Bézier.** The rectangle now has four anchor points at each corner.

4. Use the Pen tool to click the anchor points and drag them so that you are slowly converting the rectangle into a diamond, as shown in Figure 8-27.

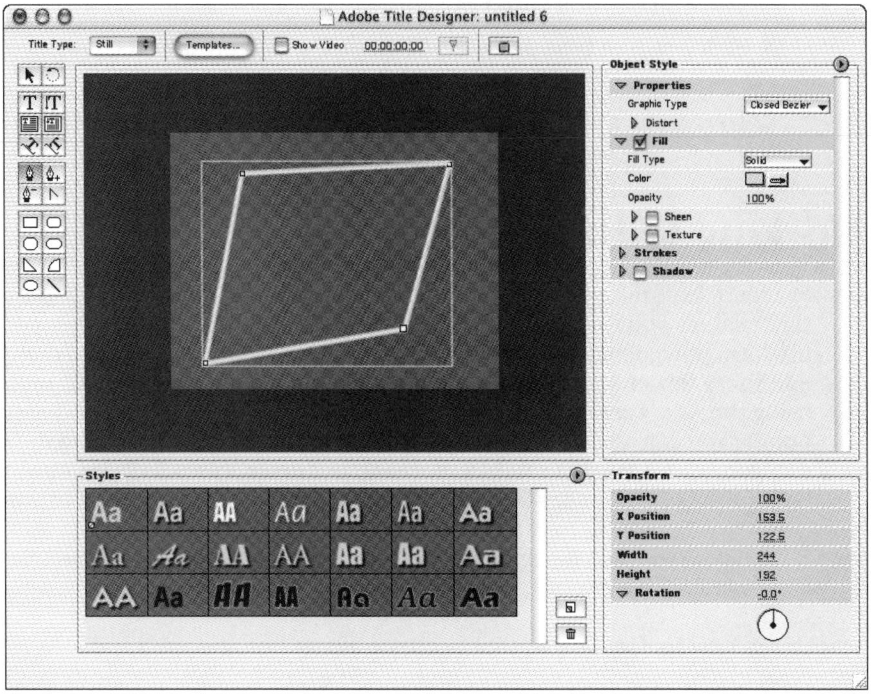

Figure 8-27: A rectangle converted to a diamond shape using the Pen tool

5. When you are done creating the diamond, you can use the Rotate tool to rotate it.

6. To fill the diamond, click the Graphic Type pop-up menu and choose Filled Beziér. Then use the Fill options to customize the fill. You can also add a shadow and strokes to the diamond using the Shadow and Stroke options.

To convert a pointed corner to a rounded corner use these steps:

1. Use the Pen tool to create four joining, small mountains (downward pointing triangles), as shown in Figure 8-28.

2. Select the Convert Anchor Point tool from the Toolbox.

3. Click and drag the anchor points with the Convert Anchor Point tool to convert a pointed corner to a rounded corner, as shown in Figure 8-28.

You can use the Add Anchor Point, Delete Anchor Point, and Pen tool to transform objects, as shown in Figure 8-29. Follow these steps to learn how to transform an object:

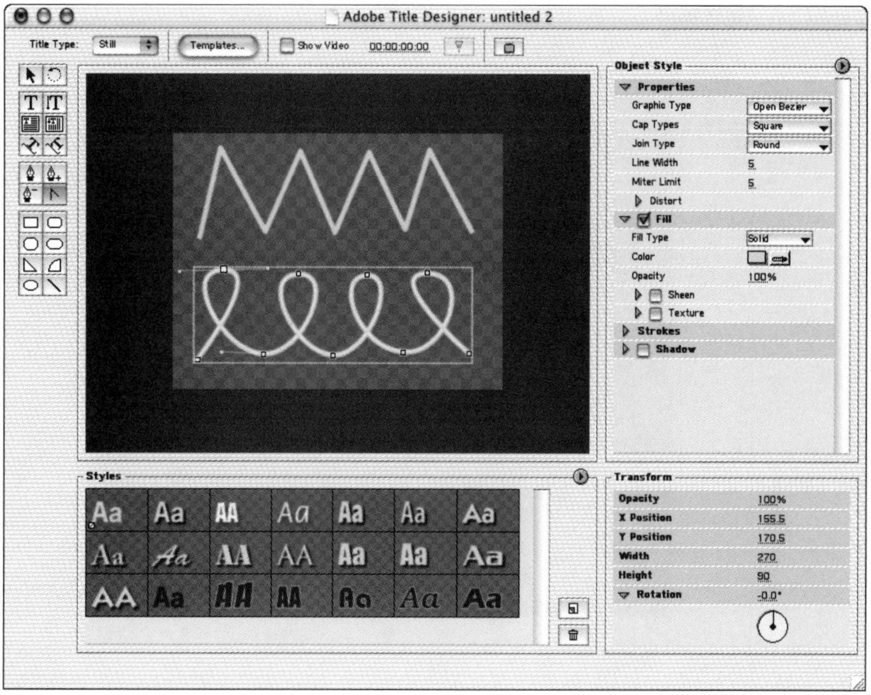

Figure 8-28: We created this path from pointed anchor points using the Pen tool and then converted to rounded anchor points using the Convert Anchor Point tool.

1. **Start by creating a square using the Rectangle tool.** As you use the Rectangle tool, press and hold the Shift to constrain the aspect ratios.
2. **To edit the object, choose Closed Bézier from the Graphic Type pop-up menu.**
3. **To turn the square into a house shape, you need to use the Add Anchor Point tool to add an anchor point in the middle of the top two anchor points.**
4. **Then use the Pen tool to drag the anchor point up, as shown in Figure 8-29.**
5. **Now use the Convert Anchor Point tool to click the new anchor point to convert it from a curve anchor point to a corner anchor point.**
6. **To convert the house shape into a triangle (shown in Figure 8-29), use the Delete Anchor Point tool to delete the two anchor points below the newly added anchor point.**
7. **To convert the triangle into a dome shape (shown in Figure 8-29), use the Convert Anchor Point tool to click and drag on the point of the triangle to convert it into a rounded anchor point.**
8. **To fill the shape, set the Graphic Type pop-up menu to Filled Bézier.** Then use the Fill, Shadow, and Stroke options to customize the fill.

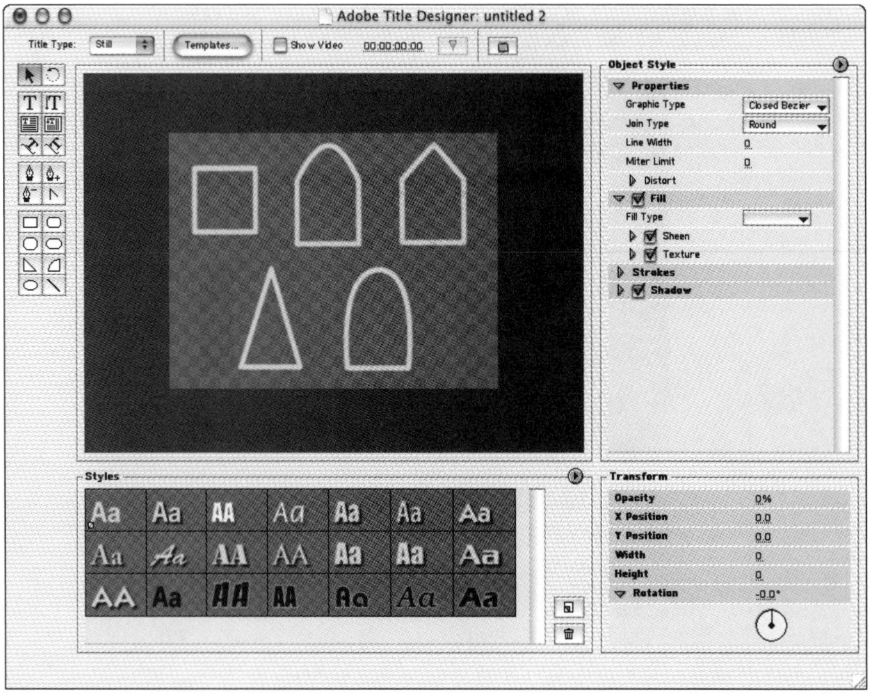

Figure 8-29: We converted a square into a house shape and then into a triangle using the Add and Delete Anchor Point tools.

To create curves with the Pen tool, follow these steps:

1. **Select the Pen tool from the Toolbox.**
2. **Move the mouse to the left side of the Adobe Title Designer window and click to establish an anchor point.** Don't release the mouse. Instead, drag straight up about half an inch (shown in Figure 8-30). Then release the mouse. The line that appears above and below the anchor point is called a directional line. The angle and direction at which the direction line is created determines the angle and direction of the curve being created. By extending the anchor point up rather than down, the first part of the curve bump will point up rather than down.
3. **Move the mouse about half an inch to the right of the anchor you created in Step 2. Then click and drag straight down about half an inch.** As you drag down, notice that a new directional line appears. Release the mouse to create a curve that has the first part of the curve bump pointing up and the last part of the curve bump pointing down. Congratulations, you've just created your first curve.
4. **If you want, you can edit the curve. Use the Pen tool to move the curve's directional lines.** As you move the directional lines, the curves shape alters.

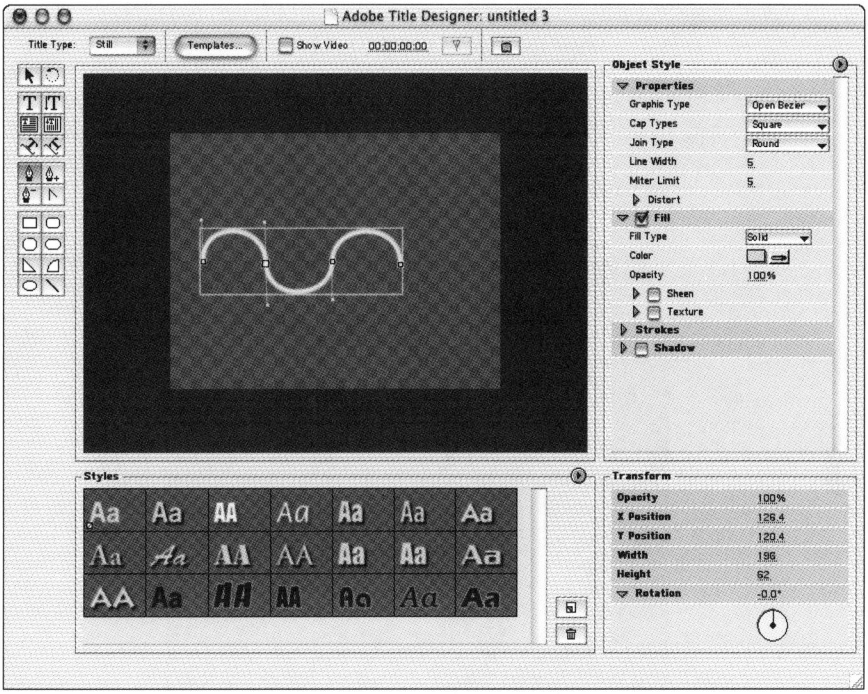

Figure 8-30: Bézier curves created with the Pen tool

5. **To continue drawing curves, move the mouse about half an inch to the right from the anchor point you created in Step 3.** Click and drag straight up about half an inch to create a curve pointing down.
6. **To draw another curve, pointing up, move the mouse about half an inch to the right from the anchor point you created in Step 4. Then click and drag straight down about half an inch.**
7. **To continue creating curves going down and up, repeat Steps 4 and 5.**

To create curves that connect to line segments, follow these steps:

1. **Select the Pen tool from the Toolbox.**
2. **Now create a curve using the Pen tool.**

   Move the mouse to the left side of the Adobe Title Designer window, click and drag straight up about half an inch. Move the mouse about half an inch to the right of the anchor you just created. Then click and drag straight down about half an inch to create a curve. If you want your curve to point down instead of up, you need to reverse the dragging part of this step. Instead of starting by clicking and dragging up, you start by clicking and dragging down, and you finish by clicking and dragging up, instead of clicking and dragging down.

3. **Connect a line to the curve, as shown in Figure 8-31.** Move the mouse over to the last anchor point you created in Step 5. Press and hold, Mac users: Option key, PC users: Alt key, and notice that a tiny diagonal line appears at the bottom of the Pen tool icon. Click the anchor point to create a corner point. To create the line segment, move the mouse pointer about half an inch to the right and click the mouse. You may need to move the directional line of the curve to adjust it.

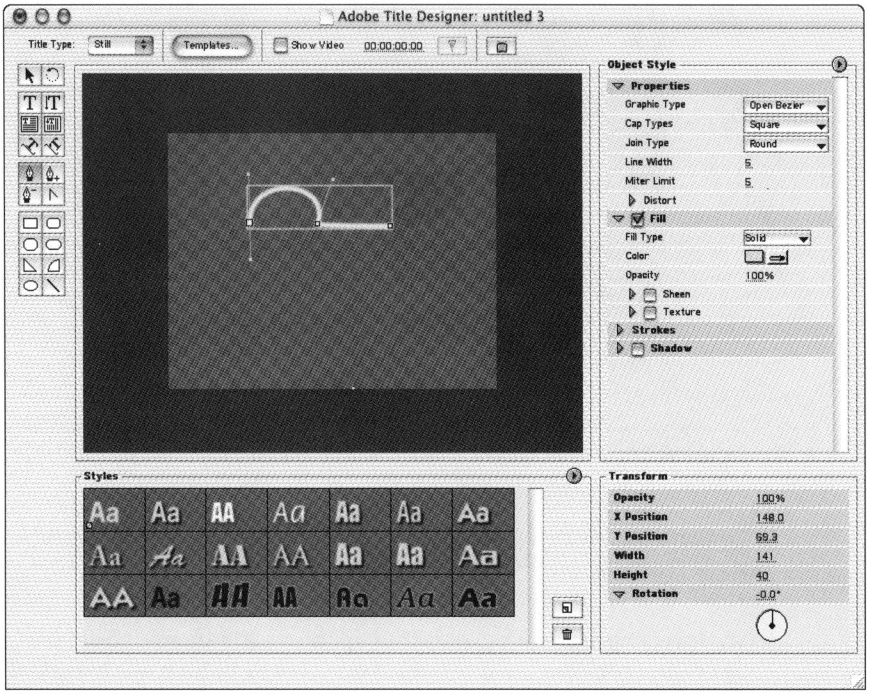

Figure 8-31: A curve connected to a line segment

To create lines that connect to curve segments, follow these steps:

1. **Click the Selection tool to deselect the curve and line segment.**
2. **Select the Pen tool so that you can create a line Bézier outline.**
3. **Use the Pen tool to create a line.** Then press and hold the Option/Alt key as you click the anchor point and drag diagonally up and to the right to establish a directional line.
4. **To connect a curve to the line you just created (shown in Figure 8-32), move the mouse straight to the right about half an inch and then click and drag down about half an inch.** The curve you created is pointing up. If you wanted the curve to point down, in Step 9, you need to make the directional line point down instead of up and then click and drag with the mouse up, instead of down.

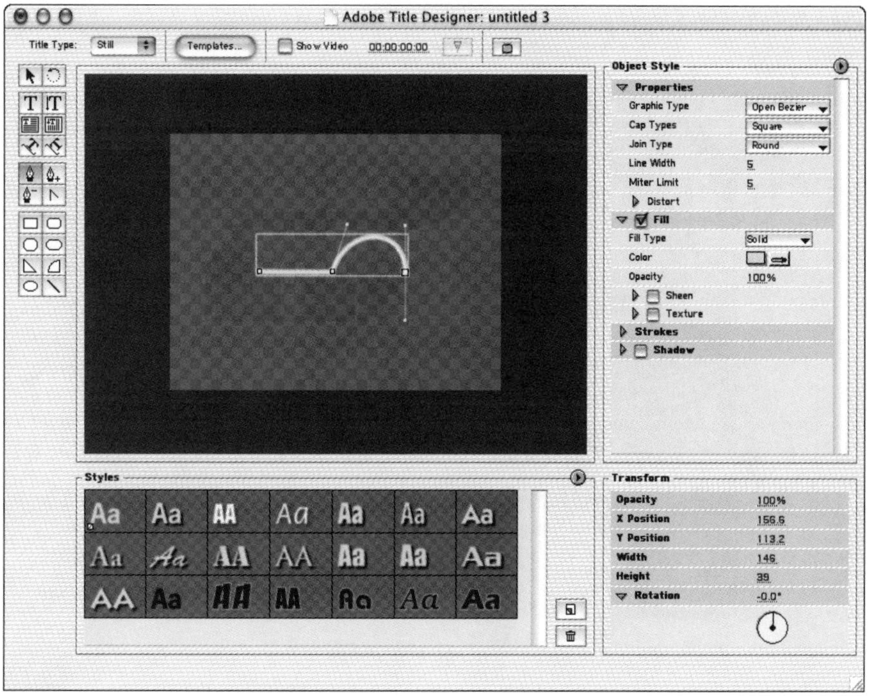

Figure 8-32: A line connected to a curve

Creating Text on a Bézier Path

To create text on a path, use the Path Type tools. To use the Path Type tool, you first need to create a path and then you can begin typing along side it. Figure 8-33 shows text along a curve path.

Here's how to use the Path Type tool:

1. **In the Adobe Title Designer window, select the Path Type tool from the Toolbox.**
2. **Use the Path Type tool to create a path.** The Path Type tool creates paths the same way as the Pen tool. To review how to use the Pen tool, go to the previous section.
3. **If you want to create a curved path and still don't feel confident in creating curves, create a path using corner anchor points.** Then use the Convert Anchor Point tool to convert the corner anchor points to curve anchor points.
4. **Use the Pen tools to make the desired path.**
5. **Switch back to the Path Type tool and start typing.**

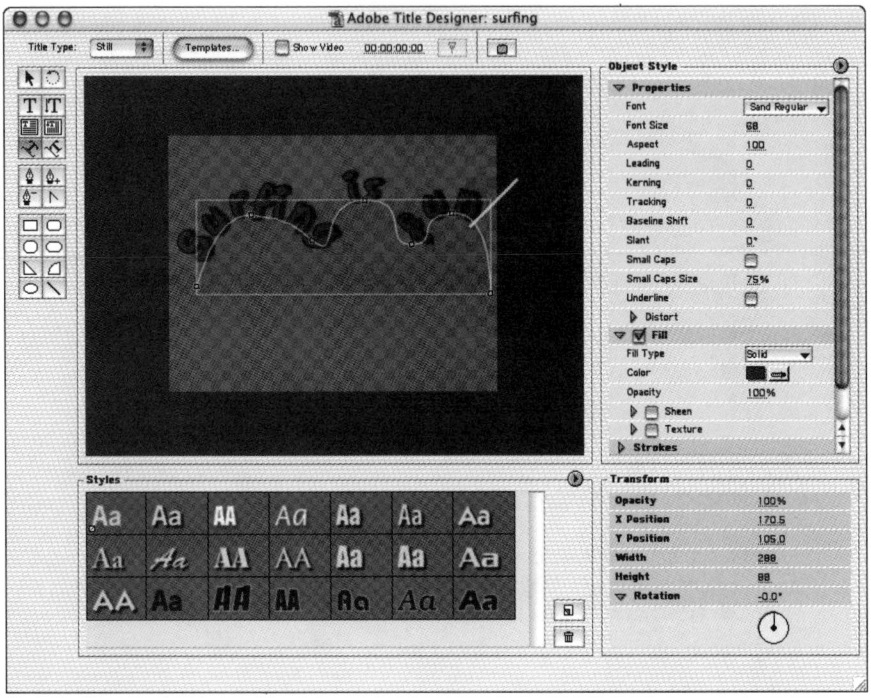

Figure 8-33: Text created along a curved path, using the Path Type tool

If you want, you can edit the text or stylize it. As you edit the text and stylize it, you may find that you need to edit the path.

Creating a Logo

Logos may appear either at the beginning of a video clip, at the end of a video clip, or throughout a video clip. You can either import a logo created from another program or create logos using the Premiere Adobe Title Designer window. Figure 8-34 shows a sample logo for a sailing school. The logo was created by using Premiere's graphic tools and by using the Type tools in the Adobe Title Designer window.

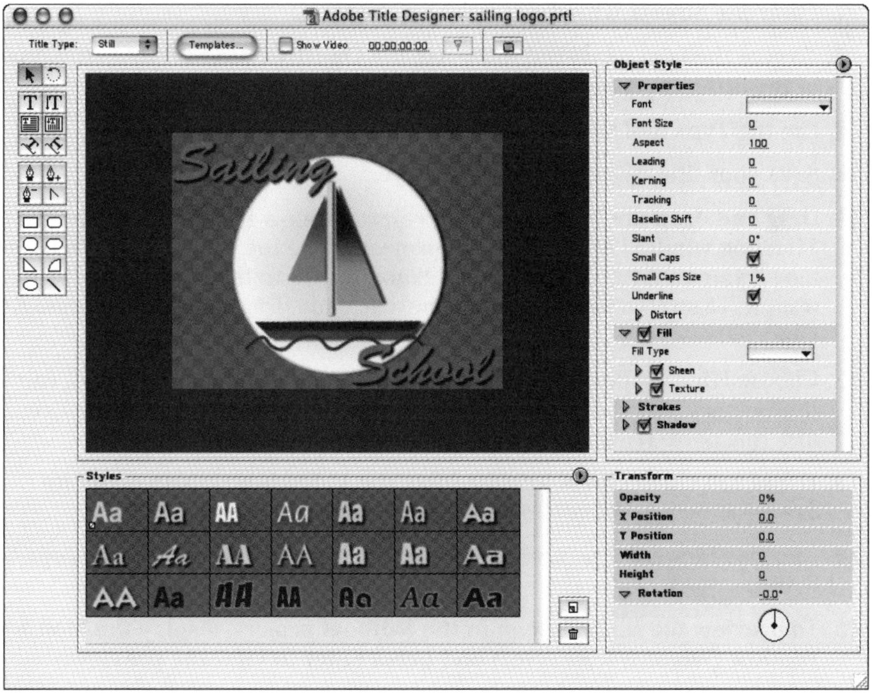

Figure 8-34: Sailboat logo created using the tools in the Adobe Title Designer window

Here's how to create the Sailboat logo shown in Figure 8-34:

1. **Choose File ⇨ New Project to create a new project using the Multimedia preset. Then choose File ⇨ New ⇨ Title to create a new title.**
2. **Use the Ellipse tool to create the circle surrounding the boat. Press Shift while clicking and dragging to create a perfect circle. Press the Option key on a Mac or the Alt key on a PC to create a circle from the center out.**
3. **Use the Rectangle tool to create the mast.**
4. **To create the sailboat shown in Figure 8-34, use the Wedge tool to create the sails.**
5. **Use the Pen tool to create the sailboat's hull.**
6. **Use the Pen tool to create small mountains (downward pointing triangles). Use the Convert Anchor Point tool to turn the mountains into waves.**

Note

Use the Title ⇨ Arrange commands to shift different shapes forward or backwards as needed. Use the Title ⇨ Position commands to horizontally and vertically center the geometric pieces.

7. **Color the objects with gradients and shadows.**
8. **To give the logo a layered look, use the Opacity field to reduce the opacity of the different shapes.**
9. **Use the Type tool to create the text. Set the attributes and color.**
10. **Save your title by choosing File ➪ Save.**
11. **Drag and drop the logo from the Project window to the Video 2 track in the Timeline window of the Sailboat project.** Move the sailboat logo to the beginning if you want it to appear there. If not, drag it to the location where you want it. To stretch the logo over time, click and drag on the right edge of the clip.
12. **Choose File ➪ Import ➪ File to import a video clip.** If you want, you can load the Sailing video clip from the Chapter 8 folder on the CD-ROM that accompanies this book. Drag the video clip to the Video 1 track.
13. **To see the video clip below the logo, the Video Key pop-up menu in Transparency Settings should be set to Alpha Channel.**
14. **Choose File ➪ Save to save the changes to the Sailboat project to your hard drive.**
15. **To preview the sailboat logo in the Sailboat project, display the Monitor window (Window ➪ Monitor) and press Enter to view the preview.**

Summary

Premiere's Adobe Title Designer window provides an easy-to-use interface for creating digital video titles. By using the Adobe Title Designer window, you can quickly create text and graphics to introduce video segments or to roll your final credits. In this chapter, you learned to do the following:

- ✦ Use the tools in the Adobe Title Designer window to create text and graphics.
- ✦ Edit object attributes by using the Title menu or the options in Object Style section.
- ✦ Drag titles from the Project window to the Timeline window.
- ✦ Create titles using styles, templates, and logos.
- ✦ Create rolling and scrolling text by using the Rolling and Crawling options.

✦ ✦ ✦

C H A P T E R 9

Creating Type and Graphic Effects

✦ ✦ ✦ ✦

In This Chapter

Using Photoshop layers to create a video clip

Using Photoshop to create text and graphics

Creating Transparency text effects

Creating Illustrator text and graphic effects for Premiere

Animating titles over graphics

✦ ✦ ✦ ✦

Adobe Premiere packs enormous power as a digital video production tool. However, if you're creating a sophisticated project, designed to appeal and impress viewers, you need to turn to other applications to create your text and graphics. During the course of production, many Premiere producers turn to such graphics applications as Adobe Photoshop and Adobe Illustrator to create eye-catching text and graphics.

This chapter provides several tutorials to teach you how to create text and graphic effects in Photoshop and Illustrator. After you see how to create the graphics effects, you integrate them into Premiere projects. After your graphics are loaded into Premiere, you use Premiere's Transparency dialog box to create some digital magic. Soon your Photoshop and Illustrator artwork appears with digital video in the background.

Creating and Importing Graphics from Adobe Photoshop

Adobe Photoshop is one of the most powerful digital imaging programs available for both PCs and Macs. Photoshop easily surpasses Premiere in its capability to create and manipulate graphics. For example, by using Photoshop you can quickly create three-dimensional text or grab a piece of text or graphics and bend, twist, or skew it. Because both Premiere and Photoshop are friendly cousins in the Adobe family of graphics products, it's not surprising that you can create graphics, text, or photomontages in Photoshop and then import them to use as titles in Premiere.

You can even use Photoshop's Web-application partner, ImageReady (free with Photoshop), to create animation for a Premiere project. For example, you can import Photoshop layers into ImageReady, create animation from the individual layers, and then export the animation as a QuickTime movie. After you've created a QuickTime movie, you can import the file into Premiere.

The following examples show two different techniques for creating animation in Photoshop. If you complete both Photoshop examples, you'll create two QuickTime movies that can be loaded into Premiere to create the Time Flies project at the end of this section.

Creating a digital movie using Adobe Photoshop and Adobe ImageReady

You can use Photoshop and ImageReady to create an animation sequence from just one digital image. Here's how:

1. **In Photoshop, choose File ➪ Open to load the digital image that you want to animate.** Load one of your own digital images or load the clock image (shown in Figure 9-1) from the CD-ROM.

   On the CD-ROM You can find the clock image in Figure 9-1 in the Time Flies folder. This folder is located in the Chapter 9 folder, inside the Tutorial Projects folder on the CD-ROM that accompanies this book.

   Note Instead of using a photograph, you can create your own graphic in Photoshop. To create your own graphic, use Photoshop's tools and colors to create an image on-screen.

   Note You may want to isolate (mask) the part of your digital image from its background before you drag and drop it into a new layer. This way, only the masked object is copied to the new file and not the background. You can use one of Photoshop's eraser tools to isolate the object from the background. If you are a Photoshop expert, you may want to use some of Photoshop's more advanced techniques.

2. **In Photoshop, choose File ➪ New to create a new file.** If your project uses square pixels, pick a resolution that matches your Premiere project, such as 320 x 240 or 640 x 480 at 72 dpi. (If you create a file whose aspect ratio does not match the aspect ratio of Premiere's project, you can prevent Premiere from distorting the image by selecting the clip in the Timeline and choosing Clip ➪ Video Options ➪ Maintain Aspect Ratio.)

   As mentioned in Chapter 3, if you are creating full-screen graphics for a digital video project (which uses nonsquare pixels), create your Photoshop file at 720 x 540. When creating the file, set the background to Transparent so that the image of the photograph remains masked.

Figure 9-1: Photoshop clock image used in Premiere animation

3. **Drag and drop the digital image into the new file you created in Step 2.** Photoshop automatically places the digital image in a new layer. If the image is too big for the file, you can scale it down by choosing Edit ➪ Transform ➪ Scale. Press Shift as you click and drag on one of the handles. By pressing Shift, the image retains its proportions.

4. **If Photoshop's Layer palette is not on-screen, open it by choosing Window ➪ Show Layers.** The digital image layer should be selected and at the top of the palette.

5. **Duplicate the layer with the photograph in it by choosing Duplicate from the Layers palette pull-down menu or by clicking the digital image layer and drag it over the New Layer icon in the Layers palette.** (The New Layer icon is to the left of the Trash icon.) Duplicate the photograph layer from 15 to 30 times (see Figure 9-2). Each layer represents a frame in Premiere. As you duplicate the image, you may want to stylize the image by applying one of the Layer ➪ Layer Style commands, such as Bevel and Emboss.

Caution

Remember that the more layers in an image, the larger the file. Make sure that your computer has enough RAM and hard drive space to handle all the layers you create.

6. **After you've duplicated the image in at least 15 layers (frames), activate each layer and use either the Move tool (the tool at the top right of the Toolbox) to gradually move the image or use the Edit ➪ Transform command to scale, rotate, skew, flip, distort, or change the perspective of your image in every layer.**

You can use the Move tool to gradually move the photograph across the frame. The photograph at the bottom of the Layers palette could start at the bottom-left side of the screen, and the photograph in the top layer could end at the top-right side of the screen. If desired, instead of using a Transform command, you can apply a special effects filter, such as Twirl or ZigZag to the image in a specific layer. Be careful not to make any drastic changes from one layer to another, or your animation may look somewhat bizarre.

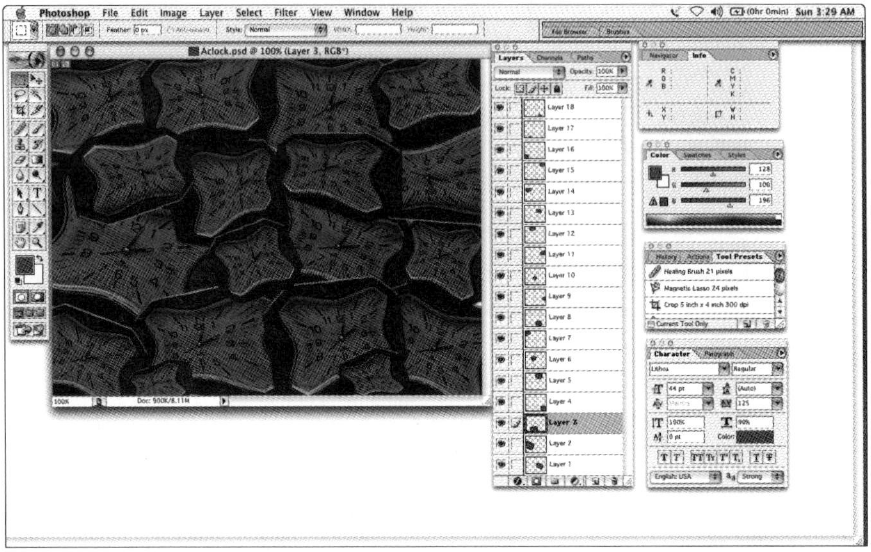

Figure 9-2: Each clock in the Layers palette eventually becomes a frame in Premiere.

Now you're ready to transform your Photoshop layers into a digital movie.

1. **Save the file in Photoshop and then choose File ➪ Jump to Adobe ImageReady.** This opens ImageReady and automatically loads the Photoshop file into ImageReady.

Note

You may not have enough memory to have both Photoshop and ImageReady open at the same time. If not, first save your work and quit Photoshop. Next, load ImageReady and choose File ➪ Open to load the clock sequence file.

2. **Open the Animation palette by choosing Window ➪ Show Animation.** To create the frames, choose Make Frames from Layers, from the Animation palette window. After you execute the command, ImageReady creates a frame with each Photoshop layer in it, as seen in Figure 9-3.

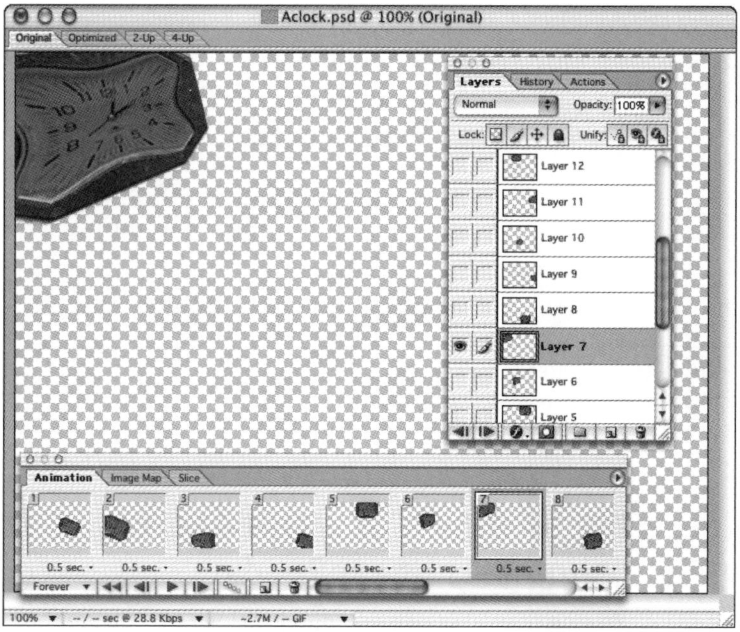

Figure 9-3: ImageReady converts the Photoshop layers into animation frames.

3. **To set a delay between frames, click Sec. at the bottom of the frame you want to change, then choose a frame delay.**

4. **Click the Play button in the Animation palette to preview the animation.**

Note

If you want to create a background video track in Premiere and the transparency of the layer is preserved, create a blue or green background for your animation. Then in Premiere, use a blue screen or green screen transparency setting in the Transparency Settings dialog box to make the background transparent.

Cross-Reference

For more information on using a blue or green screen, turn to Chapter 12.

5. **In ImageReady, choose File ⇨ Export Original to export the file as a digital movie.** In the Export Original dialog box, choose QuickTime movie from the Format pop-up menu. Name your file, locate a place to save your file, and then click Save.

6. **In the Compression Settings dialog box, (shown in Figure 9-4), choose a compression.** To save each frame with no compression, choose the Animation settings and then set the slider to Best. If you're working with digital video, you may also want to choose Apple DV-NTSC, so that the compression setting matches that of your project. Click OK to make a movie.

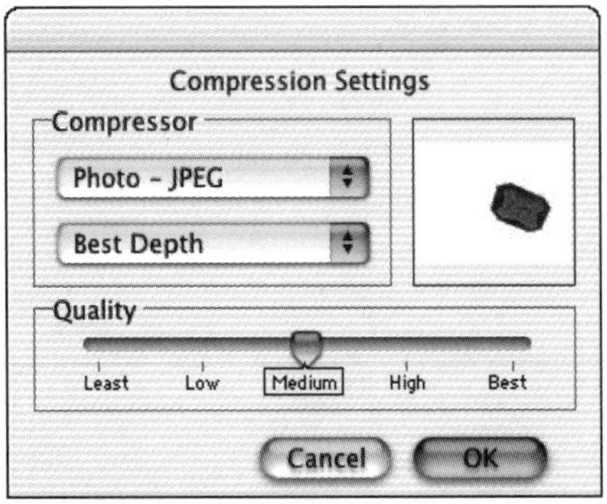

Figure 9-4: ImageReady's Compression Settings dialog box allows you to choose a compression option.

Creating a digital movie of warped text using Photoshop and ImageReady

This example illustrates how to create animated warped text, using the Photoshop warped text feature, new to Version 6.0.

1. **In Photoshop, choose File ⇨ New.** You should set the pixel resolution to the same size as you did to create the previous sequence, the Mode to RGB Color, and the Content to Transparent.
2. **Click the Type tool in the Toolbox.** Using the Horizontal Type tool, create some text and then choose a font and size (we used the font Sand) either by using the Character palette or by using the options at the Type palette. You can also change the color by using either the Colors palette or Swatches palette.
3. **Duplicate the text layer a few times.**
4. **Click one of the text layers in the Layers palette and then click the Warp button in the Type palette.** In the Warp Text dialog box, shown in Figure 9-5, pick a warp option to warp the text. Then click OK to close the dialog box and apply the effect.
5. **Edit the text in the other layers, using the Warp text dialog box.**
6. **Now use the Type tool with the vertical type button selected in the Type Options bar (Photoshop 6.0 or later) to create some vertical type.** After creating the type, make sure that you click the OK (checkmark) icon in the Type tool options bar. Again, duplicate the type layer and apply the Warp button to it.
7. **Choose File ⇨ Save to save the file in Photoshop format.**
8. **Chose File ⇨ Jump to ImageReady to load the type file into ImageReady.** Figure 9-6 shows the Photoshop time flies warped text file with its layers.

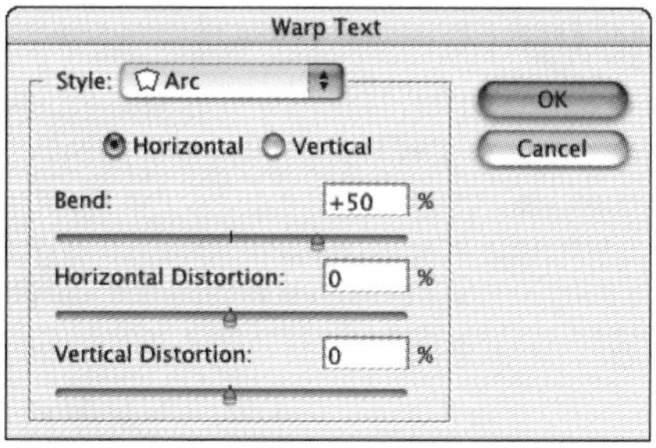

Figure 9-5: Photoshop's Warp Text dialog box

Figure 9-6: Photoshop time flies warped text with its layers

9. **In ImageReady, choose Make Frames from Layers from the Animation palette menu.**
10. **To set a delay between frames, click Sec. at the bottom of the frame you want to change and then choose a frame delay.**
11. **Click the Play button in the Animation palette to preview the animation.**
12. **To save the file, choose File ⇨ Export Original.** In the Export Original dialog box, choose QuickTime movie from the Format pop-up menu. Name your file, locate a place to save your file, and then click Save.

    Now choose a compression setting in the Compression dialog box. To save each frame with no compression, choose the Animation settings and then set the slider to Best or leave the default settings and click OK.

Creating the Time Flies project

Now that you've created QuickTime movies in both Photoshop and ImageReady, you can load the files into Premiere to create a project. Figure 9-7 shows frames from a Premiere project (Time Flies) that was created using Adobe Photoshop and ImageReady. In the Time Flies project, we imported the files that were originally created in Photoshop as a QuickTime movie created from animated clocks and the QuickTime movie of warped text.

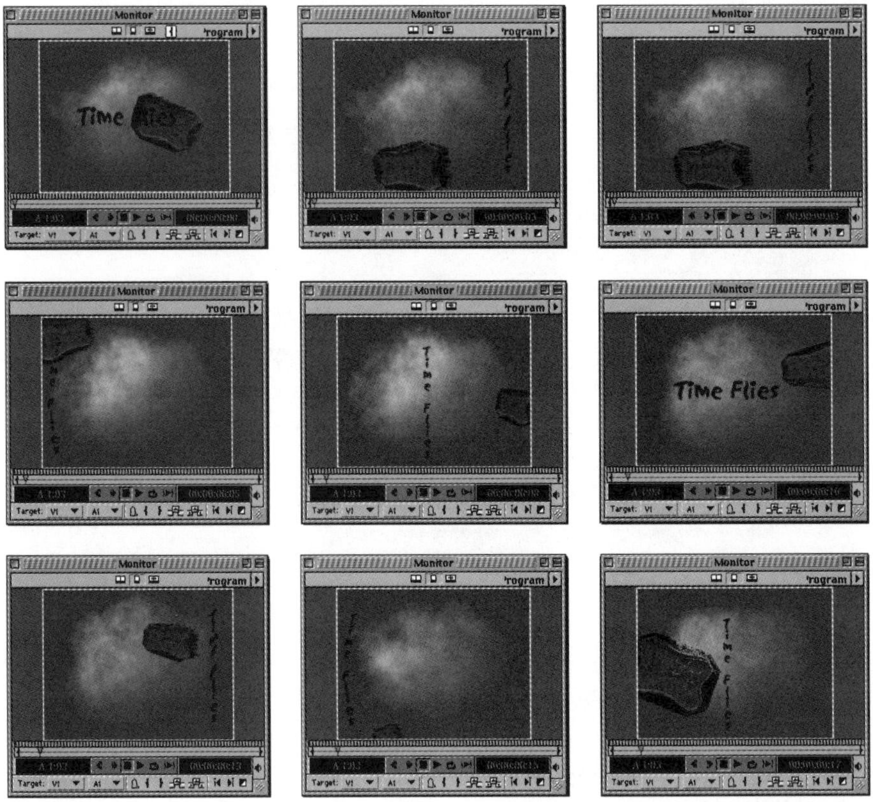

Figure 9-7: Premiere project created using Adobe Photoshop and ImageReady

Here's how to create the Time Flies project:

1. **Choose File ⇨ New to create a new project in Premiere.** Make the project size the same size as the animated sequences you just created.
2. **Now import the clips you just created into your project by choosing File ⇨ Import ⇨ File.** Make sure that you import the QuickTime movies, not the Photoshop graphic files.

On the CD-ROM

The clock sequence movie and the Time Flies sequence movie are located in the Time Flies folder, which is in the Chapter 9 folder, inside the Tutorial Projects folder on the CD-ROM that accompanies this book.

3. **Drag and drop the background QuickTime movie (the clock sequence movie) to Video 2 track.** (If the aspect ratio of the clip does not match your project, select the Clip and then choose Clip ➪ Video Options ➪ Maintain Aspect Ratio.)

4. **Create a new video track by choosing Add Track from the Timeline window menu.** Drag and drop the text QuickTime movie to the new video track (Track 3). (If the aspect ratio of the clip does not match your project, select the Clip, and then choose Clip ➪ Video Options ➪ Maintain Aspect Ratio.)

5. **Choose File ➪ New ➪ Color Matte to create a new matte.** Pick a sky blue color. Save the matte. Then drag it from the Project window to Video 1 track in the Timeline window.

6. **To animate the background matte, open the Video Effects palette.** Open the QuickTime Effects folder. Drag and Drop the QuickTime video effect to Video 1 track. In the QuickTime Effects dialog box, shown in Figure 9-8, choose Cloud.

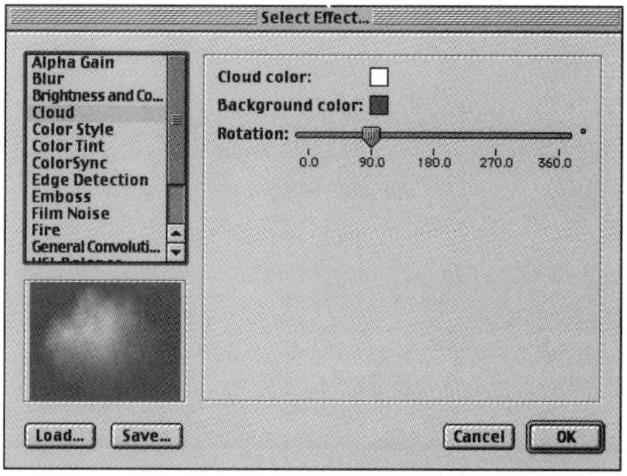

Figure 9-8: The QuickTime Effects video effect enables you to turn a blue matte into an animated cloud sequence.

7. **Select the background QuickTime movie (the clock sequence) and then choose Clip ➪ Video Options ➪ Transparency.** In the Transparency Settings dialog box, choose Chroma. Then click OK. Figure 9-9 shows the Transparency Settings dialog box with the Chroma Key Type option.

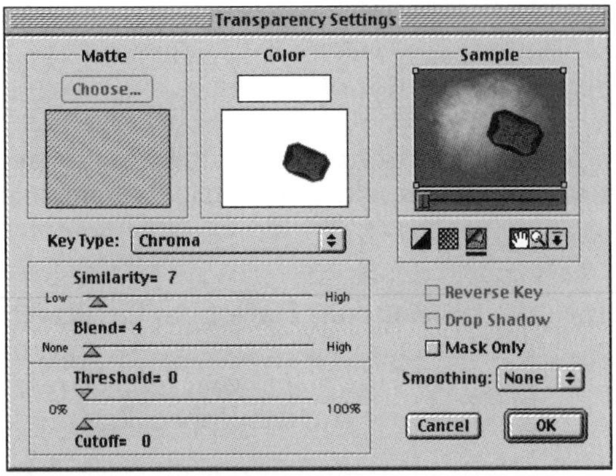

Figure 9-9: A clock over the clouds background in the Transparency Settings dialog box with the Chroma Key Type option selected

8. **Select the warped text movie and then choose Clip ➪ Video Options ➪ Transparency.** In the Transparency Settings dialog box, choose Multiple and then click OK. Figure 9-10 shows the Transparency Settings dialog box with the Multiply Key Type option.

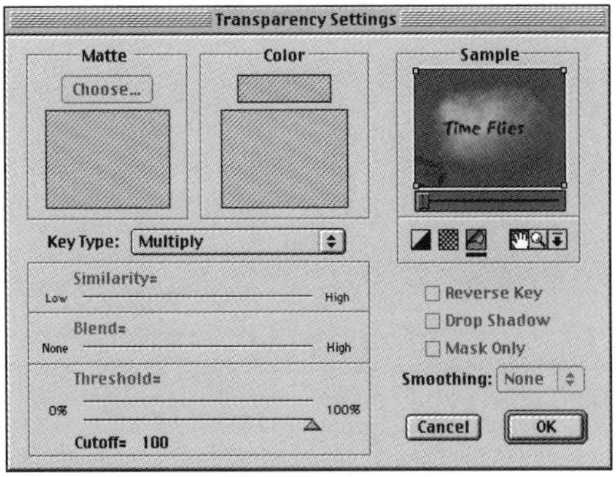

Figure 9-10: The warped text is seen over the tracks below it in the Transparency Settings dialog box when the Multiply Key Type option is selected.

9. **To see the effect, create a preview by choosing Timeline ➪ Preview or press Enter.** When the Preview runs, you see the warped text and the transformed clocks with transparent backgrounds, both against a background of clouds.

Creating Semitransparent Text

In Chapter 8, you created different title effects using Premiere's Title window. Although the Title window provides many features for creating text effects, it can't compare with the text manipulation tools, stylizes, and filters that are available in Adobe Photoshop. In this section, you use Photoshop's Layer Styles to create a beveled text effect. You create an alpha channel out of the beveled text. When the text is loaded into Photoshop, the type appears semitransparent, allowing part of the background image to show through the highlighted areas of the text. To create color for the text in Premiere, you use Premiere's Color matte command.

Creating beveled text in Photoshop

Here are the steps to create the beveled text effect shown in Figure 9-11. If you're an experienced Photoshop user, feel free to vary any of the Photoshop effects.

Figure 9-11: Beveled text created in Photoshop

1. **In Photoshop, create a new file that matches the pixel dimensions of your Premiere project.** For multimedia choose 320 x 240; for NTSC-DV choose 720 x 540; for PAL-DV, choose 768 x 576 (Premiere scales the images down without distortion when the images are imported.)
2. **Using Photoshop's Type tool, create your title text.** We typed the word Zoo at 100 points. If you want to enlarge or stretch the text, choose Edit ⇨ Free Transform and manually scale the text.
3. **Apply a beveled look to the text by choosing Layer ⇨ Layer Style ⇨ Bevel and Emboss.**
4. **In the Layer Style dialog box shown in Figure 9-12, choose the Inner Bevel from the Style menu and then use the dialog box controls to fine-tune the effect.** In the Technique pop-up menu, choose Chisel Soft and then edit the Gloss Contour.

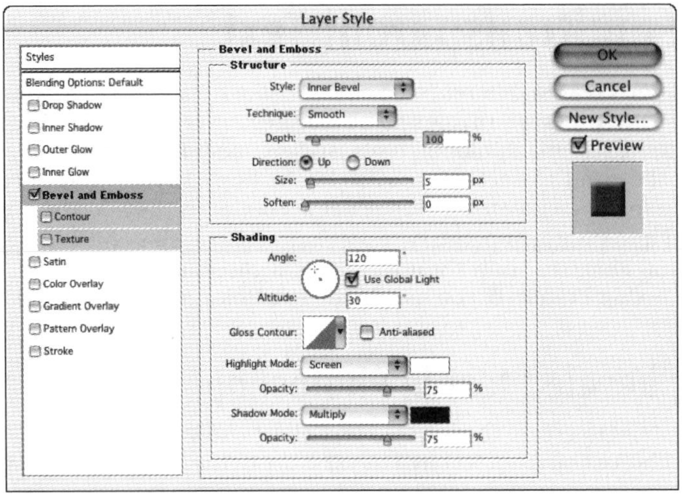

Figure 9-12: Photoshop's Layer Style dialog box is used to bevel and emboss the word Zoo.

5. **After you've finished the effect, flatten the file by choosing Layer ➪ Flatten Image.**

6. **Now you need to create an alpha channel from the text (Premiere uses the alpha channel to create the transparency effect).** To quickly create an alpha channel, convert the image to Lab color mode and then duplicate the lightness channel. To convert to Lab mode, choose Image ➪ Mode ➪ Lab. The Lightness channel is essentially a grayscale version of the RGB color image. To turn it into an alpha channel, simply drag the Lightness channel over the new channel icon in the Layers palette. After the alpha channel appears, convert the image back to RGB by choosing Image Mode ➪ RGB Color (if you don't do this, Premiere is not able to read the file).

7. **Because Premiere reads the white area of an alpha channel as the image portion of the matte, reverse the alpha channel in Photoshop by double-clicking the channel in Photoshop's Channels palette.** When the Channel Options dialog box appears, choose Masked area in the Color Indicates section. Click OK to close the dialog box.

8. **Save your file in Photoshop format.**

Creating the Zoo project

Now that you've created the text in Photoshop, you're ready to import the text into Premiere and create the Zoo project. Figure 9-13 shows frames from the Zoo project.

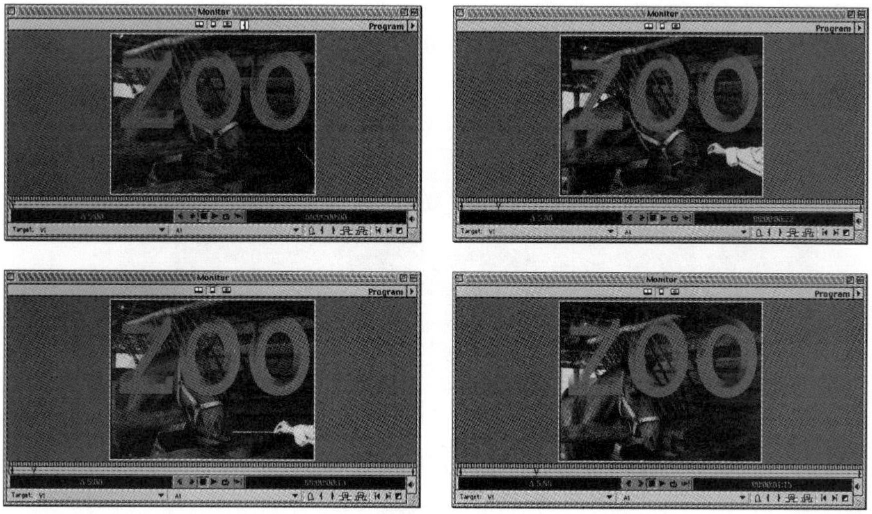

Figure 9-13: Frames from the Zoo project

1. **Choose File ⇨ New Project to create a new project in Adobe Premiere. For practice purposes use the Multimedia preset.**
2. **In Premiere, choose File ⇨ New Color Matte to create a color for the text.** After the Color Picker dialog box opens, select a color. Click OK to close the Color Picker. Then name the color matte in the Color Matte dialog box.
3. **Drag the color matte from the Project window to Video 1 Track.** Click and drag to extend the length of the graphic in the Timeline to your desired duration.
4. **Choose File ⇨ Import ⇨ File to import a clip that you want to use behind the Photoshop text graphic file.**
5. **Choose File ⇨ Import ⇨ File to import the Photoshop text graphic file you want to use.**

On the CD-ROM

To load the Horse video clip and the Zoo text file (shown in Figure 9-12), choose File ⇨ Import ⇨ Folder. Then locate the Zoo folder that is in the Chapter 9 folder, inside the Tutorial Projects folder, that is on the CD-ROM that accompanies this book.

6. **Drag the background video clip from the Project window to Video 2 Track.**
7. **Create a new track for the text by choosing Add Video Track from the Timeline window menu.**

8. **Drag the Text clip from the project palette to Video 3 Track.** Figure 9-14 shows the Timeline and Project windows for the Zoo project.

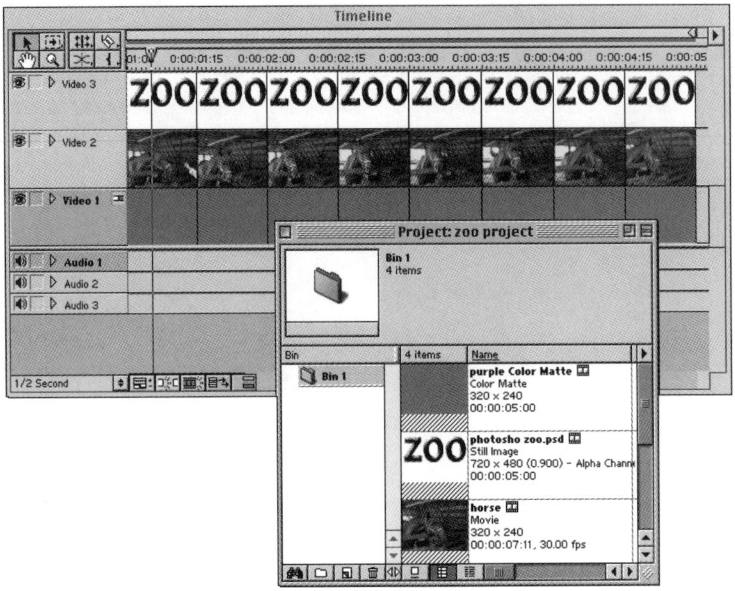

Figure 9-14: The Timeline and Project windows for the Zoo project

9. **Now create the transparency effect that allows you to see the background clip through the gray areas and light areas of the text.** Select the Animal track and then choose Clip ➪ Video Options ➪ Transparency. In the Transparency options palette, choose Track Matte in the Transparency pop-up menu.
10. **Preview the effect by choosing Timeline ➪ Preview or by pressing Enter.**
11. **If you want to add motion to the text, make sure that it is selected and then choose Clip ➪ Video Motion.** Simply click OK in the dialog box to have the text move across the screen. For more information about using the Motion Settings dialog box, see Chapter 14.

Using Video Effects to Animate Adobe Illustrator Type and Graphics

Adobe Illustrator is known as a powerful digital drawing tool. By using Adobe Illustrator, you can create precision drawings and type effects. After creating graphics in Illustrator, you can apply Effects and Filters. You can also import them into Premiere. (You can also import the graphics into Photoshop first, to apply more filters and from there, into Premiere.) This project (Hurricane Season) shows you how to create text on a curve in Adobe Illustrator and then use the Text in a Premiere project with Video effects. The Timeline for the Hurricane Season is shown in Figure 9-15. The Illustrator text is in Video 2 track and the Illustrator graphic is in Video 1 track.

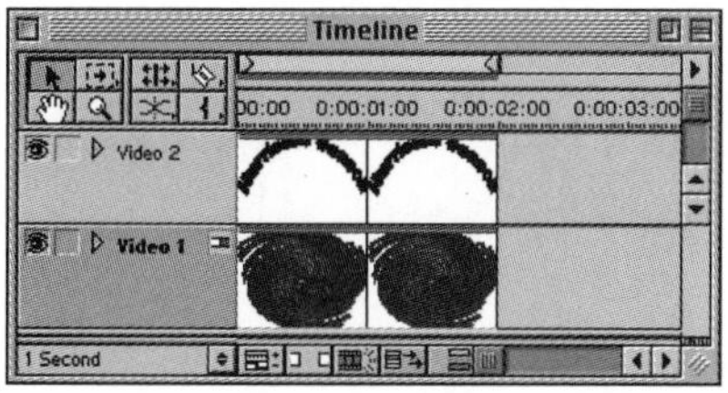

Figure 9-15: Hurricane Season Timeline window

Creating curved text in Adobe Illustrator

Figure 9-16 shows type created on a curved path in Adobe Illustrator. We imported this illustration, along with a graphic created in Illustrator (shown in Figure 9-16), into Adobe Premiere to create the Hurricane Season project. We created the distorted spiral graphic (shown in Figure 9-17) by applying filters to a spiral. This graphic was used as the background video track in the Hurricane Season project.

Figure 9-16: Curved text created in Adobe Illustrator

Figure 9-17: Graphic created in Adobe Illustrator

Here's how to create text on a curve by using Adobe Illustrator:

1. **Create a new file in Adobe Illustrator by choosing File ➪ New.**
2. **In Adobe Illustrator, use the Pen tool or the Freeform tool to create a curved path.**
3. **Use the Path Type tool to type on the curved path.**
4. **Click the Path Type tool in the Toolbox.**
5. **Drag the Path Type tool to the far-left side of the curved path that you created and then click.**
6. **When the blinking cursor appears, start typing.**
7. **After you've finished typing, select the text by clicking and dragging over it with the mouse and then choose a font and size from the Font menu.**
8. **Choose File ➪ Save to save the file.**

Creating a graphic in Adobe Illustrator

Here's how to create the distorted spiral in Illustrator used as the background to create the Hurricane Season project:

1. **Pick a Foreground and Background color.**
2. **Click the Star tool in the Toolbox.**
3. **Create a Star using the Star tool.** (Mac users: Option+click; PC users: Alt+click.) In the Star dialog box, increase the number of sides that the star has. Click OK to close the dialog box and to make a star. Feel free to experiment using various numbers of sides to your star.
4. **Distort the star by using the ZigZag and Twirl filters in the Distort submenu.** Experiment with the setting in the dialog box for the desired effect.
5. **Save the file in Illustrator format.**

Creating the Hurricane Season project

In creating this project, we used the Premiere Video Effects palette to apply the Bend effect to the background and the Strobe effect to the text. Figure 9-18 shows a few frames from the Hurricane Season project.

Figure 9-18: Frames from the Hurricane Season project

You can create still images in other programs and then import them and animate them using Premiere's Video Effects.

Here's how to animate Adobe Illustrator text and graphics using Adobe Premiere:

1. **Choose File ➪ New Project to create a new project.**
2. **Choose File ➪ Import ➪ File to import the text and background graphic (created previously).** If you don't have Adobe Illustrator, you can import these two graphics from the *Adobe Premiere 6.5 Bible* CD-ROM. They are located in the Hurricane folder, found in Chapter 9.

On the CD-ROM

To load the Hurricane text and graphic files (shown in Figure 9-17), choose File ➪ Import ➪ Folder. Then locate the Hurricane folder that is in the Chapter 9 folder in the Tutorial Projects folder on the CD-ROM that accompanies this book.

3. **Drag the (Hurricane) text to Video 2 track and the (hurricane) background graphic to Video 1 track.**

Note

If the aspect ratio of your graphics does not match the aspect ratio of your Premiere project, select the graphic clips, and then choose Clip ➪ Video Options ➪ Maintain Aspect Ratio.

4. **Click the type graphic icon in Video 2 track to select it.**
5. **To see the background behind the text, you must set Transparency options for the Text track. Select the text in the Timeline.**

   With the Text track selected, choose Clip ➪ Video Options ➪ Transparency. Select the Alpha Channel Key Type option in the Transparency pop-up menu, as shown in Figure 9-19. Click OK to close the Transparency Settings dialog box.

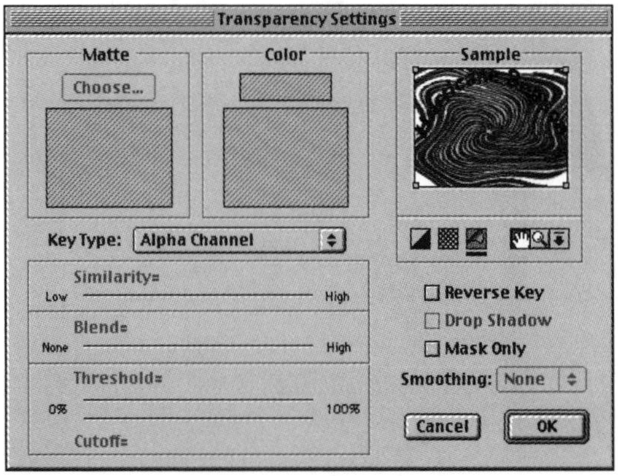

Figure 9-19: Premiere's Transparency Settings dialog box shows the background behind the text.

6. **Display the Video Effects palette by choosing Window ⇨ Show Video Effects.** The Video palette has 14 folders. Inside each folder are many effects. For more information on using the effects in the Video palette, turn to Chapter 12.
7. **Double-click the Stylize folder in the Video palette to open it.**
8. **Click a Strobe Light video effect and drag it over the icon representation in Video 2 track.**
9. **Click the background graphic icon in Video 1 track to select it.** In our example, we used the distorted spiral.
10. **Double-click the Distort folder in the Video palette to open it.**
11. **Click a Bend video effect and drag it over the icon representation in Video 1 track.** In the Bend Settings dialog box (shown in Figure 9-20), select the options you want for the pop-up menus and sliders.

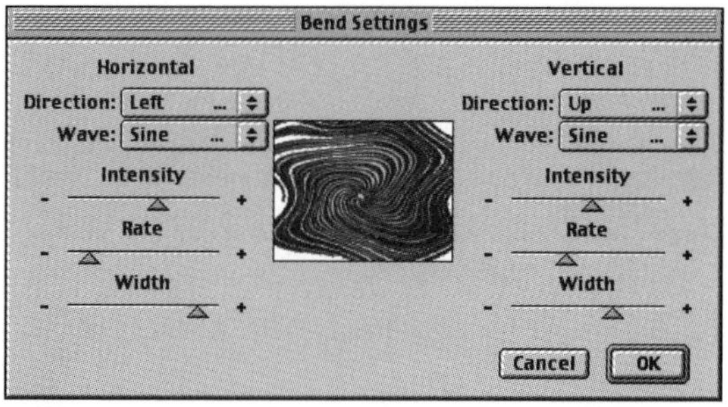

Figure 9-20: A preview of the Bend effect (Bend Settings dialog box) on the distorted graphic

12. **Choose File ⇨ Save to save the project.**
13. **Choose Timeline ⇨ Preview or press Enter to preview the Hurricane Season project.**

Animating Titles over Graphics by Using Motion and Reverse Alpha Channel Key

You can manipulate text within a video track in order to make a background (that is in a video track below the text video track) appear within the text. You can then make the text move over the same background graphic.

This effect is seen in the frames from the Mosaic project, in Figure 9-21. To create the moving text, we applied motion and a Reverse Alpha Channel key to the word Mosaic. We created the mosaic text (shown in Figure 9-22) in Adobe Illustrator. The mosaic background (shown in Figure 9-23) was created using Corel Painter.

Figure 9-21: Frames from the Mosaic project

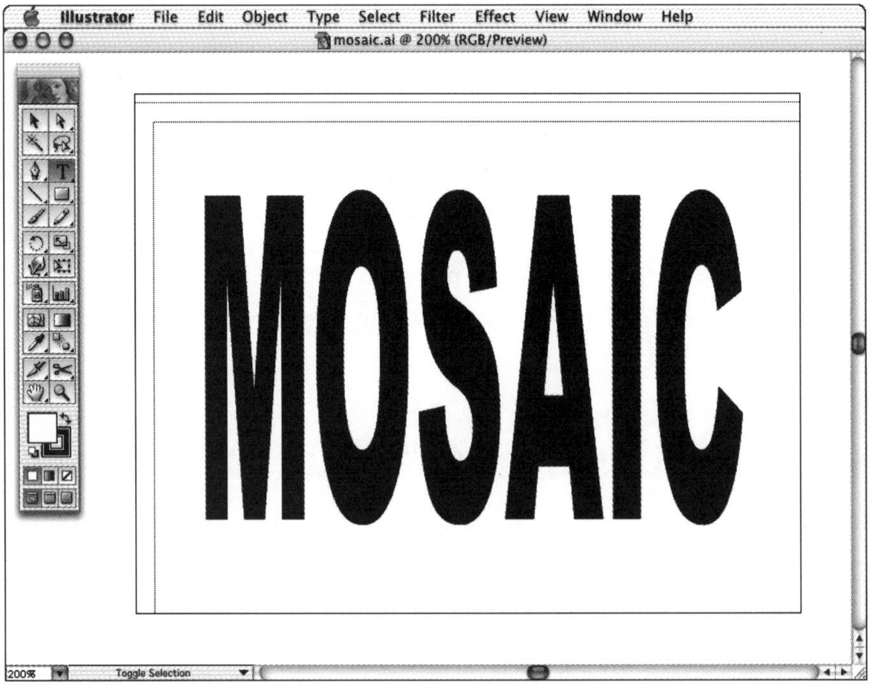

Figure 9-22: Mosaic text created using Adobe Illustrator

Figure 9-23: Mosaic background created using Corel Painter

Here's how to animate using motion and a reverse alpha channel:

1. **Create a new project in Premiere.**
2. **Choose File ➪ Import ➪ File to import a text graphic and background video clip.** You can create text using Premiere's Title Designer window or Adobe Illustrator, Adobe Photoshop, or Corel Painter. To create a background, use either Adobe Photoshop or Corel Painter.

On the CD-ROM

To load the Mosaic text and background files (shown in Figure 9-20), choose File ➪ Import ➪ Folder. Then locate the Mosaic folder that is in the Chapter 9 folder inside the Tutorial Projects folder on the CD-ROM that accompanies this book.

3. **When the text and background files have been imported, they appear in the Project window.** Click the text file and drag it to Video 2 track, so that the text file covers at least two frames. Then click and drag the text file in the Project palette to Video 2 track, next to the text frames that you just placed in Video 2 track.
4. **Click the background file and drag it to Video 1 Track.** The background file should extend over the entire text area.
5. **Choose Add Video Track from the Timeline pop-up menu.** Video 3 Track appears.
6. **Click and drag the background file from the Project palette to Video 3 Track in the Timeline window.** Again, the background file appears over the same extended text area. Figure 9-24 shows the Timeline and Project windows used to create the Mosaic project.

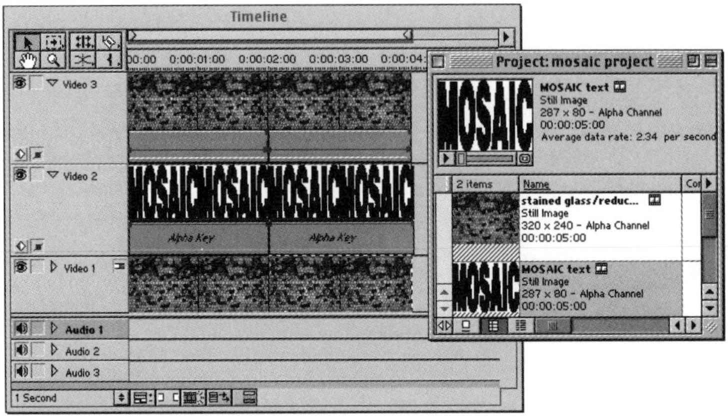

Figure 9-24: The Timeline and Project windows used to create the Mosaic project

7. **Click the first two text icon frames in Video 2 Track and then choose Clip ➪ Video Options ➪ Transparency.** In the Transparency Settings dialog box, the Key Type should be set to Alpha Channel. Click the Reverse Key option to select it. When you select the Reverse Key option, the background now appears in the text. Figure 9-25 shows the Transparency Settings option with the Reverse Key option selected.

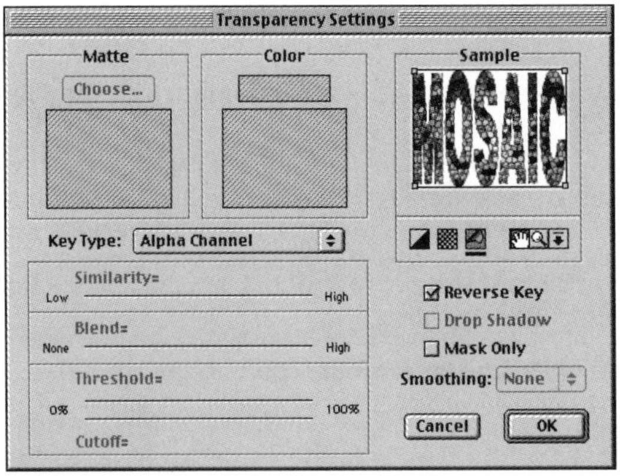

Figure 9-25: The Transparency Settings dialog box with the Reverse Key option selected

8. **Click the last two text icon frames in Video 2 track and then choose Clip ➪ Video Options ➪ Transparency.** Make sure that the Key Type is set to Alpha Channel and the Reverse Key option is selected.

9. **Click the first two text icon frames in Video 2 track and then choose Clip ⇨ Video Options ⇨ Motion to apply motion to the first two text frames.** When the Motion Settings dialog box appears (Figure 9-26), click OK to have the motion move from left to right.

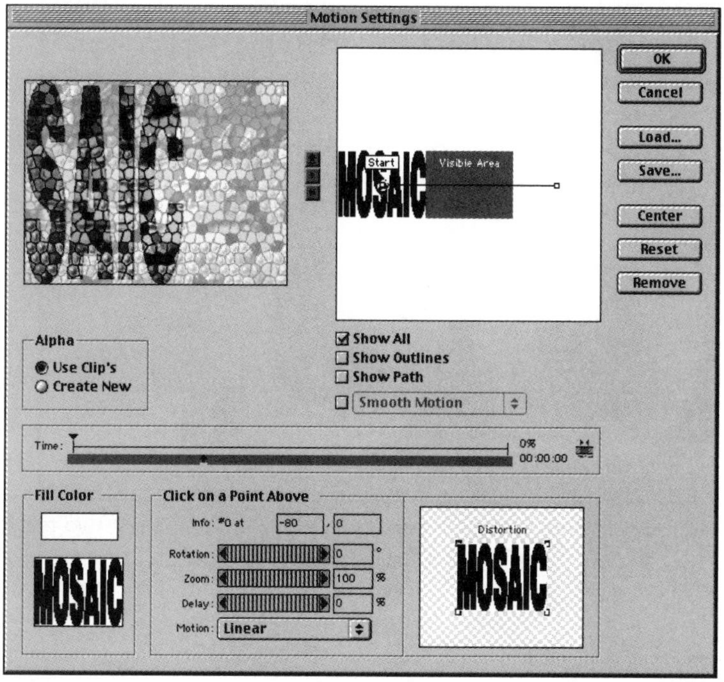

Figure 9-26: Motion is applied from left to right in the first two text frames.

10. **Click the last two text icon frames in Video 2 track and then choose Clip ⇨ Video Options ⇨ Motion to apply motion to the last two text frames.** When the Motion Settings dialog box appears, move the motion path so that it goes from top to bottom as shown in Figure 9-27.
11. **Click OK to have the motion path move from top to bottom.**
12. **Click the background icon in Video 3 track to fade the background, as shown in the Mosaic project.** Then click the Collapse/Expand track icon to expand the track. Make sure that the Opacity Rubberband icon is displayed. Then drag downward to fade the background.
13. **Save your work and then preview the project by choosing Timeline ⇨ Preview or by pressing Enter.** When the preview rolls, you should see the background graphic within the typed letters.

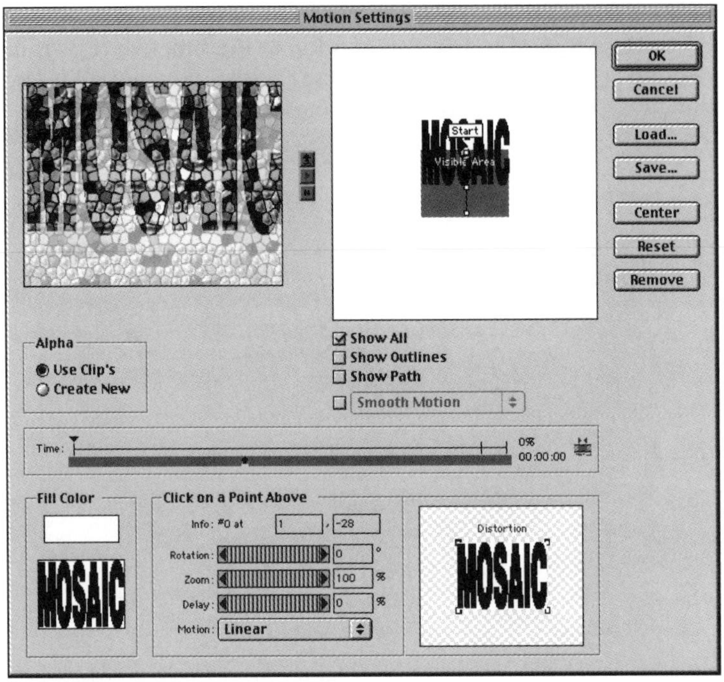

Figure 9-27: Motion is applied from top to bottom for the last two text frames.

Summary

To create the most attractive and elaborate text and graphics effects, you may need to use the digital power of such programs as Adobe Photoshop, Adobe Illustrator, or Corel Painter in conjunction with Premiere.

✦ Both Photoshop and Illustrator provide excellent text features that can be used in conjunction with Premiere.

✦ Premiere successfully interprets Photoshop transparency and alpha channels.

✦ Background transparent areas in Illustrator are automatically read as alpha channel masks in Premiere.

✦ You can create a variety of different transparency effects using Premiere and Photoshop or Illustrator.

✦ ✦ ✦

Advanced Techniques and Special Effects

P A R T

IV

✦ ✦ ✦ ✦

In This Part

✦ ✦ ✦ ✦

CHAPTER 10

Advanced Editing Techniques

✦ ✦ ✦ ✦

In This Chapter

Editing utilities

Using the Razor and Multiple Razor tools

Using paste commands

Performing ripple and rolling edits

Using the Slip and Slide tools

Three- and four-point editing

Extracting and lifting frames

Creating virtual clips

Using the clip commands

✦ ✦ ✦ ✦

Premiere is so versatile, you could create and edit an entire project using little more than Premiere's Selection tool. However, if you need to make precise edits, you want to explore Premiere's advanced editing functions.

For example, Premiere's Trim View in the Monitor window enables you to shave one frame at a time from the In or Out point of a clip by simply clicking the mouse. As you click, you see the last frame of one Out point in one side of the window, and the first frame of the adjacent In point in another side of the window. Premiere also enables you to create sophisticated three-point edits where you specify an In or Out point to maintain in a Source clip, and an In and Out point for placement in your program. When you perform the edit, Premiere calculates the precise section of the Source clip to overlay into your program material.

This chapter provides a guide to Premiere's intermediate and advanced editing features. It starts with a look at some basic editing utilities, such as the Razor and Multiple Razor tools, and then proceeds to discuss Premiere's toolbox editing tools — the Ripple Edit, Rolling Edit, Slip, and Slide tools. The chapter continues with a look at three- and four-point editing and how to trim using the Monitor window Trim mode. The chapter has been designed to enable you to quickly move from subject to subject, so that you can learn or review editing features and immediately put them to use.

Editing Utilities

From time to time you may want to edit by simply copying clips from one section and pasting them in another. To aid in editing, you may want to unlink audio from video. This section covers several different commands that can aid you as you edit your production. It starts with a discussion of the History palette, which enables you to quickly undo different stages of your work.

Undoing with the History palette

Even the best editors change their minds and make mistakes. Professional editing systems enable you to preview edits before actually recording the source material onto the program tape. However, professional editing systems can't provide as many levels of undo as Premiere's History palette, shown in Figure 10-1.

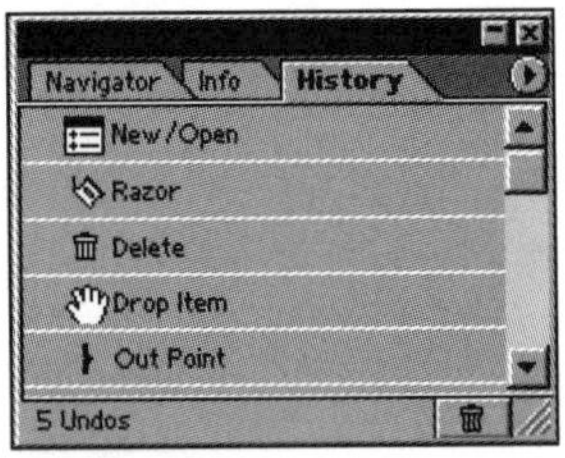

Figure 10-1: The History palette

As discussed in Chapter 2, the History palette can record up to 99 steps made while using Premiere. Each step appears as a separate entry in the History palette. If you want to return to a previous step, simply click it in the History palette, and you return to it. When you go forward with your work, the previously recorded steps after the step you returned to disappear.

Note

The default level of undo states in the History palette is 15. To raise the number of states, choose Edit ⇨ Preferences Auto Save and Undo. In the History and Undo Section, set the desired number of undo levels. The greater the number of undo levels, the more memory Premiere consumes.

If you haven't already tried the History palette, open the palette by choosing Window ⇨ Show History. In a new or existing project, drag several clips to the Timeline. As you drag, watch how the states are recorded in the History palette. Now select one of the clips in the Timeline and delete it by pressing Delete. Then delete another clip. Again, note how each state is recorded in the palette.

Now assume that you want to return the project to the state it was in before you deleted any clips. Just click in the History palette to the left of the first Delete state in the palette. The Project returns to its state before any of the deletions. Now move one of the clips in the Timeline with the Selection tool. As soon as you move the clip, a new state is recorded in the History palette, erasing the second Delete state in the History palette. After you return to one state in the History palette and begin to work, you can't go forward again.

Cutting and pasting clips

If you've ever used a word processor to edit text, you know that one of the easiest ways to rearrange your work is to copy and paste from one part of the text to another. In Premiere, you can easily copy and paste, or cut and paste, a clip from one part of the clipboard to another. In fact, Premiere has three paste commands—Paste, Paste to Fit, and Paste Attributes. Before you copy a clip, you may want to split the original clip into two pieces, and only paste one of the segments.

Splitting a clip with the Razor and Multiple Razor tools

Before copying and pasting or moving a clip, you may want to slice it into two pieces. An easy way to slice a clip is to use Premiere's Razor tool. One click of the Razor tool splits a clip into two pieces. Here's how to use the Razor and Multiple Razor tool:

1. **If you want to split one clip in one unlocked track into two pieces, select the Razor tool. To split all unlocked tracks into two separate pieces, select the Multiple Razor tool, shown in Figure 10-2.**

Figure 10-2: The Razor (left) and Multiple Razor (right) tools

Tip Press C on the keyboard until either the Razor or Multiple Razor tool is selected.

2. **Move the Edit line in the Timeline to the frame that you want to split.**
3. **Click the clip to cut it with either the Razor tool or Multiple Razor tool, as shown in Figure 10-3.** After you click with either the Razor or Multiple Razor tool, you can move the cut portion of the clip independently of the rest of the clip.

Figure 10-3: Cutting with either the Razor or Multiple Razor tool splits the clip into two clips.

Pasting clips

After you've split a clip, you may want to copy and paste it or cut and paste it to another location in the Timeline. If you want to simply copy or cut a clip and paste it in a blank area in the Timeline, select the clip or clips and then choose Edit ⇨ Cut or Edit Copy. Next, click the area in which you want the clip to appear and choose Paste. If the area into which you want to paste the clip already has clips within it, you may want to use Premiere's Paste to Fit or Paste Attributes commands.

Using Paste to Fit

Premiere's Paste to Fit command enables you to paste clips into gaps in the Timeline. It also provides options for how you want the inserted clips to fit within your production. Here's how to use Paste to Fit.

1. **Select the clip or clips that you want to copy or paste.**
2. **Choose Edit ⇨ Cut or Edit ⇨ Copy.**
3. **Click in the area that you want to paste the clips.** For example, assume that you want to paste a clip in a two-second gap between two other clips. In this situation, you click in the gap on-screen, and Premiere selects the gap.
4. **Choose Edit ⇨ Paste to Fit.** The Fit Clip dialog box appears (see Figure 10-4).
5. **Select either Change Speed or Trim Source.** If you choose Change Speed, Premiere increases or decreases the speed of the clip to fit it. If you choose Trim Source, Premiere trims the Out point of the clip to fit it.

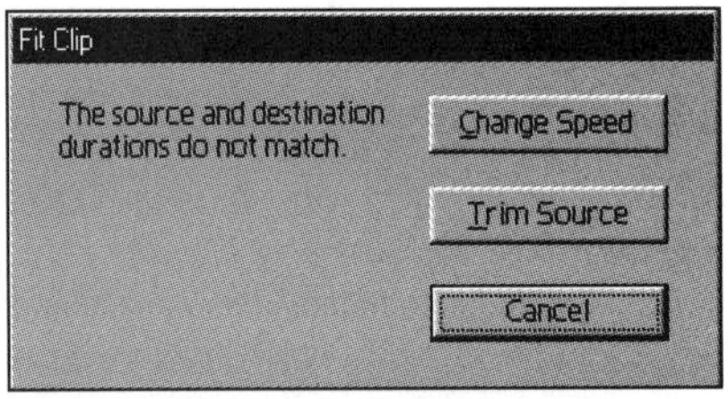

Figure 10-4: The Fit Clip dialog box enables you to either change the speed or to trim the source.

Using Paste Attributes

Premiere's Paste Attributes command provides a variety of choices for pasting clips over other clips or into gaps in the Timeline. Here's how to use Paste Attributes:

1. **Select the clip or clips that you want to copy or paste.**
2. **Choose Edit ⇨ Cut or Edit ⇨ Copy.**

3. **Click in an area in the Timeline where you want to paste the clips.**
4. **Choose Edit ➪ Paste Attributes.** The Paste Attributes dialog box appears (see Figure 10-5).
5. **Choose Content.**

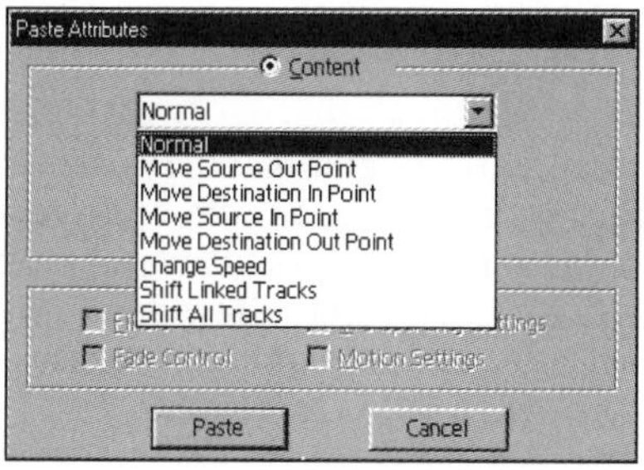

Figure 10-5: The Paste Attributes dialog box gives you different options for where and how a copied clip will be pasted.

6. **Choose an option from the Content menu:**
   - Normal
   - Move Source Out Point
   - Move Source Destination Point
   - Move Source In Point
   - Move Destination Out Point
   - Change Speed
   - Shift Linked Tracks
   - Shift All Tracks

   The Normal attribute drops the selected clip into the Timeline if it is shorter than the gap. If the selected clip is longer than the gap, Premiere trims the pasted clip to fit. For Normal and all other choices, Premiere provides an animated sequence in the middle of the dialog box, which illustrates the effect of the choice you make.

7. **Click the Paste button to execute the Paste Attributes command.**

Removing Timeline gaps

During the course of editing you may purposely or inadvertently leave gaps in the Timeline. Sometimes the gaps aren't even visible because of the time setting in the Timeline Zoom pop-up menu. If you want to remove all gaps in the Timeline, thereby snapping all clips together, choose Timeline ➪ Ripple Delete.

Unlinking and linking audio and video

While performing video edits, you may decide that you'd like to create audio effects where the audio from one clip fades into another video clip (called a *split edit*). Although editing the video is a simple chore, you may find that you need to *unlink* the audio from the video to create the effect you need. The following sections discuss tools and techniques for unlinking and linking video.

Unlinking and linking

When you capture video using the Premiere Capture command, Premiere links the video information to the audio. This marriage is evident as you work. When you drag a clip to the Timeline, its audio automatically appears in an audio track. When you move the video, the audio moves with it. If you delete the video from the track, the audio is deleted. However, during editing, you may want to separate the video from its audio to create effects or to replace the audio altogether.

Tip

If you are trying to sync audio to video, it's helpful to view the audio's waveform in the audio track. To view the waveform, expand the audio track by clicking the triangle at the front of the track.

To unlink video from audio, follow these steps:

1. **Select the audio track that you want to unlink.**
2. **Choose Clip ⇨ Unlink Audio and Video.** A white marker appears next to each clip (see Figure 10-6). These markers can aid you if you want to realign the two clips. You can move the audio and video individually and relink them after you've shifted their positions. If you want, you can also delete either the video or audio portion.

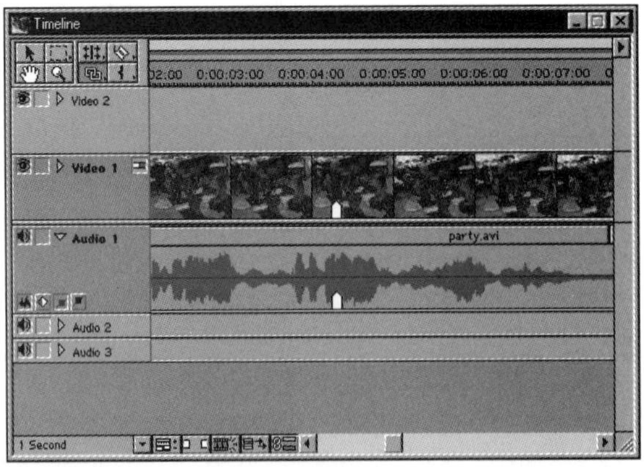

Figure 10-6: After you unlink a clip, a white marker appears in the video and audio track of that clip.

3. **Select the Link/Unlink tool to link audio and video.**

4. **Press U on your keyboard, until the Link/Unlink tool is selected.**
5. **Select the first clip you want to link (such as the video).**
6. **Clip the next clip that you want to link (such as the audio).**

Tip

If you want to unlink audio and video clips after linking them, click one of the clips with the Link tool again. If you link them, but the audio and video are not in sync, Premiere places a red triangle in front of the audio and video clips in the Timeline.

Linking and unlinking using the Timeline Sync mode

Premiere provides a quick method for unlinking and linking all clips in the Timeline. If you click the Toggle Sync Mode icon to turn sync off, you can move linked clips independently of one another in the Timeline. You can turn Sync mode back on by clicking the Sync mode icon again.

Editing Clips with the Timeline Edit Tools

After you've edited two clips together on the Timeline, you may want to fine-tune the edit by changing the Out point of the first clip. Although you can use the Monitor window to precisely change the edit point, you may prefer to use Timeline editing tools, such as the Rolling Edit tool and the Ripple Edit tool. Both tools enable you to quickly edit the Out point of adjacent clips.

If you have three clips edited together, the Slip and Slide tools provide a quick means for editing the In or Out point of the middle clip. The following sections describe how to use the Rolling Edit and Ripple Edit tools to edit adjacent clips, and how to use the Slip and Slide tools to edit a clip between two other clips. As you try out these tools, keep the Monitor window open. It provides an enlarged view of the clips. When using the Slip and Slide tools, the Monitor window also shows how many frames have been edited.

Figure 10-7 shows the Rolling Edit, Ripple Edit, Slip, and Slide tools.

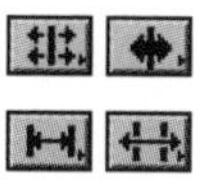

Figure 10-7: The Rolling Edit, Ripple Edit, Slip, and Slide tools

Creating a rolling edit

The Rolling Edit tool enables you to click and drag the edit line of one clip and simultaneously change the In or Out point of the next clip on the edit line. When you click and drag the edit line, the duration of the next clip is automatically edited to compensate for the change in the previous clip. For example, if you add five frames to the first clip, five frames are subtracted from the next. Thus, a rolling edit enables you to edit one clip, without changing the duration of your edited program.

Here's how to create a rolling edit:

On-screen you should have a project with at least two adjacent clips in a video track in the Timeline window.

1. **Click the Rolling Edit tool to select it or press P on the keyboard until the Rolling Edit tool is selected.**
2. **Move the Rolling Edit tool to the Edit line between two adjacent clips.**
3. **Click and drag either left or right to trim the clips.** If you drag right, you extend the Out point of the first clip and reduce the In point of the adjacent clip. If you click to the left, you reduce the Out point of the first clip and extend the In point of the next clip. Figure 10-8 shows a rolling edit.

Note If Toggle Edge Viewing (at the bottom of the Timeline window) is on, you can see the two adjacent clips in the Monitor window.

Figure 10-8: A rolling edit

Creating a ripple edit

The Ripple Edit tool enables you to edit a clip without affecting its adjacent clip. Performing a ripple edit is the opposite of performing a rolling edit. As you click and drag to extend the Out point of clip, Premiere pushes the next clip to the right to avoid changing its In point. If you click and drag to the left to reduce the Out point, Premiere doesn't change the In points of the next clips. Here's how to perform a ripple edit with the Ripple Edit tool.

On-screen you should have a project with at least two clips touching side by side in a video track in the Timeline window.

1. **Click the Ripple Edit tool to select it or press P on the keyboard until the Ripple Edit tool is selected.**
2. **Move the Ripple Edit tool to the Out point of the clip you are going to trim.**
3. **Click and drag right to increase the clip's length or left to decrease the clip's length.** The duration of the next clip remains unchanged. Figure 10-9 shows a ripple edit.

Note

If Toggle Edge Viewing (at the bottom of the Timeline window) is on, you can see the changes being made to the clip being affected in the Monitor window.

Figure 10-9: A ripple edit

Creating a slip edit

A slip edit enables you to change the In and Out points of a clip sandwiched between two other clips while maintaining the middle clip's original duration. As you click and drag the clip, the clip's neighbors to the left and right do not change; thus, neither does the project duration.

On-screen you should have a project with at least three clips side by side in a video track in the Timeline window.

1. **Click the Slip tool to select it or press P on the keyboard until the Slip tool is selected.**
2. **With the Slip tool selected, click the clip that is in the middle of two other clips.**
3. **To change the In and Out points without changing the duration of the project, click and drag left or right.** Figure 10-10 shows a slip edit.

Figure 10-10: A slip edit

Tip

Although the slip tool is generally used to edit one clip between two others, you can edit the In and Out points of a clip with the Slip tool even if it is not between other clips.

Creating a slide edit

A slide edit maintains the In and Out points of the clip that you are dragging while changing the duration of clips abutting the selected clip. As a result, the duration of the edited clip and the entire edited program do not change. Here's how to perform a slide edit with the Slide Edit tool.

On-screen you should have a project with at least three clips side by side in a video track in the Timeline window.

1. **Click the Slide tool to select it, or press P on the keyboard until the Slide tool is selected.**
2. **Click and drag on the clip that is in the middle of two other clips to move it.** Dragging left shortens the first clip and lengthens the last clip. Dragging right lengthens the first clip and shortens the last clip. Figure 10-11 shows a slide edit.

Figure 10-11: Creating a slide edit

Creating a Three- or Four-Point Edit

Three- and four-point edits are commonly performed in professional video editing studios, using a monitor set up that is similar to Premiere's Dual View in the Monitor window. In Dual View, the Source section of the Monitor window typically shows a clip that hasn't been added to the Timeline, while the Program section shows a section of the program that has already been placed on the Timeline.

Performing a three-point edit

Typically, a three-point edit is used to overlay or replace a portion of the program with a portion of the source clip. Before the edit is performed three crucial points are specified. Usually the three points are:

✦ **The In point of the source clip.**

✦ **An In point of the program clip.** This is where you want the source clip to first appear.

✦ **An Out point in the program clip.** This is where you want the source replacement to stop.

When the edit is performed, Premiere automatically calculates the exact section of the source clip needed to replace the section designated by the In and Out points of the program.

You could use a three-point edit in the following situation. Assume that you have a clip of a sailboat in the Timeline, and you want to replace two seconds of it with a clip of waves crashing. To set this up you would place the Waves clip in the Source view of the Monitor window, and set the In point for the Waves clip in the Source section. Then you'd set the In and Out points in the Sailboat clip in the monitor section of the Monitor window. When you perform the three-point edit, the Waves clip appears in the section in the Timeline designated by the area you set as the In and Out points of the Sailboat clip.

Follow these steps to perform a three-point edit. Before creating a three-point edit, you need a project on-screen containing at least one clip in the Timeline.

If you'd like to practice using one of the tutorial files, start by importing the file 705008p.mov from the Chapter 10 folder of the CD ROM. This clip shows a waitress leading diners to a table in a restaurant. After the file is imported, drag it into Track 1 in the Timeline. This clip will appear in the Program section of the Monitor window. Next import clip,705009b.mov. This clip shows chefs working in the kitchen of the restaurant. Don't place this on the Timeline, Premiere will do it for you when you create the three-point edit. The three-point edit will create a cut-away from the restaurant diners to the chefs in the kitchen for a few seconds, before returning to the diners' clip.

1. **If the Monitor window is not open, open it by choosing Window ⇨ Show Monitor.**
2. **Set the monitor to Dual View by clicking the Dual View button or by choosing Dual View in the Monitor window menu. If you click the Play button in the Monitor window, you'll see that the clip in the Timeline appears in the Program section.**

3. **Place a clip in the Source View of the Monitor window.** If you are using the *Adobe Premiere 6.5 Bible* CD-ROM tutorial files, drag clip 705009b.mov to the Source View of the Monitor window. The clip should appear in the Source View, and its name should appear in the Clip pop-up menu. Note that you may be able to choose another clip from the Clip pop-up menu, if you've already been working with Source View clips.
4. **In the Source view section, set the In point for the Source clip.** This is the first frame that you want overlaid into the program. If you are using the Tutorial files, set the In point about 3 seconds 25 frames from the beginning of clip 7005009b.mov. To move to the frame, click and drag in the scrubbing area in the Source View and then use the Frame Forward or Frame Reverse button to navigate to the precise frame.
5. **Click the In Point button.**
6. **In the Program view of the Monitor window, move to the first frame that you want to replace with the Source clip.** If you are using the Tutorial files, move to about 2 seconds from the beginning of clip 7005008b.mov To move to the frame, click and drag in the scrubbing area in the Program view and then use the Frame Forward or Frame Reverse button to navigate to the precise frame. Alternatively, you can click and drag the Edit Line in the Timeline window.
7. **Set the In point by clicking the In Point button in the Program View.**
8. **In the Program view of the Monitor window, move to the last frame that you want replaced by the Source clip.** If you are using the Tutorial files, move about 4 seconds 18 frames into clip 705008b.mov.
9. **Click the Out Point button.**
10. **To perform the edit, click the Overlay button (in the Source View, below the scrubbing area).** Figure 10-12 shows a three-point edit.

Performing a four-point edit

Three-point edits are performed more frequently than four-point edits because you only need to specify three points. In a four-point edit, you specify the In and Out points of the Source clip as well as the In and Out points of the Program clip.

Before performing the edit, make sure that the Target track pop-up menus are set correctly. If not, choose the track that you want to have the clip dropped into on the Timeline by clicking the Target pop-up menu.

Otherwise, performing a four-point edit (see Figure 10-13) is identical to performing a three-point edit, except that you must set an Out point as well as an In point in the Source side of the Monitor window. What happens if the source duration (the duration between in and out source points) does not match the duration between the program In and Out points? Premiere opens an alert enabling you to choose whether you want to trim the Source clip or change the speed of the Source clips.

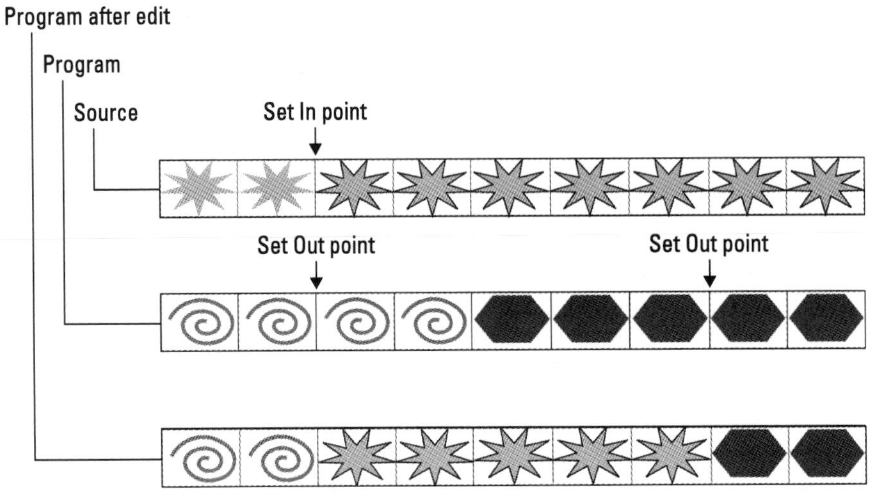

Figure 10-12: A three-point edit

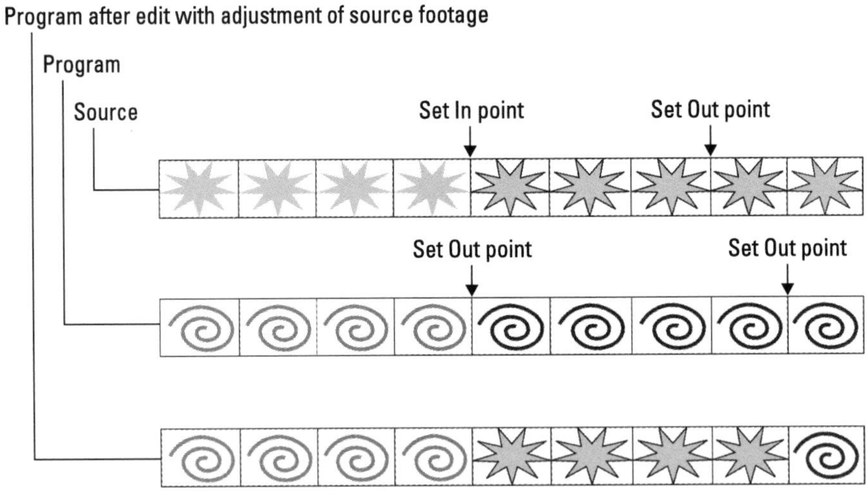

Figure 10-13: A four-point edit

Performing Lift and Extract Edits

Premiere's Monitor window provides two buttons that enable you to quickly remove sections of program material in the Timeline:

-  **Lift button.** Removes frames from the Timeline but does not close the gap created by the deleted frames.

-  **Extract button.** Removes frames from the Timeline but closes the gap that is created. This changes the duration of the project.

Before performing a Lift edit, you need to have a project on-screen with at least one clip in the Timeline window. The Monitor window should be open on-screen. The Monitor window can be in Single or Dual View. Here's how to perform a Lift edit:

1. **Using the Program's controller, find the first frame that you want removed from the program in the Timeline.**
2. **Click the In Point button.**
3. **Move to the last frame that you wish to remove from the program.**
4. **Click the Out Point button.**
5. **Click the Lift button in the Program side.** After you click, Premiere removes the frames from the Timeline, leaving a gap where the removed frames used to be.

Before performing an Extract edit, you need to have a project on-screen with at least one clip in the Timeline. The Monitor window should be open on-screen. The Monitor window can be in either Single or Dual mode. Here's how to perform an Extract edit:

1. **Use the Program side's controller to find the first frame that you want moved from the program in the Timeline**.
2. **Click the In Point button.**
3. **Move to the last frame that you want to remove from the program.**
4. **Click the Out Point button.**
5. **Click the Extract button in the Program side.** After you click, Premiere removes the frames from the Timeline. Any adjacent clips in the Timeline move to close the gap that the deletion caused.

Fine-Tuning Edits by Using Monitor Trim Mode

The Monitor window's Trim mode enables you to precisely change the edit points of clips on the Timeline. When you work in Trim mode, shown in Figure 10-14, you can click to move from edit point to edit point and then remove or add frames on either side of the edit. Trim mode enables you to create Ripple Edits and Rolling Edits. When you create a Ripple Edit, the project duration increases or decreases depending on whether frames are added to or subtracted from the edit. If you create a Rolling Edit, the project duration remains the same. Premiere accomplishes this by adding frames from one side of the edit as it subtracts from the other and by subtracting from one side of the edit while it adds to the other.

Figure 10-14: The Monitor window in Trim Mode

Here's how to use the Trim Mode to trim an edit. Before beginning, you should have at least two separate clips on the Timeline that are adjacent to each other. The Monitor window should be open on-screen.

1. **Move the Timeline Edit line close to the area that you want to fine-tune or use the Monitor window controller to move close to the area that you want to edit.**
2. **Switch the Monitor window to Trim Mode.** Click the Trim Mode button or choose Trim Mode in the Monitor window menu.
3. **Check the Target pop-up menu to make sure that the target Video and Audio tracks are correct.**
4. **Click the Next edit or Previous edit button to move to the edit that you want to adjust.** The ClipOut section of the window shows the left side of the edit; the ClipIn section of the window shows the right side of the edit (as if you were standing in the Timeline in the middle of a cut).

5. **Edit the clip.** To create a ripple edit, click the left or right Focus button depending on whether you want to edit the left side of the edit or the right side of the edit. The *ripple edit* changes the program duration. To create a rolling edit, click the Set Focus Both button. A *rolling edit* does not change program duration.

6. **Add or remove frames.** Clicking the –5 or –1 buttons removes either five frames or one frame from one side of the Edit line. Clicking the +5 or +1 buttons adds five frames or one frame from one side of the Edit Line. As you edit, Premiere displays the Time change or lack thereof, if you're using a rolling edit, next to the Delta time readout. If you set the focus to the left and subtract one frame, one frame is subtracted from the project (ripple edit). If you set the focus for both left and right, when you subtract a frame from the left side of the edit, one frame is added to the right (rolling edit).

Tip

You can change how many frames are added and subtracted in the Trim window with each click by changing settings in the Monitor Windows Options dialog box. You can also change settings to enable multiple frames to appear in the Monitor window. To access the Monitor Windows Options dialog box, choose Monitor Window Options in the Monitor Window menu.

7. **To playback the edit, click the Play button.** If you want to cancel the edit, click the Cancel edit button.

Tip

You can add a video track by clicking and dragging the track to the Timeline ruler or to the blank area at the very bottom of the Timeline window.

Duplicate and Virtual Clips

As Premiere users edit a production, most simply drag clips from the Project menu and place them into the Timeline. Doing this works well on short projects. However, if you are working on a long production with complicated edits, you may want to use Premiere clip options that enable you to duplicate clips in the Project window, create subclips, or create *virtual clips.* To understand duplicate and virtual clips, it's important to review how Premiere categorizes the clips that you use.

✦ **Master clip.** When you import a file into Premiere, the Master clip of the file appears in the Project window. The Master clip is a screen representation of the digitized material on disk.

✦ **Instance.** When you drag a clip to the Timeline, you create an *instance* of the Master clip. Premiere enables you to create multiple instances of the Master clip in the Timeline. If you delete the Master clip from the Project window, all instances are removed as well.

✦ **Duplicate clip.** Although using clip instances can be very efficient, there's one major drawback: It's difficult to keep track of all instances of the Master clip in the Timeline. The solution is to create a duplicate with a new name (you can even trim the clip before duplicating it). Each time you want to use the clip in the Timeline, you create another duplicate and drag it to the Timeline. Each duplicate remains listed separately in the Project window.

Creating duplicate clips

Instead of capturing many short clips and adding them to the Project window, it can be more efficient to capture one long sequence and then create duplicate clips from the original or Master clip. If you create a duplicate clip, it's important to understand that a duplicate clip is a copy of the Master clip that never loses its link to the original source file on disk. Thus, if you delete the Master clip in the project window, any duplicate clips created from it remain in the project.

Here are the steps for creating a duplicate clip:

1. **Select the Master clip in the Timeline.**
2. **To create a duplicate of a clip with In and Out points different than the Master clip, double-clip the Master clip in the Project window.**
3. **In the Clip window, edit the In and Out points.**
4. **To create the duplicate, choose Edit ➪ Duplicate.** The Duplicate Clip dialog box appears (see Figure 10-15).
5. **Type a name for the clip.** If desired, choose a location from the Location menu. The Location menu lists the bins in the Project window.

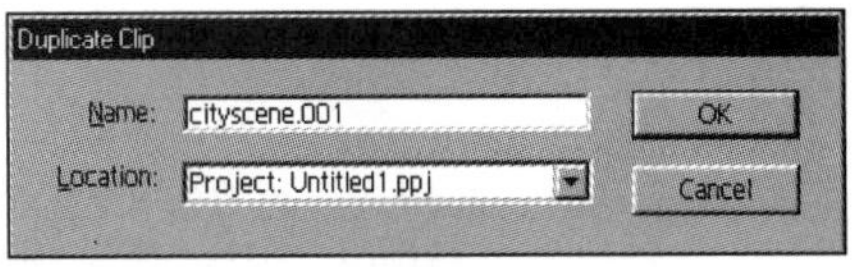

Figure 10-15: The Duplicate Clip dialog box

Tip

You can create a new name for a clip by first selecting the clip in the Project window and then choosing Clip ➪ Set Clip Name alias.

Creating virtual clips

If you plan to reuse sequences of audio, video, and effects in different areas of your program, Premiere enables you to create a *virtual clip*. A virtual clip is a visual representation of a Timeline area that you can use repeatedly.

Virtual clips have several powerful features:

✦ **Reuse.** After you create a virtual clip, you can drag it to the Timeline again and again, without re-creating the sequence. After you create multiple instances of a virtual clip, you can apply different effects to different instances.

✦ **Automatic Update.** If you use different instances of a virtual clip, updating the original Timeline area where the clip was created updates all instances.

✦ **Special Effects.** Assume that you want to create both a dissolve and a curtain wipeover to create a special effect transition. Normally, you cannot apply two transitions to the same area in the Timeline. However, you can create a virtual clip with one transition in it and then create another virtual clip and apply a transition between the two virtual clips.

✦ **Nesting.** After you create one virtual clip, you can create another virtual clip within it.

Before you create a virtual clip, it's important to understand that the original footage used to create a virtual clip must reside somewhere in the Timeline—usually away from your production area. It's a good idea to create your virtual clip at the beginning of the Timeline. That way it won't get in the way of further editing and won't be affected by future work. If you inadvertently change the position of an item in the virtual clip, it changes all instances. You may also want to create a virtual clip in tracks that aren't being used so that it doesn't interfere with your edited project. Here are the steps for creating a virtual clip:

1. **Drag all clips that you want to have in your virtual clip to the Timeline.**
2.  **Create all effects and transitions that you want to have appear in the virtual clip**. Before you can create the virtual clip, you must select the track area with the Block Select tool.
3. **Activate the Block Select tool in the Timeline toolbox.**
4. **Click and drag over all clips and tracks that you want to have included in the virtual clip.**
5. **Move the Block Select tool to the middle of the selection.** The arrow mouse pointer changes to the Virtual clip icon.
6. **Click and drag the virtual clip area to another track or to another area of the Timeline.** When you release the mouse, Premiere creates and names the virtual clip. Figure 10-16 shows a virtual clip.
7. **Rename the virtual clip by selecting it with the Selection tool and then choose Edit ⇨ Duplicate clip.** This places the virtual clip in the Project window.

Figure 10-16: A virtual clip

After a virtual clip is created, you can use it as many times as desired by simply dragging the virtual clip from the Project menu to the Timeline. If you edit the area of the Timeline that includes the footage that the clip is based on, all instances of the clip are changed accordingly. If you ever need to find the original Timeline area used to create the virtual clip, double-click any instance of the virtual clip in the Timeline. Premiere automatically selects the Timeline area that you used to create the virtual clip.

Editing a Clip Using Clip Commands

When editing a production, you may find that you need to adjust a clip to maintain continuity in a project. For example, you may want to slow the speed of a clip to fill a gap in your production or to freeze a frame for a moment or two.

Various commands in the Clip menu enable you to edit a clip. You can scale a clip by using the Clip ➪ Video Options ➪ Motion command. Premiere enables you to change the duration and the speed of a clip using the Clip ➪ Duration command and the Clip ➪ Speed command. You can change the frame rate of a clip using the Clip ➪ Video Options ➪ Frame Hold command. Or you can use the Clip ➪ Video Options ➪ Frame Hold command to freeze a video frame. Using the Clip ➪ Video Options ➪ Field Options command, you can have Premiere adjust interlaced clips. Using the Clip ➪ Video Options ➪ Maintain Aspect Ratio command enables you to have a clip maintain its aspect ratio (height and weight), even if it's different than the aspect ratio in the project. The next sections describe how to perform each command.

Using the Motion command

In this section, the Motion command is used to scale a clip. To learn more about the Motion command turn to Chapter 14, where you learn how to use the Motion command to apply motion to still images and to animate titles.

Here's how to use the Clip ➪ Video Options ➪ Motion command to scale a clip (on-screen you should have a project with a clip in a video track in the Timeline window):

1. **Click the clip in the video track to select it.**
2. **Choose Clip ➪ Video Options ➪ Motion.** The Motion Settings dialog box appears (see Figure 10-17).
3. **Click and drag the Zoom slider to the right to increase the clip size.**
4. **Move the sample image of the clip so that it is over the visible area.**
5. **Click the Start point and take note of the Info coordinates.**
6. **Click the Finish point and type in the same Info coordinates you had for the Start point.** In the preview, the start and finish points are at the same place. The clip doesn't move as it is being scaled.

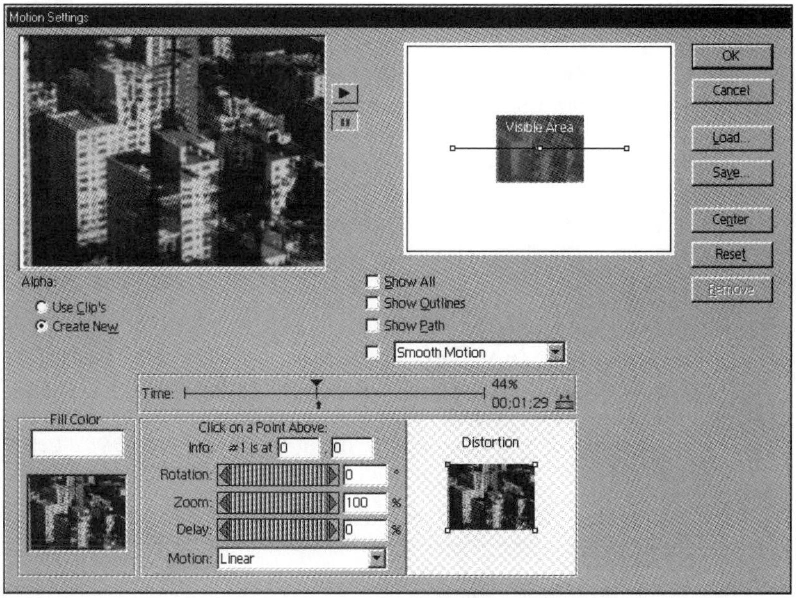

Figure 10-17: The Motion Settings dialog box enables you to scale a clip.

Using the Duration and Speed commands

You can use the Clip ➪ Duration and Clip ➪ Speed commands to change the length of a clip or to speed up, slow down, or play a clip in reverse.

Here's how to change the duration of a clip (on-screen you should have a project with a clip in a video track in the Timeline window):

1. **Click the clip in the video track to select it.**
2. **Choose Clip ➪ Duration.** The Clip Duration dialog box appears (see Figure 10-18).
3. **Type a duration.** You can't expand the clip to extend past its original Out point.

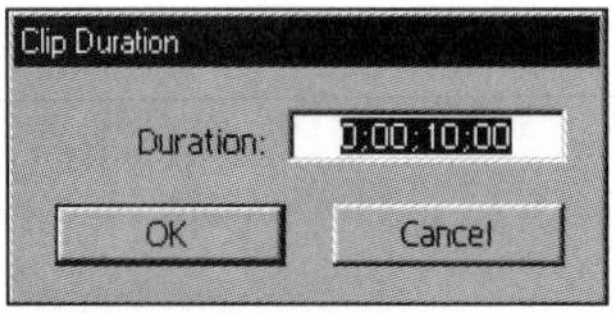

Figure 10-18: The Clip Duration dialog box

4. **Click OK to close the dialog box and set the new duration.**

Here's how to change the speed of a clip (on-screen you should have a project with a clip in a video track in the Timeline window):

1. **Click the clip in the video track to select it.**

Note: You can also change the speed of a clip that is in the Project window. To do so, select the clip in the Project window, and then choose Clip ➪ Speed.

2. **Choose Clip ➪ Speed.** The Clip Speed dialog box appears (see Figure 10-19).
3. **Type a value in the New Rate field.** Type a value greater than 100 percent to speed up the clip, or type a value between 0 percent and 99 percent to slow down the clip. Type a negative number to reverse the clip. As you change the speed, you may need to change the duration. If you want, you can type a new duration and let Premiere figure out how fast to play the clip to equal it.
4. **Click OK to close the Clip Speed dialog box and to apply the new speed.**

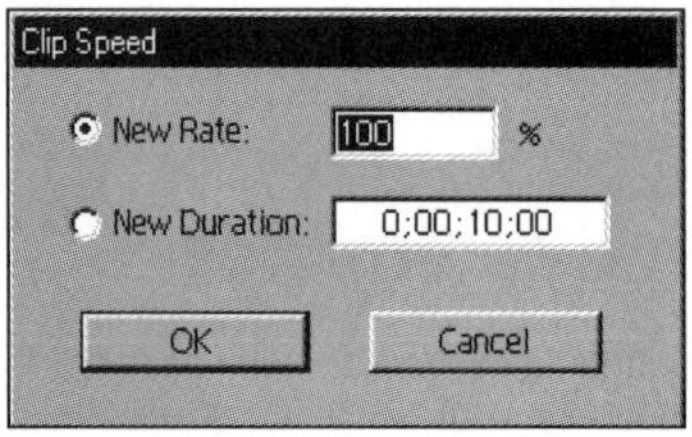

Figure 10-19: The Clip Speed dialog box

Using the Frame Hold command

You can change the frame rate (the number of frames displayed per second) of a clip by using the Frame Hold command. On-screen, you should have a project with a clip in a video track in the Timeline window. Here's how to do this:

1. **Click the clip in the video track to select it.**
2. **Choose Clip ⇨ Video Options ⇨ Frame Hold.** The Frame Hold Options dialog box appears (see Figure 10-20).
3. **Click the Alternate Rate radio button.**
4. **Type a new frame rate for the clip.** If you enter a frame rate that is lower than that of the project, action may appear jerky because Premiere repeats missing frames. To have Premiere interpolate between frames and attempt to smooth the action, choose the Frame Blending option in the dialog box.

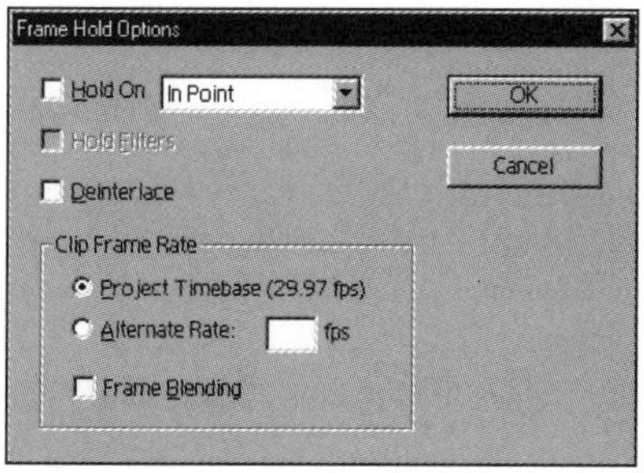

Figure 10-20: The Frame Hold Options dialog box

Note

The Frame Hold command does not change the visual speed of movement or action in a clip. To change a clip's action speed as well as its frame rate, select a clip in the Timeline or Project window and then choose Clip ⇨ Advanced Options ⇨ Interpret Footage.

The Maintain Aspect Ratio and Aspect Color commands

When an imported clip or graphic appears in a project, Premiere attempts to match the frame size of the imported clip to that of the project. If a clip or graphic was created with an aspect ratio different from that of your project, it will probably appear distorted. For example, if you create a graphic in Photoshop at 640 x 480 pixels and load it into a Premiere project that has a frame size of 732 x 480, Premiere will stretch the smaller graphic to match the larger video frame size. To prevent the distortion, you can instruct Premiere to keep the aspect ratio of the imported clip or graphic, by using the Maintain Aspect Ratio command. (Although this prevents distortion, it usually produces blank areas on two or more sides of the screen.)

Here are the steps for maintaining a clip's aspect ratio (on-screen you should have a project with a clip in a video track in the Timeline window):

1. **Click the clip in the video track to select it.**
2. **Choose Clip ➪ Video Options ➪ Maintain Aspect Ratio.** This preserves the aspect ratio of the original footage. To maintain aspect ratio, Premiere leaves an empty space in the frame. To pick a color for that empty space, choose Clip ➪ Video Options ➪ Aspect Color. In the Color Picker dialog box that appears, pick the color that you want to use.
3. **Click OK to close the dialog box and to apply the command.**

Summary

Premiere provides numerous tools and commands that enable you to quickly and precisely edit a digital video production. Premiere's editing tool can be found in the Timeline toolbox. Most other editing utilities reside in the Monitor window.

- Use the Razor and Multiple Razor tools to snip a clip into two pieces.
- Use the Ripple Edit and Rolling Edit tools to change the In and Out points of clips in the Timeline. A ripple edit changes the project duration; a rolling edit does not.
- You can click and drag with the Slip or Slide tools to edit the In and Out points of a clip in between two other clips. The Slip tool does not change project duration; the Slide tool does.
- Use the Monitor window to create three- and four-point edits.
- Use the Trim view of the Monitor window to precisely shave frames from clips.
- Use the Clip commands to change clip speed, duration, and aspect ratio.
- Creating a virtual clip enables you to reuse edited sections of a project.
- Create duplicate clips to use the same clip with different names in the Timeline.

✦ ✦ ✦

CHAPTER 11

Using Video Effects

✦ ✦ ✦ ✦

In This Chapter

What video effects can do

Using the Video Effects palette

Using the Effect Controls palette

Using video effects with keyframes

Applying video effects to specific image areas

Touring Premiere's video effects

✦ ✦ ✦ ✦

Adobe Premiere's special effects can wake up even the dullest video production. Using the effects in Premiere's Video Effects palette, for example, you can blur or skew images and add bevels, drop shadows, and painterly effects. Some effects can correct and enhance video; others can make it seem as though the video is out of control. By changing controls for the effects, you can also create startling motion effects, such as making it appear as if an earthquake or tornado has struck your clip.

As this chapter illustrates, Premiere's video effects work in sync with the keyframe track, enabling you to change effects settings at specific points on the Timeline. All you need to do is specify the settings for the start of an effect, move to another keyframe, and set the ending effect. When you create a preview, Premiere does the rest: it interpolates the video effect, editing all of the in-between frames to create a fluid effect over time.

If you haven't been adding effects to your video, this chapter provides everything you need to get up and running. You'll explore every effect in the Video Effects palette and see how the Effect Controls palette enables you to change effect settings. You'll also have a chance to practice creating effects with keyframes and image mattes with sample clips from the CD-ROM that accompanies this book.

If you've already started working with Premiere effects, this chapter shows how to use Premiere's keyframe track and provides a reference for every effect in the Video Effects palette.

Exploring Premiere's Video Effects Palette

Premiere's Video Effects palette is a storehouse of video effects. However, before you begin to use the effects, you should become familiar with the palette interface. To display the Video Effects palette, choose Window ➪ Show Video Effects. The Video Effects palette, shown in Figure 11-1, features 14 folders that contain 74 different effects.

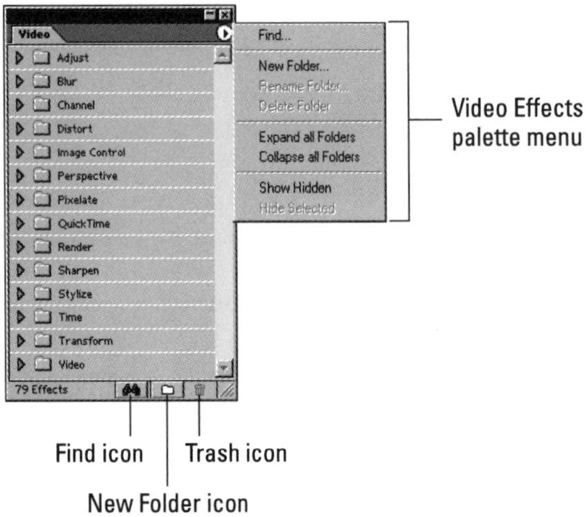

Figure 11-1: Premiere's Video palette provides access to Premiere's video effects.

Using Obsolete Effects from Previous Premiere Versions

Many of the new Premiere video effects are from Adobe After Effects and replace effects in previous versions of Premiere. If you want to continue using these obsolete effects, you must open a hidden folder in the Video Effects palette. To open this hidden folder, choose Show Hidden from the Video Effects palette pop-up menu. This reveals the Obsolete folder in the Video Effects palette. Open the folder by double-clicking it. To access an obsolete effect, select the effect. Next, choose Show Selected from the Video Effects palette pop-up menu.

To open a folder in the palette, either click the triangle to the left of the folder or double-click the folder. After the folder is open, a list of effects appears. An icon represents each effect. After you've opened a folder, you can apply an effect to a video track by clicking and dragging it over a clip.

Note: Two forms of icons appear in the palette. The turquoise icons are effects that also appear in Adobe After Effects. If you use these effects, you can safely switch between Premiere and After Effects without needing to recreate your effects.

To close a folder, either click the triangle to the left of the folder or double-click the folder.

The Video Effects palette pop-up menu

The Video Effects palette pop-up menu features commands that can help you keep organized while using Premiere's many video effects. The following is a brief description of the commands in the pop-up menu:

- **Find.** The Find command helps locate effects. After you choose Find, the Find Video Effect dialog box appears. In the field area, type the name of the effect that you want to find. If you're searching for a folder rather than an effect, deselect the Expand Folders checkbox. To start the search, click the Find button. If successful, Premiere selects the effect. If the search is not successful, an alert sounds.
- **New Folder.** Use this command to create folders that you can use to organize the effects. After you create a folder, name it and then drag the effects into it. With all of your chosen effects in one folder, you'll find that they are easier to use and locate.

Note: You can also click the Binoculars icon at the bottom of the Video Effects palette to find an effect.

- **Rename.** You can change a name of a folder at any time by clicking a folder and choosing Rename Folder. When the Rename Folder dialog box appears, type the name that you want in the Name field.
- **Delete.** If you have finished using a folder, you can delete it by selecting it and then choosing the Delete folder command. A prompt appears asking if you want to delete the selection. If you do, click Yes.

Note: You can also click the Delete icon at the bottom of the Video Effects palette to delete a folder. Click the folder you want to delete and then press the Trash icon. When the prompt appears, press Yes to delete the folder.

✦ **Expand all folders.** This command provides a quick method of opening all folders in the Video Effects palette.

✦ **Collapse all Folders.** This command provides a quick method of closing all folders in the Video Effects palette.

✦ **Show Hidden.** This command shows a folder of obsolete effects from previous Premiere versions.

✦ **Show Selected.** If you want to use an obsolete effect from the Obsolete folder, select it and then choose Show Selected.

✦ **Hide Selected.** Use this command if you want to dim a folder so that it cannot be opened.

The Effect Controls palette

When you apply a video effect to an image, the effect appears in the Effect Controls palette, as shown in Figure 11-2.

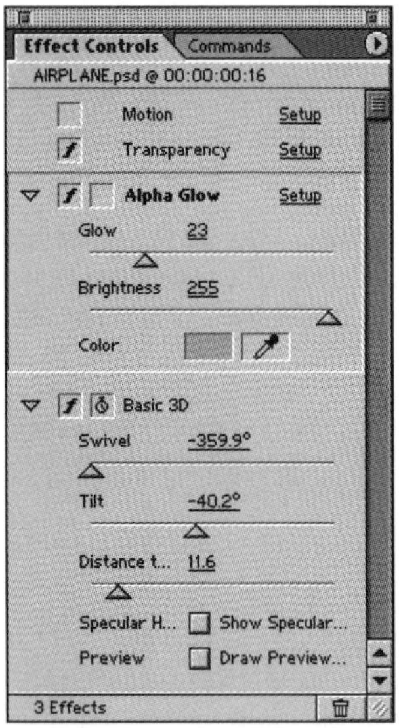

Figure 11-2: The Effect Controls palette appears after a video effect is applied to an image.

At the top of the palette, the name of the selected clip appears. Next to the clip name is a time display showing you where the clip appears in the Timeline. At the bottom left of the palette, the Effect Controls palette displays how many effects you've applied to the clip.

To the left of the effect name appears a box with an *f* in it. The *f* means that effect is enabled. You can disable the effect by clicking the *f* or deselecting Effect Enabled in the Effect Controls pop-up menu. If the effect has settings that can be adjusted, a triangle appears to the very far left. If you click the triangle, the settings for that effect appear.

Many clips also feature a dialog box that includes a preview area. If the effect provides a dialog box, you see the word Setup on the right side of the Effect Controls palette. Click Setup to access the Setup dialog box.

Many effects can be applied with Premiere's keyframe option. If so, a small box will be shown next to the name of the effect. To enable keyframing, click in the small square. After you click, a Stopwatch icon appears in the box. (Keyframing is explained later in this chapter.)

The Effect Controls menu

The Effect Controls pop-up menu provides control over all of the clips in the palette. The menu enables you to turn previewing on and off and to select preview quality as well as to enable and disable effects. The following is a brief description of the Effect Controls menu commands:

✦ **Effect Enabled.** Click this command to disable or enable effects. By default, Effect Enabled is selected.

✦ **Keyframing Enabled.** Enables you to start and stop effects based on keyframes. As mentioned earlier, you can start an effect in one keyframe and stop it in another. Premiere fills in the changes made by the effect in the frames in-between. When keyframing is enabled, a tiny stopwatch appears next to effect name in the Effect Controls menu. You can also turn keyframing on and off by clicking this icon in the palette.

✦ **Remove Selected Effect.** This command removes the selected effect from the clip.

Note: You can remove an effect from the palette by selecting it and then clicking the Trash icon in the Effect Controls palette.

✦ **Remove All Effects from Clip.** This command removes all effects from the clip.

✦ **No Previews.** This command disables previews in the Monitor window.

✦ **Preview After Adjust.** Select this command to preview the effect in the Monitor window after you adjust effect settings.

✦ **Preview During Adjust.** Select this command to review effects in the Monitor window as you adjust effect settings. This is the default selection.

✦ **Draft Quality.** This command sets the preview to Draft Quality, which is low video clarity but fast preview speed.

✦ **Best Quality.** This command sets the preview to Best Quality, which is high video clarity but slow preview speed.

Applying a Video Effect

You can apply one video effect or multiple video effects to either a portion or an entire video clip by dragging the effect from the Video Effects palette to the Timeline. You can also apply an effect to a still image that has an alpha channel. To apply an effect to just an image and not its background, it must have an alpha channel. You can use Adobe Photoshop to mask an image and save the mask either as an alpha channel or a layer. For more information on creating alpha channels using Photoshop, turn to the section, "Creating a Photoshop file with an alpha channel" in Chapter 22. Figure 11-3 shows in Video track 2 the Alpha Glow effect (from the Stylize folder) applied to an Airplane image. Because the airplane image has an alpha channel, the background is transparent. The scenic background you see in the Monitor window is from a clip that is in Video track 1A of the Timeline window.

Here's how to apply a video effect to a clip in the Timeline:

On the CD-ROM

If you want to apply an effect to an image with an alpha channel, you can apply video effects to the Airplane.psd image (seen in Figure 11-3) and use either the scenic.mov or Digital Vision's Electro 579005P.mov as the background. They are found on the Chapter 11 folder that is in the Tutorial Projects folder on the CD-ROM that accompanies this book.

1. **Choose File ➪ Import ➪ File to import a clip.** To load the airplane.psd image with its alpha channel (found on the CD-ROM that accompanies this book), choose Alpha Channel from the Choose A Layer pop-up menu in the Layer Selection dialog box.
2. **Click OK.** The airplane and its alpha channel appear in the Project window. To see the airplane alpha channel, double-click the airplane still image in the Project window. When the Clip window appears, click the Alpha Channel radio button. To return to the Project window, click the Clip window close box.
3. **Import another clip to use as the background.** If you want, you can use the scenic.mov or Digital Vision's Electro 579005P.mov video clip as the background. They are located on the CD-ROM that accompanies this book.

4. **Drag the background video clip from the Project window to Video track 2 of the Timeline window.**
5. **Drag the still image (the Airplane image) from the Project window to Video track 1 or 1A.** Place it directly above the background clip in Video track 2.
6. **Choose Window ➪ Show Effect Controls.** The Transparency dialog box appears.
7. **In the Effect Controls palette, click Set Up next to the Transparency option.**
8. **Make any necessary changes in the Transparency dialog box.**
9. **Click OK to close the dialog box.** To see a preview, click and drag the Timeline marker over the image and clip. Then, click the Enabled box that appears before the Transparency option in the Effect Controls palette. As you select and deselect the Enabled box, the airplane image appears over the background clip in the Monitor window (see Figure 11-3). Start by applying a simple effect to the background clip in Video track 1. To apply an effect to the background, you first need to select it in the Timeline window.

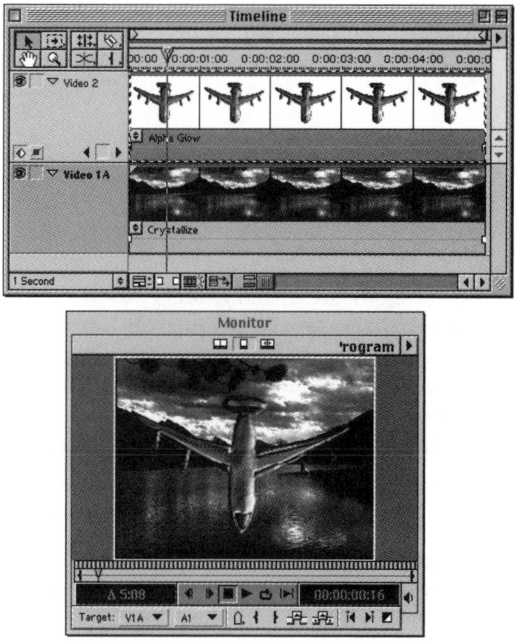

Figure 11-3: The sample Airplane image over the scenic background

10. Click the background clip in Video track 1.

11. To display a video effect, double-click one of the folders in the Video Effects palette.

12. Choose an effect, by clicking on it. For a simple effect, try the Directional blur found in the Blur & Sharpen folder.

13. To apply the effect, drag the effect from the Video Effects palette directly onto the clip in Video track 1 or into the Effect Controls palette. To adjust the settings of the effect, click and drag the sliders that are found beneath the effect name in the Effect Controls palette. As you work, watch the preview in the Monitor window. If you don't see the preview, check the Preview During Adjust option in the Effect Controls pop-up menu.

Experiment with different video effects. We used the Color Balance effect from the Adjust folder and the Crystallize effect from the Pixelate folder. To delete an effect, click the effect in the Effect Controls palette and then click the Trash icon at the bottom of the palette. A prompt asks you if you want to delete an effect. Click Yes to delete the effect.

Note

If you didn't choose the Directional Blur effect, the effect you chose may provide more settings in a dialog box. If a dialog box is provided for the effect, the word "setup" appears next to the effect in the Effect Controls palette. Click the word "setup" to open the dialog box and change the settings.

Note

You can add multiple effects to an image. You can also add the same effect with different effect settings to the same image.

14. Select the airplane image in Video track 2.

15. Drag the desired video effect from the Video Effects palette onto the background clip in Video track 2 or into the Effect Controls palette. In this example, we applied the Basic 3D effect, which is found in the Perspective folder. When applying the Basic 3D effect, we set keyframes. By setting keyframes we could change the effect over time. Proceed to the next section if you want to learn how to use video effects with keyframes.

16. To see a preview of the entire clip, choose Timeline ⇨ Preview or press Enter on your keyboard. Premiere prompts you to save your work.

17. Save your work and wait for Premiere to build a preview. When Premiere is done building a preview, the preview appears in the Monitor window. Figure 11-4 shows a few frames of the clip before and after the video effect was applied to Video track 1 and Video track 2.

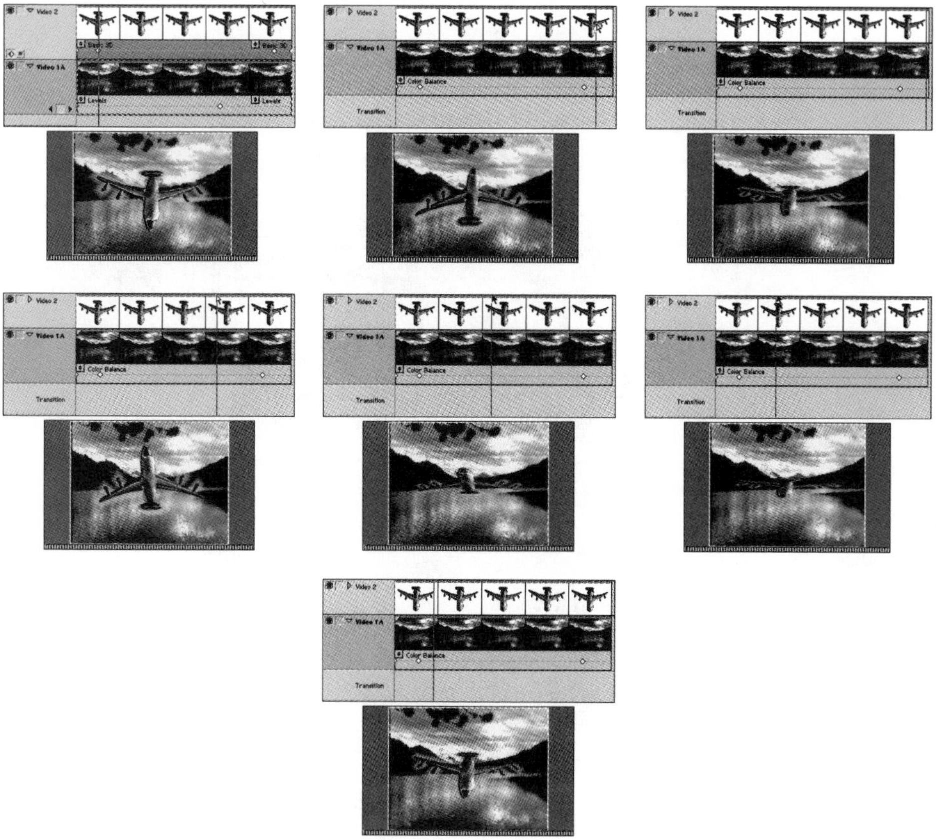

Figure 11-4: The Airplane and background files before and after application of an effect

Using Video Effects with Keyframes

Premiere's keyframe feature enables you to change video effects at specific points in the Timeline. With keyframes you can have Premiere use the settings of an effect at one point on the Timeline, gradually changing to the settings at another point on the Timeline. When Premiere creates the preview, it interpolates the effect over time, rendering all the frames that change in between the set points.

The keyframe track

Premiere 6 features a keyframe track that makes creating, editing, and manipulating keyframes quick and logical. The keyframe track is found in the Timeline window. Figure 11-5 shows the Timeline window with the keyframe track. To view the keyframe track, expand the track by clicking the track's Expand button.

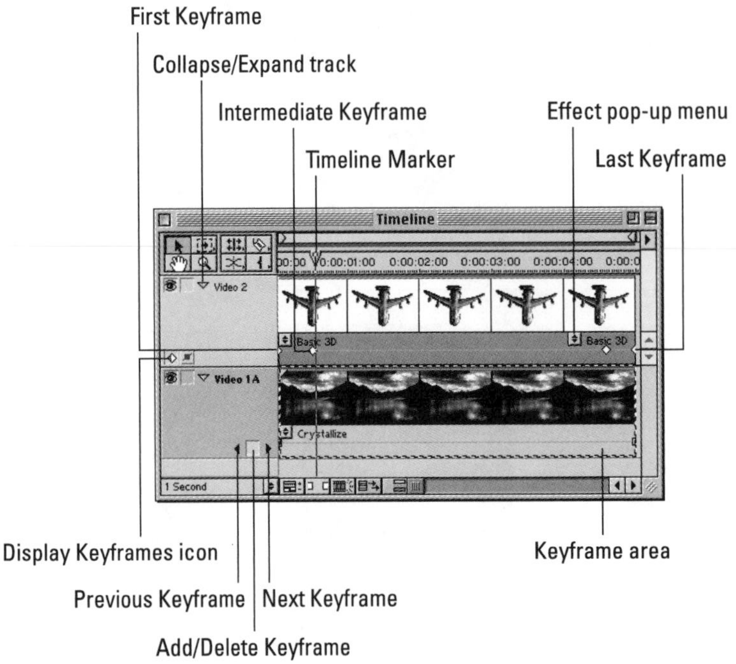

Figure 11-5: The Timeline window with Video track 1 and Video track 2 expanded with keyframes

Note

The keyframe track does not appear if you do not have a clip in the track.

In the keyframe track, a checkmark indicates a keyframe exists at the current Timeline frame. Clicking the right arrow icon jumps the Timeline marker from one keyframe to the next. Clicking the left arrow moves the Timeline marker backwards from one keyframe to the next.

Figure 11-6 shows frames of the sailing lessons logo (turn to Chapter 8 for the steps to creating the sailboat logo) animated over a background clip. The sailing lessons logo is animated using the Twirl effect. To make the logo twirl left then right and back to its original state, we set keyframes.

Note

To learn how to create the sailing lessons logo that appears in Figure 11-6, turn to Chapter 8. The logo was created using Premiere's Title Designer window.

You can use the saillogo.prtl file, which is found in the Chapter 8 and 11 folders on the CD-ROM that accompanies this book, or you can create your own logo. The Sailing Lessons logo includes an alpha channel that enables the background clip to show through it when viewed in the Monitor window.

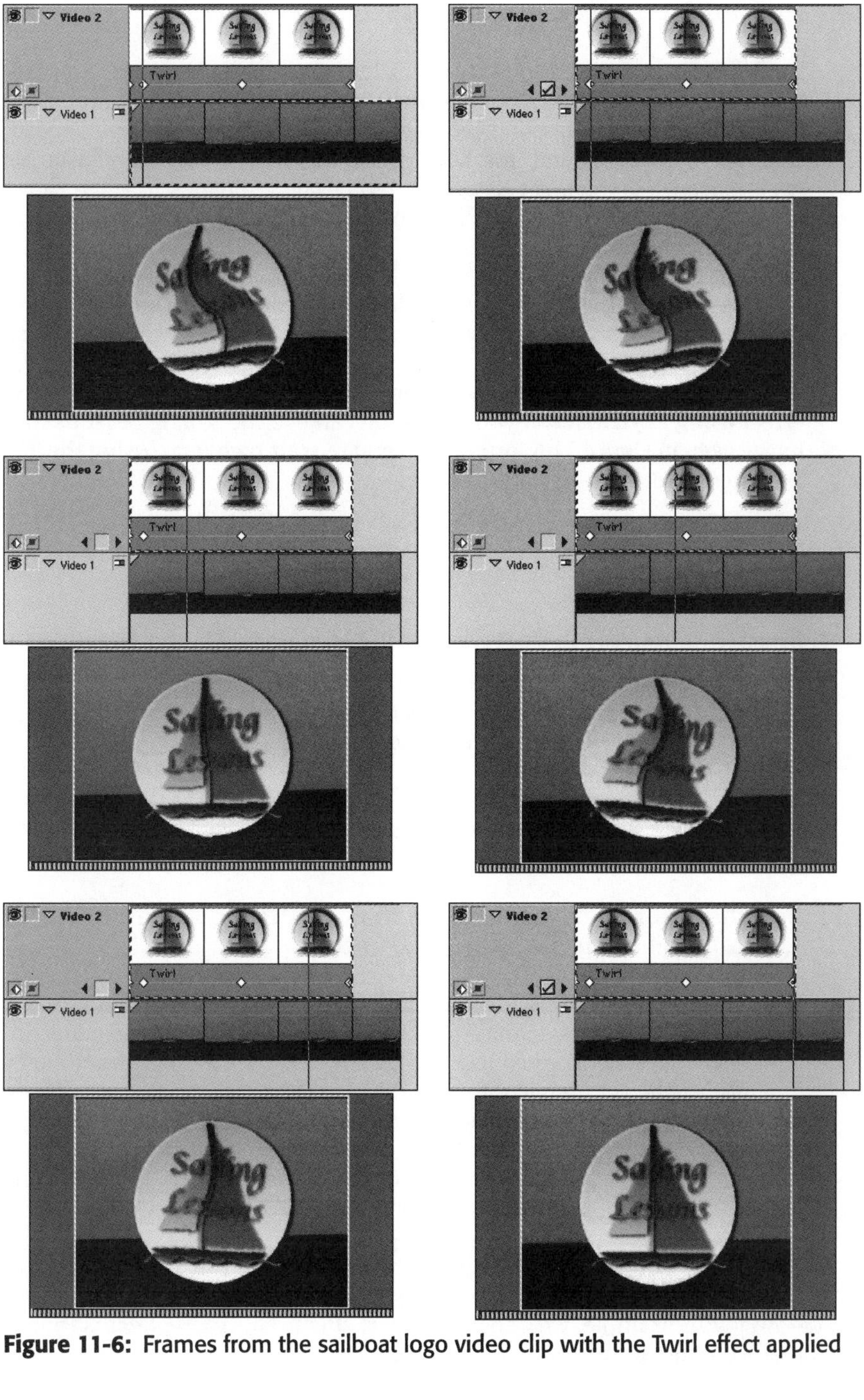

Figure 11-6: Frames from the sailboat logo video clip with the Twirl effect applied

Here's how to apply an effect to a video clip using keyframes:

Note

For this exercise, we used a logo with an alpha channel in Video track 2 and superimposed it onto the background clip in Video track 1. The logo image appears directly above the background clip in the Timeline window. To superimpose the logo over the background, the Key Type Transparency option should be set to Alpha Channel. If you want to apply effects using keyframes to video clips that transition from one track to another, you should use the A/B Editing workspace (choose Window ⇨ Workspace ⇨ A/B Editing). In the A/B Editing workspace, you can drag one video clip to Video track 1A and one to Video track 1B in the Timeline window. The video clips should overlap each other. Drag a transition to the Transition track and place it in the space where the two video clips overlap.

1. **Choose File ⇨ Import ⇨ File to import a clip that you want to apply a video effect using keyframes.** If you want, you can use the Sailing Lessons logo image seen in Figure 11-6, or you can create your own logo, using the Title Designer window.

On the CD-ROM

You can find the Sailing Lessons logo (saillogo.prtl) file in the Chapter 11 folder in the Tutorial Projects folder on the CD-ROM that accompanies this book.

2. **Drag a clip from the Project window to Video track 2 in the Timeline window.**
3. **Choose File ⇨ Import ⇨ File to import a clip to use in the background.** To create the sailing lessons logo project (seen in Figure 11-6), use Digital Vision's Electro clip 579005P.mov as the background.

On the CD-ROM

Digital Vision's Electro clip 579005P.mov, which was used as the background to create the sailing lessons logo project, is found in the Chapter 11 folder that is in the Tutorial Projects folder on the CD-ROM that accompanies this book.

4. **Drag the imported background file from the Project window to Video track 1, directly below the image in Video track 2.**

Note

The saillogo.prtl (seen in Figure 11-6) includes an alpha channel that enables the background clip to show through when previewed in the Monitor window. To see a preview in the Monitor window, choose Preview During Adjust from the Effect Controls palette. For Premiere to read the alpha channel, the Key Type option in the Transparency dialog box must be set to Alpha Channel. If the image/clip you are using in Video track 2 does not have an alpha channel, you'll have to adjust the Transparency Key Type option so that the background shows through. (Turn to Chapter 12 for more information on using Transparency Key Type options.)

5. **Add an effect to the image in Video track 2 by clicking an effect in the Video Effects palette and then dragging it to the image in the Timeline window.** In our example, we chose the Twirl effect. The Twirl effect is found in the Distort folder, in the Video Effects palette.

6. **In the Effect Controls palette, adjust the settings for the video effect.** If your effect includes a dialog box, you see the word setup next to the effect name in the Effect Controls palette. Click setup to open the Effects dialog box and set the options for the effect in the dialog box.
7. **To create a keyframe for the effect you applied in Step 7, move the Timeline marker over the first frame of the image in Video track 2.**
8. **Expand the keyframe track by clicking the Expand track icon (a triangle icon that appears before the track name).**
9. **Click the Add/Delete Keyframe box to add a keyframe.** A check mark appears.

   To add another keyframe, move the Timeline marker to a new position. Change the settings in the Effect Controls palette or the dialog box for the effect. Then click the Add Keyframe checkbox. (To add more keyframes, repeat this step as many times as desired.)
10. **Choose File ➪ Save to save your project.**
11. **To preview the video effect, choose Timeline ➪ Preview or press Enter.**

Applying Effects to Different Image Areas Using an Image Matte

You can use an image matte to show an effect only in specific areas of a clip. When you apply a matte, Premiere masks out the areas that you don't want shown.

An *image matte* is either a black-and-white image or a grayscale image. By default, Adobe Premiere applies effects to the clip areas corresponding to white portions of the matte. (The effect does not appear in clip regions corresponding to black areas.) In the gray areas, the effect is applied with some degree of transparency—which means that the areas where the effect is applied appear to be see-through to some extent.

You can use Adobe Photoshop, Adobe Illustrator, Procreate Painter, or even Adobe Premiere's Title Designer window to create an image matte. After you've created an image matte, you need two clips, one for Video track 1 and one for Video track 2. If you don't have an image matte or video clips, you can use the sample files found in the ImageMatte folder, in the Chapter 11 folder on the CD-ROM that accompanies this book.

Here's how to apply an effect using an image matte:

1. **Make sure that the project you are you're working on, is in Single-Track Editing mode.**

Cross-Reference

See Chapter 1 to select the Single-Track Editing workspace.

2. Import two video clips into the Project window.

On the CD-ROM

To use the images used to create the frames in Figure 11-7, Choose File ⇨ Import ⇨ Folder. In the Choose a Folder dialog box, choose the Image Matte Folder, from the Chapter 11 folder. In the ImageMatte folder you will find Digital Vision's Electro clip 579020P.mov and Digital Vision's CityLife clip 567017P.mov, as well as a Photoshop file called arrow.psd.

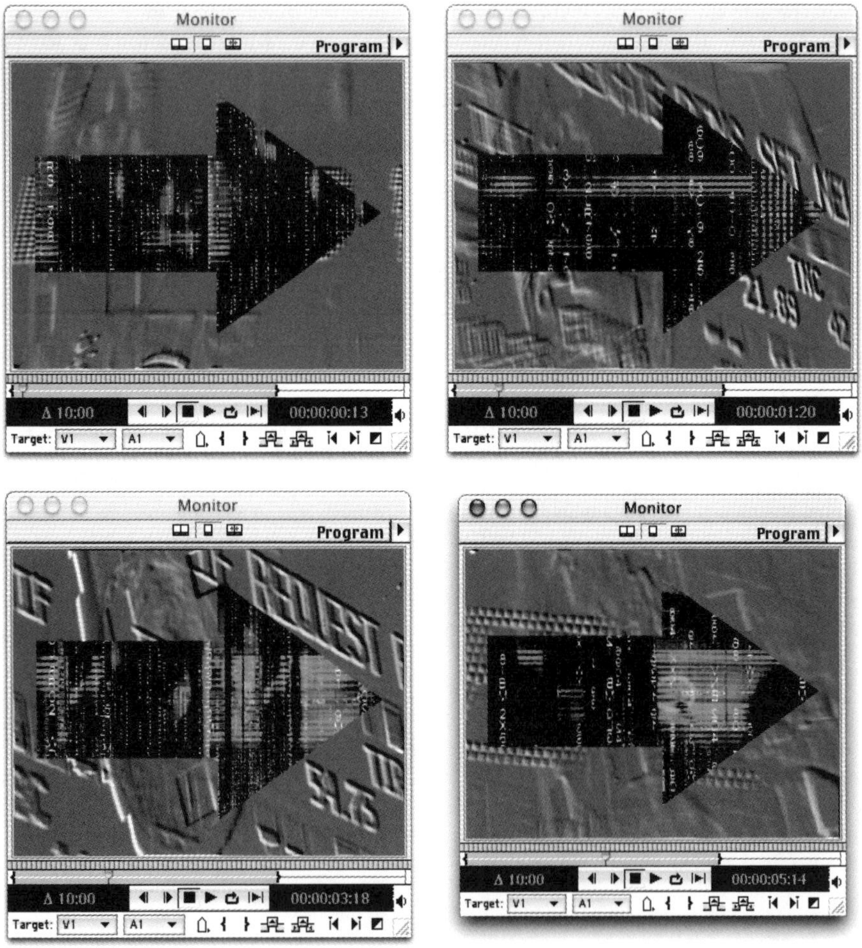

Figure 11-7: Frames from the sample image matte project using the emboss effect only on a certain area of the clip (outside the arrow)

3. **Click and drag one of the video clips from the Project window to Video track 1 of the Timeline window.** The video clip in Video track 1 will be the clip that appears inside the matte. We used Digital Vision's CityLife clip 567017P.mov, in Video track 1.
4. **Click and drag the other video clip to Video track 2.** The video clip in Video track 2 will be the clip that appears in the background of the matte. We used Digital Vision's Electro clip 579020P.mov in Video track 2.
5. **Apply an effect to Video track 2 by dragging an effect from the Video Effects palette to the clip.** If you want, you can apply a different effect to the video clip in Video track 1. If you apply the effect to Video track 2, however, the effect can only be seen outside the matte image. If you apply the effect to Video track 1, the effect is only seen in the inside of the matte image.
6. **Superimpose Video track 2 over Video track 1 by selecting Video track 2, and then choosing Video ➪ Clip ➪ Transparency.** The Transparency Settings dialog box appears.
7. **Choose Image Matte from the Transparency pop-up menu.**
8. **Click the Choose button.** The Open dialog box appears.
9. **Browse to and load the matte image.** (We used an arrow for our matte image, which can be found in the ImageMatte folder in the Chapter 11 folder on the CD that accompanies the book). To see a preview, click the Show Background icon (it looks like a page peel as seen in Figure 11-8). If you want to reverse the effect, click the Reverse Key option in the dialog box. Click OK to apply the image matte.
10. **Choose File ➪ Save to save your work.**
11. **Preview the effect by choosing Timeline ➪ Preview or by pressing Enter.**

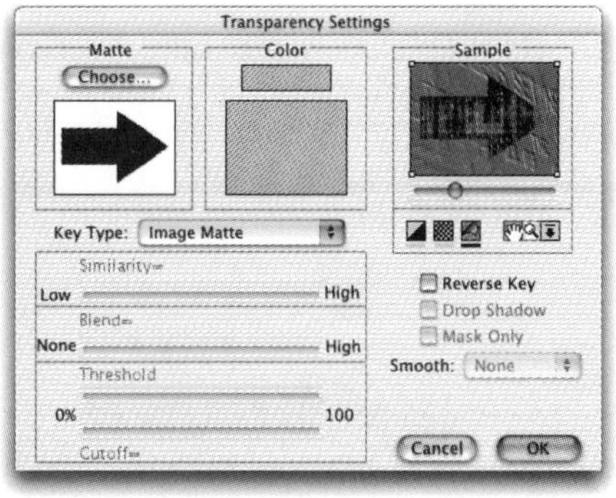

Figure 11-8: Click the Show Background icon to see a preview of your matte image.

Touring Premiere's Video Effects

Premiere boasts 78 video effects that are divided into 15 folders. The folders are; Adjust, Blur, Blur & Sharpen, Channel, Distort, Image Control, Perspective, Pixelate, QuickTime, Render, Sharpen, Stylize, Time, Transform, and Video. That's a lot of video effects to choose from. To help you deal with this overwhelming wealth of video effects, we've assembled a description of each effect according to its category folder.

Note Before undertaking a tour of the effects, remember that many effects provide previews in dialog boxes. If an effect provides a dialog box, click Setup in the Effect Controls palette to see a preview.

Tip Although most effects can be controlled by sliders that you click and drag, you can also click underlined values at the center of the slider to set effects. When you click the underlined value, a dialog box appears showing the largest and smallest values allowed in the slider setting.

On the CD-ROM If you want, you can experiment with the different video effects by applying them to one of the video clips in the Tutorial Projects folder.

The Adjust folder

The Adjust folder enables you to adjust the color attributes of selected clips, such as the brightness and contrast of an image. If you are familiar with Photoshop, you'll find that several Premiere video effects, such as Channel Mixer, Color Balance, Levels, and Posterize, are quite similar to filters found in Photoshop.

Brightness and Contrast

Using the Brightness and Contrast effects is an easy way to adjust brightness and contrast in your image. Brightness controls how light or dark your image is. Contrast controls the difference between the brightest and darkest pixels in an image. In the Effect Controls palette, click and drag the Brightness slider to increase or reduce an image's brightness; click and drag the Contrast slider to add or subtract contrast from an image.

Channel Mixer

The Channel Mixer effect enables you to create special effects by mixing colors from a clip's channels. With the Channel Mixer you create color effects, as well as turn a color image into a grayscale image or into an image with sepia tone or tint effect.

To use the Channel Mixer, click and drag any Source Channel slider in the Effect Controls palette to the left to decrease the amount of color supplied to the image. Click and drag to the right to increase it.

To convert an image to grayscale, click the Monochrome button and then adjust the sliders.

Color Balance

The Color Balance effect adds or subtracts red, green, or blue color values in a clip. Color values are easily added and subtracted by clicking the red, green, or blue color sliders. In the Effect Controls palette, dragging the sliders to the left reduces the amount of color; dragging the sliders to the right adds color. Adding equal values of red, green, and blue to your image adds gray.

Convolution Kernel

The Convolution Kernel effect uses mathematical *convolution* to change brightness values of clip. This effect can be used to increase sharpness or enhance image edges. The matrix of numbers in the Convolution Kernel Settings dialog box, shown in Figure 11-9, represents the pixels in the image. The center pixel text field is the pixel being analyzed. In the center box, enter the number that you want to use as the brightness multiplier. In other words, if you enter 2, the pixels brightness values are doubled. The same concept applies for neighboring text fields. You can enter a brightness multiplier in the surrounding boxes — you can also enter 0 to have no increase in the brightness value.

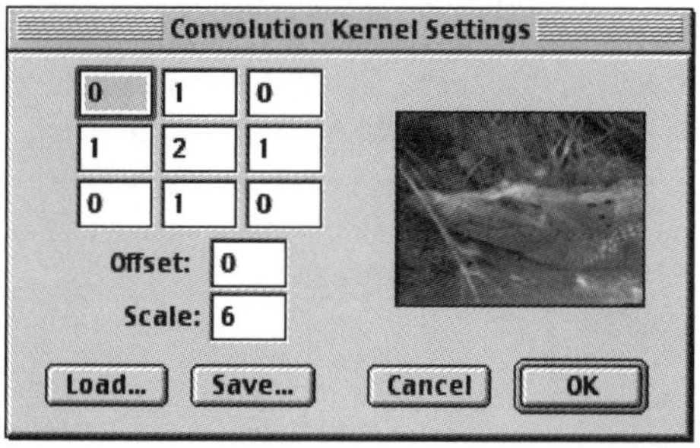

Figure 11-9: The Convolution Kernel Settings dialog box

Values entered in the Scale box are used to divide the sum of the brightness values. If desired, enter a value in the Offset field, which is the same as the value added to the Scale field.

When using the Convolution Kernel filter, you can save settings by clicking the Save button; you can reload saved settings by clicking the Load button.

Extract

The Extract filter removes the color from a clip to create a black-and-white effect. The Input and Output sliders in the Extract Settings dialog box, shown in Figure 11-10, enables you to control which image areas are affected. The Softness slider softens the effect. The preview area provides a good idea of the result of the effect.

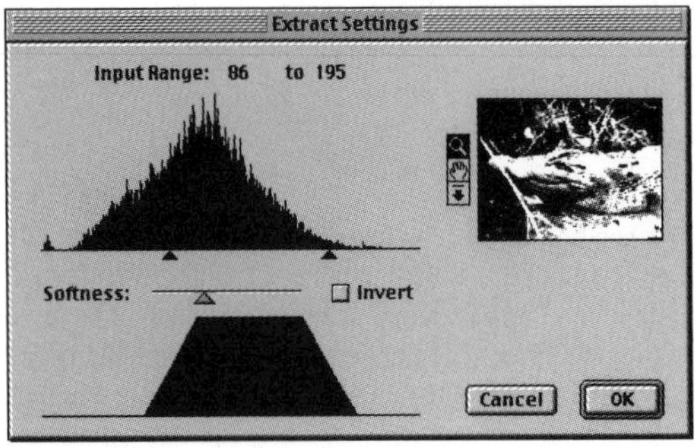

Figure 11-10: The Extract Settings dialog box

Levels

The Levels effect enables you to correct highlights, midtones, and shadows in an image. To apply the same levels to all color channels, leave the pop-up menu in the Levels Settings dialog box, shown in Figure 11-11, set to RGB. Otherwise, click to choose a red, green, or blue channel to apply the effect to.

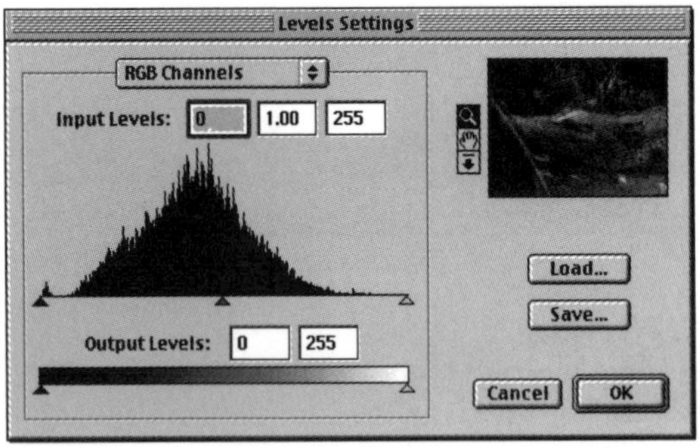

Figure 11-11: The Levels Settings dialog box

To complete your image correction, use the input slider to increase contrast. Drag the middle slider to raise or lower midtone values. Drag the output slider to decrease contrast.

Posterize

Posterize creates special color effects by reducing the tonal level in the red, green, and blue color channels. Click and drag the Levels slider in the Effect Controls palette to choose how many levels of color are in an image.

The Blur folder

The Blur folder contains effects that blur images. Using blur effects, you can create motion effects or blur out a video track as a background to emphasize the foreground.

Anti-Alias

The Anti-alias effect reduces jagged lines by blending image edges of contrasting colors to create a smooth edge.

Camera Blur

By using this effect with keyframes you can simulate an image going in or out of focus. You can also simulate a "camera bump" effect. Use the Blur slider in the Camera Blur Settings dialog box, shown in Figure 11-12, to control the effect.

Figure 11-12: The Camera Blur Settings dialog box

Ghosting

The Ghosting effect layers image areas from previous frames over one frame. Use this to show the path of a moving object — such as a speeding bullet or a pie thrown in the air.

Radial Blur

This effect creates a circular blurring effect. The Radial Blur dialog box, shown in Figure 11-13, lets you control the degree of blurring. To do so, increase the value in the Amount field by dragging the Amount slider to the right. In the Blur Method area, choose Spin to create a spinning blur; choose Zoom to create an outward blur. In the Quality section, choose Draft, Good, or Best. However, remember that the better the quality the more processing time needed to create the effect.

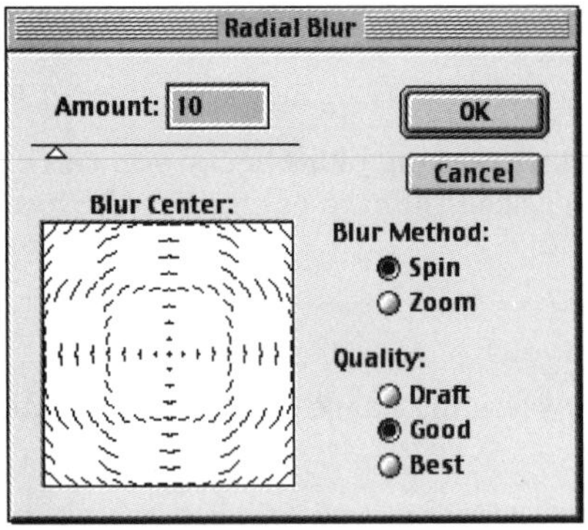

Figure 11-13: The Radial Blur dialog box

The Blur & Sharpen folder

Channel Blur

The Channel Blur effect enables you to blur an image using the Red, Green, Blue Channel, or Alpha channel. By default the Blur Dimension pop-up is set to Horizontal and Vertical. At the default setting, any blurring you do affects the image horizontally and vertically. If you want to blur only one dimension, set the pop-up menu to either Horizontal or Vertical. When the Edge Behavior/Repeat Edge Pixels option is deselected, the edges around the clip are blurred. When it is selected, they are not.

Directional Blur

The Directional Blur effect creates a motion effect by blurring an image in a specific direction. The sliders in the Effect Controls palette control the direction and the length of the blur.

Fast Blur

Use the Fast Blur effect to quickly blur a clip. Use the Blur Dimension pop-up menu in the Effect Controls palette to specify whether the blur should be vertical, horizontal, or both.

Gaussian Blur

The Gaussian Blur effect blurs video and reduces video signal noise. Similar to the Fast Blur effect, you can specify whether the blur should be vertical, horizontal, or both. The word “gaussian” is used because the filter uses a *gaussian* (bell-shaped) curve when removing contrast to create the blur effect.

Sharpen

The Sharpen effect includes a slider that enables you to control sharpening within your clip. Click and drag the Sharpen Amount slider in the Effect Controls palette to the right to increase sharpening. The slider permits values from 0 to 100; however, if you click the underlined sharpen amount onscreen you can enter values up to 4000 into the Value field.

The Channel folder

The Channel folder contains two effects — Blend and Invert. Blend, blends video clips based on color modes. Invert, inverts the color values within a clip.

Blend

The Blend effect allows you to blend Video tracks using different modes, Crossfade, Color Only, Tint Only, Darken Only, and Lighten Only. The Blend with Original option is used to specify which clip you want to blend with. For example, if you apply the Blend effect to a clip in Video track 1A and want to blend it with a clip in Video track 1B, set the Blend with Layer pop-up menu to V1B. For both clips to appear translucent, set the Blend with Original value to 50%. In order to see both clips in the Monitor window, they must be selected with the Timeline Marker. If you apply the Blend effect to a clip in Video track 1A and want to blend it with a clip in Video track 2, set the Blend with Layer pop-up menu to V2. Then hide Video track 2, by clicking on the Eye icon in the Timeline window. In order to see both clips in the Monitor window, they must be selected with the Timeline Marker and the Blend with Original value should be set to less than 90%.

Invert

The Invert effect inverts color values. You can turn black into white, white into black, and colors into their complements.

The Channel pop-up menu in the Effect Controls palette enables you to choose a color model: RGB, HLS, or YIQ. YIQ is the NTSC color space. *Y* refers to luminance; *I* refers to inphase chrominance; *Q* refers to quadrature chrominance. The alpha choice enables you to invert the gray levels in an alpha channel. Use the Blend with Original slider if you want to blend the channel effect with the original image.

The Distort folder

The Distort commands, found in the Distort folder, enable you to distort an image either by twirling, pinching, or spherizing it. Many of these commands are similar to the distort filters found in Adobe Photoshop.

Bend

The Bend effect can bend your image into goo. In the Bend Settings dialog box, which is shown in Figure 11-14, use the Intensity, Rate, and Width sliders to control effects for Horizontal and Vertical Bending. Intensity is the wave height; Rate is the frequency; Width is the width of the wave. The Direction pop-up menu controls the direction of the effect. The Wave pop-up menu specifies the type of wave: sine, circle, triangle, or square. Figure 11-15 shows a frame before and after applying the Bend effect.

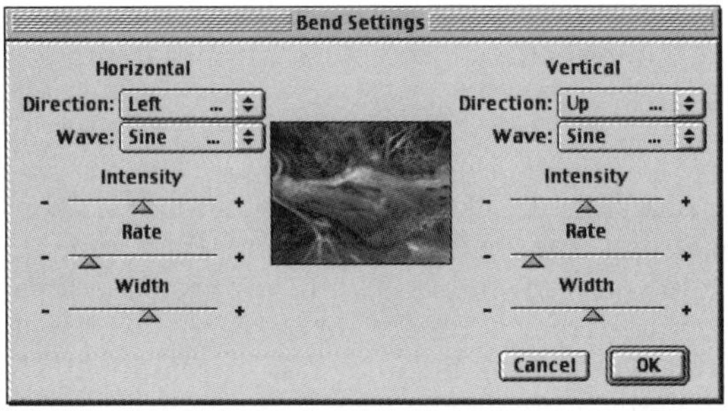

Figure 11-14: The Bend Settings dialog box

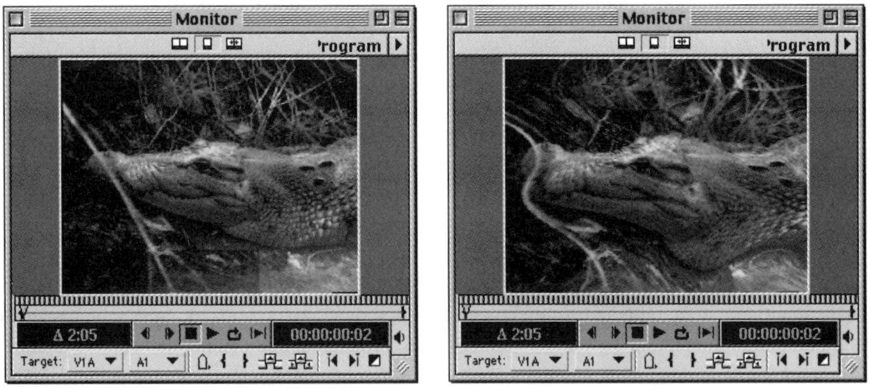

Figure 11-15: An image before and after the Bend effect is applied

Lens Distortion

Use the Lens Distortion effect to simulate video being viewed through a distorted lens.

Use the Curvature slider in the Lens Distortion Settings dialog box, shown in Figure 11-16, to change the lens curve. Negative values make the curvature more concave (inward); positive values make the curvature more convex (outward). Vertical and Horizontal Decentering sliders change the focal point of the lens.

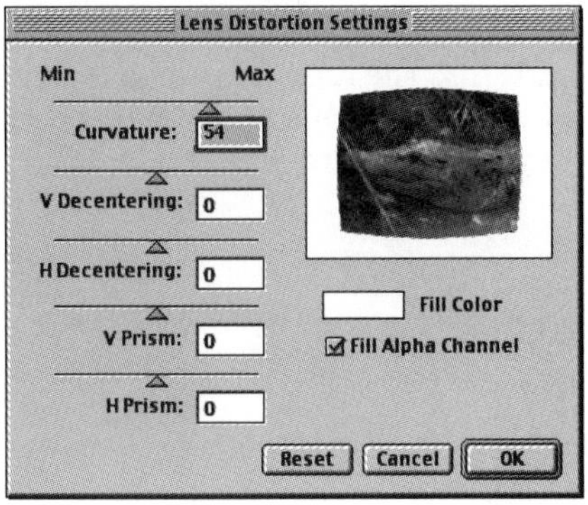

Figure 11-16: The Lens Distortion Settings dialog box

Vertical and Horizontal Prism FX creates effects similar to changing Vertical and Horizontal Decentering. Use the Fill color swatch to change the background color. Click the Fill alpha checkbox to make background areas transparent based on the clip's alpha channel.

Mirror

Mirror creates a mirrored effect. In the Effect Controls palette, click the Reflection center values to open the Edit Reflection Center dialog box to designate the X and Y coordinates of the reflection line. The reflection angle option enables you to choose where the reflection appears. The following degree settings should help orient you to how dragging the slider distorts the image:

- **0.** Left onto right side.
- **90.** Right onto left side.
- **180.** Top onto bottom.
- **270.** Bottom onto top.

Polar Coordinates

Polar Coordinates can create a variety of unusual effects by changing the clip's X and Y coordinates to polar coordinates. In the polar coordinate system, the X and Y coordinates are distances radiating out of a focal point. By using this effect, you can transform a line into a half circle or horseshoe shape.

In the Effect Controls palette, the Interpolation slider controls the amount of the distortion — 0% provides no distortion; 100 % provides the most. In the Type of Conversion pop-up menu, Rect to Polar converts horizontal coordinates to Polar; Polar to Rect converts polar coordinates to rectangular ones.

Ripple

The Ripple effect turns a clip into rippled patterns. The Ripple Settings dialog box, shown in Figure 11-17, enables you to adjust the ripples on a horizontal and vertical plane and control the intensity and frequency of the ripples.

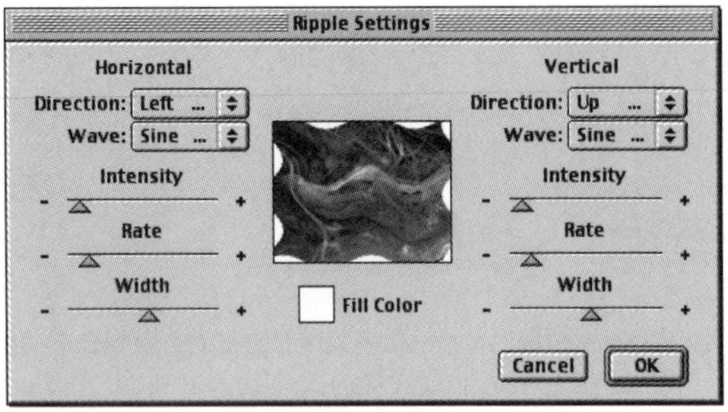

Figure 11-17: The Ripple Settings dialog box

Pinch

Pinch provides an effect similar to pinching and pulling the video image as if it were clay. In the Pinch Settings dialog box, shown in Figure 11-18, click and drag the amount slider to the right to pinch the image in; click and drag to the left to expand the image out. Figure 11-19 shows a frame after the Pinch effect is applied.

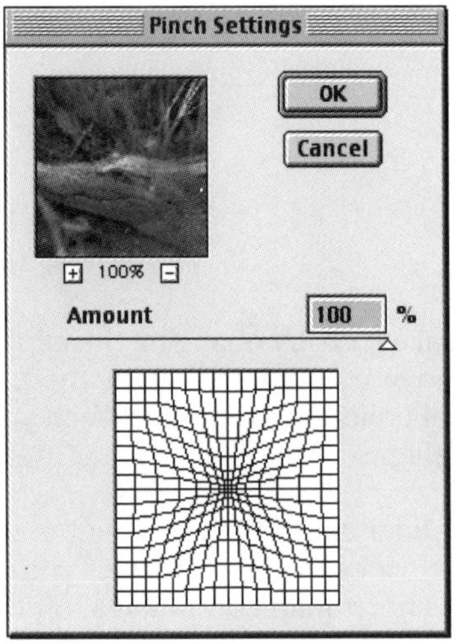

Figure 11-18: The Pinch Settings dialog box

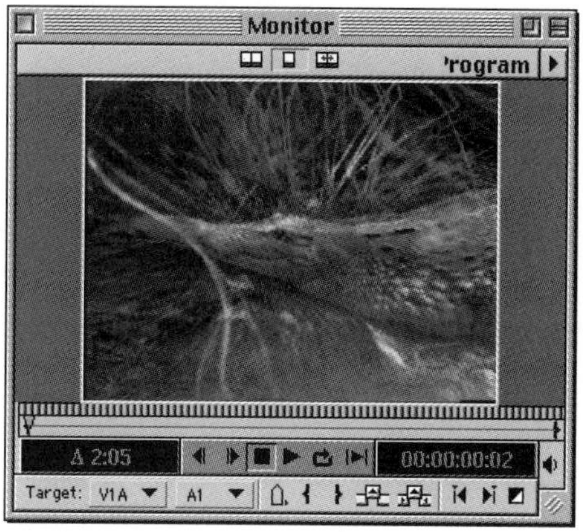

Figure 11-19: A frame after application of the Pinch effect

Shear

The Shear effect bends an image according to the curve specified in the Shear Settings dialog box, which is shown in Figure 11-20. If you shear the clip off-screen, you can choose whether to have the image wrap so that it leaves one side of the frame and returns on the opposite side. To do this, choose the Wrap Around option. Otherwise, choose Repeat Edge Pixels. This option applies extra pixels to the image edges. Figure 11-21 shows a frame after applying the Shear video effect.

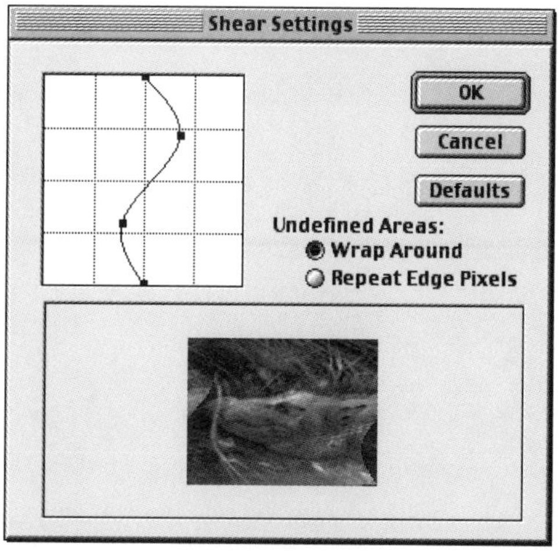

Figure 11-20: The Shear Settings dialog box

Figure 11-21: A frame after applying the Shear effect

Spherize

The Spherize effect turns a flat image into a spherical one. Use the Amount slider in the Spherize Settings dialog box (shown in Figure 11-22) to control the spherizing effect. Dragging the slider to the right increases the Amount value, providing a larger sphere. In the Mode pop-up menu, choose Normal for a standard sphere effect; choose Horizontal Only or Vertical Only to change directions. Figure 11-23 shows a frame after applying the Spherize video effect.

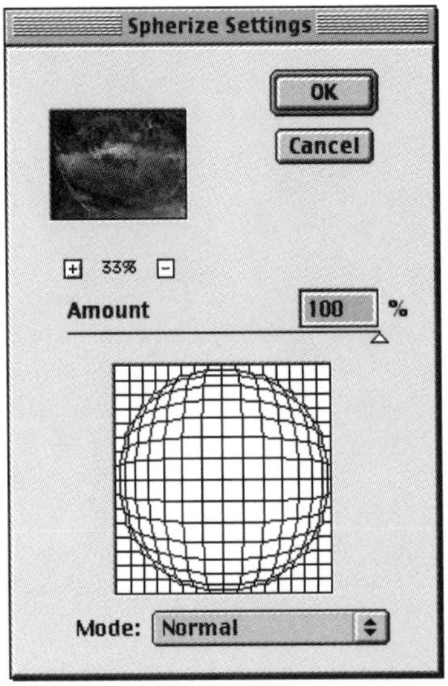

Figure 11-22: The Spherize Settings dialog box

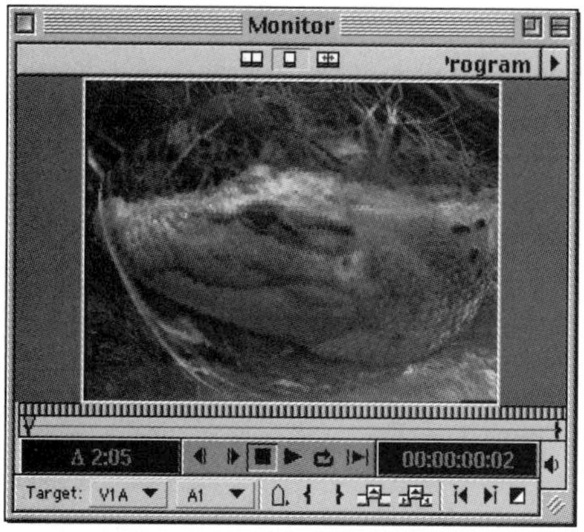

Figure 11-23: A frame of an image after application of the Spherize effect

Transform

The Transform effect allows you to move an image's position, scale its height and weight, skew or rotate, and change its opacity, as seen in Figure 11-24. You can also use the Transform effect, to change the position of a clip. To change position of a clip, click on the box next to the word, Position, in the Effect Controls palette. Then click in the Monitor window where you want the clip to move to. Use the Anchor Point option, to move a clip based on its anchor point.

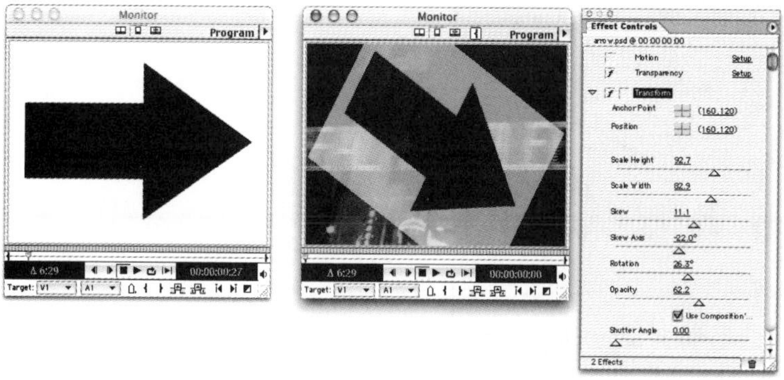

Figure 11- 24: Before Transform and After Transform with Transform options in the Effect Controls palette

Twirl

The Twirl effect can turn an image into twirling digital soup. In the Twirl Settings dialog box, shown in Figure 11-25, use the Angle slider to control the degree of twirling. Larger angle settings create more twirling. Figure 11-26 shows a frame after the Twirl video effect is applied.

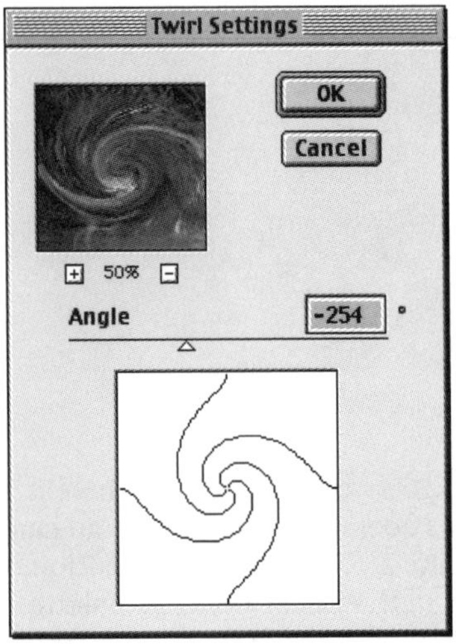

Figure 11-25: The Twirl Settings dialog box

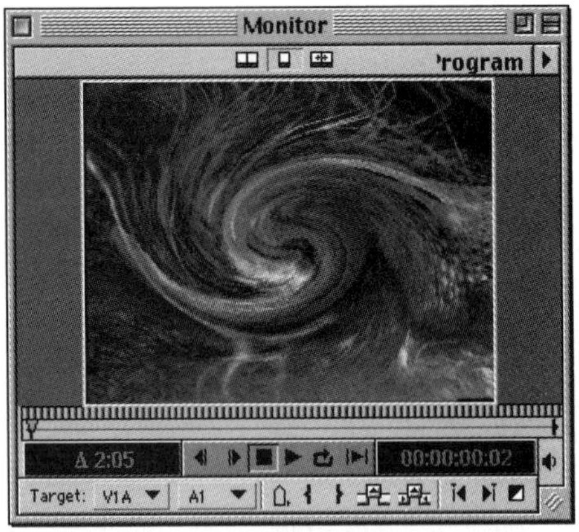

Figure 11-26: A frame of an image after application of the Twirl effect

Wave

The Wave effect creates wave-like effects that can make your clip look as if it were hit by a tidal wave. To control the effect, view the Preview window in the Wave

Settings dialog box, shown in Figure 11-27, as you click and drag the sliders. Figure 11-28 shows a sample frame with the Wave effect applied.

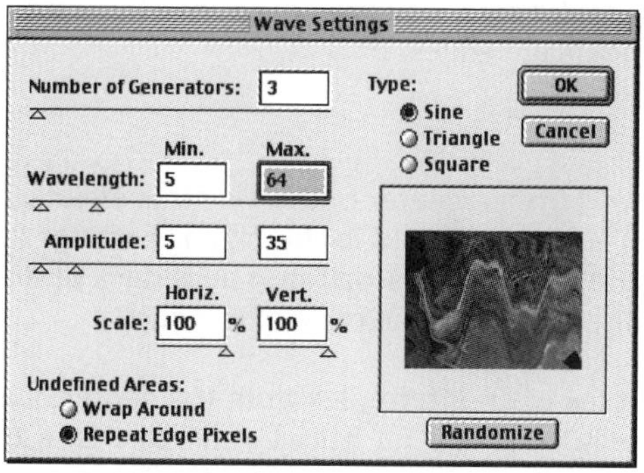

Figure 11-27: The Wave Settings dialog box

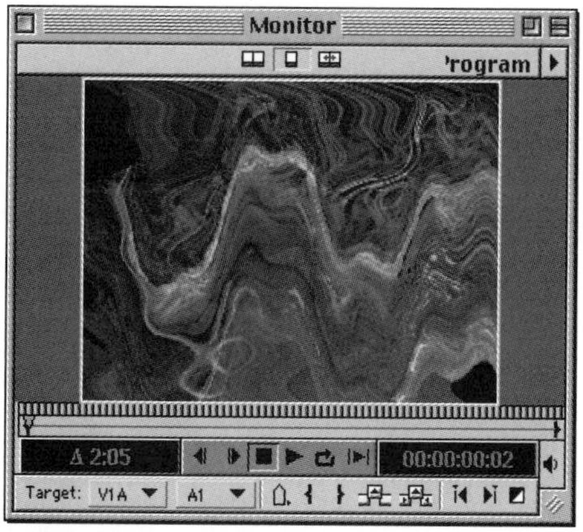

Figure 11-28: A sample frame with the Wave effect applied

Following is a brief description of the slider controls found in the Wave Settings dialog box:

- ✦ **Number of Generators.** Controls the amount of continuous waves.
- ✦ **Wavelength.** Changes the distance between wave crests.
- ✦ **Amplitude.** Changes the wave height.
- ✦ **Randomize.** Randomizes the wavelength and amplitude.
- ✦ **Scale.** Controls the amount of horizontal and vertical distortion.

✦ **Type.** Controls the type of wave crests: Sine (waving), Triangle, or Square.

✦ **Undefined Areas.** If the Wave effect spills portions of your image off-screen, choose Wrap Around to make the image wrap so that it comes out one side of the frame and returns on the opposite side. Otherwise, choose Repeat Edge Pixels to apply extra pixels to the image edges.

ZigZag

The ZigZag effect distorts a clip outward from a center point. Use this effect to create great looking pond ripple effects The Amount field in the ZigZag Settings dialog box, shown in Figure 11-29, controls the degree of distortion. The Ridges **option** controls the number of zigzags from the middle to the edge of the clip.

In the Style section, choose Pond Ripples to create ripples from the center of an image, as if a rock was dropped in a pond; choose Out from Center to create zigzags that push outward from the center of the image; choose Around Center to create zigzags that appear around the center.

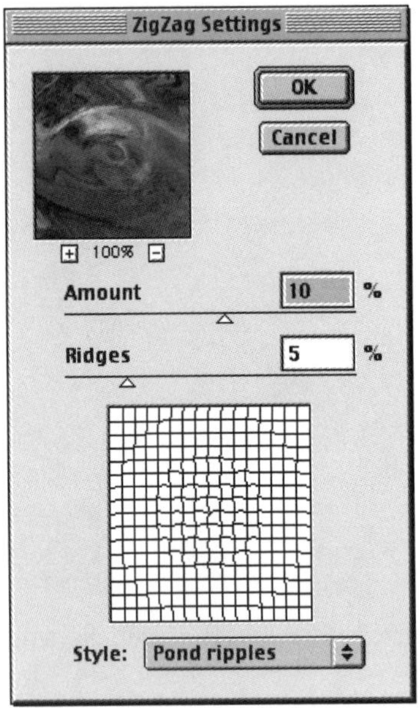

Figure 11-29: The ZigZag Settings dialog box

The Image Control folder

The Image Control folder contains a variety of color special effects.

Black & White

The Black & White effect produces a grayscale version of a selected clip.

Color Balance HLS

The Color Balance HLS effect enables you to change and adjust colors using Hue, Lightness, and Saturation sliders in the Effect Controls palette. Hue controls the color; Lightness controls how light and dark the color is; Saturation controls the intensity of the color.

Color Offset

The Color Offset effect enables you to create 3D images out of 2D artwork by enabling you to shift the red, green, and blue color channels up, down, left, and right. Use the Offset slider in the Color Offset Settings dialog box, shown in Figure 11-30, to control the distance between each color channel. Using this effect, you can set up the image for viewing with 3D glasses.

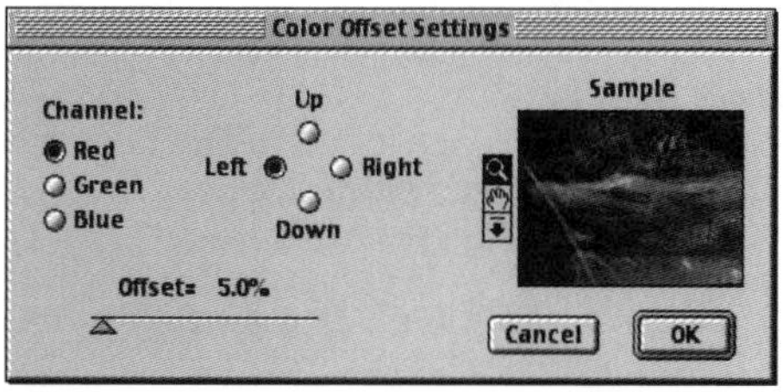

Figure 11-30: The Color Offset Settings dialog box

Color Pass

The Color Pass effect converts all but one color in a clip to grayscale — or, it can convert just one color in a clip to grayscale. Use this effect to draw interest to specific items in a clip. For example, you may want to show a grayscale party scene in which a grayscale man or woman is wearing a colored hat on his or her head, or holding a colored balloon.

Here's how to set the Color Pass color and use the filter:

1. **In the Color Pass Settings dialog box clip area (shown in Figure 11-31), click the color that you want to preserve.** Alternatively, you can click the swatch area and then choose a color in the Color Picker window.
2. **To increase or decrease the color range, drag the Similarity slider to the right or left.**
3. **To reverse the color effect (in other words, make all colors normal and gray except the selected color), click Reverse.**

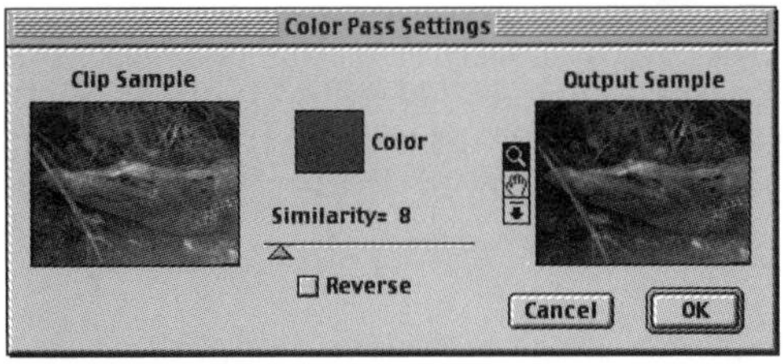

Figure 11-31: The Color Pass Settings dialog box

Color Replace

The Color Replace effect replaces one color or a range of colors with another color.

To choose a color or colors to replace, follow these steps:

1. **In the Color Replace Settings dialog box, shown in Figure 11-32, use the Eyedropper tool to click the color you want to preserve in the clip sample area.** Alternatively, you can click the swatch area and then choose a color in the Color Picker window.
2. **To choose the replacement color, click the Replace color swatch.** Choose a color in the Color Picker window.
3. **To increase or decrease the color range of the replacement color, drag the Similarity slider right or left.**
4. **Choose Solid Color to replace the color with a solid color.**

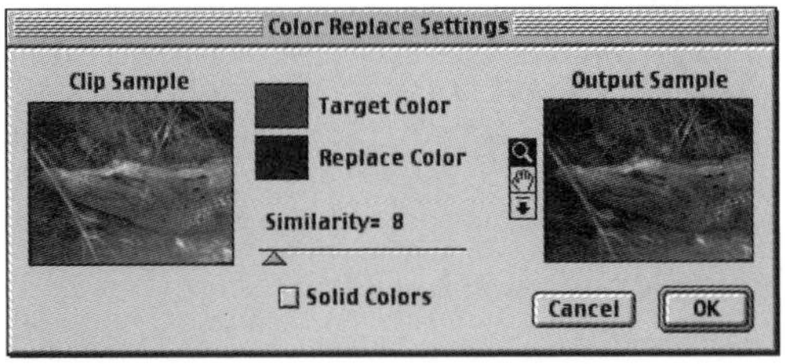

Figure 11-32: The Color Replace Settings dialog box

Gamma Correction

The Gamma Correction effect enables you to adjust the midtone color levels of a clip. In the Gamma Correction Settings dialog box, shown in Figure 11-33, click and drag the Gamma slider to make the adjustment. Dragging to the left lightens midtones; dragging to the right darkens them.

Figure 11-33: The Gamma Correction Settings dialog box

Median

The Median effect can be used for reducing noise. It creates the effect by taking the median pixel value of neighboring pixels and applying this value to pixels within the radius pixel area specified in the Effect Controls palette. If you enter large values for the radius, your image begins to look as if it were painted. Click the Operate on Alpha option to apply the effect to the image's alpha channel as well as to the image.

Tint

Use the Tint effect to apply a color tint to your image. If desired, you can reassign the black and white portions of your clip with different colors by clicking the color swatch and choosing a color in the Color Picker window. Choose color intensity by clicking and dragging the slider in the Color Picker window.

The Perspective folder

You can use the effects in the Perspective folder to add depth to images, to create drop shadows, and to bevel image edges.

Basic 3D

The Basic 3D effect creates nice flipping and tilting effects. The Swivel slider in the Effect Controls palette controls rotation. The Tilt slider adjusts the tilt of the image. Dragging the Distance to Image slider creates an illusion of distance by reducing or enlarging the image. Click the Show Specular Highlight to add a tiny flare of light to your image (indicated by a red + sign). Draw Preview enables you to view a wire-frame simulation of the effect, which provides a good idea of how the effect will look without waiting for Premiere to render it.

Bevel Alpha

The Bevel Alpha effect can add a three-dimensional effect to a two-dimensional image by beveling the image's alpha channel. This filter is especially handy for creating beveled effects with text. Sliders in the Effect Controls palette enable you to fine-tune the effect by changing bevel edge thickness, light angle, and light intensity. Change the light color by clicking the color swatch and choosing a color in Premiere's Color Picker window.

Bevel Edges

The Bevel Edges effect bevels an image and adds lighting to give a clip a three-dimensional appearance. Image edges created with this effect are sharper than those created with the Bevel Alpha effect. To determine image edges, this filter also uses the clip's alpha channel. Similar to Bevel Alpha, sliders in the Effect Controls palette enable you to fine-tune the effect by changing bevel edge thickness, light angle, and light intensity. Change light color by clicking the color swatch and choosing a color in the Color Picker window.

Drop Shadow

The Drop Shadow effect applies a drop shadow to a clip, using the clip's alpha channel to determine image edges. Sliders enable you to control the shadow's opacity, direction, and distance from the original clip. You can change the light color by clicking the color swatch in the palette and choosing a color from Premiere's Color Picker window.

The Pixelate folder

The effects found in the Pixelate folder create special effects by shifting, moving, and remapping pixels and their color values. These effects can create dramatic color distortions in your image.

Crystallize

The Crystallize effect can create a crystal-like effect in your image by shifting colors that are similar together into a grid. The size of the grid is controlled by the Cell Size slider in the Crystallize Setting dialog box, as shown in Figure 11-34. Figure 11-35 shows a frame after applying the Crystallize effect.

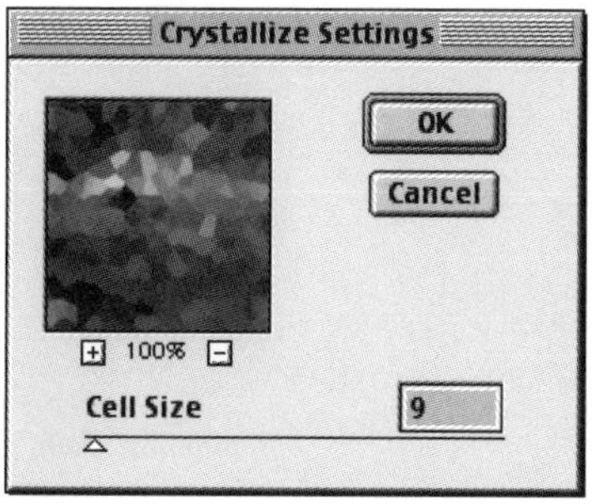

Figure 11-34: The Crystallize Settings dialog box

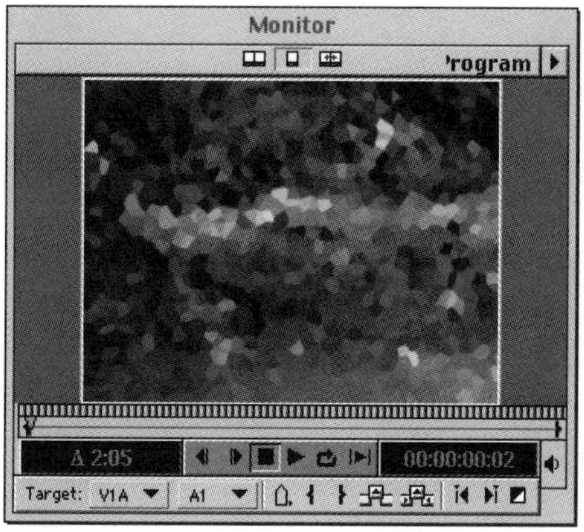

Figure 11-35: A frame after application of the Crystallize effect

Facet

The Facet effect creates a painterly effect by grouping similarly colored pixels together within a clip.

Pointillize

The Pointillize effect simulates a pointillist painting by making your clip appear as if it were created with tiny dots. You can make the dots bigger or smaller by changing the value in the Cell Size field in the Pointillize Setting dialog box, which is shown in Figure 11-36. Figure 11-37 shows a frame after applying the Pointillize effect.

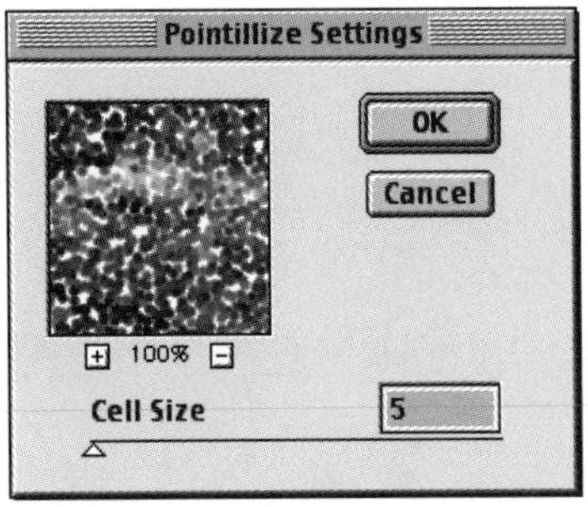

Figure 11-36: The Pointillize Settings dialog box

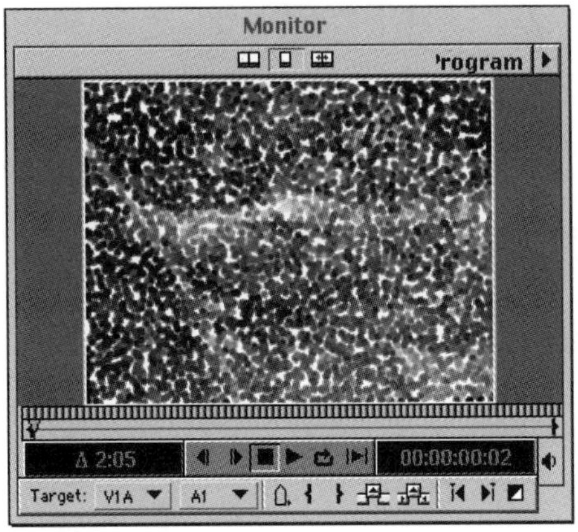

Figure 11-37: A frame after applying the Pointillize effect

The QuickTime folder

The QuickTime folder includes a variety of effects built into Apple's QuickTime digital video formats. These effects are similar to many of the effects already provided in Premiere. The QuickTime effects include Alpha Gain; Blur; Brightness and Contrast; Clouds; Color Style; Color Tint; Edge Detection; Emboss; Film Noise; General Convolution; HSL Balance; Lens Flare; RGB Balance; and Sharpen.

The Render folder

The Render folder features the Lens Flare effect, which is similar to Photoshop's Lens Flare filter.

Lens Flare

The Lens Flare effect creates a flaring light effect in your image. In the Lens Flare Settings dialog box, use the mouse to pick the image position of the flare in the Preview area. Click and drag the slider to adjust flare brightness and then pick a lens: Zoom, 35 mm, or 105 mm.

Lightning

The Lighnting effect enables you to add lightning to a clip. With the Lightning setting, you can choose a start and ending point for the lightning. Moving the Segment slider to the right increases the amount of segments the lightning has. Moving the Segment slider to the left decreases the amount of segments. Conversely moving the other Lightning effect sliders to the right increases the effect; moving the slider to the left, decreases it. You can stylize your lightning bolt, by adjusting the Segments, Amplitude, Branching, Speed, Stability, Width, Force, and Blending Mode options. Figure 11-38 shows a lightning bolt created using the Lighting effect.

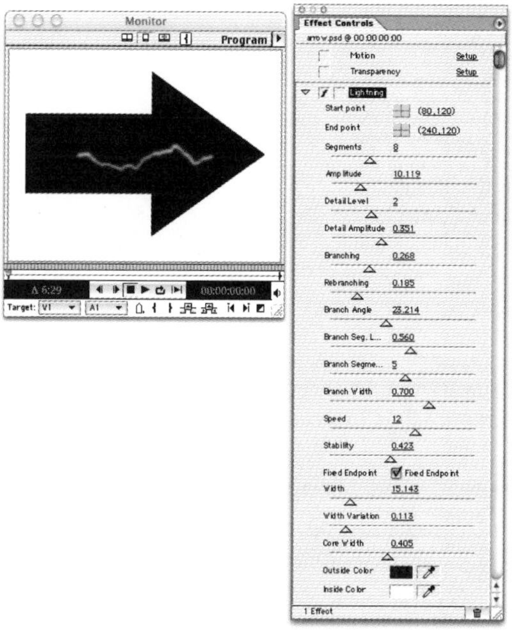

Figure 11-38: Image after applying the Lightning effect and Lighting options seen in the Effect Controls palette

Ramp

The Ramp effect allows you to create linear or radial blurs, as seen in Figure 11-39. Click the Ramp Shape pop-up menu to choose either Radial Ramp or Linear Ramp. You can set the start and end color of the blur by clicking a color in your image and using the Eyedropper tool or by clicking the color swatch and using the Color Picker dialog box. Moving the Ramp Scale slider to the left creates a smoother blend. When the Blend Witness slider is set to 50, both the blend and image clip you are applying the affect to are set to 50% translucency. Moving the slider to the right makes the image clip more opaque. Moving the slider to the left makes the blend less opaque.

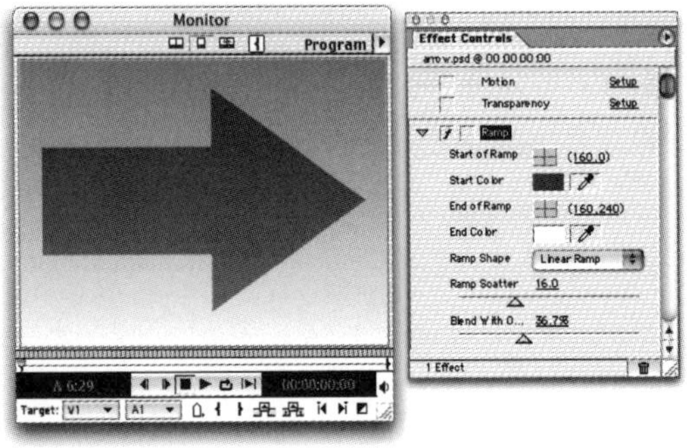

Figure 11-39: Image after applying the Ramp effect with Ramp options seen in Effect Controls palette

The Sharpen folder

The effects in the Sharpen folder enable you to sharpen images. Sharpening helps bring out image edges when digitized images or graphics appear too soft.

Gaussian Sharpen

Apply the Gaussian Sharpen effect to create strong, overall sharpening. You can obtain similar results by applying the Sharpen filter several times. This effect provides no controls.

Sharpen Edges

The Sharpen Edges effect applies sharpening effects on image edges.

The Stylize folder

The effects found in the Stylize folder create a variety of effects that change images without creating major distortions. For example, the Emboss effect adds depth throughout your image, while the Tiles effect divides your image into mosaic tiles.

Alpha Glow

The Alpha Glow effect adds a glowing effect around alpha channel edges. In the Alpha Glow Settings dialog box, shown in Figure 11-40, use the Glow slider to control how far the glow extends from the alpha channel. Use the Brightness slider to increase and decrease brightness.

In the dialog box, the Start color swatch represents the glow color. If you want to change the color, click the color swatch and choose a color from Premiere's Color Picker window.

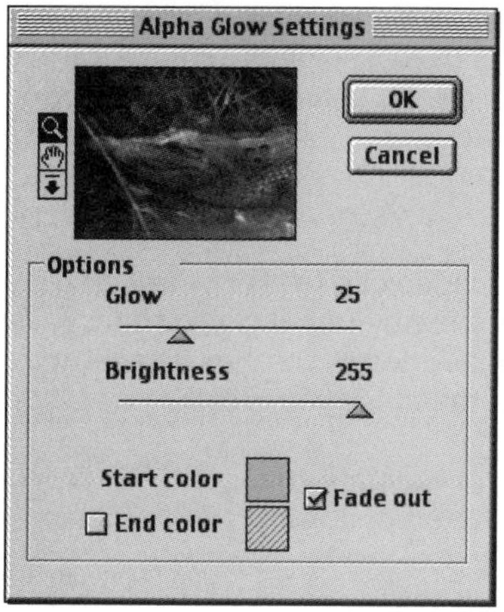

Figure 11-40: The Alpha Glow Settings dialog box

If you choose an End color, Premiere adds an extra color at the edge of the glow. To create an end color, select the end color check box and click the color swatch to pick the color in the Color Picker window. To fade the start color out, click the Fade Out checkbox.

Color Emboss

The Color Emboss effect creates the same effect as Emboss (described next), except that it doesn't remove color.

Emboss

The Emboss effect creates a raised 3D effect from image edge areas in a clip. In the Effect Controls palette, use the Direction slider to control the angle of the embossing. Drag the Relief slider to raise the emboss level to create a greater emboss effect. To create a more pronounced effect, add more contrast by dragging the Contrast slider to the right. Use the Blend with Original slider to blend shading of the embossing with the clip's original image.

Find Edges

Find Edges can make the image in a clip look as if it is a black and white sketch. The effect seeks out image areas of high contrast and turns them into black lines that appear against a white background, or as colored lines with a black background. In the Effect Controls palette, use the Blend with Original slider to blend the lines with the original image.

Mosaic

The Mosaic effect turns your image areas into rectangular tiles. In the Effect Controls palette, enter the number of mosaic blocks in the Horizontal/Vertical blocks field. This effect can be animated for use as a transition, where normally the average of the colors in the other video track is used to pick tile color. However, if you choose the Sharp color option, Premiere uses the pixel color in the center of the corresponding region in the other video track.

Noise

The Noise effect randomly changes colors in a video clip to give your clip a grainy appearance. In the Effect Controls palette, use the Amount of Noise slider to designate how much "noise," or graininess, you want added to the clip. The more noise you add, the more your image disappears into the noise you create.

If you choose the Color Noise option, the effect randomly changes the pixels in the image. If Color Noise is turned off, the same amount of noise is added to each red, green, and blue channel in the image.

Clipping is a mathematical stopgap that prevents noise from becoming larger than a set value. When the Clipping option is not selected, noise values start at lower values after reaching a certain point. If you turn Clipping off, you may find that your image completely disappears into the noise.

Replicate

The Replicate effect creates multiple versions of the clip within the frame. The effect produces this replication effect by creating tiles and placing multiple versions of the clip into the tiles. Dragging the Replicate Settings Count slider in the Replicate Settings dialog box (shown in Figure 11-41) to the right increases the number of tiles on-screen.

Solarize

The Solarize effect creates a positive and negative version of your image and then blends them together to create the solarizing effect. This can produce a lightened version of your image with darkened edges. In the Solarize Settings dialog box, shown in Figure 11-42, click and drag the Threshold slider to control the brightness level at which the Solarizing effect begins.

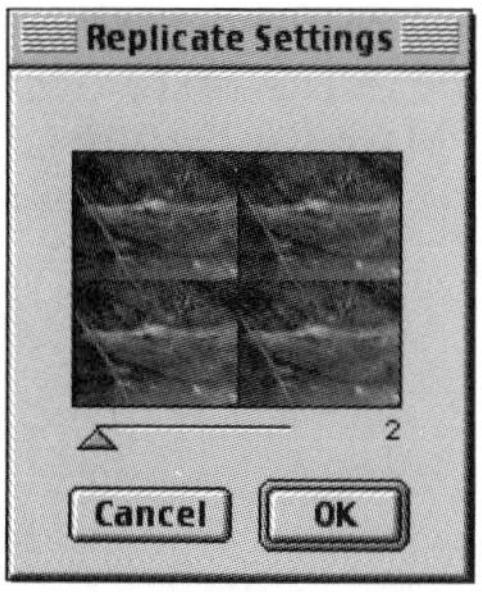

Figure 11-41: The Replicate Settings dialog box

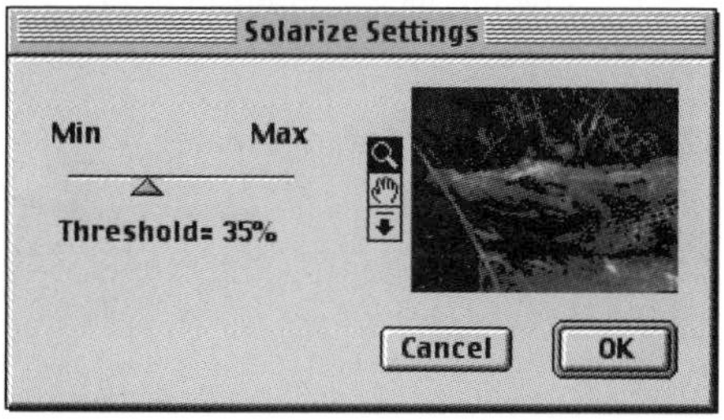

Figure 11-42: The Solarize Settings dialog box

Strobe Light

The Strobe Light effect creates the illusion of a strobe light flashing at regular or random intervals in your clip. In the Effect Controls palette, click the color swatch to choose a color for the strobe effect. Enter the duration of the strobe flash in the Duration field. In the Strobe Period field, enter the duration between strobe effect. (Duration is measured from the time the last strobe flashed—not when the flash ends.) If you want to create a random strobe effect, drag the Random Strobe Probability slider to the right. (The greater the probability setting, the more random the effect.)

In the Strobe area of the Effect Controls palette, choose Operates on Color only if you want the strobe effect to be applied to all color channels. Choose Make Layer Transparent to make the track transparent when the strobe goes off. If you choose Operates on Color, you can select an arithmetic operator from the Strobe Operator pop-up menu that can further alter the strobe effect.

Note If you set the strobe period longer than the strobe duration, the strobe will be constant – not flashing.

Texturize

The Texturize effect can create texture in a clip by applying texture, such as sand or rocks, found in one track to another track. To choose the video track supplying the texture, click in the Texture Layer pop-up menu in the Effect Controls palette and choose the track. Click and drag the Light Direction and Contrast slider to create the best effect. In the Texture Placement pop-up menu, choose Tile Texture to repeat the texture over the clip. Choose Center Texture to place the texture in the clip's center, and then choose Stretch Texture to stretch the text over the entire frame area.

Wind

As you probably guessed, the Wind effect applies a windswept look to your clip. To create a simple wind effect, choose Wind in the Method area of the Wind Settings dialog box, shown in Figure 11-43. For a tornado-like blast, choose Blast. The Stagger choice creates a bit less wind. In the Direction section, choose either From the Left or From the Right. Figure 11-44 shows a frame with the Wind effect applied.

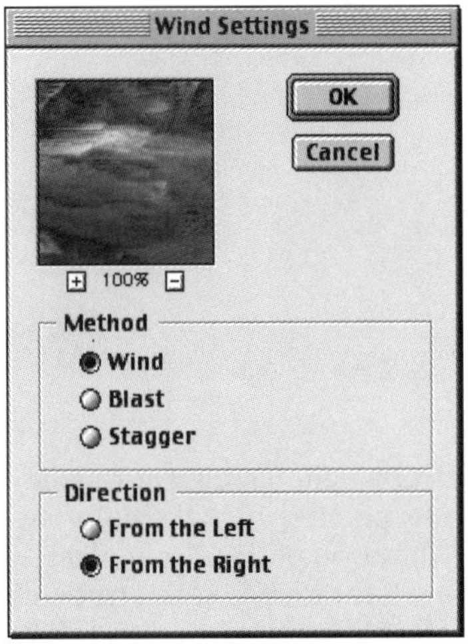

Figure 11-43: The Wind Settings dialog box

Figure 11-44: A frame with the Wind effect applied

Tiles

The Tiles effect turns your image into tiles. In the Tiles Settings dialog box, shown in Figure 11-45, choose how many tiles you wish to see and offset the tiles by entering a percentage in the Tiles Offset field. In the Fill Empty Areas With field, choose the color you wish to appear between the tiles. Background and Foreground colors fills the space between the tiles with white; Inverse Image uses a negative version of the clip to fill the space; Unaltered Image simply uses the clip. Figure 11-46 shows a frame with the Tiles effect applied.

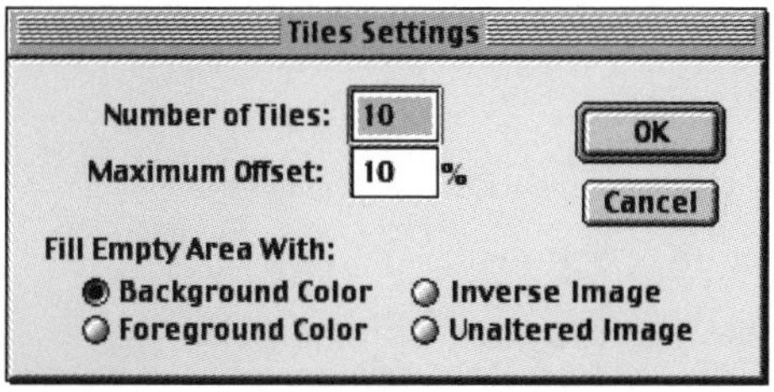

Figure 11-45: The Tiles Settings dialog box

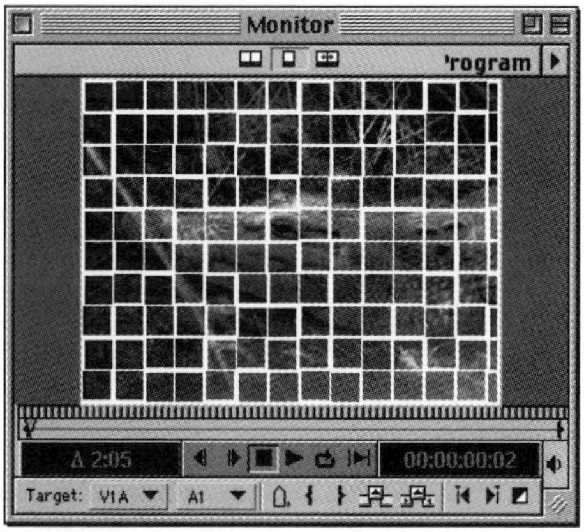

Figure 11-46: A frame with the Tiles effect applied

The Time folder

The Time folder contains effects that create effects specifically related to different frames in the selected clip.

Echo

The Echo effect creates the visual version of an echo. In other words, frames from the selected clip are repeated again and again. The effect is only effective in clips that display motion. Depending on the clip, Echo can produce a repeated visual effect or possibly a streaking type of special effect. In the Effect Controls palette, use the Echo Time slider to control the time between the repetitions. Drag the Number of Echoes to designate how many frames to combine for the effect.

Use the Starting Intensity slider to control intensity of the first frame. A setting of 1 provides full intensity; .25 provides quarter intensity. The Decay slider controls how quickly the echo dissipates. If the Decay slider is set to .25, the first echo will be .25 the starting intensity, the next echo will be .25 of the previous echo, and so on.

The Echo operator pop-up menu creates effects by combining the pixel values of the echoes. Following is a review of the pop-up menu choices:

- **Add.** Adds pixel values.
- **Maximum.** Uses maximum pixels value of echoes.
- **Minimum.** Uses minimum pixel value of echoes.
- **Screen.** Similar to Add, but less likely to produce white streaks.
- **Composite in Back.** Uses the clip's alpha channels and composites them starting at the back.
- **Composite in Front.** Uses the clip's alpha channels and composites them starting at the front.

Note: To combine an Echo effect with a Motion Settings effect, create a virtual clip and apply the effect to the virtual clip.

Posterize Time

The Posterize Time effect grabs control of a clip's frame rate settings and substitutes the frame rate specified in the Effect Controls frame rate slider.

The Transform folder

The Transform folder is filled with Transformation effects from Adobe After Effects that enable you to flip, crop, and roll a video clip, and change the camera view.

Camera View

The Camera View effect simulates viewing the clip at a different camera angle. In the Camera View Settings dialog box, shown in Figure 11-47, use the sliders to control the effect. Click and drag the Latitude slider to flip the clip vertically. Use the Longitude slider to flip horizontally. The Roll slider simulates rolling the camera, thus rotating the clip. Click and drag the Focal Length slider to make the view wider or narrower. The Distance slider enables you to change the distance between the imaginary camera and the clip. Use the Zoom slider to zoom in and out. To create a fill color to use as a background, click the color swatch and choose a color in

Premiere's Color Picker window. If you want the background area to be transparent, choose Fill Alpha Channel. (The clip must include an alpha channel to use this option.) Figure 11-48 shows a frame with the Camera View effect applied.

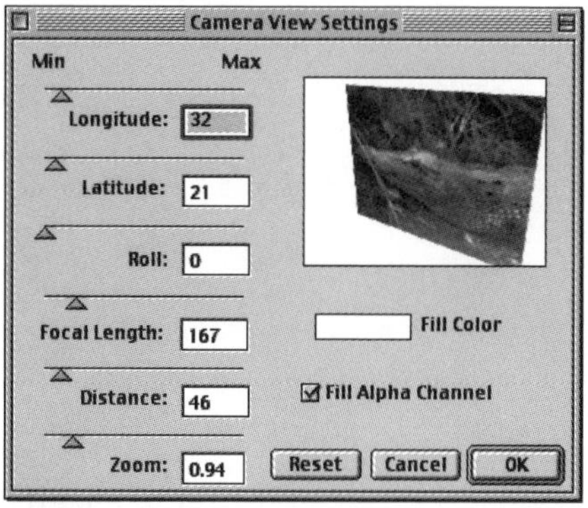

Figure 11-47: The Camera View Settings dialog box

Figure 11-48: A frame with the Camera View effect applied

Clip

The Clip effect hides the frame boundaries — similar to a Crop effect, except that the clip is not resized. The effect can be used to hide noise at image edges.

To use the Clip effect, drag the sliders in the Clipping Settings dialog box, shown in Figure 11-49, to clip the top, left, bottom, and/or right sides of the clip. Choose whether you want to clip according to pixels or percent. Click the Fill Color swatch to open Premiere's Color Picker and choose a background color.

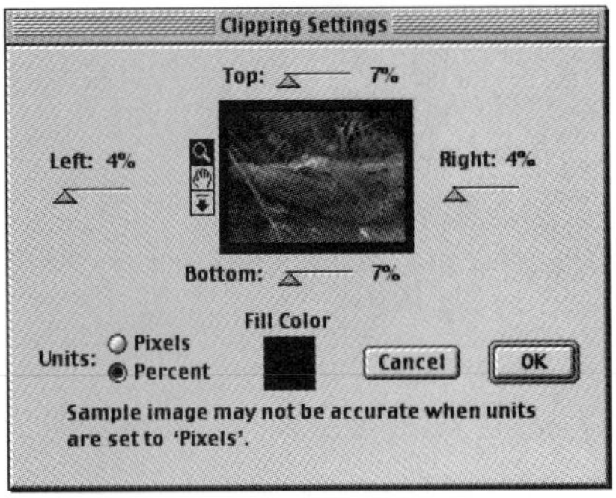

Figure 11-49: The Clipping Settings dialog box

Crop

The Crop effect provides the same settings as the Clip effect except that with the Crop effect Premiere resizes the clip according to the dialog box settings.

The Edge Feather

The Edge Feather effect allows you to create a 3D-feathered effect around the edge of the image clip you are working with. To apply a feather, edge, click "setup" in the Effect Controls palette, to display the Edge Feather Settings dialog box. In the dialog box, move the Feather slider to the right to increase the size of the edge of the feather. Figure 11-50 shows the results of the Edge Feather effect.

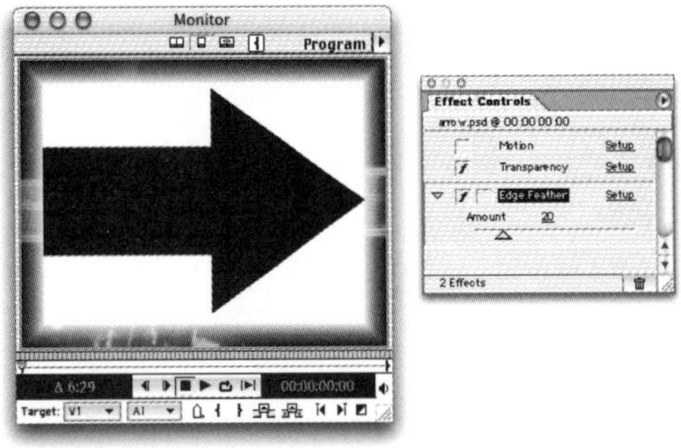

Figure 11- 50: Image after applying the Edge Feather effect with the Edge Feather options in the Effect Controls palette

Horizontal Flip

The Horizontal Flip effect flips the frame left to right.

Horizontal Hold

The Horizontal Hold effect is named after the horizontal hold knob found on a television set. As you might guess, the effect simulates turning the horizontal hold knob. In the Horizontal Hold Settings dialog box, shown in Figure 11-51, click and drag the slider to create the skewing effect.

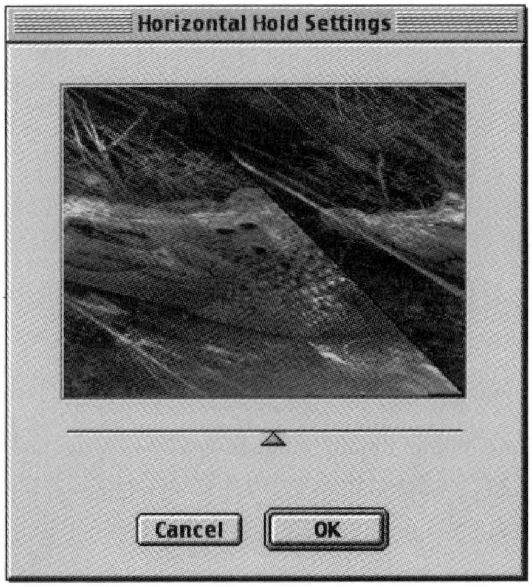

Figure 11-51: The Horizontal Hold Settings dialog box

Image Pan

The Image Pan effect creates the effect of panning the camera across the clip frame. Using the effect is quite simple. In the Image Pan Settings dialog box, click and drag any of the handles to change the Top, Width, and Height settings.

Resize

When exporting a project, the Resize effect resizes the Export Frame Dimensions. It provides better quality than both QuickTime and Video for Windows scaling.

Roll

The Roll effect provides a rotating effect. The Roll Settings dialog box, shown in Figure 11-52, enables you to roll the image left, right, up, or down.

Figure 11-52: The Roll Settings dialog box

Vertical Flip

The Vertical Flip effect flips your clip vertically. The result is an upside-down version of the original clip.

Vertical Hold

The Vertical Hold effect simulates turning the vertical hold knob found on a television set. Use the slider in the Vertical Hold Settings dialog box to create the effect you want.

The Video folder

The effects found in the Video folder simulate electronic changes to a video signal. These effects need only be applied if you are outputting your production to videotape.

Broadcast Colors

If you are outputting your production to videotape, you may wish to run the Broadcast Colors effect to improve color output quality. As discussed in Chapter 8, the gamut, or range of video colors, is smaller than the color gamut of a computer monitor. To use the Broadcast Color effect, choose either NTSC for American television or PAL for European television in the Broadcast Locale pop-up menu. Then choose a method in the How to Make Colors Safe pop-up menu. Following is an explanation of the choices available in this pop-up menu:

✦ **Reduce Luminance.** Reduces pixels brightness values, moving the pixel values toward black.

✦ **Reduce Saturation.** Brings pixel values closer to gray. (This makes the colors less intense.)

✦ **Key out Unsafe.** Colors that fall beyond the TV gamut become transparent.

✦ **Key in Safe.** Colors that are within the TV gamut are transparent.

In the Maximum Signal Field, enter the IRE breakpoint value. (IRE measures image luminance.) Any levels above this value are altered. If you are unsure of what value to use, leave the default setting of 110.

Field Interpolate

The Field Interpolate effect creates missing scan lines from the average of other lines.

Reduce Interlace Flicker

The Reduce Interlace Flicker effect softens horizontal lines in an attempt to reduce interlace flicker (an odd or even interlace line that appears during video capture).

Note

Choosing the wrong field settings in the Video ➪ Project Settings ➪ Keyframe and Rendering dialog box can increase flicker. These settings are covered in more detail in Chapter 4.

Summary

Premiere's Video Effects palette provides dozens of special effects that can add interest to or correct video.

- ✦ To add an effect to a clip, drag the effect from the Video Effects palette to the clip in the Timeline.
- ✦ Use the Effect Controls palette to specify settings for effects, to turn on and off preview, and to enable and disable keyframing.
- ✦ Use the keyframe track to set keyframes where effect settings change in the Timeline.

✦ ✦ ✦

CHAPTER 12

Superimposing

✦ ✦ ✦ ✦

In This Chapter

Understanding digital video transparency

Fading with the Fade Adjustment and Fade Scissors tools

Using the Transparency dialog box

Blending clips

Creating a split-screen effect

Creating blue-screen and green-screen effects

✦ ✦ ✦ ✦

By telling a story or providing information using innovative effects, you can ensure that you get your message across. One of the best techniques for doing so creatively is to use superimposition options. Adobe Premiere helps you create sophisticated transparency effects by enabling you to overlay two or more video clips and then blend the two together. For more sophisticated effects, the Premiere Transparency Settings dialog box provides a host of different effects that enable you to *key* out (hide) different parts of the image area in one track and fill them with the underlying video in the track beneath it.

This chapter provides a look at two powerful methods of creating transparency: the Premiere Fade command and the Premiere keying options found in its Transparency Settings dialog box. The Fade command enables you to create blending effects by changing the opacity of one video track. The Transparency Settings dialog box is home to 14 different keying options that enable you to create transparency based on color, alpha channels, or brightness levels. As you read through this chapter, think about all of the different ways that you can apply the effects in your current or next project. Using transparency creatively will undoubtedly add to its success.

Understanding Transparency in Digital Video

If you put a video clip or still in Video track 2 and another in Video track 1, you will only see the image that is in the top video track onscreen — in this case, Video track 2. To see both images, you need to either fade Video track 2 or apply the Premiere Transparency command to it.

Any video track higher than Video track 1 can be faded using Premiere's Fade option or superimposed using the Transparency Settings dialog box. Throughout this book, you find various examples of transparency effects. To review some of these examples, see Chapter 9, Chapter 14, and Chapter 23.

Fading video tracks

You can fade an entire video clip or still image over a video clip or another still image. The top video clip or still image is faded over the bottom one. When you fade a video clip or still image, you are changing the opacity of the clip or image. Any video track, except for Video track 1 can be used as a superimposed track and can be faded. Premiere's fade option appears when you expand a video track. When a video track is expanded, you can display the fade line (the Opacity Rubberband line) by clicking the Display Opacity Rubberbands icon, which is found underneath a clip or image when the track is expanded.

Note

Fading video tracks works similarly to fading sound tracks. For more information on fading sound tracks, see Chapter 6.

Here's how to fade a track:

1. **Choose File ⇨ New Project to create a new project.** For practice purposes, set the preset to Multimedia.
2. **Choose File ⇨ Import ⇨ File to import two files.** Locate either two video clips or a video clip and a still image. Press and hold the Shift key to select more than one file. Click Open to import the files.

On the CD-ROM

If you want, you can use the two video clips that we used in our fade example, seen in Figures 12-1 to 12-5. The clmwater.mov and geese.mov video clips can be found in the Chapter 12 folder in the Tutorial Projects folder on the CD-ROM that accompanies this book. In the Chapter 12 folder you will also find two Digital Vision video clips that you can use, 579023P.mov and 579024P.mov and a sound clip, 576003s.aif.

3. **When the files appear in the Project window, drag and drop one file to Video track 2 and the other to Video track 1 in the Timeline window.** Make sure that the files in the video tracks overlap each other.
4. **To expand Video track 2, click the Collapse/Expand Track triangle to the left of the word Video.**
5. **Click Display Opacity Rubberbands (the red square) to reveal the fade line (the Opacity Rubberband line), shown in Figure 12-1.** Notice that a red rubberband beneath the video clip is displayed.
6. **To decrease the opacity of the file in Video track 2, use the Selection tool (the arrow icon above the hand icon) to click and drag the red rubberband (fade line) down.**

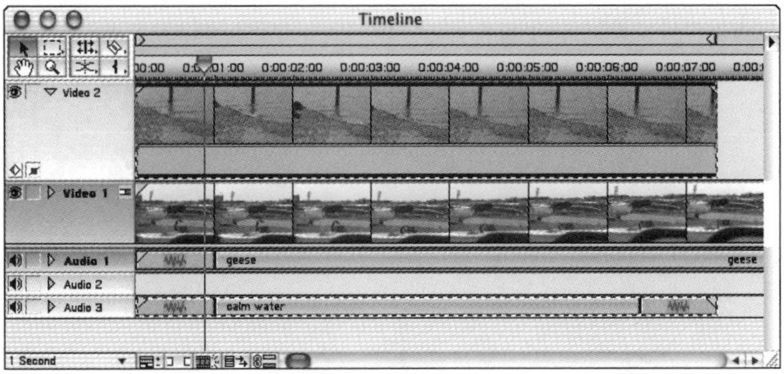

Figure 12-1: The Display Opacity Rubberbands option in the Timeline window enables you to change the opacity of a video clip.

7. **To slowly fade a video clip, set the left side of the Opacity Rubberband so that it is at the top-left position and drag the far right side down, as shown in Figure 12-2. Figure 12-3 shows a few frames of the effect of a gradual fade.** The fade in Figure 12-2 is gradual because the fade line gradually steps down. The top of the fade line indicates that the video clip is 100 percent opaque. When the fade line follows a long, slow, diagonal path from the top of the fade bar (100 percent opaque) to the bottom (100 percent transparent), the clip gradually fades out. To preview the Fade effect, choose Timeline ➪ Preview.

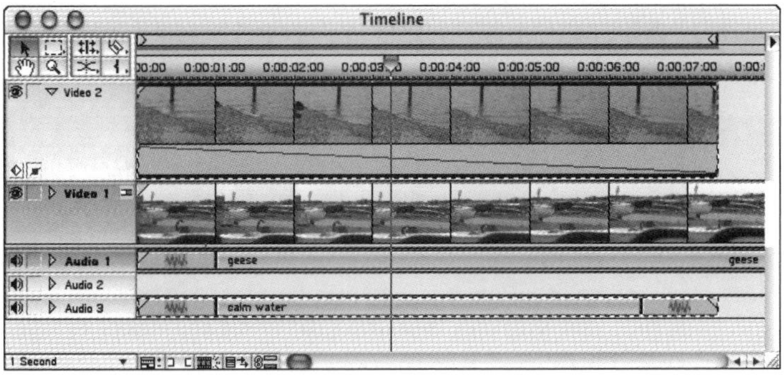

Figure 12-2: The Opacity Rubberband line displays a gradual fade.

Figure 12-3: Frames showing a gradual fade

To create more sophisticated fades, you can add handles to the Opacity Rubberband line. After you have handles, you can then drag different segments of the Opacity Rubberband line. Here's how:

1. **With the Selection tool selected, move the mouse over the Opacity Rubberband line (fade line).** Notice that the arrow icon turns into a white pointing hand icon. Then move over the area where you want to add a handle and click to create a handle. A handle appears as a small red square on the Opacity Rubberband line (fade line).

2. **To create a few handles, click the Opacity Rubberband line a few times.**
3. **Now that you have a few handles on the Opacity Rubberband line, you can drag down at different sections, as shown in Figure 12-4.**

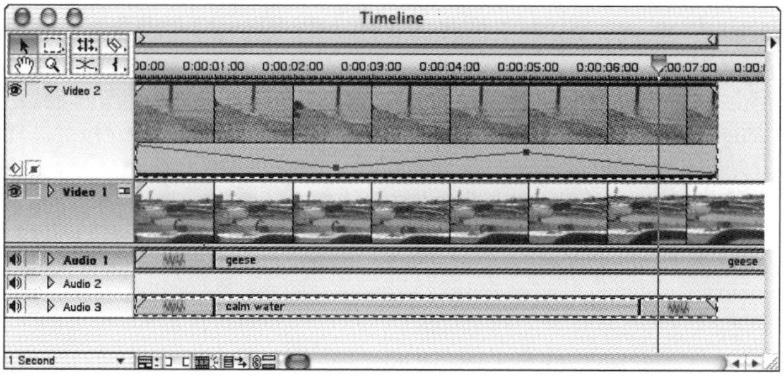

Figure 12-4: You can create handles in the Opacity Rubberband line to create a fade.

4. **Use the Info palette to display the fade level percentage shown in Figure 12-5.** To display the Info palette, choose Window ➪ Show Info. As you drag the red rubberband line, look at the Info palette and notice that the fade level percentage changes.

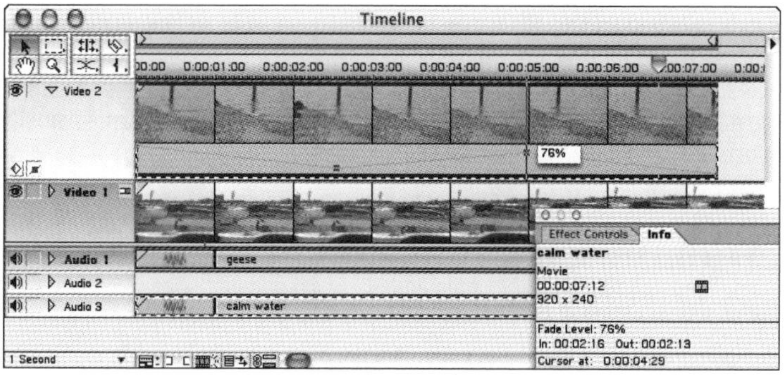

Figure 12-5: The fade level in the Info palette

5. **If you've created too many handles and want to delete one, just click and drag the handle outside the Opacity Rubberband section.**

6. **Click and drag the handle to move it.** When you click the handle, the mouse pointer should turn gray. If it turns white, you are going to add a handle when you click the Opacity Rubberband line. To make it turn gray, reposition the mouse more accurately over the handle you want to move.

7. **For a quick preview, Press and hold the Option/Alt key as you click and drag the Edit Line through the Timeline to preview the fade effect.** To save your work and build a preview choose File ➪ Save and Timeline ➪ Preview.

Note

If desired, you can fade more video tracks. Just import more video clips and/or still images into the Project window. Create new video tracks and drag the video clips and/or images into the new video tracks. Then use the fade line to fade the video tracks.

Figure 12-6 shows two images (a person and a graphic) superimposed over each other using the fade technique. We applied a 50% fade level and the Bend video effect to the graphic image. To create this advanced effect, you first need to apply a 50% fade level to the graphic image in Video track 2. Then for an added effect, you apply one of Premiere's video effects to the faded track. (For more information on using video effects, turn to Chapter 11. In Figure 12-6, we applied the Bend video effect to the faded video track (Video track 2). To create this effect, we imported a still graphic image into Video track 2 and a video clip of the lead singer, Buddy Valiante, from the band Midnight Sun Music into Video track 1. In Figure 12-7 you can see the Timeline, Project, and Monitor windows for the effect shown in Figure 12-6. The files used in the project, seen in Figure 12-7 are closeup.mov and interfrm.jpg. These files are located in the Chapter 12 folder, which is in the Tutorial Projects folder, in the CD-ROM that accompanies this book.

Note

Midnight Sun Music was formed in 1998. The group performs mostly original songs and has won several competitions.

Fading with the Fade Adjustment and Fade Scissors tools

The Fade Adjustment and Fade Scissors tools provide more fade options. These tools appear in a toolbox at the top-left side of the Timeline window. The Fade Adjustment tool is in the third slot of the toolbox's second row. Click the tool in the third slot to select the tool. The Fade Scissors tool is in the fourth slot of the toolbox's first row. Figure 12-8 shows the Fade Adjustment and Fade Scissors tools.

Figure 12-6: Buddy Valiante, the lead singer from the band Midnight Sun Music, is shown in a project using the Bend video effect on the faded video track.

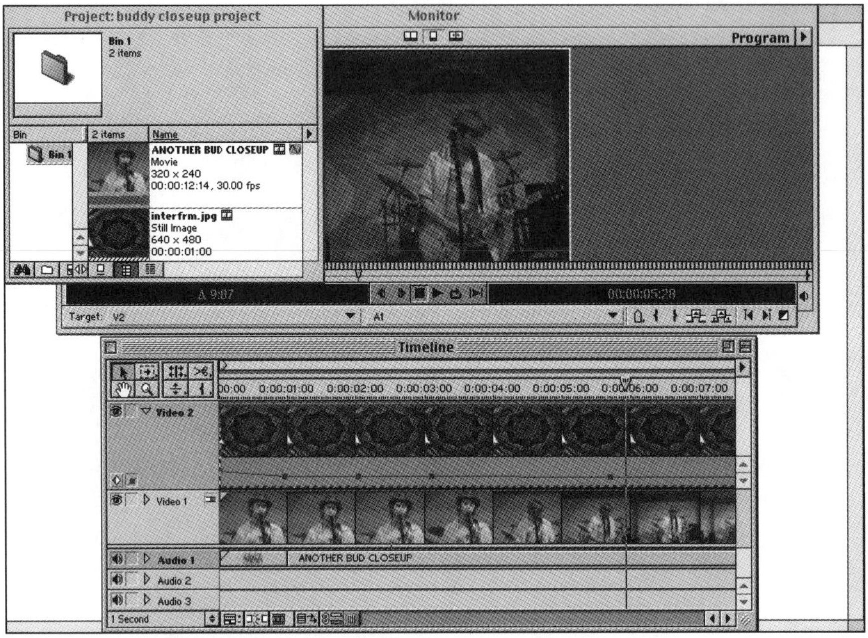

Figure 12-7: The Timeline for the project shown in Figure 12-6

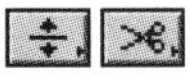

Figure 12-8: The Fade Adjustment and Fade Scissors tools

Tip

To quickly select the Fade Adjustment tool, press U on your keyboard until the Fade Adjustment tool appears. To select the Fade Scissors tool, press C on your keyboard.

Using the Fade Adjustment tool

The Fade Adjustment tool enables you to move either an entire Opacity Rubberband line as a unit or move two handles simultaneously. Follow these steps to use the Fade Adjustment tool to move an entire fade line:

Note

Before you proceed to Step 1, you should have a Premiere project with a clip in Video track 2, the track should be expanded and the fade line should be displayed. These steps are covered in the "Fading video tracks" section in this chapter.

1. **Set the Opacity Rubberband line (fade line) so that handles appear only at the beginning and end of the fade line.** If handles appear on the fade line, use the Selection tool to click a handle and drag outside the fade area to delete it.

2. **Select the Fade Adjustment tool and then press U on your keyboard until the Fade Adjustment tool appears.**

3. **With the Fade Adjustment tool, click and drag down on the Opacity Rubberband line.** If no handles appear on the line, the entire line moves as a unit.

Tip: You can use the Fade Adjustment tool to fade in one-percent increments. As you move the Rubberband line (fade line), press and hold the Shift key. Notice in the Info palette that the fade level changes at one-percent increments. To display the Info palette, choose Window ➪ Show Info.

Here's how to use the Fade Adjustment tool to move two handles simultaneously:

1. **Press V on your keyboard to select the Selection tool.**

2. **Use the Selection tool to click the Rubberband line (fade line) to add two handles.**

3. **Press U on your keyboard until the Fade Adjustment tool appears.**

4. **Click between the two handles and drag down using the Fade Adjustment tool.** When you click and drag between the two handles, the fade line between the two handles moves as a unit. The fade line outside the handles moves gradually, as shown in Figure 12-9.

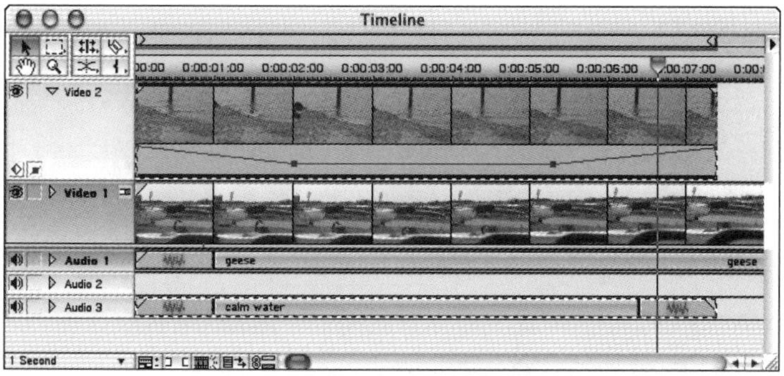

Figure 12-9: The fade line after being adjusted with the Fade Adjustment tool

Using the Fade Scissors tool

The Fade Scissors tool cuts the Opacity Rubberband, enabling you to move just a section of the rubberband line completely separate from the rest. Here's how to use the Fade Scissors tool:

Note

Before you proceed to Step 1, you should have a Premiere project with a clip in Video track 2, the track should be expanded, and the fade line should be displayed. These steps are covered in the "Fading video tracks" section in this chapter.

1. **Start with an Opacity Rubberband line (fade line) that has only a beginning and ending handle.** If handles appear on the fade line, use the Selection tool to click a handle and drag outside the fade area to delete it.
2. **Select the Fade Scissors tool, if it is not selected.** Press C on your keyboard until the Fade Scissors tool appears in the Timeline tool palette.
3. **Move the Fade Scissors tool to the middle of the fade line and click.** Notice that the Fade Scissors tool creates two handles side by side. If you want, you can use the Selection tool to move the two handles apart.
4. **To move the fade line, switch from the Fade Scissors tool to the Fade Adjustment tool.** Do this by pressing U on your keyboard until the Fade Adjustment tool appears.
5. **Move the Fade Adjustment tool toward the fade line.** Place it to the right of the start of the fade line and to the left of the handle you made with the Fade Scissors tool.
6. **Now, click and drag the fade line down.** Notice that only the line between the start of the fade line and scissors handle moves, as shown in Figure 12-10. The line moves at a constant percentage.

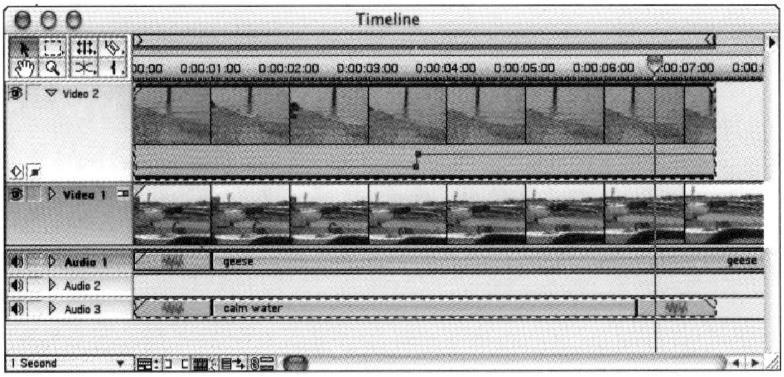

Figure 12-10: The fade line after using the Fade Scissors and Fade Adjustment tools

7. **To change the fade, use the Selection tool to move the fade line.** Switch to the Selection tool by pressing V on your keyboard to change the fade.
8. **Move the Selection tool to the right of the handle you made with the Fade Scissors tool and to the left of the end of the fade line.** Then click and drag the fade line down. As you click, notice that you create a handle and that the fade line drags down in the shape of a V, as shown in Figure 12-11.

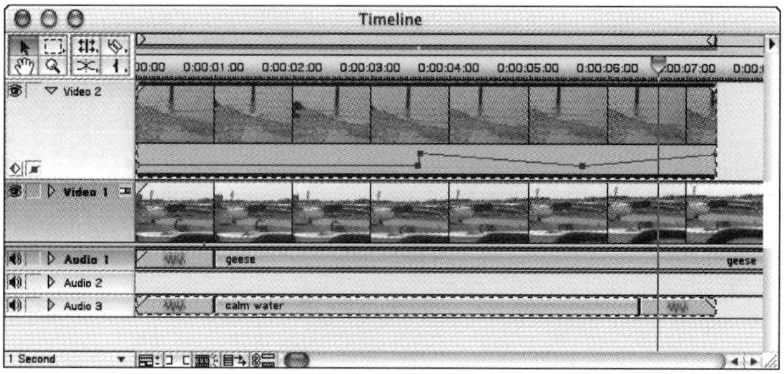

Figure 12-11: The fade line after using the Fade Scissors, Fade Adjustment, and Select tools

Superimposing Tracks Using the Transparency Dialog Box

You can superimpose a video clip and/or still image over another one using the Transparency Settings dialog box. In the Transparency Settings dialog box, you have 14 key types to pick from. Using the Key options is called *keying*. Keying makes part of the image transparent. The following sections cover how to use the Transparency Settings dialog box and the different key options.

Displaying the Transparency Settings dialog box

To display and experiment with the Transparency Settings dialog box, shown in Figure 12-12, you first need to have a Premiere project onscreen. Either load an existing Premiere project or create a new one by choosing File ➪ New Project.

To display the Transparency Settings dialog box, follow these steps:

1. **Drag a clip from the Project window to track Video 1.**
2. **Drag a clip from the Project window to track Video 2.**
3. **Click and drag the clip in Video track 2 so that part of it overlaps the clip in Video track 1.**
4. **Select the image or a video clip to which you want to apply a key.**
5. **Choose Clip ➪ Video Options ➪ Transparency.** You can also display the Transparency Settings dialog box by clicking Setup next to Transparency in the Effect Controls palette. If the Effect Controls palette is not displayed, choose Window ➪ Show Effect Controls. To learn more about the different Key Type options, read the next section, "Transparency Settings dialog box options."

On the CD-ROM

If you want, you can use one of the files found in the Chapter 12 folder that is located in the Tutorial Projects folder on the CD-ROM that accompanies this book. Most of the images seen in this chapter are located on the CD-ROM.

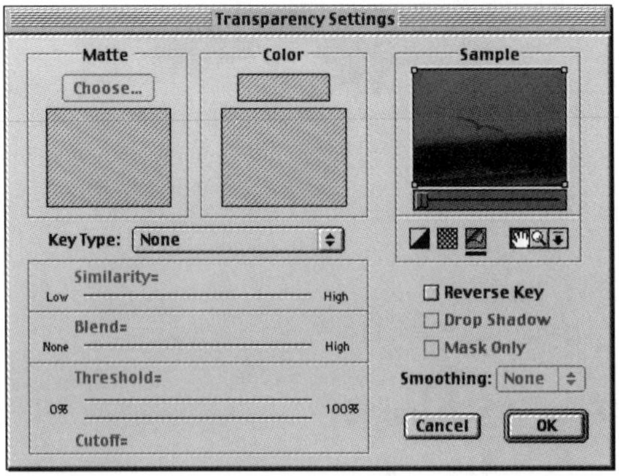

Figure 12-12: The Transparency Settings dialog box

Transparency Settings dialog box options

In the Transparency Settings dialog box, you have 14 key types to choose from: Chroma, RGB Difference, Luminance, Alpha Channel, Black Alpha Matte, White Alpha Matte, Image Matte, Difference Matte, Blue Screen, Green Screen, Multiply, Screen, Track Matte, and Non-Red.

The controls that are activated in the dialog box are based on the key option that you choose. For example, the Matte section is not available unless you have selected either the Image Matte or Difference Matte option. The Color option is not available unless you pick either the Chroma or RGB Difference key type. Also, the settings below the words "Key Type" vary depending upon which key type you use. You'll learn more about these options in the following sections.

The Sample options at the far right of the dialog box are always available. The image below the word Sample gives you a preview of what your image will look like, depending on which key type you use and what thumbnail you pick below the preview window. The following six thumbnails are available:

✦ **White/Black Thumbnail.** Clicking the first thumbnail replaces the transparent areas of Video track 2 with either a white or black color. Click once to view the transparent areas in white. Click again to view the transparent areas in black.

✦ **Checkerboard Thumbnail.** Clicking the second thumbnail replaces the transparent areas of Video track 2 with a checkerboard pattern.

✦ **Preview Thumbnail.** Clicking the third thumbnail replaces the transparent areas with areas from the clip in Video track 1.

✦ **Hand Thumbnail.** This thumbnail enables you to move around in the preview area, which is helpful when you zoom in to the preview.

✦ **Zoom Thumbnail.** This thumbnail enables you to magnify an area of the preview. To use the Zoom tool, click the preview area that you want to magnify (zoom in on). To zoom out, press and hold the Option (Mac users) or Alt (PC users) key as you click in the preview area. To return the view back to its original state, double-click the Hand tool.

✦ **Collapse Thumbnail.** This thumbnail enables you to preview the effect in the Monitor window. For you to take advantage of this effect, first display the Monitor window before using the Transparency Settings dialog box. This option is available only for Mac users.

Chroma key

The Chroma key option in the Transparency Settings dialog box enables you to key out a specific color or a range of colors. This key is often planned during preproduction so that the video is shot against one colored background. To select the color to key out, use the Eyedropper tool to click the background area of the image thumbnail. Alternatively, you can click in the color swatch (under the word Color) and choose a key color from the Premiere color picker.

To fine-tune the key click and drag the sliders, make adjustments to the following options:

✦ **Similarity.** Click and drag to the left or right to increase or decrease the range of colors that will be made transparent.

✦ **Blend.** Click and drag to the right to create more of a blend between the two clips. Dragging to the left produces the opposite effect.

✦ **Threshold.** Clicking and dragging to the right keeps more shadow areas in the clip. Dragging to the left produces the opposite effect.

✦ **Cutoff.** Clicking and dragging to the right darkens shadow areas. Dragging to the right lightens shadow areas. Note that if you drag beyond the level set in the Threshold slider, gray and transparent areas become inverted.

✦ **Smoothing.** This control sets anti-aliasing, which blends pixel colors to create smoother edges. Choose High for most smoothing, Low for some smoothing, or None for no smoothing. Choosing None is often the best choice when keying titles.

Figure 12-13 shows a few frames from a project using the Chroma key type. The frames show Donny Valiante, the drummer from Midnight Sun Music, through a blue gradient. To create the project, we imported a video clip of Donny playing the drums into Video track 1 and imported a still image of a blue gradient into Video track 2, as shown in Figure 12-14. We selected the still image in Video track 2 and chose Clip ➪ Video Options ➪ Transparency. In the Transparency Settings dialog box, we set Key Type to Chroma and adjusted the Similarity, Blend, Threshold, and

Cutoff sliders so that we could see Donny playing through the gradient. The Transparency Settings dialog box used to create the project (in Figure 12-13) is shown in Figure 12-15.

Figure 12-13: Donny Valiante, the drummer from Midnight Sun Music, in a project using the Chroma key type

Figure 12-14: The Timeline used to create a project using the Chroma key type

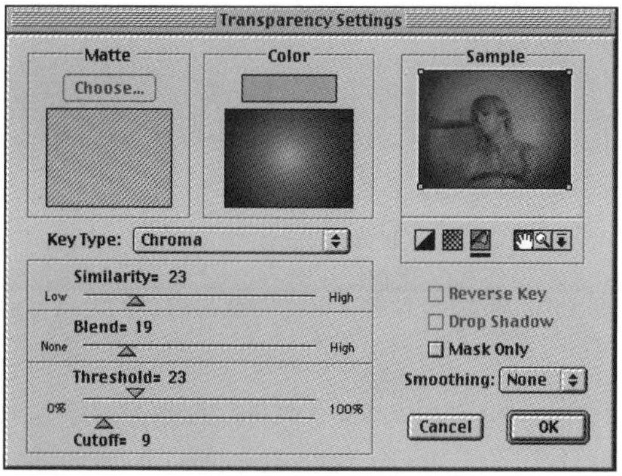

Figure 12-15: The Transparency Settings dialog box options used to create the project shown in Figure 12-13

RGB Difference key

This key is an easy-to-use version of the Chroma key option. Use this key when precise keying is not required or when the image being keyed appears in front of a bright background. As with the Chroma key, RGB Difference provides Similarity and Smoothing options but does not provide Blend, Threshold, or Cutoff controls.

Figure 12-16 shows the Transparency Settings dialog box with the RGB Difference key type chosen instead of the Chroma key type (as was shown in Figure 12-15). Notice that the edges of the gradient do not slowly fade out into soft edges but rather end abruptly.

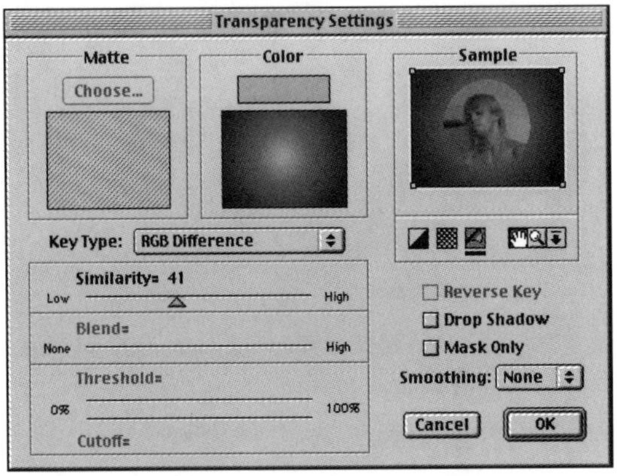

Figure 12-16: Transparency Settings dialog box with the RGB Difference key type

Blue Screen and Green Screen keys

Blue and green are traditional keys used in broadcast television where announcers are often shot in front of a blue or green background. The Blue Screen keys out well-lit blue backgrounds. The Green Screen keys out well-lit green areas. These keys have the following options:

- ✦ **Threshold.** Start by dragging to the left to key out more green and blue areas.
- ✦ **Cutoff.** Click and drag to the right to fine-tune the key effect.

Normally when using the Blue or Green Screen key type, you would videotape a person or object against either a properly lit blue or green background. This way you can import the video clip into Premiere and use either the Blue Screen or Green Screen key types to remove the background and replace it with any image your heart desires. In our example of a Blue Screen key type, we videotaped Grace singing (shown in Figure 12-17) to Steven at their wedding, using a Sony digital camcorder. Then we captured the digital video by using Adobe Premiere and a Macintosh. Steven enjoyed her singing so much that he asked us to have a special video clip created of his wife. We used Premiere to convert a few frames of the video clip in the Clip window to Filmstrip format. To shorten the clip and use only a few frames from the clip, we set the In and Out points using the In and Out buttons in the Clip window. (For more information on using the Clip window to set the In and Out points, refer to Chapter 10.) Then we chose File ➪ Export Clip ➪ Movie. In the Export Movie dialog box, we selected the Settings button. In the Export Movie Settings dialog box that appeared, we set the File Type pop-up menu to Filmstrip and the File Type pop-up menu to Range for In to Out. We clicked OK and then Save to create a Filmstrip file.

Figure 12-17: A clip of Grace singing at her wedding, shows a few frames from a project using the Blue Screen key type

We imported the Filmstrip file into Photoshop, where we used the Select ➪ Range and Lasso tool to select the background and fill it with blue (for more information on using Photoshop and Premiere, turn to Chapter 22). After all the frames had a blue background, we saved the file and loaded it back into a Premiere project. In the Premiere project, we placed the Filmstrip file of Grace singing on a blue background in Video track 2.

A photograph of a beach scene was imported into the Premiere project and placed in Video track 1. Then we selected the Filmstrip clip in Video track 2 and chose Clip ➪ Video Options ➪ Transparency. In the Transparency Settings dialog box, we used the Blue Screen Key Type option. Figure 12-17 shows a few frames from a project using the Blue Screen key type. In Figure 12-18, you can see the Timeline and Project window that we used to create the project. Figure 12-19 shows the Transparency Settings dialog box before and after choosing the Blue Screen key type.

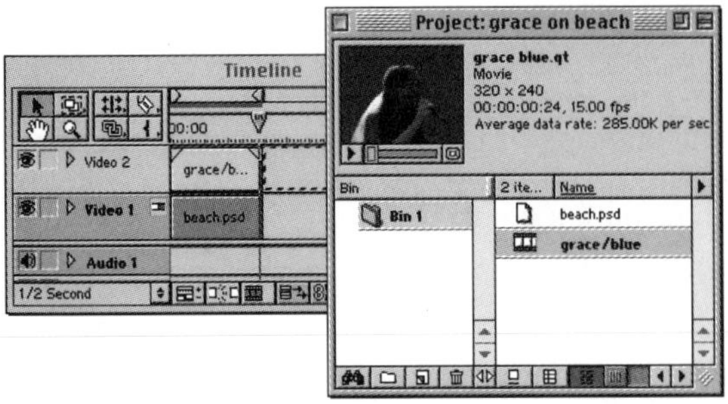

Figure 12-18: The Timeline and Project window used to create the project shown in Figure 12-17.

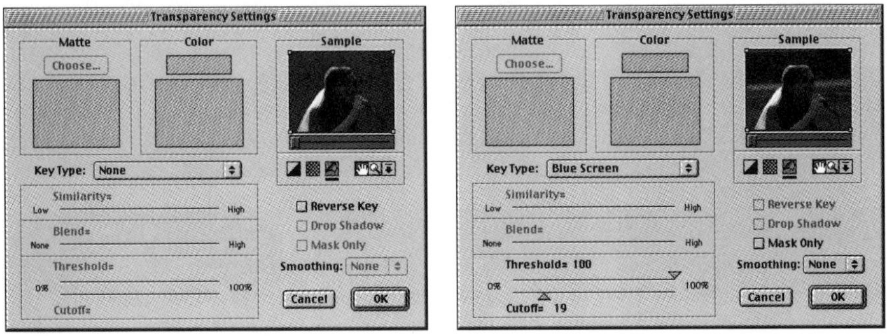

Figure 12-19: The Transparency Settings dialog box with the None and the Blue Screen key types

Non-Red key

As with the blue and green screens, the Non-Red key is used to key out blue and green backgrounds, but does both at once. This key also includes a blending slider that enables you to blend two clips together.

Luminance key

The Luminance key type keys out darker image areas in a clip. Use the Threshold and Cutoff sliders to fine-tune the effect, as follows:

- ✦ **Threshold.** Click and drag to the right to increase the range of darker values that will be keyed out.
- ✦ **Cutoff.** Controls the opacity of the Threshold range. Click and drag to the right to produce more transparency.

Figure 12-20 shows a few frames from a project using a Luminance key type. The frames show a bird flying, superimposed over a video clip of Pete Jackson, the bass guitar player from Midnight Sun Music. To create the project, we imported a video clip of Pete playing the guitar into Video track 1 and imported a video clip of a bird flying into Video track 2. We selected the video clip in Video track 2 and chose Clip ➪ Video Options ➪ Transparency. In the Transparency Settings dialog box, we set the Key Type to Luminance and adjusted the Threshold and Cutoff sliders so that we could see both the bird and Pete playing. Figure 12-21 shows the Timeline used to create the project shown in Figure 12-20. The Transparency Settings dialog box used to create the project appears in Figure 12-22. (For more Image Matte examples, turn to Chapter 24 and Chapter 9.)

Figure 12-20: Pete Jackson, the bass guitar player from the band Midnight Sun Music, in a project using the Image Matte key type

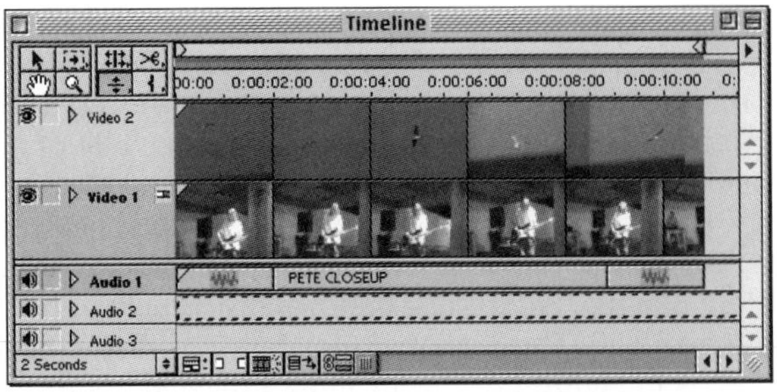

Figure 12-21: The Timeline used to create the project shown in Figure 12-20

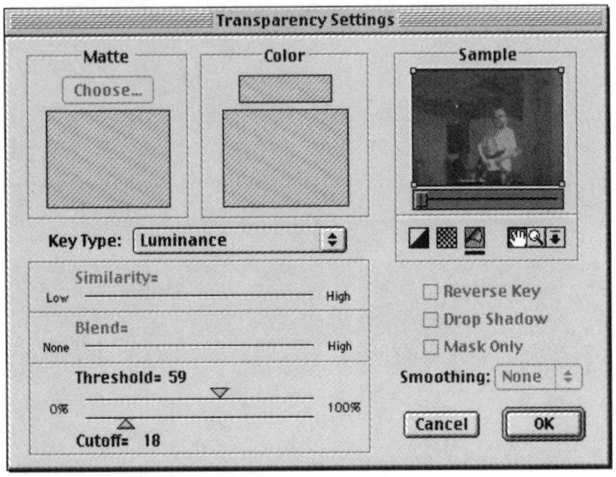

Figure 12-22: The Transparency Settings dialog box using the Luminance key type

The Alpha Channel key

Use this key to create transparency from imported images that contain an alpha channel (an image layer that represents a mask with shades of gray, including black and white, to indicate transparency levels). Premiere reads alpha channels from such programs as Adobe Photoshop and three-dimensional software programs and also translates nontransparent areas of Illustrator files as alpha channels.

Figure 12-23 shows the Project, Timeline, and Monitor windows for an Alpha Channel Key Type option. In Video track 2 is a file of a three-dimensional man that we created in Curious Labs' Poser. The man is on a white background. To mask out the white background, we created an alpha channel of the man. Video track 1 has a video clip of some waves. To animate the man, we applied the Transform video effect. Figure 12-24 shows the Transparency Settings dialog box used to create the project shown in Figure 12-23.

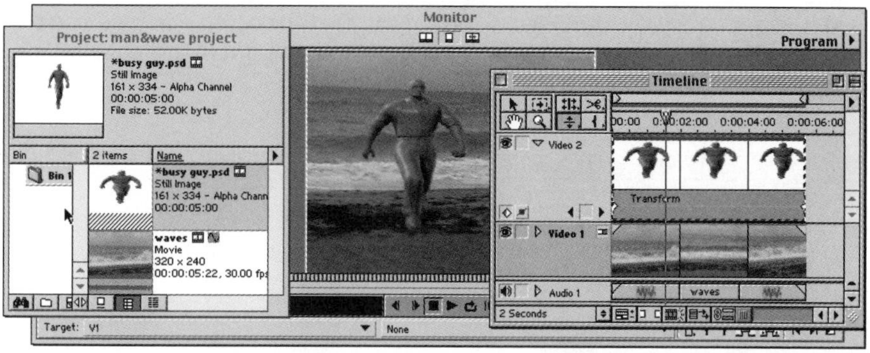

Figure 12-23: The Project, Timeline, and Monitor windows used to create a project using the Alpha Channel key type

On the CD-ROM

If you want, you can load the man image and the wave clip from Chapter 12 that is in the Tutorial Projects folder on the CD-ROM that accompanies this book.

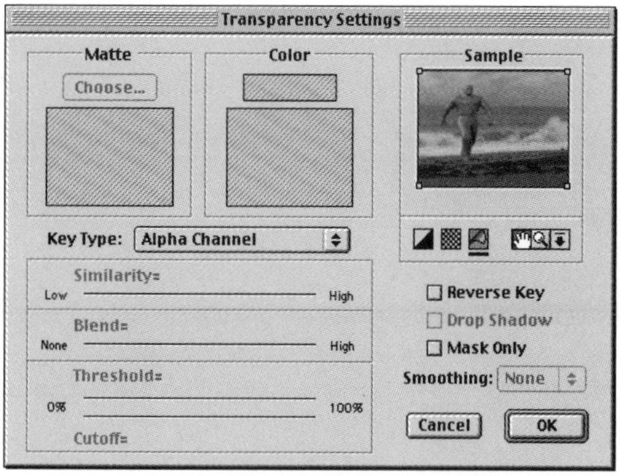

Figure 12-24: The Transparency Settings dialog box using the Alpha Channel key type

Cross-Reference

For more Alpha Channel key type examples, take a look at Chapter 23 and Chapter 9.

Figure 12-25 shows the Timeline window of a project, using a video clip in Video tracks 1 and 2, an Illustrator file in Video track 3, and a Photoshop file with an alpha channel in Video track 4. Figure 12-26 shows the Transparency Settings dialog box used to create the project in Figure 12-25. Note that the Alpha Channel key type is applied to the Illustrator file in Video track 3 and to the Photoshop file in Video track 4. Figure 12-27 shows a frame from the project in Figure 12-25.

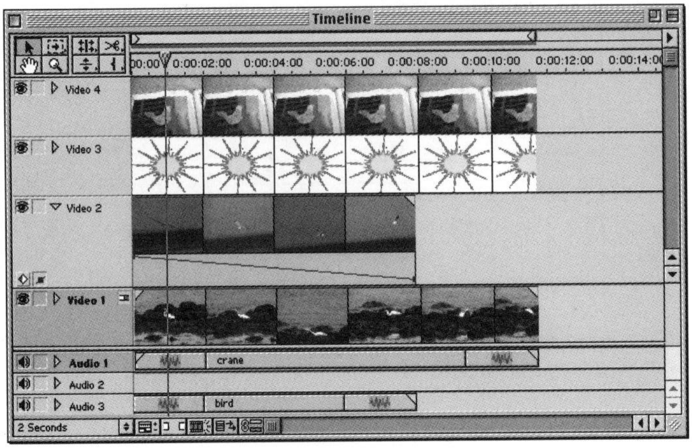

Figure 12-25: The Timeline window used to create a project using the Alpha Channel key type

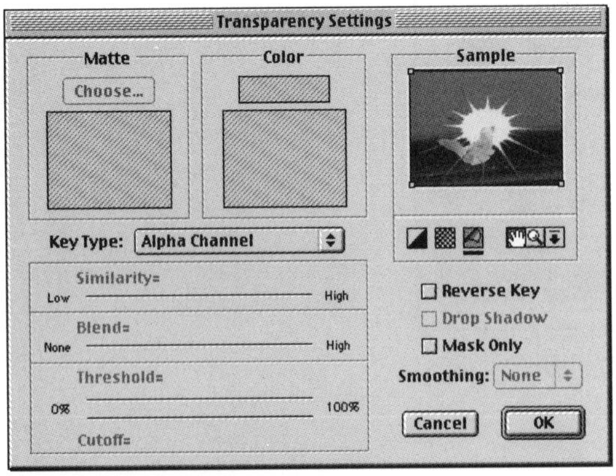

Figure 12-26: The Transparency Settings dialog box using the Alpha Channel key type

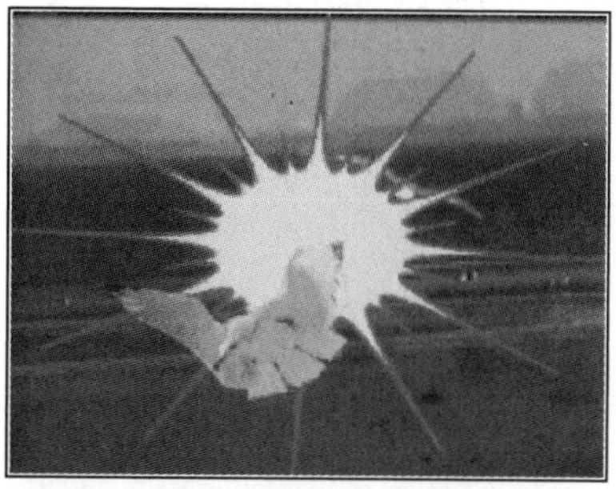

Figure 12-27: A frame from the project shown in Figure 12-26

Black Alpha Matte and White Alpha Matte keys

These keys create transparency from alpha channels created from the red, green, and blue channels as well as the alpha channel. Normally this key is used to key out the black or white backgrounds. This is useful for graphics with solid white or black backgrounds.

Image Matte key

This key is used to create transparency in still images, typically graphics. Image areas that correspond to black portions of the matte are transparent; areas corresponding to white areas are opaque. Gray areas create blending effects.

When using the Image Matte key, click the Choose button to choose an image. The final result depends upon the image you choose. If you want to reverse the key effect, making areas that correspond to white transparent, areas corresponding to black areas will be opaque.

Figure 12-28 shows a few frames from a project using an Image Matte key type. The frames show guitar player Aaron James from Midnight Sun Music superimposed over a photograph of a highway scene. To create the project, we imported a video clip of Aaron playing the guitar into Video track 2. We selected the video track and chose Clip ➪ Video Options ➪ Transparency. In the Transparency Settings dialog box, we set the Key Type option to Image Matte and clicked the Choose button and selected a photograph of a highway scene. The Transparency Settings dialog box used to create the project (in Figure 12-28) is shown in Figure 12-29.

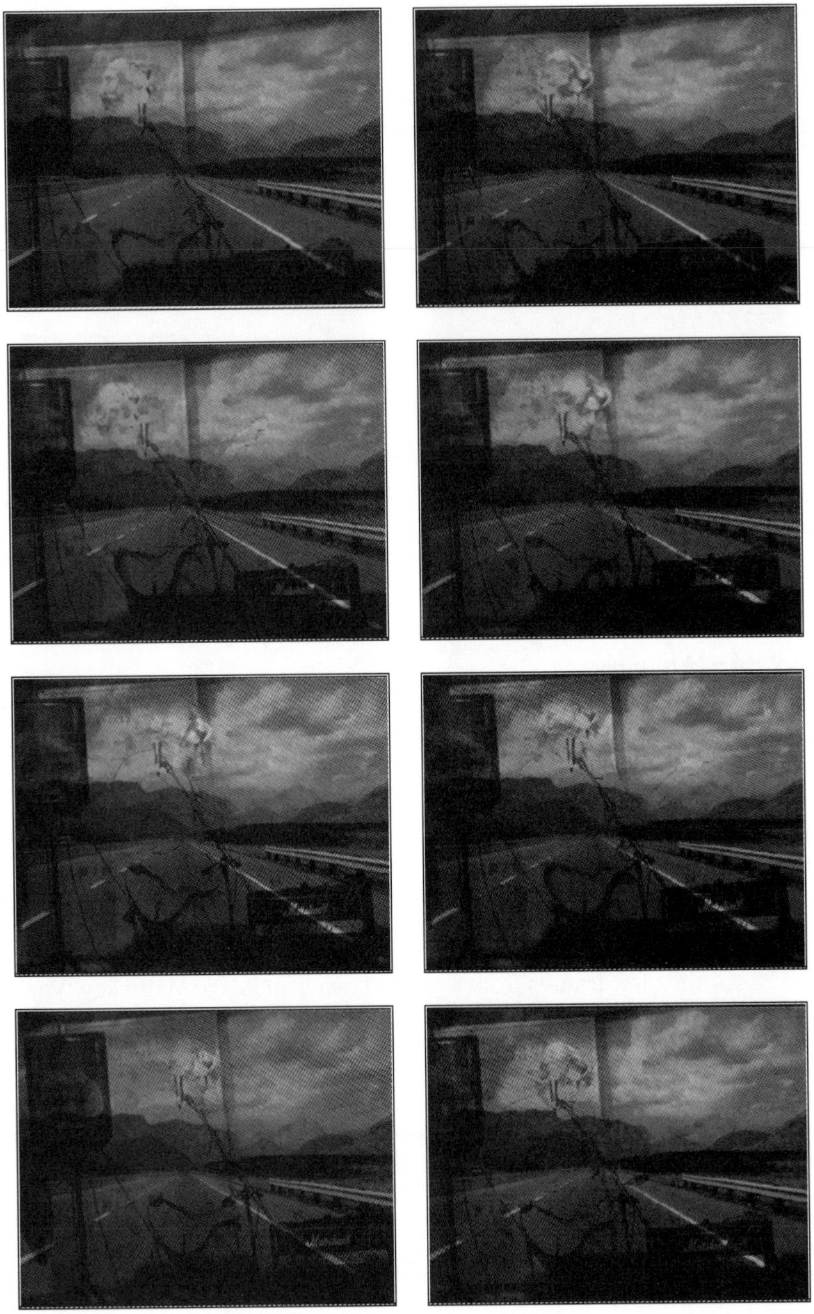

Figure 12-28: Aaron James from Midnight Sun Music playing the guitar in a project using the Image Matte key type

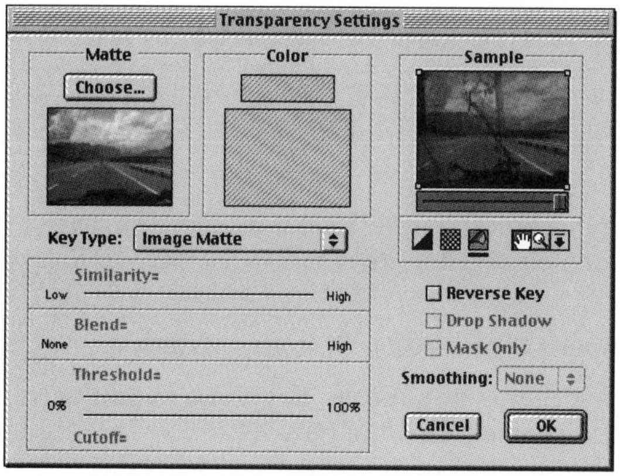

Figure 12-29: The Transparency Settings dialog box options used to create the project shown in Figure 12-29

Difference Matte key

Difference Matte enables you to key out image areas in one clip that match image areas in another clip.

Track Matte key

The Track Matte key enables you to create a moving or traveling matte effect. Often the matte is a black-and-white image that is set in motion on-screen. Image areas corresponding to black in the matte are transparent; image areas corresponding to white are opaque. Gray areas create blending effects.

Cross-Reference

For an example of Track Matte, turn to Chapter 9. See Chapter 14 for a traveling matte example.

Multiply and Screen

Multiply and Screen are transparency effects in which the lower video track image exhibits a high degree of contrast. Choose Multiply to create transparency in areas corresponding to bright image areas in the lower video track. Choose Screen to create transparency in areas corresponding to dark image areas in the lower video track. For both key effects, use the Cutoff slider in the dialog box to fine-tune the effect.

Cross-Reference

See Chapter 9 for a Multiply example.

Creating split screens using the None key type

You can use the Transparency Settings dialog box to create a split-screen effect that splits the screen between a clip in one track and a clip in another track. To create a split screen, follow these steps:

1. **If you don't have a project on-screen, either load a project or create a new project and import two video clips. Then drag the video clips to Video tracks 1 and 2.**
2. **Click Video track 2 and choose Clip ➪ Video Options ➪ Transparency.**
3. **In the Transparency Settings dialog box set the Key Type option to None.** The video clip in the preview area is from Video track 2.
4. **Move the top and bottom handles on the left side of the preview area toward the middle of the preview area, as shown in Figure 12-30.** Notice that the video clip from Video track 1 is displayed on the left side of the preview window.

Figure 12-30: An example of a split screen

Creating Garbage mattes

A video clip may contain an object that you don't want to appear in your project. When this happens, you can create a Garbage matte to eliminate (mask out) the unwanted object. At other times, you may need to create a more sophisticated mask. When this happens, you may want to use Adobe After Effects. For more information on how to create a mask using Adobe After Effects, turn to Chapter 24.

Here's how to create a Garbage matte:

1. **Choose File ➪ New Project to create a new project.**

2. **Import two video clips or one video clip and a still image.** Import a video clip in which you want to mask out an item and import another one in which you want to use to composite (or a still image).

3. **Drag the video clip that you want to use to mask out from the Project window into Video track 2 of the Timeline window.** (We used a video clip of Nancy Koehler from Musical Munchkins singing with her guitar.)

4. **Drag the video clip (or a still image) that you want to use to composite from the Project window into Video track 1 of the Timeline window.**

5. **Select the video clip in Video track 2 and choose Clip ⇨ Video Options ⇨ Transparency. In the Transparency Settings dialog box, move the handles in the preview window so that you eliminate the unwanted object, as shown in Figure 12-31.** If you want, choose a key type so that you can see the video clip in Video track 1.

6. **Click OK to preview the effect.** Figure 12-32 shows the video clip before and after using the Transparency Settings dialog box.

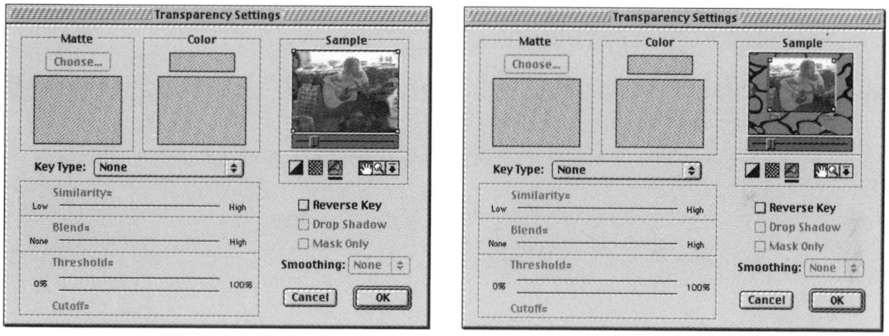

Figure 12-31: The Transparency Settings dialog box before and after moving the handles in the preview window

Figure 12-32: The video clip before and after using the Transparency Settings dialog box

Summary

Premiere's superimposition options create interesting and attractive effects that blend video tracks together or make various areas of one track transparent.

- ✦ Use the Premiere Rubberband fade control to blend a higher video track with the one beneath it.
- ✦ Click and drag on the Opacity Rubberband's handles to adjust the fading effect.
- ✦ To create key effects that make portions of a video track transparent, open Premiere's Transparency Settings dialog box by choosing Clip ➪ Video Options ➪ Transparency.
- ✦ Premiere provides 14 different keying effects: Chroma, RGB Difference, Luminance, Alpha Channel, Black Alpha Matte, White Alpha Matte, Image Matte, Difference Matte, Blue Screen, Green Screen, Multiply, Screen, Track Matte, and Non-Red.
- ✦ Use the Blue Screen and Green Screen key types to key out background image areas based on color.
- ✦ Use the Alpha Channel key to key out images based on an imported image's alpha channel.
- ✦ Use the Track Matte command to create traveling matte effects.

✦ ✦ ✦

CHAPTER 13

Using Color Mattes and Backdrops

✦ ✦ ✦ ✦

In This Chapter

✦ ✦ ✦ ✦

During the course of a video production, you may need to create a simple, colored background video track. You may need the track to be a solid color background for text, or you may need to create a background for transparency effects. This chapter looks at how to use colored background mattes and still-frame background images in Adobe Premiere. You learn to create a color background in Premiere and to export still-frames from a clip to use as a backdrop. This chapter concludes with tutorials on creating backdrops in three popular digital imaging programs — Adobe Photoshop, Adobe Illustrator, and Corel Painter.

Creating a Color Matte

If you need to create a colored background for text or graphics, use a Premiere *color matte*. Unlike many of the Premiere video mattes, a color matte is a solid matte that comprises the entire video frame. A color matte can be used as a background or as a temporary track placeholder, until you've shot or created the final track.

Note: You may want to use a black video as a background matte. To create a black video, choose File ➪ New ➪ Black Video.

An advantage of using a colored background is its versatility. After you create the color matte, you can easily change its color with a few clicks of the mouse.

Here's how to create a color matte in Premiere:

1. **With a project on-screen, choose File ➪ New ➪ Color Matte.** The Color Picker dialog box appears.
2. **Select a matte color.** If an exclamation mark appears next to the color swatches in the upper-right corner of the dialog box (see Figure 13-1), you've chosen a color that is out of the NTSC color gamut. This color cannot be reproduced correctly in NTSC video. Click the exclamation mark to have Premiere choose the next closest color.

Cross-Reference

For more information on color gamuts, see Chapter 15.

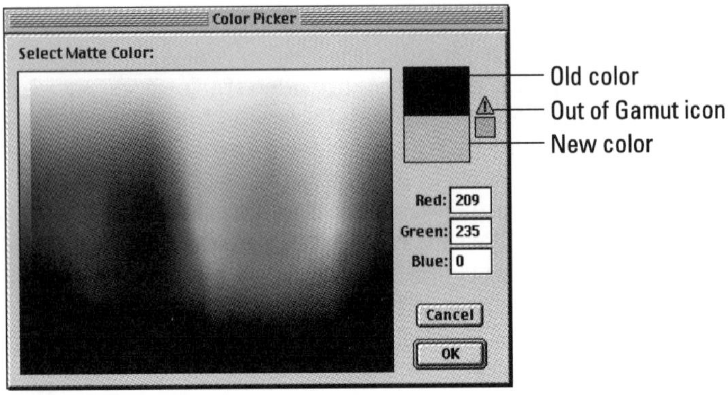

Figure 13-1: The Premiere Color Picker dialog box

3. **Click OK to close the Color Picker dialog box.**
4. **In the Color Matte dialog box, type a name for the color matte in the Name field (see Figure 13-2).**
5. **Click OK to place the matte in the Project window.**
6. **To use the color matte, simply drag it from the Project window into a video track.**

Note

The default duration of a color matte is determined by the Still Frame setting in the General & Still Image Preferences dialog box. To change the default setting, choose File ➪ General & Still Image. In the Still Image area, enter the number of frames that you want to use as the still image default.

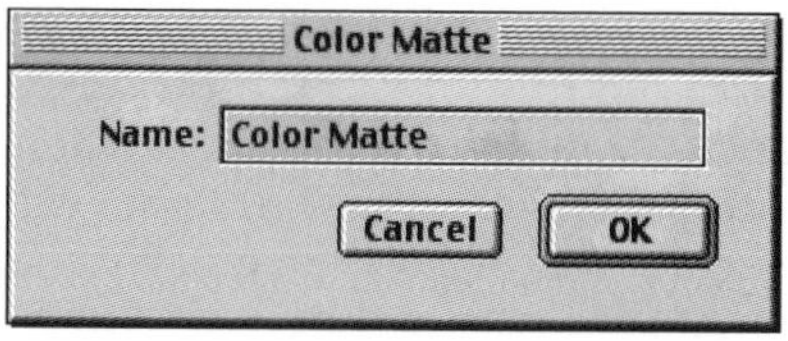

Figure 13-2: The Color Matte dialog box

Creating a Color Matte from the Project Window

Here's how to use the Project palette to create a background matte:

Note

Before you begin, you must first have a project on the screen.

1. **In the Project window, click the Create Item icon, which is located between the New Folder icon and the Trash icon.** The Create dialog box appears.
2. **Choose Color Matte from the Object Type pop-up menu.**
3. **Click OK.** The Color Picker dialog box appears.
4. **Click OK to close the box.** The Color Matte dialog box appears.
5. **Type a name for the color matte.**
6. **Click OK.** Instantly, the color matte appears in the Project window, as seen in Figure 13-3, ready for you to drag it to the Timeline window.

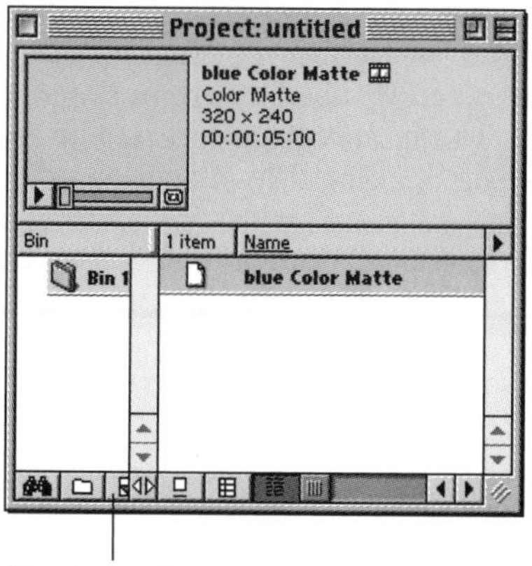

Figure 13-3: The Project window with a color matte

Editing a color matte

The Premiere color mattes have a distinct advantage over simply creating a colored background in the Title window or creating titles in another program with a colored background. If you are using a Premiere color matte, you can quickly change colors if the original matte color proves unsuitable or unattractive.

To change the colors of a color matte after you've placed it into the Timeline, simply double-click the matte clip in the Timeline. When Premiere's Color Picker appears, pick a new color and then click OK. After you click OK, the color changes, not only in the selected clip but also in all of the clips in the tracks that use that color matte.

Note: You can create a color matte in Premiere and then animate and incorporate it into a project. Chapter 9 provides two examples of creating color mattes and incorporating them into projects.

Creating a Backdrop from a Still Frame

As you work in Premiere, you may want to export a still frame from a video clip and save it in a graphic format so that you can use it in another program as part of a background. Figure 13-4 shows a collage we created using four frames from a Digital Vision, CityMix royalty-free video clip collection. The video clip 567001f from Digital Vision can be found on the CD-ROM that accompanies this book. To create the collage in Figure 13-4, we found four frames we liked from video clip 567001f. We then exported these frames from Premiere as PICT files. Then we imported the four still frames into Photoshop. Using layers we composited the collage. We added text and lines. The final collage (seen in Figure 13-4) can be used as promotional material, such as a poster for the actual video clip. The final collage can also be re-imported into Premiere and used as a backdrop of the opening title of a video production.

Following are the steps on how to export and save a portion of a video clip and use the still frame as a backdrop:

Note: Before we begin, open or create a project containing a video clip in one of the Timeline window's video tracks.

Figure 13-4: A backdrop created by exporting a frame from a video clip in Premiere into Photoshop

1. **Double-click the clip from which you want to create a backdrop in the Project window.** The clip opens in the Clip window.
2. **Use the Scrubbing tool and/or Frame Advance icon to move to the frame that you want to export.**

Cross-Reference

For more information on using the Clip window, turn to Chapter 5.

3. **Choose File ⇨ Export Clip ⇨ Frame.** The Export Still Frame dialog box appears.
4. **Choose Settings.** The Export Still Frame Settings dialog box appears.
5. **Choose TIF, Targa, PICT, or GIF from the File format pop-up menu.** If you choose GIF, your image can contain a maximum of 256 colors.
6. **Save the file.** You can now import the image into Photoshop by choosing File ⇨ Open. Photoshop enables you to enhance or manipulate your image. If you want, you can create a collage, as seen in Figure 13-4. You may also want to import the Photoshop image into Premiere by choosing File ⇨ Import.

Creating Background Mattes in Photoshop

Adobe Photoshop is an extremely versatile program for creating full-screen background mattes, or backdrops. Not only can you edit and manipulate photographs in Photoshop, but you can also create black and white or grayscale images to be used as background mattes. In this section, you create two different Photoshop projects. The first is a simple backdrop, showing you how to create a textured backdrop to use as a backdrop when superimposing titles and graphics. The second example is more complicated, but it illustrates more of Photoshop's digital imaging power.

Creating simple backgrounds with the Gradient tool

In this section, you create a project called Orchid Flower Shop. You'll use Photoshop's Gradient tool and several filters to create a background. Figure 13-5 shows the final background image created in Photoshop.

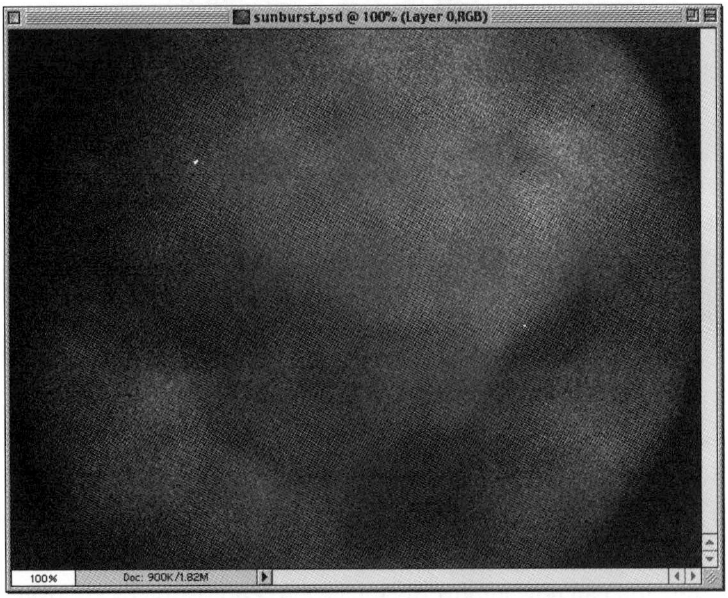

Figure 13-5: Simple background image created in Photoshop

After you create the background, you mask a flower image with a transparent background, as shown in Figure 13-6. When this file is loaded into Premiere, it reads the Photoshop file with a transparent background with an alpha channel. Text appears on top of the two Photoshop images, created by using the Premiere Title Designer window, as shown in Figure 13-7.

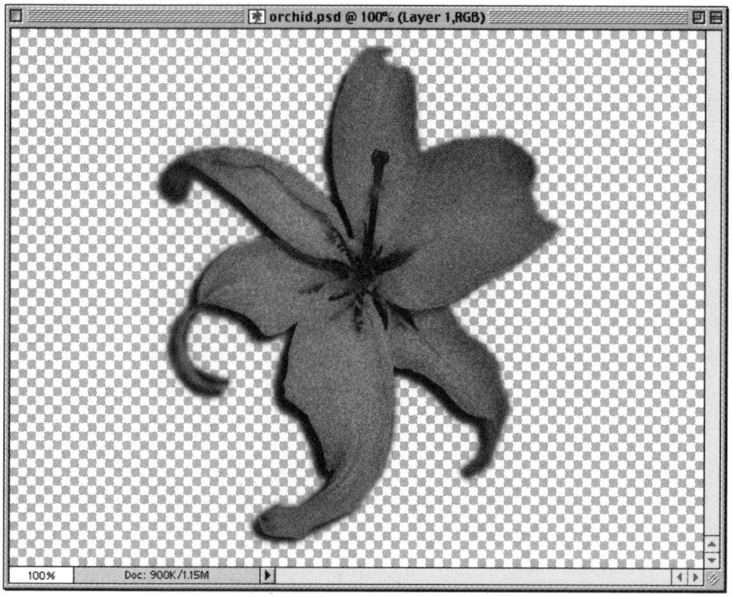

Figure 13-6: Flower image with transparent background

Figure 13-7: Orchid Flower Shop text in Premiere's Title Designer window

Here's how to create a simple background in Photoshop (shown previously in Figure 13-5):

1. **Choose File ➪ New to create a new file.**
2. **In the New dialog box, set the width and height to the dimension of your project with a resolution of 72 pixels per inch.** The mode should be set to RGB. Set the Contents to Transparent.
3. **Click OK to close the dialog box.**
4. **Set the foreground color to a light color and set the background color to a darker shade of the same color.** To change the foreground and background colors, click the foreground and background swatches in the Toolbox. In the Color Picker dialog box that appears, pick a color.
5. **Click the Gradient tool in the Toolbox.** Set the Gradient tool to use a Radial Gradient. The mode should be Normal, and the Opacity set to 100%.
6. **With the Gradient tool selected, click and drag outward from the center of your image to create a gradient.**
7. **With a radial gradient on-screen, choose Filter ➪ Noise ➪ Add Noise to add color to the gradient.**
8. **Choose Filter ➪ Render ➪ Lighting Effects to add more depth and lighting variations.** Figure 13-8 shows the Lighting Effects dialog box.
9. **Choose File ➪ Save to save your file. Save your file in Photoshop format.**

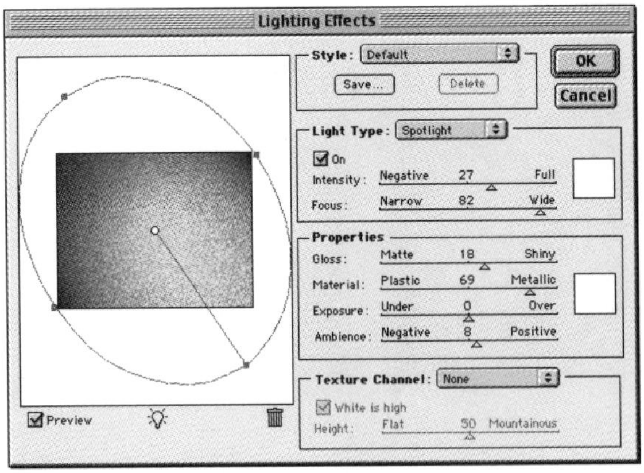

Figure 13-8: Photoshop's Lighting Effects filter is used to create a background.

Now that you've created a background, you need to mask a flower from the background so that you can import it into Premiere with a transparent background. Follow these steps to isolate the orchid flower from its background:

1. **Choose File ➪ Open to open a file with flowers.** If you don't have a picture of flowers, you can load the orchid.psd file from the CD-ROM that accompanies this book.
2. **Double-click the Background layer in the Layers palette.**
3. **In the New Layer dialog box that appears, rename the layer.**
4. **Click OK to close the dialog box.** You should now have a file with just a flower on a transparent background. (By default, Photoshop represents a transparent background with a checkerboard.) Premiere views an image on a transparent background the same way it does if the image had an alpha channel saved in the Channels palette.

Tip

If you are not familiar with Photoshop's masking features, you can use the Eraser tool to erase the background. If you make a mistake, either choose Edit ➪ Undo or File ➪ Revert. If you are familiar with Photoshop's tools, you may want to use the Lasso or Pen tool to outline the flower and select it. If you use the Pen tool, you need to convert the path into a selection by choosing Make Selection from the Path pop-up menu. Next, reverse the selection by choosing Select ➪ Inverse and press Delete on your keyboard to erase the background and isolate the flower.

5. **Choose File ➪ Save to save your file.** Save your file in Photoshop format to keep the flower isolated from the background.

Orchid Flower Shop project

Now that you have created a background and isolated an image, you're ready to create the Orchid Flower Shop project. Figure 13-9 shows a few frames from the Orchid Flower Shop project. In the frames, you can see that the orchid flower moves across the screen over the background.

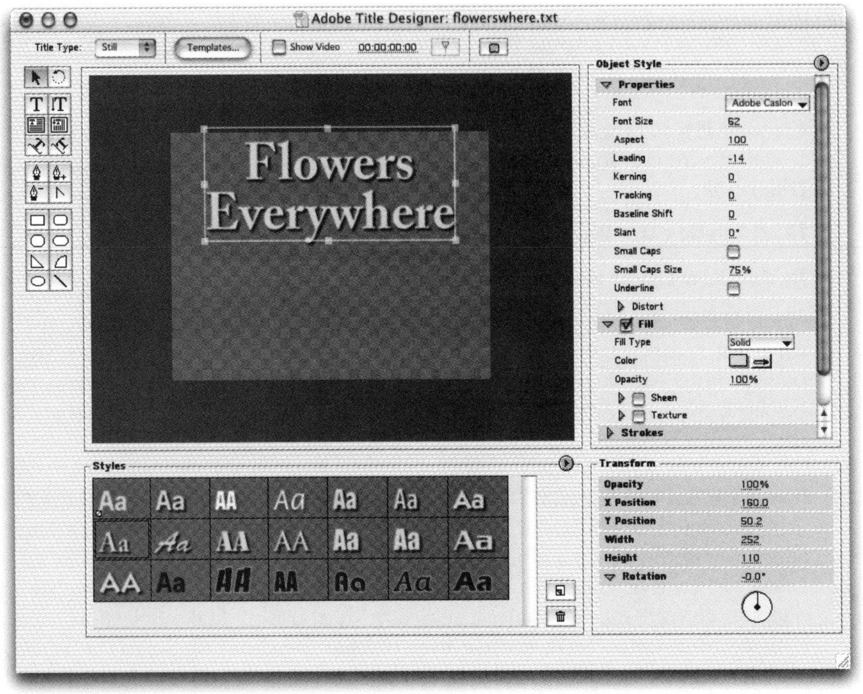

Figure 13-9: Frames from the Orchid Flower Shop project

Follow these steps to create the Orchid Flower Shop project:

1. **Choose File ➪ New Project to create a new project.**
2. **In the Project Settings dialog box, choose Multimedia.**
3. **Click OK to create a new project.**
4. **Choose File ➪ Import ➪ File to import the background and the isolated image — the gradient background image and the flower.** In the Import dialog box, find the file you want to import. If the files are in the same folder, Mac users press and hold the Command key to select more than one file at a time. PC users should press and hold the Ctrl key.
5. **When you've selected your files, click Open to import the files into the Project window.**

On the CD-ROM

If you want, you can load the images in Figures 13-4 (sunburst.psd) and 13-5 (orchid.psd) from the Chapter 13 folder, which is in the Tutorial Projects folder.

6. **Drag and drop the background image from the Project palette to Video Track 1 in the Timeline window.**
7. **Drag the image with the alpha channel (flower) in Video Track 2.**
8. **Select the graphic in Video Track 2 if it's not already selected.**
9. **Then choose Clip ➪ Video Options ➪ Motion.** The Motion Settings dialog box appears (see Figure 13-10).
10. **Click OK to apply a motion that moves from left to right.**
11. **Choose File ➪ New ➪ Title.** The Title window opens.
12. **Create some text with the Type tool.**

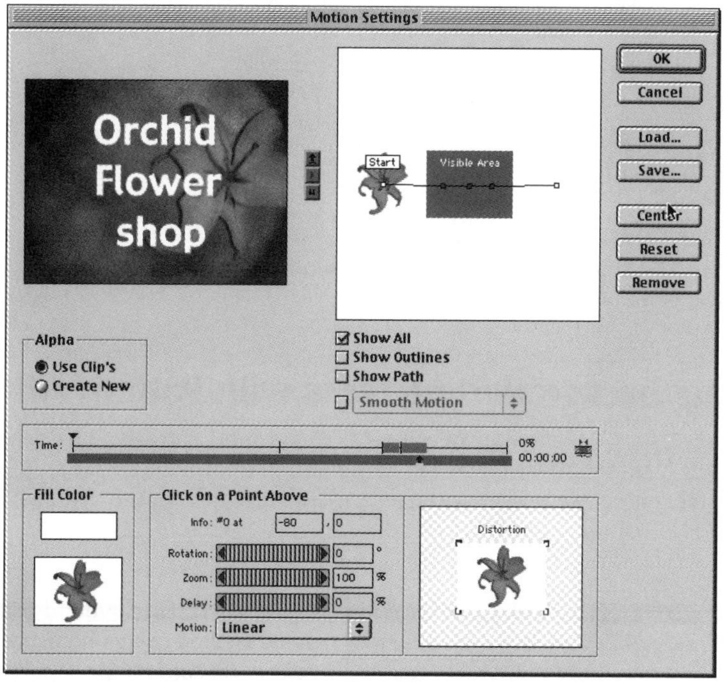

Figure 13-10: The Motion Settings dialog box adds motion to a flower image that was created in Adobe Illustrator.

Note

To guarantee that the title background is transparent, make sure that the Opaque option in the Title Window Options dialog box (File ➪ Window ➪ Title Window) isn't selected.

13. **Save the title to make it appear in the Project window.**
14. **Create Video Track 3 by choosing Add Video Track from the Timeline pop-up menu.**

15. **Drag and drop the title clip from the Project window to Video Track 3.** (See Figure 13-11.)

16. **Choose File ➪ Save to save the project.** Before previewing the clip, check that the transparency options are set for the title and the flower. Select each clip individually and then choose Clip ➪ Video Option ➪ Transparency. The transparency pop-up menu should be set to White Alpha. If it isn't, select White Alpha.

17. **Preview the file by choosing Timeline ➪ Preview.** When the preview plays, you should see the text and flower visible over the background you created in Photoshop.

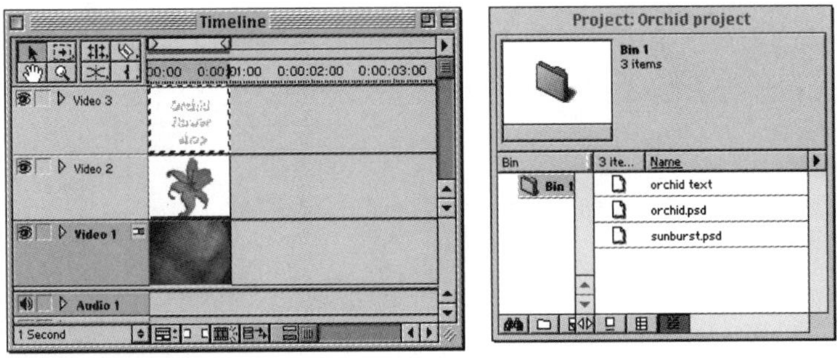

Figure 13-11: The Timeline and Project windows for the Orchid Flower Shop project

Creating background patterns with Pattern Fill

This example shows how you can create a background pattern matte (shown in Figure 13-12) using the new Layer Fill command in Photoshop 6.0. Using Layer Fill you can quickly choose preset patterns and add 3D effects. After you save the background in Photoshop, you can load it directly into Premiere.

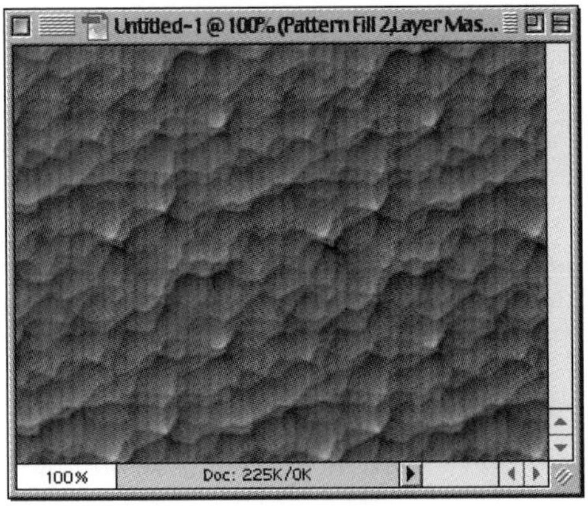

Figure 13-12: Background pattern matte created using Photoshop's Pattern Fill command

Follow these steps to create a background pattern in Photoshop using the Pattern Fill command:

1. **Create a new file in Photoshop 6.0 (File ➪ New) with the same pixel dimensions as you are using in your Premiere project.** If you're creating a project for multimedia, you may want to choose 320 x 240 pixels. When you create the project, set the mode to RGB color and the background contents to Transparent.
2. **To create the pattern in a layer, choose Layer ➪ New Fill Layer.** A pop-up menu appears.
3. **Choose Pattern.**
4. **In the New Layer dialog box, click OK.** The Pattern Fill dialog box opens (see Figure 13-13), in which you can choose a pattern from a pop-up menu of pattern thumbnails.
5. **Click OK to create the pattern.**

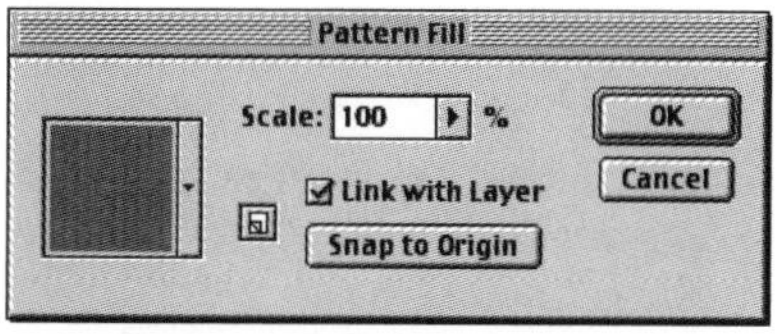

Figure 13-13: Photoshop's Pattern Fill dialog box

Note

If you want to add 3D or additional special effects to your pattern, choose Layer ➪ Layer Style ➪ Bevel and Emboss. In the Layer Style dialog box, shown in Figure 13-14, use the Depth, Size, and Soften sliders to fine-tune the effect. To add more variation to the pattern, click the Contour pop-up menu and experiment with the contours. Notice that the Layer Style changes, as shown in Figure 13-15, when you click Contour. You can also click the Texture pop-up menu to add a texture to your image. Pick a pattern and experiment with the Scale and Depth sliders, which are shown in Figure 13-16.

6. **When you've completed your background pattern, save the file in Photoshop format.** The file can then be imported into any Premiere project.

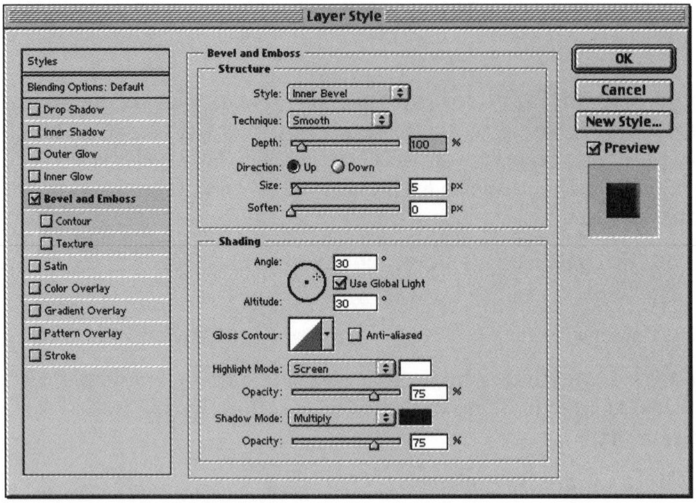

Figure 13-14: The Layer Style dialog box

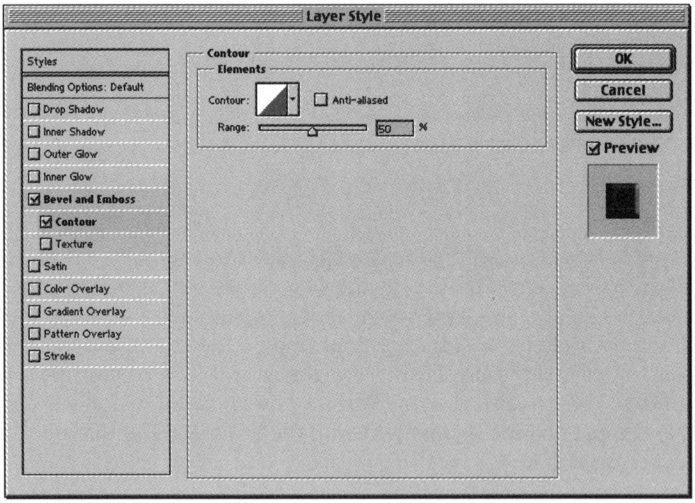

Figure 13-15: The Contour option settings in the Layer Style dialog box

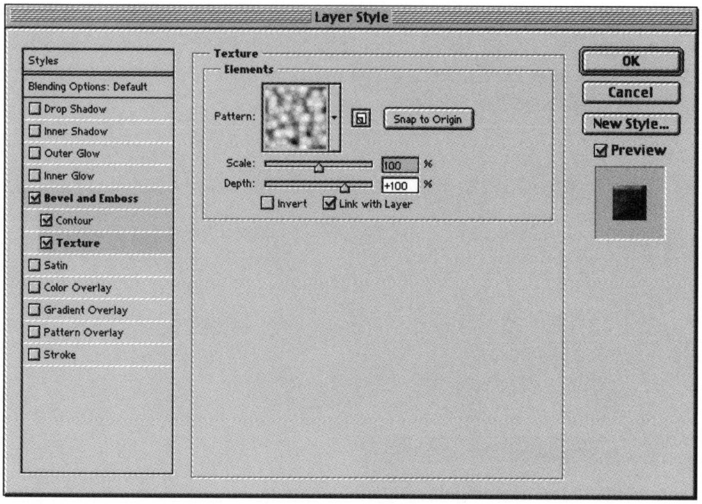

Figure 13-16: The Texture option settings in the Layer Style dialog box

Creating Background Mattes in Illustrator

In this section, you learn to create a project called Flowers Everywhere. To create this project, you use Adobe Illustrator to create a background matte, as shown in Figure 13-17.

Figure 13-17: Background matte created in Adobe Illustrator

Then you take one of the elements from the background and copy it into another file. This image, seen in Figure 13-18, appears against a background video track in Premiere. Finally, you use Premiere's Title window to create text (shown in Figure 13-19), which appears over the background and image.

Figure 13-18: Image created from one of the images from the background

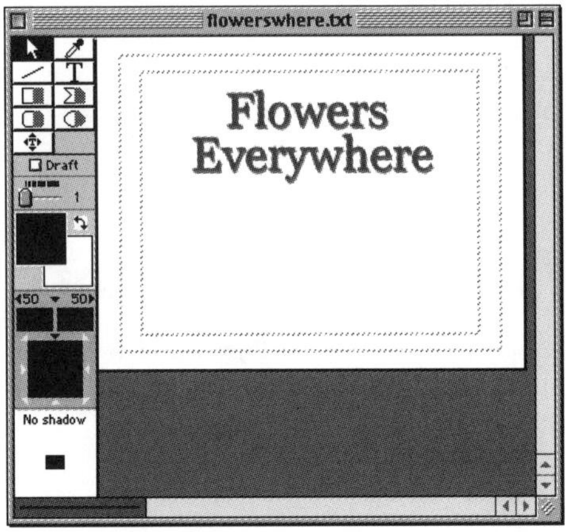

Figure 13-19: Text created in Premiere's Title window

Here's how to create a background matte in Adobe Illustrator:

1. **Load Adobe Illustrator.**
2. **Choose File ➪ New to create a new file.** Make sure that the Color Mode is set to RGB Color and not to CMYK Color. (CMYK color is for print work.)
3. **To create the flowers seen in Figures 13-17 and 13-18, click the Polygon tool in the Toolbox.**
4. **With the Polygon tool selected, move to the center of the screen.**
5. **Option/Alt+click to display the Polygon dialog box.**
6. **In the Polygon dialog box, set the Sides to 8.**
7. **Click OK to create a polygon.**

8. **Choose Filter ➪ Distort ➪ Punk & Bloat.** Illustrator converts the polygon into a flower shape.
9. **In the Punk & Bloat dialog box, drag the slider toward Bloat to about 100%.** To preview the effect before applying it, make sure that the Preview option is selected.
10. **Click OK to apply the effect.**
11. **Click the Ellipse tool in the Toolbox.**
12. **Create a circle in the middle of the flower shape.** To create a perfect circle, press and hold the Shift key.
13. **Click the Select tool in the Toolbox.**
14. **Click and drag over the flower and circle to select them.**
15. **Then choose Edit ➪ Copy and Edit ➪ Paste to duplicate the flower.** Do this a few times, until you have a few flowers on the screen.
16. **Using the Color palette, pick colors for the flowers you created.**
17. **Use the Scale tool to scale some of the flowers.** Double-click the Scale tool in the Toolbox. In the Scale dialog box, make sure that the Uniform option is selected. (Doing this prevents the flowers from being distorted when they are scaled.)
18. **Choose File ➪ Save to save the file in Illustrator format.** Now that you've created a background using Illustrator, you can easily pick one of the items from the background to use as a separate image in Premiere.
19. **Before you close this file, select a portion of your image and choose Edit ➪ Copy.**
20. **While still in Illustrator, choose File ➪ New.**
21. **Paste the flower into the file and save the file.** In Figure 13-17, shown previously, we isolated a flower from the background and copied it into a new file to create the image shown in Figure 13-18.

Flowers Everywhere project

A great feature of using Adobe Illustrator with Premiere is that Premiere translates the blank areas of the Illustrator file as an alpha channel mask. You can now import the flower files that you just created into Premiere and create the Flowers Everywhere project. In this project, the Bend video effect was applied to the background and the Bevel Alpha video effect was applied to the text in the top video track seen in Figure 13-20 (Video Track 3). Figure 13-21 shows frames from the Flowers Everywhere project.

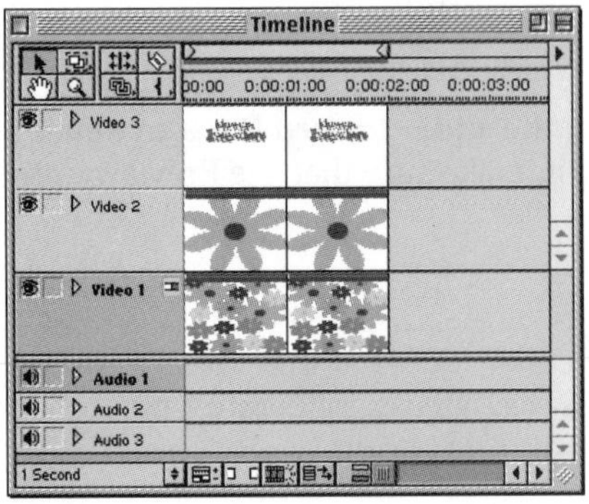

Figure 13-20: The Timeline palette used to create the Flowers Everywhere project

Figure 13-21: Frames from the Flowers Everywhere project

Here's how to create the Flowers Everywhere project:

1. **Open Adobe Premiere.**
2. **Choose File ➪ New Project to create a new project.**
3. **In the Load Project Settings dialog box, choose Multimedia.**
4. **Click OK to apply the settings to the new project.** The new project opens.
5. **Choose Window ➪ Workspace ➪ Effects.** The Effects palette displays.
6. **Choose File ➪ Import ➪ File.**

7. **Locate and select the 15flowers.ai and 1flower.ai files.**
8. **Click Open.** Premiere imports the files into the Project window.

On the CD-ROM

If you want, you can load the images in Figures 13-17 (15flowers.ai), 13-18 (1flower.ai), and 13-19 (flowertxt.prtl) from the Chapter 13 folder, which is in the Tutorial Projects folder on the CD-ROM that accompanies this book.

9. **Drag the 15flowers.ai (background file) and 1flower.ai files to Video Tracks 1 and 2, respectively.**
10. **Choose File ➪ New ➪ Title.** The Title Designer window opens.
11. **Create some text with the Type tool.**
12. **Save the Title to add it to the Project window.** To see the graphic and background below the text, make sure the background is transparent. To verify this, click the Background button in the Title Designer window. Then, in the Title background window, make sure the Background option is off. Figure 13-19 shows the Title Designer window with the text for Flowers Everywhere.
13. **Choose Add Video Track from the Timeline pop-up menu to create Video Track 3.**
14. **Drag and drop the Title to Video Track 3.**
15. **Fade the graphic in Video Track 2.**

Cross-Reference

See Chapter 12 to learn about fading clips and working with transparency.

16. **Click Video Track 2.**
17. **Drag the Bend filter from the Video Effects palette and drop it on the clip in Video Track 2.** Figure 13-22 shows the Bend Settings dialog box.
18. **Save the file.**
19. **Preview the file to view the flowers and ripple effect.**

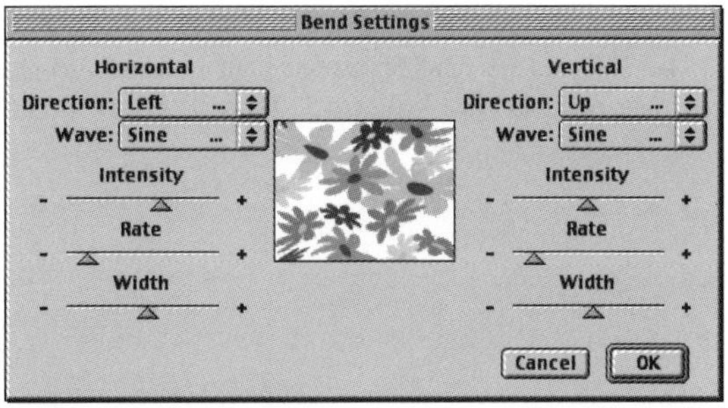

Figure 13-22: The Bend Settings dialog box with flower background file created in Illustrator

Creating Backgrounds and QuickTime Movies with Painter

You can use Corel Painter to create background mattes and QuickTime movies from graphics. Figure 13-23 displays the Timeline window for a project called Summer Fun. The Video 1 track shows a background created in Painter. The Video 2 track features an animated horse created in Painter and imported in Premiere as a QuickTime movie. The Video 3 track displays the text Summer Sun, which was created by using Adobe Premiere's Title window.

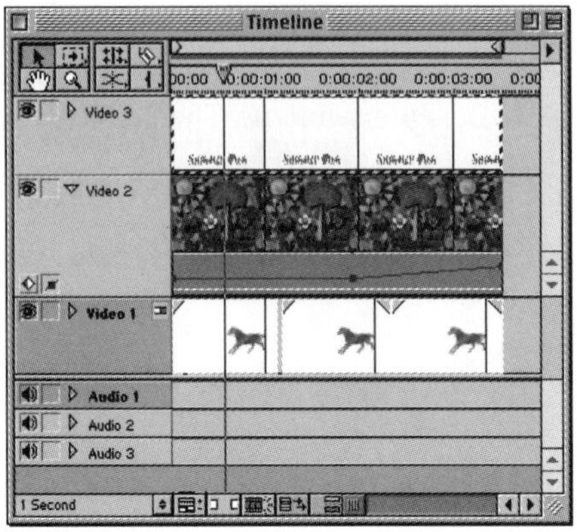

Figure 13-23: The Summer Fun project Timeline window

Here's how we created the project. To create the landscape background, we used Painter's shape tools and layers. To create the animated horse, we first created a new movie instead of a new canvas. Next, we made a horse as a layer at the far right of the screen. We filled the horse with a gold color. Then, we slowly moved the horse to the left in different frames. We saved the movie in QuickTime movie format.

In Figure 13-24, you can see the frames for the Summer Fun project. In the frames, you can see a horse moving over a faded background. To add some interest to the text, we applied motion to it.

Figure 13-24: Frames from the Summer Fun project

Here's how to assemble the graphic elements in Premiere to create the Summer Fun project:

1. **Create a new project.**
2. **Choose File ⇨ Import ⇨ Folder to import the Summer folder into the Project window.**

On the CD-ROM

You can find the files used to create the Summer Fun project in the Tutorial Projects\Chapter 13\Summer project folder on the CD-ROM that accompanies this book.

3. **Drag the horse.mov clip to the Video 1 track.**
4. **Drag sunshine.psd (background file) to the Video 2 track.**
5. **Click the Expand/Collapse icon to expand the Video 2 track.**
6. **Click the Opacity Rubber Band icon (the small red square).** A red line appears under the clip.
7. **Drag the handle at the beginning of the line downward a little, to gradually fade in the background.**
8. **To add another handle, click and drag the fade line upward, so that the background slowly appears.**
9. **Choose Add Video Track from the Timeline pop-up menu.** Instantly, the Video 3 track is created.
10. **Drag the summerfun.prtl title file to Video Track 3.** If you wish, create your own title file as shown in Figure 13-25. To create a new title in Premiere, choose File ➪ New ➪ Title. When you are done creating a title, save it so that it appears in the Project window.

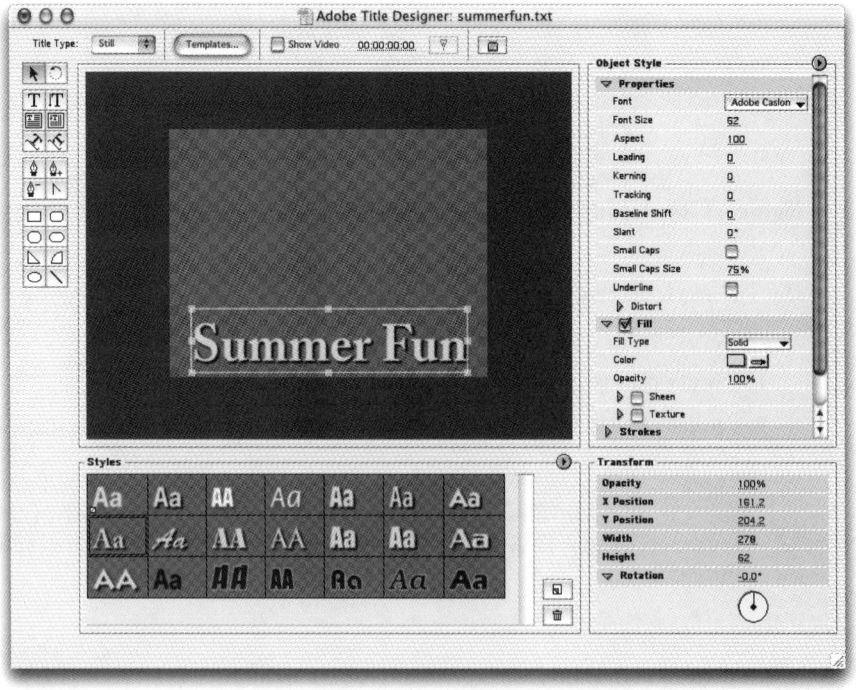

Figure 13-25: The Summer Fun Title Designer window

11. **Click the Title file icon in Video Track 3 and choose Clip ⇨ Video Options ⇨ Transparency.** In the Transparency Settings dialog box, make sure that the Key Type option is set to White Alpha Matte.

12. **To apply motion to the Title file, choose Clip ⇨ Video Options ⇨ Motion.** By default, the motion in the Motion Settings dialog box is set to move from right to left. To change the motion to move from left to right, move the start and finish points and then click OK.

13. **Save and preview your project.**

Summary

You can use Premiere's color matte command to easily create solid color backgrounds for text and graphics.

- ✦ You can use Adobe Photoshop, Adobe Illustrator, or Corel's Painter to create your own backgrounds to use as background mattes.
- ✦ Photoshop and Illustrator files can be imported directly into Premiere. You do not need to save Photoshop or Photoshop format; save Illustrator files in Illustrator format.

✦ ✦ ✦

CHAPTER 14

Creating Motion Effects in Premiere

✦ ✦ ✦ ✦

In This Chapter

Touring the Motion Effects dialog box

Adding points to the Motion Timeline

Changing size and motion speed

Creating rotation and distortion effects

Previewing motion effects

Applying alpha channels

Creating traveling mattes

✦ ✦ ✦ ✦

Motion creates interest and adds to the power of just about any presentation. In Adobe Premiere, you can send a title or logo spinning across the screen, or bounce a clip off the borders of the frame area. Using a graphic with an alpha channel, you can superimpose one moving object over another. You can also create traveling matte effects, in which one image within a shape moves across the screen over another image. This chapter not only shows you how to create traveling mattes, but also how to set graphics in motion, including how to make them bend and rotate on-screen.

To create these motion effects, you'll use Premiere's Motion Settings dialog box, which is where Premiere stores the majority of its motion effects.

Touring the Motion Settings Dialog Box

By using Premiere's Motion Settings dialog box, which is shown in Figure 14-1, you can wake up an otherwise boring image by setting it in motion. You can make any clip move and jiggle or make a still frame move across the screen. (See Chapter 9 to learn how to use Premiere's Motion Settings dialog box to add motion to your titles.)

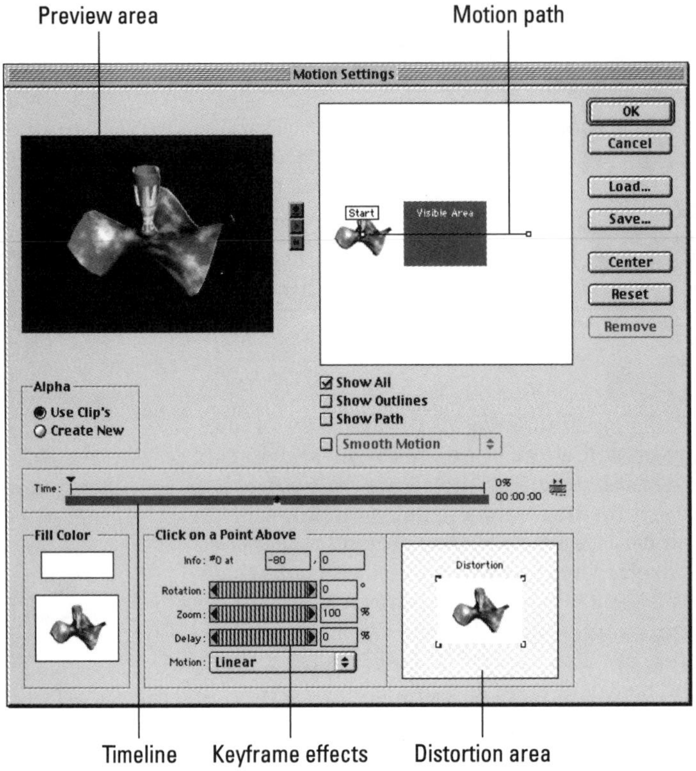

Figure 14-1: The Adobe Premiere Motion Settings dialog box

To use Premiere's Motion Settings dialog box, you need to have a project on-screen. Follow these steps to create a new project, import a clip, change clip duration, and display the Motion Settings dialog box:

1. **Choose File ➪ New Project to create a new project. In the Load Project Settings dialog box, choose the Multimedia Preset. Click OK.**
2. **Set the Timeline to show clips in one-second intervals by clicking the Time Zoom Level pop-up menu and choosing one second.**
3. **Load an image by choosing File ➪ Import ➪ File.** You can either use one of your own still images (the still image can be a Photoshop or Illustrator file), or you can use the stillLife.jpg sample file found on the CD-ROM that accompanies this book. After you import the file into your project, it appears in the Project window.

On the CD-ROM

stillLife.jpg is found in the Chapter 14 folder, which is in the Tutorial Projects folder, on the CD-ROM that is the back of this book.

4. **Next, click the file in the Project window and drag it to Video track 2 in the Timeline window.**

Note

If you have the filename option set in the Timeline Window Options dialog box, you won't see one-second intervals in the video track. If you have the filename option on and want to turn it off, choose Window ➪ Timeline Window Options. In the Track format area, select the option that does not display filenames.

5. **To view and change the duration of the imported image, select the image in the Timeline window and then choose Clip ➪ Duration.** When the Clip Duration dialog box appears, you can change the duration. Click OK to view the change in the Timeline window. To change the duration of the clip manually, click the Selection tool in the Timeline window and then position the selection tool over the right edge of the clip in the Timeline. Use the Selection tool to click the right-side clip in Video track 2. When the pointer changes to an icon with two arrows on either side of a red bar, click and drag to the right to extend the duration or to the left to decrease the duration.
6. **With the clip in Video track 2 selected, choose Clip ➪ Video Options ➪ Motion, to open the Motion Settings dialog box.**

Note

You can also open the Motion Settings dialog box by using the Effect Controls palette. Choose Window ➪ Show Effect Controls to display the palette. In the Effect Controls palette, click "Setup" next to the Motion option.

Tip

Here's a shortcut for opening the Motion Settings dialog box: Mac users press Command+Y, PC users press Ctrl+Y.

As soon as the dialog box loads, Premiere sets your clip in motion horizontally across the screen, displaying a preview of the dialog box's default motion path. Using the controls in the Motion Settings dialog box, you can alter the motion path, change the speed, and add effects, such as rotation and speed.

The key features of the Motion Settings dialog box are:

- ✦ **Preview area.** Previews the effect.
- ✦ **Motion path.** Used to edit the motion path. This shows the path and the visible area of the screen.
- ✦ **Timeline.** Used to change the speed of the motion.
- ✦ **Alpha settings.** Enables you to use an alpha channel to create transparency effects.
- ✦ **Distortion area.** Used to twist and distort the image while it moves.
- ✦ **Keyframe effects area.** Used to add rotation, zooming acceleration, and deceleration effects according to points on the motion path.

The following sections describe how to use the features in each area of the Motion Settings dialog box.

Previewing motion settings

As mentioned previously, the Motion Settings dialog box opens with a preview of your clip moving across the screen. The preview can be turned off or on by clicking the control buttons to the right of the preview area. To turn off the preview, click the Red Bars icon. To turn the preview back on, click the Triangle icon.

Note: To see a preview of the final motion in the Monitor window, click OK in the Motion Settings dialog box and then choose Timeline ⇨ Preview. Then save the project. To control the preview playback, click and drag the Timeline marker over the clip in the Timeline window.

Editing the motion path

In the motion path area of the Motion Settings dialog box, you can control the path of the moving clip. You can move the clip up or down or at different angles. By default, the motion path is set to move from left to right. The starting and ending points are displayed as tiny squares at the beginning and end of the motion path. Just in case you lose your bearings, the words Start and Finish appear if you click the starting or ending points.

It is easy to change the motion path. Just remember this: To raise or lower the image position in the video frame, click the starting or ending points and drag with the mouse.

You can also easily create the effect of the image moving diagonally from top to bottom of the frame, by dragging the starting point to the top of the visible area and dragging the ending point to the bottom of the visible area. This effect is shown in Figure 14-2.

Motion path viewing options

Below the motion path four checkboxes enable you to edit the path's appearance. One box even enables you to smooth a path so that it's not too abrupt or jerky. These checkbox options are described here:

- ✦ **Show All.** Shows the path and outline of the image and dots indicating the path.
- ✦ **Show Outlines.** Shows the outline of the image along the path.
- ✦ **Show Path.** Shows the selected path as dots. Dots that are further apart indicate faster motion; dots closer together indicate slower motion.
- ✦ **Smooth Motion.** Creates the smallest amount of smoothing. Averaging-High creates the greater amount of smoothing.

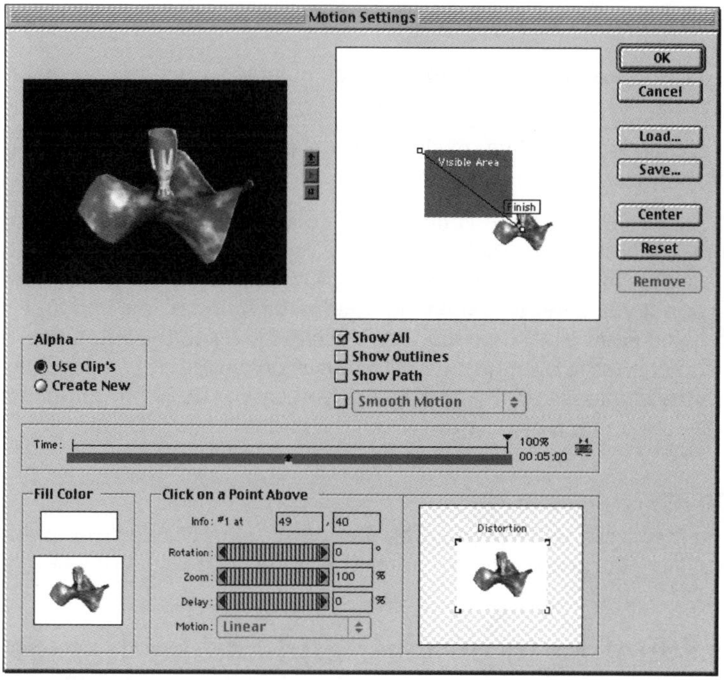

Figure 14-2: The motion path edit to move diagonally

To create motion that moves in more than one direction, or changes speed, you need to add keyframe points to the motion path. Keyframes appear as a point in the motion path and designate a change in direction or speed. To add keyframes to the motion path:

1. **Move the mouse pointer over the path.**
2. **After the pointer changes to a hand with a pointing finger, click and drag on the path.** When you click a point on the motion path, a marker appears on the Motion Timeline, displaying where that point appears. The information for that point appears in the Info readout below the Timeline.

Note

Keyframes can also be added to the motion path at specific points by clicking on the Timeline. (The Timeline is described in the next section.)

After you edit a motion path, you can return to it at any time to edit it again. To re-edit the motion path, select the point that you want to re-edit by clicking it with the mouse. After you click one point, you can select others by pressing the Tab key.

Following are tips for making intricate edits on the motion path:

- ✦ To move a keyframe on the motion path one pixel at a time, press one of the directional arrow keys on your keyboard.
- ✦ To move the motion path five pixels at a time, press Shift and press a directional arrow key on your keyboard.
- ✦ Click in the Info box below the Timeline and enter a specific coordinate for the point on the path. When you select a point, the point number appears in the Info box. For example, if you want to center the clip in the middle of the screen, enter 0,0 in the box. If you enter a positive number in the first box, the clip moves to the right. If you enter a negative number, the clip moves to the left. If you enter a positive number in the right box, the clip moves down; entering a negative number makes the clip move up. For example, if you enter **–10,10**, the clip moves ten pixels to the left and ten pixels down from the middle of the screen.

Deleting a point

As you edit, you may want to delete a point. To do this, simply select the point and press the Delete key. (PC users can also press the Backspace key to delete a point.)

Using the Timeline to preview and add keyframes

The Timeline provides a graphic view of the duration of your clip's motion effect. Why use the Timeline instead of the motion path? You can use the Timeline to create effects at specific points in time—for example, to create an effect using a graphic or video clip in motion simultaneously with a video clip. Using the timeline, the effect can occur at a specific point in your narration, and you can also add music to the effect.

Here's how to create a keyframe at a point in the Timeline:

1. **Move the mouse pointer to a point in the Timeline where you want to create a keyframe point.**
2. **Click the Timeline.** A vertical bar appears at the new keyframe position.
3. **To reposition a keyframe on the Timeline, select the keyframe point by clicking at the top of the vertical bar in the Timeline.** Then click and drag to move the keyframe to the desired location.

Previewing Timeline use

To use the Timeline to control the preview of the motion effect, click the small arrow at the bottom of the Timeline and drag. As you drag, the motion is previewed. To stop the preview at a certain point, click the mouse and hold the mouse button down. Figure 14-3 shows the Timeline with keyframe points and the motion preview in effect.

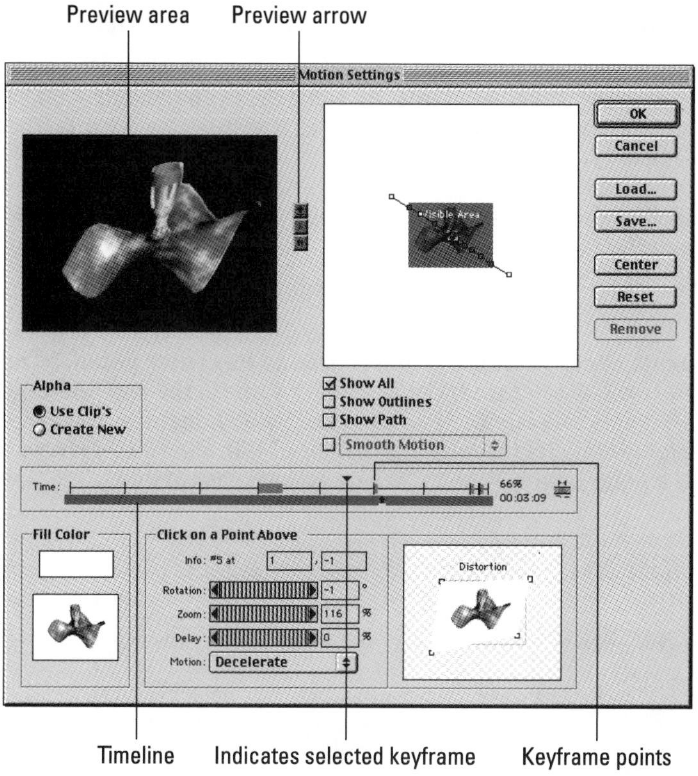

Figure 14-3: Keyframes in the Timeline and a motion preview

Changing speed

Premiere determines motion speed by the distance between keyframes. To increase the speed of motion, create keyframes that are closer together. To slow the speed of motion, set keyframes further apart.

Here's how to change the speed of motion:

1. **If you don't already have keyframes, create keyframes on the Timeline by clicking within the Timeline.**
2. **To increase motion speed, drag keyframes closer together.** To decrease motion speed, drag keyframes further apart. To move a keyframe, click the keyframe to select it and then click the black Triangle icon above the Timeline and drag.

Creating zooms, delays, distortion, and rotation

The Motion Settings dialog box provides several commands that enable you to create special effects between Timeline points. By using these commands, you can rotate, zoom, delay, and distort an image. In general, the steps for creating these effects are quite similar:

1. **Start by selecting the point on either the Timeline or motion path at which you want the effect to begin.**
2. **Use the effect slider of the effect that you want to implement to control the effect.**
   - **The Rotate slider rotates the object around its center point.** To rotate, click and drag the Rotate slider or enter a value in the rotation degree field. To create one complete rotation, enter **360** degrees. You can create up to eight rotations by entering **1440** or **–1440**. Figure 14-4 shows a preview of a point on the Timeline where an image is rotated.

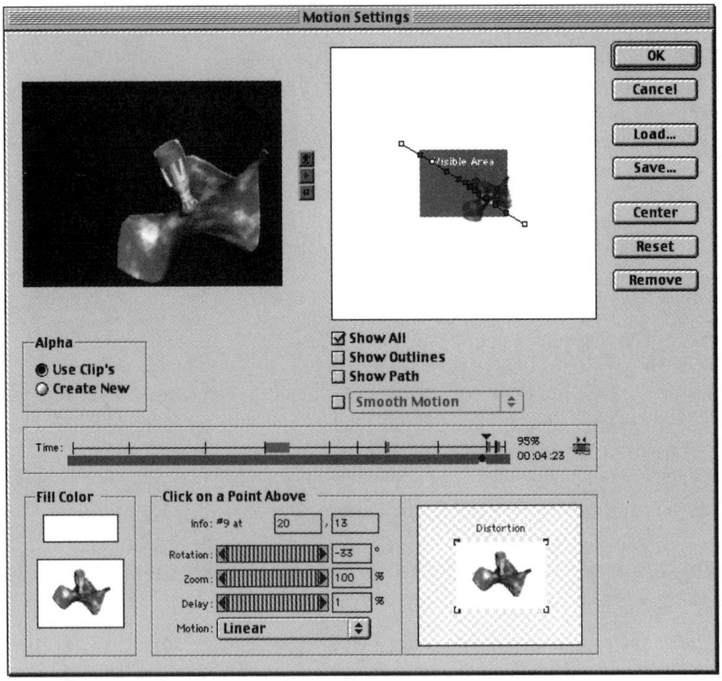

Figure 14-4: Motion settings with a rotation effect

- **The Zoom command enlarges or reduces the image at the selected keyframe.** Acceptable ranges are from 0 to 500. Enter **0** to make the clip invisible; enter **500** to enlarge the clip five times its normal size. Figure 14-5 shows a preview of a point on the Timeline where an image is enlarged using the Zoom feature.

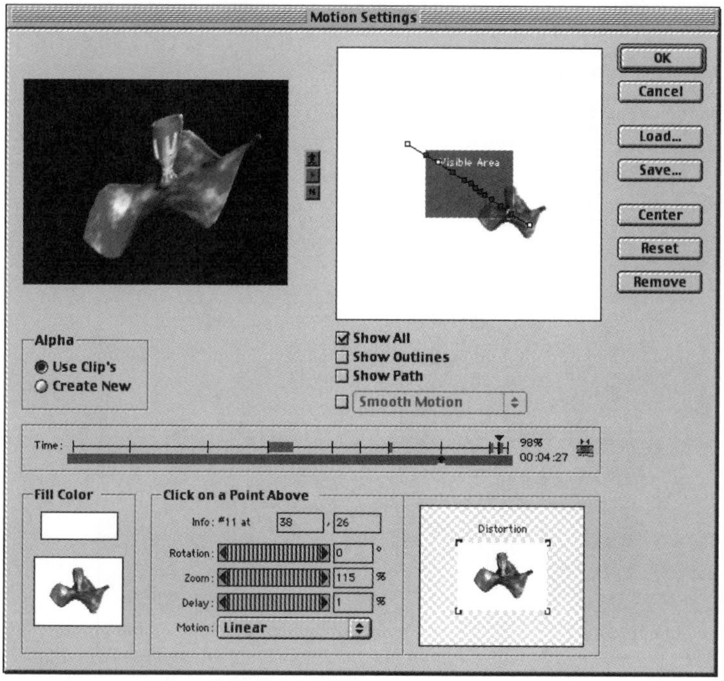

Figure 14-5: Motion settings with a zoom effect

- **The Delay slider provides a pause in the motion.** The delay is a percentage of the clip duration. (The duration is displayed at the right end of the Timeline). When creating delays, it's important to understand that the delay settings are based on keyframes. For example, you can't create a two-second delay if the next keyframe appears one second away. In other words, you cannot create a delay larger than the percentage distance between one clip and another on the Timeline. Thus, if you are creating a delay between keyframe 3 and keyframe 4, and the distance between keyframes 3 and 4 is ten percent of the total duration, you will not be able to create a delay larger than ten percent.
- **The Motion pop-up menu enables you to specify how the motion appears between the selected keyframe and the next keyframe.** The Motion pop-up menu choices are: Linear, Accelerate, and Decelerate. (Linear provides no change in settings.)

Distortion window

The Distortion window enables you to create distortion effects that occur at specific keyframe intervals. You can create unusual visual effects by distorting your image as shown in Figure 14-6.

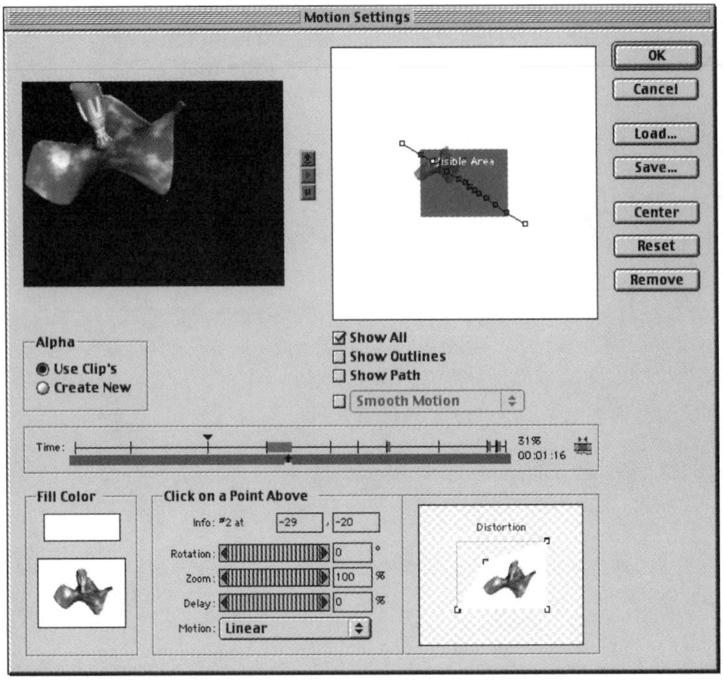

Figure 14-6: Image distorted using the Distortion window in the Motion Settings dialog box

Here are the steps for creating distortion effects:

1. **Click at the point on the Timeline where you want to distort your image.**
2. **In the Distortion section of the Motion Settings dialog box window, click and drag on a handle to distort the image.**

Note: When distorting your image, you can move the entire image by clicking and dragging in it.

Tip: To rotate the image around its center points, press Option/Alt and then click and drag on a corner point.

Fill Color

The Fill Color option enables you to add a color to the area surrounding the motion clip. To add a fill color, click the fill color patch on-screen. Doing this opens Premiere's Color Picker. In the Color Picker dialog box, click Fill Color to choose the fill color. Figure 14-7 shows an image in the Motion Settings dialog box with a fill color.

Note: In "Creating Traveling Mattes" later in this chapter, you learn to use a black fill color to make the background of a matte transparent as the matte moves across the screen.

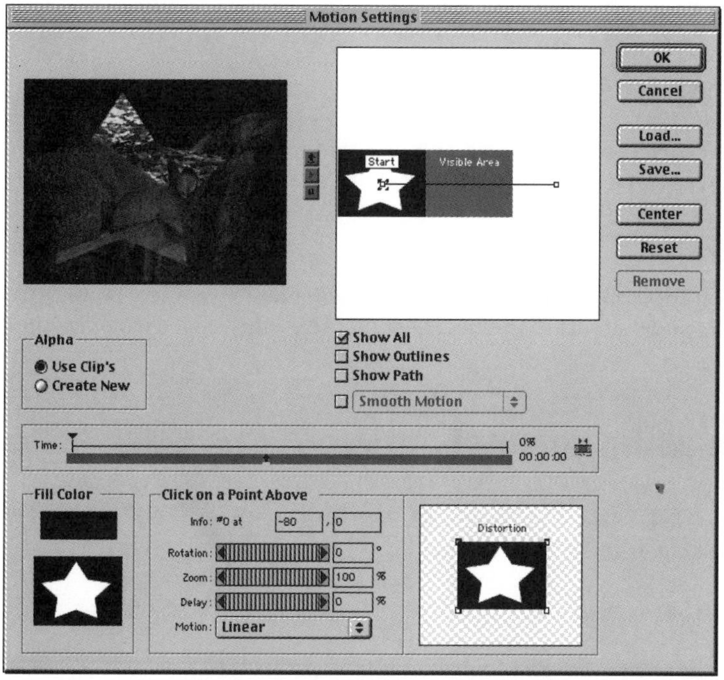

Figure 14-7: The Motion Settings dialog box with an image using the Fill Color option

Saving loading, resetting, and removing settings

The buttons at the far right of the Motion Settings dialog box enable you to save, load, remove settings, or reset a motion setting. To save a setting, simply click Save and enter a filename in the Save Motion Settings dialog box before clicking Save. To load your settings back into the dialog box, click Load. Next, select the filename that you want to load in the Load Motion Settings dialog box before clicking Open.

If you don't like the motion settings that you've created and want to restore the default settings, click Reset. To remove the motion settings from the clip altogether, click Remove. This eliminates the motion settings and closes the Motion Settings dialog box.

Editing motion settings

After you've created a motion setting and clicked OK, you can always return to the settings you created to edit them: simply select the clip and choose Clip ➪ Video Options ➪ Motion. Or, click Setup on the Motion Line in the Effect Controls palette. Either technique reopens the Motion Settings dialog box with your settings intact.

Using Alpha Channels

If you create motion effects with text or logos, you may want the text or logo to appear as if it were on a sheet of clear acetate to enable a background video track to show through in the background. The standard digital method of creating this effect is to use an alpha channel.

If the image you set in motion includes an alpha channel, Premiere can mask out the background and substitute the background area with visuals from another video track.

Using the alpha channel option

The following steps explain how to use the alpha channel option in Premiere's Motion Settings dialog box. This example uses a title with an alpha channel. We created this title using Adobe Title Designer.

Follow these steps:

1. **Choose File ➪ New Project to create a new project. In the Load Project Settings dialog box, for practice purposes, choose Multimedia. Click OK to create a new project.**
2. **Choose File ➪ Import ➪ File to import two images into the Project window.** To see the transparency effects of an alpha channel, you need two images in two different video tracks, one on top of the other. One image should be a title created using Adobe Title Designer. The other should be the background image. You can use Adobe Title Designer to create both a title and a background.

On the CD-ROM

A sample title (bella.prtl) and background file (colorfulframe.psd), seen in Figure 14-8, are found in the Chapter 14 folder, which is in the Tutorial Projects folder on the CD-ROM included this book.

What's an Alpha Channel?

Essentially, an alpha channel is an extra grayscale image layer that Premiere translates into different levels of transparency.

Alpha channels are typically used to define the transparent areas of a graphic or title. They enable you to combine a logo or text in one video track with a background video track in another. The background track surrounds the logo or text and is seen through the letters in the text. If you viewed an alpha channel of text, it might appear as pure white text on a black background. When Premiere uses the alpha channel to create transparency, it can place colored text in the white area of the alpha channel and a background video track in the black area.

Alpha channels can be created in image-editing programs, such as Adobe, Photoshop, and Corel Painter. Most 3D programs create alpha channels as well. When you create titles in the Title Designer window, Premiere can automatically create an alpha channel for the text. (For more information about alpha channels, see Chapter 13. Chapter 22 provides detailed instructions for creating alpha channels in Photoshop.)

3. **Drag the background image to Video track 1 in the Timeline window.**

Cross-Reference

To review how to create a title using Adobe Title Designer, see Chapter 8.

4. **Drag the title clip from the Project window to Video track 2 in the Timeline window.**
5. **Change the duration of the Background clip by using the Selection tool to click the right edge of the clip and drag it to the right to extend the duration image or to the left to decrease the duration. Change the duration of the Title image to match the Background clip.** The Title clip in Video track 2 should be selected. If it isn't, select it now.

Tip

To change the transparency and motion of a title in Video track 2 in the Timeline window you can use the Effect Controls palette. Choose Window ⇨ Show Effect Controls to display the Effect Controls palette. In the Effect Controls palette, click "setup" next to the Transparency option to display the Transparency Setting dialog box. Click "setup" next to the Motion option to display the Motion Settings dialog box.

6. **To specify that you want to use Transparency with the Title clip, choose Clip ⇨ Video Options ⇨ Transparency.** The Key Type setting should be set to Alpha Channel. In the Transparency Settings dialog box, you can see the background image below the Title file, as seen in Figure 14-9. This previews Premiere's use of the alpha channel it created for the text. Leave Alpha Channel setting in the Transparency dialog box selected. Click OK to close the dialog box.

Figure 14-8: The background clip appears in Title Designer window.

7. **Open the Motion Settings dialog box by choosing Clip ➪ Video Options ➪ Motion.**
8. **When using an image with an alpha channel, make sure that the Use clip's option is selected in the Alpha section of the Motion Settings dialog box.** When this option is selected, Premiere uses the clip's alpha channel to mask out its background and replace it with the background video track. To see the effect over the background image, make sure the "Show All" option is selected. This effect is shown in Figure 14-10 in the Motion Settings dialog box preview screen. Click OK to apply motion to the title.
9. **To preview the transparency and motion in the Monitor window, choose Timeline ➪ Preview.** Then save the project. When Premiere finishes building the preview, a preview appears in the Monitor window.

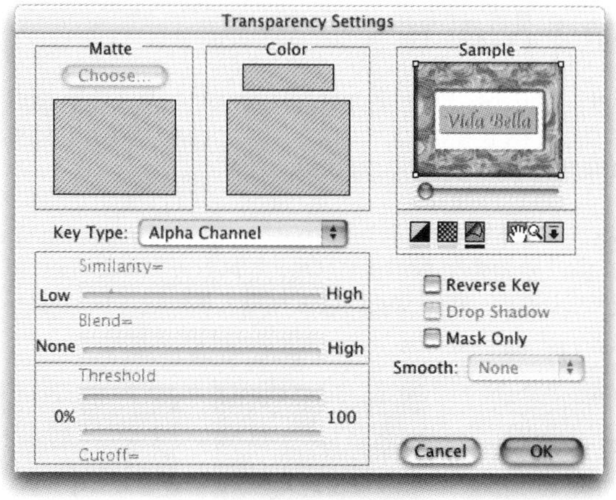

Figure 14-9: Image with an alpha channel over a background image in the Transparency Settings dialog box

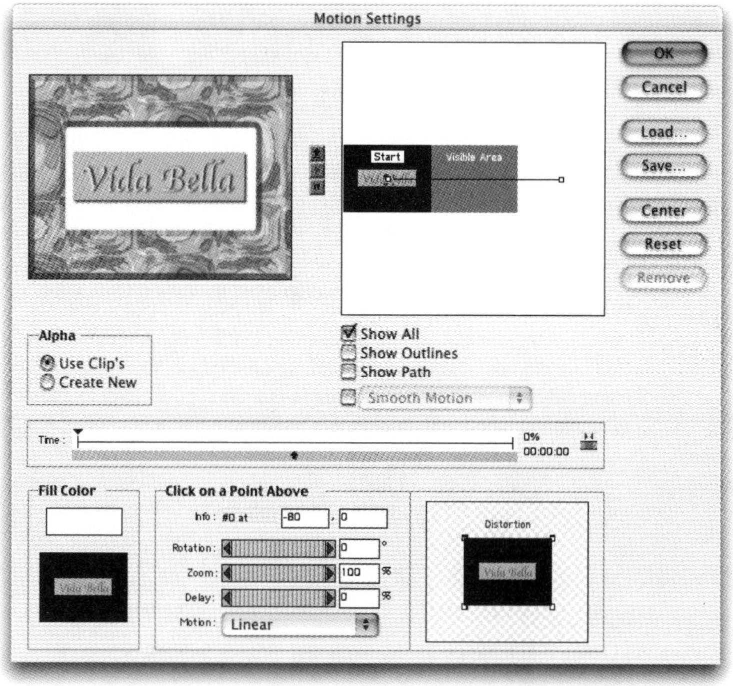

Figure 14-10: Image with an alpha channel over a background image in the Motion Settings dialog box

Creating Traveling Mattes

A traveling matte (or mask) is a special effect that combines motion and masking. Typically, the matte is a shape that moves across the screen. Within the matte is one image; outside the mask is a background image.

Figure 14-11 shows an example of the traveling matte effect. Notice that one image is seen through a star-shaped graphic pattern, which is the mask. The matte is simply a star-shaped white graphic created against a black background.

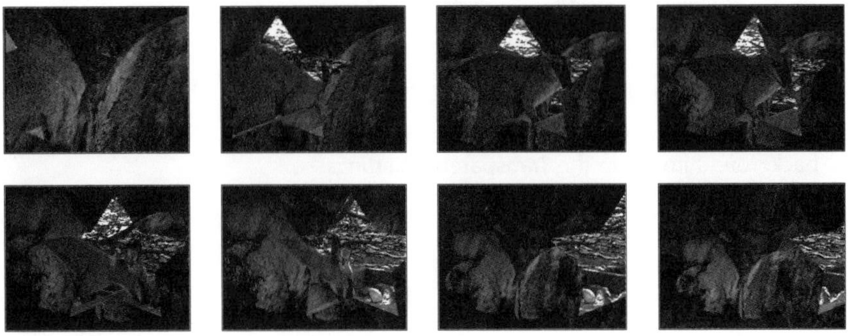

Figure 14-11: Frames for traveling matte effect.

To create a traveling matte effect you will need two video clips. One for the background and another one that will travel within the matte. You will also need a graphic image for the matte itself. Figure 14-12 shows the clips in the Timeline used to create the traveling matte effect shown in Figure 14-11. In Video track 3 is a star image. In Video track 2 is a kangaroo video clip and in Video track 1 is a video clip of water falling.

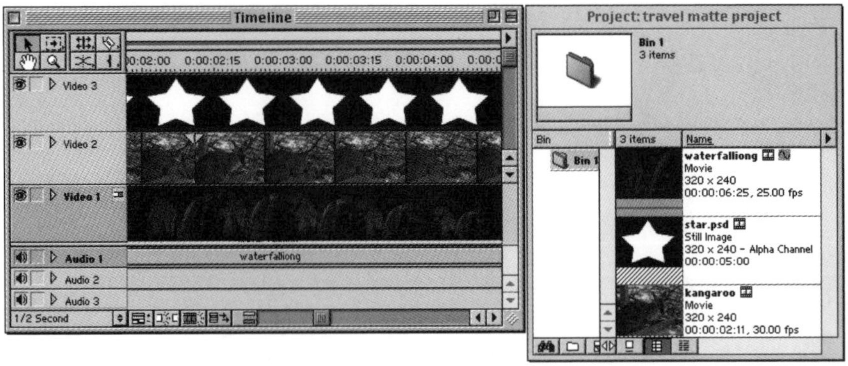

Figure 14-12: Timeline tracks used to create the traveling matte effect in Figure 14-11.

Here are the steps for creating a traveling matte effect:

1. **Choose File ⇨ New Project to create a new project.** In the Load Project Settings dialog box choose a preset. If you are using the images from the CD-ROM, choose Multimedia. Click OK to create a new project.
2. **Choose File ⇨ Import ⇨ File to import a graphic image to use as a matte.** If you want, you can create a white image against a black background to use as a matte. (We used Photoshop Shape tool to create the star. When creating the file, set the pixel dimensions to be the same as those you wish to use for your project. For more information on using Photoshop, turn to Chapter 22. For more information on using Illustrator, turn to Chapter 23.) You can also use the tools in the Title Designer window to create a matte shape. To use the Title Designer window choose File ⇨ New ⇨ Title. (For more information on creating shapes in the Title Designer window, turn to Chapter 8). Remember that once the traveling matte is complete, one clip appears within the white area. A background image appears in the black area.

On the CD-ROM

The star.psd image found in Figure 14-13 is found in the Chapter 14 folder, which is in the Tutorial Projects folder, on the CD-ROM that accompanies this book.

3. **Choose File ⇨ Import ⇨ File to import a clip to use in the background and import a file to use as the element to appear in the mask.** In Figure 14-12 we used the Waterfalling video clip as the background and the Kangaroo image to appear in the mask.

On the CD-ROM

The waterflowing.mov and kangaroo.mov video clips in Figure 14-13 are found in the Chapter 14 folder, which is in the Tutorial Projects folder on this book's companion CD-ROM. If you prefer, you can use any two video clips located on the CD-ROM's Tutorial Projects folder.

4. **Drag the image that you wish to use as your background to Video track 1.**
5. **Drag the image that you wish to appear in the matte into Video track 2.**
6. **Create a new video track for the matte by choosing Add Video Track in the Timeline pop-up menu.** This will be Video track 3. Choose Window ⇨ Workspace ⇨ Single-Track Editing to better view all three video tracks.
7. **Drag the graphic image you wish to use as a matte into video Track 3.** In Figure 14-12, we used the Star graphic.
8. **Select the matte in Video track 3 by clicking it with the Selection tool.** The transparency option should be set to Alpha Channel. To view the Transparency option, click "Setup" next to the Transparency option in the Effect Controls palette. Note that you can also use Clip ⇨ Video Options ⇨ Transparency command. In the Transparency Settings dialog box, the Key Type option should be set to Alpha Channel. Click OK to close the dialog box.

9. **To apply motion to the matte graphic, click "Setup" next to the Motion option in the Effect Controls palette.** Note that you can also use Clip ➪ Video Options ➪ Motion command. In the Motion Settings dialog box, specify the desired motion effect.

10. **In the Motion Settings dialog box, set the fill color to black by clicking the fill swatch.** When the Color Picker opens, click a black area, or set the Red, Green, and Blue fields to 0. Click OK to close the dialog box.

Note

If you don't make the background fill color black, the transparent background moves across the screen with the matte.

Now you can apply transparency to the clip in Video track 2.

1. **Select Video track 2, which is the track sandwiched between the matte and the background image.**

2. **Choose Clip ➪ Video Options ➪ Transparency.**

3. **In the Key Type pop-up menu, choose Track Matte, as shown in Figure 14-13.** Click OK. (For a detailed discussion of the Transparency Settings dialog box, turn to Chapter 12.)

Figure 14-13: Transparency Settings dialog box with the Track Matte option selected

4. **Set all tracks so that each track is the same duration.**

5. **Save your file by choosing File ➪ Save.**

6. **Preview the effect by choosing Timeline ➪ Preview or pressing Return/Enter.**

Creating Motion Settings Projects

The following projects provide the steps for integrating graphics with alpha channels to create motion effects. In the first example, a coffee cup and text move across a chart of coffee bean sales. The second example is an animated book cover — an idea that booksellers might start using on their Web sites.

Creating a presentation

You can use the Motion Settings dialog box to create an animated presentation. Figure 14-14 shows the frames used to create a sample coffee bean sales presentation. As you view the frames, notice the motion applied to the coffee cup and text clips.

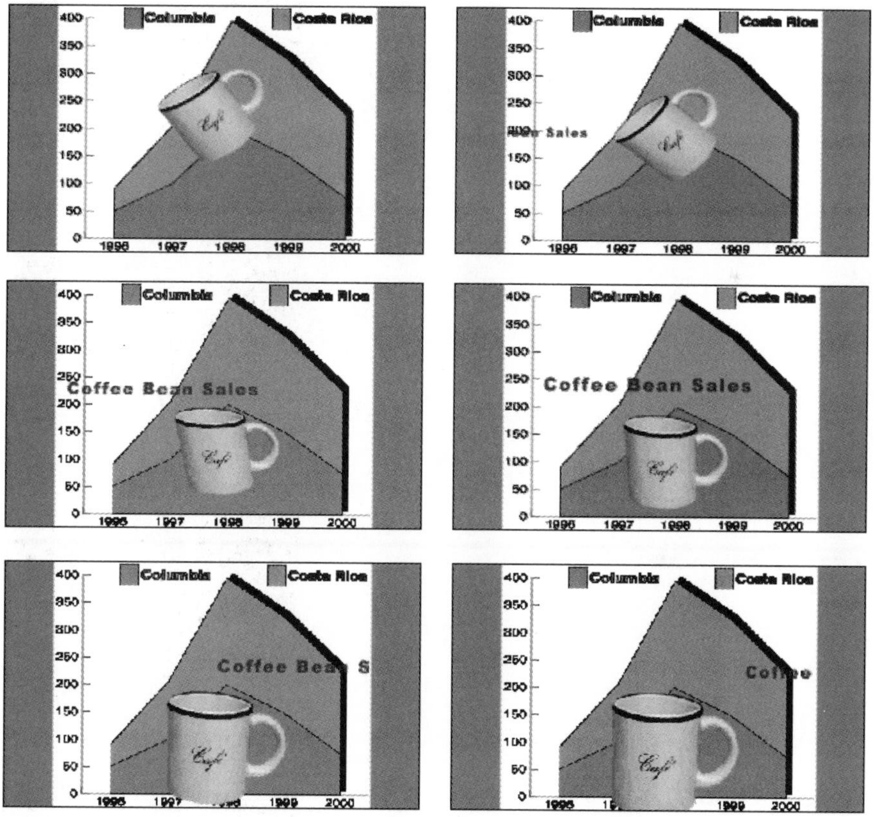

Figure 14-14: Timeline for the sample coffee bean sales presentation

We created the sample chart shown in Figure 14-15 using Adobe Illustrator and then saved it in Illustrator format. The coffee cup, shown in Figure 14-16, was scanned and manipulated using Adobe Photoshop. We used the Paintbrush and Eyedropper tools to fine-tune the edges and insides of the coffee cup. Then, a selection of the coffee cup was created using the Polygonal Lasso tool. To soften the edges of the selection, a two-pixel feather was applied to the selection (Select ➪ Feather). The selection was saved as an alpha channel (Select ➪ Save Selection). To save the coffee cup and alpha channel, we saved the file in PICT format (you can also save in Photoshop or TIFF formats). We created the text using Premiere's Title window. All the images were imported into a new project. To make the coffee cup and text overlap, we placed them into different video tracks. We set the coffee cup and text into motion, using the Motion Settings dialog box.

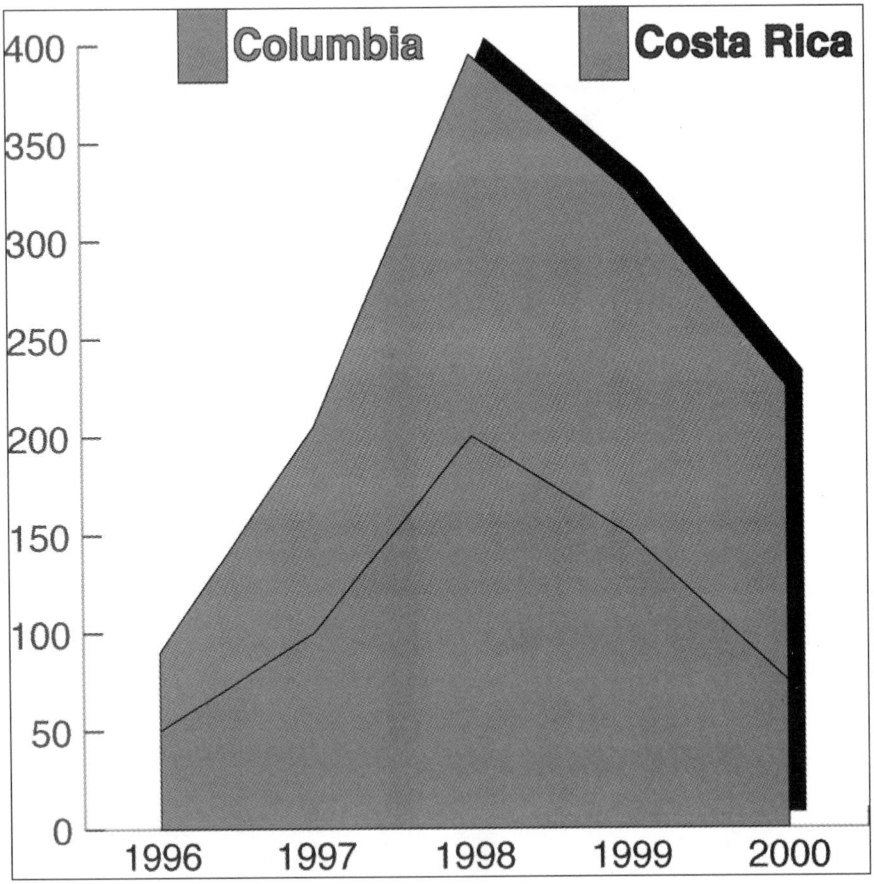

Figure 14-15: Coffee bean chart

Figure 14-16: Coffee cup

On the CD-ROM

All of the graphics used in this example can be found in the Chapter 14 Coffee folder, in the Tutorial Projects folder, on the CD-ROM that accompanies this book.

If you want to create your own graphics for a presentation, you'll need to create the following three production elements:

✦ **A background image.**

✦ **A title.** You can create a title in the Adobe Title Designer window, which is covered extensively in Chapter 8.

✦ **A graphic with an alpha channel.** Create this in a program that enables you to create alpha channels, or save masks, such as Adobe Photoshop, Corel Painter, or a 3D program.

Follow these steps to create an animated presentation:

1. **Create a new project by choosing File ⇨ New Project.**
2. **In the Load Project Settings dialog box, choose your project settings.** If you pick the Multimedia preset, Premiere chooses a frame size of 320 x 240 pixels. If you want your presentation larger, you can pick a setting with a frame size of 640 x 480. If you're creating this project for practice, you can change the frame size to 160 x 120, which consumes less disk space. To change settings, click Custom in the Load Project Settings dialog box and then choose Video from the pop-up menu in the New Project Settings dialog box. Click OK to create your new project.

Note

After you close the Load Project Settings dialog box, you can change the frame size of your project by choosing Project ⇨ Project Settings ⇨ Video.

3. **To import the sample graphic files from the CD-ROM that accompanies this book, choose File ➪ Import ➪ Folder.** Load the Coffee folder from the Chapter 14 folder on the CD-ROM.

4. **If you are importing your own files, choose File ➪ Import ➪ File.** To import more than one file at a time, press and hold the Command key (Mac users) the Control key (PC users), select the files that you want to import, and then import them. After you've imported the files, they appear in the Project window, as shown in Figure 14-17.

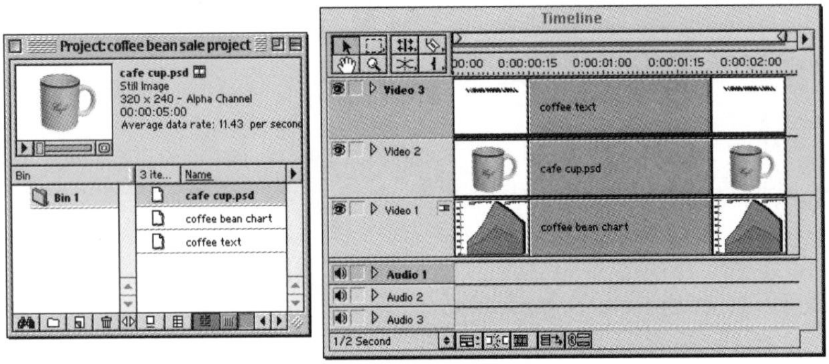

Figure 14-17: The Project window with the files needed for the Coffee Bean Sales presentation

5. **Drag the background file from the Project window to Video track 1 in the Timeline window.** Drag the chart file for the Coffee Bean Sales presentation to Video track 1.

6. **Drag the image with the alpha channel from the Project window to Video track 2 in the Timeline window.** Drag the coffee cup image to Video track 2 for the Coffee Bean Sales presentation.

7. **Now create a new video track, Video track 3, for the Title by clicking the Timeline pop-up menu (which is located to the far right of the Timeline window) and choosing Add Video Track.** Video track 3 is automatically added to the Timeline window. (Video track 3 is placed above Video track 2.) To get a better view of the video tracks, choose Window ➪ Workspace ➪ Single-Track Editing.

8. **Drag and drop the Title (Coffee Bean Sales) that you imported from the CD-ROM that accompanies this book to Video track 3.** If you want to create your own title, proceed to Step 9; otherwise, skip to Step 11.

9. **To create your own title, choose File ➪ New ➪ Title.** In the Title Designer window, make sure that the Show Video option is selected if you want to see the image in Video track 2. Then use the Type tool to type some text. Stylize the text using the commands in the Title menu or the options in the Object Style section of the dialog box.

10. **Save your title by choosing File ➪ Save.** The title is saved to your hard disk and placed in the Project window. Drag the title to Video track 3.

11. **To set the transparency option for the title, first make sure that it is selected and then choose Clip ➪ Video Options ➪ Transparency.** In the Transparency dialog box, the Key Type should be set to Alpha channel. In the Preview window in the Transparency dialog box, you should be able to see the background image in the video track. Click OK to close the Transparency dialog box. Because both the title and coffee cup images have alpha channels, choosing Clip ➪ Video Options ➪ Motion, will enable you to see the three images overlapping each other in the preview section of the Motion Settings dialog box.

12. **Set transparency for the coffee cup by selecting it in Video track 2 and then choosing Clip ➪ Video Options ➪ Transparency.** Make sure that the Key Type menu is set to Alpha Channel. Then, click OK.

Now you're ready to apply motion to the images in Video track 2 and Video track 3.

1. **Click the clip in Video track 3 in the Timeline window and then choose Clip ➪ Video Options ➪ Motion. In the Motion Settings dialog box, edit the motion using the techniques described in this chapter.** To load a preset motion setting, proceed to Step 13. To create your own motion setting proceed to Step 14.

2. **If you want to load preset motion settings from the CD-ROM that accompanies this book, click the Load button in the Motion Settings dialog box.**

   Locate the motion setting in the Coffee folder within the Chapter 14 folder on the CD-ROM that accompanies this book. Figure 14-18 shows the settings applied to the text, Coffee Bean Sales. To preview the motion settings, click the Play button (to the right of the Motion thumbnail). In the dialog box, you can see that there are three points on the Motion Timeline: a starting point, a middle point, and a finish point. At the middle point, we created a delay so that the text would stop moving long enough for the viewer to read it. The size of the text was decreased at the Start and Finish points, and the text size was increased in the middle point. Click OK to apply the settings to the clip.

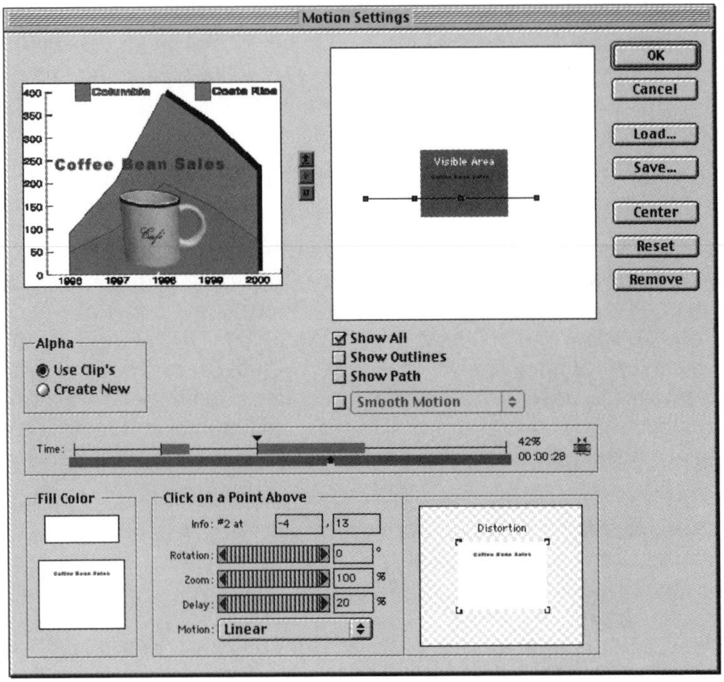

Figure 14-18: Motion settings applied to the text Coffee Bean Sales

3. **Apply your own motion settings to the image in Video track 2 by clicking the clip in Video track 2 and then choosing Clip ➪ Video Options ➪ Motion.** In the Motion Settings dialog box, edit the motion settings as desired.

4. **Load the Motion settings shown in Figure 14-19, click Load and locate the motion settings in the Coffee folder within the Chapter 14 folder on the CD-ROM that accompanies this book.** Preview the motion settings by clicking Play (to the right of the Motion thumbnail). In the Motion Settings dialog box, you can see that the coffee cup moves from the top (starting point) to the bottom (finish point). To make the cup drop to the middle of the chart and then spill into the text, we added left rotations to points on the Motion Timeline. On the points in the middle of the Motion Timeline we also added a delay for both the coffee cup and text. We also decreased and increased the coffee cup size. We used the clip's alpha channel option so that the white background would be removed from the image. Click OK to apply the settings to your video production.

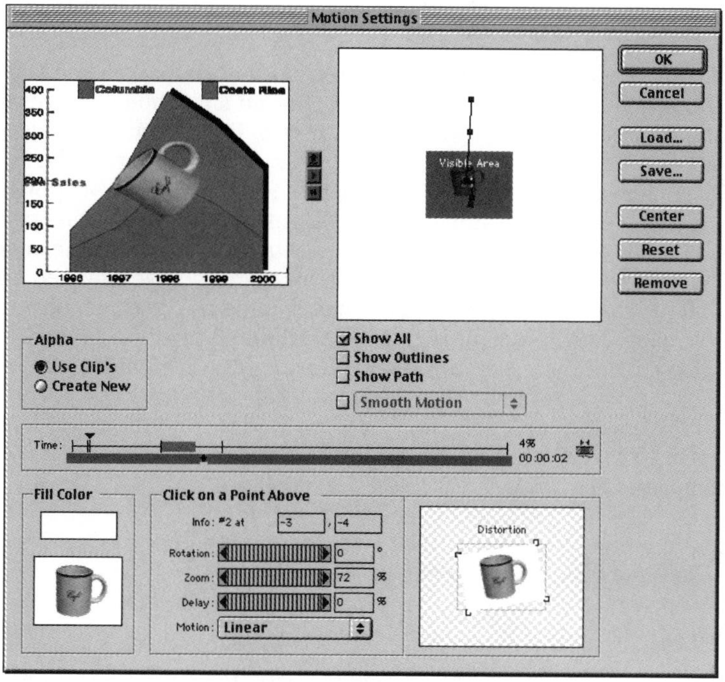

Figure 14-19: Motion settings for the coffee cup

5. **Set all tracks so that each track is the same duration.**
6. **Save your work by choosing File ⇨ Save and then name your project in the Save dialog box.**
7. **Choose Timeline ⇨ Preview or press Enter on your keyboard to preview the video production.**

Next, you need to add the audio clip to your presentation.

1. **Choose File ⇨ Import ⇨ File.** Locate an audio file from the Sound folder on the CD-ROM that accompanies this book. When the audio file appears in the Project window, drag it to the Audio 1 track in the Timeline window. (For more information on working with audio, turn to Chapter 6.)
2. **Export the current video settings by choosing File ⇨ Export Timeline ⇨ Movie.** If you want to change the export settings, click the Settings button. Otherwise, enter a filename and click Save.

Animating a book cover

In the following steps, you'll create an animated book cover. You can see the frames from the book cover project in Figure 14-20. Here an angel image moves from the top-left of the screen down to the bottom-center of the screen. The angel starts on her side and as she moves, she slowly rotates to the right, then to the left, and eventually ends in an upright position. When the angel reaches the bottom of screen, she halts for a moment while the text (Angel Stories) appears over a sky background in the middle of the screen. To create the motion for the angel, we used the Motion Settings dialog box. To create the background, we scanned a sky image and saved it in JPEG format. We used Premiere's Title Designer window to create the text. We used both Adobe Illustrator and Adobe Photoshop to create the angel image. Following are the steps for creating the angel with an alpha channel.

On the CD-ROM

All of the graphics for this example can be loaded from the Angel folder in the Chapter 14 folder, which is in the Tutorial Projects folder on the CD-ROM that accompanies this book.

If you want to create your own graphics for an animated book cover, you need to create these three production elements:

✦ **A background image.**

✦ **A title.** You can create this in Premiere's Title Designer window, which is discussed earlier in this chapter, and covered extensively in Chapter 8.

✦ **A graphic with an alpha channel.** Create this in a program that enables you to create alpha channels or save masks, such as Adobe Photoshop or MetaCreations Painter. Most 3D programs also create alpha channels.

Here's how to create the angel using Adobe Illustrator, and how to add the alpha channel using Adobe Photoshop:

1. **Create a pencil sketch of an angel image.**
2. **Scan it into Photoshop, or using your scanning software, save it in TIFF format.**
3. **Next, load the pencil sketch into Adobe Illustrator and use the Pen tool to outline the object and fill it with color.**
4. **Open the angel image in Photoshop. When the image of the angel opens in Photoshop, it opens against a transparent background, called Layer 1.** The transparent background enables you to easily create the alpha channel.
5. **To add depth to the image of the angel, apply a filter such as Texture (Filter ➪ Texture). Add depth using the Layer ➪ Layer Style ➪ Bevel and Emboss command.**
6. **To begin creating the alpha channel, you need to select only the angel onscreen.** To do this, press and hold Command (Mac users) or Ctrl (PC users) as you click in the middle of Layer 1 in the Layers palette. A selection appears around the angel image.

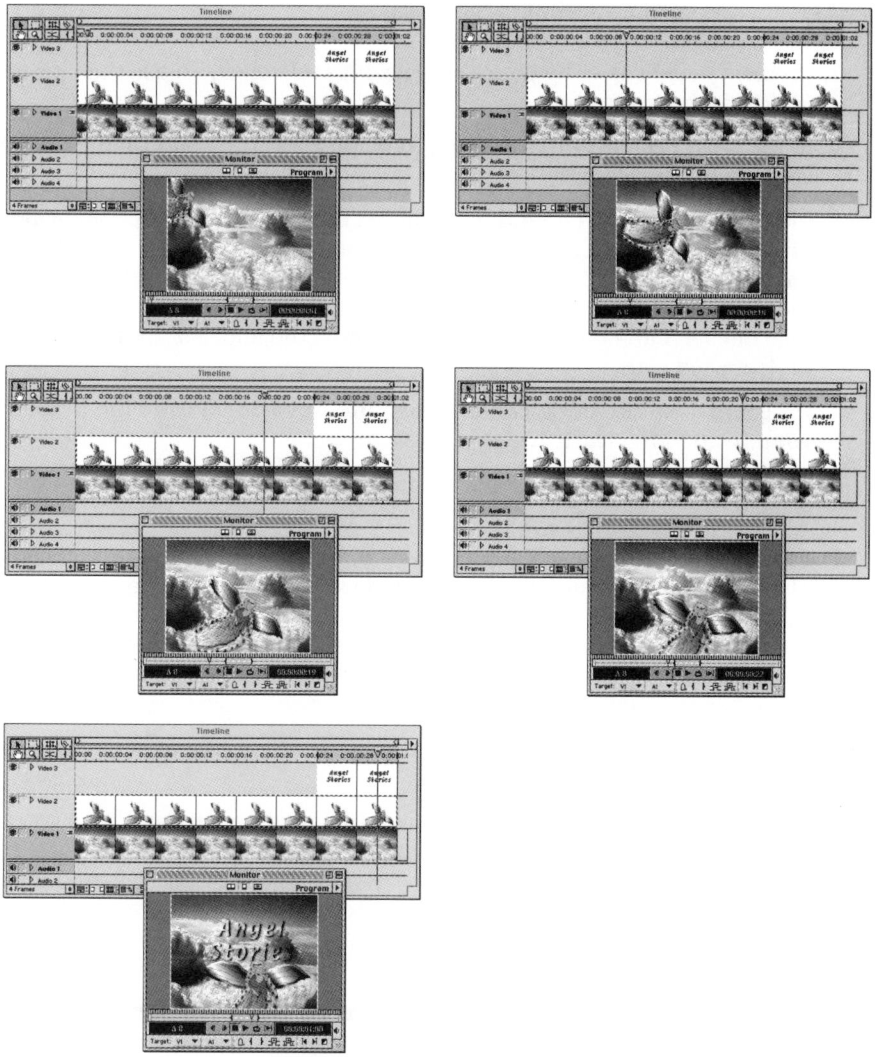

Figure 14-20: Timeline of the book cover project

7. **With the selection on-screen, choose Select ⇨ Save Selection.** In the Save Selection dialog box, enter a name for the selection and then click OK. You should now have an alpha channel in the Channels palette.
8. **To save the file with the alpha channel, choose File ⇨ Save As.** In the Save As dialog box, save in TIFF, PICT, or Photoshop format, making sure that the Save Alpha Channels option is selected.

The steps to create the animated book cover are:

1. **Create a new Project by choosing File ➪ New Project.** To use the files on the CD-ROM, choose Multimedia.
2. **In the Load Project Settings dialog box, pick a setting and then click OK to create a new project.**
3. **Choose File ➪ Import ➪ Folder to import the Angel folder that is located in Chapter 14, on the CD-ROM that accompanies this book.** To import your own images, choose File ➪ Import ➪ File to import files needed for the project. In the Import dialog box, press and hold the Command/Ctrl key to select more than one item at a time. Click Open to import the folder or files into the Project window.
4. **Drag and drop the background image (the sky image) from the Project window to Video track 1.**
5. **Drag and drop the title (Angel Stories) from the Project window to Video track 2.**
6. **Create a new Video track, Video track 3, for the title.** To do this, click the Timeline pop-up menu (which is located to the far right of the Timeline window) and choose Add Video Track. Video track 3 is automatically added to the Timeline window. Video track 3 is placed above Video track 2. If the workspace is not set to Single-Track Editing, do so by choosing Window ➪ Workspace ➪ Single-Track Editing.
7. **Drag and drop the graphic with the alpha channel (the angel image) to Video track 3.**
8. **With the graphic alpha channel image (the angel image) in Video track 2 selected, choose Clip ➪ Video Options ➪ Motion.** The Motion Settings dialog box for the angel image appears, as shown in Figure 14-21. To load the motion settings for the angel, click the Load button and locate the Angel folder in the Chapter 14 folder on the CD-ROM that accompanies this book. Click OK to apply the settings.
9. **Use the Selection tool to drag the title (Angel Stories) in the Timeline, so that it overlaps the last two seconds of the graphic in Video track 3.**
10. **To set transparency options and view a preview of the title's position relative to the angel and cloud background, choose Clip ➪ Video Options ➪ Transparency.** In the Transparency Settings dialog box, shown in Figure 14-22, the Key Type pop-up menu should be set to White Alpha Matte. If it isn't, change it. In the Sample preview box you'll see a preview of the transparency effect. Click OK to close the Transparency dialog box.

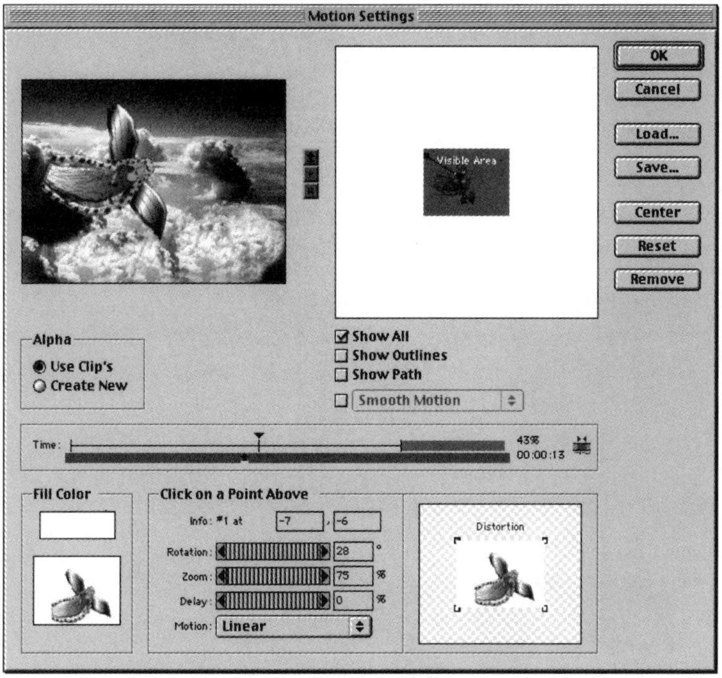

Figure 14-21: Motion settings for the angel image

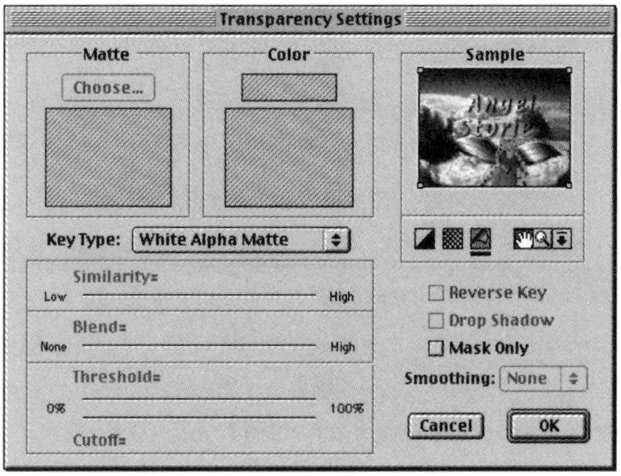

Figure 14-22: The Transparency Settings dialog box with text

11. **If you want to change the location of your text, double-click the icon representation of the title in Video track 3.** When the Title Designer window appears, as shown in Figure 14-23, click and move the text. Close the Title Designer window and save your work to update your project.

12. **Preview your project by pressing Enter or by choosing Timeline ⇨ Preview.**

13. **To export your project according to your project presets, choose File ⇨ Export Timeline ⇨ Movie. Name your file and then click Save.**

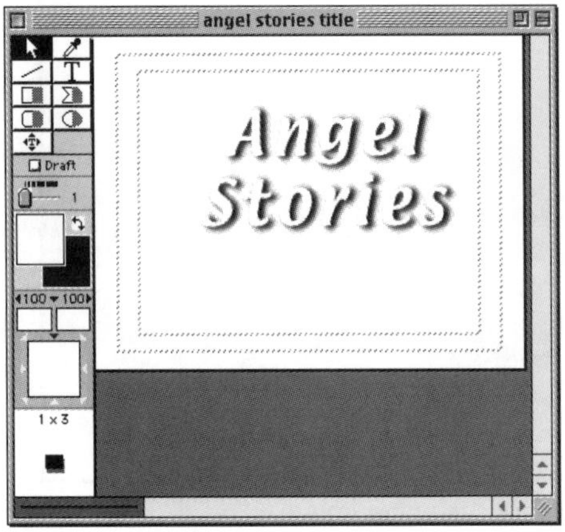

Figure 14-23: Title window for the angel text

Summary

Premiere's Motion Settings dialog box enables you to create motion effects from graphics and video clips. You can:

- ✦ Change motion speed and direction in the Motion Settings dialog box.
- ✦ Rotate, zoom, and distort images in the Motion Settings dialog box.
- ✦ Use the Motion Settings dialog box with the Transparency dialog box to create motion effects where image backgrounds are transparent.
- ✦ Use the Track Matte key type to create a traveling matte effect.

✦ ✦ ✦

CHAPTER 15

Enhancing Video

✦ ✦ ✦ ✦

In This Chapter

Reviewing color theory

Adjusting brightness and contrast

Adjusting levels

Adjusting color balance

Photoshop color-correcting commands

Adding or removing images in Filmstrip files

✦ ✦ ✦ ✦

When shooting video, you will eventually have little control over the locale or lighting conditions of a video shoot. This often results in video clips that are too dark or too bright, or that display a color cast on-screen. Fortunately, Premiere's Video Effects palette includes a number of effects specifically designed to change image brightness, contrast, and colors. Many of these effects can be previewed on-screen while you fine-tune the options in the Video Effects palette dialog box. Although there is no substitute for high-quality video shot with well-planned lighting, Premiere's Video Effects palette may be able to boost the overall tonal and color quality of your production.

However, if you find that the Premiere tools aren't powerful enough, you can import your video clip as a Filmstrip file into Adobe Photoshop. You can then use Photoshop's powerful masking and color-correcting tools to enhance your clip frame by frame. You can then import the corrected file back into Premiere.

In this chapter, we discuss the Premiere filters that can be used to enhance colors. We start with an overview of the RGB color model, and then discuss the video enhancement options that Premiere provides. We conclude with a look at how to import a file into Photoshop, correct the video, and then export it back to Premiere.

The RGB Color Model

Before you begin to correct color, lightness, brightness, and contrast in Premiere, you should review a few important concepts about computer color theory. As you'll soon see, Premiere's image-enhancement commands are not based on the basics of television engineering. Instead, they're based on the fundamentals of how a computer creates color.

When you view images on a computer display, colors are created from different combinations of red, green, and blue light. When you need to choose or edit colors, many computer programs, such as Premiere and Photoshop, enable you to choose from 256 levels of red, 256 levels of green, and 256 levels of blue. This results in over 17.6 million color possibilities (256 x 256 x 256). In both Premiere and Photoshop, each red, green, and blue color component of an image is called a *channel.*

Premiere's Color Picker provides an example of how red, green, and blue channels create color. Using the Color Picker, you can choose colors by specifying red, green, and blue values. To open Premiere's Color Picker, you must first have a project on-screen and then choose File ➪ New ➪ Color Matte. In the Color Picker dialog box, shown in Figure 15-1, notice the Red, Green, and Blue entry fields. If you click a color on the left, the numbers in the entry fields change to show how many levels of red, green, and blue are used to create that color. To change colors, you can also enter a value from 0 to 255 into each of the Red, Green, and Blue fields.

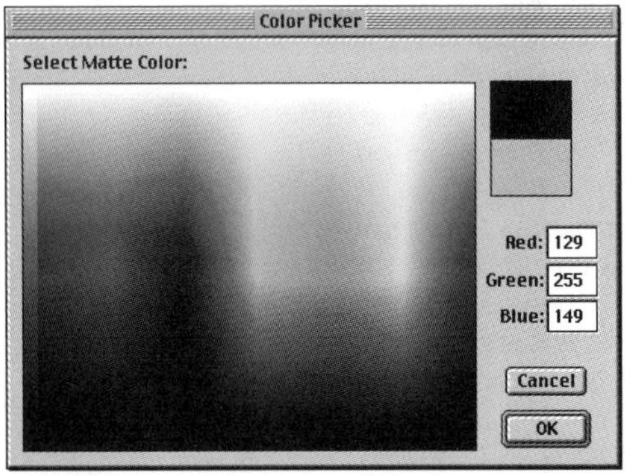

Figure 15-1: Premiere's Color Picker enables you to choose colors by specifying red, green, and blue color values.

Note

As you work in Premiere, consider your production's final export destination. If you are exporting to videotape, realize that the color gamut (the range of colors that make up an image) displayed on a computer screen is greater than the color gamut of a television screen. Your computer monitor creates colors using red, green, and blue phosphors. American Broadcast television uses the YCC standard, which uses one luminance, or brightness, channel and two color channels of color to create an image. The luminance channel was and still is based on the luminance value used for black and white television. This value was kept so those viewers with black and white television could still view the television signal when color was adapted.

If you will be using Premiere to do color correcting, you need to have a basic understanding of how the red, green, and blue color channels interact to create red, green, and blue color, and their complements (or opposites), cyan, magenta, and yellow. The following list of color combinations can help you understand how different channels create colors. Note that the lower numbers are darker, and the higher numbers are brighter. 0red, 0green, 0blue, creates black—the absence of light. If red, green, and blue values are set to 255, white is created—the most amount of light.

255 red + 255 green + 255 blue = white

0 red + green+ 0 blue = black

255 red + 255 green = yellow

255 red + 255 blue = magenta

255 green + 255 blue = cyan

Notice that adding two of the RGB color components produces cyan, magenta, or yellow. These are the complements of red, green, and blue. Understanding this relationship is helpful, because it can help provide some direction as you work. From the color calculations above, you can see that adding more red and more green to an image produces more yellow; adding more red and blue produces more magenta; adding more green and blue produces more cyan.

The above calculations also provide a basis for the results of adding or subtracting one of the Red, Green, or Blue channels from an image.

Add red = less cyan

Reduce red = more cyan

Increase green = less magenta

Reduce green = more magenta

Add blue = less yellow

Reduce blue = more yellow

As you can see from the examples in this chapter, most of Premiere's image-enhancement commands use red, green, and blue sliders or red, green, and blue channels when called upon to correct color.

Using the Premiere video effects to color correct within Premiere's Video Effects palette, the Adjust and Image Control folders contain color-correcting video effects. (You may also want to use the effects in the Sharpen folder to sharpen the video after you've adjusted its color). To display the Video Effects palette, choose Window ⇨ Show Video Effects. (For detailed descriptions on using all of the Video Effects, see Chapter 12.)

The video effects in the Adjust folder are Brightness & Contrast, Channel Mixer, Color Balance, Convolution Kernel, Extract, Levels, and Posterize.

On the CD-ROM

Before you begin exploring Premiere's color-enhancement commands, start by creating a new project. Import a color clip into Premiere and drag it into the Video 1, Video 1a, or Video 2 Track. If you don't have a video clip to use, you can use one of the clips found in the Chapter 15 folder, in the Tutorial Projects folder that is on the CD-ROM that accompanies this book.

Changing brightness and contrast

Brightness and contrast is one of the easiest image effects to correct. Brightness controls the light levels in your image, while contrast is the difference between the brightest and darkest levels. To use the Brightness and Contrast filter, click and drag it over the clip in the Video 1 track. After you drag the filter, the controls for the filter effect appear in the Effect Controls palette. To see a preview of the image in the Color Balance palette, click the Setup button in the Effect Controls palette. Take a moment to try out each of the sliders in the Brightness and Contrast Settings dialog box.

- **Brightness.** To increase overall brightness in your clip, click and drag the Brightness slider to the right. As you drag, the entire image lightens. To decrease Brightness, click and drag to the left. As you drag, the entire clip gets darker.
- **Contrast.** To see the effect of the Contrast slider, first click and drag the slider to the right. As you drag, you add contrast, increasing the difference between the lightest and darkest areas of your image. This also tends to create a sharper image. To decrease sharpness, click and drag to the left. As you drag, the entire clip begins to fade out.

Continue to experiment with the Brightness & Contrast Video effect. After you finish, you can remove the effect by clicking the trash button in the Effects palette.

Balancing colors

The Color Balance effect enables you to change the balance of a clip's red, green, and blue color channels. To use this color-enhancement effect, click and drag it from the Adjust section of the Video Effects palette and drag it over your clip in the video track.

The Effect Controls palette shows you the color slides. To see a preview of the image in the Color Balance dialog box, click Setup in the Effect Controls palette, as shown in Figure 15-2. Try experimenting with each slider. As you work, you'll put into practice the RGB color theory.

- Click and drag the red slider to the right. As you drag, you gradually pump red into your image. Drag the slider to the left to decrease red. Note that as you reduce red, you increase cyan. Cyan is added because you now have more green and blue in your image. To increase cyan, click and drag both the green and blue sliders to the right.

✦ Click and drag the green slider to the right. As you drag, you increase green in your image. Drag to the left to decrease green. As you reduce green, you add magenta. Magenta is added because you have more red and blue in your image than green. To add more magenta, click and drag both the red and blue sliders to the right.

✦ Click and drag the blue slider to the right. As you drag, you increase blue in your image. Drag to the left to decrease blue. As you reduce blue, you add yellow. Yellow is added because you have more red and green in your image. You add even more yellow by clicking and dragging both the red and green sliders to the right.

Continue to experiment with the Color Balance effect. When you're done, you can remove the effect by clicking the Trash button in the Effect Controls palette.

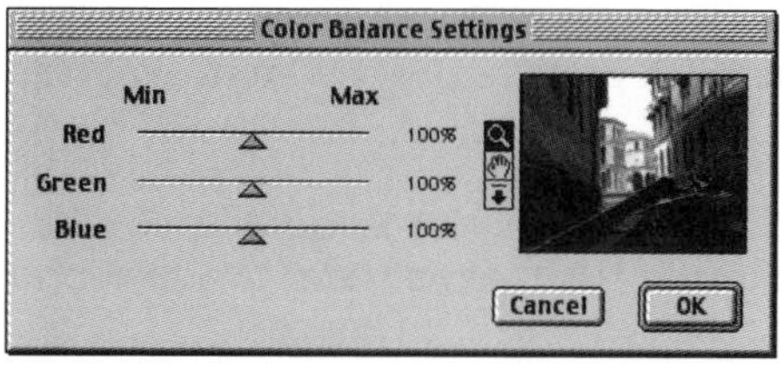

Figure 15-2: Premiere's Color Balance effect enables you to change an image's color balance by adjusting red, green, and blue color components.

Changing levels

The Levels filter is one of the most sophisticated color-correcting controls offered by Premiere. Levels can be used for fine-tuning shadows (dark image areas), midtones (mid-level image areas), and highlights (light image areas). If you've worked with Photoshop, you might recognize this command. Premiere's Levels control is virtually identical to Photoshop's. To try out the Levels effect, click and drag the Levels effect over a clip in one of your video tracks. To see the Levels Settings dialog box, as shown in Figure 15-3, click the Setup button in the Effect Controls palette.

In the Levels Settings dialog box, Premiere provides a histogram of the image. The histogram is a chart that provides a graphical representation of the brightness levels of the pixels in your image. If the darker pixel levels are shown at the left-end of the histogram, brighter levels are shown to the right of the histogram. The higher the line, the larger the number of pixels there are that occur at that brightness level. The lower the line, the fewer the pixels there are that occur at that brightness level.

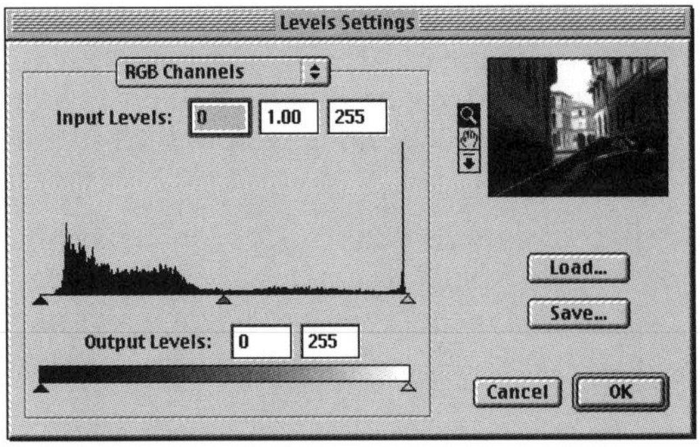

Figure 15-3: Premiere's Levels Settings dialog box enables you to adjust shadows, midtones, and highlights.

The Levels dialog box is confusing, because it provides two different sliders with five different slider controls.

The top slider is called the Input slider. The bottom slider is the Output slider. The best way to summarize the two sliders is this: Use the top slider to add contrast in an image; use the bottom slider to decrease contrast in an image.

Increasing contrast

Here's how to increase contrast in an image. Suppose that the histogram of your image shows that the darkest area of your image appears at the 10 mark on the input slider. You can increase contrast in the darkest areas of your image by clicking and dragging the black input slider to the right. When you click and drag, Premiere begins to remap the brightness levels in the image by taking all pixels that start at 10 and remapping them to 0, then remapping all corresponding pixels. The result is a darker image with more contrast. Click and drag the white slider to achieve the same effect with the brightest pixels. In other words, you can increase contrast in the lightest areas of your image.

To correct your image, you may want to move the midtone slider to the left to lighten the midtones and drag the midtone slider to the right to darken the midtones, without greatly changing the lightest and darkest parts of an image.

Decreasing contrast

If you have too much contrast in an image, you can lighten an image and reduce contrast by clicking and dragging the left black (or input) slider. When you reduce black levels, you are reducing the number of dark pixels in the image. For example, if you drag the bottom slider from 0 to 10, any pixels that were at 0 are removed from the image and remapped to 10, and the rest of the pixels in the image are adjusted accordingly.

To summarize, click and drag the left input slider to 10. Pixels that were 10 are remapped to 0. Click and drag the bottom slider to 10. Pixels that were 0 are remapped to 10.

Changing channel levels

The Levels Settings dialog box also enables you to change levels for individual Red, Green, and Blue channels. For example, to add contrast to the Red channel, choose red from the pop-up menu in the Levels Settings dialog box. When you pick a channel, the histogram displays changes to show you the pixel distribution of colors for only that channel. As you click and drag the highlight slider, you can increase contrast in the Red channel. By clicking and dragging the output slider, you can reduce contrast in the Red channel.

Note: If you frequently use the same levels settings, you can save them to disk by clicking the Save button. You can reload your settings by clicking the Load button.

Continue to experiment with the Color Balance video effect. When you're done, you can remove the effect by clicking the Trash button in the Effect Controls palette

Using other Adjust filters

The other commands in the Adjust folder that affect a video clip's color are summarized here. (For more information about these filters, see Chapter 12.)

- ✦ **Channel Mixer.** Use the Channel Mixer video effect to create special effects, such as sepia or tinted effects.
- ✦ **Posterize.** The Posterize effect enables you to reduce the number of gray levels in your image.
- ✦ **Convolution Kernel.** Use Convolution Kernel to change the brightness and sharpness of your image.
- ✦ **Extract.** The Extract video effect enables you to convert your color clip to black and white.

The Image Control effects

Adobe Premiere provides even more color effects in the Image Control folder. Two commands, Gamma and HSL Color Balance, can be used to enhance images. The other effects in the Image Control folder are Black & White, Color Pass, Color Replace, Median, and Tint. (For a description of these effects, see Chapter 12.)

Using HSL Color Balance

Although the RGB color model is used by computer displays to create colors, it's not very intuitive. For example, if you want to create a bright orange color or a light brown color, what RGB combination would you choose? To help provide more intuitive colors, the Hue Saturation Lightness (HSL) color model was created. In this color model, colors are created in much the same way as color is perceived. *Hue* is the color, *Lightness* is the brightness or darkness of the color, and *Saturation* is the color intensity. If you don't want to use Premiere's RGB Color Balance effect, you can use its HSL Color Balance effect instead.

To try out the HSL Color Balance effect, open the Image Control folder in the Video Effects palette and then click and drag the HSL Color Balance effect over a clip in a video track. Because there is no preview in the dialog box, make sure that the Monitor window is open. You can see the preview of this effect in the Monitor window.

Try experimenting with the sliders in the Effect Controls palette, which is shown in Figure 15-4. As you drag the slider to the right, it's as if you are moving around a circular color wheel. As you click and drag the slider, you see at what degree of the circle you are.

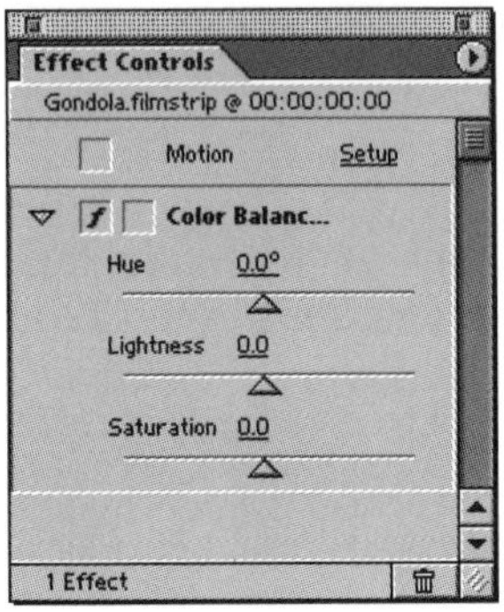

Figure 15-4: The HSL Color Balance effect enables you to adjust color balance using Hue, Saturation, and Lightness controls.

Note If you want to enter a precise number for a slider, click any numeric value above the slider. Doing so opens a dialog box in which you can enter a specific value.

The best way to see the effect of the changing hues is to add saturation to your image. Click and drag the Saturation slider to the right. To see the effect of the lightness slider, click and drag first to the right to add more light to the image, and then to the left to reduce the amount of light.

When you've finished experimenting with this filter, click and drag the Trash icon to remove it.

Gamma Correction

The Gamma Correction filter changes midtones without affecting shadows and highlights. This is an easy filter to use if you just want to make sure that the dark and light areas of your image are in good shape. To use this filter, click and drag the Gamma Correction filter from the Image Control folder in the Video Effects palette over a clip. To see a preview of the effect, click the word "Setup" in the Effect

Controls palette. To use the effect, simply click and drag the slider. As you click and drag to the right, you increase gamma, thereby darkening your image. By clicking and dragging to the left, you lighten midtones as you decrease gamma.

The Video folder effects

The effects in the Video folder are designed to improve clips that will be exported to videotape. The effects in the Video folder are Broadcast colors, Field Interpolate, Reduce Interlace Flicker. For more information on video effects, turn to Chapter 11.

Broadcast colors

To use the Broadcast Color effect, click and drag the effect from the Video folder of the Effects palette over a clip in a video track in the Timeline palette.

Note

If you are exporting your Premiere production to videotape, you can add color bars to the beginning of your production. Color bars enable a video production facility to calibrate colors when duplicating or broadcasting video. Adding color bars is discussed in Chapter 2.

The sliders and controls for the effect appear in the Effect Controls palette. To use the effect, choose either NTSC for American television or PAL for European television in the Broadcast locale pop-up menu. Then, choose a method in the How to Make Colors Safe pop-up menu. Here is an explanation of the choices:

✦ **Reduce Luminance.** Reduces pixel brightness values. As the values are reduced, colors become darker.

✦ **Reduce Saturation.** Brings pixel values closer to gray. This makes the colors less intense.

✦ **Key out Unsafe.** Colors that fall beyond the TV gamut become transparent.

✦ **Key in Safe.** Colors that are within the TV gamut are transparent.

In the Maximum Signal Field, use the slider to enter the maximum IRE (or image luminance) breakpoint value. Any levels above this value are altered. If you are unsure of what value to use, use the default setting of 110.

Note

In some video cameras, black and white stripes appear in the viewfinder when an image's brightness surpasses 100 IRE. This indicates that the image luminance is too bright.

Two other image-enhancing effects appear in the Video folder: Field Interpolate and Reduce Interlace Flicker.

✦ **Field Interpolate.** This effect creates missing scan lines from the average of other lines.

✦ **Reduce Interlace Flicker.** This effect softens horizontal lines in an attempt to reduce interlace flicker.

Note

Adobe After Effects uses many of the same color-correcting techniques as Adobe Premiere. However, After Effects has a powerful advantage: it enables you to mask or isolate areas on-screen. After you mask an area, you can choose to color correct the masked area only.

To color correct a Premiere project in After Effects, load the Premiere project into After Effects by choosing File ⇨ Import ⇨ Premiere Comp As. (For more information on working with masks in After Effects, turn to Chapter 24.) After you've completed color correcting in After Effects, you can export your file as a QuickTime or AVI movie and load it into Premiere.

Retouching and Color Correcting with Photoshop

Although Premiere provides a variety of controls for correcting colors, its powers are limited if you need to make extensive adjustments to specific image areas. Fortunately, you can export a Premiere clip to Adobe Photoshop in Filmstrip format or TIFF, PICT or Targa Sequence format. Adobe specifically designed Filmstrip format to act as a bridge between Adobe Premiere and Adobe Photoshop. When a Premiere clip is loaded into Photoshop, you can see each individual frame and use Photoshop's extensive color-correcting toolset to correct the image.

You can also use Photoshop's powerful masking utilities to isolate areas and then manipulate the shade and colors. Once in Photoshop, you can copy and paste images from one frame to another, or you can select and copy a person from a photograph, for example, and paste it into your video clip. You can also omit a person from a video clip by cloning surrounding areas or by painting over it with the Paintbrush. Figure 15-5 shows a frame from a video clip before masking and color correcting. Figure 15-6 shows the same frame after masking and color correcting.

Figure 15-5: Frame from a video clip before masking and color correcting

Figure 15-6: Frame from a video clip after masking and color correcting

Note

Before you take a person out of a video clip or add a person to a video clip, check whether you need permission to do so. This is especially so if you are going to publish or distribute the video you are creating. Make sure that you have the permission from the people who appear in the video.

Loading a video clip into Photoshop

Before you can manipulate your video clip in Photoshop, you need to convert the video clip to Filmstrip format. Here's how to export a Premiere clip to Photoshop in Filmstrip format:

1. **Load or create a Premiere project.** If you are in a new Premiere project, open a clip by choosing File ➪ Open, or import a clip by choosing File ➪ Import ➪ File.

On the CD-ROM

You can use the Gondola video clip found in Chapter 15, in the Tutorial Projects, on the CD-ROM that accompanies this book.

2. **If you used File ➪ Open to open a clip, choose File ➪ Export Clip ➪ Movie. If you used File ➪ Import ➪ File to import a file into the Timeline window, choose File ➪ Export Timeline ➪ Movie.**
3. **In the Export Movie dialog box, name your movie.**
4. **Click the Settings button to display the Export Movie Settings dialog box.** The Export Movie Settings dialog box appears (see Figure 15-7).
5. **Click the File Type option and choose Filmstrip.** Note that you can also choose to use the TIFF, PICT or Targa Sequence formats.

   Click the Range pop-up menu. If you have opened a clip, choose Entire Clip, to export the entire clip. Choose In to Out to export a clip whose In and Out points have been edited. If you have imported a clip to the Timeline window, choose Entire Project, to export the entire project. Choose Work Area to export only the area where the preview bar is located.

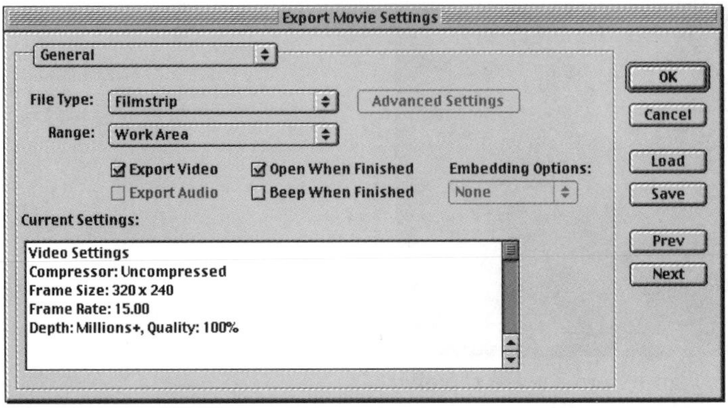

Figure 15-7: The Export Movie Settings dialog box

6. **Click OK.** Premiere exports your project into a Filmstrip file, which you can then import into Photoshop.

Note

Premiere's Export Movie Settings determine the frame size, frame rate, and other features of the exported file. The export settings are covered in detail in Chapter 17.

The following steps provide an overview of several of Photoshop's image-enhancing commands. For full details on these commands consult the Photoshop manual.

7. **In Photoshop, choose File ➪ Open.** The Open dialog box opens (see Figure 15-8).
8. **Locate the Filmstrip file.** Before you open the file, click once on the file. Notice that in the Open dialog box, next to the Filmstrip format, the size of your file appears. The file size may surprise you. Remember that when you open a Filmstrip file in Photoshop, you are opening a video clip that contains various frames at the width and height of your clip. Therefore, the Photoshop file may be very large. Make sure that your system can handle the file. If the file is too big, you may need to go back to Premiere and use the In and Out points to cut some frames out of the video clip. Then re-export the file in Filmstrip format, and reopen in Photoshop.
9. **Click Open.** The Filmstrip file loads with the file reduced in size, so that you can see all the frames in the file (see Figure 15-9). The more frames in your document, the smaller the frame preview.
10. **Choose View ➪ Zoom In a few times to enlarge the size of the frame preview.** When the Filmstrip window is enlarged, you can see the frame preview for only a few frames, as seen in Figure 15-10. Scroll down to see the rest of the frames in the video clip. Notice that below each frame appears the Timeline number. Also notice that the document size appears at the bottom left of the document.

Tip

Mac users can press ⌘+ a few times to zoom. PC users can press Ctrl+ a few times to zoom.

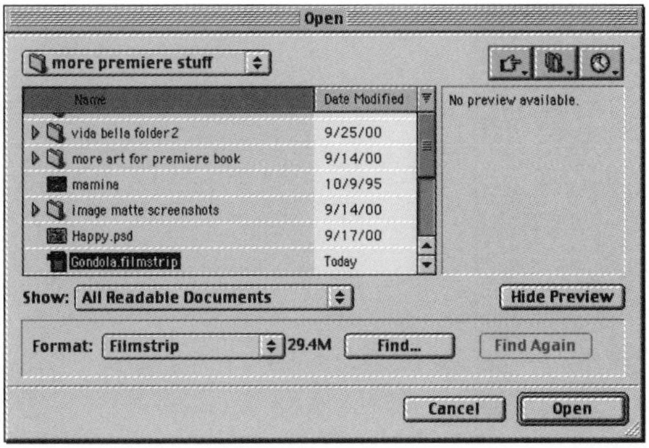

Figure 15-8: The Open dialog box shows you the size of the file you are opening.

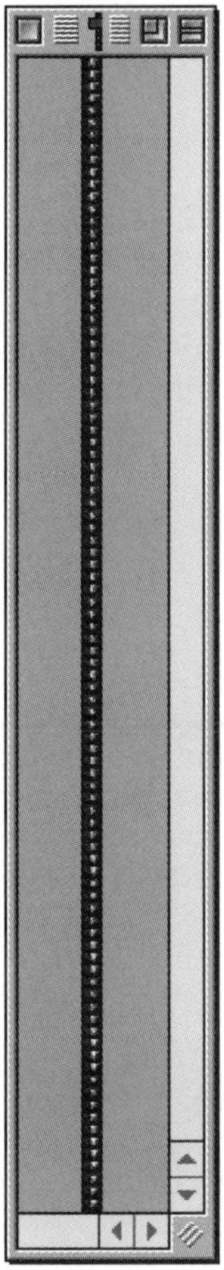

Figure 15-9: When the Filmstrip file opens in Photoshop, all of the Premiere frames are loaded.

Figure 15-10: Frames from the video clip

Using Selections in Photoshop

One of the best reasons for using Photoshop to make color and tonal adjustments is its masking capabilities. In Photoshop, you can select an image area with a selection tool, such as the Magic Wand or Lasso tool, and then execute an image adjustment command. When the command is applied, Photoshop only applies it to the selected area.

Selecting a color range

If you are selecting image areas in a Filmstrip file or sequence files, it is handy to quickly create a selection that spans multiple frames. You can easily create a selection throughout many frames using Photoshop's Color Range command. Follow these steps to select a color range:

1. **To open the Color Range dialog box, seen in Figure 15-11, choose Select ⇨ Color Range.**
2. **To select a color range, set the Select menu to Sampled Colors.**
3. **Click the Image radio button.**

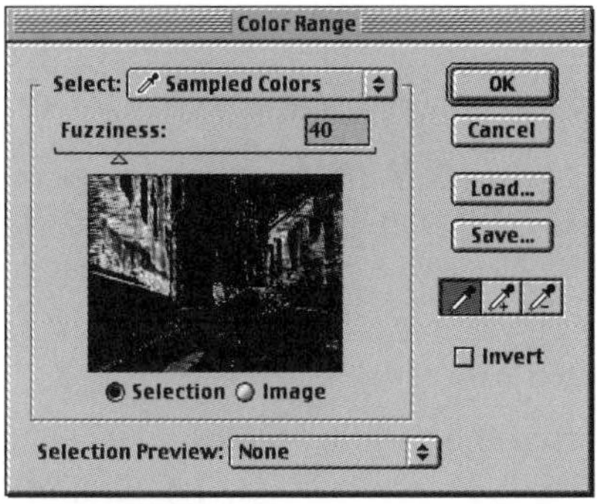

Figure 15-11: Photoshop's Color Range command enables you to select parts of an image by color.

4. **Choose Grayscale in the Selection Preview menu.** The image appears on-screen in the dialog box's preview area with the selected area in black and white.
5. **With the Eyedropper tool selected, click in the image area of the dialog box that you wish to select.** As soon as you click, all colors that match the color you clicked turn white on-screen.
6. **Click and drag the Fuzziness slider to fine-tune the selection.** To add to the selection, click the Eyedropper + tool in your image. To subtract from the selection, click in the preview image area in the dialog box with the Eyedropper tool.
7. **Click OK.** The final selection appears on-screen.

Saving selections to alpha channels

Photoshop enables you to save selections and edit them as grayscale mask images in its Channels palette. This provides a sophisticated method of creating an intricate selection. A detailed description of editing masks is beyond the scope of this book. However, the following is a quick review of the steps needed to save a selection as a mask, and to edit the mask:

1. **Create a rough selection on-screen using one of Photoshop's selection tools, such as one of the Lasso tools or the Magic Wand.**

   Tip

   While using one of the selection tools, press and hold the Shift key to add to a selection. Mac users press and hold the Option key to subtract from a selection. PC users press and hold the Alt key to subtract from a selection.

2. **To create a mask out of the selection in an alpha channel, choose Select ➪ Save Selection.** In the Save Selection dialog box, name the selection and then click Save. You can edit it using Photoshop's painting tools.
3. **Activate the mask channel so that you can still see your image on-screen.** To do this, select the channel in the Channels palette to activate the channel for editing and display the mask's eye icon. A red overlay indicates the mask edges.
4. **Select a painting tool, such as the Paintbrush or Pencil.**
5. **Choose a brush size.** Make sure that the painting tool is in normal mode, with opacity set to 100%. Try painting over your image. Try painting with white; try painting with black. If Photoshop's default settings are in effect, painting with white enlarges the mask; painting with black reduces the size of the mask. To fine-tune the mask, choose a small brush size and zoom into your image to edit it.
6. **After you finish editing the mask, reselect the RGB channel in the Channels palette.**
7. **Choose Select ➪ Load Selection.** Photoshop converts the mask into a blinking selection on-screen and is ready for use in image correction.

Note

To save a file with saved selections in channels, you must save your file in Photoshop format. When you are finished with the saved selections, you can delete the channels by dragging the channel in the Channels palette to the trash. If you don't want to delete the saved selections, you may want to make a copy of the file. Remember, you can't import a Photoshop file into Premiere as a Filmstrip; instead Premiere will import the Photoshop file as a still image. Thus, to save a Photoshop file in Filmstrip format, which can be imported into Premiere, choose File ➪ Save As. In the Save As dialog box, choose the Filmstrip format.

Using Photoshop's Image Adjust Commands

This section reviews several Photoshop image-correcting commands that can be useful if you are making color or tonal adjustments to Filmstrip files. Our goal here is to introduce you to these commands, not to make you Photoshop color-correcting experts. If you find that your video clip requires hours and hours of enhancement work in Photoshop, you should consider whether your time might be better spent reshooting or restructuring your Premiere production, so that you can use clips that don't need a lot of color correction.

Tip

To quickly retouch and/or color correct various frames in a clip, you can use Photoshop's Actions palette to process through TIFF, PICT or TARGA sequence files to open a file, apply an Image Adjust command, save, and close a file.

Using the Info palette

Before you start color-correcting a clip, you should display the Info palette, so that you can see the values of the colors that you are affecting. Choose Window ➪ Show Info to display the Info palette. The Info palette, shown in Figure 15-12, displays the individual RGB colors as you move the Eyedropper tool over an image. (If the RGB colors don't appear, click the Info palette pop-up menu and choose Palette Options. In the Info Options dialog box, choose Actual Color from the Mode pop-up menu.)

To see the values of your image, move the mouse over your image. As you move the mouse, notice the color values in the Info palette. As soon as you start color correcting, these values change. You can check the values while you are using a dialog box to color correct. In the Info palette, a before and after value appears.

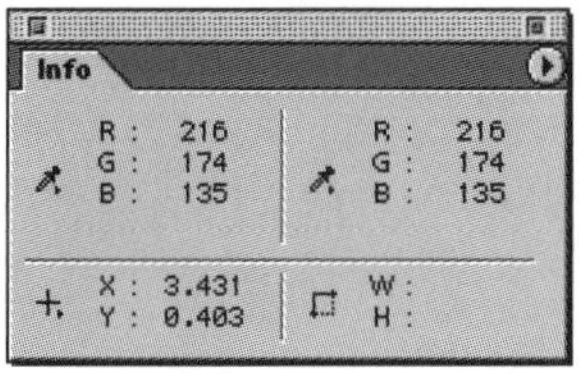

Figure 15-12: Photoshop's Info palette displays a reading of the colors in your image.

At this point, you should decide whether your image needs simple tonal adjustments or more advanced tonal and color corrections.

Brightness/Contrast

If your image needs minor color adjustments, use the Image ➪ Adjust ➪ Brightness/ Contrast command. This command works identically to Premiere's Brightness & Contrast video effect. However, in Photoshop, you can select a portion of your image and then apply the command to adjust the image.

Tip

As you are working with Photoshop's color-correcting commands, you can reset the dialog box options back to their original settings by pressing Option (PC users, press Alt) and then clicking the Cancel button.

Levels

If your image needs more sophisticated tonal adjustments or if you need to make overall adjustments to a red, green, or blue image channel, use Photoshop's Levels command. To open the Levels dialog box, shown in Figure 15-13, choose Image ➪ Adjust ➪ Levels.

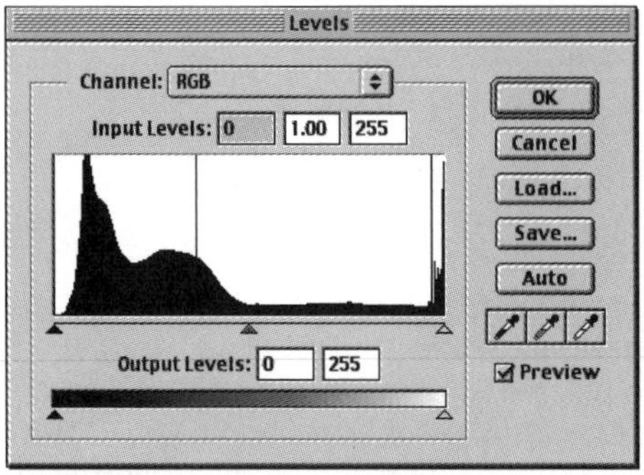

Figure 15-13: The Levels command is used to lighten the first frame of the Gondola video clip.

Photoshop's Levels dialog box works similarly to Premiere's Levels dialog box. However, in Photoshop, if you select an area on-screen, the histogram that appears charts the pixel distribution in the selected area.

In the Levels dialog box, click Save to save the settings in the Levels dialog box. In the dialog box that appears next, name the setting and then click Save. After you save the Levels settings, close the dialog box by clicking OK. Now that you've saved the Levels settings, you can add them to other clips.

Curves

Photoshop's Curves command is considered one of its most powerful tools for adjusting image tones. Unlike the Levels command, which focuses on highlights, midtones, and shadow areas, the Curves command enables you to make tonal adjustments throughout an image's brightness range. And as you make adjustments, you can lock-in up to 15 points on the curve.

To open Photoshop's Curves dialog box, choose Image ➪ Adjust ➪ Curves. In the Curves dialog box, seen in Figure 15-14, the *x* axis of the dialog box represents the original image values, and the *y* axis represents the values that are changed. Because all points are equal when you begin, the Curves dialog box opens by displaying a straight diagonal line.

To make adjustments using the curve, start by examining the horizontal axis. The left-end of the horizontal axis represents darker areas of the original image; brighter areas are represented on the right side of the horizontal axis. (This is the default setting. If the default setting has been changed, to appear in percentages rather than in a range from 0 to 255, click the middle of the curve to change the horizontal axis to its default setting.) A quick way to pinpoint where image areas are represented on the curve is to simply click in your image. As you click, a dot appears in the corresponding area on the curve.

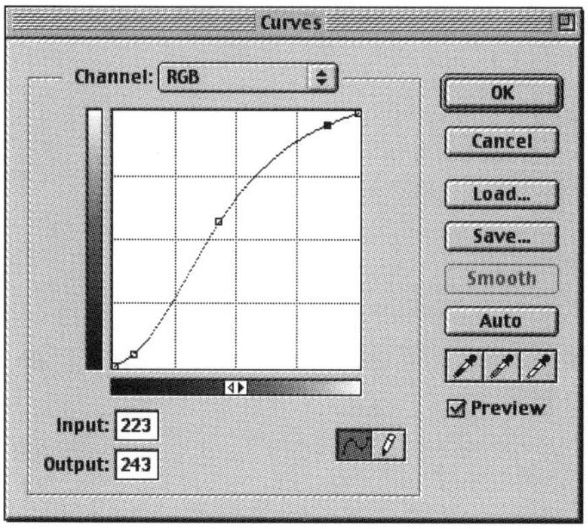

Figure 15-14: Photoshop's Curves dialog box

To lighten an image area, click and drag up on the curve; to darken an area, click and drag down. As you drag, the curve shows how the rest of the pixels in the image change. To prevent part of the curve from changing, you can click the curve to establish fixed points. As you click and drag, the fixed points lock down the curve.

As with Photoshop's Levels command, Curves also enables you to change the tonal range of individual color channels. To select a channel, choose Red, Green, or Blue from the Channels pop-up menu. If you click and drag a curve representing a channel, dragging upward increases that channel's color in the image, dragging downward reduces it and adds that color's complements. For example, if you select the Green channel, dragging up adds more green and dragging down on the curve adds more magenta.

Variations

If you want to perform a simple correction of shadows, midtones, highlights, and colors in an image, and are not a Photoshop expert, try the Variations command. This enables you to color correct visually. To open the Variations dialog box, choose Image ➪ Adjust ➪ Variations.

In the Variations dialog box, shown in Figure 15-15, move the slider at the top toward Finer so that the changes occur gradually. Then choose whether you want to adjust Shadows, Midtones, or Highlights. To lighten the frames, click the Lighter thumbnail. Notice that as the image in the current pick area changes, the original image remains the same. As you make adjustments, the current pick always shows the last change that you made. If you want to return the image to its original state, click the Original image frame.

Sometimes after lightening an image, the image may look washed out. To add color to the image, click the color thumbnails. For instance, to increase Red values in an image, click the More Red button. Keep clicking More Red until you've added the correct amount. But what if there's too much red in an image? Notice that there isn't a Less Red button. To remove red, you must click to add more of red's complement, which is cyan. Therefore, to remove red, click Add Cyan.

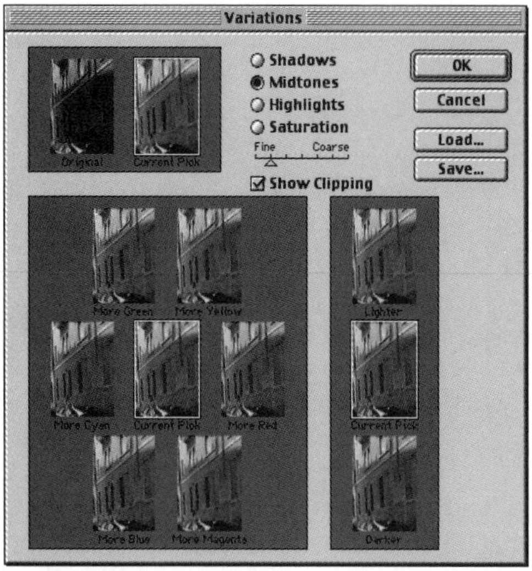

Figure 15-15: Photoshop's Variations dialog box enables you to adjust the shadows, midtones, highlights, and colors in an image.

Hue/Saturation

To adjust the lightness and intensity of a color, use Photoshop's Hue/Saturation command. This command is far more sophisticated than Premiere's HSL Color Balance command. Using Photoshop's Hue/Saturation command, you can focus on specific colors to change as well as set a hue range that you want to change.

To display the Hue/Saturation dialog box, shown in Figure 15-16, choose Image ➪ Adjust ➪ Hue/Saturation. The easiest way to use the Hue/Saturation command is to leave the Edit mode set to Master. In this mode, the Hue/Saturation is somewhat akin to Premiere's HSL Color Balance. For example, you can change image color values in the frames by clicking and dragging the Hue slider. To change the intensity of a color, move the Saturation slider. To change the lightness of the frames, move the Lightness slider.

Photoshop surpasses Premiere by providing before and after color bars at the bottom of the Color palette. The top color bar represents how colors appear before the adjustment; the bottom shows how those colors will change as you click and drag the slider.

Note: You can also use the Hue/Saturation command to colorize a grayscale filmstrip. To do this, click the Colorize button and drag the Hue slider to the desired color.

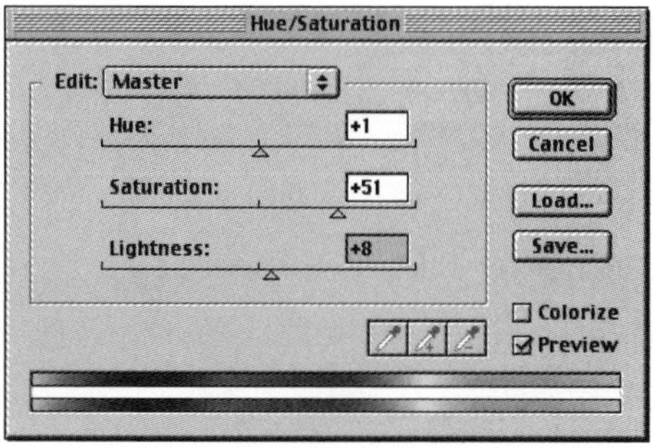

Figure 15-16: The Hue/Saturation dialog box enables you to change the lightness and intensity of colors.

The Hue/Saturation command also provides a more advanced mode, if you want to adjust a specific color range. To do this, choose Reds, Yellows, Greens, Cyans, Blues, or Magentas in the Edit pop-up menu. When you do this, the bottom color bar enables you to specify a more exact range of colors to adjust.

Note

Photoshop also features a Replace Colors command (Image ⇨ Adjust ⇨ Replace Colors). This command is a combination of the Color Range command and the Hue/Saturation command. You can use the Replace Colors command to isolate a range of colors and replace the colors with a new color chosen from the Replace Colors Hue ⇨ Saturation ⇨ Lightness sliders.

Color Balance

Photoshop's Color Balance command provides a method of changing the overall balance of colors in an image. Although Photoshop's Color Balance command is similar to Premiere's Color Balance command, Photoshop's command enables you to focus your attention on shadows, midtones, or highlights.

To open the Color Balance dialog box, which is shown in Figure 15-17, choose Image ⇨ Adjust ⇨ Color Balance. The dialog box is simple to use. Decide whether you want to focus on shadows, midtones, or highlights. Then click and drag to adjust the sliders. The dialog box clearly shows how RGB colors relate to their complements. As discussed earlier in this chapter, reducing red adds cyan; reducing green adds magenta; reducing blue adds yellow.

Note

The Preserve Luminosity checkbox helps ensure that the brightness levels of the image are maintained, as you edit the color balance.

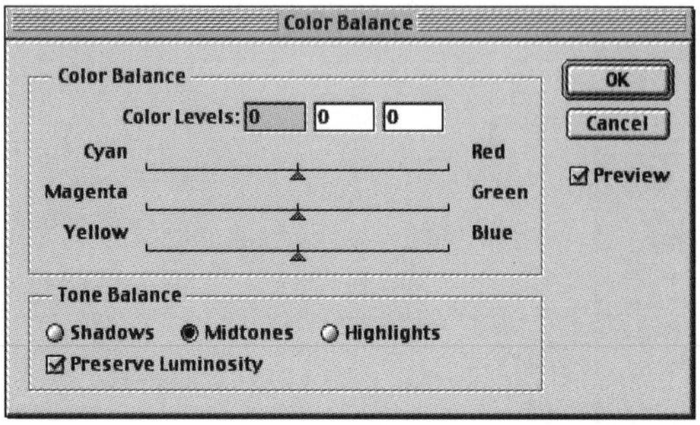

Figure 15-17: The Color Balance dialog box adjusts the RGB and CMY colors.

Using Photoshop to add and delete people from video clips

You can use Photoshop to copy a person into a video clip or to remove a person from a video clip. (However, the practicality of performing such an operation may be limited in many video clips involving action or motion.) You can use the techniques described in this section for still images, or to create interesting special effects. For instance, you may want to create or paint an object from scratch in Photoshop, and then place it in a video frame. The combination of the realistic and the artistic may be quite interesting.

Figure 15-18 shows a video clip before a person was added. Figure 15-19 shows the video clip from Figure 15-18, after the person was added.

Here's how to add a person or an object into a video clip:

1. **Load Photoshop.**
2. **Choose File ➪ Open to open a file of an image that has the person or object that you want to add to the clip.** Note that the person or object you want to add to the video clip may not be in a photograph — the person or object may be in another video clip. In that case, you need to save that video clip in Filmstrip format and open it in Photoshop.

On the CD-ROM

You can use the Mamina.psd image found in Chapter 15, in the Tutorial Projects folder on the CD-ROM that accompanies this book.

3. **Use one of Photoshop's selection tools to select the person or object.** For intricate selection, you should create a selection with a selection tool and then use Photoshop's masking tools to edit the mask with a painting tool.
4. **After you've completed the masking process, reload the selection by choosing File ➪ Load Selection.**
5. **Choose Edit ➪ Copy.**

Figure 15-18: Filmstrip video clip in Photoshop before person is added

Figure 15-19: Filmstrip video clip in Photoshop after person is added

6. **Now, choose File ➪ Open to open the Filmstrip video clip to which you want to add the object or person.**

7. **Choose Edit ➪ Paste to paste the person into the Filmstrip video clip.** You may need to reduce the size of the person. If so, choose Edit ➪ Transform ➪ Scale to scale the image. (When you paste the object or person into the file, you are pasting that person into a new layer. Choose Window ➪ Show Layers to open the Layers palette. Notice the new layer with the person in it.)

8. **Use the Move tool to move the person into the frame in which the person is to appear.** To add the person to more than one frame, you must copy the layer that the person is in. Click and drag over the New Layer icon in the Layers palette with the person to make a copy. Then use the Move tool to move it into place. When you copy and paste in Photoshop, a new layer is created. Remember to flatten the image so that you can resave the file in Filmstrip format and open it in Premiere.

Note

You may want to use the grid and/or rulers (View ➪ Show Rulers or View ➪ Show Grid) to place the person/object in the same position in every frame.

Here's how to omit or remove a person or an object from a video clip:

1. **Choose File ➪ Open to open the Filmstrip clip that contains the person or object that you wish to remove.**
2. **Locate the frame with the person or object.**
3. **Remove the person or object with one of these techniques:**
   - Use the Rubber Stamp tool to clone surrounding areas over the area that you want to remove. After you clone the object from one frame, you may be able to copy and paste that area into other frames.
   - Use the Airbrush, Paintbrush, and/or Pencil tools to paint over the area.
4. **Resave the file in Filmstrip format.** If you executed a copy and paste command, Photoshop automatically creates a new layer. Remember to remove the layers by flattening the image so that you can resave the file in Filmstrip or use the Save As command to save in Filmstrip. After the file is saved in Filmstrip format, it can be reloaded into Premiere.

Summary

If your video clips need color correction or if they need brightness or contrast enhanced, you can use Adobe Premiere's Video Effects. The Adjust, Image Control, and Video folders all contain effects that can enhance video.

✦ Use the Brightness and Contrast effect to quickly correct clips that don't need sophisticated adjustments.

✦ Use the Levels effect to add or reduce contrast and to enhance midtone areas.

✦ Use the Color Balance effect to adjust the Red, Green, and Blue channels in an image.

✦ If Premiere's image-enhancement commands aren't sufficient, you can export your Premiere file as a Filmstrip file and correct it in Adobe Photoshop.

✦ Apart from correcting colors and tonal values in Photoshop, you can also add or remove image areas from video clips.

✦ ✦ ✦

Outputting Digital Video from Premiere

P A R T

V

In This Part

CHAPTER 16

Exporting QuickTime, AVI, and MPEG Movies

✦ ✦ ✦ ✦

In This Chapter

✦ ✦ ✦ ✦

After you've completed the finishing touches on your Adobe Premiere project, you're ready to *export* the production as a digital movie. When you export the file, you can output it to videotape or you can export it to disk for viewing on another computer system. If you export your Premiere project as a QuickTime, Video for Windows, or MPEG file, it can easily be viewed on most Macs and PCs by simply double-clicking the exported video movie. Movies saved in QuickTime or Video for Windows can be integrated into other multimedia programs, such as Adobe After Effects, Macromedia Director, or Macromedia Flash. MPEG files can be used on the Web, but they're most valuable to Premiere users who want to output their projects to DVD. The Hollywood movies and music videos you see on DVD disks are encoded in MPEG format before the DVD is burned.

This chapter explains how to export Premiere projects into QuickTime, Video for Windows, or MPEG files. It covers the simple steps you need to execute to begin the export process and then focuses on key export settings, such as choosing a compressor, keyframes, and data rates.

Note

In this book, we divide the exporting procedure into different chapters—this chapter, which covers exporting QuickTime, Video for Windows, and MPEG movies, and Chapter 18, which covers exporting to the Web and creating Animated GIF files. Later, Chapter 19 discusses how to export your Premiere project using the Advanced Windows Media and RealVideo Export plug-ins. Chapter 20 covers exporting to videotape.

Beginning the Export Process

After you edit your work and preview your production, you can export your project by activating the Timeline and then choosing File ➪ Export Timeline ➪ Movie. Doing so opens the Export Movie dialog box, shown in Figure 16-1. At the bottom left of the screen, Premiere displays the current video and audio settings. If you want to export using these settings, simply name the file and click Save. The length of time Premiere takes to render the final movie depends on the size of your production, its frame rate, frame size, and compression settings.

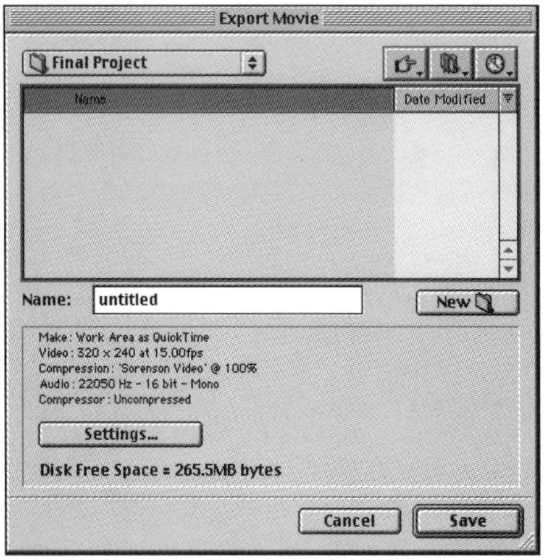

Figure 16-1: The Export Movie dialog box displays the current video and audio settings for your Premiere project.

Note You can export a video clip by opening it in a clip window and then choosing File ➪ Export Clip ➪ Movie.

If you exported the movie in QuickTime format, your movie can be viewed on any Mac or PC that has QuickTime software installed. To be viewed on the Web, the Web users' browsers must have the QuickTime plug-in installed.

If you exported the movie in Video for Windows (called Microsoft AVI in the Export Movie Settings dialog box) format, your movie can be viewed on systems running Microsoft Windows. Mac users can also view AVI movies by importing it into the latest version of Apple's QuickTime Movie player. On the Web, most Windows users are switching from AVI format to Microsoft's new Advanced Windows Media format (covered in Chapter 16). However, AVI format is still accepted as a format that can be imported into many multimedia software programs.

Note

Video for Windows files are saved with an AVI (audio video interleave) file extension. Video for Windows files are often referred to as *AVI files*.

Changing Export Settings

Although the video and audio settings used during the creation of a Premiere project may be perfect during editing, they may not produce the best quality for specific viewing environments. For example, a digital movie with a large frame size and high frame rate may not play well at slow Web connection speeds. Thus, you may want to change several export settings before saving your export file to disk, if you expect your project to be viewed on the Web. To change export settings, click the Settings button in the Export Movie dialog box. (If the Export Movie dialog box is not on-screen, you can display it by choosing File ➪ Export Timeline ➪ Movie.)

After you click Settings, the Export Movie Settings dialog box, shown in Figure 16-2, appears. When this dialog box opens, the pop-up menu at the top of the screen is automatically set to the General setting.

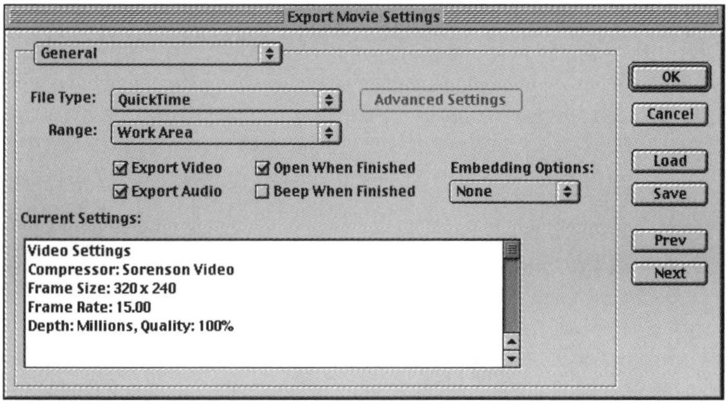

Figure 16-2: The Export Movie Settings dialog box

Following is a description of the choices available in the Export Movie Settings dialog box:

✦ **File Type.** If you want to switch file types, you can use this menu. Apart from picking a QuickTime or AVI format, you can also choose to save your digital movie as a series of still frames in different file formats, such as GIF, TIF, or Window Bitmap.

✦ **Range.** Choose to export the Entire Project or the Work Area specified in the Timeline.

✦ **Export Video.** Deselect if you do not want to export the video.

- **Export Audio.** Deselect if you do not want to export the audio.
- **Open When Finished.** When this option is selected, the final movie opens in Premiere where you can playback the finished project.
- **Save.** Click the Save button to save frequently used export settings.
- **Load.** Click the Load button to load saved project settings.

Changing Video Settings

To review or change Video settings, choose Video in the pop-up menu at the top of the Export Movie Settings screen. The video settings reflect the currently used project settings.

Choosing a QuickTime compressor

When creating a project, capturing video, or exporting a Premiere project, one of the most important decisions you can make is to choose the correct compression settings. A compressor or *CODEC* (COmpression/DECompression) determines exactly how the computer restructures or removes data to make the digital video file smaller. Although most compression settings are designed to compress files, not all of these settings are suitable for all types of projects. The trick is to choose the best CODEC for your Premiere project to produce the best quality with the smallest file size. One CODEC may be better for Web digital video, and another might be best suited to a project that contains animation created in a painting program.

The settings that appear in the Compressor pop-up menu are based upon the file type chosen in the Export Movie Settings dialog box. The QuickTime CODECs, shown in Figure 16-3, are different from the Video for Windows CODECs. Furthermore, depending on the compressor, the options in the Video section of the Export Movie Settings dialog box change.

Following is a brief review of many of the QuickTime CODEC choices available in the Export Movie Settings dialog box:

- **Animation.** Used for creating high-quality output. This setting is particularly useful for animation created in graphics painting programs. Using this compressor, you can set the bit depth to Millions+ (of colors), which enables exporting an alpha channel with the movie. If you choose the 100% option, Animation provides *lossless* compression. This results in smaller file sizes than simply choosing None in the Compression box. Choose this setting for storing high-quality animated titles.

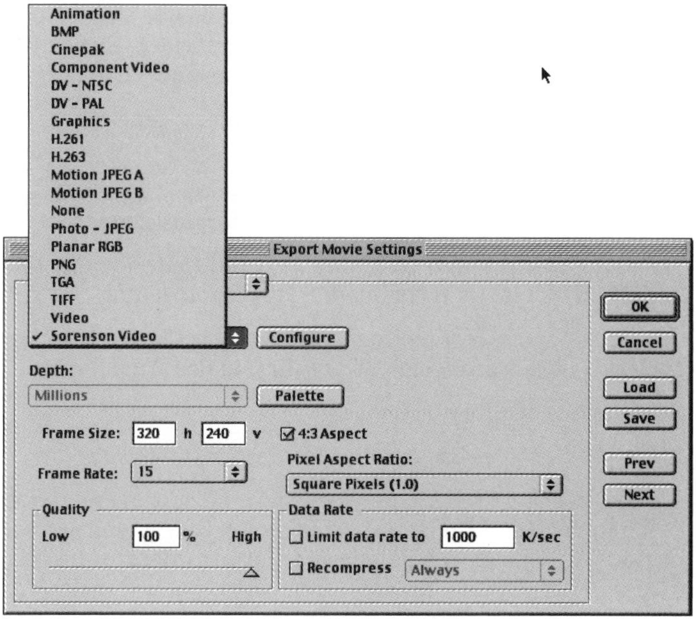

Figure 16-3: The QuickTime CODECs

✦ **Cinepak.** This is one of the most popular formats for Web and multimedia work. Working with Cinepak can be time-consuming because the compression time is sometimes long; you'll have to wait longer for previews and for final video. However, the recompression time or playback is not slow. When exporting, you can also set the data rate using Cinepak, but be aware that setting the data rate below 30K/sec can lower the quality of the video.

✦ **MJPEG-A, MJPEG-B.** Used for editing and capturing video. These CODECs can provide very good results when quality is set to 100%. Both CODECs use spatial compression, so no keyframe control is available. Also, MJPEG usually requires a hardware board for playback.

✦ **Sorenson.** Used for high-quality desktop video for the Web and for CD-ROM. This CODEC provides better compression than Cinepak. Sorenson can reduce file sizes by three to four times as much as Cinepak does. Compression can be time-consuming, so use this setting for exporting but not for editing.

Note

Sorenson also sells a high-end version of the Sorenson CODEC that provides better quality and more features.

✦ **Planar RGB.** A lossless CODEC good for animation created in painting and 3-D programs, and an alternative to the Animation CODEC.

✦ **Video.** Can be used for video editing, but not for exporting.

- **Component Video.** Generally used for capturing analog video. Not used when creating or exporting a project. When you capture video, this may be your only choice, depending on the video capture board installed in your computer.
- **Graphics.** Used for graphics with 256 colors or less; generally not used in desktop video.
- **Photo-JPEG.** Although this CODEC can create good image quality, slow decompression makes this CODEC unsuitable for desktop video.
- **H.263.** Used for video conferencing and provides better quality than the H.261 CODEC. This CODEC is not recommended for video editing.
- **PNG.** Generally not used for motion graphics. This CODEC is included in QuickTime as a means of saving still graphics in PNG Web format.
- **TIFF.** A printing format for still images.
- **BMP.** A Windows-compatible graphics format for still images.
- **DV-PAL and DV-NTSC.** Digital video format for NTSC and PAL (choose the format that applies to the geographic region for your intended audience), used for transferring digitized data from DV camcorders, or from camcorders into Premiere. Useful format for capturing video that is transferred to another video-editing system.
- **None.** No compression is used. Premiere creates preview files faster at this setting, but file sizes are very large.

Note

The QuickTime CODECs list may contain hardware-specific CODECs supplied by computer and board manufacturers. For instance, Sony Vaio computer owners see a Sony DV format in the QuickTime CODEC list. Follow the instructions provided with your capture board or computer when choosing one of these CODECs.

Choosing a Video for Windows compressor

If you are exporting a Video for Windows file, the compressor choices are different than the QuickTime choices. Following is a brief review of the AVI CODECs available:

- **Cinepak.** Originally created by Radius, provides the same features as QuickTime's Cinepak. This CODEC is primarily used for multimedia output. Compression can be time-consuming, but image quality is generally good.
- **Indeo Video 5.04.** Created by Intel (makers of the Pentium computer chip), this CODEC provides good image quality. Often used for capturing raw data. Quality is similar to desktop video produced using the Cinepak CODEC.
- **Microsoft RLE (Run Length Encoding).** The bit depth for this CODEC is limited to 256 colors, making it only suitable for animation created in painting programs with 256 colors, or images that have been reduced to 256 colors. When the Quality slider is set to High, this CODEC produces lossless compression.

Changing bit depth

After you choose a CODEC, the dialog box changes to show the different options provided by that CODEC. If your CODEC enables you to change bit depth, you can choose another setting in the Bit Depth pop-up menu. For instance, the Sorenson CODEC does not enable you to switch bit depths. However, the Cinepak CODEC enables you to choose 256 colors. Because the Cinepak CODEC allows 256 colors, clicking the Palette button enables you to either load a palette or have Premiere create a 256-color palette from the clips in the movie. However, be aware that reducing the palette to 256 could result in poor picture quality. Unless you are working with animation, created in a painting program, you probably will not want to reduce the colors in your video project to 256.

Choosing quality

The next option controlled by the selected CODEC is the Quality slider. Most CODECs enable you to click and drag to choose a quality setting. The higher the quality, the larger the file size of the exported movie.

Choosing a data rate

Many CODECs enable you to specify an output data rate. The *data rate* is the amount of data per second that must be processed during playback of the exported video file. The data rate changes, depending on which system plays your production. For instance, the data rate of CD-ROM playback on a slow computer is far less than the data rate of a hard disk. If the data rate of the video file is too high, the system will not be able to handle the playback. If this is the case, playback may be garbled as frames are dropped. Following are a few suggestions for different playback scenarios:

- **World Wide Web.** Choose a data rate that accounts for Web connection speeds. Remember, even though a modem may be capable of 56 Kbps (kilobits per second), the actual connection speed is probably slower. Also remember that the data rate field accepts data in kilobits per second, rather than bits per second. For Sorenson and Cinepak CODECs, try a data rate of 50. Adobe recommends trying a data rate of 150K/sec for movies with a frame size of 240 x180. Note that when uploading to the Web, smaller file size is more important than data rate.
- **Videotape editing.** If you are exporting video files for further editing, the data rate should be set so that it can be handled by the computer editing system. Export for further editing using a CODEC that does not reduce video quality, such as a DV CODEC, or the Animation CODEC.
- **CD-ROM.** For CD-ROM playback, specify a data rate consistent with the data rate of the CD-ROM drive. The data rate setting is especially important for older CD-ROM drives. For example, a double speed CD-ROM has a data rate at 300K per second. Adobe recommends setting the data rate in this case from 150-200. For 12 speed CD-ROMs, the recommended data rate is 1.8 MB/sec; for 24 speed CD-ROMs, the recommended data rate is 3-3.6 MB/sec.

✦ **Intranets.** The data rate speed depends upon the actual speed of the network. Because most intranets use high-speed connections, you can generally set the playback to 100K or more.

✦ **Hard disk.** If you are creating a production for playback on a computer system, try to ascertain the data rate of the audience's hard disk. The data rates for most modern hard disks are in excess of 33 million bits per second.

Note

Adobe's Support Knowledgebase document "Applying Data Rate Limits in Premiere" is available on-line at `www.adobe.com/support/techdocs/a60a.htm`.

Setting recompression

If you specify a data rate, select the Recompress check box. Doing this helps guarantee that Premiere keeps the data rate beneath the one specified in the data rate field. If you want Premiere to recompress every frame, whether or not it is below the data rate, choose Always in the Recompress pop-up menu. Better quality is produced, however, if you choose the Maintain Data Rate setting. This only recompresses frames that are higher than the specified data rate.

Changing frame rates and frame size

Before exporting video, you may want to reduce the frame rate or reduce the frame size to reduce the file size of your production. The frame rate is the number of frames Premiere exports per second. As discussed in Chapter 3, if you reduce the frame rate, it should be at a multiple of the timebase. For example, if the timebase is 30, a frame rate of 15 may provide satisfactory results. Of course, a frame rate of 30 produces smoother video.

If you change frame size, be sure to specify the horizontal and vertical dimensions in pixels. If your video was captured at a 4:3 aspect ratio, be sure to maintain this ratio to avoid distorting clips.

Specifying keyframes

Another video export setting that can control export file size is the Keyframe setting in the Export Movie Settings dialog box's Keyframe and Rendering section. (See Figure 16-4.)

Keyframe settings can be changed when choosing CODECs, such as Cinepak and Sorenson video, with temporal compression. As discussed in Chapter 3, the keyframe setting specifies how many times to save the complete video frame. If the keyframe setting is set at 15, a keyframe is created every 15 frames. As the CODEC compresses, it compares each subsequent frame and only saves the information that changes in each frame. Thus, using keyframes can significantly reduce the file size of your video.

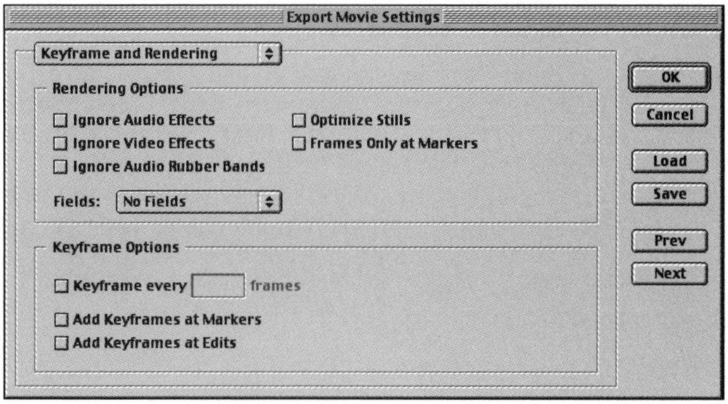

Figure 16-4: The Keyframe and Rendering section of the Export Movie Settings dialog box

A good starting point is to enter the number of keyframes per second that match the number of frames per second. Thus, if your frame rate is 30 frames per second, set the keyframe rate to 30. This creates one keyframe for every 30 frames of video. Enter 60 to create one keyframe every two seconds. If you want more keyframes, lower the number in the keyframe field. For instance, if you enter 10, a keyframe would be created every 10 frames. However, this would increase both the data rate and the file size of your production.

To help insure smooth transitions, you may want to force Premiere to create a keyframe at transitions and edits. To set keyframes at Edit points, choose the Key Frame at Edit option in the Export Movie Settings dialog box. To set key frames at specific points in your production, set Markers at points where you wish Premiere to create a keyframe, then choose the Keyframe at Markers option in the Export Movie Settings dialog box.

Tip To see a visual representation of the keyframes in a clip, select it in the Project windows, then choose Clip ⇨ Properties. Next click Data Rate. The Red Bars in the graph represent keyframes.

Other rendering options

Other options in the Keyframe and Rendering section of the Export Movie Settings dialog box can be used to change export settings. The settings are:

- ✦ **Ignore Video Effects.** The export is created without video filters.
- ✦ **Optimize Stills.** This option attempts to process stills more efficiently by creating fewer frames. When selected, Premiere creates a single frame for each second that a still frame must appear. If still images break up during playback, deselect this option.

Using the QuickTime File Exporter

Mac users who are exporting QuickTime files can also change QuickTime export settings by accessing the QuickTime File Exporter from the Export Movie Settings dialog box. First, make sure the General view is shown. Next, click the Advanced Settings button to open the QuickTime File Export Settings dialog box (see Figure 16-5). Clicking the Using menu displays presets for exporting to the Web and for exporting to CD-ROM. Clicking the Options button enables you to change compressor settings and to choose options for Hinted or Progressive Web Streaming. You can also access QuickTime filters that provide special effects, such as tinting, blurring, and embossing.

Figure 16-5: The QuickTime File Export Settings dialog box

Changing Audio Settings

When you export your final project, you may want to change the audio settings. To access the audio option, choose Audio from the Export Movie Settings dialog box. The settings in the Audio section of the Export Movie Settings dialog box, shown in Figure 16-6, are as follows. (See Chapter 6 for a complete discussion of Premiere's audio settings.)

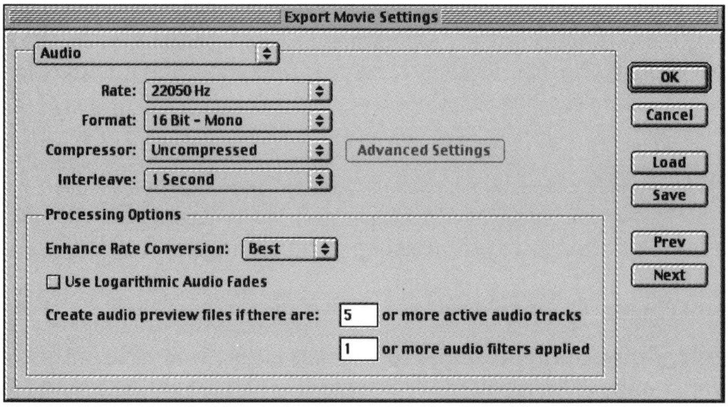

Figure 16-6: The Audio section of the Export Movie Settings dialog box

- **Rate.** Lower the rate setting to reduce file size and to speed up the rendering of the final production. Higher rates produce better quality and increase processing time. (CD-ROM quality is 44 kHz.)
- **Format.** Stereo 16-bit is the highest setting; 8-bit mono is the lowest setting. Lower bit depths produce smaller files and reduce rendering times.
- **Compressor.** In the compressor pop-up menu, choose a compressor if desired. (The Audio CODECs are reviewed at the end of this section.)
- **Interleave.** This option determines how frequently audio is inserted into the video frames. Choosing 1 frame in the pop-up menu tells Premiere to load the audio for the frame until the next frame is processed. However, this can cause the sound to break up if the computer cannot handle a lot of audio data quickly.
- **Enhanced Rate Conversion.** This option controls audio quality, as sample rates of Timeline clips are converted to the rate entered in the Rate field. The Best option produces the highest quality but results in longer processing times. Choosing Off provides the fastest processing but the lowest quality.
- **Logarithmic Audio Fades.** Selecting this check box provides the most natural changes in sounds, as they become louder or softer. When this option is selected, processing time is much longer.

Choosing QuickTime audio CODECs

Following is a brief review of several QuickTime audio CODECs. You must specify a CODEC only if you want to add compression to sound. For each CODEC, the compression ratio appears next to its name.

- **ULaw 2:1.** Used as a common audio format on Unix platforms. ULaw is used for digital telephony in both North America and Japan.
- **16-bit Endian and 16-bit Little Endian.** Not used for video editing. Used by hardware engineers and software developers.
- **24-bit integer and 32-bit integer soft.** Not used for video editing. Used by hardware engineers and software developers.
- **IMA Designed by the Interactive Multimedia Association.** This cross-platform format can be used to compress audio for multimedia.
- **32-bit floating point and 64-bit floating point.** Not used for video editing. Used by hardware engineers and software developers.
- **ALaw.** Used for European digital telephony.
- **Qdesign Music codec.** Can be used for high-quality Web output. Can provide CD-ROM quality over a modem.
- **Qualcomm Pure Voice.** A speech format. Shouldn't be used at an audio rate higher than 8 kHz.

- **MACE 3:1 and MACE 6:1.** Macintosh audio CODEC that can be used for QuickTime movies for PCs and Macs. MACE 3:1 provides better quality because it uses less compression.

Choosing other audio settings

Other audio export settings are available in the Keyframe and Rendering section of the Export Movie Settings dialog box. These include:

- **Ignore Audio Effects.** This exports audio without using audio filters. Use this for roughcuts.
- **Ignore Audio Rubber Bands.** When this option is selected, fades and pans created with the Timeline rubber band icons are not processed.

Choosing Video for Windows audio CODECs

Premiere offers the following audio compression options when exporting a project as a Video for Windows file:

- **Indeo audio software.** Good for Web output of music and speech. Created for use with Indeo video CODECs.
- **Truespeech.** Used for speech over the Internet. Works best at low data rates.
- **Microsoft GSM 6.10.** Used for speech only. Used for telephony compression in Europe.
- **MS-ADPCM.** Microsoft's version of an Adaptive Differential Pulse Code Modulation compressor. Can be used for CD-ROM quality sound.
- **Microsoft IMA ADPCM.** Used for cross-platform multimedia. Developed by the Interactive Multimedia Association.
- **Voxware codecs.** Can be used for speech output on the Web. Best at low data rates.

Exporting MPEG Files

The Windows version of Adobe 6.5 features an MPEG export module that enables you to export MPEG files specifically set for playback on different formats that can be played on a DVD. If you don't wish to export your Premiere project to DVD, but wish to create an MPEG, you can edit the Adobe presets to create an MPEG file with the frame size, frame rate, and data rate of your choice. To create an MPEG file, you need do little more than click a few buttons and name your file. Using the MPEG encoder, you can export both single clips or the entire Timeline.

Note

Mac users who have DVD Studio installed can load Premiere projects exported in DV format directly into DVD Studio. DVD Studio users can also create an MPEG file directly from Premiere's Timeline by using Apple's MPEG Encoder accessed through Apple's QuickTime File Exporter. To view the QuickTime File Exporter, click Settings in the Export Movie dialog box. In the File type menu, choose QuickTime File Exporter.

Using the Adobe MPEG Encoder

Adobe's MPEG encoder provides an efficient means of creating quality MPEG files for a variety of DVD formats that can be viewed on DVD players. The different DVD formats described below are options available in software that burns DVD disks. The different formats allow for different screen sizes and different data rates. Some enable subtitles, links, and menus to be integrated into the DVD production.

Using the Adobe Encoder is quite simple: To create an MPEG from the Timeline, first click the Timeline and then choose File ⇨ Export TimeLine ⇨ Adobe MPEG Encoder. To export a clip, select it and choose File ⇨ Export Clip ⇨ Adobe MPEG Encoder. Choosing either command opens the Adobe MPEG Encoder, shown in Figure 16-7.

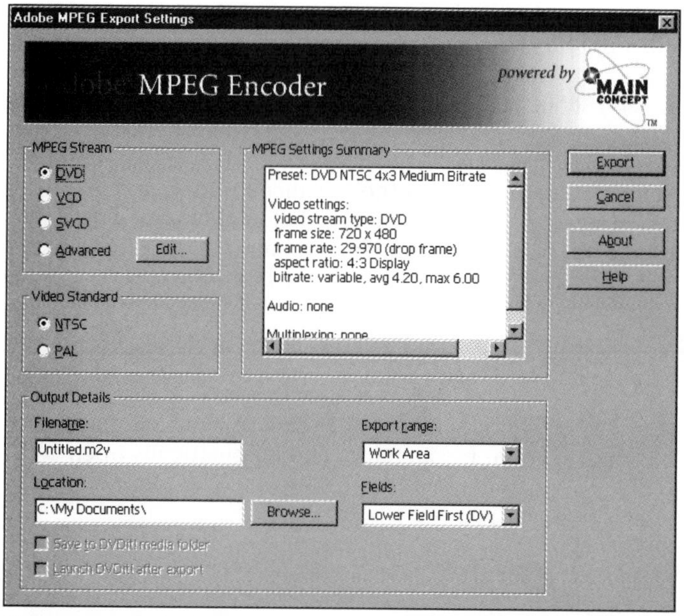

Figure 16-7: Windows users can create MPEG files using the Adobe MPEG Encoder.

The Adobe MPEG Encoder dialog box enables you to choose these disc options in the MPEG stream section:

✦ **DVD.** This option is the Hollywood standard, which can provide over two hours of entertainment. This format utilizes a full frame of 720 x 480 pixels. When the file is exported, audio and video are separated into two MPEG-2 files. The video file extension is m2v; the audio file extension is a .wav file (NTSC), or .mpa (for PAL systems).

✦ **VCD.** This format uses MPEG-1 encoding and provides a frame size of 352 x 240 (NTSC). VCD disks can be played in standard CD-ROM drives, yet can play as much as 74 minutes of audio and video.

✦ **SVCD.** Use MPEG-2 encoding. Provides a frame size of 480 x 480. This format can provide titles, manuals, and links. It's a fairly new format supported by major electronics companies such as Sony, Phillips, Matsushita, and JVC.

✦ **Advanced.** Enables you to choose your own settings.

After you select the MPEGstream, enter the output stream section. In this area, you choose whether to use NTSC or PAL and whether to export your work area or the entire project. Next, name the file and set the export location. The field setting you choose is usually determined by the video-capturing process. Some video boards specify the upper field first and others specify the lower field. If you're unsure, choosing the no fields option can produce good results.

Cross-Reference For more information about field options when exporting video, see Chapter 19.

If you want to edit the MPEG settings, click the Advanced button and then choose Edit. Doing this provides access to a series of tabs that enable you to not only create your own settings but to also save and load them from your hard disk. Figure 16-8 shows the Advanced MPEG Settings dialog box's Basic Settings screen, where you can change the data rate at which the video and audio are streamed. If you are creating DVD discs, however, you should use only the presets — unless you're very familiar with the DVD file format.

If you have DVDit! installed (DVDit LE ships with Premiere), you can have Premiere save the files to the DVDit media folder and automatically open DVDit! by choosing the Save to DVDit! Media folder, and Launch DVDit! after export options.

Cross-Reference For a detailed discussion of the DVD formats, see `www.afterdawn.com/glossary/terms`.

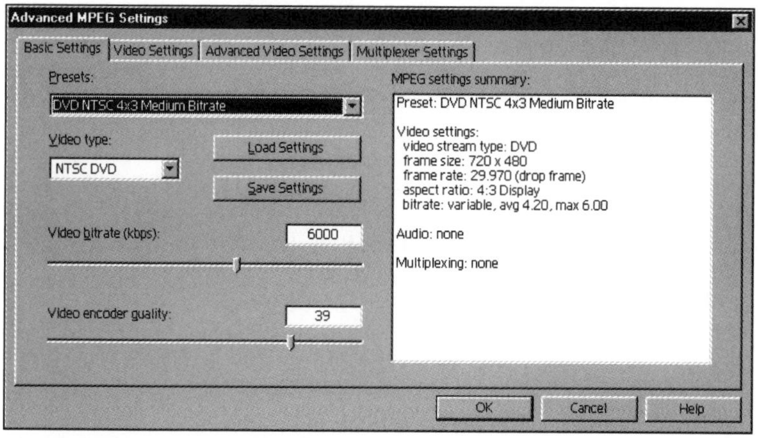

Figure 16-8: Adobe MPEG Encoder enables you to edit, save, and load your own output settings.

Creating a DVD

There's hardly any doubt that DVD discs will replace videocassettes as the chief delivery media for entertainment, education, and advertising. DVD provides high-quality, crisp images that surpass those viewed on videocassettes. Because DVD program material is digital, viewers easily jump from one scene to another, rather than viewing the production linearly, from start to finish. DVDs viewed on computers can also be set-up to access Web sites, which can add to the information provided on the DVD.

If you want to create DVDs from the MPEG movies you create in Premiere, you'll need DVD authoring software and a DVD writer connected to your computer. Mac users who want to create DVDs should investigate Apple's iDVD and the full featured DVD Studio Pro. Windows users can take advantage of the DVDit! LE, included in the PC version of Premiere 6.5.

This section provides a step-by-step guide to creating a DVD disc using DVDit LE. This software not only creates DVDs, but cDVDs that can be created on a regular CD-RW drive.

The DVD production process

Before you get started creating a DVD, you should have an understanding of the features provided in DVD-authoring software. If you're fully versed in the DVD software, you'll be able to take advantage of the interactivity that DVDs provide, and thus create an enriching and educational experience for the viewer. For example, DVDit! enables you to integrate your Premiere MPEG files with text and other graphics. Using DVDit!, you can also create menu screens that feature interactive buttons. When you click on a button, you can trigger a movie to play or jump to another menu screen.

For Premiere users, your first step is to create a project in Premiere and export it using the Adobe MPEG Encoder. If you have a DVD recorder connected to your computer, you should export using the DVD option. If you want to use DVDit! to burn the MPEG files using a CD-RW, you should export your file, choosing the Video CD choice. When exporting, choose the Save to DVDit! Media folder. This tells Premiere to save the file in the Media folder. On most systems the path to this folder is C:\Program Files\Sonic Solutions\DVDit! LE\Themes\Default\Media.

Before you get started creating your DVD, collect any graphics or audio files that you want to use as buttons or background images. These can easily be added to your DVD production in DVD Light.

Creating a DVD with DVDit!

DVDit! is a production environment that enables you to integrate video, graphics, sound, and interactive buttons in a DVD production. After you've set up your production and previewed it, you can also use DVDit! to write or *burn* a DVD.

Although DVDit! is not difficult to use, Premiere users will probably find themselves in unfamiliar territory. The program's interface is quite different from Premiere's. However, once you get used to the DVDit! interface, you'll find that you can quickly set-up and burn a DVD. The following sections lead you step by step through the process of creating an interactive DVD using DVDit! If you follow the steps, you'll create a DVD, an opening menu, and an interactive button that plays a movie.

Creating the project

Your first step is to create a new project in DVDit! If you didn't click the option that automatically opens DVDit! in the Adobe MPEG encoder, start by loading DVDit!

The first screen that appears enables you to start a new project or open an existing project. Click Create New Project. The next screen, shown in Figure 16-9, enables you to set up your initial project settings. If your video standard is not NTSC, click the TV Standard pop-up menu and choose PAL. Next, choose the type of DVD you want to create. If you are creating a DVD from Premiere, choose the MPEG-2 DVD video format. If you chose the Video CD option in Premiere, select MPEG-1 for the cDVD choice. Then click Finish to enter the DVDit! studio environment.

Working with themes

To work efficiently in DVDit!, it's important to understand the concept of *themes*. The easiest way to conceptualize a theme is to consider it as a means of categorizing the different production elements in DVDit!. The program includes a Theme window for backgrounds, buttons, text, video, and audio.

Figure 16-9: To create a project, specify MPEG settings.

As a Premiere user, you're undoubtedly most interested in viewing the MPEG files you created in Premiere. These are available in one section of the Theme window.

Here's how to access video production elements and preview them.

1. **To view video clips, click the film icon at the bottom of the Theme palette.**
2. **To work with movies, you must change the Theme choice from Menu to Movies. Click the word Menus (at the bottom of the screen, above the Time readout) and choose Movies.** After you click, you should see an icon representing the MPEG file that you exported from Premiere, as shown in Figure 16-10.

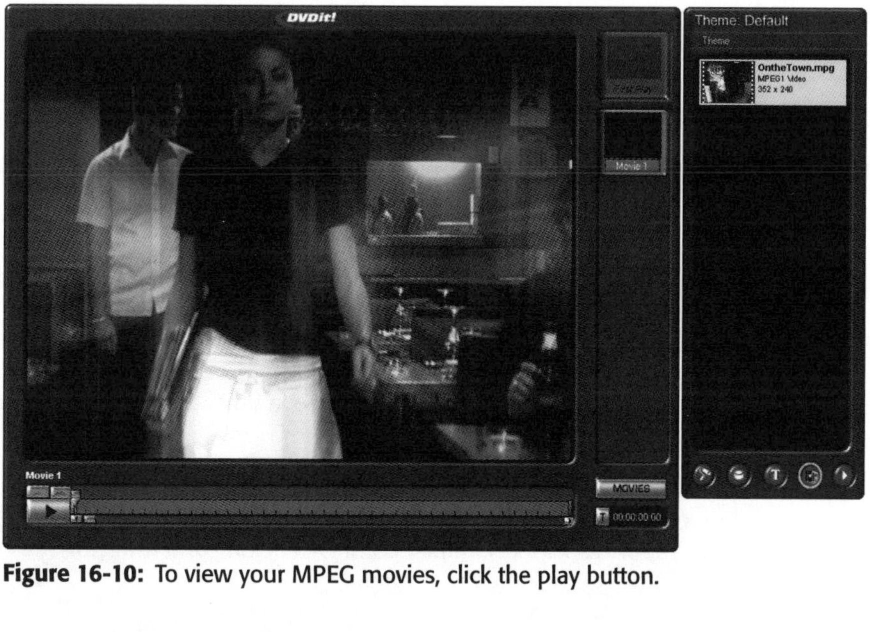

Figure 16-10: To view your MPEG movies, click the play button.

3. **If you don't see it or if you want to add other files (including audio) to the list, click the Theme menu below the words Theme: Default and choose Add Files to Theme.**

4. **To play your movie, simply right-click its icon and choose Play from the menu that appears.**

Note

You can also click and drag video and audio files to the Movie 1 icon. (Later, you can rename the Movie 1 icon.) You can then play your movie by clicking the Play button at the bottom of the DVDit! monitor screen. However, linking a button to Movie 1 is a bit more complicated than the steps provided later.

Adding a background image

Menus provide a stopping point for movies and allow for interactivity. In this section, you create a First Play menu and add a background image and text. The menu is a full screen area that can contain graphics, text, and interactive buttons. It is called first play because it is the first one that appears when the DVD starts to play.

1. **If the Theme window is set to Movies, click the word Movies and select Menus.**

2. **Switch to the background screen theme area by clicking the paint roller icon at the bottom of the Theme palette.**

3. **Choose a background image for your opening menu by clicking one of the images in the list.** We chose the waterfall background. To access it, click the 3D ball icon and drag down.

4. **Next, add the background image to your menu by clicking and dragging the image to the First Play icon.** After you release the mouse on the First Play icon, the background image appears full screen in the DVDit! Monitor window, as show in Figure 16-11.

Adding text

Now you're ready to add text to the First Play menu. At this point, you'll probably want to create some title text. In our example, we created the text, "My First CD." Here's how to place text and a button on-screen.

1. **To add text to the First Play menu, you need to access the Text theme area.** Click the Text button (it has a *T* on it) at the bottom of the Theme palette. A list of fonts is displayed.

2. **Click a font (we chose Arial Rounded MT) and drag it to the full screen menu area.** When you release the mouse, a box appears in which you can type your text.

3. **If you need to expand the text box, click a corner and drag.**

4. **If you want to change text color, choose Effects ⇨ Text Properties.** In the Text Properties window, adjust color by clicking and dragging the color slider. Only text that is selected is altered.

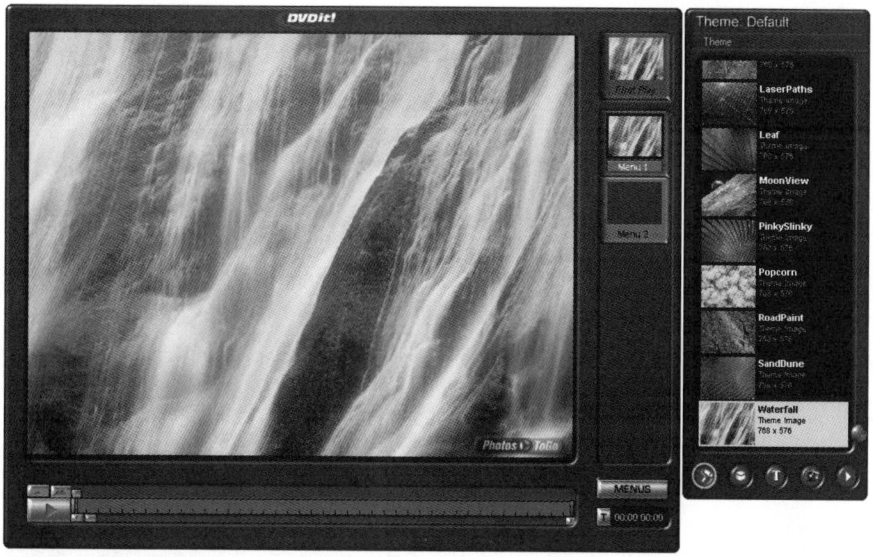

Figure 16-11: Background added to First Play menu screen

Linking to an interactive button

Undoubtedly, one of the most important features of DVD menus is to provide a home for buttons that play movies or jump to other menus. In this section, you create a simple interactive button with a link to your Premiere movie. Clicking this button plays the movie. The easiest way to create a button is to choose one from the DVDit! Theme palette. Here's how to choose a button, add it to the menu, and link it to your movie.

1. **To access the DVDit! buttons, click the button icon at the bottom of the Theme palette.**
2. **Click a button and drag it to the DVDit! Monitor window.** (We used the Blue Glassware button.)
3. **Now you must access the Theme that displays your Premiere movie.** Click the Film icon at the bottom of the Theme palette. After you click, your Premiere movie should appear.
4. **Now select the movie in the Theme palette and drag it over the button in the DVDit! Monitor window.** Release the mouse. A musical audio cue indicates the link has been made.
5. **To add audio, click and drag any audio files that you want to play as a sound track for the movie.**
6. **View the Link. If you want to be sure that the link has been created, right-click your button in the DVDit! Monitor window and choose Show Button Links.** The button disappears and is replaced by a box indicating the name to which the movie is linked. To return to Button view, right-click again on the button area and choose Hide Button Link.

At this point, you'll probably want to add some instructional text to the button.

7. **Select the text icon in the Theme palette.**

8. **Click a font and drag it over the button.** After you release the mouse, type the words that you want to appear on the button. In our example, we typed Click Here to Start, as shown in Figure 16-12.

Note

If you dragged your movie to the Movie 1 icon when the Movie Theme palette was opened, you can choose Movie 1 from a drop-down list near the Start button at the bottom of the DVDit! Monitor window. You can then link the movie to the button by dragging the chapter marker (downward pointing triangle) to the button in the DVDit! monitor window.

Figure 16-12: Interactive button with text

Previewing the DVD.

After you've finished creating your menu, you're ready to preview the DVD. To preview the DVD, you need to open the DVDit! Remote Control window

1. **To open the Remote Control window, click the Remote Control icon (right triangle at the bottom-right side of the Theme palette).** The Remote Control window opens as show in Figure 16-13.

   Notice that the time readout in the remote control window changes to indicates that the remote control window is in play mode.

2. **Test the functionality of your button by simply clicking the button you created in the DVDit! window.** Your Premiere MPEG movie starts to play.

Figure 16-13: The Remote Control window enables you to preview DVD interactivity.

Burning the DVD

After you've tested and previewed your work and find that the production runs to your satisfaction, you can burn your DVD. Before you begin the process of burning the DVD, remember that DVDit! has other features that you haven't explored. For example, you can link a menu to a button: When the user clicks the button, a new menu appears.

1. **To burn a DVD, choose Build ⇨ Make DVD Disc.** The build screen, as shown in Figure 16-14, appears.
2. **In the Make a DVD Disc dialog box, set the options for burning your DVD. For instance, select your DVD or CD-RW recorder in the Recorder pop-up menu.** Set the recording speed in the Write pop-up menu. If you want to test to see if your source materials can be written to Disc, click the Test button. If you want to test source material and then write to the disc if the test is successful, choose Test and Create Disc. Otherwise, choose Create Disc.
3. **If you are writing to a CD-RW drive, click the Include DVD Player to add DVD software to the CD-ROM.** Next, click the Advanced Tab and make sure that Enable Joliet and Use Long File Names are selected.
4. **To create the DVD, click OK.**

If you want to learn more about DVDs and other Sonic Software products, see Sonic's Web site, `www.sonic.com`. If you are creating cDVDs using DVDit!, go to the technical support page and read the white paper on cDVDs. The white paper lists the recommended hardware requirements, which include a minimum of 350 MHz Pentium and a 10x CD-ROM (or 1x DVD-ROM).

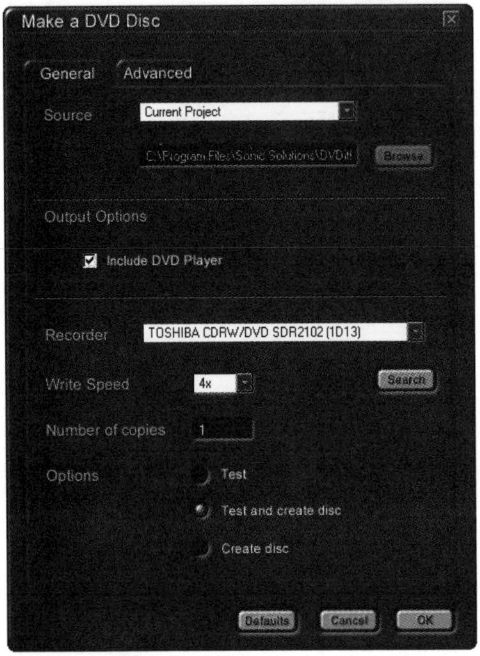

Figure 16-14: Set Build settings before burning a DVD

Summary

To view a Premiere movie on a CD-ROM or the Web or to view it on a computer system that does not have Premiere installed, you must export the Premiere file in QuickTime, AVI, or MPEG format.

- To change export settings, click the Settings button in the Export Movie dialog box.
- When exporting, you can change Video, Keyframe and Rendering, and Audio settings.
- Choosing the correct CODEC and reducing frame rates and frame size, reduces file size of the exported production.
- Windows users can create MPEG files by using Adobe MPEG Encoder. They can also create DVDs with Sonics DVDit! LE, included in the Windows package of Adobe Premiere.

✦ ✦ ✦

CHAPTER 17

Outputting to the Web and Intranets

✦ ✦ ✦ ✦

In This Chapter

Streaming or progressive download

HTML overview

Web movie file formats

Adding a digital movie to a Web page

QuickTime HTML options

Adding QuickTime tracks to Web movies

✦ ✦ ✦ ✦

If you're a video producer or Web designer, at some point, you'll undoubtedly want to show one of your Adobe Premiere video productions on your Web page, on a client's Web page, or on a company intranet. Before you start creating digital movies for the Web or intranet pages, however, it's helpful to have an idea of exactly how a browser loads a digital movie onto a Web page and what options are available to you. For instance, when a QuickTime movie is displayed on a Web page, you can have it play immediately or you can add controls to have the user start and stop the movie. This chapter provides an overview of the movie file formats for the Web as well as discusses how to add a digital movie to the Web and the QuickTime HTML options available.

Web Delivery Options

You don't need to be a Webmaster or Java programmer to play a Premiere movie on a Web or intranet page. To get started, all you need to know is a little HTML. As you'll find out from reading this chapter, movies can be displayed by using a simple HTML *embed* tag. For instance:

```
<EMBED SRC="mypremiereproject.mov", WIDTH=320,
HEIGHT=240 >
```

In this case, the name of the movie is my mypremiereproject.mov. Its frame size is 320 x 240.pixels The embed command tells the browser to load the movie from a Web server and use a plug-in to play the movie. Although this technique works, it can lead to poor playback. Unless the movie is saved so that it can stream or use progressive playback, the viewer needs to wait until the entire movie is downloaded to his or her hard drive, before he or she can view it. It's almost like having to wait for a VCR to play the program once, before you can view it. If you want to display digital movies on a Web or intranet page, you should investigate two delivery choices designed to enhance playback quality: *streaming* and *progressive download.*

Streaming video

If you can afford it, streaming is the best vehicle for delivering digital video over the Web or an intranet. In many ways streaming is similar to cable TV. You see the program as it arrives at your home or office. No portion of the file is downloaded before or during playback. Instead it is *buffered* to memory first and then displayed on-screen. Typically, the video is streamed at different data rates: a data rate for modems (narrow band connections), as well as data rates for faster connections (broadband).

Often the view clicks an on-screen button to request a data stream based upon whether they have a slow or fast connection. This "on demand" Web broadcasting comes at a price. To handle the streams of video and audio, a high-speed connection, such as T1, is required.

Furthermore, special server software is needed to stream the video. Often, the server software and video content are on a separate computer that just handles video streaming.

The three primary producers of streaming media software are Apple, Microsoft, and Real Networks. Apple's QuickTime streaming software is part of its OS X server package. Microsoft provides Windows Media server software with its Windows 2000 server package. Real Networks servers software must be purchased from RealMedia (`www.quicktime.com`; `www.microsoft.com/windows/windowsmedia/default.asp`;`www.realnetworks.com`).

Progressive download

For short video clips, progressive download often can provide a suitable alternative to streaming media. Although progressive download doesn't provide video and audio quality as high as streaming, it allows the beginning of the video clip to be played before it is downloaded. For most producers, this is key to preventing viewers from surfing away while the video downloads. However, unlike streaming media, the video is actually downloaded to the viewer's hard drive, which allows the viewer to keep a copy of the production. A further drawback: playback can become distorted if the data rate of the Web connection slows. In contrast, streaming media removes portions of the video to keep the playback consistent (often the viewer doesn't notice. To use progressive download, you don't need server software. Discreet's Cleaner 5 software allows QuickTime progressive downloading, as does Apple's QuickTime export mode, (covered in Chapter 18).

Note

For an in-depth discussion of streaming media, see www.adobe.com/smprimer. For the latest on streaming media as well as a few streaming media tutorials, check out: www.Streamingmedia.com. If you're looking for a job in the streaming media industry, click the careers link on this page.

Web File Formats

Before you begin planning to output your digital movies to the Web or an intranet, you should be familiar with the different movie file formats that can be viewed in a browser connected to the Web or an intranet. The file formats listed here all require that some form of plug-in be installed in the browser software. Saving QuickTime Windows Media and Real Video files for the Web is covered in Chapter 18.

- **QuickTime.** Apple's QuickTime format is one of the most popular Web video file formats. It is cross-platform and provides good quality. QuickTime provides numerous HTML options that can change how the movie appears on the Web. Different QuickTime tracks (discussed later in this chapter) can also be added to Web-based movies.

  Although not a requirement for Web playback, for best results QuickTime movies should be streamed by Apple's QuickTime streaming software. This software is included with Apple's Mac OS X server package.

- **Windows Media Format.** Video created in Windows media format is loaded on a Web page into Microsoft's Window's media player. Windows users can output projects in Windows Media format by choosing File ➪ Export ➪ Advanced Windows Media Export. The Windows export module creates three flavors of Windows files: ASV files are audio only, ASM files can be saved on a Web server, and ASF files must be delivered by a Windows Media server, which is part of the Windows 2000 server package. Because ASF provides high-quality output and streaming video, this format is a good choice for Windows-only intranets that must display high-quality video presentations.

- **RealVideo.** RealNetworks' streaming video format is probably the most popular format available. For true high-quality video, the RealVideo encoded movies must be created with RealNetworks streaming software CODEC. Premiere's Export Timeline ➪ Advanced RealMedia Export enables you to export Premiere movies in RealVideo format.

- **Audio Video Interleave (AVI).** All Windows computers are equipped to read Microsoft AVI files; however, because AVI is not cross-platform, it is not often used on the Web. Furthermore, Microsoft has dropped the format and replaced it with the more sophisticated, Windows Media Format. For intranets composed of Windows-only computers, AVI is a viable option for short digital movies.

Understanding HTML

If you plan to output digital video to the Web, you should have an understanding of how digital movies are loaded onto a Web page. With this knowledge, you'll be able to control how your movie is displayed and when it begins to play. Your first step is to understand how Hypertext Markup Language (HTML) can be used to load text and images on a Web page.

How a movie is loaded onto a Web page

When you see a QuickTime movie on a Web page, it appears because the HTML code instructs the browser to load the movie from a Web server. HTML is a series of text codes or tags that tell the browser what to do. Although there are numerous programs that write HTML code for you, you could construct an entire Web page using a simple text editor. For example, this HTML code snippet `<b>Web Movies</b>` tells the Web browser to put the words "Web Movies" on a page in bold type.

As an example, we created a simple Web page with a QuickTime movie on it. (See Figure 17-1.) To create the page, we used Adobe GoLive, which automatically created the following HTML instructions. (Loading a QuickTime movie into GoLive is covered later in this chapter.)

```
<html>

<head>
  <meta http-equiv="content-type"
content="text/html;charset=iso-8859-1">
  <meta name="generator" content="Adobe GoLive 5">
  <title>Web Movie Center</title>
 </head>

 <body bgcolor="#ffffff">
 <div align="center">
  <h1>WEB MOVIES</h1>
  <h1><embed src="mymovie.mov" width="310" height="348"
type="video/QuickTime" controller="false" autoplay="true"></h1>
 </div>
 </body>
</html>
```

To those unfamiliar with HTML, the code may look complicated. However, after you become familiar with the syntax, you will find HTML coding quite easy. If you scan through the code, you'll see several HTML *tags*, such as `<head>` and `<body>`. Each tag designates a specific area or formatting section in the page. Most tags begin with a word, such as `<title>`. At the end of the section, the tag is repeated with a / (forward slash) in front of it. For example, the end tag of `<title>` is `</title>`.

Here's a review of the some of the more important elements in the HTML code, shown previously:

✦ <html> This tag simply tells the browser that the HTML coding system will be used.

✦ <head> The "head" area of the page provides the browser with information concerning the character set used (within the meta tag). If scripting languages such as JavaScript will be used, this information normally appears in the "head" area as well.

✦ <title> The window title of the browser page appears within the title tag.

✦ <body> The main elements of a Web page are found within the body area. Notice that the body tag ends just above the ending </html> tag. Within the body is the information that loads the QuickTime movie.

✦ <embed> The embed tag loads the digital movie plug in. The SRC section provides the name of the digital movie that will be loaded from the Web server. The height and width sections show the width and height of the movie on the page.

The Type section tells the browser that a QuickTime movie is being loaded. Controller false tells the browser not to place the QuickTime controller. Autoplay true tells the browser to start playing the movie as soon as the page loads.

To enable the movie to be seen on the Web, the page must be named. If we name the page Index.htm, most Web servers will load this as the home page for a Web site. For the page and movie to appear, both must be copied to the Web server that hosts the Web site.

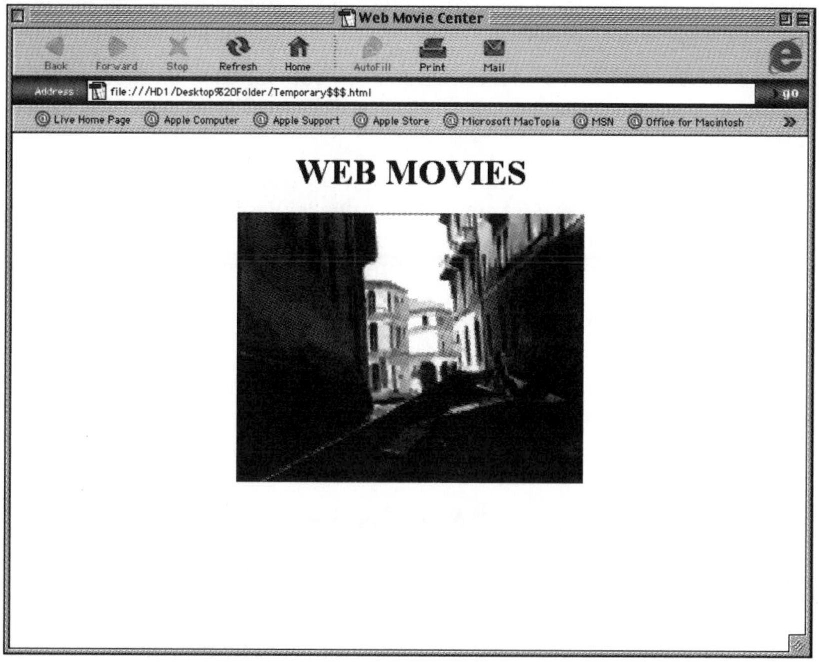

Figure 17-1: A sample Web page that contains a QuickTime movie

QuickTime settings for Web pages

Because QuickTime is the most popular digital video Web format, we've provided a list of HTML tags that enable you to customize how a QuickTime movie appears on a Web page. Many of the tags are simple true/false statements, such as `Loop=True` or `Loop=False`. These tags, described below, are easily inserted using a word processor that saves files in standard text format. However, it's easiest to insert these tags using a Web-page layout program, such as Adobe GoLive.

- `Bg color` Background color for the movie. Example: `bg color="#FF0000"` (colors are created in hexadecimal code when assigned in HTML. FF0000 displays red).
- `Cache=`**True/False.** Caches the movie. (Netscape browsers read the cache setting; Internet explorer does not.) This allows the movie to be loaded faster if the user returns to the page.
- `Controller=`**True/False.** Adds the QuickTime controller, which enables the user to start and stop the movie.
- `Hidden=`**True/False.** Hides the QuickTime movie but plays the audio.
- `HREF` Enables you to enter a clickable link. When the user clicks the QuickTime movie, the browser jumps to the specified Universal Resource Locator (URL), or Web address. (Example: `HREF=http//:myhomepage.com/Page-3.com`.)
- `Target=`**.** This option is related to the `HREF` tag. When the movie jumps to a URL, it tells the movie which frame to play in. (Note that frame is an HTML frame, not a digital video frame.) You can include a frame name or common frame tags, such as `_self`, `_parent`, `_top`, or `_blank`. (Example: `target = _ top`.)
- `Loop=`**True/False.** Plays the movie nonstop. You can also choose `Loop=Palindrome`, which plays the move from beginning to end then from end to beginning.
- `Play every frame=`**True/False.** Forces every frame to be played. If this option is activated, every frame of the movie is played. This option is usually not turned on primarily because it could slow movie playback and it could throw the sound track out of sync or turn it off entirely.
- `Scale`**.** Enables you to resize the movie. (Example: `Scale=2` doubles the movie size.)
- `Volume`**.** Enables you to control the volume. Uses values from 0 to 256. By default, the value is set to 256. To turn off the sound, use `Volume=0`.

Placing a QuickTime Movie into a Web Page with Adobe GoLive

Adobe GoLive is one of the best Web-page layout programs for QuickTime movie producers. GoLive even features a QuickTime tab, which enables you to edit the tracks of a QuickTime movie and add special effects. GoLive's palettes allow you to quickly and easily place a QuickTime movie on a page.

Following are the steps for adding a QuickTime movie to a Web page and for editing its attributes with Adobe GoLive:

1. **Create a new window in GoLive for the Web page by choosing File ➪ New.**
2. **If the Objects palette is not opened, open it by choosing Window ➪ Objects.** Click the QuickTime icon in the basic palette, shown in Figure 17-2, and drag it to the page. GoLive provides a placeholder for the QuickTime movie. The position of the placeholder determines where the movie appears on the page.

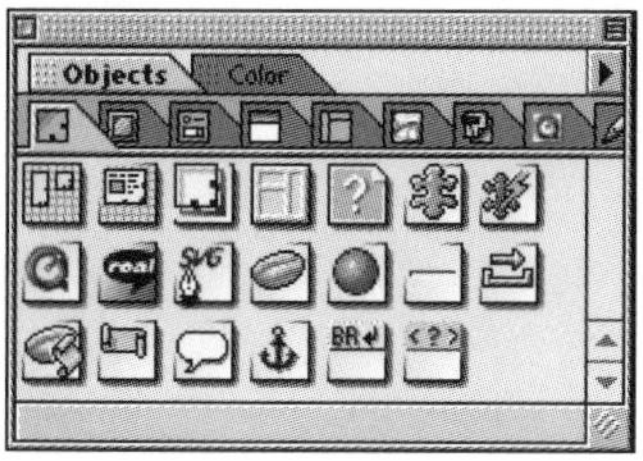

Figure 17-2: Adobe GoLive's Objects palette includes a QuickTime icon.

3. **To specify the filename and attributes, open the Inspector palette by choosing Window ➪ Inspector.**
4. **In the Inspector palette, click the Basic tab button, shown in Figure 17-3.**

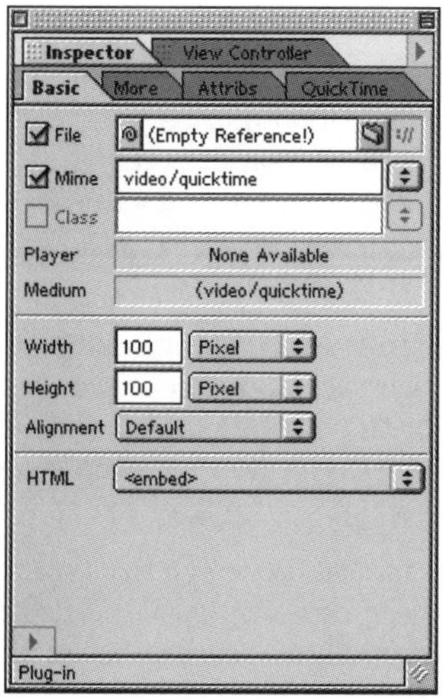

Figure 17-3: The QuickTime movie Basic tab

5. **To select the QuickTime movie you want to load, click the folder icon in the Basic tab section.** Doing this opens a dialog box in which you can choose the QuickTime movie from your hard disk. (Alternatively, if you have a Web site already designed, you can drag the Point-and-shoot icon directly to the file your Adobe GoLive site window on your computer's desktop.)
6. **After the movie is placed in a Web page, the width and height attributes are set automatically.**
7. **Click the More tab in the Inspector palette, shown in Figure 17-4.**

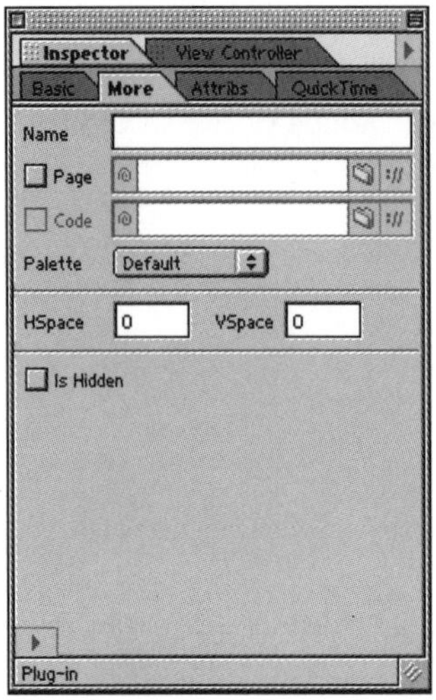

Figure 17-4: The QuickTime movie More tab

8. **If you want to enter a name for your movie (for HTML coding use only), type a name in the Name field.** The Page section enables you to designate a page from which to download the QuickTime plug-in. If you want to add padding between the movie and surrounding text, enter a value in pixels in HSpace, for horizontal space and/or VSpace, for vertical space. To hide the movie and only playback audio, click the Is Hidden button.
9. **To specify more HTML controls specific to QuickTime, click the QuickTime tab, shown in Figure 17-5.** Clicking check boxes and entering data into fields automatically creates the HTML codes for the options described. For example, clicking the Link check box and then typing **myhomepage.com/page 2** tells the browser to switch to page 2 on the Web site if the user clicks the movie.
10. **If you want to preview the movie while in GoLive, click the Open Movie button at the bottom of the tab.** When the movie appears, the Basic tab provides track, size, and data rate formation about the movie, as shown in Figure 17-6.

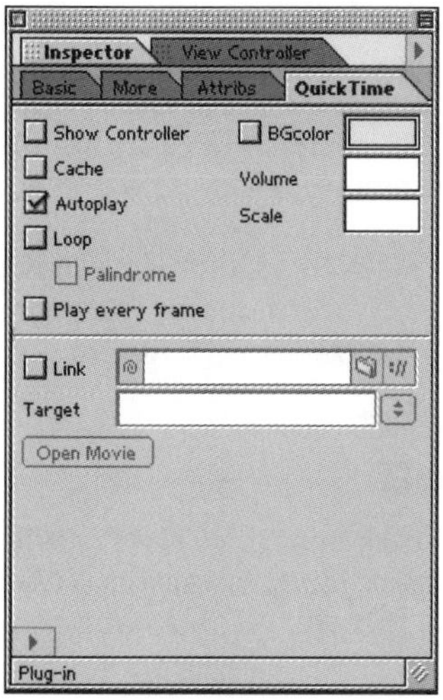

Figure 17-5: GoLive's QuickTime tab

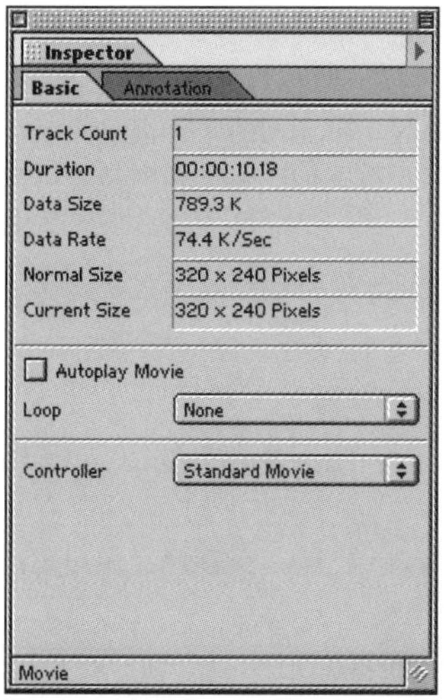

Figure 17-6: The Basic tab provides track, size, and data rate information.

Using QuickTime Tracks for the Web

QuickTime provides several hidden movie tracks that can add to the versatility of the Web and intranet movies. For example, QuickTime enables you to create an *HREF track* that can make the browser jump to another Web page at a specific point in the movie. QuickTime also provides a *chapter track*, which enables a user to click a chapter name and jump to that section of the movie. Perhaps the most unusual

QuickTime track is the *sprite track*. The sprite track enables you to add graphics and provide interactivity to the QuickTime movie. For example, by using a sprite track, you can add a button that is assigned an action to your QuickTime movie. When the user clicks the button, the action occurs, such as restarting the movie, going to another Web page, or turning up the volume.

The following sections show you how to add tracks to a QuickTime movie. The first section shows how to add an HREF track with Adobe Premiere. The sections that follow show you how to create chapter and sprite tracks with Adobe GoLive.

Creating a Web link in Premiere

Adobe Premiere enables you to add an HREF track in a QuickTime movie. Using the HREF track, you can make the users' browsers jump to another Web location while the QuickTime movie plays. In Premiere, this QuickTime feature is called a *Web link*.

You set up a Web link within Premiere using markers. Your first step is to add a marker to either a clip or a Timeline.

Before you can add a Web link to a Premiere QuickTime movie, you must add a marker to the Timeline. A marker adds a visual clue on the Timeline for specific important points in a movie. Following are the steps for adding a marker to the Timeline. (Before following these steps, you should have at least one clip in the Timeline.)

1. **Activate the Timeline window by clicking it.**
2. **If a clip is selected in the Timeline, deselect it.**
3. **Click and drag the Edit Line marker in the Timeline to move to the frame where you want to set the Web link.**
4. **Choose Timeline ⇨ Set Timeline marker and then select a number from 0 to 9.** The marker appears on the Timeline.

   Now that you've created a marker, you need to open the Marker dialog box, shown in Figure 17-7, to specify the URL you want to jump to.

5. **To open the Marker dialog box, double-click the marker in the Timeline.** In the marker dialog box, enter a URL in the Marker dialog box, such as `http://myhomepage.com/page_2.htm`. You can enter a frame in the Frame Target field if you are using HTML framesets. Frames are handy tools if you want to create an effect in which the QuickTime movie begins in one section of the Web page and then jumps to and plays in another section. To create this effect, you need to enter the name of the URL and the filename for the frame in the Frame Target area.

Note

Web links can only be created from Timeline markers. You cannot create a Web link from a clip marker.

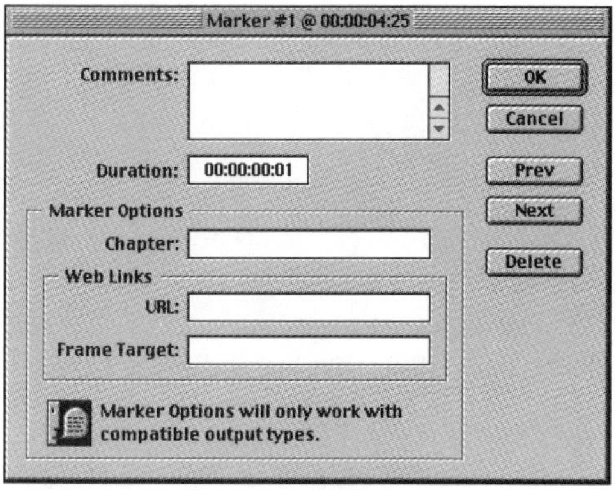

Figure 17-7: Premiere's Marker dialog box allows the movie to open a Web page at a specific point in the movie.

Using Adobe GoLive to edit and create QuickTime tracks

Adobe GoLive provides extensive support for QuickTime tracks for use on the Web. Using GoLive, you can add HREF links as well as chapter tracks and sprite tracks.

The following sections show you how to create and edit QuickTime video tracks in Adobe GoLive. Before you begin, here are the basic steps for loading a QuickTime movie and viewing its tracks so that they can be edited. (For a complete explanation of GoLive's QuickTime editing options, see the online help manual or the GoLive users' guide.)

Note

GoLive also enables you to create QuickTime movies and to add effect tracks to them.

1. **To open a QuickTime movie in GoLive to edit tracks, choose File ➪ Open.** In the Open dialog box, use the mouse to navigate to the QuickTime movie you want to open and then click OK. This opens the movie in GoLive's Preview tab.

   To edit or add tracks to use on the Web, you must view the QuickTime movie in a Timeline. (Figure 17-8 shows a Timeline with HREF, chapter, and sprite tracks.)

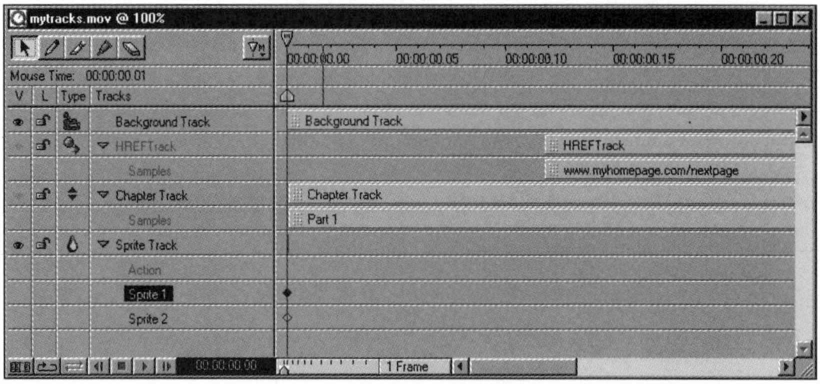

Figure 17-8: QuickTime Timeline with HREF, chapter, and sprite tracks

2. **Select the QuickTime tab in the Objects palette (Window ⇨ Objects).** The different icons that appear enable you to edit and add tracks (see Figure 17-9).

Figure 17-9: The QuickTime Objects palette with track icons

Adding an HREF track

QuickTime's HREF track can be used to create Web links. Unlike Premiere, GoLive enables you to create both clickable and nonclickable Web links.

You can use this feature in a page with HTML frames. When the movie plays, you can send it to the URL of the frame and specify that it play in the top part of a frame or in a new window.

Here's how to add a QuickTime HREF track and to specify a Web link with Adobe GoLive:

1. **To create a new HREF track, click and drag the HREF icon from the QuickTime section of GoLive's Object palette to the Tracks section of the Timeline.**

2. **Activate the New Sample tool (Pencil icon) and click the triangle next to the HREF track to open the samples track.**
3. **Create a new samples track by clicking and dragging with the New Sample tool in the blank sample HREF area of the Movie Timeline (which is beneath the background track).**
4. **Position the HREF track in the area where you want to have the Web link occur.** To shorten or lengthen the track, click and drag the edge of the track.
5. **Open the Inspector palette, shown in Figure 17-10, by choosing Window ➪ Inspector.** The time readout in the Inspector palette shows the start and stop times for the Web link action.
6. **If desired, use the Divide Sample tool to divide the track into the specific number of HREF segments you want.** (Do this only if you want to create multiple clickable links.)
7. **Select the sample area of the track that you wish to assign to the URL. In the Inspector palette enter the linking HREF.** You can use the GoLive Point-and-shoot icon to link to a Web site. If you are using frame sets, enter the frame that you want to use in the target box. You can click the Target pop-up menu to open a list of standard frame set locations, such as _top, _parent, _self, and _blank. For example, _top loads the movie into a full browser window and replaces any framesets; _blank opens the movie into a blank browser window.

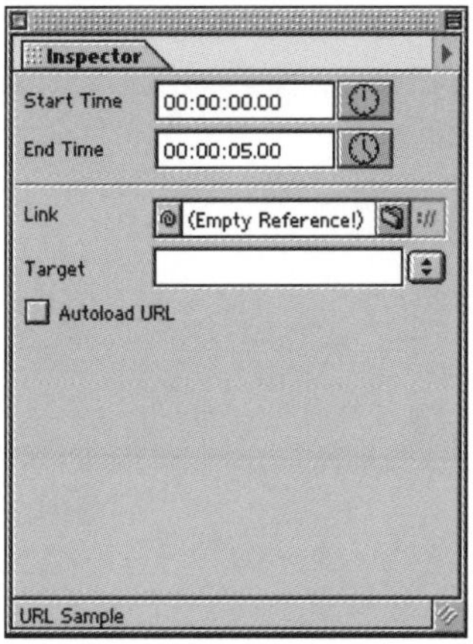

Figure 17-10: The Inspector palette

8. **If you want to have the URL load automatically so that the user does not have to click the QuickTime movie, select Autoload URL.**

Creating a chapter track

QuickTime chapter tracks enable Web page visitors to jump to different areas of a QuickTime movie. When a chapter track is created, QuickTime adds a pop-up menu with the different chapters in it. All the Web page visitor needs to do is click the pop-up menu to move to that segment of the movie.

Here's how to add a chapter track to your QuickTime movie:

1. **To create a new chapter track, click and drag the Chapter icon from the QuickTime section of the Object palette to the Tracks section of the Timeline.**
2. **Activate the New Sample tool (Pencil icon) and click the triangle next to chapter track to open the samples track.**
3. **Create a new samples track by clicking and dragging with the New Sample tool in the blank samples area of the Movie Timeline (which is beneath the background track).**
4. **Open the sample area of the chapter track and then click and drag in the Timeline area in the sample track to create the new sample.**
5. **To create multiple chapters, activate the Divide Sample tool and click along the sample track to divide it into different segments.**
6. **Choose Window ⇨ Inspector to open the Inspector palette.**
7. **Activate the Arrow Inspection tool and then select each chapter.** After you select the chapter, enter a name in the Chapter Title field in the Inspector palette, as shown in Figure 17-11. Do this for each segment in the chapter samples track.

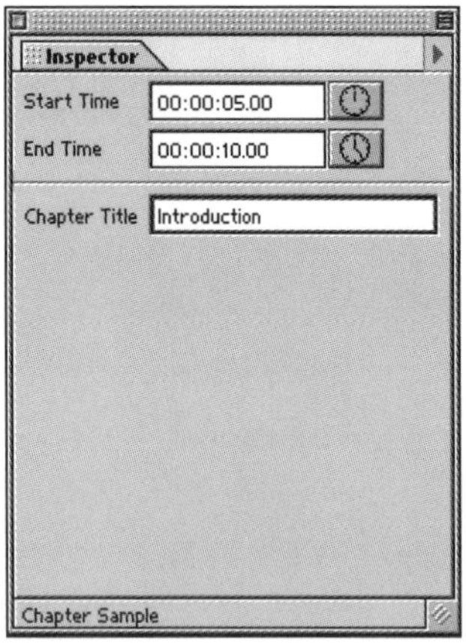

Figure 17-11: Entering a chapter name in the Inspector palette

8. **To edit the time for each track, use the Arrow tool to click and drag the position of the sample or edit the track length by clicking the edge.** As you click and drag, the time readout in the Inspector palette changes.

Creating interactivity with sprite tracks

Interactive sprites are the most sophisticated effect that you can add to a QuickTime movie in Adobe GoLive. (The term *sprite* is often used to represent a graphic or object that can be used repeatedly.) After you add a sprite track to a QuickTime movie, you can import graphics and use the graphics for added visual effect, or even as interactive buttons.

There are countless ways to use sprites and interactive behaviors. Following is a short example to give you an idea of the possibilities. This example shows you how to import a graphic into a QuickTime movie and have the image change when the user moves the mouse over it. We also show you how to assign an action to the graphic. Because creating and using sprites can be a time-consuming process, we've broken the project into three short sections.

Adding sprite tracks

1. **To create a new sprite track, click and drag the Sprite icon from the QuickTime section of the Object palette to the Tracks section of the Timeline.**
2. **If you want to rename the track, double-click it and enter a new name.**

Importing graphics

You can import graphics to use as sprites in the sprite track of a QuickTime movie. For example, you can create tiny buttons or characters that appear and disappear while the QuickTime movie plays. After the graphics are imported, you can load them into the sprite track and create interactivity. In this example, you'll import two graphics into the sprite track. However, after the graphics are added to the sprite track, they do not appear until you place them into a sprite subtrack. (Creating sprite subtracks is discussed later in this section.)

Note: You can load the following graphic formats into sprite tracks: JPEG, GIF, PICT, BMP, and PSD (Photoshop native format).

1. **Select the sprite track in the Tracks section of the Timeline.**
2. **If the Inspector palette is not opened, open it by choosing Window ⇨ Inspector palette.**
3. **Click the Images tab in the Inspector palette, as shown in Figure 17-12.**
4. **Before importing graphics, deselect multiple layers (otherwise you may import layers with nothing in them).** To import graphics, click the Import button in the Images tab. When the Open dialog box appears, select the graphics you want to add and then click Add for each graphic. Click Done when finished.

5. **Importing graphics opens the Compression Settings dialog box, shown in Figure 17-13.** If desired, change the Quality settings and the Compressor.

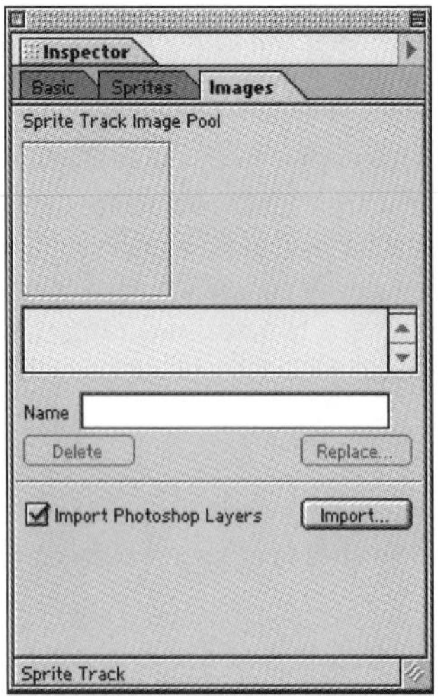

Figure 17-12: The Images tab in the Inspector palette

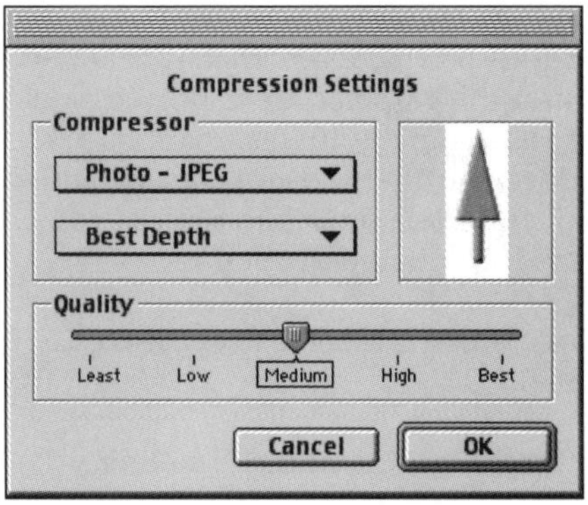

Figure 17-13: You can change compression settings in the Compression Settings dialog box.

Creating sprite subtracks

Importing sprites adds them to the Tracks sprite pool. Now they can be used as many times as desired in sprite subtracks. In a sprite subtrack, you can control sprite positioning and switch from one sprite to another.

1. **Select the sprite track in the Tracks section of the Timeline.**
2. **Click the Sprites tab in the Inspector palette.**

Note You can change the background color of the sprite track by clicking the background color check box in the Sprites tab and then clicking the color swatch. (By default, the sprite track is black.) You can also set a blending mode for the track by clicking the Basic tab In the Inspector palette.

3. **Click in the Add New Sprites field, as shown in Figure 17-14.** Enter the number of sprite subtracks that you want to add and then press the Tab key. If you want to create a simple rollover effect or a simple action, type **1**. Doing this adds a sprite subtrack to the Timeline and creates a keyframe for the sprite. (A diamond in the subtrack area of the Timeline represents the keyframe.)

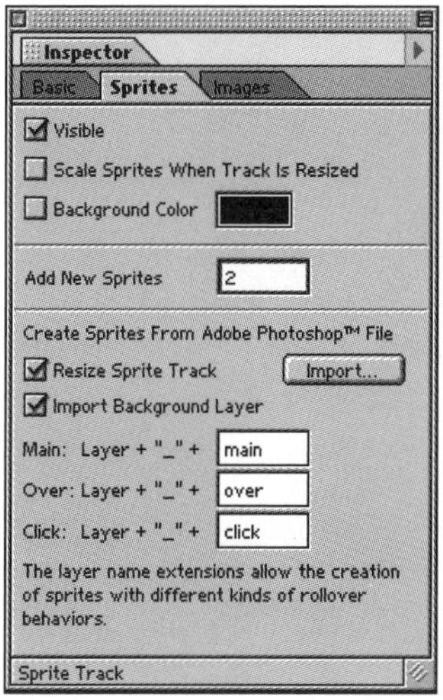

Figure 17-14: Type the number of subtracks that you wish to add in the Add New Sprites field.

Changing location and creating simple behaviors

If you want the sprites to switch sprite images or sprite positions in the subtrack as the movie plays, you must create more keyframes and then use the Inspector to switch images or locations. Here's how:

1. **In the Timeline, select the keyframe for the subtrack.**
2. **If you want to change the positions of the sprite, enter the new coordinates in the position section of the Basic tab in the Inspector palette.**

Note You can also make a sprite invisible at a keyframe by deselecting the Visible check box in the Basic tab of the Inspector palette.

3. **If you want to switch graphic images, select the image from the Image pop-up menu in the Basic tab of the Inspector palette.**
4. **To create a new keyframe, press Option/Alt, click and drag the keyframe in the Timeline track to the right, and then release the mouse.**

   After creating a keyframe, you can change images or image positions.
5. **If you want to create interactivity or a rollover effect, click in the Over swatch (for a rollover) or in the Click Inside or Click Outside boxes in the Basic tab of the Inspector palette.** Then choose the image that you wish to switch to when the mouse rolls over or clicks inside or outside of the image. A click inside effect is shown in Figure 17-15.

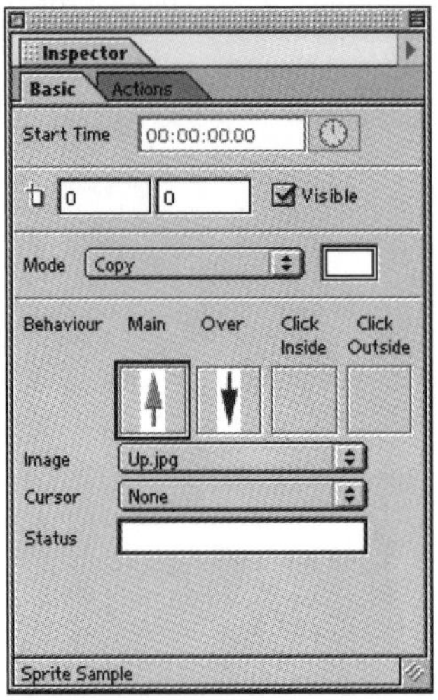

Figure 17-15: Switching images with a mouse click in the Basic tab

Assigning actions to a sprite

GoLive enables you to assign an action when the user clicks or moves the mouse over a sprite. For instance, when the user clicks a sprite you can have the movie increase volume, return to its beginning, or jump to another Web page. While assigning actions, remember that actions only occur at keyframes. Therefore, you may need to create many keyframes to give the user enough time to click the sprite.

Here's how to assign actions to a sprite:

1. **Select the keyframe where you want the action to occur.**
2. **Click the Action tab in the Inspector palette.**
3. **Choose an event in the event list, such as Mouse Down, Mouse Click, or Mouse Enter.**

4. **Click the New Action icon (which is to the left of the Trash Can icon).**
5. **In the pop-up menu at the bottom of the screen, choose an action, such as Movie Set Volume, Movie GoTo Time, or Movie GoTo Beginning, as shown in Figure 17-16.**
6. **Click the Apply button.**

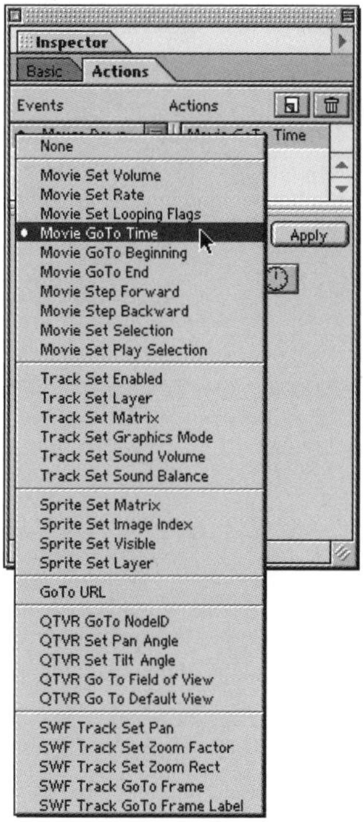

Figure 17-16: Assigning an action to a sprite

Previewing and saving your work

When you are finished creating sprites and assigning actions to them, you can preview your work by clicking the Play icon (triangle) at the bottom of the Timeline. You can also slowly preview your sprite work by clicking and dragging the Edit Line marker over the Timeline.

At this point, you can save your movie by choosing File ➪ Save. Then choose Movie ➪ Export Movie. In GoLive's Save Exported File dialog box, click the Options button to review or change the QuickTime video settings and then click OK to save the movie.

If you will be importing the movie into Premiere, see Chapter 18, which discusses how to use Premiere's Web export plug-ins.

Summary

If you will be exporting a movie to the Web or to an intranet, knowing the HTML options available to you can help you add features to your movies. A program such as Adobe GoLive can simplify the task of loading a digital movie onto a Web page and the task of writing the HTML code. QuickTime movies enable you to add many features that can be utilized on the Web, including the following:

- You can add a clickable HREF track to a QuickTime movie.
- You can add a chapter pull-down menu that appears on a Web page. When a user clicks the chapter name, the movie jumps to that section.
- You can add sprite graphics to a QuickTime movie and add interactivity.

✦ ✦ ✦

CHAPTER 18

Exporting Video to the Web

✦ ✦ ✦ ✦

In This Chapter

Using the Advanced RealMedia Export plug-in

Using Discreet Cleaner

Exporting Streaming QuickTime movies

Exporting Progressive QuickTime movies

Using the Advanced Windows Media Plug-in

✦ ✦ ✦ ✦

Undoubtedly, slow connection speeds prohibit more video streaming off the Web. For many video producers, the solution is to create Premiere projects with small frame dimensions and low frame rates. This enables home users who have modems to download the video in a reasonable amount of time.

Fortunately, Adobe Premiere provides solutions for outputting video to both the Web and to local intranets. If you are using Premiere to create video productions for the Web or an intranet, you can set the output of your movies for streaming or progressive download by using the RealNetworks Advanced RealMedia Export plug-in. (Streaming and progressive downloading are discussed in Chapter 17.) The RealNetworks package enables you to export your Premiere projects in RealVideo format. Discreet's Cleaner outputs in QuickTime format and also enables you to create files for Windows streaming media. Both packages enable you to export one clip optimized for multiple bandwidths. In other words, you can export a high-quality file to the Web or an intranet and have the plug-in create versions for users with either high- or low-bandwidth connections.

The chief advantage of many of Premiere's export utilities is that they take the guesswork out of choosing output settings. For example, when using Advanced Windows Media, choosing a preset for a 28 Kbps modem automatically chooses the best frame size and data rate for this connection. Choosing a broadband connection choice (such as DSL) produces a setting with a larger frame size, faster frame rate, and faster data rate. When you output to an intranet or the Web, the utilities discussed in this chapter can save you time and help ensure quality playback for users who view your videos.

Note

Web users will need either the QuickTime or RealMedia plug-in installed in their browser to view your video from the Web. If you are using Windows Media files, users need the Windows Media Player.

Exporting with the Advanced RealMedia Plug-in

The Advanced RealMedia plug-in from RealNetworks enables you to create digital movies in RealMedia format, one of the most popular streaming video formats used on the Web. RealMedia became popular because it was one of the first true streaming video formats. *Streaming media* enables users to watch a video program as it downloads. Before streaming media existed, Web users had to wait for the entire clip to download before the video actually started to play. When media is streamed, information packets are sent by special streaming software (in this case the RealNetworks RealVideo server), enabling the viewer to watch the video section by section as it downloads. As the data streams, the RealPlayer (or newer RealOne Player) software and the Real Media server communicate to ensure that the data is sent at the best data rate. The RealMedia plug-in enables you to create one video clip for multiple audiences. For example, you can record a clip for viewers using different modem speeds. When the clip is downloaded, RealMedia switches to either the faster stream for faster modem users or the slower stream for slower modem users.

After you've finished your production work, you can start the export process by choosing File ➪ Export TimeLine ➪ Advanced RealMedia Export. Doing this opens the Advanced RealMedia Export dialog box shown in Figure 18-1.

Specifying file details

Before choosing video quality or target audience settings, your best bet is to start by deciding whether you want to export the entire Timeline or just the work area. In the Export Range pop-up menu, choose whether you want to export the Work Area or the Entire Project.

At this point, you should also decide whether you want to change your project's frame size. You may want your frame dimensions smaller to accommodate Web users who connect to the Web at slow speeds. If so, enter the new width in the Width field. The height changes automatically, as long as you keep the Maintain Aspect Ratio check box selected.

Specifying clip settings

The dialog box's Clip Setting section enables you to specify audio and video quality.

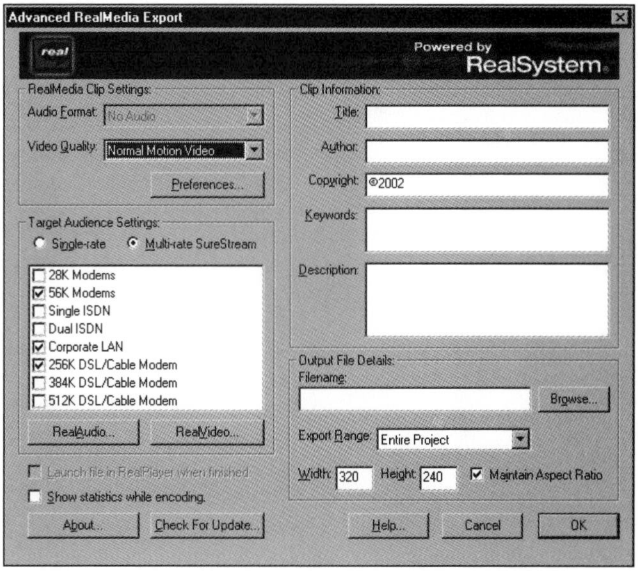

Figure 18-1: The Advanced RealMedia Export dialog box

If your Premiere movie includes audio, start by choosing an audio format from the Audio pop-up menu. The choices are self-explanatory: Voice Only, Voice with Background Music, Music, and Stereo Music.

Next, choose one of the video settings, which are described here. Choosing the correct setting helps provide better video quality.

- ✦ **Normal Motion.** Use this for clips that include some motion and stills.
- ✦ **Smoothest Motion.** Select this option for clips that feature limited motion.
- ✦ **Sharpest Motion.** Use this option for sporting events and other action clips.
- ✦ **Slide Show.** This makes your video appear as a series of still-frames.

Changing preferences

The default export settings are suitable for most projects. From time to time, however, you may wish to change these settings. To change the default settings, click the Preferences button. This opens the Preferences dialog box shown (see Figure 18-2).

The Preferences dialog box is divided into five tabs. The sections that follow describe each tab's functionality.

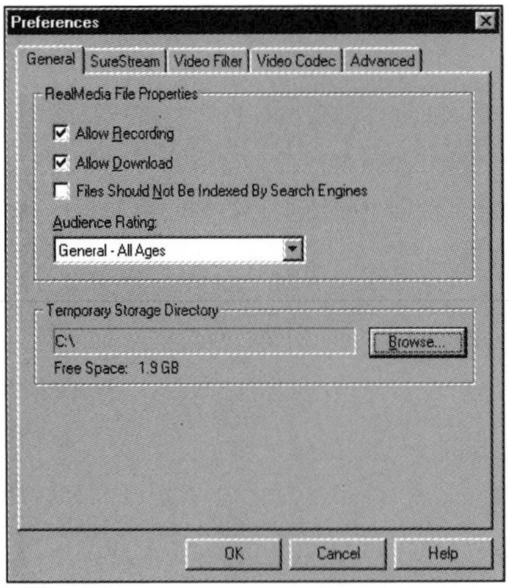

Figure 18-2: The General tab of the Preferences dialog box

General

The General tab enables you to set the following download specifications:

✦ **Allow Recording.** Select this option to enable users to save the clip on their computers, by clicking a Record button that appears in the browser. If you don't select this option, the Record button is grayed.

✦ **Allow Download.** Select this option to enable users who don't have the RealPlayer plug-in to save the clip directly to their hard drives.

✦ **Files Should Not Be Indexed by Search Engines.** If you leave this box deselected, search engines can search for your clip using the keywords specified in the Advanced RealMedia Export dialog box.

If you wish to provide a rating for your clip, choose the following from the pop-up menu:

✦ **General all ages.** Suitable for everyone.

✦ **Parental Guidance Recommended.** May not be appropriate for children 13 or younger.

✦ **Adult Supervision Required.** Audience should not include children under 18.

✦ **Adults Only.** Not appropriate for anyone under 18.

The temporary storage section provides a location where the plug-in stores temporary files before exporting the clip.

SureStream

The SureStream tab, shown in Figure 18-3, enables you to save clips in older formats, emphasize audio rather than video, or vice versa.

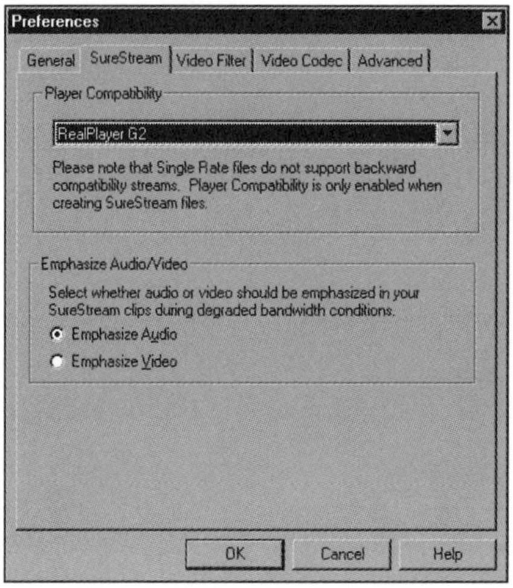

Figure 18-3: The SureStream Preferences tab

Video Filter

The Video Filter tab, shown in Figure 18-4, enables you to turn on filtering if your clips contain noise. The word *noise* refers to static or blotching that may have been produced by capture cards or cameras. Choose Filter Low Noise for low-noise situations. If your video contains much noise, specify the Filter High Noise option.

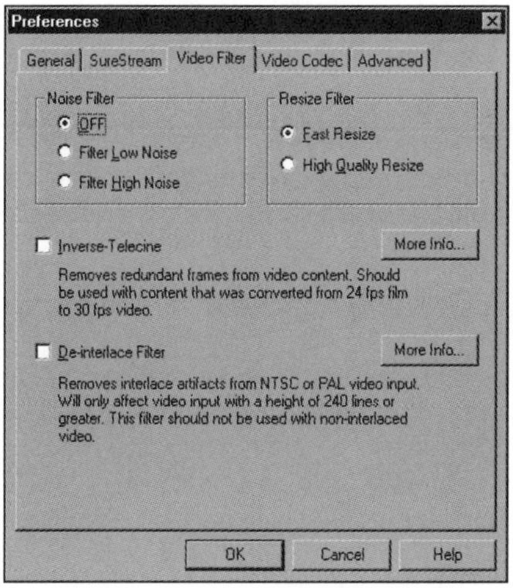

Figure 18-4: The Video Filter Preferences tab

If you choose to resize your video clip in the RealNetworks dialog box, you may want to click the High Quality Resize to produce sharper video. Using this filter slows the export processing time, however.

Video Codec

The Video Codec tab, shown in Figure 18-5, enables you to choose a compression format. By default, the RealVideo G2 with SVT is selected. This format is chosen because it is compatible with RealVideo 8.0 (the latest version) but does not require as much processing power on the user's machine. However, for the highest-quality video, RealVideo 8 is the best option. If users do not have RealVideo 8, a message appears that enables them to upgrade.

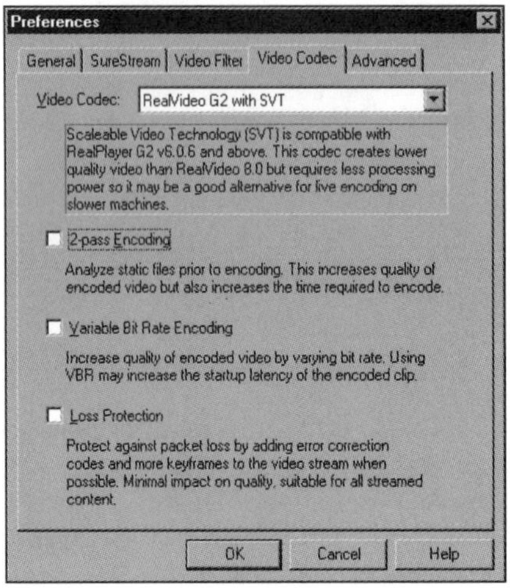

Figure 18-5: The Video Codec Preferences tab

Advanced

The Advanced tab should only be of concern to advanced users. It's best to leave these settings at their defaults, because the best settings for most users are already chosen. For example, if you lower the maximum time between keyframes too low, higher bandwidths may be needed to download the video.

Providing clip information

The clip information section of the Advanced RealMedia Export dialog box enables you to enter information into the Title, Author, Copyright, Keywords, and Description fields. (Keywords can be used by search engines to locate the clip on the Web.) The other text fields actually appear as your movie is playing. You do not need to enter any information into any of these fields.

Choosing a target audience

Before exporting your presentation, be sure to choose a target audience in the Advanced RealMedia Export dialog box's Target Audience Settings section. If you are exporting a small movie, such as one created at 15 frames per second, you may want to simply choose Single-rate, and pick one modem setting. If, however, you want to have RealMedia create different streams for different bandwidths, select the available bandwidth choices by clicking your mouse. The lowest available bandwidth option is 28K Modems; the highest is 512K DSL/Cable Modem.

Note

Bandwidth is measured in *kilobits* per second, not kilobytes. Eight bits equal one byte.

Creating the export file

When you've selected all export options and preferences for your video production, you're ready to create the export, or output, file:

1. **Click the Browse button.**
2. **Using the mouse, navigate to a folder in which to save your export file.**
3. **Type a name for your file then click Save.**
4. **Click OK in the Advance RealMedia Export dialog box.** The plug-in creates the export file with a .rm extension, which you can then send to your Web server.

Exporting with Discreet Cleaner

Cleaner creates high-quality streaming files from Premiere movies. As mentioned earlier in this chapter, streaming technology enables a digital video movie to be sent over a network in packets so that the viewer can watch the video as it downloads. Without streaming, viewers must wait for the entire production to download before they can see the downloaded video. Cleaner also presents a very efficient and quick method for both Mac and Windows users to create QuickTime Streaming and Progressive Download files. Cleaner is available for purchase online at `www.discreet.com/products/cleaner/`.

Cleaner enables you to load a digital movie on screen by simply clicking and dragging it to the program's opening Batch window. Double-clicking the filename opens the movie in the Project window, as shown in Figure 18-6. To change settings, you click one of the Edit buttons on-screen.

For files that you wish to export to the Web, click a WWW setting and then click a button labeled Continue. If you choose a QuickTime option on the next screen, you can access the streaming choices, shown in Figure 18-7, by simply clicking another Continue button.

Figure 18-6: Discreet Cleaner enables you to load QuickTime and AVI movies and choose export settings.

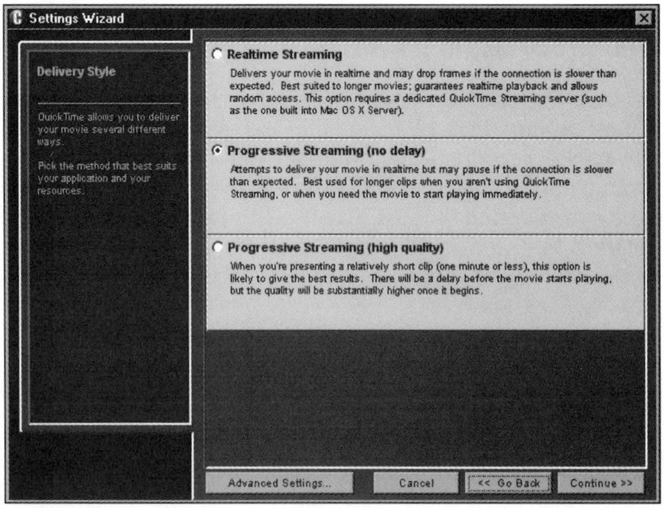

Figure 18-7: QuickTime Streaming choices presented by Discreet Cleaner

You should only use the Realtime Streaming choice if your video will be streamed by a QuickTime Streaming Server. QuickTime Streaming Server software provides faster streaming than a standard QuickTime download. It also provides random access capabilities, enabling viewers to click the mouse to jump to specific points in the video, without waiting for the entire video clip to be downloaded.

Progressive downloading enables users to view the video as it downloads, but the video quality is not as high as that of Realtime Streaming. In progressive downloading, the media file is actually downloaded to the user's hard disk, whereas in Realtime Streaming it is not. If you click Next again, you can choose alternate settings to specify the creation of different versions of the file for different viewers, as shown in Figure 18-8. Thus, you can create one high-quality video production for viewers with high and low-speed connections. Viewers with high-speed connections would see a high-quality version; viewers with lower speed connections would see a lower-quality version of the production. To export for the broadest range of connection speeds, select the 28.8k Modem, 56k Modem, ISDN (Dual), and 'Broadband' settings. (Broadband/LAN is the highest setting speed.)

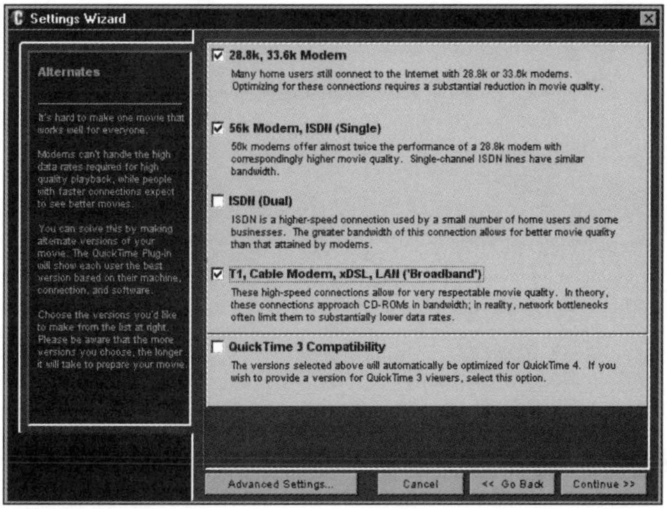

Figure 18-8: Cleaner enables you to choose alternate streaming options.

After you've clicked through the various choices, Cleaner displays a summary dialog box in which you can view all choices and change them, if needed, before exporting the file. After the file is created, you can save the file to your Web server.

Exporting with the Advanced Windows Media Plug-In

Premiere's Advanced Windows Media plug-in can output Premiere files in Windows Media format, Microsoft's newest audio and video format. A .wmv extension designates video files created in Windows Media format. WMV files can be read by Windows Media Player version 7 and higher. To use the Advanced Windows Media plug-in, choose Export ➪ Timeline ➪ Advanced Windows Media. The dialog box shown in Figure 18-9 appears. The options in this dialog box help you optimize your exported file and adjust how it appears when viewed.

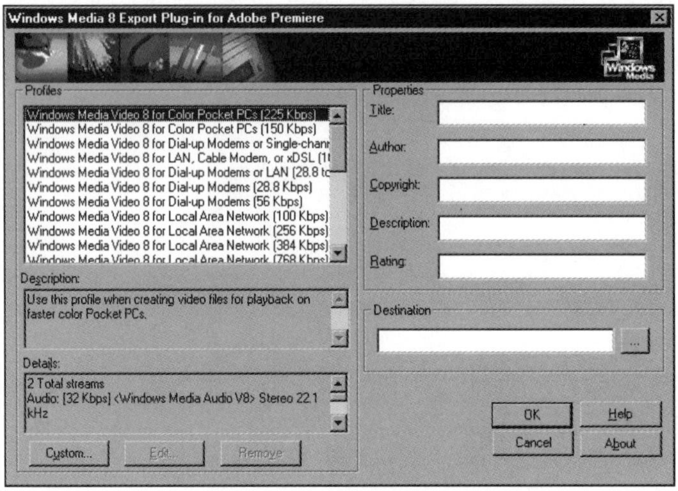

Figure 18-9: The Advanced Windows Media dialog box

Selecting a streaming profile

Before exporting a program as a Windows Media file, you must first specify a streaming profile for the file. Each profile represents a specific bandwidth or playback device. Video files designed to be played over high-bandwidth connections typically employ faster frame rates, larger frame sizes, or a combination of both. The opposite holds true for video files created for low-bandwidth transmission. When you click a profile, its description appears beneath it.

The details section of the dialog box shows how many streams will be created and at what speed. For example, if you choose settings for cable modem and DSL connections, Windows Media picks five streams. The slowest stream is 15 frames per second and a keyframe every 8 seconds, 320 x 240 pixels; on the other hand, one stream is 30 frames per second with a keyframe every 4 seconds. The data rates for the streams range from 64 to 464 kilobytes per second. Notice the data rate for 28.8

mode: 15 kilobytes per second; with a frame size of 160 x 120 pixels. If you wish to edit the stream, click the Custom button. This command opens the Manage Profiles dialog box, shown in Figure 18-10. To display information on data rate and frames per second and frame size, click the detail button. If you want to edit a stream, select it, copy it, and then type a new name for it. After renaming, you can edit the frames per second and data rate options.

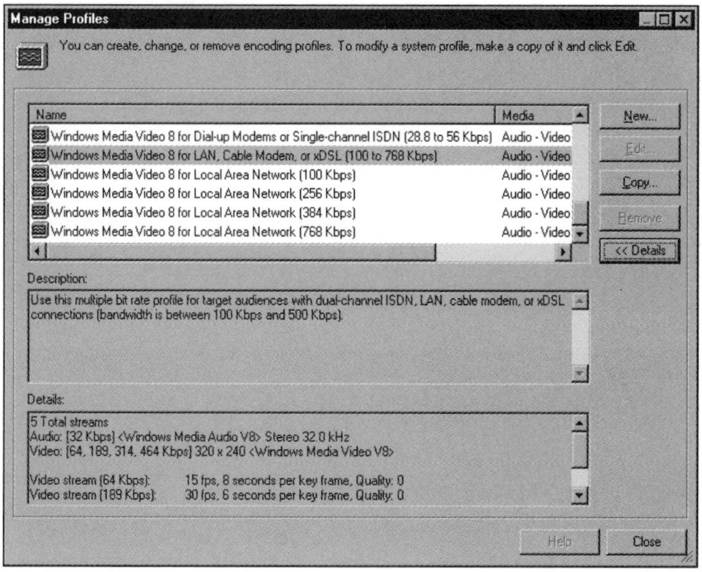

Figure 18-10: The Advanced Windows Media plug-in enables you to edit streaming parameters.

Assigning file properties

Before exporting your file, you can enter title and copyright information, if desired. You may also want to display information such as the author, rating, and a brief description. When the WMV file is loaded in Windows Media Player, the Properites information appears both in the program window and in the Properties dialog box (choose File ➪ Properties).

Creating the export file

After you've selected a profile and entered any properties for the file to be exported, you must click the Destination button (3 dots) and browse to a folder in which to save the file. Then type a filename for your file and click Save. The Save dialog box closes. Finally, to export your file as Advanced Windows Media, click the OK button in the Windows Media dialog box.

Summary

Slow Web connection speeds can make downloading digital video a time-consuming task. Premiere includes two packages that take advantage of video streaming and help optimize download times: the RealNetworks' Advanced Video plug-in and the Advanced Media Plug-in (Windows only).

- Use the RealNetworks Advanced Video plug-in to export files for different target audiences in RealVideo format.
- Use the Advanced Media Format plug-in to create streaming Advanced Windows Media files.

✦ ✦ ✦

CHAPTER 19

Exporting to Videotape and Edit Decision Lists

✦ ✦ ✦ ✦

In This Chapter

Preparing to output to videotape

Setting playback options

Outputting by using Device Control

Outputting without Device Control

Creating an EDL

✦ ✦ ✦ ✦

Despite the excitement generated by outputting video to the World Wide Web, videotape still remains one of the most popular mediums for distributing and showing high-quality video productions. Provided you have the right hardware, Adobe Premiere enables you to both export clips and complete projects to videotape.

Professionals who demand high-quality output can also have Premiere export an Edit Decision List to be used at an edit session at a video post-production facility. An *Edit Decision List*, or EDL, is essentially a text file with the timecode In and Out points of all edits in the production. After the text file is loaded into a professional editing system, the system can automatically create a final program that conforms to the edit decision list.

This chapter discusses the steps you need to take to output your Premiere files to videotape or to an Edit Decision List.

Preparing to Export Video

Two methods exist for exporting your Premiere project to videotape: You can manually control your videotape equipment during the export, or you can use device control, which enables you to start and stop a videotape recorder or camcorder directly from Premiere. If you have a DV camcorder and your computer has an IEEE 1394 port, chances are you'll be able to use device control. If you have a capture board that does not support device control, or if you have a FireWire/IEEE1394 port with equipment that does not support device control, you can start the process of recording from Premiere by manually starting and stopping your recording equipment. The following sections explain how to export to video by using both methods.

Checking project settings

Before exporting to videotape, review your production's project settings by choosing Project ➪ Project Settings ➪ General. Review the Video, Audio, and Keyframe and Rendering sections. (During the editing process, you may have lowered frame rates or frame size to speed up the previewing process.) As you view the settings in these dialog boxes, make sure that they are set to the highest quality output because Premiere uses these settings when exporting to videotape.

Note

The video settings in Premiere are explained in several chapters in this book, so we do not repeat them here. You may, however, wish to review the Fields setting option in the Keyframe and Rendering section, as shown in Figure 19-1.

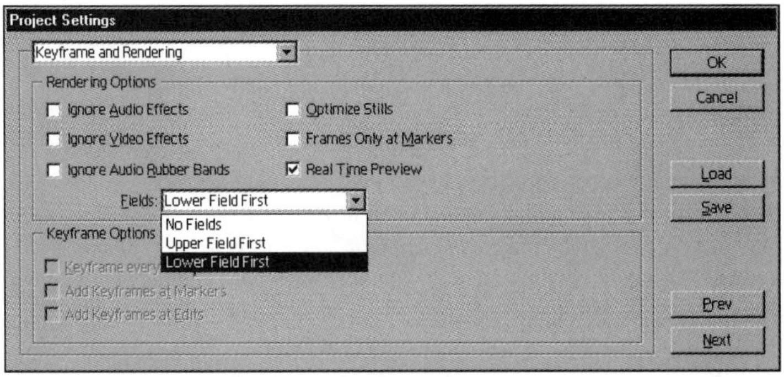

Figure 19-1: The Keyframe and Rendering options in the Project Settings dialog box

Fields are only relevant when exporting to videotape. The NTSC, PAL, and Secam standards divide each frame into two fields. In NTSC video, where the frame rate is approximately 30 frames a second(one video frame appears each 30th of a second. Each frame is divided into two fields that appear for a 60th of a second. PAL and Secam display a video frame every 25 frames, and each field is displayed each 50th of a second.

When the field is displayed, it displays alternating scan lines. Thus, the first frame may scan lines 1, 3, 5, 7, and so on. After the first field is scanned, the frame then scans lines 2, 4, 6, 8, and so on. Thus, in some respects you might conceptualize a video frame to be like a child's puzzle with the video fields being two zigzagging, interlocking pieces. If you only view one of the pieces, you don't get a sharp picture. In fact, if you could freeze a field on screen, you'd see an image with blurry lines.

When setting export settings, you can choose Upper Field First or Lower Field First, depending on which field your system expects to receive first. If this setting is incorrect, jerky and jumpy video may be the result.

Note If you don't know what order your equipment expects fields, run a quick export of a project that includes motion. Export the project set to Upper Field First and then export it set to Lower Field First. The correct field setting should provide the best playback. Use this setting when you export your video project.

Previewing at final project speed

While working in Premiere, different preview options in the Keyframe and Rendering Preferences dialog box provide different playback quality. To ensure that you view previews at final playback speed, select From Disk from the Rendering section's Preview pop-up menu.

Checking scratch disk and device control settings

Before you begin exporting your project to videotape, check that your scratch disk settings are correct and that your device control options are properly installed. Both settings appear in the Premiere program's Preferences dialog box. To open the Preferences dialog box and access the Scratch Disk and Device Control section directly, choose Edit ➪ Preferences ➪ Scratch Disks and Device Control.

In the Scratch Disk area, make sure that the Video and Audio previews are set to the correct disks. If your hardware supports device control, click the Device pop-up menu and choose the Device Control option for your equipment. (If you have digital video (DV) equipment, you may be able to choose DV Device Control 2.0.) Next, click the Options button. Doing this opens the DV Device Control Options dialog box, as shown in Figure 19-2.

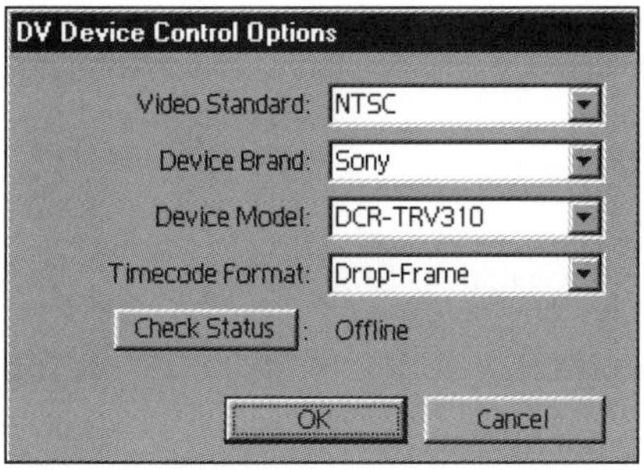

Figure 19-2: Choose your camcorder in the Device Model section.

In the DV Device Control Options dialog box, choose the correct video standard (NTSC or PAL). Choose a Device Brand and a Device Model. Next, pick the timecode format you want to use in the Timecode Format menu.

Setting playback options

After you've checked your video and device control settings, your next step is to establish playback options. The choices are different, depending upon the hardware you are using.

Digital video playback

If you are using digital video equipment, start by connecting the IEEE1394 cable from you camcorder or tape deck to your computer.

Now, set the playback to your camcorder by following these steps:

1. **Turn on your camcorder or recording device. If you are using a camcorder, make sure that it is set to the VCR or VTR setting.**
2. **To set the playback to a digital video recording device, choose Project ➪ Project Settings.** In the General dialog box, choose DV Playback in the Editing Mode pop-up menu; for most Mac users, the Editing Mode is set to QuickTime (the only choice).
3. **Click the Playback Settings button.**

If you choose DV Playback in the Editing Mode field, the DV Playback Options dialog box, as shown in Figure 19-3, appears.

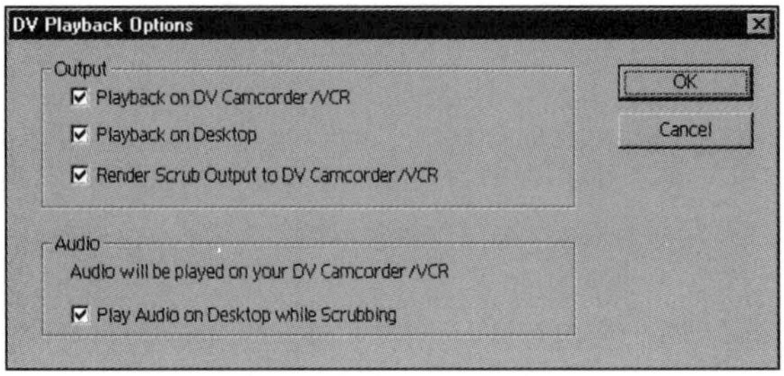

Figure 19-3: Setting Playback options to a DV camcorder or VCR

Following is a list of the options in the DV Playback Options dialog box:

- ✦ **Playback on DV Camcorder/VCR.** Select this option to play back on your camcorder or VCR.
- ✦ **Playback on Desktop.** If you wish to see the output on your desktop as well as on your camcorder, choose Playback on Desktop. (Poorer quality output may result when this option is selected.)

✦ **Render Scrub Output to DV Camcorder/VCR.** If you want to see *scrubbing* (clicking and dragging your mouse on a slider control dialog box to move from location to location in your footage) on your camcorder or VCR, select this option.

✦ **Play Audio on Desktop while Scrubbing.** Select this option to play back audio on your computer while scrubbing.

If you chose QuickTime playback, the playback options are different than the DV playback options. The options found in the Playback Settings dialog box, as shown in Figure 19-4, are these:

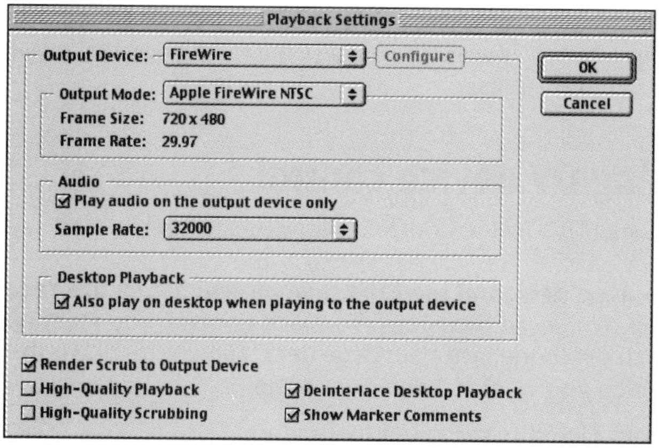

Figure 19-4: Playback Settings dialog box for DV playback with QuickTime

✦ **Output Device.** Select FireWire.

✦ **Output Mode.** Select NTSC or PAL. Frame size and Frame rate appears below. Mac users see these choices: Apple FireWire NTSC or Apple FireWire PAL.

✦ **Play Audio on Output Device Only.** Select this option to play audio on the output device only. If this option is not selected, audio plays through your computer.

✦ **Sample Rate.** Select the audio sample rate supported by your DV camera. (32 or 48khz are common sample rates. Check your equipment documentation for details.)

✦ **Render Scrub Output to Output Device.** If you want to see scrubbing (clicking and dragging you mouse in on a slider control dialog box to move from location to location in your footage) on your camcorder or output device.

✦ **High Quality Playback/High Quality Scrubbing.** Only select these items if necessary. If you select high quality, video plays back slower.

✦ **Deinterlace Desktop Playback.** This option makes image edges less blurry when playing back to the desktop. It has no effect on output.

✦ **Show Marker Comments.** This option enables marker comments to appear on output device.

Exporting with Device Control

The following sections describe how to export to videotape with device control for DV hardware and analog hardware.

Before starting the export session, make sure that you have set the DV control options in the Preferences Scratch Disks and Device Control dialog box, and that you have reviewed your video settings.

Exporting by using DV device control

To export to videotape using DV Device Control, follow these steps:

1. **Turn on your videotape deck and load the tape on which you are recording into your tape deck.** To record by using DV Device Control, you must insert a tape pre-striped with timecode into your tape deck; then write down the timecode location at which you want to begin recording.
2. **Choose File ⇨ Export Timeline ⇨ Export to Tape.**
3. **In the Export to Tape dialog box, as shown in Figure 19-5, select Activate Recording Deck.** This tells Premiere to take control of the recording device.

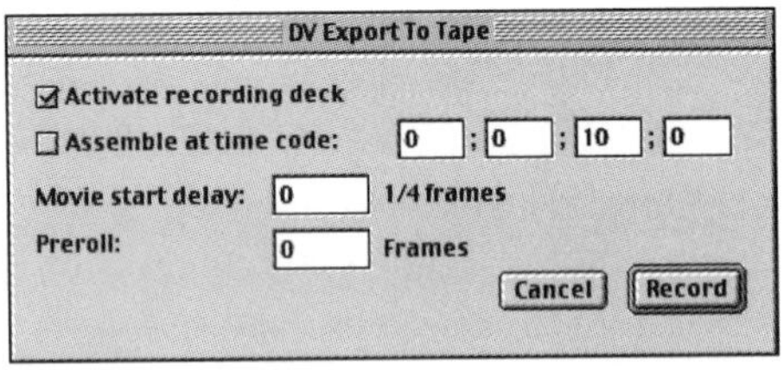

Figure 19-5: The DV Export to Tape dialog box instructs Premiere to take control of the recording device.

4. **If you don't want the recoding to begin at the current location, choose Assemble at Timecode; then enter the timecode where you want recording to begin.**
5. **In the Movie Start Delay dialog box, enter a delay in quarter frames.** (Some devices need this delay to sync the recording device with the movie after starting the recording process.)

6. **In the Preroll field, enter the number of frames you want to back up before the specified timecode.** This enables the tape to attain the proper speed before recording.

7. **Click OK.**

Exporting by using analog device control

To use device control with analog boards, choose File ➪ Export Timeline ➪ Export to Tape. In the dialog box that appears, enter the options as described by your capture board.

Exporting Without Device Control

If you wish to record your Premiere production without Device Control, you must use the Premiere Print to Video command. Print to Video plays your Premiere production centered on a television or camcorder monitor. If your frame size is smaller than the monitor, Premiere places the video against a black background. Print to Video also enables you to double the size of the frame when you export to videotape.

To Print to Video without using Device Control, follow these steps:

1. **In the Timeline window, make sure that the Work Area bar appears above the Timeline section you want to export to videotape.**

2. **Create a preview by pressing the Enter key.** The preview should appear on your DV monitor or camera. If not, review the section earlier in this chapter on Setting Playback options.

3. **Cue the tape recorder to the tape location before the area at which you want to record.**

4. **Make sure that the Edit Line is at the beginning of the Timeline. If it isn't, drag it to the beginning of the Timeline or press the Home key.**

5. **Press the Record button in your camera or tape deck.**

6. **Click the Play button in the Program Video in the Monitor window.** The Print to Video dialog box shown in Figure 19-6 appears.

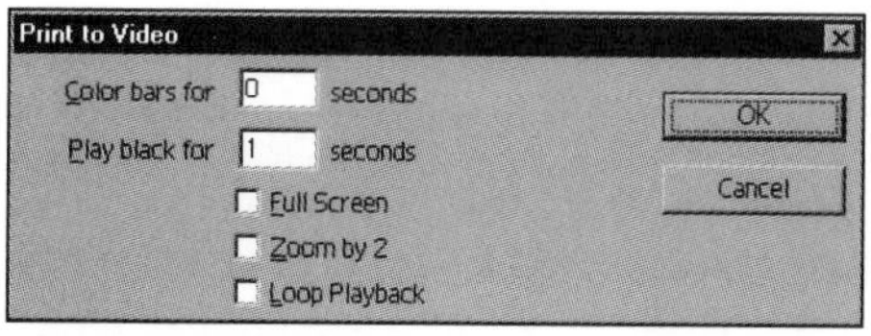

Figure 19-6: The Print to Video dialog box

7. **In the Print to Video dialog box, type in how many seconds of color bars and how many seconds of black you wish to be recorded before your video is output.**
8. **Select Zoom Screen (Macs) or Full Screen (Windows) if you wish to enlarge the frame to fill the screen.** Mac users choose Hardware from Zoom Screen if your hardware enables zooming. If not, choose Software from Zoom Screen. Windows users can choose Zoom by 2 to enlarge frame sizes smaller than 320 x 240 pixels.
9. **Select Loop Playback if you wish to have the video play back constantly.**
10. **Click OK.**
11. **To stop the playback, press the Esc key.**

Exporting an Edit Decision List

Video producers who require the highest quality video may decide to create an Edit Decision List (EDL) from their Premiere project rather than use their own equipment to export to tape. The EDL is a text-based computer file that contains the names of clips as well as the In and Out points of all edits. Premiere provides EDL translation for numerous professional systems, including CMX, Grass Valley, and Sony BVE.

If you are going to be using an EDL, it's important to realize the differences between the digital effects Premiere can provide and the effects that can be interpreted by the EDL. For example, the Premiere program's video effects and motion settings cannot be translated by the EDL. Premiere also provides many audio mixing features that cannot be exported to EDL. Nonetheless, using an EDL can be the most efficient way to conform original source material to a program you've created in Premiere. The following sections provide the steps for creating an EDL as well as information on how to translate Premiere transitions and audio settings to an EDL.

Note: If you are planning to use an EDL to create your final production, contact your production facility to discuss your project. Most systems do not accept Mac OS disks. CMX and Grass Valley systems require specially formatted disks. If you are using an NTSC system, make sure that your project timebase is set to 29.97.

Creating the Edit Decision list

After you've finished your production work in Premiere, the steps for creating an EDL are quite simple:

1. **Choose File ⇨ Export Timelines ⇨ EDL. In the EDL submenu, as shown in Figure 19-7, chose the editing system used by your production facility.**

Note: The EDL list represents plug-ins loaded from the Premiere plug-in folder. You may be able to obtain other EDL plug-ins that are Premiere compatible.

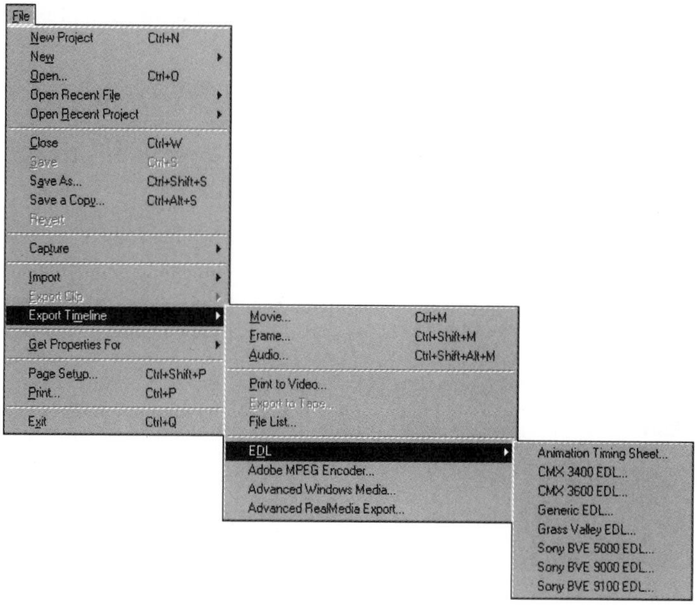

Figure 19-7: The EDL submenu

2. **In the EDL Output dialog box (see Figure 19-8), enter the specifications that describe your production.** Following are options that appear in most dialog boxes:

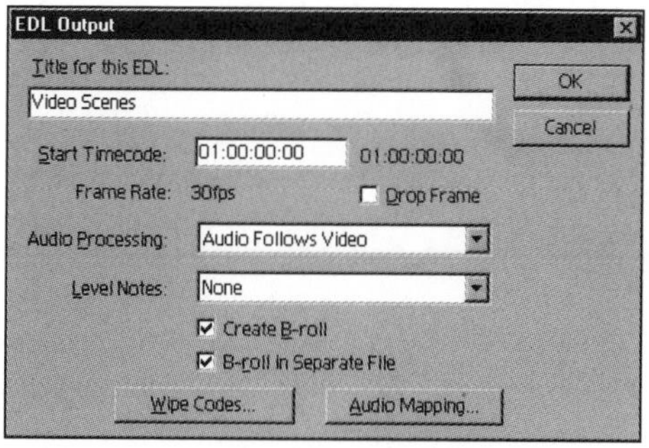

Figure 19-8: The EDL Output dialog box

✦ **Title.** Enter a title name that appears at the top of the EDL.

✦ **Start Time.** Enter the Recording reel start time in this field.

✦ **Drop Frame.** Select this check box only if you want drop frame timecode instead of non-drop frame timecode (the default). Chapter 4 describes the difference between drop frame and non-drop frame timecode.

✦ **Audio Processing.** The Audio Processing pop-up menu provides the following choices:

  - **Audio Follows Video.** Audio and video are listed as one in the EDL. (Pans and fades are not listed.)
  - **Audio Separately.** Audio is listed separately. Note that Premiere can only provide a listing that the EDL can interpret.
  - **Audio at End.** The edit list is the same as Audio Separately but appears at the end of the list.

✦ **Level Notes.** The Level Notes pop-up menu enables you to provide the following editing notes options:

  - **None.** No editing notes are provided.
  - **Audio Only.** Only notes about audio are included.
  - **Keys Only.** Provides notes about keys only.
  - **Audio and Keys.** Provides notes about audio and keys.

✦ **Create B-roll.** If the production requires footage for transitions and keys from the same source reel, a B-roll conform list is created. The production facility creates a separate video reel from the B-roll conform list.

✦ **B-roll in Separate File.** If you select Create B-roll, this option enables you to create a B-roll conform list in a separate file.

3. **Click the Wipe Code button.** The EDL Wipe Codes dialog box, as shown in Figure 19-9, appears.
4. **In the EDL Wipe Code dialog box, enter the wipe codes used by your production facility, if needed.**

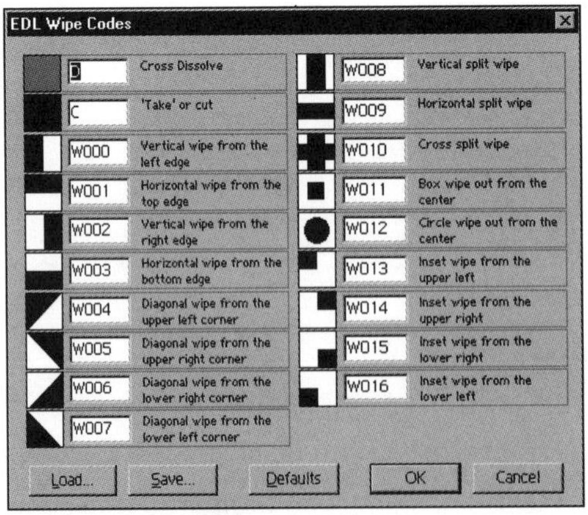

Figure 19-9: Enter the wipe codes used by your post-production facility in the EDL Wipe Codes dialog box.

5. **If desired, load a list of wipe codes from disk by clicking the Load button in the EDL Wipe Codes dialog box and click Save to save the wipe codes settings.** If you want to return to the default settings, click Defaults.
6. **Click OK to close the EDL Wipe Codes dialog box.**
7. **In the EDL Output dialog box, as shown in Figure 19-8, click Audio Mapping.** This opens the Audio Mapping dialog box, as shown in Figure 19-10.

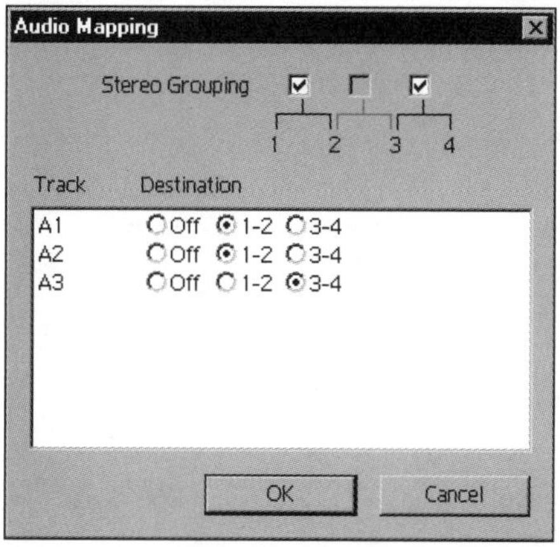

Figure 19-10: The Audio Mapping dialog box

8. **Assign Premiere audio tracks to EDL tracks in the Audio Mapping dialog box. In the dialog box, choose whether you wish to group stereo tracks in two EDL tracks. Assign Premiere audio tracks to EDL tracks. Click Off if you do not wish to output the audio track.**
9. **Click OK to close the Audio Mapping dialog box.**
10. **To save the EDL file to disk, click OK in the EDL Output dialog box.** You are prompted to supply a name for the file. If you asked to create a B-roll, you are prompted to provide a name for the B-roll as well. After you click Save, the EDL opens in a window for your review.

Note Not all options are available with every EDL choice.

Using transitions in Edit Decision Lists

The Premiere superimposition effects and many transitions cannot be directly interpreted by an EDL. For instance, the EDL describes superimposition effects as keys and only allows cuts between keys. Transitions other than cuts used in keys are dropped from the EDL. Despite these drawbacks, many Premiere transitions can be replaced by adequate EDL wipes. Table 19-1 describes the EDL transitions and some of the Premiere equivalents.

Note

In the EDL, Premiere transitions appear as notes. The transition codes are C: Cut, W: Wipe, K: Key, and D: Dissolve.

Table 19-1
EDL Translations of Premiere Transitions

EDL Wipe	***Premiere Transition***
EDL Box Wipe	Iris Cross, Iris Diamond
EDL Circle Wipe	Clock Wipe, Iris Wipe, Peel Back
EDL Cross Dissolve	Additive Dissolve, Cross Dissolve, Dither Dissolve, Curtain, Cross Zoom
EDL Cross Split Wipe	Center Merge, Center Peel, Center Split
EDL Diagonal Wipe	Page Peel, Page Turn, Radial Wipe
EDL Horizontal Wipe	Checkerboard, Random Wipe, Wedge Wipe, Zig-Zag Blocks
EDL Horizontal Split Wipe	Stretch Over, Venetian Blind
EDL Inset	Inset
EDL Vertical Wipe	Cube Spin, Pinwheel, Push, Roll Away, Slide, Sliding Boxes, Stretch, Swing In, Swing Out, Wipe
EDL Vertical Split Wipe	Band Slide, Band Wipe, Barn Doors, Doors, Sliding Bands, Spin, Spin Away, Split

Summary

Premiere provides two menu commands for outputting projects to videotape. If you are using Device Control, use File ➪ Export Timeline ➪ Export to Tape. If your hardware does not support device control, use File ➪ Export Timeline ➪ Print to Video.

✦ Premiere uses the settings in the Project Settings dialog box when outputting to videotape.

✦ If you are outputting by using an analog board, many dialog box options are specific to the hardware in your system.

✦ If you want to create an Edit Decision List, choose File ➪ Export Time ➪ EDL; then choose the editing system you are using.

✦ Most Premiere effects and motion settings cannot be translated into an EDL.

✦ ✦ ✦

CHAPTER 20

Outputting to CD-ROM and Using Macromedia Director

✦ ✦ ✦ ✦

In This Chapter

Exporting Premiere movies to CD-ROM

Creating behaviors in Macromedia Director

Using Discreet Cleaner to output to CD-ROM

Using Macromedia Director to add interactivity to Premiere movies

Importing Premiere movies into Macromedia Flash

✦ ✦ ✦ ✦

Although the number of digital movies appearing on the World Wide Web seems to grow each day, the most widely used medium for distributing digital movies is CD-ROM. Virtually every computer sold today includes a CD-ROM drive, and many sold today are at least 12 times faster than those sold just five years ago. A standard CD-ROM holds 650MB of data, usually enough space for at least 30 minutes of compressed digital video. CD-ROM disks also are among the cheapest and most durable digital media available.

Many multimedia producers who distribute their work on CD-ROM find that to truly take advantage of the medium, they need to add interactivity to their Adobe Premiere presentations. A popular interactive multimedia program is Macromedia Director. If you import a Premiere movie into Director, you can create buttons that start, stop, and rewind your Premiere movie. You can also put several Premiere movies into different Director frames and create buttons that enable the viewer to move from one movie to another.

This chapter guides you through the steps for exporting your Premiere movie to CD-ROM. The chapter begins with the steps for choosing compression settings for Premiere movies that will be exported to CD-ROM. It includes an overview of how to use Macromedia Director to create interactive behaviors to control digital movies. Because many multimedia producers will soon be moving their interactive productions to the Web, we've included a section on Macromedia Flash—undoubtedly the most popular application for creating interactive productions on the Web.

Exporting Premiere Movies to CD-ROM

Outputting Premiere movies to CD-ROM often presents the multimedia producer with a dilemma: The higher quality settings that are necessary when exporting a Premiere movie can result in poor quality playback. This problem is especially true if you export your Premiere project for viewing on older computer systems that have slow CD-ROM drives. When you export, you may need to make small compromises in quality to ensure that your Premiere movie plays back well on older systems.

Before you begin the process of exporting a movie for CD-ROM output, understanding what is involved in the process is a good idea. Here is an overview of the process:

1. **Complete all editing in Premiere.** Decide whether you want to export the entire Timeline to one movie, or export it to several movies.
2. **Select the platform.** Premiere can export in AVI or QuickTime formats.
3. **Assign Premiere export settings, including the frame size, frame rate, and compressor.**
4. **Choose File ⇨ Export Timeline to export the movie.** If you are importing your Premiere movie into Director or another multimedia program, such as Macromedia Authorware, import the Premiere movie into the program. Then complete the final production in Director or Authorware.
5. **Record the final production to a CD-ROM disk using a CD-ROM recorder.** Most Mac CD-ROM recording software enables you to partition the CD-ROM to create a Mac version and a Windows version.

Project settings for CD-ROM

When you first create a project, Premiere provides suggested multimedia presets for both QuickTime and AVI movies. The settings Premiere suggests are often used for digital movies output to CD-ROM. The settings are as follows:

- ✦ **Compressor.** Cinepak.
- ✦ **Frame Size.** 320 x 240.
- ✦ **Frame Rate.** 15.00.
- ✦ **Color Depth.** Millions.

The audio presets are as follows:

✦ **Rate.** 22050.

✦ **Format.** 16-bit mono.

When you start your project, you may decide to change the multimedia presets so that you edit using higher quality settings. For example, if you captured video at 30 frames per second, you may want to keep editing at 30 frames per second. If you captured audio in stereo at a higher rate, you may want to maintain this higher quality setting while you work. You may want to keep these higher settings particularly if you are exporting very short video movies to CD-ROM.

The downsides of working with high-quality settings are that the file size of your project is larger, and the rendering is slower. However, when you export, you can create a new movie with a lower frame rate, and, if desired, a smaller frame size, which usually results in lower video quality.

When you are ready to export your final Premiere movie to CD-ROM, you can choose your own project settings. Discreet Cleaner guides you through the process. (See the section that follows for steps on how to use Discreet Cleaner to export your movie to CD-ROM.) If you want to export to CD-ROM and choose your own settings, the steps are virtually identical to exporting your production as a digital movie, as described in Chapter 16.

Here's a summary of the steps:

1. **Complete your editing.**
2. **Choose File ⇨ Export Timeline ⇨ Movie.** If you want to export your movie at the current settings, simply name your file and click Save. If you want to change settings, click the Settings button in the Export Movie dialog box.
3. **Change settings as desired in the General, Video, Audio, Keyframe and Rendering, and Special Processing sections.** If you're exporting QuickTime movies, you may want to choose Sorenson Video, rather than Cinepak, as your compressor. Sorenson can provide higher-quality movies in smaller file sizes. (However, Cinepak is still considered the best compressor for older computers. Cinepak also allows color reduction to 256 colors, whereas Sorenson does not.) Figure 20-1 shows the Sorenson Video settings in the Export Movie Settings dialog box. One of the most import options in this dialog box is the Data Rate. The value entered in this dialog box limits the flow of data so that the video doesn't pour out at a rate the CD-ROM can't handle. Typical data rates for double-speed CD-ROM is between 200K and 250K per second. If you know that your project will be played on a 12-speed (12X) CD-ROM drive, Adobe recommends using 1.8MB/Sec; for a 24X CD-ROM, 3–3.6MB.

Note

To view a tech note on limiting data rates in Premiere from Adobe's support knowledgebase, point your browser to www.adobe.com/support/techdocs/a60a.htm.

Tip

If you reduce the number of frames per second in the Frame Rate menu, you can usually increase the data rate.

4. **When you are done editing settings in the Export Movie Settings dialog box, click OK.**
5. **In the Export Movie dialog box, name your file.**
6. **Click Save.** If you are using Cinepak compression and are exporting a long movie, the compression process may take quite some time.

Note

Mac users who don't want to deal with choosing data rate and other export options can let QuickTime handle settings. In the Video dialog box, choose QuickTime File Exporter in the File Type pop-up menu. Then click Advanced Settings. In the QuickTime Export settings dialog box, choose one of the CD-ROM choices in the pop-up menu.

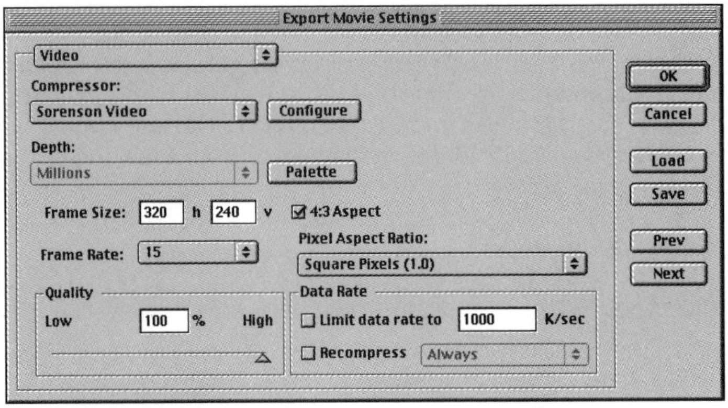

Figure 20-1: The Sorenson Video settings in the Export Movie Settings dialog box

Using Discreet Cleaner to output to CD-ROM

Although being familiar with export settings is always a good idea, some Premiere users may prefer Cleaner to walk them through the exporting process step by step.

The following steps walk you through the process of exporting a movie using Cleaner EZ:

1. **Complete all editing in Premiere.** View a final preview to make sure that all edits and effects appear as desired. If you want to export a specific area of the Timeline, edit the work area bar above the Timeline so that it is above only the area that you want to export.

2. **Choose File ➪ Export Timeline ➪ Movie.** Since Cleaner will create the final version of your file, you can export the project using your default project settings. Thus even though you are exporting to CD-ROM, you can still export using DV settings. Discreet will change the frame size and CODEC for CD-ROM output.
3. **Open Discreet cleaner, and drag the movie you created in Premiere to Cleaner's opening batch screen.** You can also add a file to the screen by choosing File ➪ Add to Batch.
4. **Double-click the file to open it on screen, then click the Edit button to the right of the word Settings.** This opens the Delivery Medium screen as shown in Figure 20-2.

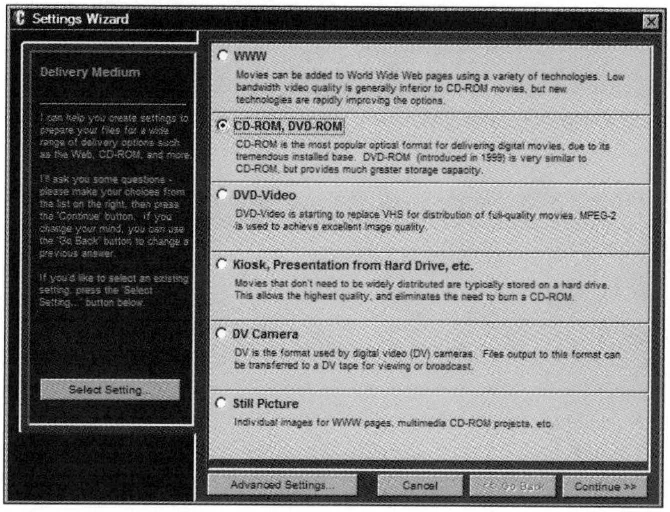

Figure 20-2: The Cleaner Delivery Medium screen

5. **Choose the CD-ROM, DVD-ROM radio button and then click Continue.** The next screen, shown in Figure 20-3, enables you to pick a target machine. By default, High-end and Midrange are selected. If you are working on a project that is to be viewed on home computers, you may want to change the settings to include low and midrange systems. Note the warning that movies compatible with low-end machines may not be high quality.
6. **Click Continue.**
7. **In the CD or DVD-ROM Speed screen (see Figure 20-4), choose the CD-ROM playback speed.** Virtually all CD-ROM drives sold today are higher than 12x speed. Many users, however, own machines with slower CD-ROM drives. When choosing a setting, note the duration of video possible at the 4x speed settings is approximately half an hour.

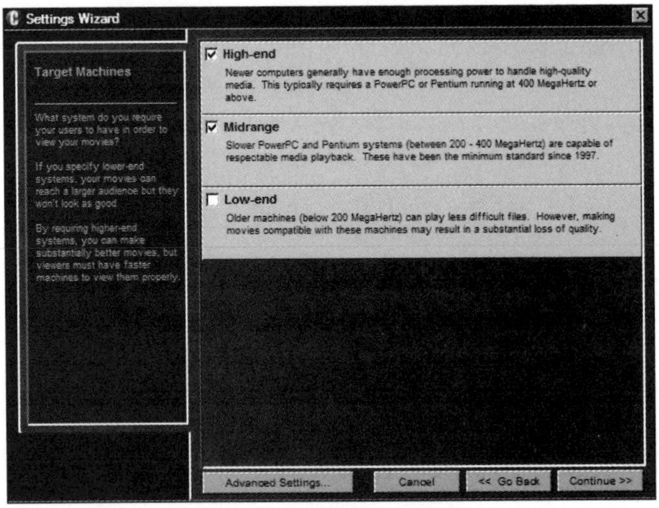

Figure 20-3: Cleaner's Target Machine Screen

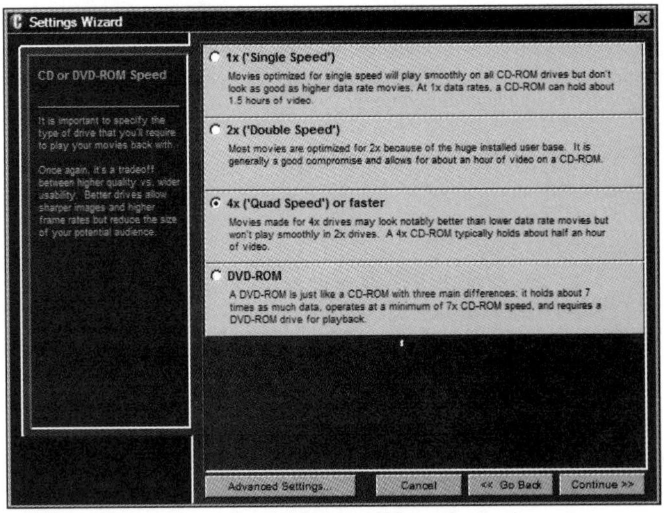

Figure 20-4: Cleaner's CD or DVD-ROM screen

8. **Click Continue.** The File Format screen appears (see Figure 20-5).
9. **Select either QuickTime or AVI formats.** The recommended format for both Mac and PC users is QuickTime; Microsoft no longer recommends the AVI (Video for Windows) format. However, you may need to import your Premiere movie into a program that only accepts AVI files. If this is the case, choose AVI.
10. **Click Continue.** The Preferences screen appears (see Figure 20-6).

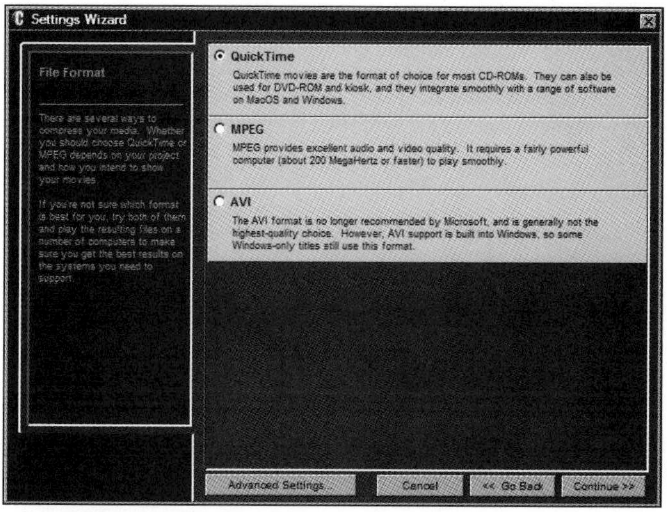

Figure 20-5: Cleaner's File Format Screen

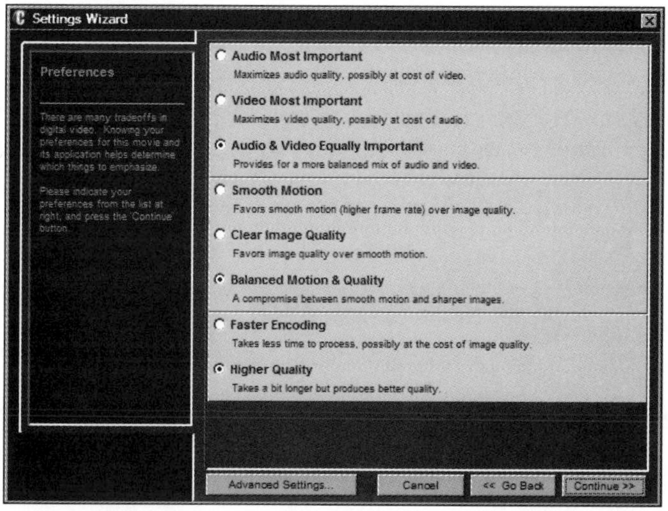

Figure 20-6: The preferences screen enables you to choose whether video or audio is most important.

11. **Specify whether audio or video is most important, or whether smooth motion is more important than image quality.** Make your choices based on the specifics of the project that you are exporting.

12. **Click Continue.** The Options screen appears (see Figure 20-7).

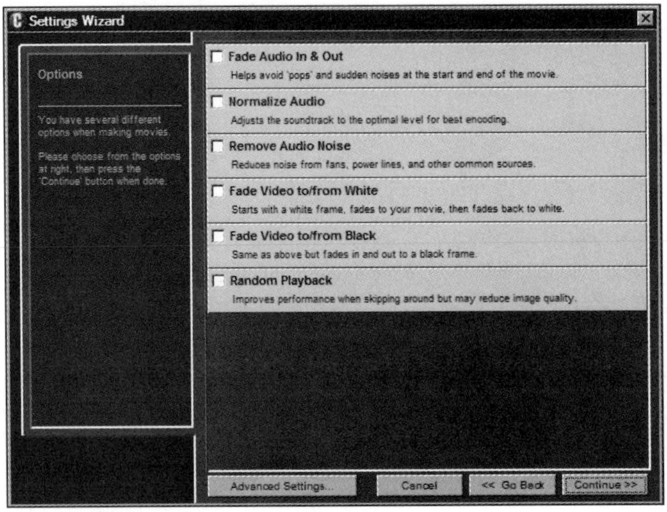

Figure 20-7: The Cleaner EZ Options screen

13. **Select from settings that improve audio.** Here, you can also choose whether to fade your movie from black or to black. Most users will probably select the first three options to help improve audio quality.

14. **Click Continue.** The final screen presents you with the video and audio settings chosen by Cleaner EZ, as shown in Figure 20-8. Note that the CODEC chosen is Sorenson, and that Cleaner has automatically chosen a frame size of 320 x 240. (We had started with a DV file whose frame size was 720 x 480.)

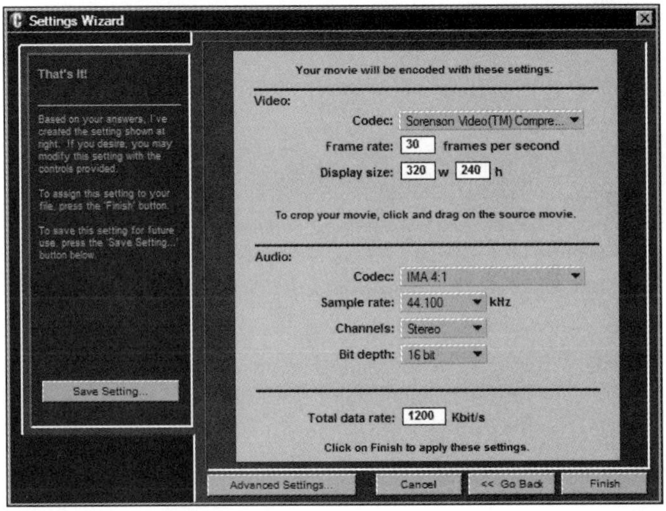

Figure 20-8: CD-ROM export settings chosen by Discreet Cleaner

15. **Click the Go Back button to change your choices or click Finish to create the movie.** If you click the Advanced Settings button, you can add further adjustments to the video. For instance, you can sharpen, blur, change hues, as well as add audio effects. After you click Finish, Cleaner begins compressing and exporting the movie for CD-ROM output.

    After the movie is created, you can record it to a CD-ROM, or you can import it into a production that will later be saved on CD-ROM, such as one created in an interactive multimedia program like Macromedia Director.

Using Macromedia Director

Macromedia Director is a powerful and widely used multimedia-authoring program. Like Premiere, Director enables you to import graphics files from such programs as Adobe Photoshop and Adobe ImageReady. It also enables you to import source images from Macromedia FireWorks and Macromedia Flash.

Although Director is often used for creating animated sequences, to Premiere users it offers the power of adding interactivity to digital movies. Unlike Premiere, Director features a powerful programming language, which is called *Lingo*. By using Lingo, you can create scripts or behaviors that enable the user to jump from frame to frame or to start and stop Premiere movies imported into Director. For instance, using both Premiere and Director you can create educational productions that enable users to choose what areas they want to learn and what video segments they want to see.

Director overview

To understand how Premiere movies can be integrated into a Director presentation, you should become familiar with the various elements of the Director interface. Director makes use of three primary screen areas: the Stage, the Score, and the Cast windows (see Figure 20-9). The *stage* is where all animation and activity take place. You might view this as equivalent to Premiere's Monitor window. The *score* is somewhat similar to Premiere's Timeline. In the Director score, each frame is represented by a tiny rectangle. Each track in Director is called a channel. All program elements imported or created in Director are automatically added to its *cast*. To start the process of creating a production, cast members are dragged from the cast window to the stage. Cast members can include graphics such as buttons, digital movies, text, audio, and behaviors.

Importing Premiere movies into Director

For Premiere users, one of Director's most valuable features is that it enables you to import and control QuickTime and AVI movies. Before you can use a Premiere movie in Director, you must first import it into the program.

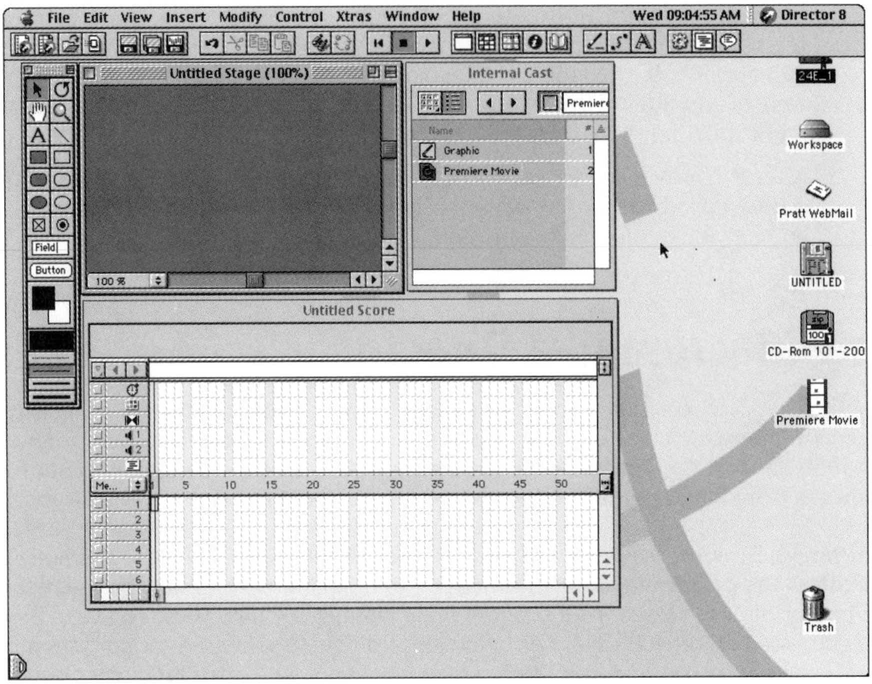

Figure 20-9: The Director Stage, Score, and Cast windows

To import a QuickTime or AVI movie into Director, follow these steps:

1. **If you have multiple casts in Director, start by selecting the cast you want to import the digital movie into, and then choose File ➪ Import.**
2. **In the Import Files dialog box, select the digital movie that you want to import.**
3. **If you are only importing one file, click the Import button. Otherwise, select another digital movie and then click Add.**
4. **When you are done adding movies, click Import.** After the movie is imported, it is loaded as a cast member in the Cast window.

Changing movie properties

Although you most likely will control digital movies in Director using Lingo, you can easily change settings that affect playback in the Cast Member Properties windows. To open the Property Inspector window shown in Figure 20-10, select the digital movie in the Cast tab and then click the Info button. The digital movie's properties window (in the Property Inspector) enables you to choose to playback both video and sound, or one or the other. Perhaps the most important choice in the dialog box is the Paused checkbox. This enables you to prevent the movie from playing as soon as the viewer enters the frame that contains the video. If you select the Paused button, you can use Lingo to have the user start and stop the movie. If you select Loop, the digital video movie plays continuously.

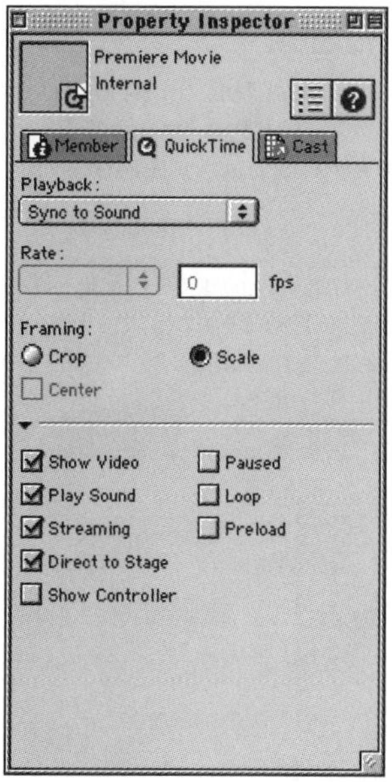

Figure 20-10: The Property Inspector window

QuickTime movies enable the QuickTime controller to appear on-screen as a device for starting and stopping QuickTime movies. Many multimedia producers choose not to show the controller, preferring to create their own interface and controlling it with Lingo.

Usually, the Sync to Soundtrack option is selected. The other choice in the pop-up menu — Play Every Frame (can result in video playing without audio. If the Director to Stage option is selected, you can place other cast members over QuickTime movies.

Placing the movie onstage

For a digital movie to be viewed in Director, it must be positioned in Director's Stage window. Before dragging the movie from the Cast window to the Stage window, most Director users select the frame that the QuickTime or AVI movie will reside in. Typically, a background and buttons are created in Director or Adobe Photoshop. After the frame in the Score window is selected, clicking and dragging the movie from the Cast window to the Score window puts the movie on that frame.

At this point, the Director producer must decide whether he or she wants the movie to play in one Director frame or if the movie should play over multiple Director frames. Projects are often easier to manage if the movie plays in one Director frame. When movies play in one frame, Director must stop its own playback head and turn the processing over to the QuickTime or AVI movie.

Pausing the playback head with the Tempo channel

If you set up Director to play a movie in one frame, you must tell Director to halt and wait for the end of the QuickTime movie or wait for a button to tell it to move off the frame. The easiest way to tell Director to wait for the end of a movie is to specify this in Director's Tempo channel.

To access the Tempo channel controls for the movie, simply double-click the Tempo channel frame directly above the movie frame. In the Tempo channel dialog box, shown in Figure 20-11, select Wait for Cue Point and then click {End} in the Cue Point pop-up menu.

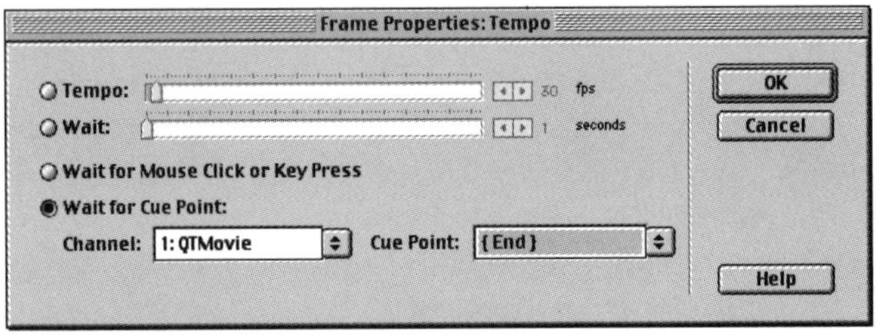

Figure 20-11: Director's Tempo channel dialog box enables you to pause the playback head while a digital video movie plays.

Pausing the playback with a behavior

Although the Tempo channel provides a quick way of stopping Director's playback head, most experienced Director users don't use it because it does not provide as much power as does Lingo. To pause the playback head while a digital movie plays, you can use a Lingo behavior instead of the Tempo channel. Fortunately, for non-programmers, Director comes packaged with prewritten behaviors. You can use a prewritten behavior to pause the playback head by dragging the Hold on Current Frame behavior from Director's Behavior Library (in the Navigation section) into the Score channel frame that appears directly above the digital movie frame. (The Score channel appears above channel 1.)

Using Lingo

Although it's quite easy to play QuickTime and AVI windows from within Director, learning a few Lingo commands to control navigation and start and stop QuickTime movies is helpful. Director provides a simple interface to get you started creating Lingo scripts. The following section shows you how to create a simple navigational script using Director's Behavior Inspector. After you learn how to use the Behavior Inspector, you can create scripts that control QuickTime and AVI moves.

Creating behaviors

Director *behaviors* are Lingo scripts that can be used to control navigation and to control QuickTime movies. After you create a behavior you can click and drag it over an on-screen object, such as a button. If the behavior includes commands for mouse events, you can program the behavior to execute when the user clicks the mouse on the object that contains the behavior.

The following are steps for creating a simple navigational behavior:

1. **Choose Window ➪ Inspectors ➪ Behavior.**
2. **To create a new behavior, click the + button, and then choose New Behavior.**
3. **In the New Behavior dialog box, enter a name for your behavior and then click OK.**
4. **To utilize the Behavior Inspector window's automatic scripting features, click the arrow in the middle of the dialog box to expand it.** The dialog box is shown in Figure 20-12.

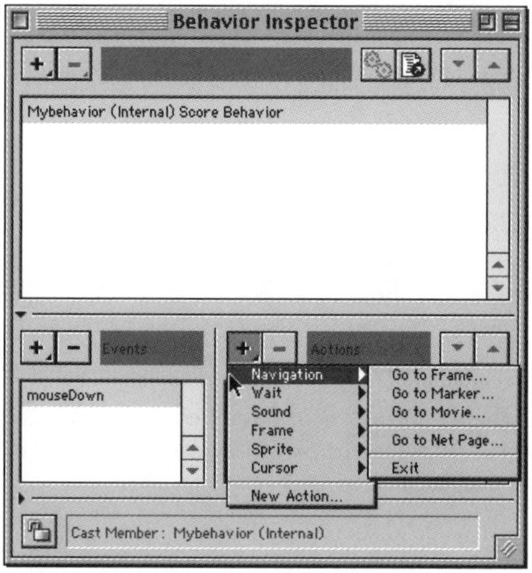

Figure 20-12: Create behaviors in the Behavior Inspector dialog box.

5. **In the Events section in the Behavior Inspector dialog box, click the + sign and choose an event to trigger your behavior.** For most button-triggered programs, choose Mouse Up or Mouse Enter. Choose Mouse Up instead of Mouse Down to enable the user to release the mouse. If a Mouse Down triggers the event, the user cannot cancel after clicking the mouse. If you use a Mouse Up event, the user can cancel the event by moving the mouse off the button before releasing the mouse.
6. **In the Actions section, select an Action category.** For example, if you are creating a navigational button, choose Navigation.
7. **In the menu that appears, pick a specific action such as Go To Frame.** If you choose Go To Frame, enter the frame number you want to go to.
8. **Click OK.**
9. **If you want to see the Lingo script that was created, click the Script window icon.**
10. **Close the Behavior Inspector window by clicking the Close box.**
11. **To use your behavior, drag it from the Cast window and release it over an object such as a button graphic in the Stage window.**

Creating your own Lingo

When you know the basics of creating behaviors, you can begin using Lingo to control QuickTime and AVI movies. Most of the Lingo that controls QuickTime and AVI movies refers to the movie by the channel the movie is in, or its cast member name or number. When you drag a movie from the Cast window to the Stage, the movie becomes know as a *sprite*. Lingo addresses different sprites according to the channel the sprite is in. Thus, if you dragged a digital video movie into channel 1, you often refer to it as *Sprite 1*.

To create your own behaviors that control QuickTime movies, you can use the Behavior Inspector dialog box to get you started and then enter the Lingo commands that control digital video movies by opening the Script Window dialog box and entering them there. The following sections review some commonly used Lingo commands that control digital video movies.

Playing movies with Lingo

If you wish to create Lingo buttons that start, stop, and reverse QuickTime movies, you can set and change the sprite's MovieRate property and the MovieRate function. The following are common movie rate values:

Play	1
Stop	0
Reverse	–1

(You can slow down the movie by setting the movie rate to .5.)

Here's a simple script that starts a QuickTime movie in Channel 3 when the user clicks the mouse on an object containing the following behavior:

```
On mouseUp
 Set the movieRate of Sdprite 3 to 1
End MouseUp
```

Or in Director 7 and above, you can use "dot syntax":

```
On mouseUp
 sprite(3).movieRate=1
End mouseUp
```

Checking movie duration

Director's `MovieTime` and `Duration` commands are more helpful Lingo utilities. Use `MovieTime` to check how much of a QuickTime movie has played. Duration measures the length of a QuickTime movie. Both Duration and `MovieTime` are measured in *ticks* (one tick equals one-sixtieth of a second), not frames. By constantly comparing the `MovieTime` property of a QuickTime movie to its duration, you can tell when the movie actually stops playing. When the movie stops playing, you can then send Director's playback head to another frame. The following Lingo is an example. A movie script that is executed when the production starts puts the duration of a QuickTime movie into a *variable* called `gmovduration`. In this example the QuickTime movie is in Director's third channel (like a video track). In Lingo this is designated as Sprite 3.

```
Global gmovduration
Put the Duration of Sprite 3 into gmovduration
```

Another script, executed when the playback head exits a frame, compares the current `MovieTime` of the QuickTime movie to its duration. If the `MovietTime` is less than the duration, then the movie hasn't ended yet. Thus, the Lingo script keeps Director playback on the current Director frame. The Lingo command "go to the frame" keeps the playback head in the current frame. When the QuickTime movie finishes, its `MovieTime` is no longer less than its duration. At this point the "go to the frame" section of the code is not executed, so Director's playback moves on to the next frame in the Director production.

```
Global gmovduration
On Exit Frame
 Put the MovieTime of Sprite 3 into myMovieTime
 If myMovieTime < gmovduration then go to the frame
End
```

You can also change the `MovieTime` of a digital movie with a script like this:

```
Set the Movietime of Sprite 3 to 360
```

The dot syntax version would be

```
sprite(3).Movietime=360
```

The above Lingo code results in the playback of the QuickTime movie jumping to the new time position you have assigned.

Changing digital movie settings

The movie settings in the Cast Properties window that controls looping and whether the movie pauses when the playback head enters the frame are easily controlled with Lingo commands.

For example, at the beginning of a movie or at a certain point in a movie, you can turn off looping with the following line of Lingo code:

```
Set the loop of member "Mymovie" =True
```

Or you can stop the movie from playing when the playback head enters the frame with this Lingo:

```
Set the PauseAtStart of Member "Mymovie"=TRUE
```

Playing a portion of digital movie

Director also enables you to start and stop a digital video movie from any point in the movie using its `StartTime` and `StopTime` commands. Using these Lingo commands, you can create a button labeled Show intro or Show interview. When the user clicks the button, only the specified segment is played. `StartTime` and `StopTime` are measured in ticks. For example, this Lingo snippet tells Director to start the digital movie one minute into the digital movie:

```
Set the startTime of sprite 1=360
```

or:

sprite(1).startTime=360

To set the stop point of the movie you could use this Lingo snippet:

```
Set the StopTime of sprite 10=720
```

or:

```
Sprite(10).stoptime=720
```

Other Lingo commands

Director includes numerous Lingo commands that work with QuickTime movies. For example, Lingo includes commands that can turn QuickTime sound tracks on and off. Lingo can determine whether QuickTime or Video for Windows is installed on a computer, and it can tell the video producer when keyframes occur. Lingo commands are well documented in Director's Lingo dictionary. However, if you are a Director beginner, be forewarned: You won't become a Lingo expert overnight.

Using Macromedia Flash with Premiere movies

Macromedia Flash is undoubtedly responsible for livening more Web pages with animation and music than any other computer application. It doesn't take many mouse clicks in a Web browser to land in a Flash-centric site. In fact, throughout the world, Flash movies appear on thousands of Web sites. Flash is used for virtually everything that moves on animated logos, full-featured cartoons, and interactive games. Many sites even use Flash to create interactive forms that post data to databases and display the results as animation. Fortunately, Premiere users can take advantage of all that Flash has to offer. The current version of Flash can import QuickTime, AVI, MPEG, and Windows Media files.

The Flash production process

Like Director, Flash is an animation program that features a powerful authoring language designed to provide interactivity that goes well beyond the simple links provided by HTML. Unlike Director and Premiere, graphics created in Flash are not based on pixels; they are based on vectors. *Vector images* are based on mathematical coordinates, not pixels. Vector images are the foundation of programs like Adobe Illustrator and Macromedia Freehand. In Illustrator and Freehand, you can click and drag the mouse to create an image; move it and bend it with ease. The image transformations are quickly processed by mathematical computations. To display the image on a computer screen, Flash renders the vector-based data to a screen image. When a Flash movie is viewed in a Web browser, the vector graphics scale to fit the user's window.

In Director and Premiere, on the other hand, a grid of pixels comprises every frame. When you change the color of a pixel-based image, you change individual pixels in the image. When you tilt or transform the image, the pixels need to be mathematically rearranged in the pixel grid. This grid-like foundation means that pixel-based image files are larger than vector-based image files and take longer to download.

To create its vector-based images, Flash features a rich set of drawing and color tools. However, if the developer needs graphics created in other programs, such as Photoshop or Illustrator, he or she can easily import them. Images are animated in a timeline interface, somewhat similar to Premiere's. Instead of video tracks, however, Flash supports a multitude of superimposition effects using layers.

When the developer is finished creating graphics and animation, and has added interactive buttons or forms, he or she "publishes" a Flash movie. Publishing creates an SWF file that can be saved to a Web server. During the publishing process, Flash can write an HTML file containing the scripting code that loads flash onto a Web page. The movie appears in a Web browser courtesy of a Flash plug-in that must be installed in the user's browser. Fortunately for Flash developers, the Flash plug-in is one of the most popular in the world. According to Macromedia, it is installed in more than 400,000,000 browsers.

Integrating Premiere Movies into Flash

Although an in-depth discussion of working with Flash is beyond the scope of this book, this section shows how you can easily import a Premiere movie into Flash and create a simple script attached to a frame that sends the movie's playback head to another frame.

To load a Premiere movie into Flash, choose File ➪ Import. After you select the movie from your hard drive, Flash enables you to choose whether to embed the movie into Flash or simply link to it (see Figure 20-13). If you want to use Flash to create another QuickTime movie, you can choose the link option; otherwise, you want to embed the movie into the Flash file for use on the Web.

Figure 20-13: Flash enables you to embed a Premiere movie into a Flash project.

After you choose to embed the movie in Flash, the Import Video Settings dialog box appears (see Figure 20-14). This dialog box enables you to specify quality settings and to synchronize the imported movie's frame rate to the Flash frame rate.

After the video is imported, it appears in the Flash timeline. You can access each of the movie's frames by clicking a frame in the Timeline. As the movie plays, you can use Flash's graphic creation and text tools to embellish your production. For example, you can add a new layer by clicking an icon in the Timeline. To keep yourself organized, name your layers. Figure 20-15 shows a QuickTime movie in a layer beneath a Text layer. (You can add text to Flash without creating a new layer.) To tilt the text, we simply clicked and dragged a text handle. Changing text styles is simply a matter of selecting the text and choosing an option from Flash's text menu. You can create simple animation just by creating a keyframe (Insert ➪ Keyframe) and moving objects that appear on stage.

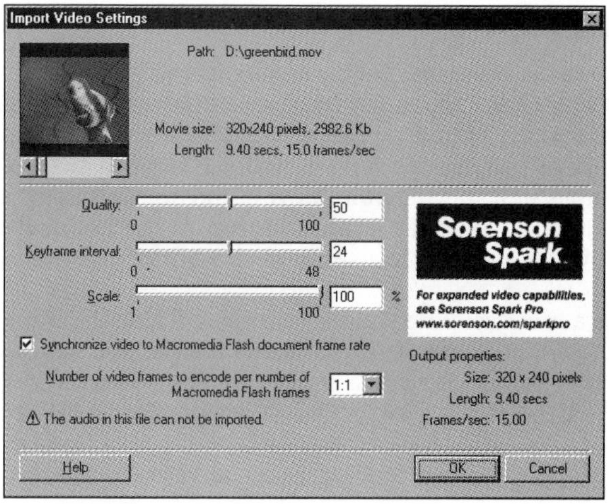

Figure 20-14: Flash enables you to embed a Premiere movie into an animated project.

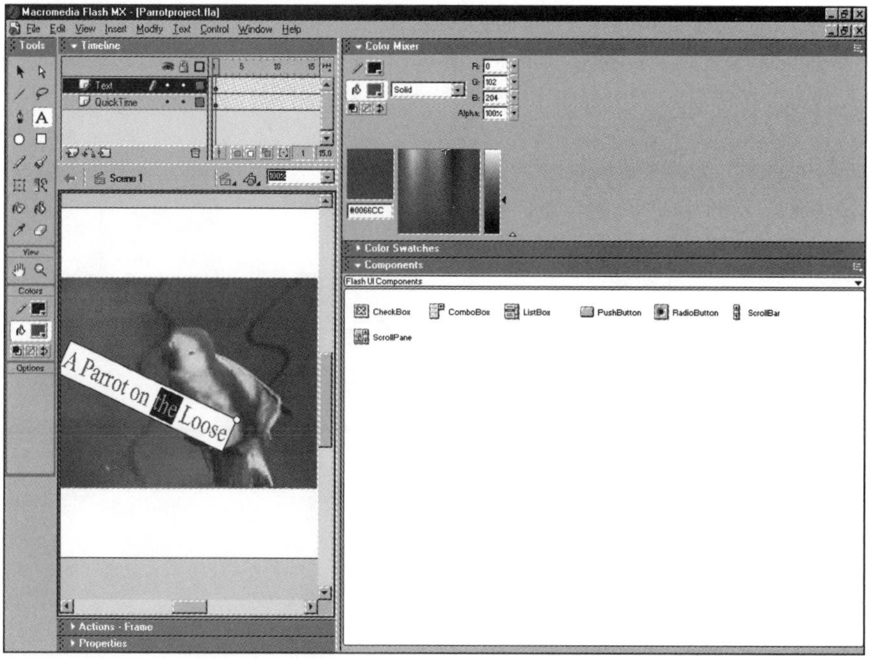

Figure 20-15: Text and QuickTime movie layer in Flash

Creating an ActionScript

Flash's ActionScript language is the key to producing sophisticated Web interactivity. If you know JavaScript, you won't have too much trouble wading into the enticing waters of ActionScript. Like Director's Lingo scripting language, Flash's ActionScript can create interactive buttons and objects on screen. ActionScript can also control how a movie plays. For example, at a specific point in your movie, you can attach a script that tells the movie to jump to a specific frame and stop. At the stopping point, you can start up another movie or wait for the user to click a button to proceed.

Attaching an ActionScript to a frame is quite simple. Start by clicking the frame where you want to trigger the ActionScript. Next, you need to open the Action window by choosing Windows ➪ Actions. To create a script that controls a movie, click the Actions icon and then click the Movie control icon. Flash displays a list of choices for your ActionScript. Figure 20-16 shows the `gotoAndStop` option chosen. You can use this script command to go to a specific frame and stop to wait for more commands.

After you've completed your Flash work, you can choose File ➪ Publish Preview to preview your work in Flash, viewing your work locally in your default Web browser.

To learn more about Flash, visit the Macromedia Web site, `www.macromedia.com`. Premiere users who want to fully explore integrating interactivity with digital video will certainly want to investigate all that Flash has to offer.

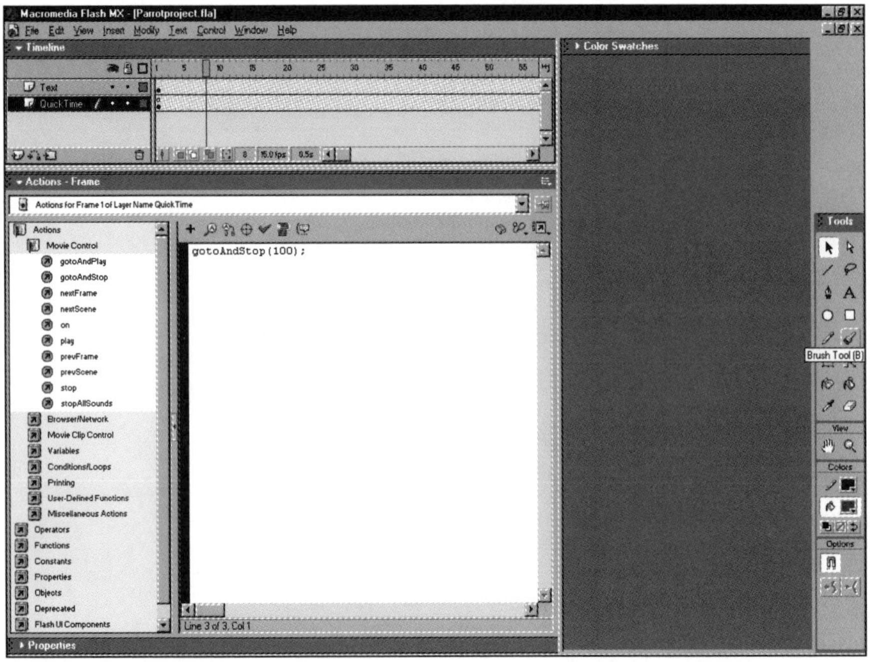

Figure 20-16: Creating an ActionScript that goes to a frame and stops

Summary

The most widely used medium for distributing digital movies is CD-ROM. Many Premiere movies are imported into interactive multimedia programs, such as Macromedia Director, before the project is saved to CD-ROM. When exporting a movie that will play on CD-ROM, your export settings should be based on the system that will be playing your movie. This chapter covered the following:

- Lower quality settings must often be used to playback digital video movies on slower systems.
- The most common compressor used for exporting digital video for CD-ROM has been Cinepak. Sorenson Video is now commonly used for exporting movies that will be played on mid- to high-end machines.
- To quickly determine the Export settings for a QuickTime or AVI movie, Mac OS 9.2 users can choose Premiere's Save for Web command. This enables you to use Cleaner EZ's Export Wizard.
- If you want to add interactivity to a Premiere movie, you can export your movie into Macromedia Director or Macromedia Flash.
- Macromedia Director's programming language, Lingo, features many commands that enable on-screen clickable buttons that can start and stop digital video movies.
- Macromedia Flash enables you to integrate Premiere movies in Web multimedia projects.

✦ ✦ ✦

Premiere and Beyond

PART

VI

✦ ✦ ✦ ✦

In This Part

✦ ✦ ✦ ✦

CHAPTER 21

Trimming Clips in After Effects

✦ ✦ ✦ ✦

In This Chapter

Trimming using the Time Layout window

Trimming using the Layer window

Exporting your After Effects work

Importing After Effects files to Premiere

✦ ✦ ✦ ✦

Adobe Premiere features a complete set of video editing tools. However, from time to time, you may need to make a few quick edits in Adobe After Effects. Adobe After Effects is another digital video editing application created by Adobe Systems. It provides certain functionality that Premiere does not, such as working with layers (discussed in Chapter 21), creating Beziér masks in the Composition window (see Chapter 24), creating motion paths, and composite projects (see Chapter 25). You can go to `www.adobe.com` for details on purchasing the product. If you import a video clip into After Effects to create masks or special effects, you may find it more convenient to change the clips' In and Out points while you work in After Effects.

Cross-Reference

See Chapter 24 to learn how to create special effects in After Effects; Chapter 25 covers creating masks in After Effects.

After you trim clips in After Effects, you can save your work as a QuickTime movie. Later you can import the QuickTime movie into Adobe Premiere for more video editing and compositing. You can also export your After Effects work as a sequence of separate graphic files. Later you can import the sequence folder into Premiere.

Many digital video producers use both Premiere and After Effects to create a project. This chapter introduces you to trimming a video clip in After Effects using the Layer Window, as well as trimming in the Time Layout window area. The chapter also shows you how to export clips from After Effects as QuickTime movies and graphic sequences.

Cross-Reference

For information on editing video clips using Adobe Premiere, turn to Chapters 5 and 10.

Trimming in After Effects: What's It All About?

In Adobe After Effects, you can use either the Layer window or the Time Layout window to trim a video clip from a Premiere project. You can trim a clip at the beginning or at the end of a video clip. When you trim at the beginning, you change the clip's *In point*. When you trim at the end of the video clip, you change the clip's *Out point*. As in Premiere, even though the In and Out points change after editing, the original In and Out points are always accessible. You can re-edit the clip at any time.

Note

When you trim the In point in the Layer Window, the clip is edited in the Time Layout window, but its starting time in the composition doesn't change. Also, when you trim a still image, only the duration of the still image changes, not the actual still image.

Creating an After Effects Project

Trimming video clips in After Effects' Time Layout window is easy. To trim a video clip using After Effect's Time Layout window, you need to have an After Effects project on-screen with at least one video clip in the Time Layout window. You can also import a Premiere project into After Effects and trim the Premiere project using After Effects Time Layout window.

Here's how to create an After Effects project and import video clips and Premiere projects:

1. **Choose File ⇨ New Project to create a new project.** You can also choose to load an existing After Effects project, or you can load a Premiere project. (If you want to import a Premiere project into After Effects, skip Steps 2, 3, 4, 5, and 6 and jump to Step 7.)
2. **Choose Composition ⇨ New Composition to create a new composition.** The Composition Settings dialog box appears (see Figure 21-1).
3. **Set the Frame Size the same size as the size of the project**. Choose a preset and notice that the Width and Height values automatically change. If you want, you can change the Frame Rate and Resolution settings. If you are working with a Premiere project that uses the Multimedia preset, select the Medium preset in the Compostion Settings dialog box.
4. **Click OK to close the dialog box.**
5. **Choose File ⇨ Import ⇨ File or Multiple Files.** Locate a video clip to use. After Effects imports the video clips and still images you are going to use in the project.

On the CD-ROM

If you want, you can follow along using any of the video clips found in the Chapter 22 folder on the CD-ROM that accompanies this book.

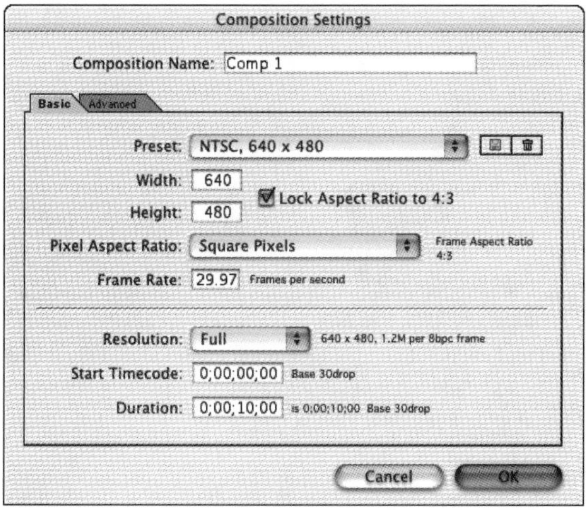

Figure 21-1: The Composition Settings dialog box enables you to set the frame size of your project.

6. **Drag the clips from the Project window to the Composition window.** The items will appear in layers in the Time Layout window. To change the order of the clips, just drag one layer above another.
7. **To load a Premiere project into After Effects, choose File ⇨ Import ⇨ File (older versions of Premiere, choose Premiere As Comp).** The Import File dialog box appears (see Figure 21-2).
8. **Locate the Premiere project you want to import.**
9. **Set the Import As menu to Composition.**
10. **Click Import.** After Effects imports the Premiere project, which appears in the After Effects Project window.
11. **Double-click the Premiere project Composition file to display the Composition window and the Time Layout window.** The Time Layout window appears with layers. The layers are the video and sound tracks from the Premiere project as seen in Figure 21-3.

On the CD-ROM

You may want to follow along using the Premiere project found in the Chapter 22 folder on this book's companion CD-ROM. The Premiere project video clips are from Digital Vision's City Mix collection file; 567012p.mov, 567006p.mov, and 567019p.mov, and Digital Vision's Track 32.cdda from City Life/Urban Moods collection.

Note

You can also load a Photoshop layered file into After Effects by choosing File ⇨ Import ⇨ File (older versions of Photoshop, choose Photoshop As Comp). In the Import File dialog box, choose a file and then set the Import As menu to Composition. For more information on working with Photoshop, turn to Chapter 22.

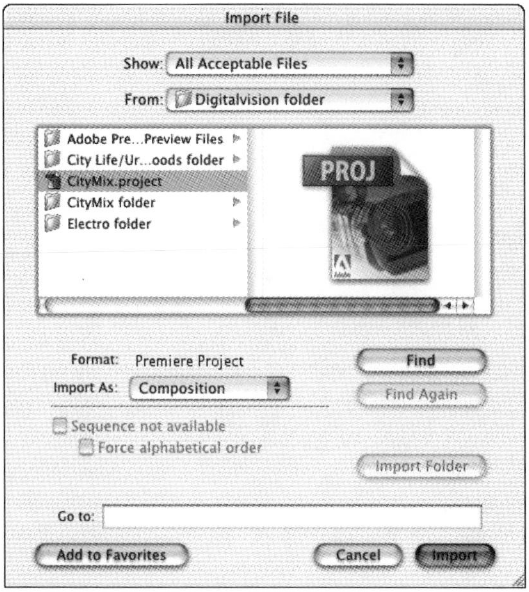

Figure 21-2: To import a Premiere project into After Effects, set the Import As menu to Composition in the Import File dialog box.

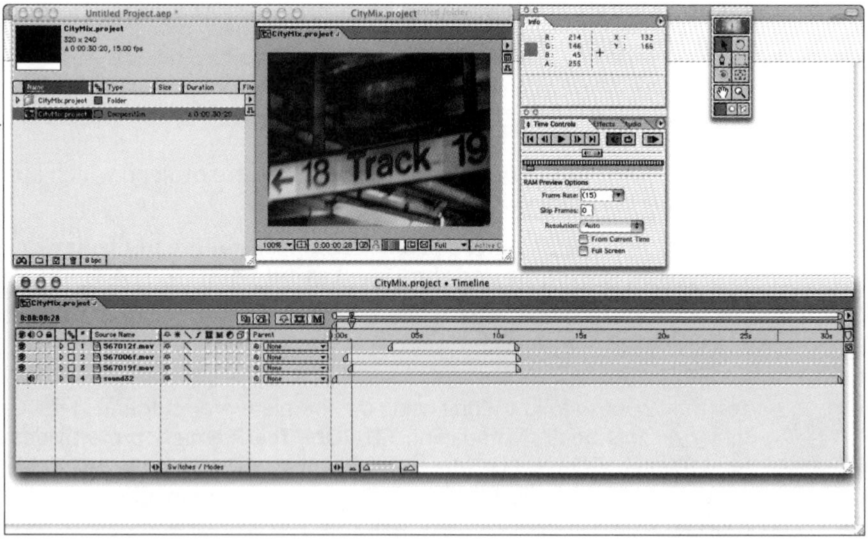

Figure 21-3: The Time Layout window with video and sound clips from a Premiere project created using Digital Vision royalty-free stock clips. The Premiere project is included on the CD-ROM that accompanies this book.

Trimming Using the Time Layout Window

When you have an After Effects project with the items you need in the Time Layout window, you can trim them using the Time Layout window. Trimming using the Time Layout window is easy. You can trim using the Time Layout window by either dragging the In and Out point in the layer duration bar or by using the current-time marker.

Trimming with the layer duration bar

A video clip's duration in the Time Layout window is displayed as a layer duration bar (see Figure 21-4). Here's how to trim using the layer duration bar:

- **To trim the In point.** Click at the beginning of a clip and drag to the right to change the In point and to trim the video clip.
- **To trim the Out point.** Click at the end of a clip and drag to the left to change the Out point and to trim the video clip.

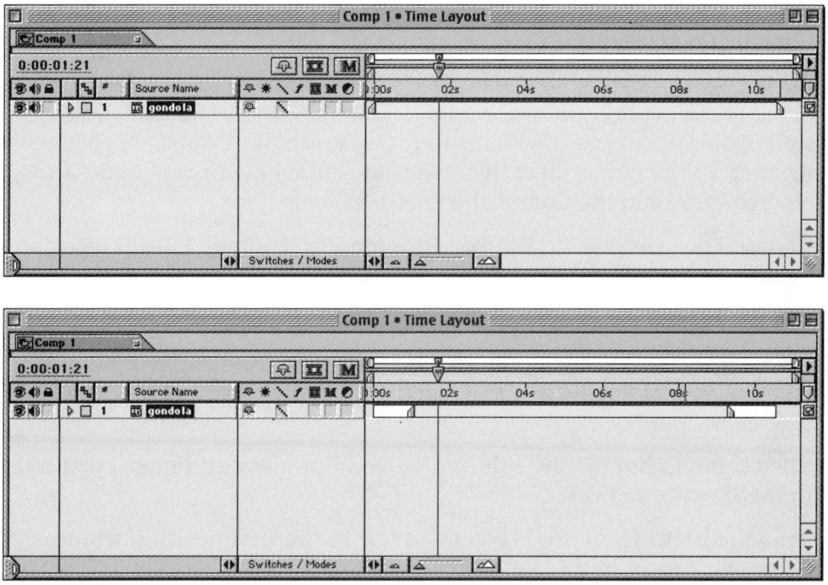

Figure 21-4: Trimming the In point and Out point with the Time Layout window

Trimming with the current-time marker

Follow these steps to trim a clip at the current-time marker:

1. **Click the layer in which your video clip resides.**
2. **Move the current time marker to the point you want to trim.**

3. **Trim the In or Out point:**
   - To trim the In point, press Option/Alt + [.
   - To trim the Out point, press Option/Alt +].

Trimming Using the Layer Window

Trimming in the After Effects Layer window is similar to trimming in Premiere's Clip window except that trimming a clip's In point in the Layer window doesn't affect the clip's relative starting position in the Time Layout window. In other words, no gap appears in front of it when you remove frames from the clip's In point.

Here's how to trim using the Layer window:

1. **Choose File ⇨ New Project to create a new project. You can also choose to load a project.** If you want to import a Premiere project into After Effects, skip Steps 2, 3, and 4 and jump to Step 5.
2. **Choose Composition ⇨ New Composition to create a new composition.** The Composition Settings dialog box appears.
3. **Set the Frame Size to be the same size as the size of the project.** Choose a preset, noticing that the Width and Height values automatically change. If you want, you can change the Frame Rate and Resolution values. If you are working with a Premiere project that uses the Multimedia preset, choose the Medium preset in the Compostion Settings dialog box.
4. **Choose File ⇨ Import ⇨ Multiple Files (choose Footage Files if using an older version of Premiere).** The Import File dialog box appears.
5. **Set the Import As menu to Footage.**
6. **Click Import to select the file to import.** Continue selecting files and choosing Import until you've imported all the files you need. To close the dialog box, click Done.
7. **Click Done to import the selected video clips and still images you selected to use in your project.**
8. **Drag the items from the Project window to the Composition window.** The items will appear in the Time Layout window.
9. **To load a Premiere project into After Effects, choose File ⇨ Import ⇨ File.** If using an older version of Premiere, choose Premiere As Comp.
10. **In the Import File dialog box, set the Import As menu to Composition.**
11. **Click Import to import the Premiere project into After Effects.** The Premiere project then appears in After Effects' Project window.

12. **Double-click the Composition file to display the Composition window and the Time Layout window.** The Time Layout window appears with layers representing the video and sound tracks from the Premiere project.

13. **To display the Layer window (seen in Figure 21-5), either double-click the layer you want to use or click the layer and choose Layer ➪ Open Layer Window.** The Layer window opens.

14. **Click the In and Out buttons, shown in Figure 21-5, to trim the clip.** Just move the Time Marker to where you want to set either the In or Out point and then click the In or Out button in the Layer window.

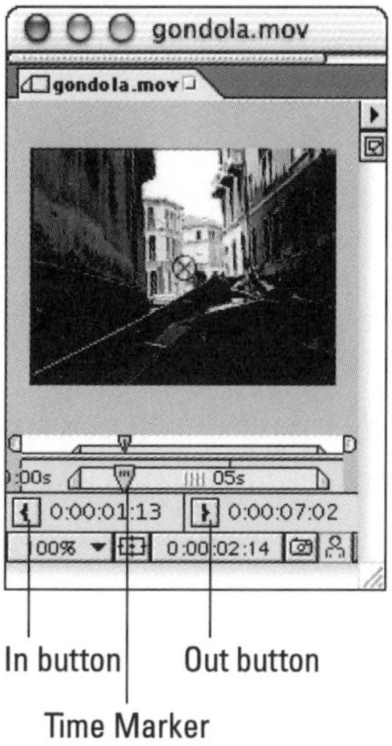

Figure 21-5: Trimming Gondola clip using the In and Out buttons in the Layer window

The trimmed portion of your video footage appears in the Time Layout window as outlines, as shown in Figure 21-6.

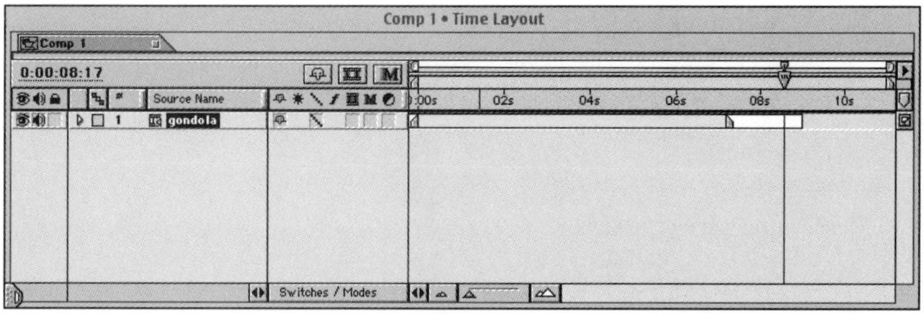

Figure 21-6: A trimmed clip appears in the Time Layout window as outlines

Exporting Your Adobe After Effects Files

To export your After Effects projects, you can choose either the File ➪ Export command or the Composition ➪ Make Movie command. If you want to export your After Effects work so that you can import it into Adobe Premiere, you must save the After Effects file as either a QuickTime movie or as an *image sequence*, a series of separate graphic files, rather than a stream of video frames.

Note You can choose to export either the entire After Effects project, or you can just export a section of the After Effects project. To export a portion of your After Effects work, click the Time Layout window and move the work area bar (this bar appears where the Time Marker is located) over the area you want to save.

Exporting a QuickTime movie from After Effects

QuickTime movies can be read by almost any machine. To quickly save your After Effects project as a QuickTime movie, follow these steps:

1. **Make sure the Time Layout window is the active window.** Click the Time Layout window to activate it.
2. **Choose File ➪ Export ➪ QuickTime Movie.** The Save dialog box appears.
3. Name your movie, then click Save. The Movie Settings dialog box appears (see Figure 21-7).

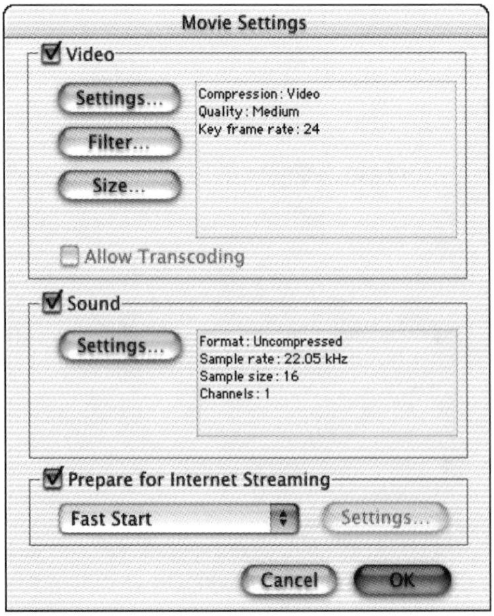

Figure 21-7: The Movie Settings dialog box

4. **Click the Settings button.** The Compression dialog box appears.
5. **Click the Video menu to choose a type of compression.**
6. **Click OK to set the compression and close the Compression dialog box.**
7. **Set any desired options in the Movie Settings dialog box.**
   - Click the Filter button to apply a filter (video effect) to your work.
   - Click the Size button to apply a custom size to your work.
   - Click the Sound Settings button to change the sound settings.
8. **In the Movie Settings dialog box, click OK to save your work as a QuickTime movie.**

Exporting an image sequence from After Effects

A quick way to save your After Effects work in a sequence format is to use the File ⇨ Export command. You can save your sequence file in Photoshop format. A Photoshop sequence file can be imported into Premiere or Photoshop for more editing.

Here's how to save your work as an image sequence using the File ⇨ Export command:

1. **Make sure that the Time Layout window is the active window.** Click the Time Layout window to activate it.
2. **Choose File ⇨ Export ⇨ Image Sequence.** The Save dialog box appears.
3. **Create a new folder and name it.**
4. **Save your sequence image in the new folder you created.** All the sequence files will be saved in the folder.
5. **Click Save.** The Export Image Sequence Settings dialog box appears (see Figure 21-8).

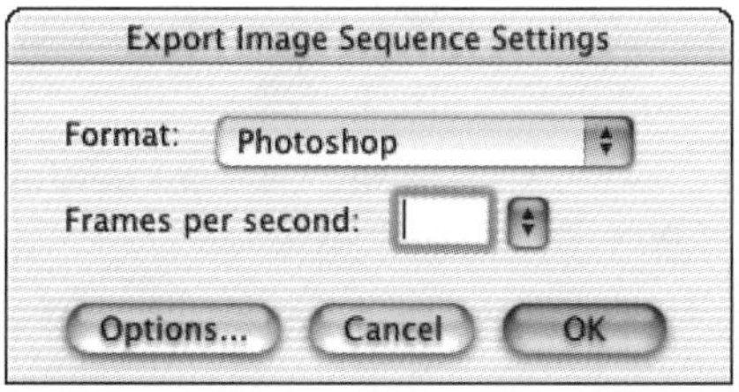

Figure 21-8: The Export Image Sequence Settings dialog box

6. **Select a format option type (BMP, JPEG MacPaint, Photoshop, PICT, PNG, QuickTime Image, SGI, TGA, or JPEG).** You can also set the frames per second. By default the Frames per second option is set to Best. If you want to use a different option, click the menu.

Tip

For best results, save your image sequence in Photoshop format if you will be importing it into Adobe Premiere.

7. **Click the Options button in the Export Image Sequence Settings dialog box to view and set the compression and color options.** Click OK to exit compression and color options and return to the Export Image Sequence Settings dialog box.

8. **In the Export Image Sequence Settings dialog box, click OK to create a sequence.** The Export dialog box displays how long the sequence will take and how many frames will be created in the sequence.

Note

Turn to the end of this chapter to learn how to import the sequence into Adobe Premiere.

The Make Movie command

The Composition ➪ Make Movie command offers precise control of your rending options. For better quality files, use this command to save your After Effects project as either a QuickTime movie or an image Sequence.

Note

You can choose to export either the entire After Effects project, or you just a section of the After Effects project. To export a portion of your After Effects work, click the Time Layout window and move the work area bar (this bar appears where the Time Marker is located) over the area you want to save.

Follow these steps to save your work using the Composition ➪ Make Movie command:

1. **Click the Time Layout window to activate it.**

2. **Choose Composition ➪ Make Movie.**

3. **In the dialog box that appears, name the movie.**

4. **Click Save.** If you are outputting to a sequence, create a new folder in which to save your sequence frames before naming and saving your file. The Render Queue dialog box appears (see Figure 21-9), enabling you to change the Render Settings and the Output Module.

5. **To view and change the Render Settings, click the Current Settings to display the Render Settings dialog box.** (See Figure 21-10.)

6. **Choose the resolution with which you want your work to be saved by clicking the Resolution menu.** Be careful not to use a resolution higher than what you are working with, because your work will appear blurry. You can choose a resolution lower than what you are working with. You may want to reduce the resolution of your work if you want to reduce the file size of the final movie, which may be an issue if you are outputting to the Web, or e-mailing your movie to someone.

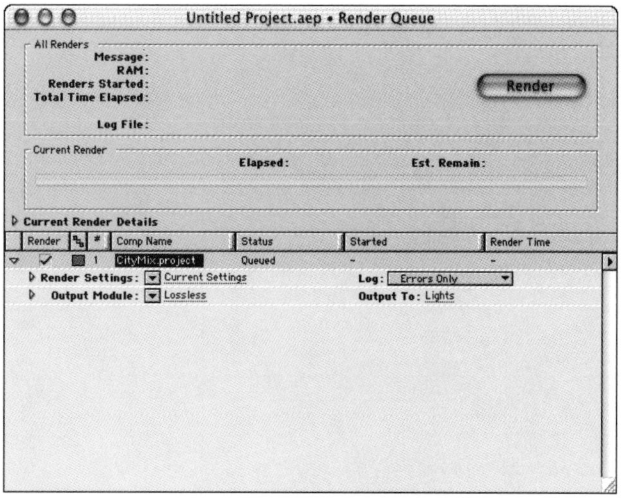

Figure 21-9: The Render Queue dialog box

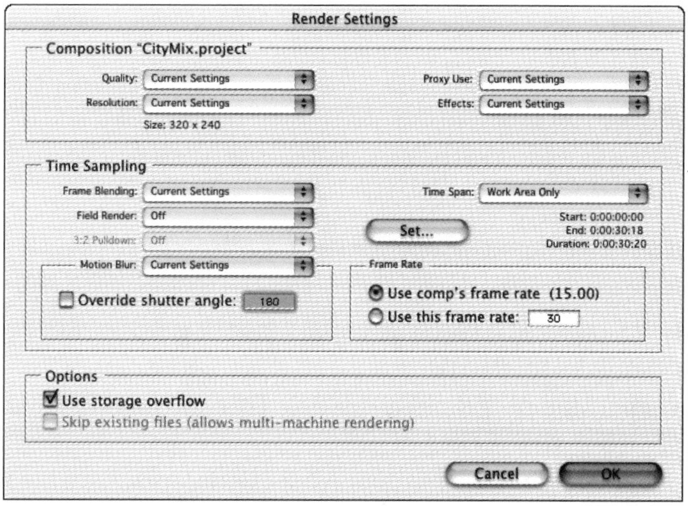

Figure 21-10: The Render Settings dialog box

7. **Click the Time Span menu to specify whether you want to output a designated work area or an entire composition.**

8. **To view and change the Output Module, click Lossless.** The Output Module Settings dialog box appears (see Figure 21-11).

9. Click the Format menu to save your work as either a QuickTime movie or as a sequence.

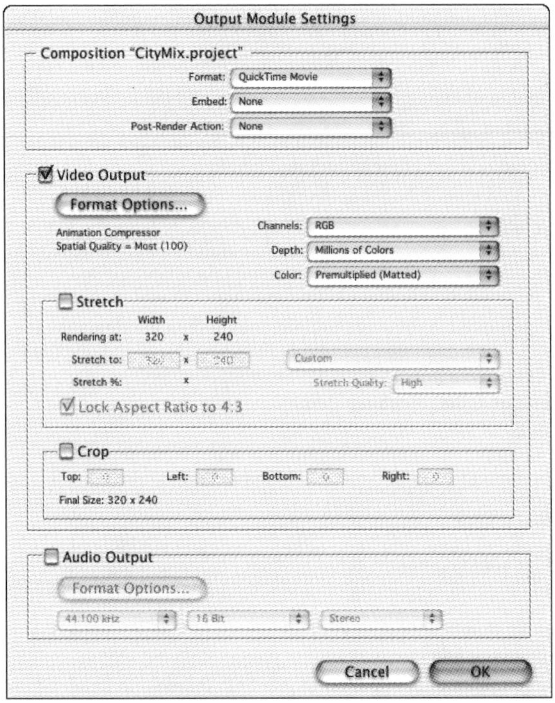

Figure 21-11: The Output Module Settings dialog box

10. Click the Channels and Depth menus to select how many colors you want your movie to be saved with.

11. In the Output Module Settings dialog box, click the Audio Output section to select the audio output you want.

12. When you are ready to output your After Effects work, click the Render button in the Render Queue dialog box.

Importing After Effects Files into Premiere

You may want to load the QuickTime Movie or Sequence you exported from After Effects into Premiere. Here's how to import a file:

1. **In Adobe Premiere, choose File ➪ New Project to create a new Premiere Project.**
2. **Choose File ➪ Import ➪ File.**
3. **Locate the QuickTime file.**
4. **Click Open.** The QuickTime file appears in the Project window, ready for you to drag it to a video track in the Timeline window.

Follow these steps to import a sequence:

1. **In Adobe Premiere, choose File ➪ New Project to create a new Premiere Project.**
2. **Choose File ➪ Import ➪ Folder.** The Choose a Folder dialog box appears.
3. **Locate the sequence folder.**
4. **Click Choose.** The Sequence folder appears in the Project window, as shown in Figure 21-12. You can now drag it to a video track in the Timeline window.

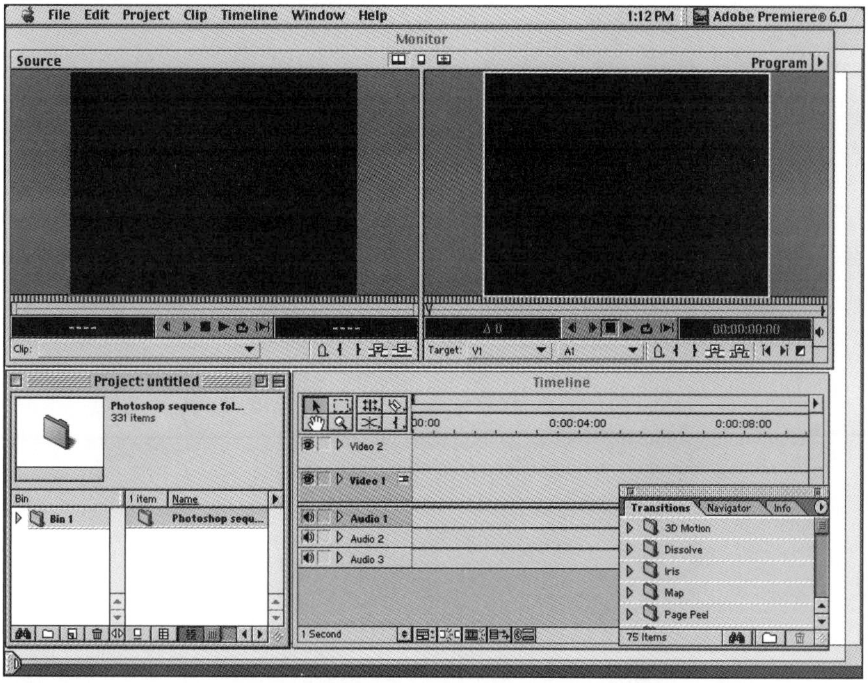

Figure 21-12: The Premiere Project window contains a Sequence folder.

Summary

If you import clips into After Effects to create special effects, you may want to also edit the In and Out points of the clips while you are in After Effects. Later you can import the clips into Adobe Premiere as QuickTime movies or as a sequence of separate graphic files.

- In After Effects, you can time clips in the Time Layout or Layer Window.
- Clips can be trimmed by clicking the edge of a clip and dragging, or by pressing a keyboard command. To trim the In point, press Option/Alt + [. To trim the Out point, press Option/Alt +].
- To import a sequence of graphics created in After Effects into Premiere, choose File ➪ Import ➪ Import Folder.

✦ ✦ ✦

CHAPTER 22

The Photoshop Connection

In This Chapter

Exporting a Premiere frame to Photoshop

Exporting an After Effects frame to Photoshop

Exporting Photoshop layers to Premiere

Exporting Photoshop alpha channels to Premiere

During video production, you may want to export still frames from your Adobe Premiere project for use on a Web page or in a print document, such as a brochure. If you export the still frames to Adobe Photoshop, you can prepare them for print and optimize them for the Web. You can even export an entire Premiere project with all of its video tracks into After Effects. Once in After Effects, each track appears as a separate layer. A frame exported from After Effects to Photoshop retains its layers. A frame exported from Premiere to Photoshop does not.

Photoshop can also be used as an image data source. You can use Photoshop to create backgrounds, titles, or images with alpha channels. These images can then be integrated into a Premiere project.

Exporting a Premiere Frame to Photoshop

Although Premiere is primarily used for creating desktop video projects, you can easily export a video frame from your project to use as a still image. The frame can be any individual frame from a clip, or it can display a frame from a transition or video effect.

In addition to using the still frame for print purposes, you can also use the still frame to create or enhance a Web site, or to create a background scene in an interactive presentation. After the frame is in Photoshop, you can edit the clip's colors, convert the clip to grayscale or black and white, and even add or delete items or people from a clip.

Cross-Reference

To learn how to export an entire video clip as a QuickTime or AVI movie, see Chapter 16. To learn how to export a Premiere video clip to Photoshop as a Filmstrip file, see Chapter 15.

Here's how to export a frame from Adobe Premiere:

1. **Open or create a Premiere project.**
2. **After you have a Premiere project on-screen, locate the frame you want to export.** Start by opening the Monitor window. To display the Monitor window, choose Window ➪ Show Monitor.

Note

If an X is in the Monitor window's upper-left corner, as shown in Figure 22-1, you need Premiere to build a preview of all the effects and video tracks in the Timeline. To have Premiere build a preview, choose Timeline ➪ Preview or simply press Enter on your keyboard. Remember that the time it takes Premiere to build a preview depends on the speed of your computer and the length of your project.

Figure 22-1: An X in the Monitor window's upper-left corner indicates that Premiere needs to build a preview.

3. **Use the Frame Forward and Frame Back buttons in the Monitor window to locate the frame you want to export.** Figure 22-2 shows the frame that we want to export in the Monitor window.

Figure 22-2: The still frame that will be exported

4. **After you have chosen the frame you want to export, choose File ➪ Export Timeline ➪ Frame.**

5. **In the Export Still Frame dialog box, shown in Figure 22-3, you can name your frame.** Also notice that below the Name field, the frame's make and video size appear. Click the Settings button if you need to change the file format and image size.

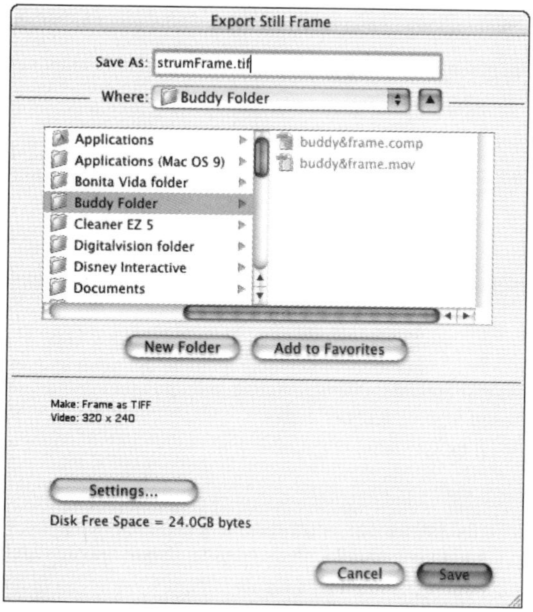

Figure 22-3: The Export Still Frame dialog box enables you to export a still frame.

6. **In the Export Still Frame Settings dialog box, shown in Figure 22-4, the pop-up menu should be set to General.** To choose a file format, click the File Type pop-up menu. You can choose TIFF, Targa, PICT, Windows Bitmap, or GIF. If you are going to use the still frame for print, you'll probably want to save your file in TIFF format. Use the Targa format if you are going to import this frame into a 3D program. If you are going to use this frame for multimedia purposes, choose PICT format or Windows Bitmap.

   If you are going to use the frame for the Web and want to reduce the number of colors in the image to 256, use the GIF format. When you pick the GIF format, an Advanced Setting button appears. You can click this button and choose whether you want your GIF file to be dithered, and whether you want the image to contain a transparent background.

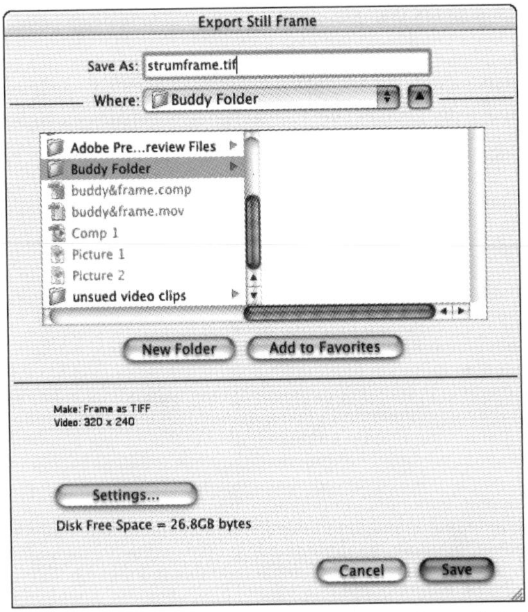

Figure 22-4: The Export Still Frame Settings dialog box General settings enable you to export a still frame as a TIFF, Targa, PICT, or GIF file.

Note

If you are going to use this frame for multimedia purposes, you may want to import the still frame into MacroMedia Director. To learn more about using Premiere and MacroMedia Director, turn to Chapter 20.

7. **In the Export Still Frame Settings dialog box, click the General pop-up menu and select Video. Notice that the settings change.** Figure 22-5 shows the Export Still Frame Settings dialog box with the Video settings available. When you use TIFF, Targa, or PICT formats, you can change the number of colors in the image by clicking the Depth pop-up menu. If you use the GIF format, you can choose what color palette you want the frame to have. The Video settings also enable you to change the size of your frame. (Reducing frame size results in no loss of quality. However, if you make the frame size larger, your image may become blurry and pixelated.)
8. **When you are finished adjusting the General and Video settings, click OK to return to the Export Still Frame dialog box.**
9. **In the Export Still Frame dialog box, click Save to save the frame in the format chosen.** The frame just saved appears on-screen. Figure 22-6 shows the frame that exported. If this is the right frame, you can close the file and export another frame or quit Premiere and load Photoshop to import the frame.

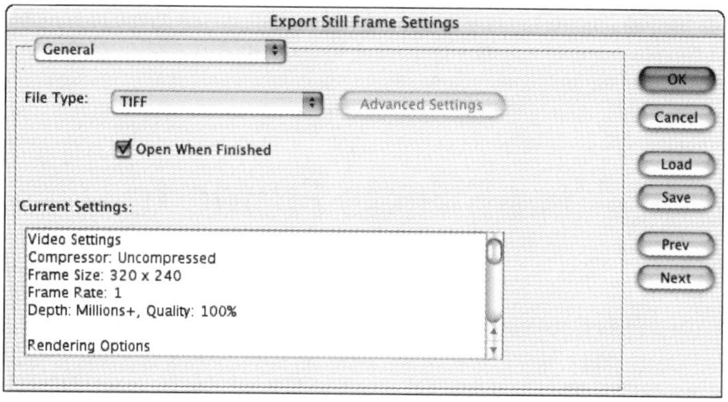

Figure 22-5: The Export Still Frame Settings dialog box Video settings enable you to change the color depth and choose a color table and frame size for the exported still frame.

Figure 22-6: The still frame captured appears on your screen after you click Save in the Export Still Frame dialog box.

Importing a still frame from Premiere into Photoshop

After you've exported a still frame from Premiere, you'll probably want to import it into Photoshop to either color correct it and/or incorporate it into a collage or other project.

Here's how to import a still frame from Premiere into Photoshop:

1. **Load Adobe Photoshop.**
2. **Choose File ➪ Open.**
3. **Locate the Premiere file you just saved as a still image and choose Open.**
4. **When the Premiere still image file opens in Photoshop, you see all of the tracks flattened in one layer.**

If you want to load a Premiere frame into Photoshop and have the tracks appear as separate layers, you must export the frame to Adobe After Effects first, which is discussed in the following section.

Exporting an After Effects Frame to Photoshop

You can use After Effects to export a frame from a Premiere project to Photoshop. If you import a Premiere project into After Effects, then you can export a frame from the Premiere project that is in After Effects to Photoshop. In After Effects, the video tracks from a Premiere project appear as separate layers. Following are the steps to import a Premiere project into After Effects, then exporting a frame from the Premiere project that is in After Effects to Photoshop:

1. **Load Adobe After Effects.**
2. **Choose File ➪ New ➪ New Project.**
3. **Choose File ➪ Import ➪ File (older versions of Premiere, choose Premiere As Comp).** In the Import File dialog box that appears, locate the Premiere project you want to import. Then, set the Import As pop-up menu to Composition. Click Import to import the Premiere project into the After Effects project.
4. **Double-click the Composition file in the Project window to display the Time Layout window and Composition window.** In the Time Layout window, all Premiere tracks appear as layers. In the Composition window, you see the layers as a composite.
5. **Move the Time Marker in the Time Layout window to the frame you want to export.**
6. **Choose Composition ➪ Save Frame As ➪ Photoshop Layers to save the still frame with all of its layers.** To save a still frame as a composite without the layers, choose Composition ➪ Save Frame As ➪ File.
7. **To open the file in Photoshop, load Adobe Photoshop and choose File ➪ Open to open the file.** When the file opens, the video tracks from Premiere appear in different Photoshop layers.

Working with Photoshop Layers and Channels

Many users consider Photoshop to be one of the most powerful digital imaging programs available for personal computers. Its ability to manipulate images, colors, and text far surpasses Premiere's. Therefore, you may want to use Photoshop to create or enhance graphics for eventual loading into Premiere. The following project, called Ski Bariloche, leads you through the steps of creating text and alpha channels in Adobe Photoshop and then, once created, you can use the text and alpha channels in Premiere.

Figure 22-7 shows a few frames from the Ski Bariloche Premiere project that we created, using three Photoshop files. The three files used in the project include a digitized image of two skiers on the slopes (used as the background), the text ("Ski Bariloche"), and an image of a bird. We animated the bird (shown in Figure 22-8) using Premiere's Motion Setting command. To set the bird and not the background in motion, we had to select the bird and then save the selection. When you save a selection, Photoshop saves the selection as a mask in an alpha channel.

Figure 22-7: A few frames from the Ski Bariloche project, which was created with Photoshop files

Because the bird starts moving from behind the text, we had to create the text and the background in two separate Photoshop files. Originally, the text was created in the same file as the background file (the skiers), as shown in Figure 22-9, so that we could use the background for positioning of the text. We duplicated the text layer into a new file so that the text could be in a separate video track when we imported it into Premiere.

With the text and the background in separate video tracks, the bird could move between the two images in the two tracks. You may be wondering, why didn't we just use Premiere to create the text? We used Photoshop to create the text, and not Premiere, because Photoshop has powerful layer style features that enable you to create 3D text effects.

Figure 22-8: Photoshop file of a bird used in the Ski Bariloche project

Figure 22-9: Photoshop file of skiers and text used in the Ski Bariloche Premiere project

Creating a Photoshop Layer file

To create the Ski Bariloche project, we created a Photoshop layer file of two skiers and some text. This section describes how to create the layer and duplicate it as a file.

Here's how to use Photoshop to add text to another layer in a background file:

1. **Load Photoshop.** Choose File ➪ Open and open a file you want to use as the background.

   On the CD-ROM

   To use the skiers' image (seen in Figure 22-9), load the Skiers file found in the Chapter 22 folder on the CD-ROM that accompanies this book.

Note

You can also choose File ➪ New to create a new file. In the New dialog box, set the width and height to the same size as your Premiere project. Set the Resolution to 72 ppi (pixels per inch). Set the Mode to RGB Color. Then click OK to create a new file. In the new file, use the Gradient tool to add color. Then use Photoshop filters, such as the Artistic, Brush Strokes, Pixelate, Sketch, or Texture filters, to create a background.

2. **Click the Type tool in the Toolbox to create text.**
3. **Choose whether you want to create horizontal or vertical text.**
4. **Move the mouse to the place on the image you want the text to appear and click the mouse once.** Begin typing.
5. **With the text selected, select a font and size.** You can also add tracking (spacing between the letters). To do so, use the Character palette. Choose Window ➪ Display Character, to display the Character palette as shown in Figure 22-10.
6. **To move the text on-screen, drag it with the Move tool.**
7. **To add interesting effects to your text, choose Layer ➪ Layer Style.** Then choose an effect. To create the text effect seen earlier in Figure 22-9, we used the Layer ➪ Layer Style ➪ Drop Shadow, Layer ➪ Layer Style ➪ Inner Shadow, and Layer ➪ Layer Style ➪ Stroke commands. After you apply the effects, the effects appear in the Layers palette, as shown in Figure 22-11.

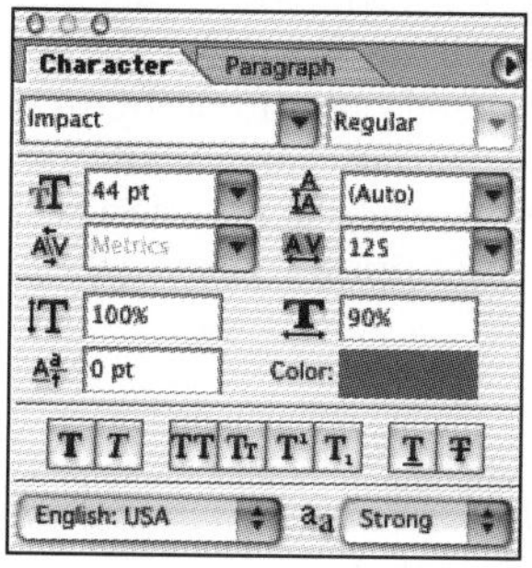

Figure 22-10: Photoshop's Character palette enables you to pick the font, size, tracking, and so on for your text.

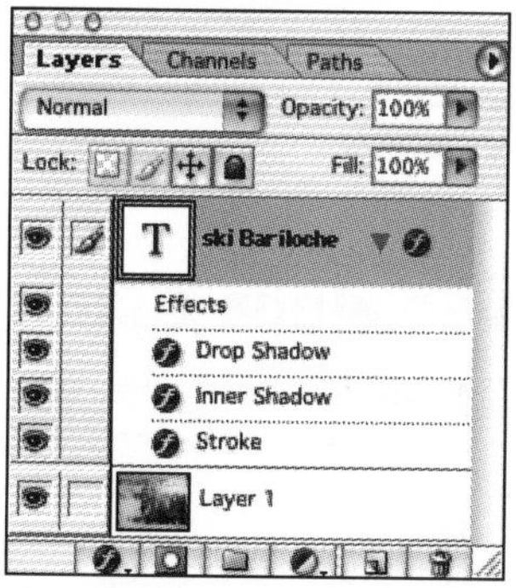

Figure 22-11: The text effects appear in the Layers palette with the text layer.

8. **When you are done creating and stylizing the text, save your file by choosing File ➪ Save.** Save the file in Photoshop format to save the background and text layer. Also, by saving in Photoshop format, you can always go back to the text layer and move the text, edit the text, or edit the text effect.

Now that you've used the background for the positioning of the text, you can either save the file in Photoshop format with two layers, or you can duplicate the text layer into another file.

Duplicating a layer

You should have a file onscreen with a layer. If you want, use the file you created from the Previous section, "Creating a Photoshop layer file." If the Layers palette isn't visible, open it by choosing Window ➪ Layers. Make sure that the layer you want to duplicate is selected.

You can duplicate a layer by following these steps:

1. **Choose Layer ➪ Duplicate Layer or choose Duplicate Layer from the Layers palette pop-up menu.**
2. **In the Duplicate Layer dialog box, shown in Figure 22-12, click the Document pop-up menu and choose New.**
3. **Click OK to create a duplicate layer in a new document.** In the new file, the duplicated layer appears in the Layers palette. Notice that the layer is on a transparent background. You need the layer to appear in Premiere on a transparent background, if you want Premiere to read only the item on the layer. To save the file with a transparent background, rather than a white background, you need to save the file in Photoshop format. Choose File ➪ Save. In the Save dialog box, make sure to set the Format menu option to Photoshop.

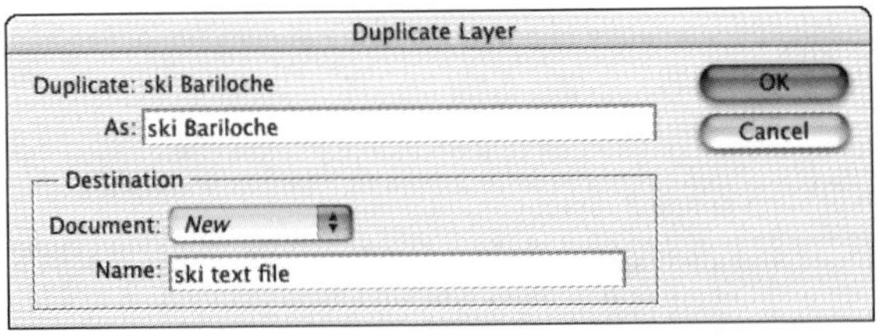

Figure 22-12: The Duplicate Layer dialog box

Creating a Photoshop file with an alpha channel

To have the bird.psd file (shown previously in Figure 22-8) appear in Premiere without its background, we must select the bird and then save the selection to an alpha channel. When we loaded the file into Premiere, the alpha channel enabled us to use the Motion Setting dialog box to animate the bird, without its background appearing.

After you load Photoshop, follow these steps to select an image and save the selection to an alpha channel:

1. **Open the file with the image you want to isolate.**

   On the CD-ROM

   To use the bird image (seen in Figure 22-8), load the bird.psd file found in the Chapter 22 folder on the CD-ROM that accompanies this book.

2. **Use a Photoshop Selection tool (the Pen tool, the Magic Wand, or the Lasso tool) to select the image you want to isolate from the background.** We used the Polygonal Lasso tool to select the bird. For a soft-edged selection, we set the Lasso tool to have a feather radius of 1.

3. **With the selection on-screen, choose Select ⇨ Save Selection.** In the Save Selection dialog box, shown in Figure 22-13, we clicked the Channel pop-up menu and set it to New and left the Operation radio button set to New Channel. Then we clicked Save to save the selection to an alpha channel.

   Note

   To load a saved selection, choose Select ⇨ Load Selection.

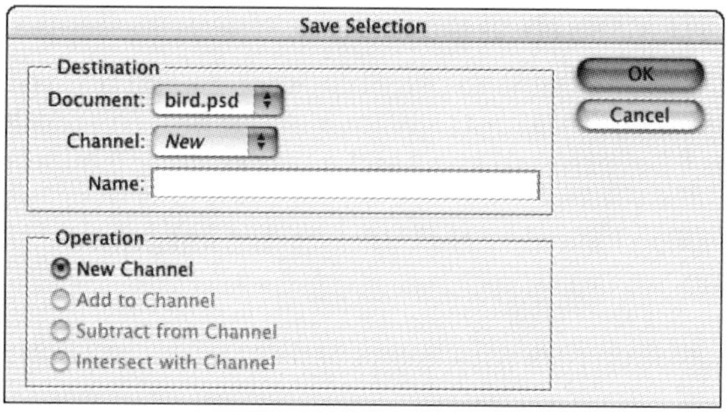

Figure 22-13: The Save Selection dialog box enables you to save a selection to an alpha channel.

4. **To see the alpha channel, choose Window ⇨ Show Channels.** In the Channels palette, you see a Red, a Green, a Blue, and an Alpha channel. Click Alpha 1 in the Channels palette to display the alpha channel. The alpha channel, shown in Figure 22-14, displays the white area as the selected area. The white area is the only area that Premiere reads. The black area represents the area that Premiere won't read. (This happens only if the Color Indicates option, in the Channel Options dialog box, is set to Masked Areas — the default setting. To display the Channel Options dialog box, double-click Alpha 1 in the Channels palette.)

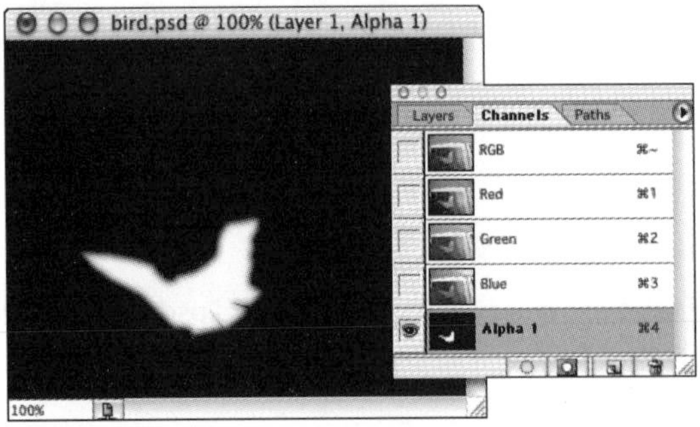

Figure 22-14: The Photoshop file with the alpha channel selected

5. **To import this file into Premiere with the alpha channel, you must save the alpha channel with the file.** Choose File ➪ Save As. In the Save As dialog box, click the format pop-up menu and choose either [ES1]Photoshop. In the Save section, only the Alpha Channel option should be selected. Click Save to save the file.

Importing Photoshop layers and alpha channels to Premiere

Earlier in this chapter, you learned how to use Photoshop to add text to a background and then duplicate the text layer to create another file. The result was two Photoshop files, one with a background layer and a text layer, and another with just a layer with some text. In the previous section, you learned how to select part of an image and save it to an alpha channel so that the selected image could be read separate from the background.

Here's how to import Photoshop files with layers and channels into Premiere's Project window:

1. **Load Adobe Premiere.**
2. **In a new or existing Premiere project, choose File ➪ Import.**
3. **In the Import dialog box, locate the Photoshop file with the two layers (the skier and the text) then click Open.** When the Layer Selection dialog box appears, shown in Figure 22-15, click the pop-up menu and choose Background Layer to import just the background layer without any other layer.
4. **Click OK to have Premiere store the file in the Project window.**
5. **Choose File ➪ Import ➪ File.**

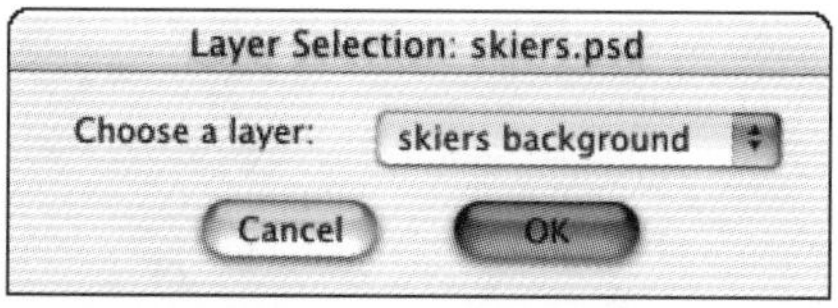

Figure 22-15: The Layer Selection dialog box enables you to either open a layer or merge and open the layers.

6. **In the Import dialog box, shown in Figure 22-16, locate the Photoshop file with the text layer and click Open.** When the Layer Selection dialog box appears, click the pop-up menu and choose the text layer, as shown in Figure 22-16. (Make sure not to choose Merged Layers. If you choose Merged Layers, the text layer merges with the background, preventing you from seeing below the text.) Click OK to have Premiere store the file in the Project window.

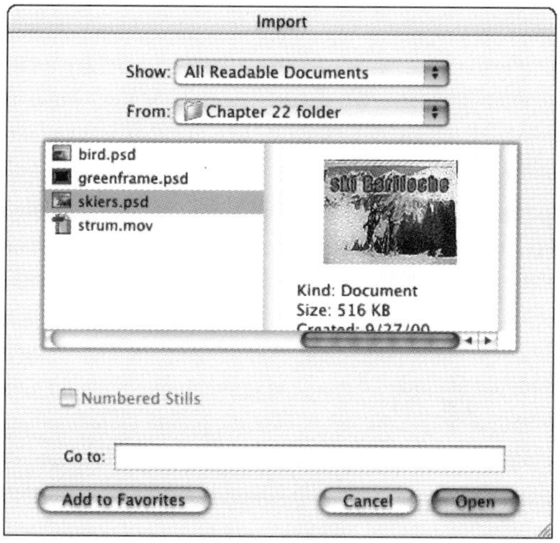

Figure 22-16: The Import dialog box

7. **Choose File ⇨ Import ⇨ File.** Locate the Photoshop file with an alpha channel (the bird file), and click Open to have Premiere store the file in the Project window. To see the alpha channel, double-click the file with an alpha channel in the Project palette. When the Clip window appears, click the alpha channel radio button. Figure 22-17 shows the alpha channel file in the clip window.

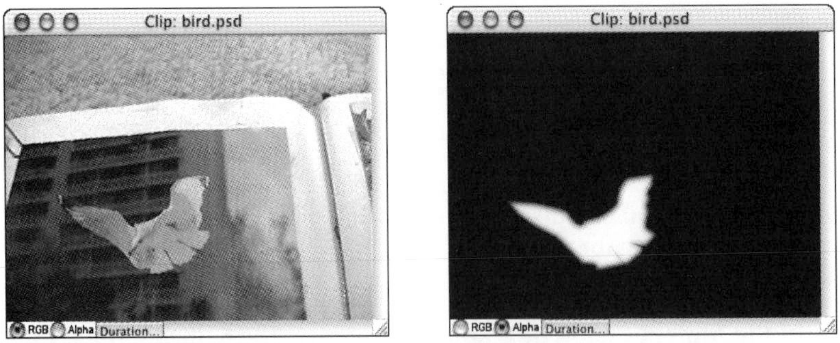

Figure 22-17: You can view a file's alpha channel in the Clip window.

Placing Photoshop layer and alpha channel files in video tracks

Now that you've created the clips for the Ski Bariloche project, you have to assemble them in the Timeline window:

1. **Drag the background file (the skiers) from the Project window to Video Track 1 in the Timeline window, the bird to Video Track 2, and the text to Video Track 3.** Figure 22-18 shows the Project and Timeline windows for the Ski Bariloche project.

2. **To see the text's Transparency effect, click the text image in Video Track 3 and choose Clip ⇨ Video Options ⇨ Transparency.** The Video Track 3 Transparency Settings dialog box appears, as shown in Figure 22-19.

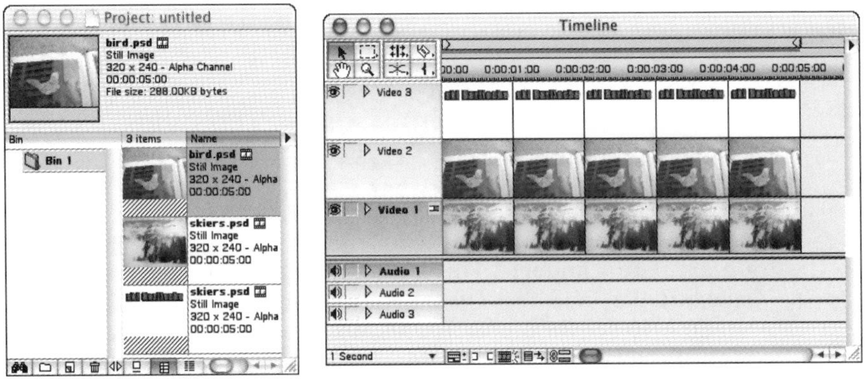

Figure 22-18: The Project and Timeline windows for the Ski Bariloche project

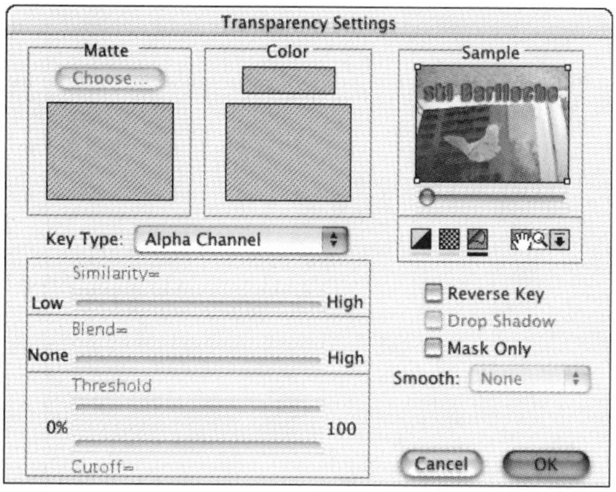

Figure 22-19: The Transparency Settings dialog box shows the text file's transparent background.

3. **To see the bird's alpha channel Transparency effect, click the bird image in Video Track 2 and choose Clip ⇨ Video Options ⇨ Transparency.** The Video Track 2 Transparency Settings appear, as shown in Figure 22-20.
4. **To animate the bird, click the bird icon in Video Track 2 and choose Clip ⇨ Video Options ⇨ Motion.** In the Motion Settings dialog box, shown in Figure 22-21, notice that the bird starts to move from behind the text on the upper-left corner and moves down to the middle, and ends in the upper-left side under the text again.

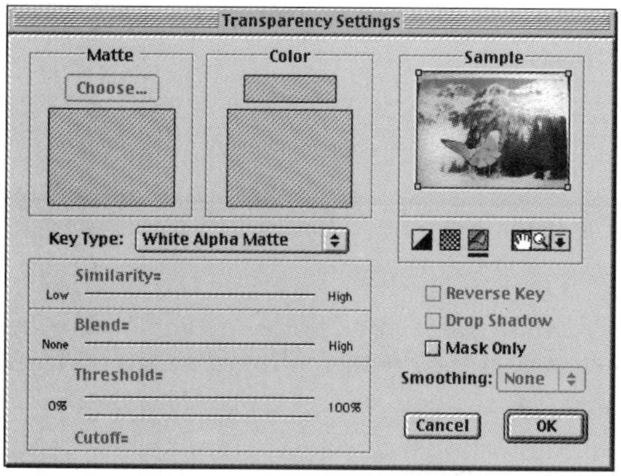

Figure 22-20: The Transparency Settings dialog box shows the bird alpha channel's transparency effect.

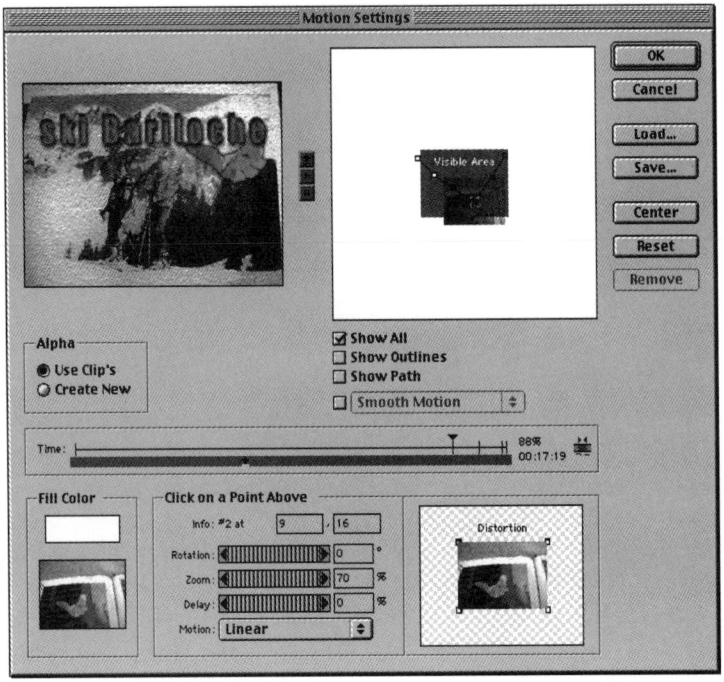

Figure 22-21: The Motion Settings dialog box with the settings used on the bird image to create the Ski Bariloche project

5. **To preview the video clip, choose Timeline ➪ Preview.**
6. **Save your work.**

Summary

You can easily export a frame from Premiere to Photoshop or export Photoshop files into Premiere.

- ✦ If you want to load a Premiere frame into Photoshop and have a Premiere frame appear as a layer, export the Premiere Project to After Effects first.
- ✦ Premiere automatically reads the background transparency of Photoshop layers. It does not convert Photoshop transparency into a white background.
- ✦ Premiere can use Photoshop alpha channels to create transparency effects.

✦ ✦ ✦

CHAPTER 23

Using Adobe Premiere and Adobe Illustrator

✦ ✦ ✦ ✦

In This Chapter

✦ ✦ ✦ ✦

Adobe Illustrator is one of the most powerful desktop illustration programs available for personal computers. Using Illustrator, graphic designers can place text on a curve or bend and reshape the letters in a word. Illustrator, which is a *vector-based* program, provides designers with the power they need to create virtually any shape that can be drawn. In vector-based programs, shapes are defined mathematically and can easily be moved and reshaped. In Illustrator, shapes appear as *paths* filled or outlined with color. On-screen, a path resembles a wireframe outline with tiny squares called *anchor points*. Editing the anchor points edits the path.

For Adobe Premiere users, Illustrator opens up a new world of possibilities. Illustrator type and shapes can be imported directly into Premiere. When Premiere opens an Illustrator file, it automatically converts it from Illustrator's vector format to Premiere's *raster* format, and appears with transparent backgrounds. This conversion enables you to not only use the Illustrator text but also to use shapes created in Illustrator as masks.

Working with Illustrator Type

You can create type effects in Adobe Illustrator and then import them into Adobe Premiere for use as title effects, logos, credits, and more. You can also import Illustrator type into Premiere and use the type as a mask and have a video clip run through the shape of the text, as described later in this chapter. Adobe Illustrator features six tools with which to create type.

 The Type tool enables you to create text that reads horizontally, from left to right.

 The Area Type tool is used to create type inside a shape. You can select the Ellipse, Polygon, Star, or Rectangle tools to create a shape. To create more elaborate shapes, you can apply one of Illustrator's Effect commands to a shape, such as the Punk & Bloat command (Effect ➪ Distort & Transform ➪ Punk & Bloat). With a shape on-screen, click inside the shape with the Area Type tool and then start typing. Your text appears on-screen in the shape of the path shape and reads from left to right.

 The Path Type tool creates text on a path. To use the Path Type tool, you first need to create a path. You can create a path using the Pen, Pencil, Paintbrush, or Ellipse tool. You can also use the Spiral tool to create a spiral path on which the text can appear (see Figure 23-1).

After you've created a path, click it with the Path Type tool and start typing. The text appears on the path as you type (as seen in Figure 23-1). In some cases, the font size may be too big to appear on the path. In this case, you may need to scale the font size down. To do so, click and drag over the text with the Path Type tool to select it. Then, select Type ➪ Size and pick a size, or click the Font Size menu in the Character palette. To display the Character palette, choose Type ➪ Show Character.

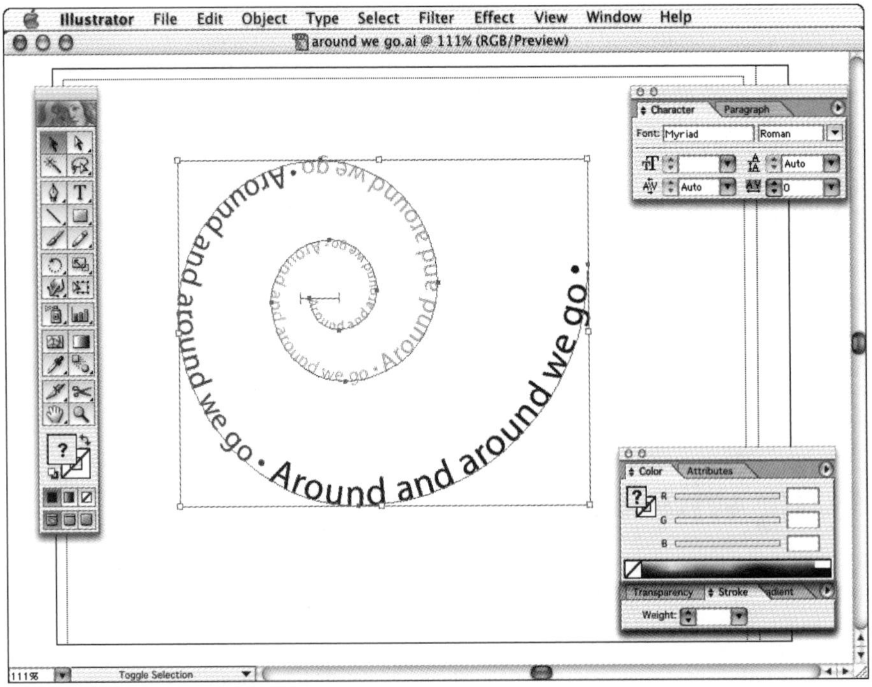

Figure 23-1: A spiral path with text

The Vertical Type tool flows text from top to bottom (vertically) rather then from left to right (horizontally), as the Type tool does. To create vertical text, click the Vertical Type tool in the Toolbox, click in the document where you want the type to appear, and then start typing.

The Vertical Area Type tool works like the Area Type tool. Both type tools create type within a path. When type appears while using the Vertical Area Type tool, it appears from top to bottom (vertically) inside the path instead of from left to right (horizontally), as it does when using the Path Area Type tool.

The Vertical Path Type tool works similar to the Path Type tool. Both type tools create type on a path. However, instead of the type appearing left to right (horizontally), as it does when using the Path Type tool, it appears top to bottom (vertically).

Follow these steps to learn how to use Illustrator's type tools.

1. **Load Adobe Illustrator, if it is not already loaded.**

2. **Choose File ➪ New to create a new document.** The New Document dialog box appears (see Figure 23-2).

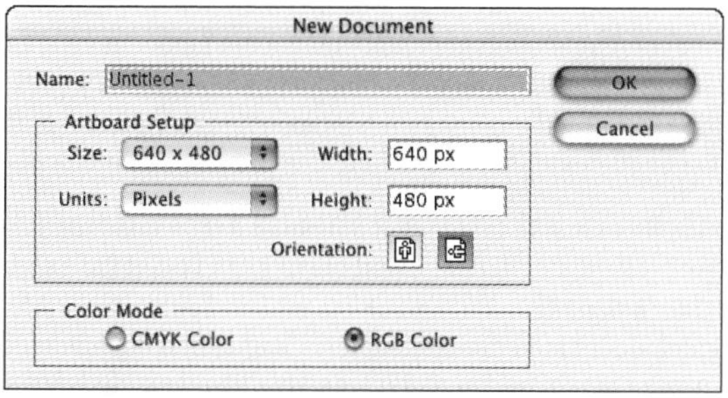

Figure 23-2: Adobe Illustrator's New Document dialog box

3. **Set the Artboard Size to 640 x 480 pixels (or the frame size that you will be using in Premiere), set Color Mode to RGB Color, and then click OK.** A new document appears.

Note

If you are creating a Premiere project with an NTSC DV frame size of 720 x 480 pixels, your best bet is to create an image in Illustrator at 720 x 540 pixels (768 x 576 PAL) to compensate for the non-square pixels used by DV. When Premiere imports the file into your project, it downscales the image to properly match the frame size without distorting it. If you create an image in Illustrator at a small size that doesn't match the image aspect ratio, you can prevent distortion by selecting the clip in Premiere and choose Clip ➪ Video Options ➪ Maintain Aspect Ratio. If you choose this option, Premiere will not have the clip fit the frame but will instead resample using non-square pixels.

4. **Set the Fill color to the desired type color.** Double-click either the Fill swatch in the Tools palette (the top, overlapping square toward the bottom of the Tools palette) or the Fill swatch in the Color palette (the top, overlapping square at the top, left side of the Color palette). The Color Picker dialog box appears.

Tip

By default, Illustrator uses the Fill color as the type color. If you set the Fill color to the color you want the text to be, you won't have to worry about changing it later.

5. **Click a color in the Select Color area or on the color slider next to it.** If you are creating a project for the Web, make sure to select the Only Web Colors option.
6. **Click OK.** The Fill color changes to the newly selected color. If you decide to change the Fill color, the easiest way to pick a new color is to use the color bar in the Color palette. To display the Color palette, choose Window ➪ Show Color. In the Color palette, click a color in the color bar at the bottom of the palette to change the Fill color. To create a new color, move the sliders in the middle of the palette.
7. **To apply a stroke to the text, click the Stroke swatch (which is below the Fill swatch) and pick a color.** Select a color by either using the Color Picker dialog box—accessed by double-clicking the Stroke swatch in the Tools or Color palette—or by dragging the sliders and/or color bar in the Color palette. To set the size of the stroke, click the Weight menu in the Stroke palette and then pick a size. To display the Stroke palette, choose Window ➪ Show Stroke.
8. **Set the Fill color to black.** Click the Default Fill and Stroke Color icon, which is below the overlapping Fill and Stroke swatch in the Tools palette. This sets the Stroke swatch to black and the Fill color to white. Next, click the Swap Fill and Stroke icon (the curved arrow next to the Fill and Stroke swatch) to set the Fill to black and the Stroke to white. To use the Illustrator text as a mask with a video clip run through the shape of the text, you must set the Fill color to black. Now you are ready to use a Type tool to start creating some type.
9. **Select one of the Type tools in Illustrator.**
10. **Move the cursor to the middle of the document.**
11. **Click the document and type a word or two.**
12. **Choose Window ➪ Type ➪ Character and Window ➪ Type ➪ Paragraph to display either the Character or Paragraph palette.**
13. **Click and drag over the area you want to stylize.** You can stylize either an entire word or a letter or two in the word.

For a more interesting text effect, you can use one of the Effect commands to alter the text path. Figure 23-3 shows the Effect ➪ Distort & Transform ➪ Free Distort command when applied to text.

Figure 23-3: The Free Distort dialog box can be used to distort text.

Converting Illustrator type to path outlines

You may want to convert your Illustrator type into outline paths, so that you can manipulate it further as seen in Figure 23-1. To manipulate path outlines, click the type path's anchor points using the Direct Selection tool (the white arrow), and move the anchor points to alter the type path and the type itself. Essentially, this enables you to create your own type designs.

Note

When you convert text to outline format, it is no longer considered a font. The outline paths now appear as art, not text. So if you send an Illustrator file to another person, that person won't need to have the font on their machine.

Here's how to convert your type into outline type paths:

1. **Create text with one of Illustrator's type tools.**
2. **Use the Selection tool to select the type.**
3. **Choose Type ➪ Create Outlines to convert the text from type to art.**

Editing path outlines

After you have converted your text into outlines, Illustrator views the text as art (a path that is in the shape of text). You'll probably manipulate, distort, or enlarge the text so that when you import it into Premiere you can run a video clip through the text, as seen in Figure 23-6. Type path outlines are enlarged with the Scale tool, rotated with the Rotate tool, and moved with the Selection tool. Using Adobe Illustrator 10, Type path outlines can be manipulated using the Reflect, Shear, and Free Transform tools. They can be distorted using the Warp, Reshape, and Twist tools.

Here's how scale, rotate, and move path outlines:

- **Enlarging text.** Make sure that the text is selected (use the Selection tool; the black arrow). To use the Scale dialog box, double-click the Scale tool in the Toolbox. When the Scale dialog box appears, as shown in Figure 23-4, make the adjustments you want and then click OK to scale the text.
- **Scaling a single letter.** Click the outline path of the letter with the Group Selection Type tool (the white arrow with the plus sign). Next, select the Scale tool in the Toolbox and click once on your document. Now click and drag on the letter with the Scale tool selected to scale the letter.
- **Rotating type.** Select the path outline of the letter you want to select. Next, click the Rotate tool in the Toolbox (next to the Scale tool in the Toolbox) and click in your document. Next, click and drag on the letter to rotate it. If you want to display the Rotate dialog box, press and hold the Option/Alt key while you click the text with the Rotate tool.
- **Moving type.** Click inside the letter using the Group Selection tool and then drag the letter to where you want to move it. You can also use the arrow keys on your keyboard to move the letter on-screen. By default, the arrow keys are set to move in 1-pixel increments. You can change the increments in the Keyboard Increment section, located in the Preferences ⇨ General dialog box.

Editing with anchor points

Type outlines can be manipulated so that you can create new typefaces. You manipulate type path outlines by moving either anchor points or directional lines. Figure 23-5 shows a type path outline before and after manipulation.

To move an anchor point, click on it with the Direct Selection tool (the white arrow) and then drag. Illustrator also enables you to move multiple anchor points at one time. To select more than one anchor point, press and hold the Shift key as you select anchor points. You can also click and drag over the anchor points you want to select.

Tip

You can also press the arrow keys on your keyboard to move a selected anchor point. Anchor points move keyboard increments that are set in the General Preference dialog box. To display the General Preference dialog box, choose Preference ⇨ General.

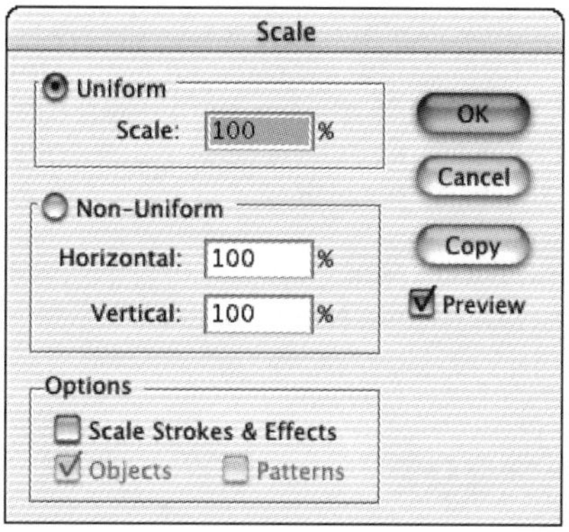

Figure 23-4: The Scale dialog box enables you to scale paths.

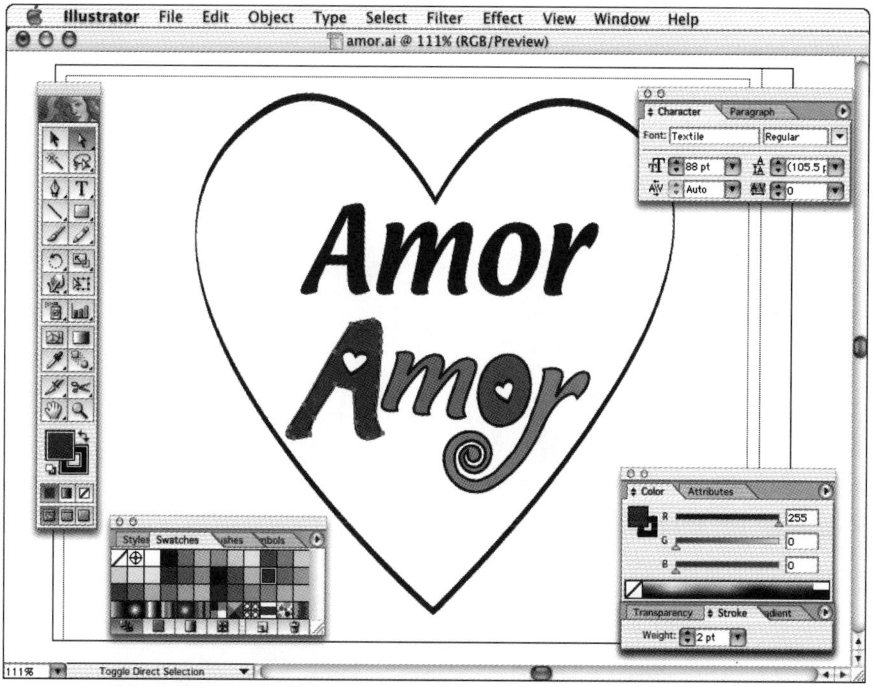

Figure 23-5: Path type outline before and after manipulating

Editing with directional lines

Curves on a path are created from a *curve anchor point*. Curve anchor points have *directional lines*, which determine the size and arc of your curve. Clicking and dragging a directional line changes the form of the curve.

Other ways to adjust the type path outline include using the Pen + tool, Pen – tool, and the Convert tool. Use the Pen + tool to click the path to add an anchor point. This anchor point can then be manipulated. Clicking an anchor point with the Pen – tool deletes it. Use the Convert tool to click on a corner anchor point to convert the corner anchor point to a curve anchor point, and vice versa.

Adobe Illustrator 10 enables you to create some interesting distortions with theWarp tool. You can convert plain path outlines into interesting and unusual ones.

Using an Illustrator Text Shape in a Premiere Project

Earlier in this chapter, you learn how to use Illustrator to create type and then convert the type into type shapes. This section shows you how to use Illustrator's Type tool to create text, convert it into a type shape, and then import it into a Premiere project that uses the text shape as a mask. The Premiere project in this chapter's examples features a video clip playing through and behind the Illustrator text shape. Figure 23-6 shows frames from a Premiere project that has a video clip running inside and behind an Illustrator text shape.

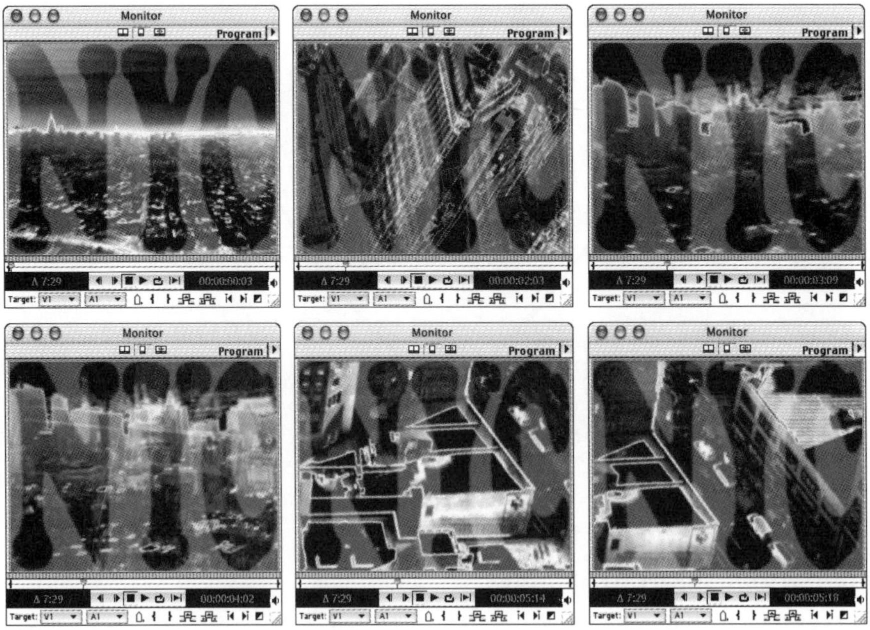

Figure 23-6: Illustrator text shape used in a Premiere project

The following steps show how to create an Illustrator text shape and then import it into a Premiere project and use it as a mask:

On the CD-ROM

The Images seen in Figure 23-6 are on the CD-ROM that accompanies this book. The images are an "NYC" text shape created in Illustrator, a black-and-white video clip of New York City from Digital Vision's CityMix collection, and a sound clip from Digital Vision's City Life/Urban Moods collections.

1. **Load Adobe Illustrator and create a new document.** The document should be the same size as your Premiere project. If you don't have access to Adobe Illustrator, skip Steps 1–4.
2. **Select one of Illustrator's type tools.**
3. **Choose a font and type size.**
4. **Set the foreground color to black so that the text you create is black.** The black text is used later as a mask in Premiere.
5. **Create some text.**

Cross-Reference

To learn about using the different Illustrator type tools, see the "Working with Illustrator Type" section earlier in this chapter.

6. **Manipulate the text in Illustrator.** Either choose Effect ➪ Distort & Transform or convert the type into outlines using the Direct Selection tool. To convert the type into outlines, select it with the Selection tool and choose Type ➪ Create Outlines. Figure 23-7 shows the Illustrator text shape we created for the project seen in Figure 23-7. We converted the NYC text into outlines and then manipulated the text by using the Direct Selection tool.
7. **After you've created an Illustrator text shape, save your file in Illustrator 8 format.** Premiere can then read the file information. If you want, you can quit Adobe Illustrator.
8. **Load Premiere and create a new project.** For practice purposes, use the Multimedia preset.
9. **Import an Illustrator text shape, a video clip, and a sound clip.** Choose File ➪ Import ➪ File to import the files needed for this project. If you want, you can import the files used to create the frames seen in Figure 23-6. You can find them on the CD-ROM that accompanies this book. They are Digital Vision's video clip 576005p.mov and sound clip 576002s.aif.
10. **Drag the video clip to the Video 2 track, the Illustrator text shape to the Video 1 track, and if you want, a sound clip to the Audio 1 track.** If the text shape is not as long as the video clip, you can click the end of the text shape in the Timeline window and drag to the right until it's the same duration as the video clip. (For more information on basic editing, turn to Chapter 5.) If the sound clip is longer than the video clip, you can use the Razor tool to cut it. (For more information on editing sound clips, turn to Chapter 6.)

Figure 23-7: Illustrator text shape created in Illustrator

11. **Select the text shape in Video 1.**
12. **Choose Clip ➪ Video Options ➪ Transparency.** The Transparency Settings dialog box appears.
13. **Set the Key Type menu to Screen.** In the Sample window, the video appears inside the text shape.
14. **Drag the Cutoff slider to the left to have the video clip also appear in the background.**
15. **Click OK to apply the effects to your project.** Figure 23-8 shows the Transparency Settings dialog box.

Note

Choosing the Multiply Key Type option, results in the opposite effect of the Screen Key Type option. If you move the Cutoff slider halfway to the left, however, both options have similar effects. Using the Alpha Channel Key Type option enables you to either run the video clip inside or behind the text shape. Whether the video clip is seen inside or outside the shape depends on whether you have the Reverse Key option selected in the Transparency Settings dialog box. For more information on using Key Type options, turn to Chapter 12.

16. **To soften the edges of the text shape, blur it by using the Gaussian Blur video effect.** To do so, select the text shape in track Video 1. Next, choose Window ➪ Show Video Effects. In the Video palette, open the Blur & Sharpen folder and then drag the Gaussian Blur video effect over the text shape in Video 1. The Effect Controls palette will appear on-screen if it is not already on-screen. Drag the Blurriness slider a little to the right. Figure 23-9 shows all the windows and palettes used to create the frames for the NYC project.

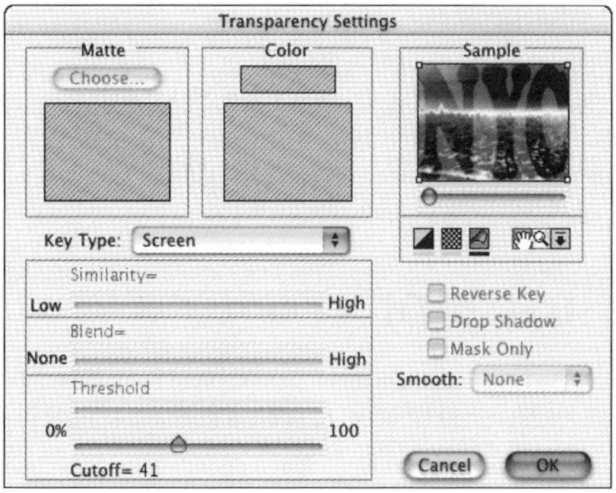

Figure 23-8: The Transparency Settings dialog box used to create the project in Figure 23-6

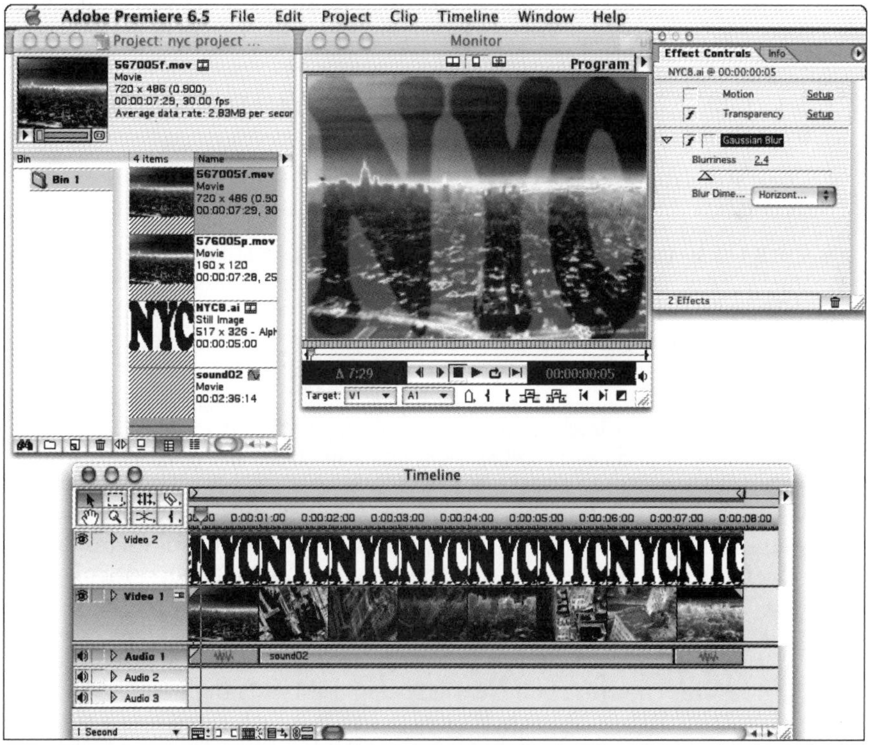

Figure 23-9: The Premiere windows and palettes used to create the project in Figure 23-6

17. **Choose File ➪ Save to save your project.**

18. **Choose Clip ➪ Preview to preview the project.** If you want, you can make a movie by choosing File ➪ Export Timeline ➪ Movie. Click the Settings button if you want to change the settings of your movie. For more information on outputting your Premiere projects to movies, turn to Chapter 16.

Creating Masks in Illustrator

The Illustrator drawing capabilities make it the perfect place to create intricate masks for Premiere. This example shows you how to create a simple shape in Illustrator that can be used as a mask in Premiere.

Here's how to create a simple mask:

1. **Load Adobe Illustrator, if it isn't running already.**

2. **Choose File ➪ New to create a new document.** In the New Document dialog box, set the Artboard Size to 640 x 480 pixels and choose RGB Color for the Color Mode.

3. **Select the Rectangle, Ellipse, Polygon, or Star tools (shown in Figure 23-10) from the Toolbox.**

4. **Click and drag to create a shape or Option/Alt-click to display the tool's dialog box.** In the dialog box that appears, make your adjustments.

5. **Click OK to create the shape.** The shapes you create are filled with whatever the Fill and Stroke colors are in the Toolbox. If you want, you can change the Fill and Stroke color by double-clicking the Fill or Stroke swatch in the Toolbox. When the Color Picker appears, make your adjustment and then click OK. Figure 23-11 shows the Star dialog box and a star it created.

Note

Experiment using different fill shades. Filling with black, white, and different shades of gray and colors will result in different effects in Premiere.

6. **When you have a shape on-screen, experiment with creating a few different shapes using one of the Effect commands.** Figure 23-12 shows how we transformed a star shape into a blob shape using the Effect ➪ Distort ➪ Roughen dialog box. Figure 23-13 shows the star transformed into a snowflake using the Effect ➪ Distort ➪ dialog box. An interesting effect was created when we used the Effect ➪ Distort ➪ Photocopy command, which is shown in Figure 23-14. The star shape twirled using the Twirl command, shown in Figure 23-15. Figure 23-16 shows how a star is transformed into a sun shape using the Effect ➪ Distort & Transform ➪ Punk & Bloat command. Figure 23-17 shows how a black star is transformed into a grayscale star using the Effect ➪ Sketch ➪ Note Paper command. Figure 23-18 shows how a star shape is converted to an ellipse using the Effect ➪ Convert to Shape ➪ Ellipse command. Figure 23-19 shows the Blur ➪ Gaussian Blur command applied to the ellipse shape we created from a star shape.

Figure 23-10: Illustrator's Rectangle, Ellipse, Polygon, and Star tools

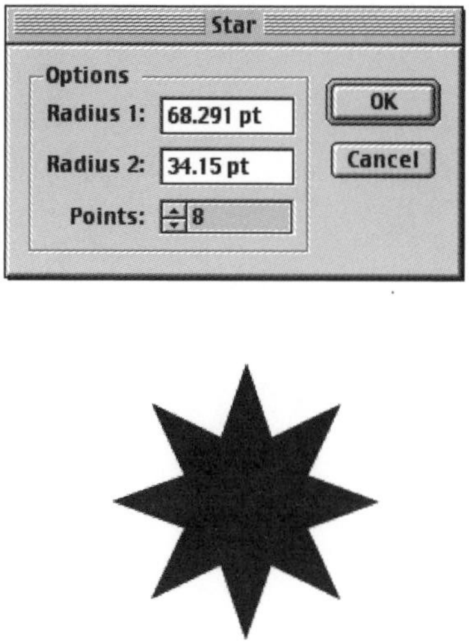

Figure 23-11: The Star dialog box and the star it created

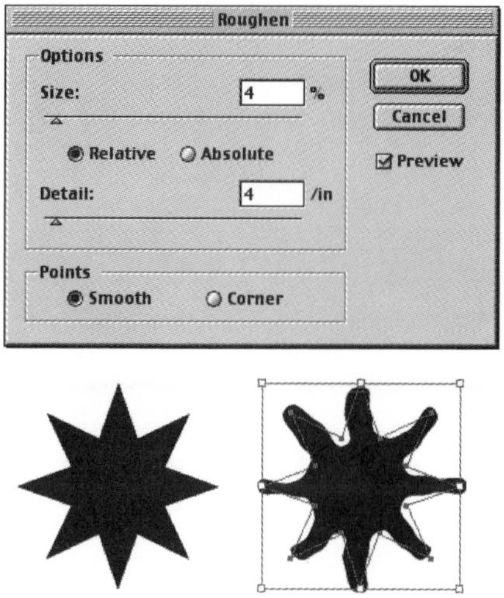

Figure 23-12: A star before and after applying the Roughen command

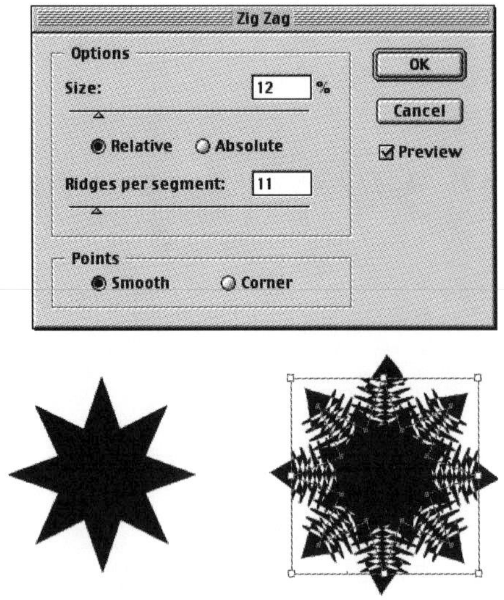

Figure 23-13: The Zig Zag command transformed a star into a snowflake.

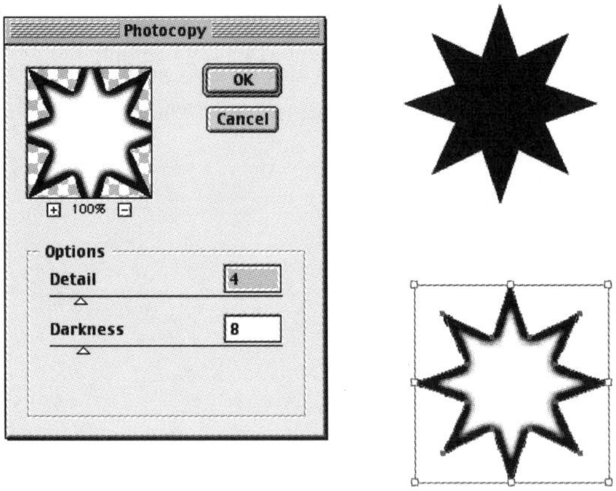

Figure 23-14: The Photocopy command copied and altered the star.

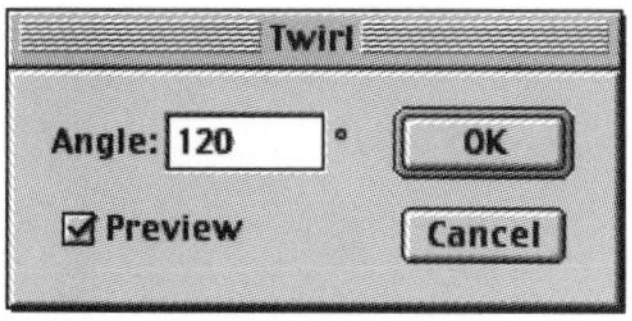

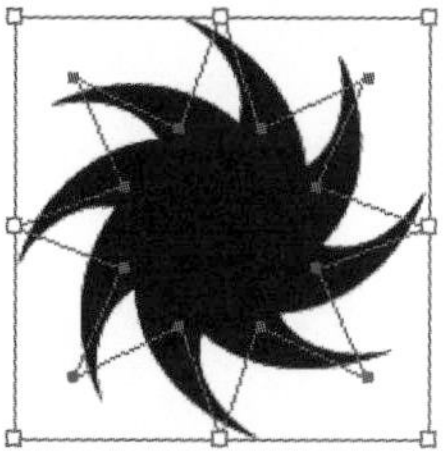

Figure 23-15: The Twirl command twirled the star.

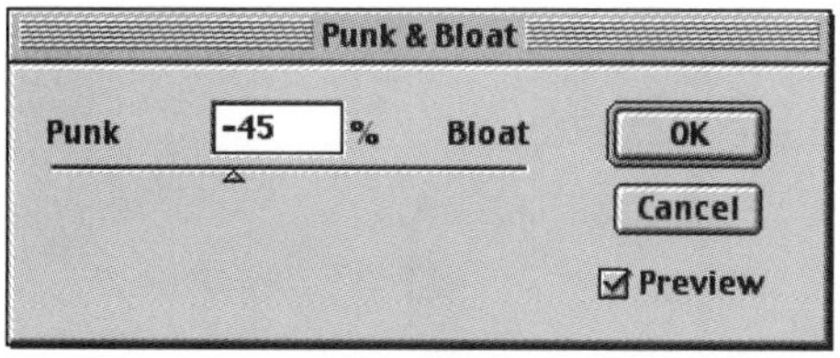

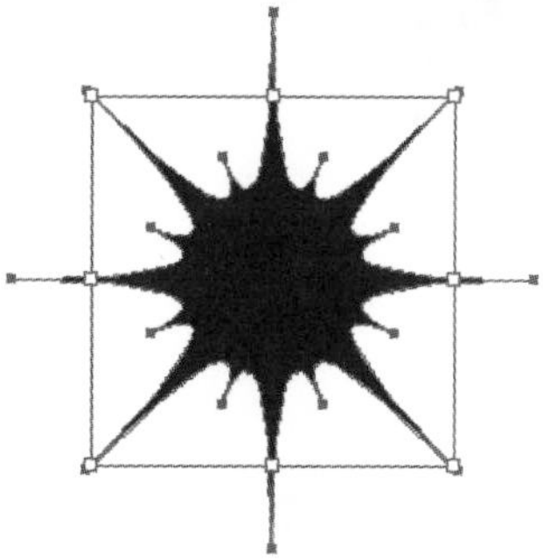

Figure 23-16: A star is transformed with the Punk & Bloat command.

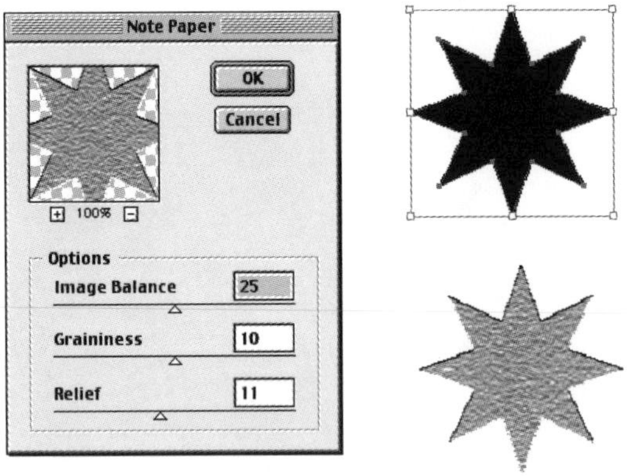

Figure 23-17: A black-and-white star is transformed with the Note Paper command.

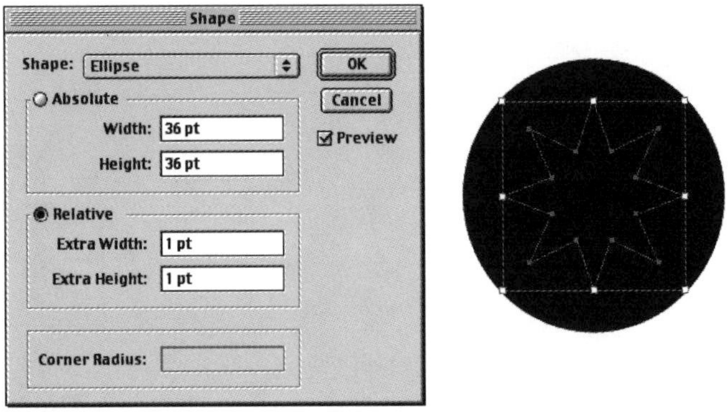

Figure 23-18: A star shape is converted to an ellipse with the Ellipse command.

Note

You can also transform simple shapes created in Adobe Illustrator 10 into more elaborate shapes using the Reshape, Twist Warp, Twirl, Pucker, Bloat, Scallop, Crystallize, and Wrinkle tools.

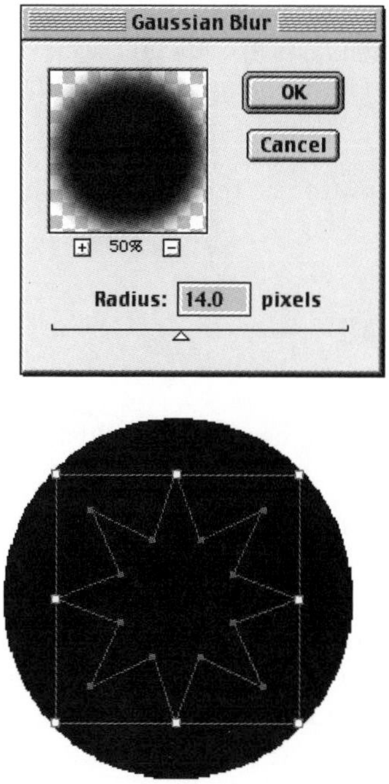

Figure 23-19: The Gaussian Blur command applied to an ellipse shape

Importing an Illustrator File As a Mask

After you know how to use Illustrator to create type and manipulate it into type shapes, you can import them into Premiere and use them as masks. You can import an Illustrator file as a mask into Premiere one of two ways: directly into the Video 2 track (as seen in Figure 23-9). Or you can import it into the Transparency Settings dialog box.

The first way of importing an Illustrator file as a mask entails importing the Illustrator file and placing it in track Video 2 of the Timeline. In Video 1, you place the video clip you want to use in your project. Then, you need to Select the Illustrator file in track Video 1 and Apply the Transparency Settings to it. In the Transparency Settings dialog box set the Key Type pop-up menu to Alpha Channel, Screen, Multiply, or Luminance Key Type. The second way of importing an Illustrator file as a mask, entails first importing a video clip and placing it in track Video 2. Then you need to select track Video 2 and apply the Transparency Settings to it. In the Transparency Settings dialog box set the Key Type to Image Matte Key Type.

When you select the Image Matte option, the Choose button becomes available. By selecting the Choose button, you can import the Illustrator file you want to apply to the video clip in track Video 2. The effect is seen in the Sample window of the Transparency Settings dialog box.

The following sections take you step-by-step on how to use the Luminance and Image Matte Key Type.

Applying the Luminance Key Type

1. **Create a new project in Premiere.**
2. **Choose File ➪ Import ➪ File.** Select a video clip to use with the Illustrator mask, then click Open.
3. **Choose File ➪ Import ➪ File.** Select the Illustrator file you want to import and then click Open.

On the CD-ROM

If you don't have a video clip, use one from the CD-ROM that accompanies this book. If you don't have an Illustrator shape, you can use one of the Illustrator shapes seen in Figures 23-12 through 23-19. The CD-ROM's Chapter 23 folder contains these Illustrator files.

4. **Drag the Illustrator file from the Project window to track Video 2 in the Timeline window.**
5. **Drag the video clip from the Project window to track Video 1 in the Timeline window.** You should now have a video clip in Video track 1 and an Illustrator file in the Video 2 track in the Timeline window.
6. **Click the Illustrator icon in the Video 2 track.**
7. **Choose Clip ➪ Video Options ➪ Transparency.** The Transparency Settings dialog box appears.
8. **Click Alpha Channel in the Key Type menu.** Notice that only the black or colored areas show through. The rest of the file is transparent.

   When working with Illustrator gray paths, you'll want to use the Luminance Key type so that the image is translucent. Here's how:

   1. **Import and then drag a gray Illustrator shape to Video track 2 in the Timeline window.**
   2. **Choose Clip ➪ Video Options ➪ Transparency.** The Transparency Settings dialog box appears.
   3. **Click Luminance in the Key Type menu, as shown in Figure 23-20.** Notice that the video clip shows through the Illustrator shape at whatever percentage to which the gray color is set. Click and drag the Cutoff slider to display more of the background of the video clip in track Video 1. (For more information on using the Transparency dialog box, turn to Chapter 13.)

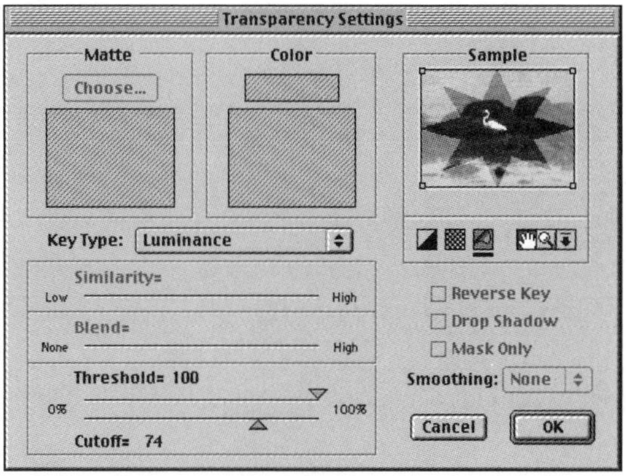

Figure 23-20: The Transparency Settings dialog box can be used to make a video clip translucent, based upon the gray level of the Illustrator shape used.

9. **Choose Clip ➪ Preview to preview the project.** Notice that the Illustrator shape appears above the video clip. You can see the video clip beneath the shape because all Illustrator backgrounds are transparent unless you put something in it.
10. **Choose File ➪ Save to save your work.**

Applying the Image Matte Key Type

The Image Matte Key Type option is a good choice to use when you would like a video clip to be seen through an Illustrator image. For this section, you can use any of the star images, or the ellipse image you created in the previous section.

On the CD-ROM

If you want, you can load the star.ai image and the ellipse.ai image from the Chapter 23 folder on the CD-ROM that accompanies this book.

Follow these steps to apply the Image Matte Key Type option on the Illustrator file:

1. **Choose File ➪ New Project.**
2. **Choose File ➪ Import ➪ File.** Locate a video clip and then click Open. We used the crane.mov video clip, which is found in the Chapter 23 folder on the CD-ROM that accompanies this book.
3. **Drag the video clip from the Project window to track Video 2 in the Timeline window.** Figure 23-21 shows the Timeline window with the Crane clip in track Video 2.
4. **Click the video clip in the Video 2 track.**

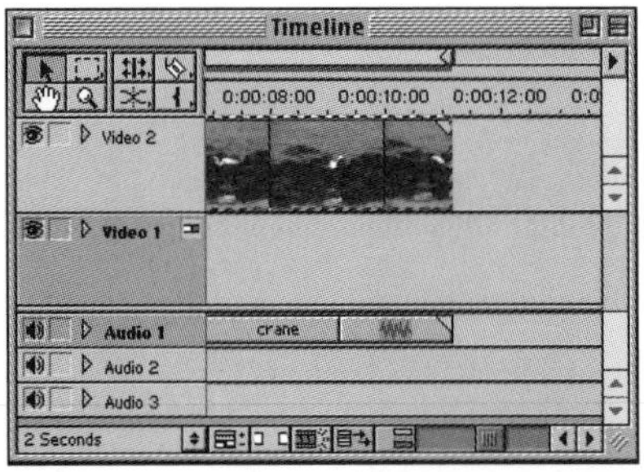

Figure 23-21: The Timeline window with the crane.mov clip in track Video 2

5. **Choose Clip ⇨ Video Options ⇨ Transparency.** The Transparency Settings dialog box appears.
6. **Click Image Matte in the Key Type menu.**
7. **Click the Choose button and locate an Illustrator file to use.** Figure 23-22 shows an Illustrator path type displayed in the Sample area. Figure 23-23 shows a star shape in the Sample area. Notice that the white areas in the star and on the outside of the star don't show up in the preview. Only the black areas show through. The video clip shows through the areas that are beneath the white areas.

Note

You can put an image or video clip in the Video 2 track and another one in the Video 1 track. Next, choose Clip ⇨ Video Options ⇨ Transparency. In the Transparency Settings dialog box, select the Image Matte Key Type and choose a file to use as a matte. If you are using a black-and-white image, the file from the Video 1 track appears in the black areas, and the file from the Video 2 track appears in the white areas. If you click the Reverse Key option, track Video 1 shows through the white areas and track Video 2 shows through the black areas. If the file you choose has gray in it, the file in either track shows through at a translucent value, which depends upon the shade of gray. If the shade is set at 50%, the file in the video track shows through at a 50% translucency.

8. **To experiment using the Image Matte option, click the Choose button in the Transparency dialog box.** Select another Illustrator file. After you've chosen an Illustrator file, click the Reverse Key option to activate it.

Note

Figure 23-24 shows the crane video clip through an Illustrator ellipse shape with a blur at the edges. Try choosing another Illustrator shape and using the Reverse Key option. Figure 23-25 shows the Crane video clip through an Illustrator twirled star shape. Figure 23-26 shows the Crane video clip through an Illustrator blob shape. Figure 23-27 shows the Crane video clip through an Illustrator snowflake shape. Figure 23-28 shows how gray shapes work using the Image Matte and Reverse Key options. In Figure 23-28 the outer circle is made with a 25% gray fill. The middle circle is filled with a 50% gray fill, and the square in the center is filled with

100% black. Notice how the Crane video clip shows through at 100%, through the square shape. At the 50% gray circle, the video clip shows through at 50%. At the 25% gray circle, the video clip shows through at 25%.

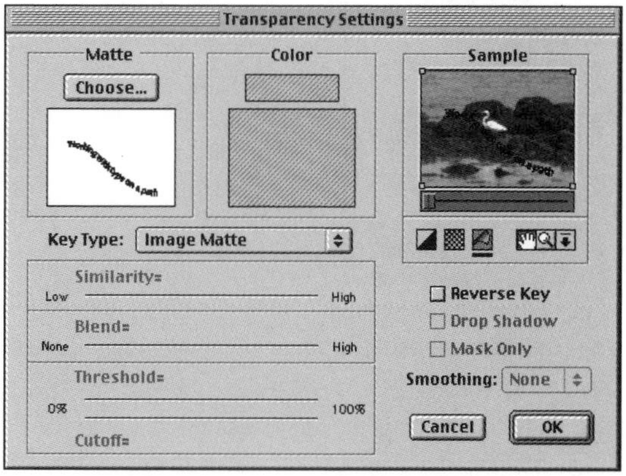

Figure 23-22: The Transparency Settings dialog box shows how you can use the Image Matte Key Type option on Illustrator path type.

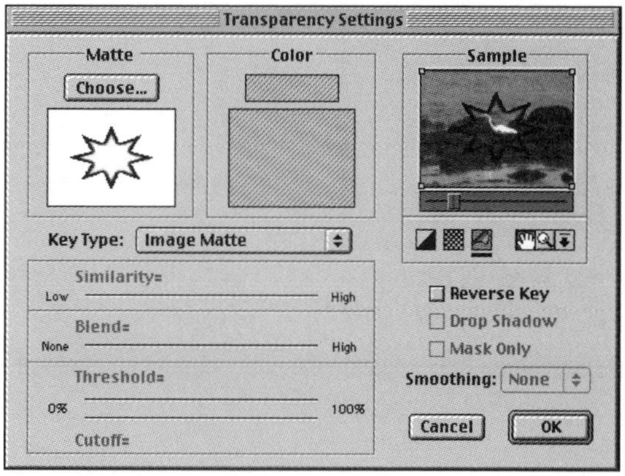

Figure 23-23: The Transparency Settings dialog box shows that only the Image Matte's black areas show through. The white areas are replaced by the video clip.

9. **When you finish experimenting with the Image Matte and Reverse Key option, click OK to close the dialog box.**
10. **Choose File ⇨ Save to save your work.**

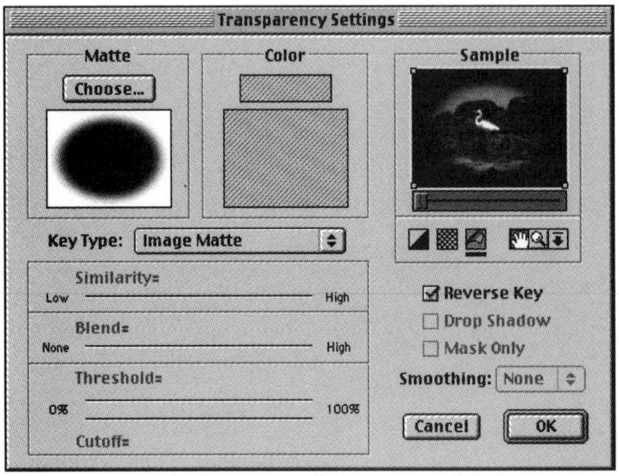

Figure 23-24: The Transparency Settings dialog box shows a video clip through an Illustrator ellipse shape.

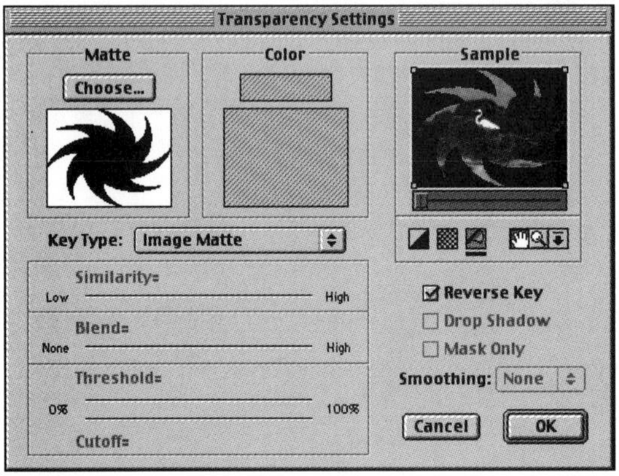

Figure 23-25: The Transparency Settings dialog box shows a video clip through an Illustrator twirled star shape.

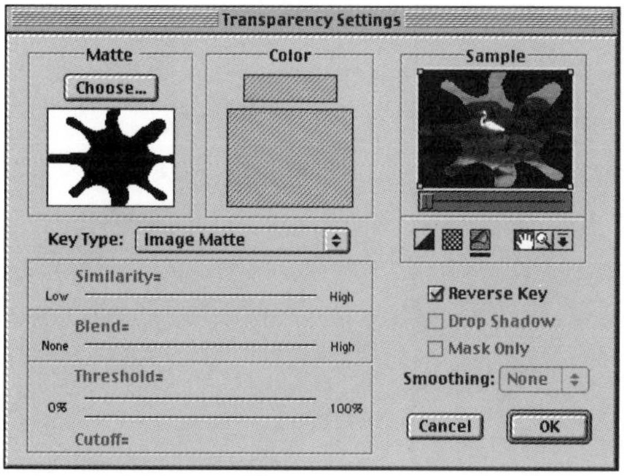

Figure 23-26: The Transparency Settings dialog box shows a video clip through an Illustrator blob shape.

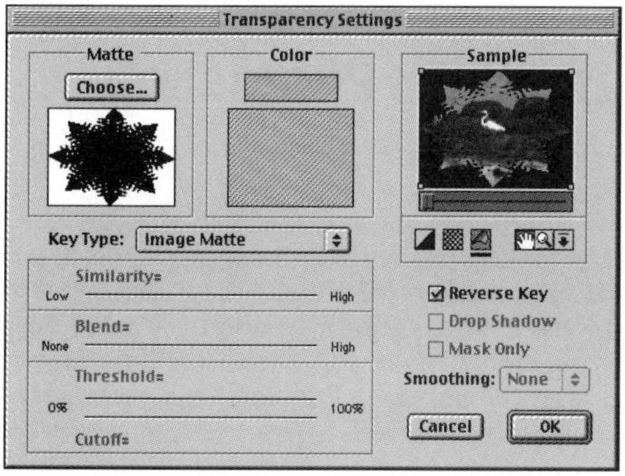

Figure 23-27: The Transparency Settings dialog box shows a video clip through an Illustrator snowflake shape.

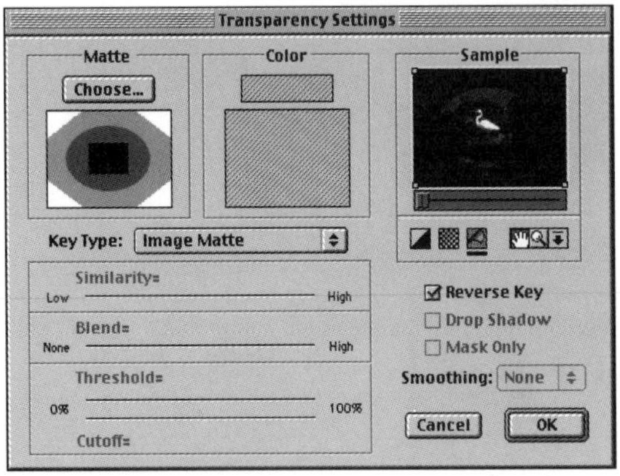

Figure 23-28: Illustrator gray shapes using the Image Matte and Reverse Key options

Creating a Mask Using Both Photoshop and Illustrator

Combining the strengths of Adobe Photoshop and Adobe Illustrator, you can create elaborate masks. Start by using Photoshop to save a scanned photograph, an image captured with a digital camera, or a stock image. Then load the file into Illustrator and use one of the path creating tools to create a path around the area in the photo you want to import into Adobe Premiere. In Figure 23-32, we used Illustrator's Paintbrush tool to create a path. After the path is in Premiere, you can have a video clip running in the background, as seen in Figure 23-33.

Here's how to create a complex mask using both Adobe Photoshop and Adobe Illustrator:

1. **Scan or capture an image into Adobe Photoshop with a scanner, digital camera, or a digital camcorder.**
2. **Save the file in either Photoshop or TIFF format.** Many photo-finishing labs can develop your film as well as archive the pictures on a CD-ROM or floppy disk.

Note: Figure 23-29 shows the sample image (girl.psd) we used in this section. If you want, you can load this image from the Chapter 23 folder on the book's CD-ROM.

3. **Load Adobe Illustrator.**
4. **Chose File ➪ Open.** Locate the digitized Photoshop image and open it.

Figure 23-29: Sample photo used to create a mask in Photoshop and Illustrator

5. **Choose Window ⇨ Show Layers.**
6. **In the Layers palette, double-click the layer in the Layers palette.** The Layer Options dialog box appears (see Figure 23-30).
7. **Click both the Lock and Dim image options to lock and dim the layer.** Make sure that the Dim option is set to 50%.
8. **Click OK for the effects to take place.**

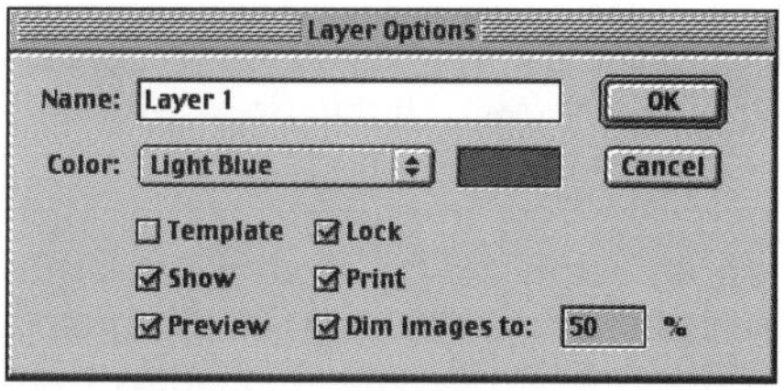

Figure 23-30: The Layer Options dialog box enables you to lock and dim a layer.

9. **Click the New Layer menu in the Layers palette to create a new layer.** In the Layer Options dialog box that appears, name the layer and then click OK.
10. **Select the Pen, Pencil, or Paintbrush tool.**
11. **Trace the dimmed image's outline.** If you use the Pen tool, a small circle appears next to the tool when the starting and finishing points meet. When this happens, click to close the path, if you want to create a closed path. Figure 23-31 shows the sample image dimmed in a layer and a few path strokes created with the Paintbrush in another layer.

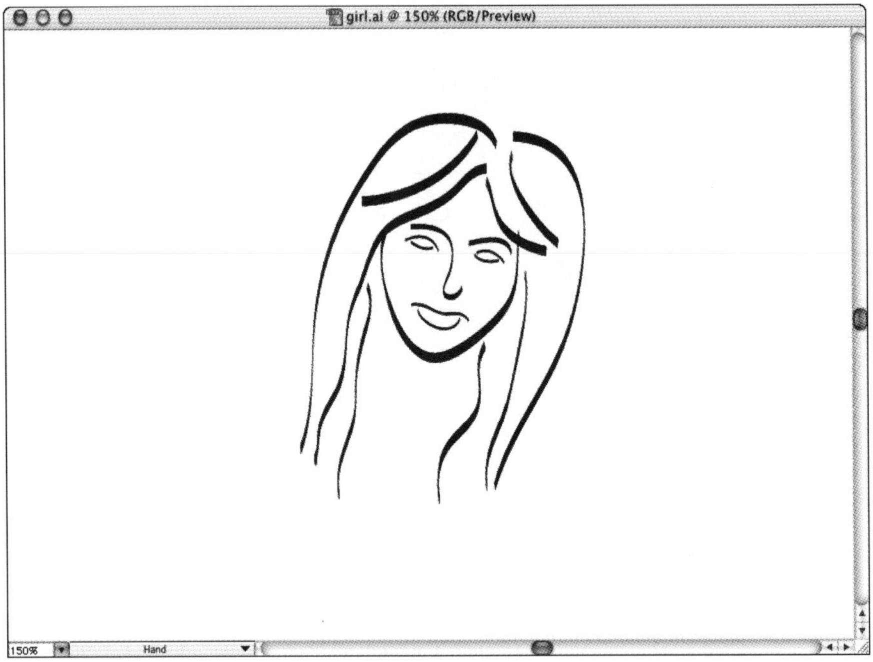

Figure 23-31: The dimmed image is in one layer and the Paintbrush paths are in another layer.

When you are drawing, it's easier to see the image you are tracing if you trace with a stroke and no fill, as seen in Figure 23-32. If you draw with a fill, you won't see the image in the layer below. To set the Fill to none, click the Fill swatch (the top overlapping square) in the Toolbox and then click the third small square (the one with the dialog line) below the Fill swatch. Click the Stroke swatch (behind the Fill swatch) and then click the first small square to set the stroke color to black. Choose Window ⇨ Show Stroke to display the Stroke palette. The Stroke palette enables you to choose the width of your stroke.

12. **After you've created a few paths, you may want to hide the bottom layer with the image in it to see how your path strokes are appearing.** Click the eye icon next to the layer you want to hide.
13. **After you have a path, fill it with black if you want to use it as a solid mask in Premiere.** You may want to fill the path with a shade of gray to create a translucent mask. (See the section "Applying the Luminance Key Type" for more information about how to do this.)
14. **When you finish tracing over the dimmed image, you can delete it.** You may, however, first want to use the File ⇨ Save As command to duplicate the file.
15. **Save your final file in Illustrator format.**

Figure 23-32: The traced image created in Illustrator

Note

If you are using Illustrator 9 or 10, you'll need to save your file in Version 8 format for it to be read in Premiere, because Premiere 6.5 won't read Illustrator 9 or 10 format.

16. **Load Adobe Premiere and then create a new project.**
17. **Choose File ➪ Import ➪ File.** Locate the Illustrator file you want to import and then click Open.

Note

The screen shots in this section feature the traced image created in the preceding section. If you want, you can load the file, girl.ai from the Chapter 23 folder on the book's CD-ROM. Or, if you prefer, you can import an Illustrator file that has text.

18. **Drag the Illustrator file from the Project window to track Video 2 in the Timeline window.**
19. **Choose File ➪ Import ➪ File.** Locate a video clip and then click Open. We used a video clip called cruising.mov, which we've included in the Chapter 23 folder on the CD-ROM that accompanies this book.
20. **Drag the video clip from the Project window to track Video 1 in the Timeline window.** You should now have a video clip in the Video 1 track and an Illustrator file in the Video 2 track (see Figure 23-33).

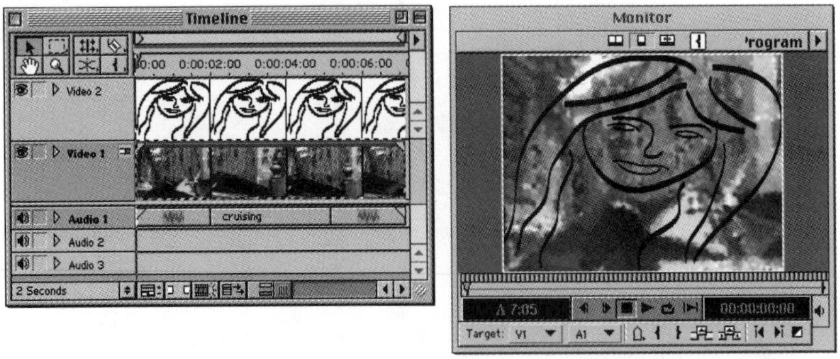

Figure 23-33: The Monitor and Timeline windows with the Illustrator file and video clip

21. **Click the Illustrator icon in the Video 2 track.**
22. **Choose Clip ➪ Video Options ➪ Transparency.** The Transparency Settings dialog box appears (see Figure 23-34).
23. **Click Alpha Channel in the Key Type menu.** Notice that only the black or colored areas show through. The rest of the file is transparent.
24. **Click OK when you are ready to close the Transparency Settings dialog box.**

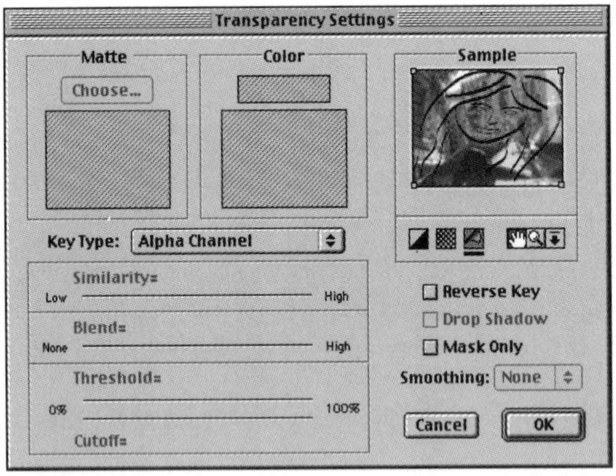

Figure 23-34: The Transparency Settings dialog box shows the Alpha Channel Key Type option used on an Illustrator document.

Summary

You can use Adobe Illustrator to create text and masks for Premiere projects.

- Illustrator features six type tools: the Type tool, Area Type tool, Path Type tool, Vertical Type tool, Vertical Area Type tool, and the Vertical Path Type tool.
- You can create shapes in Illustrator using the Rectangle, Ellipse, Polygon, and Star tools.
- When creating masks using Illustrator, the Alpha Channel, Screen, or Multiply keys are best used when you only want the black or colored areas of the mask to appear.
- The Luminance or Image Matte Key Type option is the best option when you want a video clip to be seen through an Illustrator image.
- You can create complex masks by using both Adobe Photoshop and Adobe Premiere.

✦ ✦ ✦

CHAPTER 24

Working with Masks in Adobe After Effects

✦ ✦ ✦ ✦

In This Chapter

Creating oval and rectangle masks in After Effects

Editing a mask with the Layer command and the Layer window

Creating Bézier masks

Editing a mask with the Time Layout window

✦ ✦ ✦ ✦

Matte effects are undoubtedly one of the more interesting special effects provided by Adobe Premiere. In Chapters 12 and 13, you've learned how mattes can be used to hide portions of one video clip in a track behind the masked area of a shape in another video track.

If you want to create a matte effect in Premiere, one technique is to create a shape in another program to use as a mask and import it into Premiere. Although this is a rather straightforward and simple process, it does not enable you to create the mask at the same time as previewing the clip with which it will be used. Nor does it enable you to change the matte's shape as the clip runs.

If you need to create sophisticated matte effects, you can turn to Adobe After Effects. In After Effects you can create masks using the After Effects Pen tool, edit them, and animate them over time. You can also import Adobe Illustrator and Adobe Photoshop files into After Effects to be used as masks. After Effects also enables you to import Illustrator and Photoshop paths or Photoshop alpha channels to be used as masks.

This chapter looks at Adobe After Effects's masking options. It also discusses the features that Premiere lacks but which you still may want to use to add interesting and unusual matte effects to Premiere. To do this, you can import a Premiere project into After Effects and use After Effects's masking capabilities to add pizzazz to your clips.

After Effects Masks: An Overview

In Adobe After Effects, you can load a video clip or an entire Premiere project into After Effects and isolate an area by using a mask so that the viewer only sees a portion of the video clip or project. In After Effects, masks are created using *paths*. A path is similar to a wire frame line on-screen that can be used to create anything from shapes with sharp corners, to flowing waves created from perfect curves. After Effects features three types of masks: Oval, Rectangle, and Beziér. When you want to create or use an oval-shape mask, you work with an oval path. When you want to create or use a rectangular-shape mask, you work with a rectangular path. If you are creating any other shaped mask, you work with a Beziér mask.

To create a Beziér mask, you need to use the After Effects Pen tool, which is found in the Toolbox. The Pen tool in After Effects is quite similar to the Pen tool in Adobe Illustrator and Adobe Photoshop. You can edit the path using the Pen +, Pen -, and Convert tools. All of these tools reside in the same location in the Toolbox as the Pen tool. You can use the Selection tool (arrow tool) in the Toolbox to edit a point on the path by clicking the point and dragging it to the position you want. If you double-click the path with the Selection tool, you can move, scale, or rotate the path as a whole. The effects of a mask are displayed in the Composition window. Masks are edited in the Layer window. Masks can be altered over time by using the Time Layout window.

Creating Oval and Rectangle Masks

You can have a lot of fun creating interesting effects with masks. Figure 24-1 shows a frame with a video clip before applying a rectangular mask. Figure 24-2 shows the same frame after an oval mask was used on the video clip's perimeter. We then placed a still image in the background. For an added effect, we applied the Twirl command (Effect ➪ Distort ➪ Twirl) to the background still image.

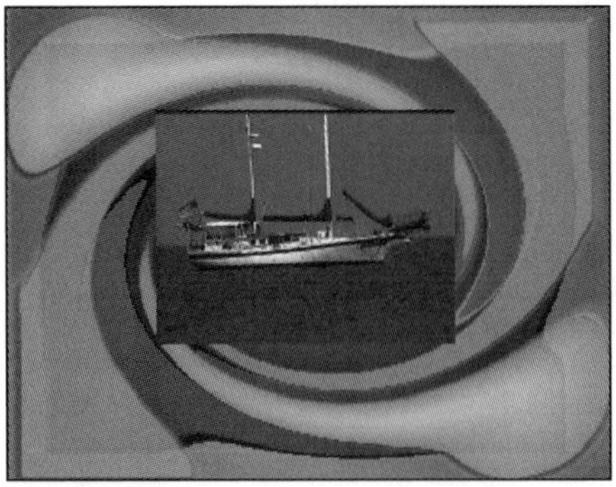

Figure 24-1: An After Effects frame before using a mask

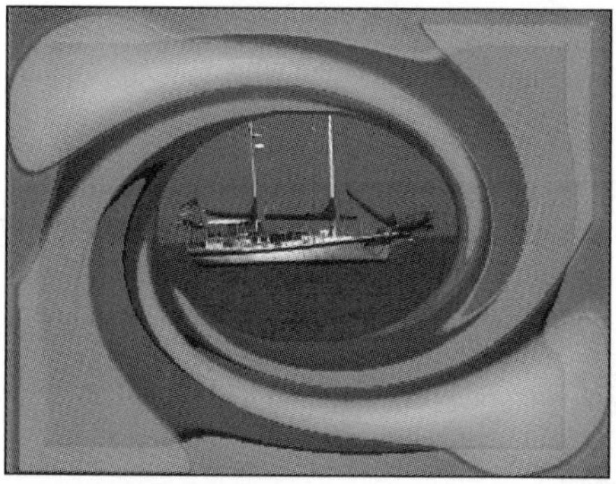

Figure 24-2: An After Effects frame created using an oval mask

Here's how to create an oval or rectangle mask in After Effects:

1. **Load After Effects.**
2. **Choose File ➪ New ➪ New Project to create a new project.**
3. **Choose Composition ➪ New Composition to create a new composition.**
4. **In the New Composition dialog box, set the frame size.** To create the frame shown in Figure 24-1, we set the width and height frame to 320 x 240 pixels and imported a video clip that was 160 x 120. That way, we had plenty of room to see the background beneath the video clip.
5. **Choose File ➪ Import ➪ File.**
6. **In the Import File dialog box, choose a file and then set the Import As menu to Footage.** You can use one of the video clips found in the Chapter 24 folder on the CD-ROM that accompanies this book.
7. **Click Import to import a video clip you want to mask.** The imported video clip appears in the Project window.

Note

When creating a mask in After Effects for the first time you may want to use just a simple video clip that doesn't have too much action, rather than an action-packed video clip or an entire Premiere project. If you want, you can use the video clip of the sailboat we used in this section. The sailboat video clip is found in the Chapter 24 folder on the CD-ROM that accompanies this book. If you would like to import a Premiere project, choose File ➪ Import ➪ File (older versions of Premiere choose Premiere As Comp). In the File Import dialog box, click Composition in the Import As menu. Click Import to import a Premiere project into After Effects.

8. **Click and drag the imported video clip to the middle of the Composition window.** Not only does the video clip appear in the Composition window, but it also appears in the Time Layout window.

9. **Choose Layer ➪ Mask ➪ New Mask to add a mask to your clip.**

10. **Choose Layer ➪ Mask ➪ Mask Shape.** The Mask Shape dialog box appears (see Figure 24-3).

11. **Click either the Oval or Rectangle Shape option.** Leave the Units menu set to pixels and then click OK to see the effects of the mask in the Composition window.

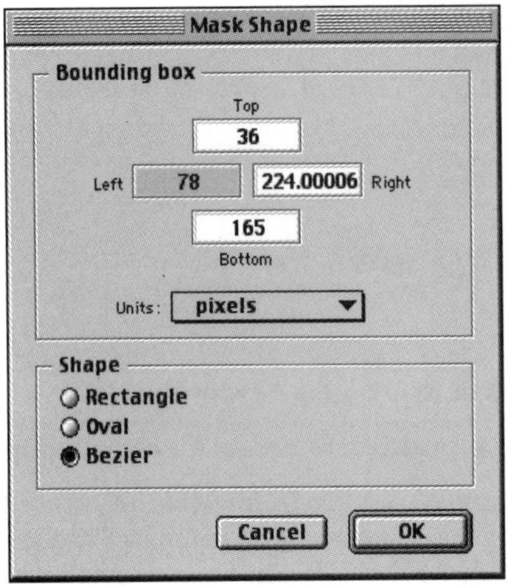

Figure 24-3: The Mask Shape dialog box enables you to pick a shape for your mask.

12. **Choose File ➪ Import ➪ File to import another video clip to use in the background or import a still image to use as the background.** You'll be better able to view the effect of the Oval/Rectangle mask. Locate the still image or video clip that you want to import. If desired, you can use the still image that appears in the background in Figures 24-1 and 24-2. This file, shapes.psd, is found in the Chapter 24 folder on the CD-ROM that accompanies this book.

13. **Click and drag the imported clip from the Project window to the Time Layout window.** Make sure that you place the image or clip beneath the video clip that has the mask. If it isn't, click and drag it in the Time Layout window and place it below the masked video clip.

14. **To preview the effect of the mask, move the Time Marker along the Timeline.**

15. **Save your file by choosing File ➪ Save.** After saving the file, if you want, you can continue editing the mask.

Editing a Mask with the Layer Window and Layer Menu

After you've created a mask, you can use the Layer menu and the Layer window, along with the Selection tool in the Toolbox, to edit the mask. Here are a few mask-editing tips:

✦ **To edit the mask, the mask must be selected.** If the mask isn't selected, you can select it by double-clicking the name of the clip you are working on in the Time Layout window. In the Layer window that appears, click the path to select it.

✦ **Keep the Layer and Composition windows side by side.** As you change the path in the Layer window, you'll be able to see the effect of the mask on the video clip in the Composition window. Figure 24-4 shows the path in the Layer window and the mask in the Composition window.

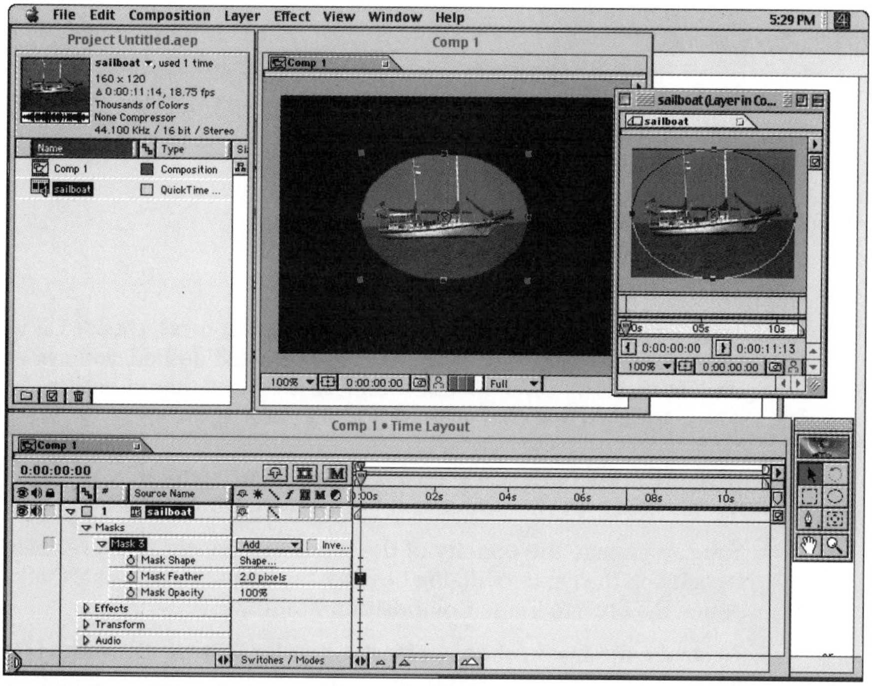

Figure 24-4: The Layer window shows the mask as a path. When the path is edited, the mask is edited in the Composition window.

Here's how to edit a mask:

1. **To soften your mask's edges, you can apply a feather by choosing Layer ➪ Mask ➪ Feather.** In the Feather Mask dialog box, type in a small value to create a small feather. A large value results in a large feather.
2. **To resize a rectangle or oval mask, start by double-clicking the video clip's name in the Time Layout window.** The mask appears as a path in the Layer window. To edit the path, click an anchor point (shown in Figure 24-5) using the Selection tool found in the Toolbox. Then press an arrow key on your keyboard to move the anchor point up, down, or to the right or left. As you edit the path, the mask in the Composition window is affected. Clicking and moving the directional line in the oval path changes the shape of the curve.

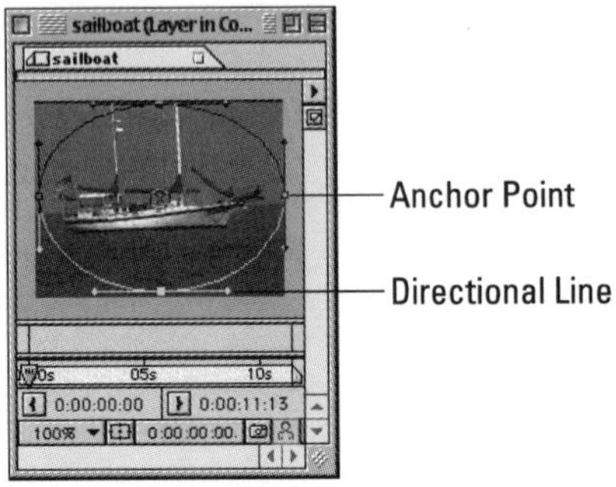

Figure 24-5: You can edit an oval path by moving anchor points and directional lines.

Tip

If you want to cancel the changes you made to your mask, choose Layer ➪ Mask ➪ Reset Mask to reset the mask to its original state. If desired, you can remove the mask by choosing Layer ➪ Mask ➪ Remove Mask and then choosing Layer ➪ Mask ➪ New Mask to create a new mask and start over again.

3. **With the mask path still selected in the Layer window, you can choose Layer ➪ Mask ➪ Free Transform Points to continue editing.**
4. **You can change the opacity of the mask by choosing Layer ➪ Mask ➪ Opacity.** In the Opacity dialog box, set the opacity you want. Click OK and notice the change in the Composition window.
5. **To stroke the mask, choose Effect ➪ Render ➪ Stroke.** Use the Effect Controls palette to set the stroke color and width. You can also set a fill color, by choosing Effect ➪ Render ➪ Fill. Again, use the Effect Controls palette to set the fill color and opacity.

6. **To invert the mask (reverse the effect of the mask), choose Layer ➪ Mask ➪ Inverse.** To bring the mask back to the state it was before you inverted it, choose Layer ➪ Mask ➪ Inverse.
7. **To change the mode of the mask, choose Layer ➪ Mask ➪ Mode and then choose a mode.** By default the mode is set to Add.

Creating a Beziér Mask

The Pen tools used in programs such as Illustrator, Photoshop, Macromedia Freehand, and Corel DRAW provide digital artists with the power to draw virtually any shape imaginable. The After Effects Pen tool provides similar power — except instead of using the Pen tool to create works of art, After Effects users can use the Pen tool to create masks.

Figure 24-6 shows the first frame of a video clip without a Beziér mask. Figure 24-7 shows the same frame with a Beziér mask applied to the chipmunk in the clip. In order to isolate the chipmunk from the background, we used a Beziér mask — because using an oval or rectangle obviously wouldn't provide the desired effect. After we isolated the chipmunk from its background by applying the mask, we added a background still image. To make the background image more interesting, we applied the Effect ➪ Stylize ➪ Mosaic command. Finally, we added type, using After Effects's Effect ➪ Text ➪ Path Text command.

Cross-Reference

To use After Effects's Path Text command, you first need to create a New Solid (Layer ➪ New Solid). For more information on creating and animating text in After Effects, turn to Chapter 25.

Figure 24-6: A frame from a video clip without a Beziér mask

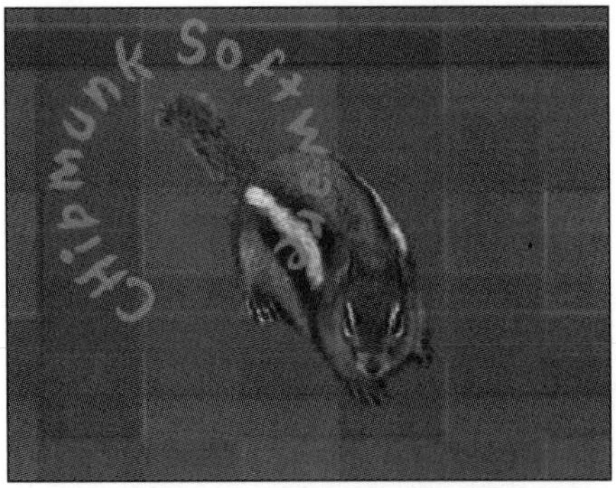

Figure 24-7: A frame from a video clip with a Beziér mask

Here's how to create a simple Beziér mask using the After Effects Pen tool:

1. **In After Effects, create a new project by choosing File ➪ New ➪ New Project.**
2. **Choose Composition ➪ New Composition to create a new composition.**
3. **In the New Composition dialog box, specify a frame size.** To create the frame shown in Figure 24-6, we set the width and height frame size to 320 x 240 pixels.
4. **Choose File ➪ Import ➪ File to import a video clip you want to mask.** In the File Import dialog box choose a file and then set the Import As menu to Footage. Choose Import to import the selected video clip. The imported video clip appears in the Project window.

On the CD-ROM

If you want to use the video clip of the chipmunk.mov shown in Figure 24-6, it can be found in the Chapter 24 folder on the CD-ROM that accompanies this book.

5. **Drag the video clip to the middle of the Composition window.** The video clip not only appears in the Composition window, but it also appears in the Time Layout window.
6. **Double-click the video clip's name in the Time Layout palette.** When the Layer window appears, click the menu to make sure Masks is selected.
7. **Select the Pen tool in the Toolbox.**
8. **Create a path around the image.** Click in the image you want to isolate. Keep clicking the perimeter of the image with the Pen tool to create a path around the image. When the first and last points meet, a tiny circle appears next to the Pen icon. Click the mouse to close the path. As you create a Beziér path in the Layer window, the effect of the mask appears in the Composition window. Figure 24-8 shows the mask path in the Layer window and the effect of the mask in the Composition window.

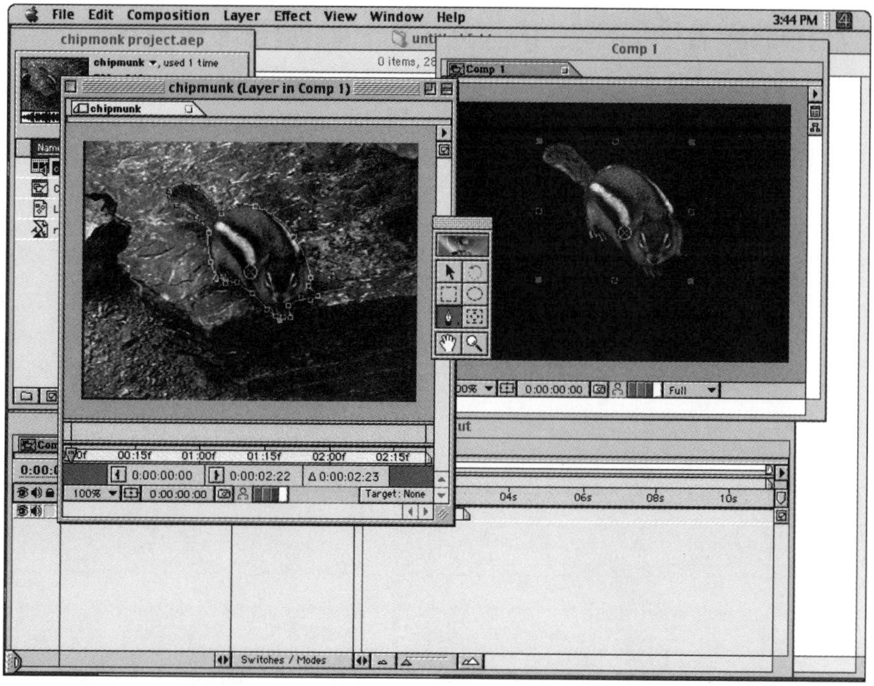

Figure 24-8: The mask path in the Layer window and the mask effect in the Composition window

Note

If you find the Pen tool difficult to use, you can start by using the Oval or Rectangle tools to create a path and then use the Pen and Selection tools to edit the path.

9. **After you've created the Beziér mask, you can import a still image or video clip to use as the background. Choose File ⇨ Import ⇨ File to import a file.**
10. **To add text to your image, choose Layer ⇨ New Solid, then choose Effect ⇨ Text ⇨ Basic Text or Path Text.**
11. **Save your file by choosing File ⇨ Save.**

Editing Paths with the Pen Tool

You can edit a path in After Effects by using the Selection tool to select an anchor point and move it, or you can click on a directional line with the Selection tool to change the shape of a curve. You can use the Convert tool, which is found in the same location as the Pen tool, to convert a curve to a corner point, or vice versa. If you need more anchor points, select the Pen + tool and click the path to add a point at that location. To omit a point, click it with the Pen tool.

Editing a Mask with the Time Layout Window

You can edit a mask's shape, location, feather, and opacity over various time intervals using After Effects Time Layout window. Figure 24-9 shows the Layer window, the Composition window, and the Time Layout window at different points in time. Notice that the mask shape changes as the video progresses.

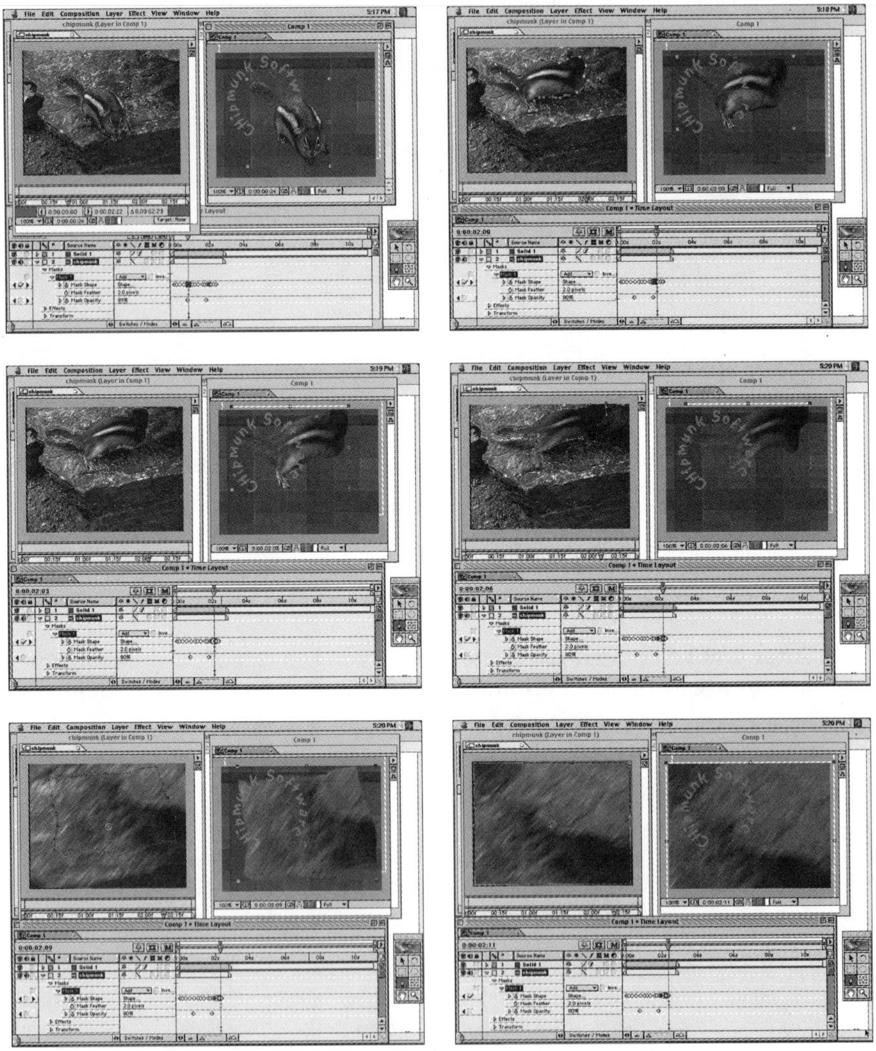

Figure 24-9: The frames above show that the mask shape changes over time in the Time Layout, Composition, and Layer windows.

To use the Time Layout window to edit a mask over time, follow these steps:

1. **Click the triangle next to the video clip's name in the Time Layout window.**
2. **Click the triangle in front of the word Masks to display the mask.**
3. **Click the triangle in front of the mask to show the mask options.**
   - **Mask Shape.** Allows you to set the shape to either Rectangle, oval, or Beziér.
   - **Mask Feather.** Allows you to apply either a horizontal and/or vertical feather to the edges of a mask.
   - **Mask Opacity.** Allows you to change the opacity. To make the mask translucent, set the Opacity, less than 100%.
   - **Mask mode.** By default the mode is set to Add. (Next to the modes, After Effects provides an area that you can click if you want to invert the mask.)
4. **Move the Time Marker to the beginning of the Timeline.**
5. **Click the stopwatch next to the option you want to change.** In Figure 24-9, we changed the mask's shape so that it would follow the chipmunk as it moved over time.
6. **Move the Time Marker over to the right just a bit and edit the mask shape, feather, or opacity.** To follow an image the way we did, you need to move and edit the mask path in the Layer window.
7. **When you've finished editing the mask path, move the Time Marker again to the right.**
8. **Now edit the shape.** Continue until you've reached the end of the Timeline.

You can also edit a mask option from a point other than the beginning. For Figure 24-9 we started editing the Opacity at the middle of the Timeline.

Follow these steps to edit mask options from within the Timeline:

1. **Move the Time Marker to the middle of the Timeline.**
2. **Edit the mask options.** First, click the stopwatch in front of the option. Next, click the desired option value. When that option's dialog box appears, type in a number and then click OK.

   In the example, we changed the Opacity setting. The opacity in the Timeline starts at 100%.
3. **Preview the project by choosing Composition ⇨ Preview.** When the Time Marker reaches the middle of the Timeline, the option you edited changes to whatever value you entered in Step 2.

4. **Make the mask option gradually change from the middle of the Timeline to the end of the Timeline.** Move the Time Marker to the end of the Timeline. Next, click the desired option and type in a new value in its dialog box.

5. **Click OK for the value to take effect.**

Importing Masks from Illustrator or Photoshop

You can import a black-and-white Illustrator or Photoshop file into After Effects to use as a mask. The Illustrator or Photoshop file can be used to isolate areas in a video clip, as shown in Figure 24-10. Figure 24-11 shows the black-and-white Illustrator file used as a mask.

Figure 24-10: The effect of an Illustrator file used as a mask on a video clip in After Effects

Figure 24-11: The black-and-white Illustrator file used as a mask

Here's how to use Illustrator and Photoshop to create a mask in After Effects:

1. **In Illustrator, create a shape using the Rectangle, Oval, Star, or Polygon tool.** Fill the shape with black. Then apply a filter or effect to the shape to create a more interesting shape.
2. **In Photoshop, create a new file and make the background color white.** In Photoshop, you can use one of the Selection tools to create a selection and fill it with black, or you can use a Painting tool to create a shape. You can also use Photoshop's filters to make an unusual shape.
3. **After you have created a black-shape in Illustrator or Photoshop, load After Effects and create a new project and a new composition.**
4. **Import the Photoshop or Illustrator file, as well as a video clip, into the project.**
5. **Drag the video clip to the Time Layout window.**
6. **Drag the Photoshop or Illustrator black-and-white file to the Time Layout window.**
7. **Click the Mode column that appears next to the file's name.** Click either the Lighten or Darken mode. (In Figure 24-10 the Lighten mode was used to lighten the dark areas.) The light (white) areas are not affected; only the dark areas (black areas) are. If you use the Darken mode, the dark area (black) in the image is not affected, but the light (white) area is affected.

Using Illustrator Paths as Masks

Hardcore Illustrator users will most likely prefer to create their masks in Illustrator, which provides more path-editing commands than does After Effects. Fortunately, importing an Illustrator file into After Effects is a simple copy-and-paste operation. Here are the steps:

1. **In Illustrator, select the path and all of its anchor points and then choose Edit ⇨ Copy.**
2. **Switch to After Effects, open the Layer window for the target layer and then choose Edit ⇨ Paste.**

Summary

Although Adobe Premiere provides numerous matting effects, it does not enable you to create sophisticated masks or edit masks over time. Adobe After Effects enables you to do both.

- ✦ After Effects enables you to create Oval, Rectangle, and Beziér masks.
- ✦ You can edit After Effects masks with its Pen +, Pen -, and Selection tools.
- ✦ After Effects masks can be edited over time.

✦ ✦ ✦

CHAPTER 25

Adding Special Effects in Adobe After Effects

✦ ✦ ✦ ✦

In This Chapter

How After Effects works

Importing Premiere clips

Animating Photoshop layers

Animating Illustrator layers

Animating text

Working with motion paths

Creating a composite video clip

✦ ✦ ✦ ✦

Although Adobe Premiere is packed with powerful video effects, at times you may want to create composite motion or text effects; that may not be possible within the confines of Premiere's menus and palettes. If your project requires a bit more pizzazz than Premiere seems able to produce, consider using Adobe After Effects.

After Effects can create dozens of effects that aren't possible in Premiere. For example, you can fine-tune a motion path's shape as you would a curve in Adobe Illustrator or Photoshop. You can also rotate text 360 degrees along a curve over time. After Effects enables you to run multiple clips simultaneously in the video frame — creating a three-ring circus of video effects.

This chapter's goal is not to persuade you to use After Effects over Premiere, but to show you how the two can work together to create the ultimate video production. Both programs have their strengths, and you can use this to your advantage.

How After Effects Works

After Effects combines some of the features of Photoshop and Premiere. To start a project in After Effects, first create a new *composition.* A composition determines the type of movie you will be creating. In the Composition Settings dialog box, you pick your settings for width, height, and frame rate. Then, you import all the images, sounds, titles, and video clips you need to create your video production. Like Premiere, After Effects stores all of these imported items in a Project window. As you need footage items, you drag them from the Project window into the Time Layout window. Unlike Premiere, the items in the Time Layout are not stored in video or sound tracks. Video and sound clips don't appear in different tracks; instead, they are organized as layers. In this way After Effects works like Photoshop. In both programs, you also can apply transformations (scale, rotate, and so on), effects, and masks to the layers. After Effects, however, enables you to animate the transformation, effects, and masks over time; in Photoshop, each layer's properties remain static.

Cross-Reference

If you import a Photoshop file into Adobe ImageReady, you can make animation frames from your layers and output the file as a QuickTime movie. See Chapter 9 for an example of how to do this.

Importing Premiere Projects

You can import an entire Premiere project along with its transitions and effects directly into After Effects to take advantage of the program's powerful features, such as animating transformations and masks over time.

Follow these steps to import a Premiere project into After Effects:

1. **In After Effects, choose File ➪ Import ➪ File (older versions of Premiere, choose Premiere As Comp).** The Import File dialog box appears.
2. **Select the Premiere project you want to import and set the Import As menu to Composition.**
3. **Click Import.** After Effects imports the Premiere project. The video and sound tracks now appear as layers in the Time Layout window. The first layer in the Time Layout window is the first video or sound track that appears in the Premiere Timeline window.
4. **If needed, you can now click a layer and animate it over time, using either one of the Effect commands, Layer ➪ Mask commands and/or one of the Transform options seen in the Time Layout palette.** These options can be animated over time using keyframes — similar to the way Premiere uses keyframes with video effects.

Note

Not only can you import a Premiere project into After Effects, but you can also output your Premiere project as a QuickTime movie and then import the QuickTime movie into After Effects by choosing File ➪ Import ➪ File (older versions of Premiere, choose Footage File). In the Import File dialog box, select a QuickTime movie to import. Set the Import As pop-up menu to Footage. Then choose Import to import the movie into After Effects.

Importing and Animating Photoshop Files

To animate a Photoshop file in After Effects, you can either create a folder and place all of the Photoshop files in it and import it as a Photoshop Sequence, or you can import a Photoshop file with layers like the one shown in Figure 25-1. When you use import a Photoshop file with layers as a compostion, a folder is created in the Project window, with the layers inside of it.

Here's how to import a Photoshop file with layers into an After Effects project:

1. **Create a Photoshop file that has layers, as the image in Figure 25-1, and save it in Photoshop format.** Follow these steps to create layers in Photoshop:
   a. **Load Photoshop.**
   b. **Choose File ➪ New to create a new file.**
   c. **In the New dialog box, set the width and height to the size you want your After Effects movie to be.**
   d. **Set the Mode to RGB Color and the Contents to Transparent.**
   e. **Create a background with the painting tools and filters.** You can also scan or digitize one with a digital camcorder.
   f. **Click the Create New Layer icon in the Layers palette or choose New Layer from the Layers palette pop-up menu.** To open the Layers palette, choose Window ➪ Show Layers.
   g. **Create an image in the new layer.** You could also copy and paste a digital image into a new layer.
   h. **Create another new layer.** Keep creating layers until you have all of the layers needed.
   i. **Save the file in Photoshop format.**

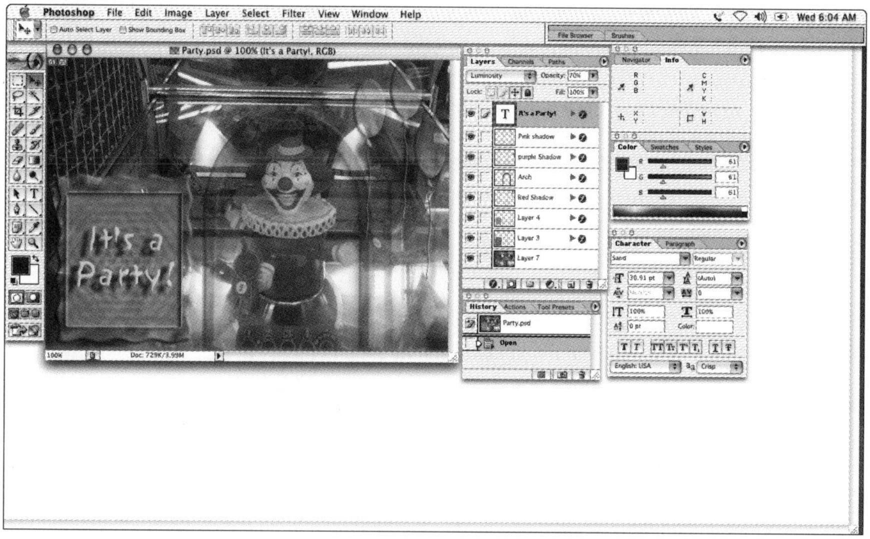

Figure 25-1: "It's a Party" file in Photoshop with its layers

2. **Quit Photoshop and load After Effects.**

3. **In After Effects, choose File ➪ New ➪ New Project**. The Project window appears.

4. **Choose File ➪ Import ➪ File. (If using an older version of Premiere, choose As Photoshop Comp.)** The Import File dialog box appears.

5. **Locate the Photoshop file you want to import.** Set the Import As menu to Composition.

6. **Click Import.** In the Project window, folder and composition icons appear in the Project window (see Figure 25-2). The Photoshop file (Party.psd) seen in Figure 25-2 can be found on the CD-ROM that accompanies the book.

   - **To see the Photoshop layers, either double-click the folder or click the triangle.**
   - **To view the layers in the Composition window and Time Layout window, double-click the composition icon in the Project window.** Notice that the layers appear in the Composition window and the Time Layout window. The layers also appear in the Time Layout window in the same order as they did in Photoshop's Layers palette. You don't have to drag each layer to the Time Layout window. After Effects automatically places them there.
   - **To either decrease or increase the view of the Composition window, choose Zoom out or Zoom in from the View menu.**

Note

To import various Photoshop files as a sequence, create a folder to hold all of the Photoshop files. Then, choose File ➪ Import in After Effects. When the Import dialog box appears, click the Photoshop Sequence option to import all of the Photoshop files as a sequence.

After importing a Photoshop file, you can *animate* its layers. When you animate a layer, you either transform it (scale, rotate, or change opacity and/or position), apply an effect (such as distortion), or apply a mask to the entire layer or just a portion.

Note

In Photoshop, you can use the Modes menu to create composite effects between layers. To display the modes, click the Switches/Modes option at the bottom of the palette until you see the word "Mode" next to the Source Name column.

Follow these steps to animate Photoshop layers in After Effects:

1. **Click the triangle beside one of the layers in the Time Layout palette.** When you expand the layer, the Transform option appears.

2. **Click the triangle next to Transform.** Notice that the Anchor Point, Position, Scale, Rotation, and Opacity options are visible. You can animate the layer's anchor point, position, scale, rotation, or opacity.

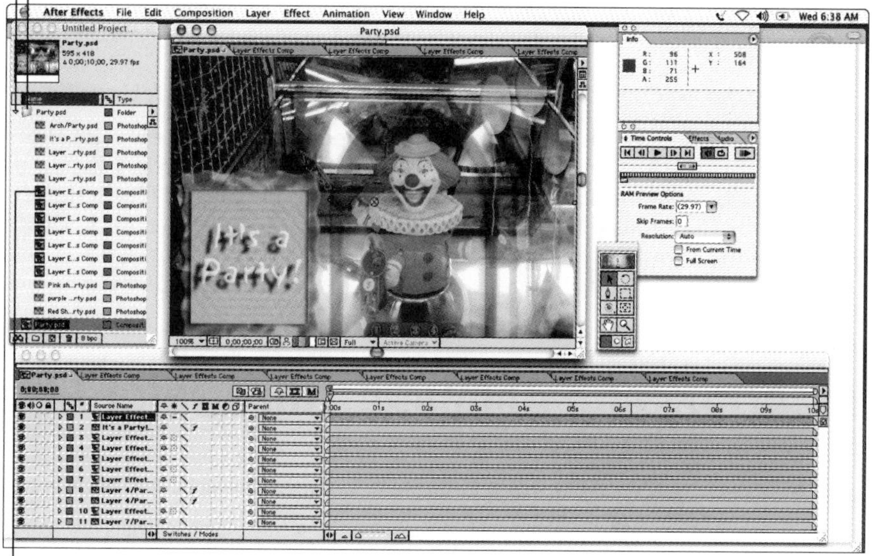

Figure 25-2: "It's a Party" layers shown in After Effects

3. **To animate the layer's position, click the stopwatch icon in front of the word *Position*.** A keyframe is created.
4. **Move the Time Marker to a new location by clicking and dragging on it.**
5. **Move the layer in the Composition window by clicking and dragging on it.** A new keyframe is created.
6. **To animate the position of the layer over time continue moving the Time Marker on the Timeline in the Time Layout window and then move the layer to create a new keyframe.**
7. **When you are done, click the Transform triangle.**
8. **To animate a layer using an effect, choose a layer in the Time Layout window.**
9. **Click the Effect menu and choose an effect.**
10. **Click the Effects triangle in the Time Layout window.** The name of the effect you choose appears on-screen. In front of the effect name is a stopwatch icon.
11. **Move the Time Marker to the beginning of the Timeline in the Time Layout window.**

12. **Click the stopwatch icon and then alter the effect in the Effects Control palette.** Notice that a keyframe is created.

13. **Again, move the Time Marker and alter the effect to create another keyframe.**

14. **When you are done, click the Effects triangle.**

15. **Choose File ➪ Save to save your work as an After Effects project.**

16. **To preview your work, choose Composition ➪ Preview ➪ RAM preview.** To export your work as a QuickTime movie, choose File ➪ Export ➪ QuickTime Movie. In the Save dialog box that appears, name the file. In the Movie Settings dialog box, make the necessary adjustments and click OK to save the file. After you've saved your work as a QuickTime movie, if you want, you can import it into a Premiere project as you would any other file in Premiere.

Importing and Animating Illustrator Files

In this section, you learn how to import an Illustrator file with layers into After Effects and animate it. We used this technique to create a project filled with butterflies.

Here's how to import an Illustrator file with layers into After Effects:

1. **Using Illustrator, create a file with layers, like the one shown in Figure 25-3, and save it in Illustrator format.** Here is a summary of the steps:

   a. **Load Illustrator.**

   b. **Choose File ➪ New to create a new file.** In the New dialog box, name the file and then set the Color mode to RGB Color.

   c. **Set the artboard width and height to your After Effects project size pixel dimensions.**

   d. **To create the Butterfly project, click the Paintbrush tool in the toolbox.**

   e. **Choose Window ➪ Brush Libraries ➪ Animal Shapes.**

   f. **Click the butterfly shape.**

   g. **Click in the artboard area to create a butterfly.** Click again and again.

   h. **Choose Window ➪ Layers to open the Layers palette.**

   i. **To create a new layer, click the Create New Layer icon in the Layers palette or choose New Layer from the Layers palette pop-up menu.**

   j. **In the new layer, click the artboard to create a butterfly in the new layer.** Then create another new layer and create another butterfly. Repeat the process until you have nine layers with butterflies, as shown in Figure 25-3.

k. **Create another new layer.** This should be your tenth layer. In this layer use the Pencil tool to create a curve.

l. **Create some type using the Path Type tool.** We typed "Summer time brings butterflies" for the image in Figure 25-3.

m. **Save your file in Illustrator format.** We saved ours in Illustrator 8 format because After Effects 4 does not read Illustrator 9 files.

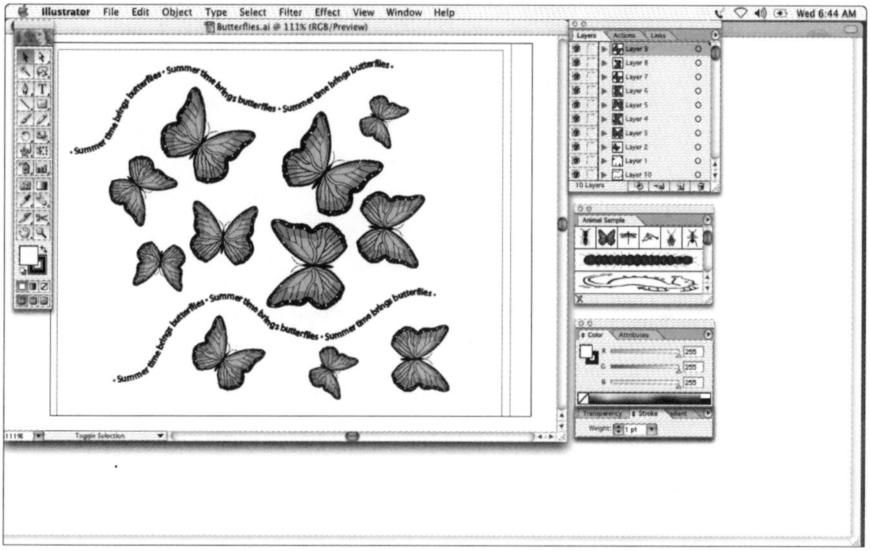

Figure 25-3: The Butterfly project as seen in Adobe Illustrator

2. **To import the Illustrator file choose File ⇨ Import ⇨ File (older versions of Premiere, choose Premiere As Comp).** In the Import File dialog box, set the Import As pop-up menu to Composition. Locate the Illustrator file you want to import and choose Import. Notice that a folder icon and composition icon appear in the Project window as shown in Figure 25-4. To see the Illustrator layers, either double-click the folder or click the triangle. To view the layers in the Composition and Time Layout windows, double-click the preview in the Project window. Notice that the layers appear in the Composition window and the Time Layout window. To either decrease or increase the view of the Composition window, choose Zoom out or Zoom in. The layers also appear in the Time Layout window in the same order as they appeared in Illustrator's Layers palette. You don't have to drag each layer to the Time Layout window(After Effects automatically places them there.

3. **To animate the Illustrator layers, click the triangle of one of the Time Layout palette's layers.** You can either choose to animate that layer's masks or effects or transform the layer itself.

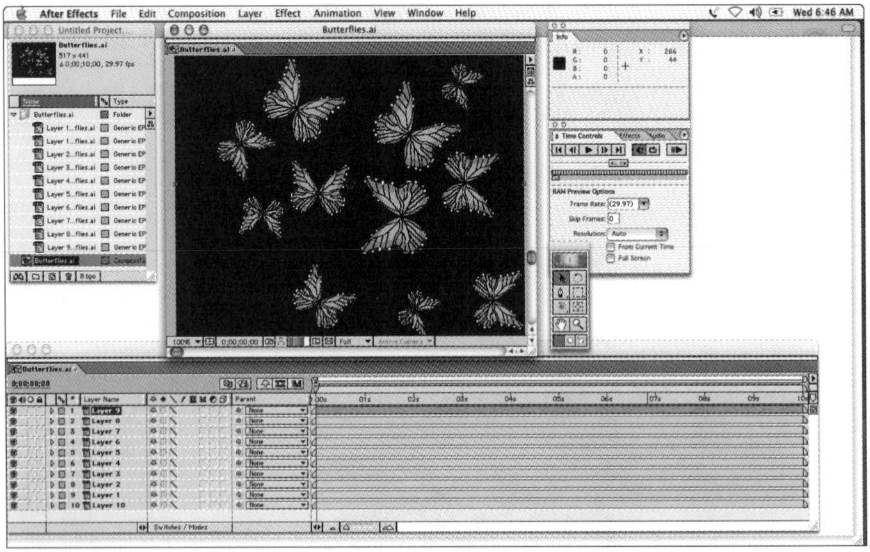

Figure 25-4: The Butterfly project as seen in Adobe After Effects

4. **Try animating the butterflies by rotating, moving, and scaling them and applying effects over time.**
5. **Choose File ➪ Save to save your work.**

Creating and Animating Type

In After Effects, you create type by choosing Layer ➪ New Solid. After Effects recognizes three different types of text: Basic Text, Numbers, and Path Text. When you select the Basic Text option, you can create horizontal or vertical text. You can also use the Basic Text option to animate one letter of a word at a time. The Numbers option enables you to create numbers. Path Text creates text on a path.

Because you cannot create type on a path or around a circle in Premiere, the following example covers creating Path Type. Figure 25-5 shows a frame from the Path Type project along with the Layer, Composition, and Time Layout windows. We used the Rotate option, found in the Time Layout palette, to animate text around the curve to create the text in this example.

Follow these steps to create and animate Path Text in After Effects:

1. **Choose File ➪ New ➪ New Project.** Instantly the Project window appears.
2. **Choose Composition ➪ New Composition.** The Composition Settings dialog box appears (see Figure 25-6).

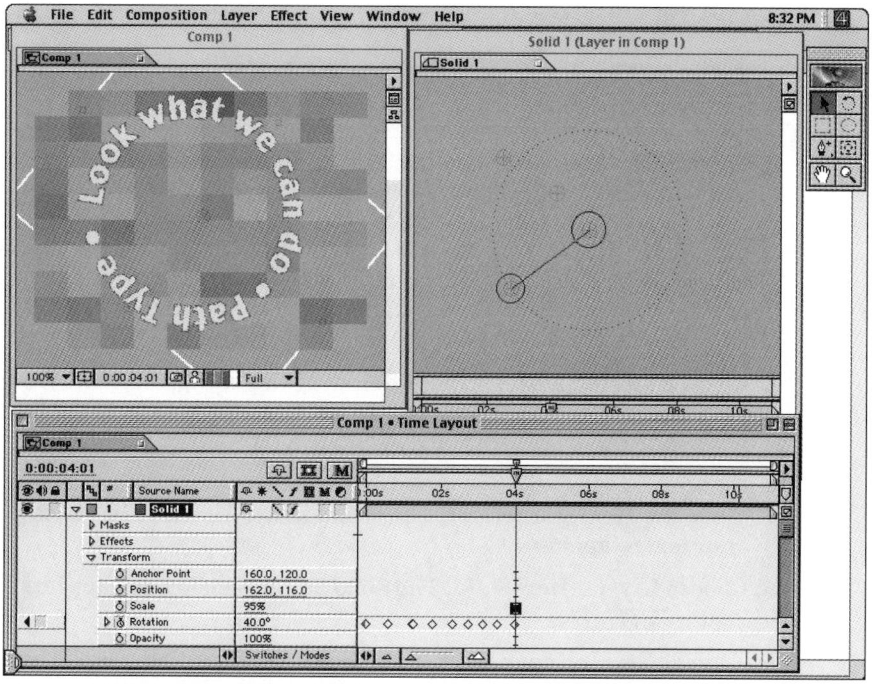

Figure 25-5: A frame from the Path Type project along with the Layer, Composition, and Time Layout windows

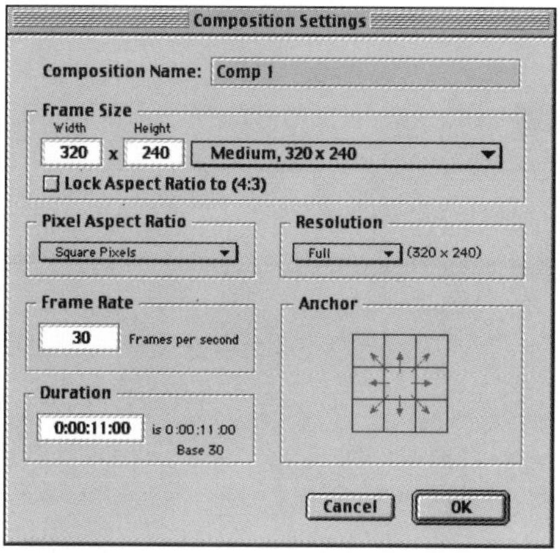

Figure 25-6: The Composition Settings dialog box

3. **Name your composition and then choose the width and height that you'll be using.**

4. **Click OK to create a new composition and to display the Time Layout palette.**

Note

If you want to change the settings in the composition, choose Composition ➪ Composition Settings.

5. **Choose File ➪ Import ➪ Footage File or Footage Files to import a file that will work as a background for the path text.** In Figure 25-6, we created a new solid layer by choosing Layer ➪ New Solid. (Before you create a new solid, make sure that the Time Marker is at the Timeline's beginning because the new solid appears at the Timeline.) After we created a New Solid layer, we applied the Effect ➪ PS Tiles command and the Effect ➪ Stylize ➪ Mosaic command to create the background.
6. **If you imported a background file, drag the background file from the Project window to the Time Layout palette.** The background file immediately turns into a layer. Before you can create a type effect, you must have a new solid layer in your project.
7. **Move the Time Marker to the position in the Timeline in which you want your text to appear.**
8. **Choose Layer ➪ New Solid.** The Solid Settings dialog box appears (see Figure 25-7).
9. **Type a name for your layer in the Solid Settings dialog box.** Leave the width and height alone and click OK to create a new solid. (Usually the width and height are the same as the composition.) Notice a new solid layer appears in the Time Layout palette. The new solid layer also takes up the entire size of the Composition window. As soon as you add text, the solid turns into text on a transparent layer.

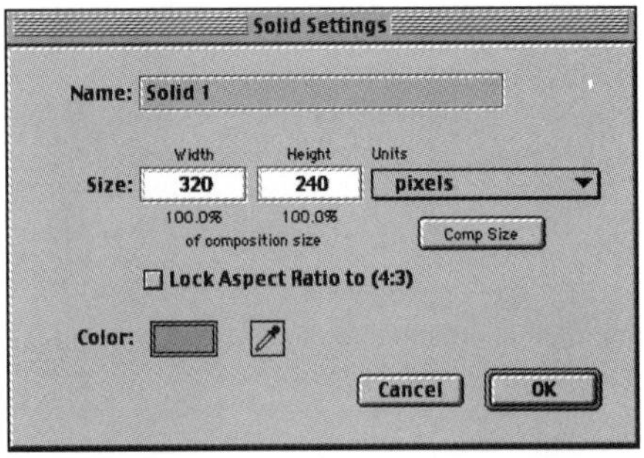

Figure 25-7: The Solid Settings dialog box

Note

If you want to change the settings in a layer, click the layer in the Time Layout palette and then choose Layer ➪ Solid Settings.

10. **Choose Effect ➪ Text ➪ Path Text to create text on a path.**

11. In the Type dialog box, shown in Figure 25-8, type some text and pick a font.

Note

If you can't see the text, you may need to click the background file and drag it below the text icon in the Time Layout palette.

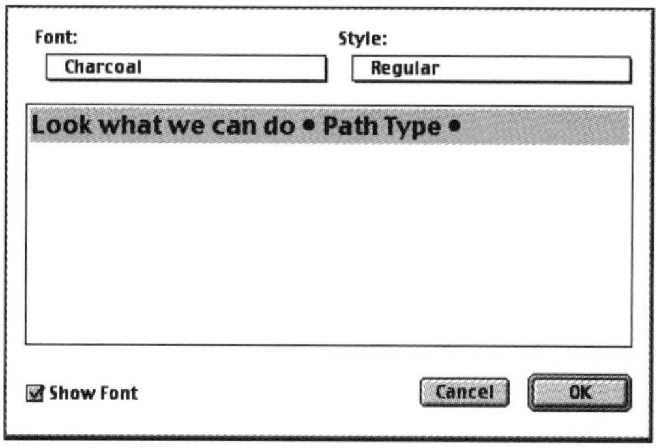

Figure 25-8: Type some text in the Type dialog box.

12. Click OK to close the dialog box and view your text on a curve in the Composition window. The Effect Controls palette appears at the same time as the text on the curve appears in the Composition window (see Figure 25-9).

13. Use the Effects Control palette to change the size, tracking (letter spacing), fill, and stroke color, or edit the text you just wrote.

- **To change the size of the text, click and drag the Size slide in the Effect Controls palette.**
- **To edit the text on the curve, click the word Options at the top of the palette.** When the Type dialog box appears, you can edit the text. Click and drag over the letters you want to change.
- **To choose whether you want your text to be filled, stroked, or be filled with a stroke surrounding it, click the Display Options menu.** To change the fill or stroke color, click the color swatch next to the word *Fill* or *Stroke* at the bottom of the palette. When the Color dialog box appears, pick a color and then click OK. You can also use the Eyedropper tool to change a color. To change the fill or stroke color to the color you've selected with the Eyedropper, click the Eyedropper next to either the word *Fill* or *Stroke* and then click a color from the background file. To change the stroke color's width, click the Stroke Width option and then type a number.
- **Clicking the Shape Type pop-up menu lets you choose a Béziér, Circle, Loop, or Line.**

Note

If the Effect Controls palette is not on-screen, you can display it by first clicking a layer you want and then choosing Layer ⇨ Open Effect Controls.

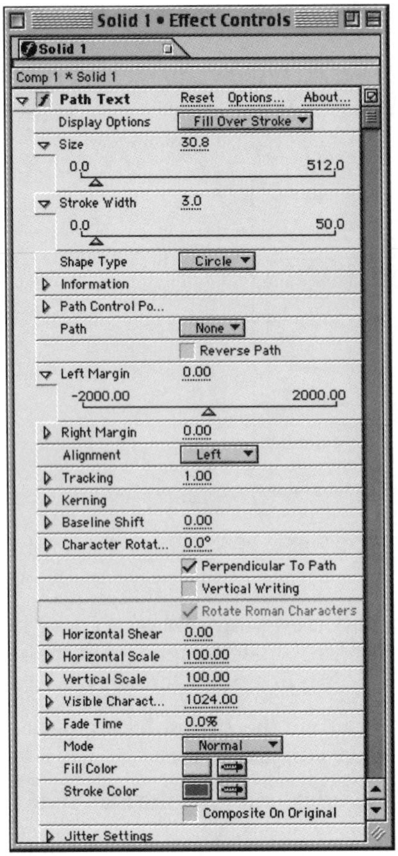

Figure 25-9: The Effect Controls palette can be used to adjust the text in the composition.

14. **To adjust a circle's size, open the Layers window by either double-clicking the layer in the Time Layout palette or by choosing Layer ⇨ Open Layer Window.** In the Layer window, choose Path Text from the Layer pop-up menu. Click the circles to adjust the curve. (Note that any change you make in the Layer window is automatically updated in the Composite window. The Layer window for the Path Text project can be seen in Figure 25-5, shown previously.)

15. **You can rotate text around a curve to animate it.** To do so, click the triangle in front of the Path Text (Solid) layer to display its features. Then click the Transform triangle to display the Rotation option. Move the Time Marker to the Timeline's beginning and then click the stopwatch icon next to the Rotation option to create your first keyframe. Then move the Time Marker

over on the Timeline and click the degree amount next to the Rotation option. When the Rotation dialog box appears, type in a degree amount and click OK to create another keyframe. Continue moving the Time Marker on the Timeline and changing the Rotation degree to create keyframes. Continue until you have a number of keyframes, or until you've created a complete rotation.

16. **Choose File ➪ Save to save your work.** To preview your work, choose Composition ➪ Preview ➪ RAM Preview. You can import this project into Premiere by creating a QuickTime movie. To do so, choose File ➪ Export ➪ QuickTime Movie. In the Save dialog box that appears, name the file. In the Movie Settings dialog box, make the necessary adjustments and click OK to save the file.

Working with Motion Paths

After Effects provides more control of motion effects than does Premiere. In After Effects, you can create motion along a path by moving an object along the objects anchor point. When moving an object along its anchor point, you are essentially using a path similar to Illustrator and Photoshop paths. Figure 25-10 shows a butterfly that's been animated in After Effects using its *anchor point*. Notice that the path is visible in the Layer window.

Cross-Reference

For more information on using the Motion Settings command in Premiere, turn to Chapter 14. To learn how to use Premiere's Motion Transformation, turn to Chapter 7.

Animating with anchor points

Here's how to animate an object in After Effects using its anchor point:

1. **Load or create a new project in After Effects.**
2. **Import a Photoshop or Illustrator object.** If you want, use the butterflies.ai file from the companion CD-ROM's Chapter 25 folder.
3. **Select a layer.**
4. **Expand the layer by clicking the triangle next to the layer in the Time Layout palette.** The Masks, Effects, and Transform options are displayed.
5. **Click the Transform triangle to display the Transform options.**
6. **Move the Time Marker to the Timeline's beginning, or to where you want to start animating your object.**
7. **Click the stopwatch icon next to the words "Anchor Point."**

8. **Double-click the layer in the Time Layout window to display the Layer window.**

9. **In the Layer window, choose Anchor Point Path.**

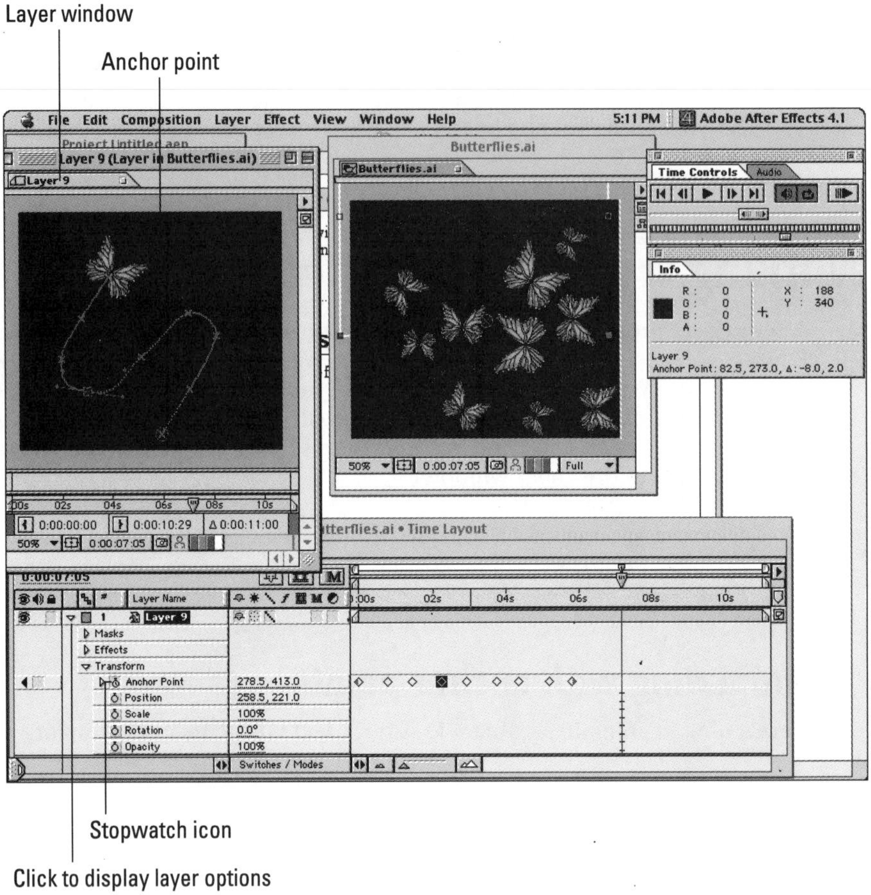

Figure 25-10: In the Layer window you can see a motion path created.

10. **Click the circle and move it to where you want the path to begin.**

11. **Move the Time Marker to a new position in the Timeline and then move the circle again to start creating the motion path.** Continue moving the Time Marker and move the circle in succession until you've finished creating your motion path. To edit the motion path, you can move the layer keyframe, Direction handles, or Direction lines.

Depending upon the path you've created, you may want to use the Layer ➪ Transform ➪ Auto-Orient Rotation command. The Auto-Orient Rotation command enables you to rotate an object along a path, so that the object is facing a different direction.

12. **Preview the motion you just created.** You can choose one of three commands:
    - Composition ➪ Preview ➪ Motion with Trails (fastest)
    - Composition ➪ Preview ➪ Wireframe Preview
    - Composition ➪ Preview ➪ RAM Preview (slowest)
13. **If you want to keep your work, save it.**

Animating with Sketch a Motion

The Sketch a Motion option enables you to draw your path freehand.

Here's how to animate using Sketch a Motion:

1. **Load or create a new project in After Effects.**
2. **Import a Photoshop or Illustrator object.** If you want, use one of the butterfly files from the companion CD-ROM's Chapter 25 folder.
3. **Select a layer from the Time Layout window.**
4. **Choose Window ➪ Plug-in Palettes ➪ Motion Sketch to display the Motion Sketch palette.**
5. **Click the Start Capture button in the Motion Sketch palette.**
6. **Move the mouse to the Composition window.**
7. **Press and hold the mouse button while you draw your motion path.** As soon as you let go of the mouse button, After Effects stops creating the motion sketch. The motion sketch is displayed in Figure 25-11.
8. **Click the triangle in front of the layer you have selected in the Time Layout window.**
9. **Click the triangle in front of the word Transform.** Notice that the Motion Sketch command has created keyframes in front of the Position section of the Time Layout window.
10. **Preview the motion.** Choose the Composition ➪ Preview ➪ Motion with Trails command, the Composition ➪ Preview ➪ Wireframe Preview command, or the Composition ➪ Preview ➪ RAM Preview command.

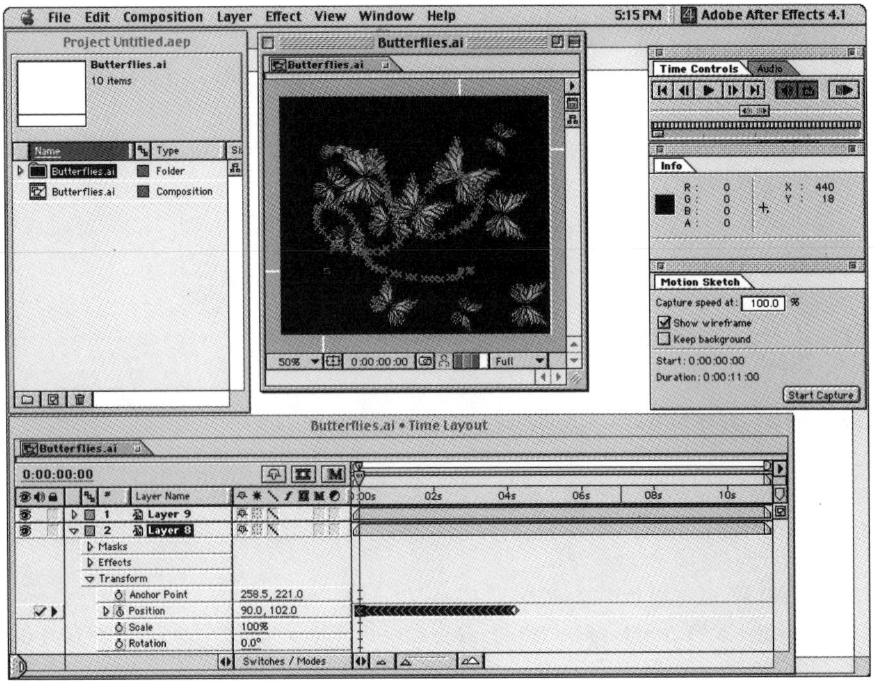

Figure 25-11: The motion sketch appears in the Composition window. The motion sketch is created with the Motion Sketch palette.

Creating a Composite Video Clip

You can use After Effects to create a *composite video clip*. A composite video clip consists of a few video clips displayed side by side on the screen at the same time, as shown in Figure 25-12. To create the Venice project illustrated in Figure 25-12, we placed two video clips side by side and then added some text below the two clips. If your project called for it, you could have three or four video clips. The video clips that you use to create a composite clip can be Premiere projects, video captured from your digital camcorder, or even stock video clips.

Here's how to create a composite video clip in After Effects:

1. **Choose File ➪ New ➪ New Project.**
2. **Choose Composition ➪ New Composition.**
3. **In the New Composition dialog box, name your composition.** Pick the correct frame size for your project's width and height. If you are working with video clips that are 160 x 120, you should set the width and height to 320 x 250 pixels.

Figure 25-12: The first frame from the Venice project is an example of a composite clip.

4. **Click OK to create a new composition.**
5. **Choose File ➪ Import ➪ Multiple Files.**
6. **In the Import File dialog box, set Import As option to Footage.**
7. **Select the video clips and then Click Import.** If you want, you can use the clips seen in Figure 25-12 (Italy.mov and Cruising.mov), which is found in the Chapter 25 folder on the CD-ROM that accompanies this book.
8. **Drag the video clips you imported from the Project window to the Composite window.** If you want your composite to appear as it does in Figure 25-12, place the video clips so that they are side by side. You can also place two clips on top of each other on the left side of the Composition window and place text to the right of the video clips. You can also fill the Composite window with video clips and have no text.
9. **If you want your composite to include text, as shown in Figure 25-12, first create a new solid layer.** To create a new solid, you first need to click the Composite window to activate the layer. Choose Layer ➪ New Solid. In the Solid Settings dialog box that appears, name your solid and leave the size set to the same size as the Composition window. Click OK. The new solid appears in the Time Layout window.
10. **With the New Solid layer selected in the Time Layout window, choose Effect ➪ Text ➪ Basic Text.**
11. **In the dialog box that appears, type the text and pick a font.** Click OK to have the solid turn into the text you just created. If desired, use the Effects Control palette to continue editing your text.
12. **To bevel and add a drop shadow to your text, choose Effect ➪ Perspective ➪ Bevel Alpha and Effect ➪ Perspective ➪ Drop Shadow.**

13. **To create the background that appears behind the text, as seen in Figure 25-12, you first need to create another solid layer.** Choose Layer ➪ New Solid. Click the Eyedropper tool and pick a color from one of the video clips. This is the color that appears in the solid. Leave the other settings as they are. If you want, name the solid. Then click OK to create the new solid. When the new solid appears in the Time Layout window, it appears in front of the text you just created

14. **To see the text, click the new solid layer in the Time Layout window and drag it below the text.** The background solid layer should still be selected. Figure 25-13 shows the Project, Composite, and Time Layout windows for the Venice composite project.

Figure 25-13: The Time Layout window for the Venice composite project

15. **Click one of the handles that appears around the background to scale the solid so that it appears only in the empty space behind the text.**

16. **Give the background a little texture by using an effect or two.** To create the effect shown in Figure 25-12, we chose the Effect ➪ Stylize ➪ Tiles command. In the Tiles dialog box, we set the Fill Empty Area With to the Foreground. In the Effects Control palette, we used the Foreground Eyedropper tool to pick a color from one of the video clips. We then applied the Effect ➪ Distort ➪ Ripple command.

17. Choose File ➪ Save to save your work.

Tip

You can save a frame of your After Effects project as a Photoshop file, either with or without layers. To do so, choose Composition ➪ Save Frame As ➪ Photoshop Layers or choose Composition ➪ Save Frame As ➪ File.

18. To preview your work in RAM, choose Composition ➪ Preview ➪ RAM Preview.

19. To export your work as a QuickTime movie, choose File ➪ Export ➪ QuickTime Movie. When the Save dialog box appears, name your movie. When the Movie Setting dialog box appears, click the Setting button to set the compression, color depth, and frames per second. Click the Filter button if you want to apply a filter to your clip. Click the Size button to either leave the size as is, or change your movie's size. You can also adjust sound settings and choose whether you want to stream for the Web. Make the necessary adjustments, then click OK to create a QuickTime movie.

Note

To export your movie in a different format, choose Composition ➪ Make Movie. In the Render Queue dialog box, click the triangle in front of the Composition being rendered. Next, click Lossless, next to the Output Module option. In the Output Module Settings dialog box, click the Format pop-up menu and choose a format. Available format options include Animated GIF, BMP Sequence, Cineon Sequence, ElectricImage IMAGE, FLC/FLI, Filmstrip, IFF Sequence, JPEG Sequence, MPS, PCX Sequence, PICT Sequence, PNG Sequence, Photoshop Sequence, Pixar Sequence, QuickTime Movie, SGI Sequence, TIFF Sequence, and TARGA Sequence.

After you've created a QuickTime movie, you can import the QuickTime movie into a Premiere project for further editing.

Summary

Although Adobe Premiere features many video effects, Adobe After Effects provides more motion and compositing effects.

- ✦ You can import a Premiere movie directly into After Effects.
- ✦ You can animate text over time in After Effects.
- ✦ You can open multiple QuickTime movies into After Effects.

✦ ✦ ✦

CHAPTER 26

Third-Party Special Effects Software

✦ ✦ ✦ ✦

In This Chapter

An introduction to third-party software

Installing third-party software

Overview of different third-party plug-ins

✦ ✦ ✦ ✦

This chapter focuses on creating special effects with third-party software. Every day, third-party companies are producing new software, enabling you to not only create more and more special effects with your digital video clips but also to save a lot of time and money. As an overview of third-party plug-ins, we've picked some examples that extend the effects built into Adobe Premiere:

- **SpiceMaster.** A transitions plug-in
- **Boris FX 6.1.** A video effect plug-in
- **Boris Graffiti.** A titling effects plug-in
- **SFX Machine.** An audio plug-in

Introduction to Third-Party Software

Third-party software companies make plug-in software for Adobe Premiere and Adobe After Effects that enable you to create stunning special effects. These plug-ins become accessible from Premiere's Transitions and Effects palettes, and add to Premiere's own capabilities of creating video and audio effects as well as transitions. If you want to start using plug-in software, check out the plug-ins section in Appendix B. We've listed a variety of Web sites from plug-in developers. These Web sites provide the most up-to-date information on products and features. Many of them enable you to download demos and manuals.

Installing third-party software

Third-party software is usually installed in Premiere's Plug-in folder. During the installation process, some plug-ins automatically hunt down Premiere on your hard drive, and then you click a button to have the software installed in the correct folder. Others simply install files on your hard drive. After the files are installed, you then drag them to Premiere's Plug-in folder. Typically, on both Mac and Windows systems, the installation process is simply a matter of following on-screen instructions.

When you load Premiere, you can find third-party software in either the Video palette or the Transitions palette in a folder called 3rd Party. If you have any questions about installing third-party software, check with the software's manual or contact the software company.

Caution Before installing any third-party plug-ins, check with the manufacturer to ensure that the software you are installing is compatible with your version of Premiere. Furthermore, check that the software is compatible with your computer's operating system.

Using third-party software

To use third-party software, you must first create a project on-screen with video clips in the Timeline window. Then, choose Window ➪ Show Video Effects (for audio effects, choose Window ➪ Show Audio Effects) and Window ➪ Show Transitions to open the Video and Transitions palettes. Choose an effect or suite of effects from the Video palette and then drag the effect onto the clip to which you want to apply the effect. In the Transitions palette, click and drag a transition to the Timeline window's Transition track and place the transition in the Timeline where you want the transition to occur. After you release the mouse, the plug-in opens on-screen, as shown in Figure 26-1.

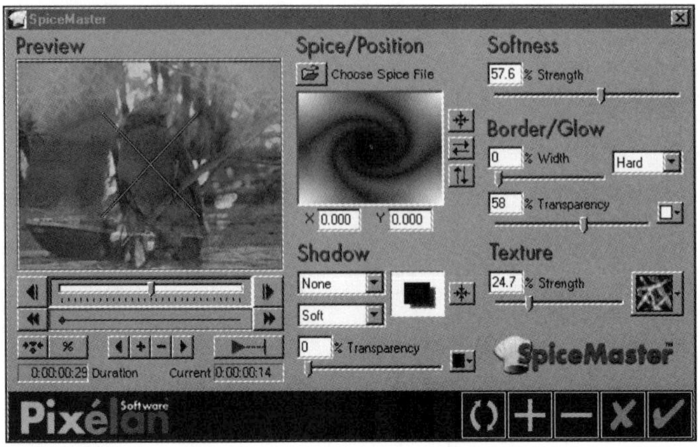

Figure 26-1: Pixélan's SpiceMaster transitions plug-in

Pixélan SpiceMaster

Pixélan's SpiceMaster is a collection of video plug-ins that provides numerous unusual transitions. Figure 26-2 shows some of the different types of effects that SpiceMaster creates. The transitional effects can create the illusion of one scene exploding into another, one scene dripping into another, or one scene being gradually revealed through fog. If you like the effects and want more, you can order more effects that load into the main SpiceMaster window (see Figure 26-1).

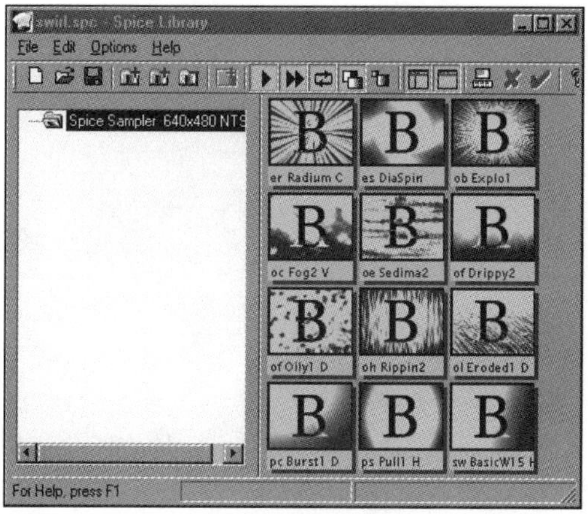

Figure 26-2: Sample SpiceMaster transitions

SpiceMaster's appeal and versatility is based on the many options the plug-in provides. At the center of the plug-in window is a grayscale image previewing the shape of the effect. To change effects, click the folder icon at the top of the window. This opens a window to your hard drive where you can load other Spice files. The button icon on the bottom-right corner of the window enables you to load saved settings or to apply or cancel the transition effect.

The SpiceMaster transition options go beyond most of the transition controls found in Premiere. For example, as you create the transition, you can create keyframes. At different keyframes you can change the transparency of the effect by clicking and dragging the Transparency and Softness sliders. With these two sliders you can turn a harsh transition into a soft ephemeral blend between one clip and another. SpiceMaster also enables you to add textured patterns to transitions. Clicking the Texture menu in the bottom-right corner of the transition window opens a palette of patterns. After you choose the pattern, it is mapped to the effect, adding text to the transitional area on-screen. To preview the effect, you can click and drag the slider below the Preview window. For more information about SpiceMaster, check out Pixélan's Web site at `www.pixelan.com`.

Boris FX

One of the most well-known software developers of digital video plug-ins is Boris, makers of Boris FX and Boris Graffiti. Boris FX provides an elaborate suite of special effects that can rotate, spin, distort, change the lighting, or explode a video clip or still image. The interface Boris provides enables precise control over the numerous effects in the plug-in package. Figure 26-3 shows the Timeline on the right side of the screen along with a preview of the Particle filter being applied to an imported still image of a clock. The list of effects appears on the left side of the screen.

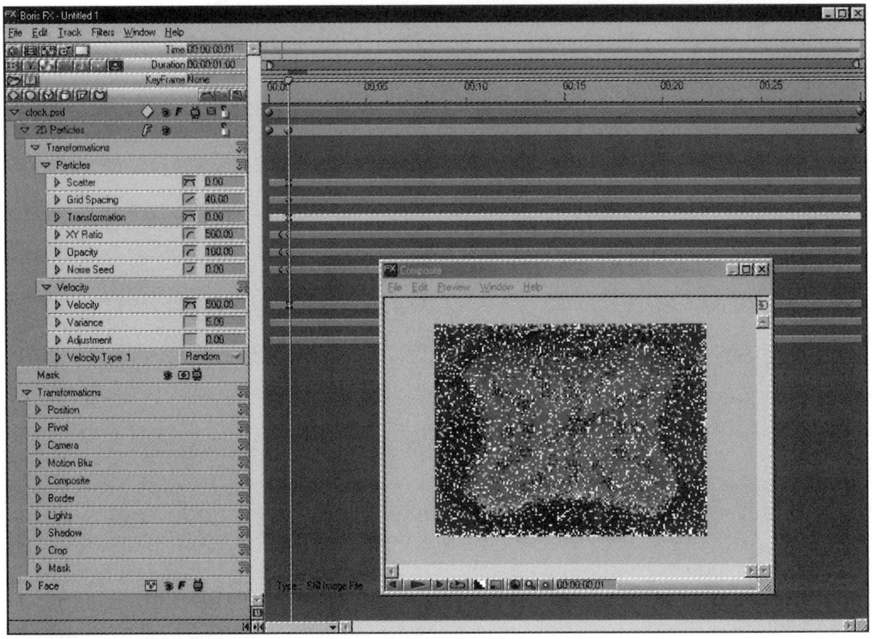

Figure 26-3: Boris FX track and Timeline view

The Timeline provides an overview of all the effects and different effects tracks. The dots on the Timeline indicate keyframes, easily created by choosing Track ➪ New Keyframe. Previewing the effect is simply a matter of clicking and dragging the thin vertical bar in the Timeline. Effect controls can be accessed from the Expanded track layer, or they can be controlled from the Controls window shown in Figure 26-4. Here you can see the controls for rotating, tumbling, and spinning an image. As you can see from Figure 26-4, the effect is previewed in the Composite window, which shows not only the effects of the Tumble Spin and Rotate controls, but the Border effect, as well. Using the Border effect, we gradually faded out the edges of the image. The buttons at the bottom of the Composite window enable you to move forward and backward one frame at a time.

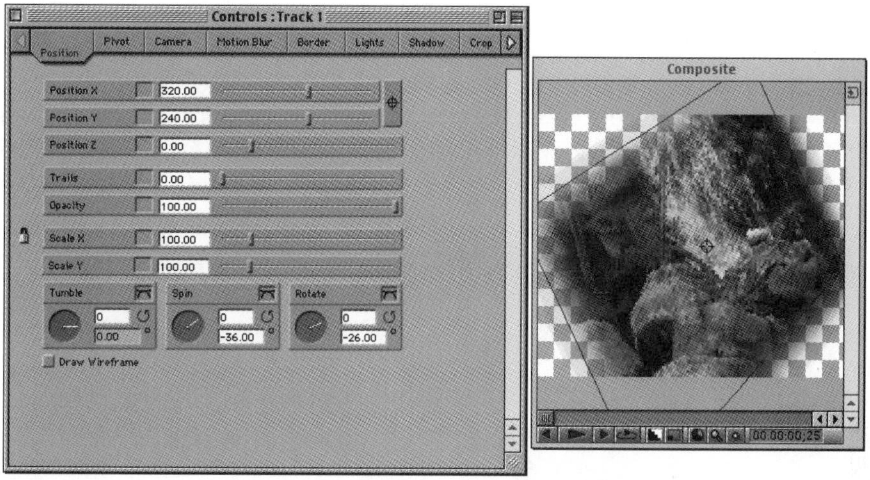

Figure 26-4: An image being rotated and tumbled in Boris FX

Boris FX also provides a variety of different image filters accessed from its Filters menu. Using filters, you can distort images, and apply color, keying, and lighting effects. One of the more unusual filters, Particle Group, provides 2D and 3D Particle commands as well as a Scatterize command that shatters an image. Figure 26-5 provides some idea of how an image can be distorted with the 3D Image Shatter command; in case you can't recognize it, the image in the Composite window is a waterfall.

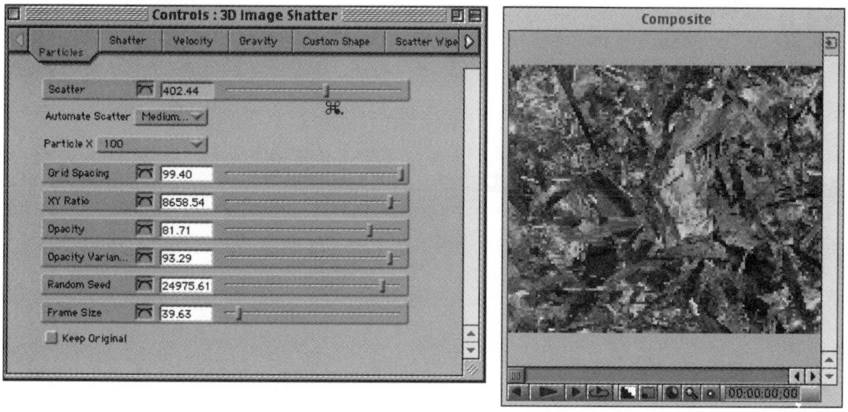

Figure 26-5: A 3D Image Shatter effect applied to a waterfall image

Boris Graffiti

Boris Graffiti is a text-based special-effects package. Figure 26-6 shows the Boris Graffiti Text Window. Notice that the window includes advanced text-formatting options such as tracking, leading, and kerning. You can even set tabs in the Text window.

Figure 26-6: Text created in the Boris Graffiti text window

The user interface for Boris Graffiti is similar to Boris FX. Figure 26-7 shows the Timeline and track layers that provide an idea of the different transformations and effects that you can apply to text. Using these commands, you can rotate and extrude text as well as create page rolls and crawls. As with Boris FX, the Timeline in Boris Graffiti enables you to click and drag to preview the effect, set keyframes, and access menu commands.

As with Boris FX, the Boris Graffiti effects feature their own individual Control windows. Figure 26-8 shows a preview of the text typed in the Text window being tumbled, rotated, and spun.

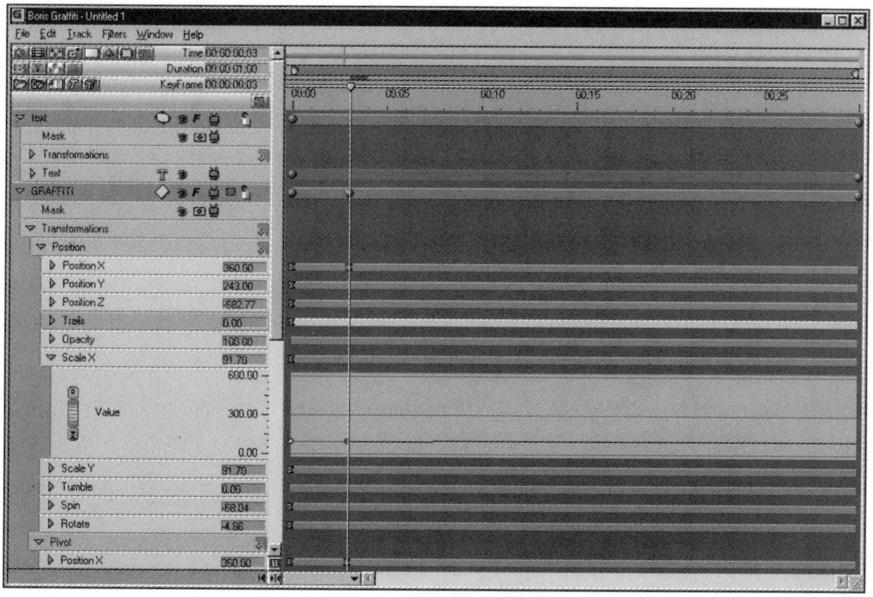

Figure 26-7: Timeline and track layers in Boris Graffiti

SFX Machine

Berkeley Integrated Audio Software's SFX Machine is a Macintosh audio effects plug-in that provides many audio effects with more than 300 presets. Figure 26-9 shows a sampling of effects in the SFX Effects main window. To choose an effect such as Flanger, Feedback, Chorus, or Multitap, you simply click it. After you select the effect, the presets are shown as a list. To select preset, you click it. After choosing the preset, you can edit the window controls and save your settings to disk.

Apart from those visible in Figure 26-9, the SFX package includes some unusual effects with descriptive names such as Drums Gate Brass, Guitar Tuning, Bleep-a-thon, Bubble Synth, and H2-Oh. As you might guess, these create the effects implied by their name. For example, for bubble sounds, use Bubble Synth; for water effects, try H2-Oh. SFX also features a DSP Construction Kit that enables you to create your own effects. The SFX Machine enables you to chose from 9 different sources, apply 11 different DSP processes, and perform 13 different modulations. Multiply all of these combinations, and you have a plug-in that can create countless new sound effects.

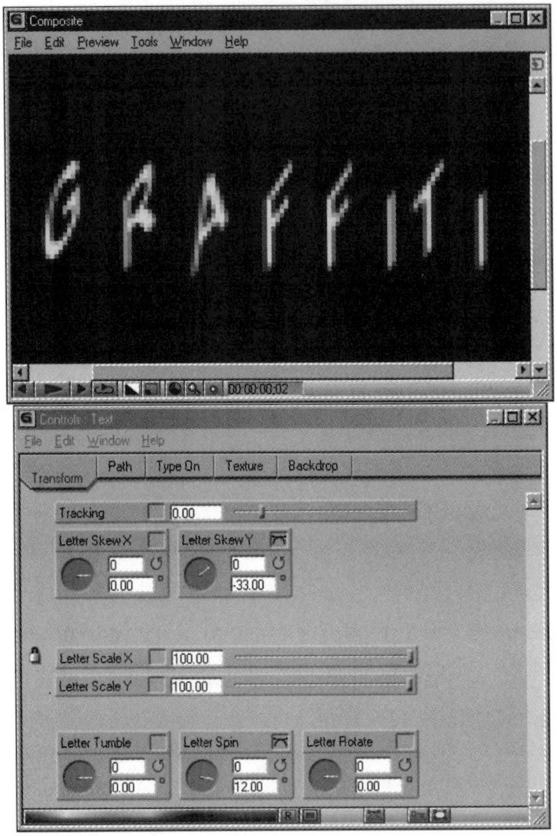

Figure 26-8: Text being transformed in Boris Graffiti

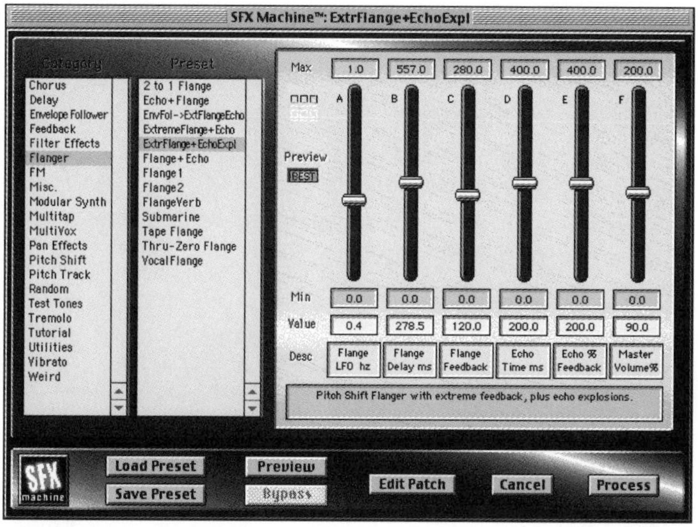

Figure 26-9: SFX Machine enables you to create and edit numerous audio effects.

Summary

A variety of software companies have created third-party plug-ins that extend the special effects capabilities of Premiere. Third-party plug-ins appear in Premiere's Transitions, Video, and/or Audio palettes in a folder labeled 3rd Party.

✦ Most third-party plug-ins are installed in Premiere's plug-ins folder.

✦ When you apply a third-party plug-in, a window often opens on-screen offering you a suite of effects.

✦ Most third-party plug-ins provide preview screens and enable you to save settings.

✦ Most plug-in manufacturers provide demos that you can download from the Web.

✦ ✦ ✦

Appendixes

PART

VII

In This Part

APPENDIX A

What's on the CD-ROM

✦ ✦ ✦ ✦

This appendix provides you with information on the contents of the CD-ROM that accompanies this book. For the latest and greatest information, please refer to the ReadMe file located at the root of the CD-ROM. Here is what you will find:

- System requirements
- Using the CD-ROM with Windows and Macintosh
- What's on the CD-ROM
- Troubleshooting

System Requirements

Make sure that your computer meets the minimum system requirements listed in this section. If your computer doesn't match up to most of these requirements, you may have a problem using the contents of the CD-ROM.

For Windows 98 Second Edition, Windows 2000, Windows Me, or Windows XP:

- PC with a Pentium processor running at 120 MHz or faster
- At least 128MB of total RAM installed on your computer; for best performance, we recommend at least 256MB
- Intel Pentium III 500 MHz processor (Pentium 4 or multi-processor recommended)
- 600MB of available hard-disk space for installation
- A CD-ROM drive

For Macintosh:

- ✦ Mac Power PC G3 or faster
- ✦ Mac OS 9.2.2 or OS X v.10.1.3
- ✦ 64MB of RAM (128MB recommended)
- ✦ 600MB of available hard-disk space for installation
- ✦ A CD-ROM drive

Using the CD-ROM with Windows

To install the items from the CD-ROM to your hard drive, follow these steps:

1. Insert the CD-ROM into your computer's CD-ROM drive.
2. A window will appear with the following options: Install, Browse, eBook, Links and Exit.

    Install: Gives you the option to install the supplied software and/or the author-created samples on the CD-ROM. To access specific files, select the Explore option instead.

    Explore: Allows you to view the contents of the CD-ROM in its directory structure and copy only the files that you want to your hard disk.

    Links: Opens a hyperlinked page of Web sites.

    Exit: Closes the autorun window.

If you do not have autorun enabled or if the autorun window does not appear, follow the steps below to access the CD-ROM.

1. Click Start ➪ Run.
2. In the dialog box that appears, type ***d*:\setup.exe**, where *d* is the letter of your CD-ROM drive. This will bring up the autorun window described above.
3. Choose the Install, Browse, Links, or Exit option from the menu. (See Step 2 in the preceding list for a description of these options.)

Using the CD-ROM with the Mac OS

To install the items from the CD-ROM to your hard drive, follow these steps:

1. Insert the CD-ROM into your CD-ROM drive.
2. Double-click the icon for the CD-ROM after it appears on the desktop.

3. Most programs come with installers. For those, simply open the program's folder on the CD-ROM and double-click the Install or Installer icon. Note: To install some programs, just drag the program's folder from the CD-ROM window and drop it on your hard drive icon.

What's on the CD-ROM

The following sections provide a summary of the software and other materials you'll find on the CD-ROM.

Tutorial files

In the Tutorial Projects folder are still images, video, and sound clips for following along with the exercises in the book. The still images are in Photoshop and Illustrator formats. The digital video clips are in either Premiere project formats or in QuickTime format. Many of the files used are from Digital Vision, providers of royalty-free still and moving images. The sound files are in AIFF format. The files are divided into chapter folders that are associated with the chapters in the book. Please note that the images in the Tutorial Projects folder are for instructional purposes only. They are not for commercial use.

Adobe Premiere 6.0

Adobe Systems, Inc.

Thirty-day trial version for Macs and Windows.

Although the tryout verison of Adobe Premiere 6.5 was not available when the *Adobe Premiere 6.5 Bible* went to press, we have included the tryout version of Adobe Premiere 6.0. Not all features discussed in this book are available in Premiere 6.0, but many similarities exist. In fact, most core features in 6.5 are identical to those in 6.0.

See `www.adobe.com/products/premiere` for more information.

Shareware programs are fully functional, trial versions of copyrighted programs. If you like particular programs, register with their authors for a nominal fee and receive licenses, enhanced versions, and technical support. *Freeware programs* are copyrighted games, applications, and utilities that are free for personal use. Unlike shareware, these programs do not require a fee or provide technical support. *GNU software* is governed by its own license, which is included inside the folder of the GNU product. See the GNU license for more details.

Trial, demo, or evaluation versions are usually limited either by time or functionality (such as being unable to save projects). Some trial versions are very sensitive to system date changes. If you alter your computer's date, the programs will "time out" and will no longer be functional.

Troubleshooting

If you have difficulty installing or using any of the materials on the companion CD-ROM, try the following solutions:

- **Turn off any antivirus software that you may have running.** Installers sometimes mimic virus activity and can make your computer incorrectly believe that it is being infected by a virus. (Be sure to turn the antivirus software back on later.)
- **Close all running programs.** The more programs you're running, the less memory is available to other programs. Installers also typically update files and programs; if you keep other programs running, installation may not work properly.
- **Reference the ReadMe file.** Please refer to the ReadMe file located at the root of the CD-ROM for the latest product information at the time of publication.

If you still have trouble with the CD-ROM, please call the Customer Care phone number: (800) 762-2974. Outside the United States, call (317) 572-3994. You can also contact Customer Service by e-mail at `techsupdum@wiley.com`. Wiley Publishing, Inc. will provide technical support only for installation and other general quality control items; for technical support on the applications themselves, consult the program's vendor or author.

✦ ✦ ✦

APPENDIX B

Places to Visit on the Web

You can use the following list of Web resources as a guide to digital video software and hardware manufacturers and distributors. Also included are a variety of resources that should prove valuable to digital video producers.

Software

www.apple.com

This site offers access to Apple's QuickTime site as well as useful information about MPEG-4 (`www.apple.com/mpeg4`).

www.adobe.com

Check Adobe's site for Premiere upgrades and tech support. The site also includes Premiere tutorials, as well as samples from professionals in the digital video field. Be sure to sign up for an e-mail newsletter that provides updates and important Premiere technical information.

www.discreet.com

Find out more about Discreet Cleaner as well as other Discreet programs for editing and creating special effects and animation.

www.eovia.com

Go to this site, to learn more about creating 3-D images using Carrara 2 and Amapi 3D.

www.macromedia.com

This site is maintained by Macromedia, the makers of Director, Authorware, and Flash. Many Premiere digital movies wind up in Director and Authorware projects. Download free trial software at this site, which includes lots of tech notes for Macromedia projects.

www.microsoft.com/windows/windowsmedia

Get updates on the latest Microsoft Windows Media and streaming video products.

www.procreate.com

Go to this Web site to find out more about ProCreate Painter, discussed in Chapter 13.

www.quicktime.com

Download the latest version of QuickTime or upgrade to QuickTime Pro. The site includes developer and licensing information as well as links to many sites using QuickTime.

www.realnetworks.com

Find out about RealNetworks audio and video streaming products. Download the latest plug-ins.

www.wwug.com/forums/adobe_premiere

A users group forum for Adobe Premiere. You can ask questions or scroll through other users' questions and answers. Also helpful is `www.wwug.com/digital_video_editing`.

Plug-ins

The following Web sites represent software manufacturers and distributors of Premiere plug-ins. Check these sites for downloadable samples and Premiere compatibility questions. Note that many of these software companies are small, and it may take them time to upgrade their products as Premiere evolves. Also, note that some plug-ins are Mac- or Windows-specific.

www.accessfx.com

AccessFX are the creators of Lord of the Wipe, a dynamic transition plug-in that features seemingly endless options for changing transitions.

www.bias-inc.com

Bias produces SFX Machine, an audio plug-in for advanced sound effects on Apple Macintosh.

www.borisfx.com

The Boris FX plug-in package includes numerous 3D effects, including 3D extruded text. Boris also produces Boris Factory and Graffiti, which creates 3D effects as well as particle explosions and motion blurs.

www.digieffects.com

Makers of TransFX; 40 transitions for Adobe Premiere are available.

www.digigami.com

Digigami offers three plug-ins for Adobe Premiere. MegaPEG exports MPEG-1 files to the Internet. MovieScreamer enables you to create streaming *fast-start* QuickTime movies. MegaPEG exports MPEG movies from Premiere.

www.focusinfo.com

This site provides information about a variety of video products, including MediaMotion, a VCR control plug-in for the Macintosh.

www.panopticum.com

Panopticum Fire is a plug-in for creating real-time burning images and flames. Panopticum also created Rich Typing, which creates text and titling effects.

www.pixelan.com

Pixélan Software's Video SpiceRack Pro provides over 350 broadcast-quality transitions and effects for both Adobe Premiere and Adobe After Effects. Pixelan also produces Organic FX, which includes over 250 burst, erosion, and fluid effects.

www.smartsound.com

SmartSound Quicktracks enables users to quickly create precise custom soundtracks from within Premiere. The company also produces Sonicfire Pro, a standalone soundtrack creation program that enables you to import QuickTime and AVI files. The package includes music and music sound effects.

www.thepipe.com

Pipeline Recorder is frame-accurate, print-to-tape software for VideoVision Studio and Telecast, and the Truevision TARGA line of video digitizers. Pipeline Recorder controls Sony compatible RS-422, RS-232, and VISCA videotape decks.

The Pipeline Digital ProVtr is a device-control plug-in for deck control on both the Macintosh and Windows. ProVtr controls Sony compatible RS-422, RS-232, and VISCA videotape machines, stamps time code, and enables batch capture of clips to disk.

www.ultimatte.com

Home of Ultimatte, a plug-in that provides masking and noise reduction.

www.xentrik.demon.co.uk

At this site, you find the creators of Vixen Video Enhancer, a plug-in that provides professional video adjustment and color-correction tools.

General Resources

www.aftra.com

This is the American Federation of Televison and Radio Artists. Here you can find out about using union talent, contacts, and industry news.

www.dv.com

This is the digital video Web magazine, an excellent source of hardware and software information, as well as technical articles. It features news, tutorials, and a buyer's guide. The site enables you to search back issues for product information and technical articles.

www.dvpa.com

This is the Web site for the Digital Video Producers Association. Membership enables access to thousands of stock clips available online for instant download.

www.digitalmedia.net

This site is a hub for accessing multiple sites about digital media hardware, software, and production.

www.ieee.org

This is the Web site for the Institute of Electrical and Electronics Engineers. It contains information on products and services for engineers.

Hardware

www.adstech.com

Check out this site for info on ADS Pyro video card. Here you can purchase products and download drivers.

www.apple.com

Virtually all new Macs include FireWire ports for transferring digital video directly to desktop or laptop. Purchase a Mac here or find out the latest from Apple's tech support library.

www.canon.com

At this sight you can find out about Canon DV cameras and other products.

www.dell.com

Several Dell computers include digital video cards. Purchase a computer or video board for your computer.

www.digitalvodoo.net

Find out more about the Iridium HD video board, which was designed for high-end compositing.

www.epson.com

Learn more about Epson's color printers.

www.guitarcenter.com

This Web site has information on music hardware and software.

www.harman-multimedia.com

Learn more about powered satellite speakers and subwoofers for your computer.

www.hp.com

At this site you can learn more about Hewlett-Packard's color printers.

www.jvc.com

Details about JVC professional and consumer video equipment are available at this site.

www.matrox.com

Matrox are the creators of video boards and video capture boards (Millennium, Marvel, and so on). Find out prices and compatibility information.

www.olympus.com/digital

At this site you can learn more about Olympus's digital cameras.

www.pinnaclesys.com

Find out tech specs for Pinnacle's PC video boards and editing systems; also broadcast-quality equipment.

www.shure.com

This site includes information on Shure's audio products as well as downloadable technical guides.

www.sony.com

Most Sony laptops include i.LINK digital video ports that conform to the IEEE 1394 standard. Find out about the latest Sony computers, monitors, digital camcorders, and professional video equipment.

Stock Image, Sound, and Video Clips

www.digitalvisiononline.com

Many of the video and sound clips in this book are from Digital Vision. At their site you can learn more about their products.

www.smartsound.com

Visit this site to learn more about stock sound clips.

✦ ✦ ✦

APPENDIX C

Licensing QuickTime

If you plan to distribute a Premiere movie on a CD-ROM as a QuickTime movie, you probably want to include QuickTime along with your production on the CD. Because QuickTime is available at no charge from Apple's Web site, you may be tempted to just copy the QuickTime installers to your CD. However, to legally distribute QuickTime, you must obtain a software license from Apple.

Optaining a license is easy and usually free of charge. To obtain a license, start by visiting the QuickTime Web site, `www.quicktime.com`. On the main QuickTime page, click the Developer tab, which is on the Developer link at the top of the page. Under ADC resources, click the Software Licensing link.

Doing this opens up a page describing why you need to license Apple's software products. Next, click the Agreements On Line link and then click the QuickTime choice. This brings you to: `http://developer.apple.com/mkt/swl/quicktime.html`

Next, you need to download a PDF file that includes the licensing contract and licensing information. Most multimedia producers need to click the QuickTime Software SDA Agreement link. If you need to license QuickTime within your business or organization, click the QuickTime Site License link.

Print out the PDF forms, fill them out, and then send them to Apple:

Apple Computer, Inc.
Software Licensing M/S 198-SWL
2420 Ridgepoint Drive
Austin, TX 78754

✦ ✦ ✦

APPENDIX D

The Digital Video Recording Studio

Setting up a small studio to create desktop digital video movies often involves the purchase of computer, video, and sound equipment. For digital video producers, editors, and graphic designers without a technical background, evaluating hardware can be a frustrating and confusing undertaking.

This appendix provides a hardware overview, describing some of the hardware you may consider purchasing. The sections here are meant to provide you with a general idea of the hardware components that you may need to purchase or rent when shooting a video production. For a thorough analysis of using digital video hardware, you might check several resources: Web sites of hardware manufacturers (such as `www.sel.sony.com`, `www.canon.com`, `www.apple.com`), magazine Web sites (`www.DV.com`), or publishers of books specializing in DV and file production (`www.focalpress.com`). Another good resource is your local library. Many video books written over the past 20 years include video shooting, sound, and lighting chapters that are still relevant today. Finally, you might wish to investigate television production workshops and classes provided by local colleges and universities.

Computers

For most Premiere users, the most important element in their digital studio is their computer. For both Mac and PC users running Premiere, the general rule is to get the fastest system you can afford.

The minimum system requirements for Premiere include the following: Please remember that these are the minimum specifications. They may not be adequate for your needs if you are outputting professional video productions.

Macintosh Requirements

- PowerPC processor G3 (G4 recommended)
- Apple System software OS 9.2.2 or 10.1.3
- 64MB of RAM (128MB or more recommended)
- 600MB hard drive space required for installation
- Apple QuickTime 5.0.2 or later

For digital video capture:

- Apple FireWire 2.7 or later
- QuickTime-compatible FireWire (IEEE 1394) interface
- Large-capacity hard drive capable of sustaining 5MB/sec

Note that digital video typically consumes 13GB per hour of footage

Windows Requirements

- 500 MHz Pentium-class processor
- Microsoft Windows 98, Windows 98 SE, 2000, Me, NT4 Sp4
- 128MB RAM or more recommended
- 600MB of available hard drive space for installation (40MB for application)
- 256-color video display adapter
- Adobe Premiere-certified capture card
- Large-capacity hard drive or disk array

Note that digital video typically consumes 13GB per hour of footage

For digital video capture:

- 500 MHz Pentium-III processor (800 MHz for Real Time Preview)
- Windows 2000 Pro, Windows 98 Second Edition, or Windows Me
- Microsoft DirectX-compatible IEEE 1394 interface
- Large-capacity hard drive capable of sustaining 5MB/sec
- Adobe Premiere-certified capture card

Processing speed

A computer system's central processing unit (CPU), as well as the speed of its hard drive (or disks), determines its overall speed when working with multimedia projects.

Many consider the computer's CPU to be the brains of the system. Modern Processors, such as the Pentium 4 are faster and more sophisticated than the Pentium III chips, just as the Macintosh's PowerPC G4 CPU is faster and more sophisticated than the G3. For both Macs and PCs, chip speed of the chips is measured in *megahertz* (MHz) — a million clock cycles per second — where a higher number indicates a faster chip. Thus, a 900 MHz chip is faster than an 800 MHz chip. As this book goes to press, 2-gigahertz (GHz) processors are the state of the art in processors.

Co-processors

For both PCs (Windows NT, Windows 2000, and Windows XP) and Macs, two CPUs are better than one. Premiere, unlike many computer programs, takes full advantage of computer systems with two or more processors. Preview rendering speeds should be dramatically increased in both Mac and Windows systems with multiple processors.

Hard drive speed

Hard drive speed is generally evaluated by the revolutions per minute, seek speed, and data transfer rate. Most of the faster hard drives provide a rotational speed of at least 7,200 RPM (revolutions per minute). Some high-capacity drives have a rotation speed of 10,000 RPM.

Seek speed essentially measures the time it takes to seek out the section of the hard drive that it needs to read to or write to. Seek time is measured in milliseconds. Thus a seek time of 8.5 ms is faster than 9.5 ms. A hard drive's transfer rate determines how fast the drive can transfer data. Transfer rates for IEEE 1394/FireWire drives are often advertised to be between 15 to 200MB per second.

IEEE boards

All new Macs and most high-end PCs are now sold with built-in IEEE 1394 cards. The IEEE standard has been pioneered by Apple computer, which calls the IEEE 1394 standard FireWire (Sony calls it i.LINK). As discussed in Chapter 4, IEEE 1394 ports enable you to copy digitized audio and video from a DV camcorder or DV tape recorder directly to your computer. The actual digitization process takes place in the camera. The IEEE 1394 port enables transferring data at high speeds from the camcorder to the computer, or from computer to hard disk. The top transfer rate for the IEEE 1394/FireWire standard is a blistering 400MB per second. FireWire supports up to 63 connected devices and cables up to 14 feet long.

If your computer does not have an IEEE port, you may be able to purchase an add-in IEEE card for $50, and sometimes even less. The IEEE 1394 port can also be used to attach a hard disk or CD-ROM recorder. Prices of IEEE 1394/FireWire peripherals have been dropping steadily. You should be able to purchase a 30GB drive for less than $500. (Drives for portables are more expensive.)

Companies such as Pinnacle Systems and Miro sell high-end IEEE 1394 video boards, which can cost over $1,000. High-end DV cards usually enable you to export files in MPEG-2 format. MPEG-2 is a high-compression video format that provides extremely high-quality output. Most MPEG-2 boards enable you to export your files to DVD-ROM format. A further benefit of high-end cards is that most processing chips are built into the cards and, therefore, can create and/or render digital effects at high speeds.

Video cards

A third-party video card can speed the display of video effects in real time, and often improve image quality. While you're taking a break from your video production work, these cards also speed the processing of 3D games. Newer, faster boards are AGP, Accelerated Graphics Port, which can deliver high performance graphics to Pentium-based motherboards. One of the chief advantages of the AGP bus is that it delivers four times the bandwidth of the PCI bus. (The PCI, peripheral component interconnect, is a high performance system that handles the transfer of data from the CPU to expansion slots. It is standard on most newer computers, including PowerPC Macs.) Furthermore the AGP bus reduces bottlenecks between the computer's CPU and RAM, providing very high transfer of graphics data.

If you're interested in AGP boards, check out Radeon9700 Pro AGP, which retails for under $400. On its manufacturer's website (`www.ati.com`) the card is championed as the "world's fastest and most advanced graphics board." According to the manufacturer (ATI), the 9700 Pro can process 8 pixels simultaneously, twice as many as competing products. If you are looking for a lower priced card, take a look at the PNY's Verto GeForce4 Ti4600 AGP card, which retails for about $300 or less. (See `www.pny.com` for more details.)

Go to `www.intel.com/technology/agp` for a technical review of AGP technology.

Raid arrays

To help attain extremely high transfer rates, many multimedia producers have installed raid array systems, in which data is shared among several hard drives. Raid systems can split the data transfer over two or more hard disks in a procedure known as *striping*. Because the computer can read and write from multiple drives, transfer rates are increased. Many raid systems use Ultra-SCSI connections (IDE-RAID systems are also available), which provide faster transfer than standard Mac and PC ATA connections or standard SCSI connections.

Peripheral Storage Devices

As you work with digitized video and sound, you are consuming large amounts of storage space. Where do you store clips and sounds that you no longer need to access directly from your hard disks? If you want to quickly save and reload files, you should consider purchasing an Iomega Jaz Drive, which stores 2GB of data. Jaz cartridges are removable and are easy to insert and remove. The cartridges conveniently appear on your desktop, as though they are a separate hard drive.

For long-term storage, yet slower recording and slower loading, consider purchasing a CD-ROM recorder to record directly onto CD-ROM, or a DVD drive. Many high-end computer models include a DVD drive that allows you to record on DVD rewritable DVD-ROM disks, which can store about 4.7GB on a single drive. CD-ROM disks store about 650MB.

Analog Capture Boards

Analog capture boards accept an analog video signal, and digitize video to a computer's hard disk or other storage device. On the PC, most analog boards are add-in boards that must be purchased separately from the computer system. On the Mac side of the fence, for several years Apple sold several computer models with built-in analog cards. If you are not shooting video using a DV system, you may consider purchasing an analog board. The three formats used by analog boards are *composite video*, *S-video,* and *component video.*

✦ **Composite video.** Provides good quality capture. In this system the video brightness and color components are combined into one signal. Most composite boards have three cables, one video, and two sound cables. Many of the older DV Camcorders that are still on the market enable you to place analog tape in them and transfer data using composite signals. Many VHS tape recorders allow input from composite video.

✦ **S-video.** Provides a higher quality video signal than composite video, because luminance and color are separated into two different signals. Most analog boards that provide S-video also allow composite output. S-video is considered better quality than VHS. Most VHS tape recorders allow input from S-video. (Many DV cameras provide an S-video port to enable you to transfer DV footage to VHS tape decks.)

✦ **Component video.** Component video provides broadcast quality video. In component video, two channels handle color and one channel handles luminance. Although Composite and S-video boards enable connections to camcorder and consumer tape decks, component boards enable a connection to broadcast quality Beta SP tape decks.

Digital Video Cameras

Every few months, a new crop of digital video camcorders hits the market with more features than the last group. If you are considering purchasing a camcorder, you have many options to consider. If you already have a camcorder, should you upgrade to a DV camcorder? If your budget allows, the answer should be yes, definitely.

DV camcorders, especially the newer ones that use mini-cartridges, provide higher quality video and sound output than Hi-8 and 8mm format camcorders. DV cameras provide more lines of horizontal resolution images than older cameras, thus color is better and images are sharper.

DV cameras digitize and compress the signal directly in the camera. The DV compression uses a data rate of 25 megabits (Mb) per second; thus the compression standard is often known as DV 25. As mentioned earlier, one chief advantage of a DV camera is that you can connect it directly to a computer with an IEEE 1394 port.

Your best bet is to survey the Web pages of camcorder manufacturers, such as Sony, Canon, and JVC. Look at the features listed and compare prices. (Canon's Web page currently allows you to download user manuals, which can help you understand all features in the camera.) The more you pay, the better the camera and the more features offered.

Better DV Camcorders usually create pictures with more pixels. For example, the Canon Elura has a ¼-inch CCD (charge coupler device, responsible for converting the image into a signal that can be digitized) that provides 380,000 pixels; however some cameras—such as the Canon XL1, Canon GL1, Sony TVR900, and Sony DCR-VX2000—provide 3 CCDs with 27,000 pixels per CCD, which provides a sharper image. (More expensive cameras boast over 500 lines of horizontal resolution.)

Another consideration is accessories. Some cameras enable you to change lenses and have more control for changing exposure and shutter speed. If audio is important, you might check whether your camera can connect to a wireless microphone or to an audio mixer. Another feature to consider is whether you want to be able to use older analog tape formats. Some models can take a Hi-8 or 8mm tape and digitize the video right in the camera, so it can be transferred to the computer's IEEE 1394 port (rather than to an analog capture board). Most models feature an S-video port, so that the digital video data can be transferred to a consumer VHS tape recorder.

Lenses

Most casual users of video equipment simply purchase a camera and use whatever lens is mounted on the camera. If you keep working with video equipment, you should learn a bit about lenses. Virtually all camcorders sold today include zoom lenses. For example, Canon's XL1S, one of the more expensive prosumer cameras on the market, features a 16x zoom. The modifier 16x indicates that the camera can zoom in to make the focal length 16 times greater. This enables you to alter the built-in focal length of the XL1S from 5.5mm to 88mm (this lens is interchangeable with other lenses).

The focal length is the middle of the lens to the point where an image begins to appear, usually measured in millimeters. The focal length indicates exactly what image areas can appear in the lens. If the focal length is low, the viewing area is large; if the focal length is large, the viewing area is correspondingly smaller. Thus, if you focus on a subject with a smaller focal length, such as 10mm (a wide angle lens), you see more of the subject than at 50mm (telephoto). At 10mm you might see an image of a person from head to toe, at 50mm only the person's face is seen in a close-up.

Many cameras provide digital zooms of up to 50x. Although this provides further zooming capabilities, the picture quality usually isn't as good as optical zooming. When viewing the specs of high range cameras, you frequently see the f-stop range. The f-stops control the iris opening of the camera. The lower the f-stop, the greater the amount of light allowed in. Higher f-stops allow less light in. Canon's XL1 provides a range of 1.6-16 (you can also adjust the shutter speed on this camera as well). This enables you to set manual exposure and provides greater control over depth-of-field.

Depth-of-field is typically defined as the area from the nearest point in focus to the furthest point in focus. Having sufficient depth-of-field is especially important if a subject you are shooting is moving. You don't want the subject moving in and out of focus. The focal length of the lens, the distance of the subject from the camera, and the f-stop setting all determine depth-of-field.

Microphones

Although most camcorders feature a built-in microphone, you may want to purchase an external microphone to capture better quality audio. For sophisticated audio recording, you may want to purchase a mixer that enables you to accept multiple sound inputs and enables you to monitor and set recording levels.

If you are purchasing a microphone, you want to become familiar with several common audio terms. The first one is *frequency response*, which describes the pick up or sensitivity range of sound for the microphone, from low to high sounds. Sound waves are measured in cycles per second (Hz). The human ear is sensitive to a range from 20 Hz to 16,000 Hz. A microphone frequency response determines the range of sounds it can record. An expensive studio microphone could have a range from 20 to 20,000 Hz.

Microphones are divided into different categories, according to the inner electronics that control the capture of sound. The primary categories are *condenser*, *dynamic*, and *crystal*.

Condenser mics are generally used as studio mics. They are usually expensive. But, you get what you pay for. They are sensitive and provide a broad frequency response. Electret condensers are a subcategory of condenser microphones, which can be powered with a small battery provider. They are good for reproduction of narration. Because these microphones are especially sensitive to heat and humidity, care must be taken when using and storing them.

Dynamic microphones are often used as external mics for camcorders. They are inexpensive and usually quite durable. Although the sound quality recorded from dynamic microphones is not excellent, it is generally good enough for most DV taping sessions.

Crystal mics are the least expensive. They do not record a large frequency range and should generally be avoided.

Another basic audio concept to understand about microphones is that they utilize different pick up patterns. Mics can be omnidirectional or unidirectional.

- **Omnidirectional.** These mics pick up sounds from all directions. If you are not recording in a noisy area and want to capture all sounds from the recording site, you probably want to use an omnidirectional microphone.
- **Unidirectional.** These microphones pickup sound primarily from one direction. If you are recording in a noisy room and want to record someone speaking, a unidirectional can help eliminate background sounds.

To further specify how microphones pick-up sounds, microphone manufacturers provide polar graphs showing the response of a microphone. A polar graph is plotted over 360 degrees with the center of the graph depicting the center of the microphone. The round curves depict the area from which the microphone picks up sound. The graph patterns are described as cardioid, super-cardioid, and bidirectional.

- **Cardioid.** Picks up sounds primarily from the front of the mic. They eliminate sounds from the back of the mike and can pick up some sounds from the side. If you stand in front of the mike, most cardioids accept a 30-angle range.
- **Bidirectional.** Picks up sounds primarily from the front and back of the microphone.

On a more technical level, mics are considered either high or low *impedance*. Measured in ohms, impedance is an electrical term indicating resistance in the circuit. Most professional (and thus high quality) audio/video equipment and studio equipment is low impedance. Low impedance equipment is often called Low-Z. Less expensive equipment is generally high impedance (called Hi-Z). Generally short-cabled microphones are Hi-Z; long cable microphones are Low-Z (15 feet or longer).

As you work with audio, also see the terms balanced and unbalanced to describe audio cabling. Short cables with high impedance equipment using RCA mini plugs are using unbalanced lines. Most nonbroadcast camcorders provide unbalanced lines. Balanced lines feature XLR and cannon plugs (shielded cables), which eliminate buzzing sounds and other electronic noise. Expensive prosumer camcorders, such as the Cannon l XL1, provide a connection to a CLR plug for hookup to an audio mixer.

Tip You may also want to visit audio equipment manufacturer Shure's Web site, which includes technical publications such as "Guide to Audio Systems for Video Production" by Shure engineer Christopher Lyons. This publication—which reviews microphones and mixers, and covers topics such as "Connecting a Mixer to a Camcorder" and "How to Handle Some Common Miking Situations"—can be downloaded from Shure's Web site, at `www.shure.com`.

Lighting

Lighting is one of the crucial factors determining video quality. If you are shooting indoors, you should investigate lighting equipment and learn the basics of setting up lights. If you're new to video, you might take a basic studio production course, or read a book on television lighting (the Focal press offers a variety of books on this subject).

If you are primarily going to be shooting interior scenes and want to produce high-quality video, you should investigate purchasing a lighting kit, along with lighting utilities, such as scrims and barn-doors (these can limit and control lights).

Although this appendix is not designed to serve as a lighting guide, to properly light a scene, you typically include a key light and a fill light, with a backlight added to provide more depth. The key light is the main source of illumination. Often the key light is set at a 45-degree angle between the camera and the subject. The fill light, often placed on the opposite side of the camera from the key, helps lighten shadow areas produced by the key.

If you are setting up lights on-location, be wary of blowing out a fuse. A typical US consumer circuit is a 15-amp line and does not handle more than 1,800 watts (multiply total amps times voltage to obtain the total watts used, 120 x 15 = 1,800). It's a good idea to add up all the watts you are using, including any camera equipment, before you start plugging in electrical equipment. Also remember that other electrical equipment may be using the circuit as well.

✦ ✦ ✦

Index

Continued

Continued

E

Continued

M

Continued

O

P

Q

Continued

T

Continued

Continued

W

Y

Z

Wiley Publishing, Inc.
End-User License Agreement

5. **Limited Warranty.**

(a) WPI warrants that the Software and Software Media are free from defects in materials and workmanship under normal use for a period of sixty (60) days from the date of purchase of this Book. If WPI receives notification within the warranty period of defects in materials or workmanship, WPI will replace the defective Software Media.

(b) WPI AND THE AUTHOR OF THE BOOK DISCLAIM ALL OTHER WARRANTIES, EXPRESS OR IMPLIED, INCLUDING WITHOUT LIMITATION IMPLIED WARRANTIES OF MERCHANTABILITY AND FITNESS FOR A PARTICULAR PURPOSE, WITH RESPECT TO THE SOFTWARE, THE PROGRAMS, THE SOURCE CODE CONTAINED THEREIN, AND/OR THE TECHNIQUES DESCRIBED IN THIS BOOK. WPI DOES NOT WARRANT THAT THE FUNCTIONS CONTAINED IN THE SOFTWARE WILL MEET YOUR REQUIREMENTS OR THAT THE OPERATION OF THE SOFTWARE WILL BE ERROR FREE.

(c) This limited warranty gives you specific legal rights, and you may have other rights that vary from jurisdiction to jurisdiction.

6. **Remedies.**

(a) WPI's entire liability and your exclusive remedy for defects in materials and workmanship shall be limited to replacement of the Software Media, which may be returned to WPI with a copy of your receipt at the following address: Software Media Fulfillment Department, Attn.: *Adobe Premiere 6.5 Bible,* Wiley Publishing, Inc., 10475 Crosspoint Blvd., Indianapolis, IN 46256, or call 1-800-762-2974. Please allow four to six weeks for delivery. This Limited Warranty is void if failure of the Software Media has resulted from accident, abuse, or misapplication. Any replacement Software Media will be warranted for the remainder of the original warranty period or thirty (30) days, whichever is longer.

(b) In no event shall WPI or the author be liable for any damages whatsoever (including without limitation damages for loss of business profits, business interruption, loss of business information, or any other pecuniary loss) arising from the use of or inability to use the Book or the Software, even if WPI has been advised of the possibility of such damages.

(c) Because some jurisdictions do not allow the exclusion or limitation of liability for consequential or incidental damages, the above limitation or exclusion may not apply to you.

7. **U.S. Government Restricted Rights.** Use, duplication, or disclosure of the Software for or on behalf of the United States of America, its agencies and/or instrumentalities "U.S. Government" is subject to restrictions as stated in paragraph (c)(1)(ii) of the Rights in Technical Data and Computer Software clause of DFARS 252.227-7013, or subparagraphs (c) (1) and (2) of the Commercial Computer Software - Restricted Rights clause at FAR 52.227-19, and in similar clauses in the NASA FAR supplement, as applicable.

8. **General.** This Agreement constitutes the entire understanding of the parties and revokes and supersedes all prior agreements, oral or written, between them and may not be modified or amended except in a writing signed by both parties hereto that specifically refers to this Agreement. This Agreement shall take precedence over any other documents that may be in conflict herewith. If any one or more provisions contained in this Agreement are held by any court or tribunal to be invalid, illegal, or otherwise unenforceable, each and every other provision shall remain in full force and effect.